The Royal Geographical Society with the
Institute of British Geographers
Special Publications Series

33 Space and Social Theory

The Royal Geographical Society with the Institute of British Geographers
Special Publications Series

GENERAL EDITOR: **Chris Philo**

Space and Social Theory
Interpreting Modernity and Postmodernity

Edited by Georges Benko and Ulf Strohmayer

BLACKWELL Publishers

for Ken and Sebastian

First published 1997

Blackwell Publishers Ltd
108 Cowley Road
Oxford OX4 1JF
UK

Blackwell Publishers Inc
350 Main Street
Malden, MA 02148
USA

British Library Cataloguing in Publication Data
A CIP catalogue record for this book is available from the British Library.
Library of Congress Cataloging in Publication Data
Space and social theory: interpreting modernity and postmodernity /
   edited by Georges Benko and Ulf Strohmayer.
      p. cm. – (Special publications series (Institute of British
   Geographer) ; 33)
      Includes bibliographical references and index.
      ISBN 0–631–19466–5 (alk. paper). – ISBN 0–631–19467–3 (pbk. :
   alk. Paper)
      1. Human geography–Philosophy. 2. Postmodernism–Social aspects.
   3. Civilization. Modern. I. Benko, Georges. II. Strohmayer, Ulf.
   III. Series.
   GF21.S69 1997
   304.2'01–dc20   96–25628
                                                            CIP

Typeset in 10.5 on 12 pt Plantin
by Archetype, http://ourworld.compuserve.com/homepages/Archetype
Printed in Great Britain by T.J. Press Limited, Padstow, Cornwall.

This book is printed on acid-free paper

Contents

List of Plates

List of Figures

List of Contributors

Georges Benko is professor of Geography at the University of Pantheon-Sorbonne in Paris. A member of the editorial boards of *Economic Geography, GeoJournal, Espace et Societés* and of *Society and Space* (1987–92), Benko is also the author of numerous books in French and English, including *Industrial Change and Regional Development* (Belhaven/Pinter; with Mick Dunford) and *Les régions qui gagnent* (P.U.F.; with Alain Lipietz). Together with Ulf Strohmayer, he also edited *Geography, History and Social Science* (Klumer).

Augustin Berque is professor of Cultural Geography at the École des Hautes Études en Sciences Sociales in Paris, where he is the director of the Center for Contemporary Japan. A member of the editorial boards of *Géographie et Cultures* and *L'Espace Geographique*, Berque has authored numerous books in French and English on Japanese culture, urban formation and landscape, and has edited the influential *Dictionnaire de la civilisation japonais* (Hachette). His latest book is *Etre humains sur la terre* (Gallimard).

Philip Cooke is professor of Regional Development and Director of the Centre of Advanced Studies in the Social Sciences at the University of Wales, Cardiff, and editor of *European Planning Studies*. His primary research interests are regional innovation studies, institutional networks and the management of technopoles. His most recent project was the EU-funded study of Regional Innovation Systems (with K. Morgan). His other publications include *Towards Global Localisation* (UCL Press), *Back to the future and Localities* (Unwin Hyman) and an edited volume on *The Rise of the Rust Belt* (UCL Press).

Tim Cresswell is a lecturer in Geography at the University of Wales, Lampeter. He has published papers on Geography and transgression in numerous geographical journals and is the author of *In Place/Out of Place: Geography, Ideology and Transgression* (Minnesota). Currently, he is working on a book on mobility, power and identity.

Michael Curry is a member of the faculty of the Department of Geography at the University of California, Los Angeles. He holds degrees in liberal arts, philosophy and Geography. His work concerns the interrelationships among geographical ideas and technologies, and the cultural and institutional contexts within which they are applied. He is the author of numerous articles and of two books, *Understanding geographical writing: Putting the work in its place* (Minnesota), *The paradox of geographical information systems* (Routledge), and *The Work in the World. Geographical Practice and the Written Word* (Minnesota, 1996).

Michael Dear is professor of Geography and director of the Southern California Studies Center at the University of Southern California. He is the founding editor of *Society and Space (Environment and Planning D)*, and his most recent book is entitled *Malign Neglect: Homelessness in an American City* (with J. Wolch). He was recently a Fellow at the Center for Advanced Studies in the Behavioral Sciences at Stanford and is currently preparing a book on postmodern urbanism.

Derek Gregory was educated in England and is currently professor of Geography at the University of British Columbia in Vancouver. The author and editor of numerous books and articles in geography and social theory (the last of which was *Geographical Imaginations*), he is currently exploring the connections between information circulation, the production of 'imagined geographies' and the impress of imperial power with the British Empire.

Matthew Hannah is assistant professor of Geography at the University of Vermont. His interests include the historical Geography of race relations in the United States, the history and philosophy of social science and critical social theory. He is currently researching the links between early American social science and the elaboration of national government power during the Gilded Age.

John Paul Jones III is associate professor of Geography and Co-Director of the Committee on Social Thought at the University of Kentucky, Lexington, and the editor of the *Annals of the Association of American Geographers*. His research interests include the history of twentieth-century geographic thought, poststructuralist theories of space and representation and applications of textual and discourse analysis in Geography. He is the co-editor, with Wolfgang Natter and Theodore Schatzki, of *Postmodern Contentions* and *Objectivity and its Other* (Guilford).

Julie Kathy Gibson-Graham is the pen name of Katherine Gibson and Julie Graham, who are currently in the Department of Geography and Environmental Science, Monash University, and the Department of Geosciences, University of Massachusetts-Amherst, respectively. Their book *The End of Capitalism (as we knew it)* was published with Blackwell in 1996.

Alain Lipietz is professor, director of research, influential member of the French Green Party and member of the French Centre National de la Recherche Scientifique (CNRS). One of the chief proponents of the regulationist theory of capitalist development and crises, Lipietz is the author of countless articles and books, most of which have been translated into English. Possibly best known among the latter are *Mirages and Miracles* (Verso), *Towards a New Economic Order*

(Polity) and *Green Hopes* (Polity). His latest book, *La societé en sablier* was recently published.

Wolfgang Natter is associate professor of German and Co-director of the Committee on Social Theory at the University of Kentucky. His published work has addressed intersections of literary, cultural and spatial theory, and they include Germany, essays on democratic theory, U.S. and German film, and implications for both space and representation that devolve from poststructuralism. He is co-editor of *Postmodern Contentions* and *Objectivity, its Other and The Social and Policitical Body* (Guilford).

Richard Peet is professor in the Graduate School of Geography at Clark University, Worcester, Massachusetts and co-editor of *Economic Geography*. His interests lie in social theory, development, discourse, ideology and he has been known to canoe on occasion. Recent and future publications include, among other projects, a co-edited book (with Michael Watts) on *Liberation Ecology* (Routledge) and *Philosophy, Social Theory and Geographic Thought* (Blackwell, forthcoming).

Allan Pred is professor of Geography at the University of California at Berkeley. Principally concerned with modernity and the historical Geography of the present, his recent books include *Reworking Modernity: Capitalisms and Symbolic Discontent* (with Michael J. Watts; Rutgers University Press) *Recognizing European Modernities: A Montage of the Present* (Routledge).

Rob Shields is the author of *Places on the Margin: Alternative Geographies of Modernity* (1989) and *Henri Lefebvre, A Critical Introduction* (forthcoming) and has edited several books including *Lifestyle Shopping: The Subject of Consumption* (1991); *Cultures of Internet* (1995). Recent research includes: methodological work on dialogism, *verstehen* and the ethics of qualitative methods; the spatialization of settler societies and changing patterns of consumption. He lectures in the Culture and Communications programme, University of Lancaster and maintains close ties with Carleton University, Ottawa, where he is associate Professor of Sociology and Anthropology.

David Slater is professor of Social and Political Geography at the University of Loughborough, England, and formerly he was a Senior Research Associate at the Interuniversity Centre of Latin American Research and Documentation in Amsterdam. His most recent publications include 'Exploring other zones of the Postmodern: Problems of Ethnocentrism and Difference across the North-South Divide' in A. Rattansi and S. Westwood (eds) *Racism, Modernity and Identity* (Polity Press), and he has edited two special issues on 'Social Movements and Political Change in Latin America', published in *Latin American Perspectives*.

Edward W. Soja currently teaches in the Department of Urban Planning, School of Public Political Research, UCLA. He is the author of *Postmodern Geographies* (Verso) and *Thirdspace: Journeys to Los Angeles and other Real-and-Imagined*

Places (Blackwell). He is also co-editor (with Allan J. Scott) of the forthcoming *The City: Los Angeles and Urban Theory at the end of the Twentieth Century* (U of California P).

Ulf Strohmayer studied at the Universities of Munich, Freiburg, Paris-Sorbonne, the Fernand Braudel Center (SUNY Binghamton), NORDPLAN, Stockholm, and received his doctorate from Penn State University. He is currently lecturer in human Geography at the University of Wales, Lampeter. He is the author of numerous articles, co-editor of two books and author, with Matthew Hannah, of *Gnostic Materialism, Cosmology and the Ruins of Social Theory* (forthcoming).

Preface

The essays in *Space and Social Theory* were collected with the principal aim in mind of making key geographical interpretations of 'postmodernity' or 'postmodernism' and their respective notions of space accessible to a wider readership. With the idea of 'a postmodern turn' having almost acquired an historical weight since first it entered into our respective academic orbits, we felt it necessary and fruitful to survey its impact on the intellectual landscape in which we live and work. For, truth be told, this 'landscape' has been altered dramatically through the confrontation with 'postmodernity': more than other disciplines, with the possible exception of Cultural Studies, it was Human Geography that came away from this encounter with a renewed sense of mission, vindication, even of pride. Our mention of 'landscape' in this context is thus by no means accidental: the problems geographers assumed to be inherent in their (spatially relativist) *Weltanschauung* were now revealed to be a common problem across the human and social sciences. The infamous 'crisis of representation' did not stop at disciplinary boundaries, thus again confronting scholars everywhere with the indivisibility of the social world. Arguably, though, human geographers had had to labour with the (still largely implicit) consequences of this non-reducibility of the social world for the longest time already and were thus, if only in hindsight, better equipped to respond to emerging questions with extraordinary zeal and fervour. Human geography, after all, never was granted anything like the straightforward delimitation of a subject area so common to other academic subjects; the eagerness by which it acknowledged what used to be problems particular to geography as general quandaries is quite telling in its own right. The resurgence furthermore of 'cultural geography' – to wit, the emergence of journals like *Ecumene* and *Géographie et Cultures* – over the course of the last decade or so is only the most visible aspect of this response.

And yet, to speak of 'a response' in the singular can only be misleading. The 'crisis of representation', and the ensuing thorough critique of established scientific categories developed under the banner of 'deconstructive' practices, caused an even greater fragmentation of geographic approaches than we had to contend with before. What was increasingly lacking was the sheer power of persuasion that had hitherto surrounded accepted scientific paradigms and analytical terms like say 'Location Theory' or 'Marxism'. Split open to critique, our inherited scientific vocabulary ceased to *function* in the manner we had come to expect. The result was either the prompt abandonment of such vocabularies – and 'Marxism' surely suffered most in this respect – or else an ongoing process of even finer specification of the categories under scrutiny.

Alongside this 'epistemological' response to the engagement between 'postmodernism' and Human Geography we can identify a distinct 'ontological' one. This latter strand of thought, rather than departing from a foundational 'crisis in representation', took the crisis to be the epiphenomenal result of an increasingly fragmented world. Here, the 'world' refused incorporation into accepted categories by simple virtue of no longer obeying rules that we made for another, 'modern' world. Modern technologies in particular had rendered what had once been a more or less 'legible' world increasingly incomprehensible. New approaches, new categories were thus needed to cope with a world that continued to change while we watched. Needless to say, this 'ontological' response to 'postmodernism' served to further, rather than eliminate, the aforementioned tendency towards fragmentation with geography's attempt to answer 'the postmodern challenge'.

The present collection of essays is intended both as an expression of, and as a first attempt at repudiating, this fragmentation of our approaches. We hope to achieve the former by virtue of the sheer breadth of the topics addressed and through the careful selection of general and of particular voices. How successful we have been in the pursuit of a new sort of cohesion will have to be judged by the reader. As such, the *collection* serves to illustrate how little is actually achieved when debates within the human sciences have finally settled on some common denominator (à la 'postmodernism') or another. What is evident in this volume is a wide spectrum of not merely topical dimensions but, and even more strikingly, an almost eclectic compilation of diverging views on the subject. Both 'deficiencies' are intentional. For us, they exemplify the problem that we see at the core of the debate around 'postmodernism', namely the question of how to conduct debates, academic and otherwise, in the absence of a pregiven, unquestioned 'centre'.

Human Geography, like any other human and social science, has witnessed a succession of these 'centres' over the course of the last century, and it is these, as much as the analytical concepts they gave birth to, that are put into question by the essays in this book. First and foremost among these problematic 'centres' are the disciplinary subdivisions to which we have all become accustomed. If once geographers thought that designations like 'economic' or 'cultural' geography could circumvent the problem of a generally accepted indivisibility of the world and thus render geography more scientific a subject, this belief no longer reigns within the field. It is hence no accident that the majority of authors assembled here refuse an easy go at subdisciplinary categorization. A second type of 'centre' that we are all familiar with comes in the form of the contested (often generational) paradigms that have ruled the roost at various periods within the short history of Human Geography. But even such a form of 'difference' between approaches and paradigms can become a centre by its own right, provided that we can document some accepted form of 'progress' that works through a succession of theoretical trends or fashions. Here the change from, say, a straightforward 'Marxist' position to a 'Structurationist' manner of arguing so popular a decade ago provided a welcome structural 'centre' for discussions within Human Geography and elsewhere. Taken together, these 'centres' all seemed to guarantee in one form or another the internal coherence and the argumentative strength of groups within the discipline while simultaneously immunizing debates within these various groups against outside interference. No longer do these outdated mechanisms of coherence produce the desired results, one of the changes wrought by the encounter between Geography and 'Postmodernism'.

All of this has implifications that clearly extend beyond geography. What we encounter in these debates are questions associated with the wide field of multiculturalism in today's Western societies. In a strikingly analogous manner to the problems encountered in discussions about the politics of 'multicultural' societies, Human Geography now stands at a crossroads. The question we have to ask ourselves is just how 'particular' or 'different' our knowledges, or how 'multi' our cultural practices, can become before they no longer constitute a meaningful whole. Or, in other words, lurking beneath the surface of current debates around 'postmodernism', we find a series of questions: What it is it that constitutes 'public' debates within our contemporary democratic societies? Who is allowed to speak? On what grounds does he or she claim 'expertise'? What counts as 'evidence' (of rigour, of honesty, of responsibility, of 'the real', of 'the past', etc.) in any of these debates? It is these questions that will increasingly push to the forefront of our academic and civil debates. We hope that the present collection of essays will serve to illuminate such questions. Does this mean that indeed we accept as a fact that we live in a 'postmodern' world? Far from it. In fact, we have barely begun to explore the conditions of possibility of *answering* that question.

We need to be aware, however, that however tentative such an exploration is intended to be, the moment it becomes a public document is simultaneously the moment it forms a centre of its own right and thus at least partly violates the tentative character of its own intentions. The present collection is not an exception: there is a finite number of voices in here which have been grouped into coherent subdivisions. The reader will furthermore find introductory thoughts at the beginning of each of these groups of articles. Uniformity stops here, however. As editors, we consciously refrained from superimposing a style (of length, of referencing, of subheadings, etc.) binding for all contributors. While such a uniformity serves a distinct purpose in other collections, a book addressing the absence of communally binding 'centres' within the debate around postmodernism could not but make pretensions towards unity where the visibility of differences is what is needed most. We do hope that our decision not to homogenize the book in the manner that we all have become accustomed to will serve this latter need.

Finally, words of gratitude are in order. First of all, we would like to thank a host of colleagues who took the time to eliminate stylistic oddities that continue to plague the products of our writing efforts in the medium of English. We would also like to thank John Davey, Anna Harrison and Neil Curtis at Blackwell for their patience, skill and subtle pressures, Felix Driver for encouraging the project all along, the contributing authors for (mostly) delivering their promised essays on time and our respective home institutions for tolerating our at times excessive fax habits. Lastly, Ulf Strohmayer would like to thank the Deutsche Forschungsgemeinschaft for financing the final stages of this project.

G.B. Benko
Paris

Ulf Strohmayer
Lampeter

Introduction: Modernity, Postmodernity and the Social Sciences

Georges Benko

Le thème du postmoderne se prête merveilleusement à l'activation de la bêtise.
J.-F. Lyotard

Modernity and postmodernity are not primarily concepts of the social sciences. Rather, the terms are to be understood as characteristic modes of civilization. Symbolic and geographic diversity notwithstanding, the terms have gained wide acceptance in the West; yet the notions behind them remain confused and diversely interpreted, and in their most general sense denote a historical evolution and change in mentalities. An oscillation between myth and reality has characterized developments over the last 20 years in every domain: the arts, architecture, ideology, politics and so on. Modernity and postmodernity are the products of far-reaching upheavals in our social, economic and political organization, the consequences of which are registered at the level of morals, life-style, and day-to-day activity.

Modernity and postmodernity are not analytical concepts, so they possess no laws; each has merely a set of particular features, the canonical rules of conflicting processes of change. If anything, modernity and postmodernity thus enact 'the tradition of the New' (Harold Rosenberg, 1960). They act as '*idées forces*' and dominant ideologies, giving expression to the contradictions of history in socio-cultural forms. They are linked to the historical crises of structures. Modernity and postmodernity are the ambiguous expressions of crises of civilization and of knowledge, engaged in a headlong flight from the present. Each represents an attempt to impose a new cultural regime. For this reason they occupy a central position in the present debates in all fields of the social sciences.

I

Modernity can have no single meaning, since modernity is itself a search for meaning.

Meschonnic, 1988.

The notion of modernity is indissolubly paired with the term tradition: what is modern is defined in relation to its occurrence in time as of the 'present'. The word *modernus*, which began to be used in Latin at the end of the fifth century, stemmed from *modo*, 'just now, recently, now'. Thus *Modernus* refers not to what is new but to what is current, contemporary with whoever is speaking. By contrast, aesthetic or intellectual references to tradition belong to a system of values in which the achievements of the past are treated as definable and unchanging, and hence able to serve as a model for present-day literature, art, and thought. Use of the term modernity carries with it the idea of a temporal discontinuity between past and present, and a discontinuity between the models of the past and the models that the present can or should construct.

To adapt an Althusserian formula, modernity is perhaps a failed concept which attests to an absence of concept: a widely employed term for which its status as an autonomous epistemological object has not been established. This is certainly the conclusion suggested by the theoretical weakness of attempts to define modernity as a concept (use of the same term to describe different concepts, low theoretical content of the word, inconsistency, etc.).

The notion of modernity can be treated as:

1   a distinct form of temporality;
2   a social and aesthetic experience inextricably linked to the modernization of capitalism;
3   a project (unfinished), understood as the result and instrument of a particular balance of power, and for this reason subject to a constitutive tension.

A normative interpretation of modernity does not mean simply that it generates its own norms within its own space, that it 'can and will no longer borrow the criteria by which it takes its orientation from the models supplied by another epoch' (Habermas, 1988). Such an interpretation also suggests, first, that the *degree of modernity* is to be measured in terms of divergence from the 'traditional' forms of social life, and second, that historical time is itself normatively structured, identified with a homogeneous and continuous movement of a progressive character.

A survey of the accumulated consequences of modernity is enough to dispel any such progressive vision. The singular adventure of modernity is littered with discontinuities and changes, turning points and false starts. It presents neither the linearity of the *tradition of the new* in which discontinuity becomes accepted as the norm, nor the 'conservatism through change' described by Baudrillard. Just as the notion of modernity presents ambiguities which reflect the range of topics covered by the term, so the attempt to *date* the emergence of the modern and to identify stages in its formation is far from straightforward.

One attempt to give a precise meaning to the term 'Modern' is that provided by Habermas (1988). He begins by observing that 'the term "modern" was first used at the end of the fifth century, in order to distinguish the Roman and pagan past from the Christian present which had just obtained official recognition'. According to this definition, the *Modern* is distinguished from the concept of the *Modern Period*:

> A belief that one was Modern existed at the time of Charlemagne, in the twelfth century, and during the Enlightenment – that is at each time a new relationship with Antiquity produced an awareness of a new epoch in Europe. In addition, the lay concept of the modern period expresses the belief that the future has already begun: it designates the epoch which lives in relation to the future which is open to the new that is coming [...]. Only during the eighteenth century was the historical threshold situated around 1500 perceived, with hindsight, as the start of a renewal.

The three major historical events that marked the beginning of the modern period were the discovery of the New World, the Renaissance and the Reformation.

According to Wolin (1984), the emergence of the Modern: 'corresponds to a world-historical process of crystallization that transpires over the course of the 15th, 16th and 17th centuries or the "early modern" period. However, its definite form is not achieved until the 18th century, with the transition from the absolutist to democratic eras.'

A second phase can be identified in the nineteenth century, with the development and ramification of the modern, to the point of becoming (about the middle of the nineteenth century) aesthetic modernity, which was conceived as a break from, and rejection of, the Classical tradition. This also seems to be Baudrillard's point of view, when he asserts that modernity 'is only identifiable in Europe from the 16th century onwards and only assumes its full significance from the 19th century'.

For Habermas (1988) it is really the Enlightenment which transformed the Modern from an amorphous sensibility to the spirit of the age: '... it is only with the ideal of perfectability advocated by the French Enlightenment, with the vision, inspired by modern science, of an unlimited advance of knowledge and progress to a better, more just society, that perception was gradually freed from the fascination with the classical works of antiquity which had characterised each of the successive modern epochs'.

This liberating of Modernity from a fascination with the classical world coincided with the growing awareness of its *historical project*. Habermas observes that the adjective 'modern' began to be used as a substantive only 'very late in European languages of the modern period – approximately since the middle of the 19th century – and then only in the realm of the fine arts'. But while the advent of aesthetic modernity was the undoubted product of the nineteenth century, the break from the model of classical art had in fact begun at the start of the eighteenth century with the famous 'Querelle des Anciens et des Modernes'. This saw the *modernes* reject the tenets of French classicism and assimilate the Aristotelian concept of perfection to that of progress, such as had been suggested by modern science (Habermas, 1988).

Whereas the terminological itinerary of *Modern* occupies a long historical span and is generally associated with the sense of a radical break with the past, the *modern period* refers to a temporally specific historical configuration (in particular, since the Renaissance). The *project of modernity* took shape intellectually in the course of the eighteenth century, but it was only in the nineteenth century that modernity acquired a social and aesthetic substance (modernism). From this standpoint, the nineteenth century marks a turning point.

Clearly, then, the problem of chronology cannot be separated from that of defining and conceptualizing the notion of modernity. Moreover, an approach based on proposing hypotheses of historical periodization would carry the risk of ignoring all the divergences within a given historical period and thus of excluding all the elements that conflicted with modernity's hegemonic course of development. As Jameson reminds us, ' one of the concerns frequently raised by periodizing hypotheses is that these tend to obliterate difference, and to project an idea of the historical period as massive homogeneity (bounded on either side by inextricable chronological metamorphoses and punctuation marks)'.

The greatest danger, however, lies in considering modernity (and the process of modernization) in terms of *essence* (rational, contractual, logic of complexification) objectively embodied in historical structures. This point is capital for a criticism of the Habermasian conception of modernity. The diversity of the changes that signal the 'massive presence' of modernity cannot be interpreted simply as concrete evidence of the liberating finality of the modern project (modernity as application of the modern project, the Modern becomes modernity, that is, the concrete realization of the Modern, the state of the Modern, in other words: the adjective replaced by the noun). Modernity is not the application or realization of a predetermined project. If it was, it would appear as governed, and indeed driven, by the action of modern historical logocentricity. The ideals of the modern project would emerge as the essential and propulsive force for the process of *mise en modernité*. Acknowledging the present failures (the defeat of modernity on all fronts) would automatically signify the bankruptcy of the modern project. Such an interpretation is favourable to the emergence of 'post'-modern positions which condemn the modern project as intellectually outdated and ethically flawed, even reactionary.

Yet modernity as a historical experience is not an inexorable order spawned by the modern project and the development of which this project determines. On the contrary, the modern project is itself an organic element of the modern historical formation; it is formed in an *agonale* process, the result of a balance of power, or rather as the expression of tensions which discursively amplify the fractures inherent to modernity. In other words, only by conceptualizing modernity in terms of *capitalist modernity* can we account for the contradictory character of this historical experience and construe the itinerary of the modern project in the light of the contradictions observed in the real world.

Viewed thus, the modern project appears as the product of compromise, ambiguity and even of muddle. It constantly encounters resistances and counter-tendencies, and is continually under attack from the established material or intellectual forces, while the dynamic of its own internal divisions is responsible for transmutations and translations. As A. Wellmer (1985) observes, 'from early on, modern society has repeatedly mobilised strong counterforces against the Enlightenment as a processus of rationalization: examples are the German Romantics, the young Hegel, the early Marx, Adorno, the anarchists; a large part of modern art belongs to these counter tendencies'. Meanwhile, the socialist movement itself gradually compromised the unity of Enlightenment reason by introducing *a class dimension* into capitalist modernity: 'there are strong objections even within modernism (think of Chaplin's *Modern Times*) to the idea that the machine, the factory and the rationalized city provide a sufficiently rich conception to define the eternal qualities of modern life' (Harvey, 1989).

In short, if the modern project does not possess the assumed homogeneity, this is because it is part of the shifting (and hence unfinished), transient and elusive reality which is characteristic of capitalist modernity. The fields and modes of action of this reality remain to be identified.

The classification of this historical experience of modernity I propose is three-fold:

1 modernity as a *global social experience*, inextricably linked to the process of capitalist modernization of the productive and politico-juridico space, and which today has become a hegemonic and universal form;
2 modernity as an experience in day-to-day life, or better as the *capillary logic of everydayness* and dominant line of development of actual experience, and even as a mode of perception of historical time;
3 modernity as a cultural quest (and cultural uncertainty), a reference which fascinated Rimbaud ('il faut être absolument moderne') and Baudelaire, in other words, a heritage linked to avant-garde aesthetic production (modernism).

Discussions of 'modernity' are all too often based on imprecise ideas, imperfect knowledge and unjustified extrapolations. What clearly has to be established is whether the word 'modern' is merely a convenient label for a few centuries of history, or does not rather designate the metamorphosis of an entire culture, that is of our relations with each other and with our natural surroundings, and, consequently, of our conception of the divine.

'Modern', in fact, describes what followed a radical change, and applies as much to humankind as to its environment. The modern world is what followed the agrarian world; with it emerged a new world-view that was wholly unlike its predecessor. Modernity first changes humankind, then its world. A single meaning can therefore be given for the word modernity: it is a new logic of a new world-view. To be modern is to inhabit a world which is no longer that of yesterday and apprehension of which requires recourse to different methods.

It is important to note that this new world-view manifests itself in a number of fields, where the new logic produces structures which have nothing in common. Awareness of the changes occurring in each of them develops at different rhythms.

The four revolutions responsible for the passage to modernity are the following: scientific, political, cultural, and technical and industrial. Each of these revolutions occurs in stages, and it is perfectly possible to be more or less modern in each domain. Equally, experiencing one or more of these revolutions by no means implies experiencing all the others. These four revolutions can be examined as a whole if the purpose is simply to identify the components of modernity. It is quite another matter to identify the new logic and the intellectual changes it produces, though it is this shared logic that defines modernity from among the range of modernities. Our purpose here is simply to identify the places in which it occurs.

These four revolutions are interlinked but only loosely, and they affect each individual differently. Even when two domains are linked, it is possible to be modern in one and traditional in the other. Thus, one can be modern in politics yet be committed to a more traditional mode of production, for example. And the disparity can be greater still when the two domains are less interdependent. A scientist, for instance, may be modern in his or her own sphere of activity while remaining culturally traditional; a theologian may have accepted the cultural revolution while knowing nothing of the challenge to the logical foundations from the scientific revolution. The interplay of these different modernities, which affect different individuals at different speeds, becomes itself a political problem in modern society. And the problem is further complicated by the fact that one can be more or less modern in each of the spheres touched by a revolution occurring in stages. There have already been so many successive modern world-views, that some speak of postmodernity.

Evidently, the problem is that modernity as a cultural system, appeared definitive in the nineteenth century, but today is challenging its own foundations (Jeannière, 1987).

But can we speak of postmodernity? Is there a critical point in the contrasted history of these four distinct fields, and above all in the socio-cultural milieu produced by their interaction, which clearly points to a new beginning? Has a new world recently emerged, one as different from the modern world as the world of Newton and Einstein was different from the symbolic world of the medieval peasant?

Those who speak of postmodernity usually focus their attention on the cultural and industrial revolutions. They discern in the already lengthy history of these two revolutions an essential discontinuity between a before – modernity – and an after – postmodernity.

Though it cannot be dated with precision, the cultural break becomes clearly apparent around 1968. What is observed concerns primarily a transformation in values: anarchy is preferred to order, and play to organized activity, 'deconstruction' replaces creation, individual liberty takes precedence over collective values, and so on. The turning point in the economic domain is marked by the crisis of the 1970s. Industrial society becomes post-industrial, and the productive system based on Fordism gives way to post-Fordism. Technologies of information and communication invade the economy and the household. In the political realm, the welfare state declines, the communist states disappear; the liberal state and the free market economy dominate. It can also be said that postmodernity is characteristic of the transition from the certainty generated by a triumphant positivist science to a condition of generalized uncertainty.

In short, all who employ the term postmodernity agree that the contemporary world is experiencing an acute crisis. How realistic is it to speak of modernity when all the certainties that characterized modernity have collapsed, including in the scientific field? For the epistemology of the sciences is also undergoing a serious crisis, of which Paul Feyerabend (1979) is one of the best commentators. The crisis of scientific epistemology is certainly symptomatic of a far-reaching change. But does such a crisis, however deep and however widespread, necessarily herald a new historical era? Can it be that the crisis is too severe to fail to produce a new world-view? Perhaps ...

It is hard to say whether postmodernism does indeed correspond to an authentic change of episteme or paradigm in the Kuhnian sense of the term, and has been responsible for creating original forms, or whether it has merely recycled established procedures in a different context. Is there continuity or rupture with modernism, and if there is, is it in a positive or negative sense?

The logic of modernity is that of three great axes and of the constraints upon them: production-organization-power; its rhetoric is that of movements of change and experimentation, of tensions that favour the new and the untried. From the interaction and confrontation of these forces there resulted a crisis of representation, a blurring of existing norms, a fracturing within society and culture, which as a result became increasingly fragmented. And it was through the fissures thus opened up that the postmodernist current took hold in the 1960s and 1970s, from the outset demonstrating an affinity with contradiction which ultimately questioned its own credentials. How is it possible to be situated in the present time while at the same time transcending immediate modernity?

At the origin of this development was a criticism of the conventions, forms and aims which made up the theory and practice of architecture. The attack focused on the first generation of modernists, and in particular the founders of the Bauhaus – the great studio of the twentieth century – and all their followers. The rejection of tradition, the production of new forms and the systematic use of new materials, 'absolute functionalism' and the attempt to integrate all 'the activities of a place' were no longer accepted as rules. The process was described by C. Jencks (1986) as 'the inversion and partial modification of the established architectural language'. That phrase could appear moderate given the extent of the 'contradictions in architecture' which quickly became apparent. Particularly characteristic of postmodern architecture is its allusions to the past and its historical references. Exemplary in this respect is the new brand of religious architecture in the United States: this has broken with the 'authentically national' production which, until recently, was 'profoundly rational, empirical and utilitarian'; its allusions are to the medieval cathedrals, the basilicas of Renaissance Italy, and English country churches; it makes extensive use of religious symbolism and liturgical references. Its promoters – 'the architects of the metaphysical school' – are claimed to have opened the 'doors of a postmodern era coloured by romanticism'.

Postmodernist thought has been influential in the arts, culture in the broad sense, literature, and certain branches of social theory and philosophy. In its most theoretical version, it owes much to the negative dialectic of the Frankfurt School and the work of J. Habermas who, in a recent contribution, spoke of those 'who believe they have left behind them all the paradigms and entered the anarchist glade of postmodernity'. Habermas draws attention to the 'scepticism towards the grand theories and generalizations', and with regard to philosophy notes the development of a syncretism which leads to incorporating into knowledge 'sometimes hastily and with a simultaneousness unguided by choice ... what had hitherto been rejected'. J.-F. Lyotard contrasts a 'critical' modernity with a postmodernity that is 'more empirico-critical or pragmatic'. For Lyotard, postmodernism is to be seen as a 'state of mind', as a way of describing the social, cultural and intellectual changes since the turning point of the 1950s, which marked the end of the post-war period and opened a period of expansion in all fields of activity and generalized social change. This state of mind encourages rejection: be it of one-way representations of the world, of totalizing visions, of dogmas, and also of the effort to identify and articulate meaning. It manifests itself as an erosion of landmarks, a blurring of established ways of seeing and understanding, and a loss of confidence in theories. In Lyotard's view, the priority for philosophy is to avoid both the 'ambiant positivist pragmatism' and dogmatism. Both are hegemonic; for the moment the only solution is to operate by 'micrology'.

Postmodernism presents itself as a movement of deconstruction, intent on dismantling the hierarchy of knowledge and values, undermining all that gives meaning and all that has been erected as paradigm or model. It has been said that 'it explains nothing, while asserting that it is possible to live happily in a universe without explanation'. For its detractors, postmodernism represents a cynical brand of compromise and opportunism, a widespread and affected nihilism, an acceptance born of passivity and commonplace effects; it is content with ambiguity; and has nothing to contribute to a political or utopian programme. For its adepts, however, it stands for the liberation of expressive potential, for the free exercise of the creative urge; it favours a profusion of styles, an openness to experimentations that are multiple, disparate and indifferent to their place in posterity. An illustration of this last aspect is supplied by the rapid succession of movements of young painters. The 'Graffitistes' draw inspiration from the aggressive graffiti of the suburbs to produce a savage art that combines the naïve and the trivial. Incompleteness, incompetence and confusion are the techniques used by practitioners of 'Bad Painting' to reconstitute an image in its raw rate, provocatively indifferent to the criteria of realism. The 'New Expressionism' exploits violence, blackness, and unbounded derision and emotional force, playing with false grandeur, displaying affinities with the literature of horror stories and cruelty. The 'Trans-avant garde', in reaction to conceptual art, seeks to re-establish 'the sovereign exercise of painting' as a vehicle for anecdote and personal expression, associated with mythical and fantastical themes; according to the movement's founder, it has 'moved things' and shattered the unitary world-view by 'advocating a fragmentary vision and a nomadic experience'. The most recent of these movements, 'Anachronistic Painting', exploits tradition, making allusions to the great periods in art history and rediscovering neo-classicism and fantastical realism; it is a painting in which nostalgia is relieved by discrete humour.

This brief survey of new painting indicates many of the lines of fragmentation and recomposition that delineate modernity and postmodernity. The new directions in fiction are equally revealing. Over and above the thematic of ideals, ideologies and ambitions, there is a new emphasis on literary experiment, relating the experience of fragmented existences and employing an extreme mobility to convey the richness of events with self-confidence and irony. A certain continuity can be discerned linking modernity to postmodernity. The latter accentuates some aspects of the former, pushing its rhetoric to extremes. Both attest to an upheaval in social and cultural landscapes, to a breaking of the established bonds between individuals and their groups and their works, and to an attempt to identify the significant fragments of a future to be informed. They are attempts to explore spaces that are ill- or undefined, unknown or nearly unknown. They disorient. Ulysses' words on returning to Ithaca seem apposite at this point: 'what are the people whose land I have come to ... where shall I myself be driven?'

'Yet, if postmodernism is a historical phenomenon, then the attempt to conceptualize it in terms of moral or moralizing judgement must finally be identified as a category-mistake'

(Jameson, 1984).

In the space of 20 years, postmodernity has become one of the most widely used concepts in discussions about art, literature and social theory. The notion of 'postmodernity' is part of a whole network of concepts and modes of thought labelled with the 'post' prefix. A list of the most commonly cited includes: post-industrial society (Bell, 1973; Touraine, 1969), post-structuralism (Bonnet, 1989; Dews, 1987; Harland, 1987; Pratt, 1993), post-Fordism (Amin, 1994; Harvey, 1989), post-communism (Fejtö, 1992), post-Marxist (Peet, Watts, 1993), post-Christian (Poulat, 1994; Lambert, 1995), post-hierarchical

(Mills, 1994), post-bureaucratic (Heckscher, Donnellon, 1994), post-liberalism (Gray, 1993), post-development (Escobar, 1992), post-Freudian (Ameret et al., 1995), post-imperialism (Schuurman, 1993), post-philosophical (Fougeyrollas, 1994), post-urban (Kling et al., 1991), post-colonial (Harasym, 1990; Aschcroft et al., 1994), post-capitalist (Vakaloulis, 1994a). Many theories are 'modernized' by becoming 'post': post-modernized Simmel (Weinstein, 1993), post-Weberian industrial location (Scott, 1988; Benko, 1991), post-impasse theory (Schuurman, 1993), post-television culture (D'Agostino, Tafler, 1994), and post-Lazarsfeldian sociology (Pasquier, 1994), and even public administration and marketing have become postmodern (Fox, Miller, 1995, Brown S., 1995). Postmodernity has been coupled with feminism (Bondi, 1990; Nicholson, 1990; Soper, 1990), ecology (Beck, 1992; Ferry, 1992), environmental problems (Gandy, 1996), religion (Bhatt, 1996; Gellner, 1992), planning (Dear, 1986, 1991; Soja, 1993), space (Bonnet, 1992; Harvey, 1990). Geography, sociology, philosophy, literature, architecture, the plastic arts – have all entered their postmodern period. As the twentieth century draws to its close, the term 'post' has become unavoidable. An atmosphere of crisis and renewal hangs over the social sciences, arts and philosophy.

It is hardly surprising that the term 'post-' is ambiguous in all these contexts. Is it not simply 'after' that is meant? That term can imply continuity or change. But if it is continuity that is meant, why use a prefix and a new term? Objectively, it separates; yet semantically it fails to establish a difference. Continuity and rupture are evoked simultaneously. An authentic break with the past would have a name of its own. 'Post-' is suggestive of the continuous, and the linear.

Postmodern. In modernity's mythology of change, to break from the past is the modern act *par excellence*. So, to break with the modern, the postmodern has to repeat the modern.

As an umbrella term for a wide variety of tendencies, postmodern suffers from a definitional imprecision that reflects its heterogeneous content (elliptical, cryptic, partial and transient etc.). As one of the leading theorists of postmodernism has explained, it is an 'equivocal, disjunctive category, doubly modified by the impetus of the phenomenon itself as by the shifting perceptions of its critics' (Portoghesi, 1982).

The origins of the term remain unclear. Ihab Hassan has reminded us that 'Frederico de Onis used the word *postmodernismo* in his *Antologia de la poesia espanola e hispanoericana* (1882–1932) published in Madrid in 1934; and Duelly Fitts picked it up again in his *Anthology of contemporary Latin-American poetry* of 1942. Both meant thus to indicate 'a minor reaction to modernism already latent within it, reverting to the early 20th century' (Hassan, 1982: 260–1). The term also appeared in Arnold Toynbee's *A Study of History* as early as D C Somervell's first volume abridgement in 1947. For Toynbee, Postmodernism designated a new historical cycle in Western civilization, starting about 1875, which we now scarcely begin to discern.

Daniel Charles (1985:138) has found the term used by the English painter Chapman who, in 1880, defined himself as 'postmodern', by which he understood 'more modern', modern in a different way, as compared to the French impressionists. Wolfgang Welsch (1988) has noted the use of the adjective 'postmodern' by the German writer Rudolf Pannwitz, a 'nietzscheist' of the start of the present century, who in a text written in 1917 proclaimed: 'Postmodern man, toughened by sports, trained militarily, and fired by metaphysics, is a hardshelled creature, an equal mix of decadent and barbarian, swept along on the outpourings from the fertile vortex of the final decadence of the radical revolution of European nihilism'.

It was in the mid-1960s, however, with the growth of a climate hostile to modernism throughout the Western world, that the term 'postmodern' came into general use, albeit unevently (Habermas, 1981b: 965). Artistic and intellectual currents now began to conflict with the established modernist positions, invading architecture, theatre, cinema, music and dance, philosophy, psychoanalysis, theology and historiography, literature and literary criticism, and lastly cybernetics, science and epistemology.

The problem common to all these fields, however, can be formulated as follows: is this change limited to the *emergence* of a new constellation of ideas, combined with new aesthetic practices? Or is it not evidence of an authentic revolution initiating an epoch marked by the rule of simulacrum and the near total derealization of the world ('and end of the world without tragedy' as Baudrillard has formulated it)? Indeed, what are the phenomena of which postmodernity is the translation? A series of propositions suggests itself:

1 A change in the social function of the cultural sphere, an inflation of the aesthetic form which completely invades the social practices of everyday life (the *Image Ridden World*)?
2 The decline in the self-legitimating power of speculative narratives, the implosion of the idea of progress, and the obsolescence of a unitary representation of a subject as the sole bases for the production of meaning?
3 Political and social changes of historic dimensions, namely the new phase of social modernization of the capitalist system and the consequent increase in the tensions of global modernity?

Postmodernism embraces all these phenomena. It combines a *cultural logic* which favours relativism and diversity, a set of *intellectual processes* which provide extremely fluid and dynamic structures of meaning to the world, in contrast to the modern categorization of the world, and lastly a *configuration of social traits* which signifies the development of a movement of fundamental change within the modern condition (crisis of productive systems and rise in unemployment, demise of historicity before the atemporality of the ephemeral, crisis of modern individualism and omnipresence of narcissistic mass culture etc.). In other words, the postmodern condition evokes a cultural complex, an intellectual change within Western humanism, and a particular historical experience, which is rooted in turn in a specific historical context. In particular, it is the expression of an overt reconciliation with the world of commodity fetishism, a freeing from guilt about the contradictions of modernity, even the *tradition of the 'exhaustion' of the modern heritage*.

This pluridimensional presence precludes a *unified* meaning for the post-modern. The postmodern appears confused, a prisoner of its imbricated semantic sedimentations; it appears variously as a cultural tonic for post-industrial society, a 'radical' version of 'post-history' or an intellectual configuration loosely linked with poststructuralism etc. Its usefulness as a chronological and typological schema is in consequence diminished.

Umberto Eco (1985) argues that the postmodern is not a tendency to which chronological limits can be attached, but rather a spiritual category, or rather a *Kunstwollen*, a way of doing. It could be said that every epoch has its postmodern, just as each epoch will have its mannerism (so much so that I wonder if postmodern is not the modern word for mannerism as a metahistorical category).

Eco goes on to give a critical defence of postmodernity. The postmodern response to modernity involves recognizing that, because the past cannot be destroyed, because its destruction would produce silence, it must be revisited; but in an ironical, not innocent way. Eco illustrates what he has in mind by an example from everyday life and literature. He draws an analogy between the postmodern attitude and that of someone in love with a highly cultured woman who knows that he cannot say 'I am desperately in love with you' because he knows that she knows (and she knows that he knows) that these words have already been written by Barbara Cartland. A solution exists, however: he can say: 'As Barbara Cartland would say, I am desperately in love with you'. In this way, while avoiding false innocence, by stating clearly that it is impossible to speak in an innocent way, he will nonetheless have told the woman what he wanted to tell her: that he loves her and that he loves her in an epoch of lost innocence. If the women plays the game, she will accept this as a declaration of love. Neither interlocutor will feel innocent, both will have accepted the challenge of the past, that of what has already been said and cannot be eliminated, both will have played consciously and with pleasure in the game of irony ... And both will have managed once again to speak of love.

In contrast to Eco, the American neomarxist critic Frederic Jameson (1991), seeks to identify postmodernism as an historically well-defined stage in the evolution of systems of thought and analyses the change in relation to modernist thought. As cultural dominant of the logic of late capitalism, postmodernism is characterized by its critique of 'deep models': the dialectical model of essence and appearance, and its concepts of ideology and false consciousness; the existentialist model of authenticity or lack of authenticity, based on the opposition between alienation and disalienation. And lastly the great semiological opposition between signifier and signified which dominated the 1960s and 1970s.

What has taken its place is a 'surface model' or rather a 'multiple surfaces model'. According to Jameson, the world is loosing its depth and is in danger of turning into a brilliant surface, a stereoscopic illusion, a flow of film-like images lacking in density. Signalling the triumph of space over time and the disappearance of the sense of history, this surface model is in phase with the new scale of the global expansion of transnational capital, its instantaneous movement through electronic networks, and the flow of images that are both universal and fragmented.

For Jameson, postmodernism reinforces the logic of capitalism, by denying the autonomy of art which offered, as Adorno argued, the last guarantee of independence from bourgeois, commercial culture. Postmodernism has abandoned modernism's subversive and critical stance, in favour of an uncomplicated cohabitation with post-industrial society. Jameson does, it is true, admit the possibility that postmodernism may also defy the logic of capitalism, though without specifying how.

Gianni Vattimo also discerns a strong link between postmodern theory and, if not Baudelaire, at least the critiques of classical philosophy represented by the Nietzschean doctrine of eternal recurrence and by Heidegger's 'going beyond' of metaphysics. The essential feature of postmodernity is in fact the denial of what is the modern notion *par excellence*, that of 'going beyond', just as Nietzsche and Heidegger challenged European thought 'while refusing to offer a critical "going beyond" which would have imprisoned us within its own logic of development'. For Vattimo (1987), postmodernity thus represents a genuine turning point in relation to modernity: 'The "post-" in post-modern in fact indicates a new departure which, by attempting to avoid the logics of development of modernity, and in particular the idea of a critical "going beyond" towards a new foundation, continues the efforts of Nietzsche and Heidegger in their "critical" relation with western thought.'

Of all the theorists of the postmodern, Vattimo appears to accord it the greatest philosophical value, that of a taking leave of modernity, not by a 'going beyond' or a renewal, but, as he puts it, by an 'overcoming', in the sense of recovering from an illness. In this perspective, postmodernity is not just another crisis among those that have punctuated the history of modernity, the latest of the modern negations, the most recent episode in modernism's revolt against itself; but rather the actual conclusion of the modern adventure, the awareness that the 'modern project', to use Habermas's term, will never be finished. Yet the end of the belief in progress does not automatically mean an apocalyptic descent into irrationality. Postmodernity, according to Vattimo, is a 'weak thought'; it offers no more than a different way of conceptualizing the relations between tradition and innovation, one in which originality is not systematically favoured over imitation. A whole series of modern dichotomies now loose their sharpness: new–old, present–past, left–right, progress–reaction, abstraction–figuration, modernism–realism, avant-garde–kitsch. The postmodern mind also makes it possible to reinterpret the modern tradition, without having to see it in terms of the conveyor-belt image and the great adventure of the new. And with the Messianic vision discarded, so become apparent the contradictions, the role played by chance, and all the obstacles thrown up by modernism to its own forward march. That the teleological interpretation of modernism has been abandoned does not mean that 'everything is good'; just that a work can no longer be rejected on the grounds that it is outdated or retrograde. If the orthodox modernist view of art as heading inexorably, through successive critical leaps, towards an apotheosis of abstraction, is no longer acceptable, then we enjoy a degree of liberty unprecedented in the last 100 years or so. Such freedom is not, it seems, easy to exploit.

II

I would argue that something of the notion of modernity has been swept away by the postmodern current. The main interest of postmodernity may reside ultimately in the fact that it is no longer possible to speak of modernity without asking oneself questions.

The idea of modernity dominated thinking only up to the construction of industrial society. The rejection of the past and the absolute confidence in the power of reason gave the image of modern society a force and consistency which were quickly to disappear when hope was replaced by experience, when the new society was no longer merely the other face of that one sought to destroy or replace but had become reality (Touraine, 1988).

The history of modernity is that of the emergence of social and cultural actors who increasingly lost faith in modernity as the concrete definition of good. The first to reject modernity, following the examples of Nietzsche and Freud, were the intellectuals; and the most influential current of modern thought, from Horkheimer and the Frankfurt School to Michel Foucault, has always been highly critical of a modernity it saw as responsible for isolating the intellectuals in what they referred to contemptuously as mass society. In addition to the intellectuals, however, sometimes in a sense that echoed their criticisms, but more often very remote from them, an increasingly important role was occupied by the nation states, whose struggles for their independence, history and identity dominated the twentieth century in the modernized world in much the same way that the class struggle had dominated the nineteenth century. Later to come on the scene was the enterprise, first in the United States, then in Japan and in Europe, developing into an actor whose power sometimes exceeded that of the nation state, thus becoming authentic centres of political decision-making rather than mere economic agents. Finally, starting in the United States, then in Europe and subsequently in Japan, there developed mass consumption, followed by mass communication, which opened public life to realms of desire, imagination and sensuality that modern rationalism had hitherto rejected or repressed. As long as instrumental rationality established a network of relations between these social and cultural actors, however, modernity remained intact, and we can speak of industrial society and even of neo- or hyper-industrial society. The importance of techniques in the functioning of most modern societies enabled them to respond to the threat of disintegration by combining technical training with defence of a certain asceticism; their strongest defence came from the school which, especially in France, was seen as the champion of Enlightenment reason before, in its turn, being overwhelmed by the resurgence of what the post-revolutionary bourgeoisie had eliminated during its long period in power.

At what point did the disintegration of modernity become complete rather than partial? When the universe of instrumental rationality became totally divorced from that of the social and cultural actors. Sex, consumption, enterprises and nations were now free to evolve in any direction, rather like icebergs after the break up of the ice floe, moving apart, colliding, moving together again for a while. More specifically, we can be said to have emerged from modernity when a behaviour or form of social organization is no longer defined according to its place on a tradition–modernity axis or, as it is usually described for the less modernized countries, on an underdeveloped–developed axis. Awareness of this coming-out of modernity has increased steadily since at least 1968. Social facts are no longer explained by their place in a history which has a meaning and direction; spontaneous social thought, ideologies and the prevailing ethos have abandoned all historical references. This is in fact the main meaning of the postmodernism theme which is, above all, a post-historicism.

Two responses are possible to this crisis of the classical idea of modernity and of modernist ideology: the first, which is that of the postmoderns, argues that the process of decomposition is irreversible; the second holds that modernity can and must be defended and even extended. Before considering these positions, we must go to the end of the path which runs from the classical idea of modernity to its crisis, decomposition and, ultimately, disappearance. Following Alain Touraine (1992), we can say that postmodernity has four main axes of thought, representing the different types of breaks from modernist ideology.

1—The first defines postmodernity as a *hypermodernity*, in the same way that Daniel Bell defined post-industrial society as hyper-industrial. The movement of modernity accelerates ever faster, the avant-gardes become increasingly ephemeral and, as Jean-François Lyotard observes, all cultural production becomes avant-garde by an increasingly frenetic consumption of languages and signs. Modernity consumes itself. Baudelaire defined modernity as 'the presence of the eternal in the instant', in opposition to the idealism of cultures intent on extracting eternal truths from the grubbiness of everyday experience and emotion; a century later, however, it seems to be a prisoner of the instant and caught in the increasingly complete elimination of meaning. What is left is a kaleidoscopic culture which, while it does not abandon modernity, reduces it to the production of technical improvements the sole interest of which resides in a novelty and technical virtuosity that are rapidly outdated.

2— Very different – though easily complementary – is the critique, not of technical modernism but of the social and political modernism responsible for inventing countermodels of societies the realization of which supposed such a radical break with the past that the action of an absolute power was needed to bring it about. As was pointed out earlier, the idea of revolution has always been closely associated with that of modernity. The intellectual success of postmodernism at the end of the 1970s was a direct result of the crisis of revolutionary leftism. The neo-liberalism that triumphed in economics and politics during the 1980s and cultural postmodernism are in fact parallel products of the disintegration of leftism. This was an extreme form of modernism, especially as exemplified by the Trotskyists who, since the start of the Soviet revolution, had cultivated the Utopia of the central machine, which became the central plan, and more recently the central computer, whereby the government of people was to be transformed into the administration of things, thus liberating them from the damaging consequences of the political subjectivism embodied by Stalin and Hitler. The clearest example in France of this transition from leftist criticism to the postmodernist criticism of leftism, and even to the negation of the social domain, is that of Jean Baudrillard.

3 — The hyper-modernist and antimodernist approaches can produce a radical departure from modernity, but it may be in opposing directions. The most frequently encountered is the break from historicism, that is, when cultural forms no longer exist in succession but simultaneously. A work holding strong religious and social significance for a traditional society has to coexist in our museums and in our imaginations alongside an example of pure abstraction, a direct expression of an emotion, and a work charged with commercial or political significance. Not because all are expressions of eternal values, but because nothing enables us to choose between experiences, all of which, claims Habermas, must be accepted when they possess a certain authenticity. This cultural pluralism, this return to a polytheism mixed with atheism, pushes to the extreme the idea that Weber took from Kant: if modernity is based on the separation of essences and phenomena, and if technical and scientific action is confined exclusively to the latter sphere, our cultural and political space is necessarily polytheist, since the unicity of the rational explanation of phenomena is dissociated from a world of the gods which no longer has any unifying principle. Postmodernism here becomes post-historicism, which is its main meaning and the source of its importance.

4 — But once cultural works are divorced from the historical context in which they appeared, their value can be defined only by the *market*. Hence the new importance assumed by the art market, in contrast to the traditional situation in which works of art were selected either by monarchs or by amateurs who represented the cultural demands of the aristocracy and bourgeoisie. This takes us back to our analysis of liberal society and the victory of two of the elements of fragmented modernity, the enterprise and consumption, over the other two, sex and the nation-state; a victory therefore of movement and change over Being.

The postmodernist movement pushes the destruction of the modernist representation of the world to the extreme. It rejects the functional differentiation between the different domains of social life – art, the economy, politics – and its corollary, the use by each of instrumental reason. In so doing it rejects the distinction between high culture, be it social, political or aesthetic, which expresses the metasocial foundations of the social order – reason, history, modernization, emancipation of the working class – and mass culture. Hence the strong 'anti-aesthetic' content stressed by Frederic Jameson [especially in the book edited by Hal Foster (1983), *The Anti-Aesthetic*]. At an even deeper level, what is rejected is the construction of images of the world, to use the term that Heidegger believed to be the most significant in modernity. Postmodern thought refuses to place humankind before the world, to observe it, reproducing humanity in images; instead it puts humanity in the world, with no distance between them, or rather replacing this distance, which assumes the existence of the object, by the construction of a network of communications, of a language between painter, architect, or writer, and objects.

This evocation of a new system of historical action, that of the programmed society, with its actors, its social movements, the cultural dimensions of their conflicts and negotiations, is far removed from the images of our society that are currently dominant, those associated with the idea of postmodernism. This leads me to identify what distinguishes this idea from the post-industrial or programmed society. Postmodernism proclaims the complete dissociation of system and actor: the system is self-referential, *autopoétique* (*self-poetical*) according to Luhman, and the actors are defined not by social relations but by a cultural difference. While I do not deny that these analyses correspond to a part of the reality, they are as misleading as the early nineteenth-century descriptions of industrial society as the rule of money and merchandise. What had yet to be defined as the working class was represented as the alien or sublime world of the *faubourgs*, workshops and wineshops, in which capital and labour appeared to occupy wholly distinct realms. Only with the development of trade unions and socialist ideas were the relations of production that lay behind these extreme differences recognized. Contemporary society has such a high degree of control over itself and over its historicity that the possibility does indeed exist of a cultural break which leaves no scope for social conflict. But the opposite evolution is more likely. Our society is referred to as an information society, just as it used to be described as an industrial society or the machine age. How much longer is it going to take to rediscover that behind the techniques there are human beings and social relations, and to recognize that information and communication can be used and organized in socially opposing ways, either 'abstractly' to reinforce those flows of information which are also flows of money and power, or 'concretely' to promote dialogue between actors who occupy unequal positions in the relations of power and authority.

More than anything else, I see postmodern ideas offering a sociologically superficial interpretation of changes which, in fact, call for analyses that are closer to, not radically different from, those employed for industrial society. In my view, the phenomena emphasized by postmodern thought are more akin to crisis situations than to lasting innovations. Consider, for example, the extreme differentiation of the political and social systems described by Luhman: is this not symptomatic of the crisis of political representation that is widely recognized and which will be resolved only when new social demands have been organized and our democracies made representative again? Similarly, the call for absolute difference is merely a crisis behaviour when not accompanied by recognition of social conflicts and their cultural dimensions.

We are living through the transition from one society to another. Most of the nineteenth century was taken up with the transition from a mercantile society to an industrial society, and from the republican spirit to the working-class movement. Luhman rightly reminds us that a society cannot be defined by just one of its dimensions: industrial, capitalist or democratic. This is true today, but it was also true in the past.

The main interest of this debate lies in reminding us that the idea of the subject is indissociable from that of social relations. In the programmed society, the individual, reduced to the status of consumer, human resource or target, opposes the dominant logic of the system by asserting himself or herself as a subject, against the world of things and against the objectivation of his or her needs by market forces. This is why the idea of the subject cannot be separated from an analysis of present-day society, not as postmodern but as post-industrial or programmed. Postmodern theories show us the decomposition of the subject, but also the growing demands of minorities as well as the development of cybernetic systems. Instead of considering only the mutual alienness of these two phenomena, however, why not consider the conflict between them, since neither is defined in isolation, technologically or culturally; each must be defined socially, and more specifically by their opposition to each other.

No upheavals! Just vogues

The heroes of post-modernity, be they painters, architects or philosophers, are all agreed that the crises currently afflicting social and artistic practices can now lead only to an unqualified rejection of any large-scale collective project. Let us all get on with our own business, preferrably using the same standards and practices as our contemporaries. No upheavals! Just vogues, shaped by the markets in art and opinion via advertising campaigns and opinion polls.

But what are the grounds for the view that the 'socius' can thus be reduced to matters of language and these in turn to signifying chains in binary and 'digital' form? On this point the post-moderns are scarcely original but belong squarely in the highly modernist tradition of structuralism, whose influence on the social sciences appears to have been relayed in the worse conditions by Angle-Saxon systems theory. The secret link between all these doctrines, it seems to me, lies in the fact is that they have all been underground – influenced by simplistic views and vehicled in the immediate post-war period by information theory and early research in cybernetics. The conclusions repeatedly drawn from the new technologies of communication and information were so hasty and so ill-conceived, that they represent a major regression on earlier phenomenological research.

We have to get back to a simple but far-reaching truth, namely that concrete social arrangements – not to be confused with the 'primary groups' of American sociology which have yet to acquire objective form – involve far more than linguistic exploits. There are ethological and ecological dimensions, semiotic, economic, aesthetic, corporal, fantasmic components that cannot be reduced to the semiology of language, a multitude of incorporal universes of reference, which are not easily accommodated by the dominant empiricity ...

The post-modern philosophers may well undertake pragmatic research, they remain faithful to a structuralist conception of speech and language with which it will never be possible to articulate subjective facts to the formations of the unconscious, to aesthetic and micro-political problematics. Not to beat about the bush, I don't think this philosophy is in fact a philosophy; merely a prevailing state of mind, a 'condition' of opinion whose ideas are drawn from the mood of the time. Why, for example, take the trouble to produce a serious speculative argument for its hypothesis about the inconsistence of the 'socius'? Doesn't the current omnipotence of the mass-media largely make up for a demonstration that any social link can be used, with no obvious resistance, for the desingularising and infantilizing destruction of capitalistic productions of the signifier. The old Lacanian saying that 'a signifier represents the subject for another signifier' could well stand as the motto for this new ethic of noncommital. For that's where we've ended up! Contrary to what the postmoderns seem to believe, however, this is really no reason to get excited. Indeed, the question is rather to find a way out of such a dead end!

Félix Guattari (1986).

III

And then there was Lyotard ... He was the first to describe the intellectual crisis caused by philosophy as 'postmodern'. What does this magic word mean for him? *The Postmodern Condition*, his most widely read text and, probably, the least understood for what it is (a sociological report rather than a philosophical analysis) says roughly this: because philosophy can no longer legitimate the pragmatics of political and juridical discourse, the natural sciences or the arts – the analytical vocabulary of the linguistic turning-point that Lyotard uses here is symptomatic of this legitimacy crisis which is ultimately a crisis of meta-physical thought of the platonic or Cartesian variety – it provokes an intellectual crisis that disorients all fields of human activity. The question now is to know where to find legitimacy.

Lyotard's elaboration of the notion of the postmodern begins as a reworking of what, in the critical theory of the Frankfurt School, is known as the dialectic of enlightenment. Thus it shares the shortcomings common to all theories based on the logical Manicheism of reason and its Other. The dialectic of enlightenment operates on a pair of concepts: reason and myth. For Lyotard, postmodernity is identified with a generalized state of crisis in the legitimacy of knowledge, a destabilization of the governing social theories. He distinguishes two theoretical models which were, until recently, dominant, one organic, the other dialectical: functionalist sociology, or systems theory, and Marxism. But these models have become intertwined and mutually neutralized; class struggle has been integrated as a regulatory principle of liberal capitalism, while communist societies strove to reduce differences in the name of Marxism. The master narrative of emancipating humanity and winning freedom has ceased to provide a source of unification and legitimacy: this was the discourse of progress and of the Enlightenment which had been ascendant since the eighteenth century. Beyond its aesthetic aspects, postmodernity re-examines the thought of the Enlightenment but without accepting the idea of a single meaning to history, and challenging the rationalist ideal by pointing to its disastrous effects in modern experience, including Nazism.

Lyotard does not hesitate to use the most orthodox narrative of the modern tradition to explain the ambivalence he sees as inherent to the postmodern. In 1982 he wrote:

> So what then is the postmodern? What place does it or does it not occupy in the great task of the questions posed to the rules of image and narrative? It is certainly part of the modern. All that comes from the past, even if only from yesterday (*modo, modo*, wrote Pétrone), must be challenged. What space did Cézanne attack? That of the Impressionists. What object did Picasso and Braque attack? That of Cézanne. From what presupposition did Duchamp break in 1912? That it was necessary to produce a painting, even a cubist painting. And Buren challenges another presupposition he believes the work of Duchamp has left intact: the place in which the work of art can be represented. With an astonishing acceleration, the 'generations' are rushing by. A work cannot become modern unless it is first of all postmodern. Postmodernism in this sense is not modernism at its end, but in its nascent state, and this state if constant.

A few lines later, Lyotard (1982) adds that he will not be satisfied with this 'somewhat mechanical meaning of the word', which is something of an understatement, in that it contains the dogma of evolution without any qualification. Lyotard goes further. If modernity is the refusal of realism, bounded only by the limits of the presentable and conceivable, then he says 'the postmodern would be that which, in the modern, puts forward the unpresentable in presentation itself: that which denies itself the solace of good forms [...] *Postmodern* would have to be understood according to the paradox of the future (*post*) anterior (*modo*). It seems to me that the essay (Montaigne) is postmodern, whereas the fragment (the Athenaeum) is modern'. The postmodern conceives itself as the true modern, as the realization of the still unrealized potential of the modern, and thus as yet another 'going beyond' towards the essence of art.

Postmodern philosophy respects the incommensurability of the games, prevents the encroachment or excess of one on the other, by maintaining the right distance, the 'abyss' which exists between each of the language games. This preoccupation is inspired not just by Wittgenstein but, still more clearly, by Kant. It is that of the Kantian 'critique' as the judge of a 'court' which rules on the 'territory' or 'domain' in which phrases and language games are validated. In another sense: 'Being just means making a hypothesis about what is to be done'. This 'hypothesis' supposes 'an idea and a practice of justice which is not that of consensus' (Lyotard, 1979). Consequently it requires a 'policy of judgement' (Lyotard, Thébaud, 1979), the programmatic outline of which ends *The Postmodern Condition*. This policy implies that the infinity of history, time and the Idea are to be judged according to the 'imagination of effects' (Lyotard, Thébaud, 1979), in short that 'judgement precedes all rules' (Lyotard, 1981). In these conditions, the act of judging is a political and not just a juridical faculty. It is hence the entire Kantian problematic which is re-examined by Lyotard.

He considers the concept of the sublime to belong to the postmodernity whose characteristics he was one of the first to describe (Lyotard, 1979). In the postmodern condition, the judgement of taste is replaced by the sense of the sublime. Experience, in the Hegelian sense, gives way to experimentation. The artist and the philosopher, partners in experimentation, invent using words, colours and sounds, or sentences and the rules of their structure. They both 'play' with a displeasure combined with satisfaction, with the effort of presenting what is unpresentable and unlimited in thought. Contemporary painting presents only the invisible, never the accepted reality or absence of reality: there is, says Lyotard, an 'unpresentable' for thought (the absolute, infinite, etc.). His studies of the work of contemporary artists reveal how the end of experience and the question of time are central to postmodern painting as they are to capitalism (Lyotard, 1984): the postmodern painter paints in monochrome or, by colour, on the contrary, 'constitutes time'. The aesthetic of the sublime that is with everything is thus in constant conflict based closely or loosely on the real world, realism and reality. The subjugation of thought to ends other than its own, to an assumed unique and unitary finality of history or of the subject, to a present or future given, is heavy with the threat of the Terror. None of the participants in the confrontation (*agôn*) of sentences and language games is authorized to inflict a 'blow', to employ 'even indirectly or even symbolically, the death threat towards his audience' (Lyotard, 1973). It is doubtless a feature of the postmodern condition that the act of thinking is equated with 'making sentences'. To think is to produce and string together sentences. It is to seek the rule 'without already being able to state what this rule says' (Lyotard, 1981). It is also to mark the incommensurability of sentences, of the 'abyss' which separates them, and to take the side of the *différend*. The outline of an ontology can be discerned: no longer the 'being-in-the-world' of the phenomenologists, but the 'being-with-sentences which is not a being-as, nor a being-together, nor again a being-without' (Lyotard, 1981).

IV

Ecology and modernity. The wave of ecological movements continues to grow throughout the world. The demise of strong political ideologies has been accompanied by an extraordinary increase in the search for authenticity and individual identity. A singular feature of the ecological movement is that it is the first political movement to believe that it is our duty to be afraid of the future and, above all, of our inability to turn the clock back. Parallel to this, is an awareness of the global dimension of environmental problems such as the greenhouse effect, nuclear disasters, pollution.

Ecology is not a homogenous movement. It contains three main currents, which have in common a critical attitude towards *modernity*. A right- (and even extreme-right) wing current which claims to represent a lost past: the quasi-romantic myth of the golden age, of cultural diversity, of rural society, of humanity living in harmony with nature. Their discourse plays on an ambiguous register by qualifying materials as 'stateless' which therefore do not harmonize with the natural framework. Unconsciously, they valorize membership of the national entity. A number of similar themes is present in the ideology of the second ecological current, that of the extreme left, which was dominant in France in the 1960s, and exemplified by the Parti Socialiste Unifie (PSU). They claim inspiration from Félix Guattari and his book *Les Trois Ecologies* (1989). In place of the one-dimensional and universal capitalist world denounced by Marcuse (1964), they advocate a new diversity for individuals and lifestyles. Their analysis goes further: the destruction of the environment is the result of the free market economy and the liberal society, and thus of the democracy of which these are the expressions. Both the extreme right and extreme left currents in ecology challenge, more or less explicitly, the foundations of Western society. Their analyses focus not on man with a capital M, the universal man of the *Declaration of the Rights of Man*, but on the concrete individual situated in a specific context: such as the Breton, the Corsican, though also women, blacks, immigrants; even Nature itself. Michel Serres, taking up the ideas developed in the United States by the 'deep ecologists', has defended the idea that nature (forests, valleys, animals, etc.) has rights, just as humanity has. A transition is being formed from an anthropocentric vision of the world to an ecocentrist vision. When Serres (1990) calls for the social contract to be replaced by a natural contact, he is in effect arguing for an end to the humanist tradition in which humankind is the only subject for law, and for acceptance of the idea that nature itself can be considered as a partner in a contract and thus as a subject for law. These ecologists offer no consistent policy or model, simply a central idea: that the present evolution must be stopped at all cost. In the 1970s in Germany, Hans Jonas (1990) in *The responsibility principle* argued that the methods available to liberal democracy are ineffective to control technology, the source of all the problems, and that an authoritarian control is necessary. Others, from Dany Cohn-Bendit to Cornélius Castoriadis and Félix Guattari, continue to put their faith in the fantasy of auto-gestion.

The third current in ecology accepts the democratic system, advocates harnessing science to offset the negative effects of science and technology, and wants to see democracy integrate ecology at every level of decision-taking. The political discourse of this current remains vague and combines elements of the other two currents. Generally speaking, this part of the ecologist movement does not contest the advantages of the welfare state, and while the industrial world is criticized, there is no suggestion that we should abandon air travel, health care, modern communications, in short all that technology has to offer. This is what accounts for the complexity of this tendency, because it embraces many disparate elements and draws on both modernity and postmodernity.

Ecology is a reaction to the crisis currently being experienced by the industrial societies, as is confirmed by the fact that ecological protests are heard only in these societies. In all its various forms, ecology is the expression of a sense of emptiness specific to the liberal industrial democracies of the West. What are the sources of this feeling? Does it stem from the 'democratic melancholia, that the philosopher Pascal Bruckner has linked to the collapse of totalitarianism which has left democracies without enemies? From the decline of the great ideologies which had hitherto supplied powerful ideals? From the lack of a grand scheme? From a heightened form of individualism? From the decline of traditional and 'secular' (that is, political) religions? Whatever the explanation, if ecology as a whole is the response to a sense of emptiness, it is clear that each current within ecology has its own critique of modernity.

V

Space, place, non-place, hypermodernity, globalization ... much effort has gone into explaining, often in a very technical way, the contemporary transformation of places; a modernity pushed to the extreme, towards a hypermodernity or *surmodernité*. A journey beyond the modern, beyond place.

Space can be apprehended as a category and as a material reality. For philosophers it is a principle of understanding, one of the forms of knowledge, a tool of theory on a level with time, to which of course it is linked. Sociologists consider space in a double light, as a product of society and as a factor of social production. In its relationship with space, by the work of present and past generations, humankind creates places. For their part, anthropologists have concentrated their attention on the most qualified spaces, to which they ascribe a triple function: identificatory, relational and historical. In its active relationship with space, hypermodernity can be envisaged from three standpoints regarding its most significant effects: dequalification, derealization, and virtualization. Derealization corresponds to mobility, to networks, to a 'counter-space'; virtualization is responsible for a rupture, blurring the distinction between the real and the virtual real, which is the hallmark of the universe of televirtuality. Dequalification is applied to spaces that have a low specificity. Non-places illustrate the counter-type of the anthropological place, presented by Marc Augé (1992). Non-places combine the characteristics of those spaces which people simply move through and of imposing a form of behaviour on their users that can be described as machine-like, reducing individuals to the status of operators.

What is a geography of nowhere? It is, of course, the opposite of somewhere, that is of a place or of a milieu. (Indeed, in French it might even be described as 'mi-lieu', that is half place, half non-place). It is a space devoid of the symbolic expressions of identity, relations and history: examples include airports, motorways, anonymous hotel rooms, public transport ... Never before in the history of the world have non-places occupied so much space. But we are not dealing with a contrast between a good place, human, and a bad non-place, dehumanized. Living in a small village, where everyone is watching you, is not always a pleasant experience. A place can have too much 'soul'. This 'soul' shapes the milieu, and the results can be oppressive. Conversely, a non-place is not necessarily unpleasant. Waiting in an airport lounge for one's flight can be an occasion for calm reflection.

On the side of place, there is meaning, but also non-liberty or constraint. On the side of non-places, there is an individual liberty which can reach absurd levels and produce a loss of identity. When nationalists speak of cosmopolitanism, they are setting places against non-places, that is against the spaces of movement. Having said that, non-places can occur in inappropriate contexts. The salespeople in supermarkets and garage forecourt attendants are also elements in day-to-day social contact. Similarly, many people prefer to go to a café rather than drink their coffee in front of a vending machine!

These spaces belong to the second half of the twentieth century. Speed, transport (Virilio, 1993, 1995), the globalization of trade, circulation, consumerism – are all responsible for the production of interchangeable places, identical throughout the world, through which people move without stopping and without meeting anyone. The examples are legion: motorways, turnpikes, giant car-parks, airports, automatic dispensers (money, drinks, tickets, etc.), shopping centres, supermarkets, multiple and brandname stores (Benetton, Lacoste, Hugo Boss, Ralph Lauren, etc.), hotel and restaurant chains (Novotel, Hilton, MacDonalds, etc) … People move past each other in airports and hypermarkets without there being any communication between them. A latter-day Jules Verne would not write *Around the World in Eighty Days* – his traveller would really have to slow down – but *Around the World Without a Word*. It would be safe to bet that the hero could go around the world in 72 hours and without having a conversation. A smile, perhaps, or some rudeness, being all that is necessary.

The logic of the economy does not escape the logic of 'nowhere'. Companies also make use of these spaces that are free of history (in every sense of the word). Companies are attracted to distant suburbs by economic considerations (tax reductions, an easing of planning and ground-use restrictions), and today they are moving out beyond the public transport networks to the zones called 'Nowherevilles'. The phenomenon was described by Garreau in 1992 (quoted by Galletti, 1992) in his work on the shift of companies to what he dubbed 'nowheres'. One such 'nowhere' is '287/78', a zone one hour west of Wall Street in a lightly wooded area of New Jersey, which takes its name from the interstate highways 287 and 78 which intersect at this point. These road links encouraged a number of big American companies to abandon the disadvantages of the city centre (land prices, congestion and other diseconomies) for recently created wider spaces. The zone '287/78', for example, has more buildings than the centre of New Orleans, and firms installed there include Johnson & Johnson, A.T.&T and Bristol Myers. In his 1992 report, Jérôme Galletti shows that the strength of such spaces lies in responding to the needs of the motor car, the jet plane and the computer. What confers identity on these 'Edge Cities' is in fact a function, not the visual image of a well-defined urban centre and tall buildings. The connotations of 'nowhere' would thus seem to be those of an extreme functionalism.

Altered, too, is the way in which we look at the world. Mass tourism, for example, is often associated with an abstract way of seeing that remains detached from others. The same people who delight in relating their holiday stories of Marrakesh are horrified by the supposed difficulties created by North

Africans in suburbs they have only heard of. Likewise, the constant stream of images gives us the illusion of being familiar with Texas or Kurdistan. Another instance of this artificial relation to place is the signposts along the motorways which tell you what you would see if you stopped. In reality, you don't stop, but you watch the signposts go past announcing 'Vézelay, eternal hill', 'Fortified village, 12th century'. This is the world turned into spectacle.

We are living in an unprecedented epoch. Everything is changing. Faith in the dogmas of the traditional systems of belief has been shaken, political parties and trades unions are in crisis. Commitment to certain values used to provide a real degree of regulation in day-to-day life. Party activists do not all discuss Ideology every day, any more than Roman Catholics continually speculate about the meaning of the Real Presence; but their practices did serve to invest social life with meaning. Between absolute individualization on the one hand, and globalization on the other, holes have appeared in the ideological layer.

Excesses of space, time events, information have consequences. Fifty or a hundred years ago, people did not live with the constant impression of being part of history. Nowadays, by contrast, radio and television create the impression that historically important events are occurring daily. History seems to be on our heels, and the result is a confusion between history and news. These three excesses, of time, space and events, foster the sense of a loss of meaning. What is new, however, is not that the world has little or no meaning, but that we should feel the constant need to give it a meaning. In traditional society, meaning could be taken for granted. Today, we are expected to find a meaning for everything, from terrorism in Peru to Islamic fundamentalism in Algeria.

We are in a situation of *solitary communication*, as seems to be indicated by the proliferation of non-places. Individuals can no longer simply coexist. The social bond is necessarily being reshaped. The question is under what conditions? There is a danger of seeking simplistic principles of identity, such as the demand for ethnic identity, thereby, as it were, creating the foreigner, fascism. But it is also possible – and in this respect the question of Europe is very important – to add together the increasing rights of the individual, the greater personal responsibility of each citizen. The effort for a renewal in France or in Europe requires talking in terms not of national identity but of relations with each other. The world has changed. The Other now either arouses less interest or is viewed with suspicion. Why is immigration immediately viewed as a problem? To do so is to admit that there are Others who are still more Other than the Others, the foreigners. To exclude people as foreigners because we are no longer able to conceive of the Other attests to a social pathology. The status of foreigners in France, of these who wish to remain foreigners and those who do not, is a central question. It is a question which in the past has always been resolved satisfactorily but over which there now exists a real political division. It is not the case that there is a consensus to which the extreme right is the only exception. Today, we think of the other in terms of foreignness, not of alterity. To think in terms of alterity is also to think in terms of identity, relation, bond. We are creating categories for exclusion, yet we are made to live together.

A far-reaching change has occurred at the level of day-to-day life. Homes are now self-sufficient in sounds and images, and in information. This development has two related consequences: an opening up to the rest of the planet thanks to the availability of instantaneous information from anywhere in the world, and at the same time a deeper personal isolation and an individualization in the experience of communications; this is a phenomenon I refer to as solitary communication. Habitat is becoming remote from urban life and space, though without becoming isolated. People thousands of kilometres apart can experience the same event at the same time, transmitted by CNN or another television channel, while sitting in the same model of IKEA armchair, in the same Holiday Inn room, and while eating a McDonald hamburger. Place and milieu have ceased to have a significance.

Geographers have always been concerned by at least two spaces: that of the place they are studying (a region, a town, etc.) and the larger one, to which this place belongs and in which operate the influences and constraints which have consequences for the internal structure of local relations. The geographer is thus condemned to a methodological double vision: he or she must keep one eye on the immediate place of observation, and the other on the frontiers of its external influence. In the postmodern world, a part of this exterior is composed of non-places and a part of these non-places of images. The frequenting of non-places today provides a historically unprecedented experience of solitary individuality and non-human mediation between the individual and the collectivity. The geographer of contemporary societies now finds individual presence in the surrounding universe where he/she was used to finding general criteria which bestowed meaning on particular configurations and unique features.

In the 'hypermodern' world, the individual is always and yet never 'at home', frontier zones no longer open on to wholly unfamiliar worlds. It is in non-places that hypermodernity – which results simultaneously from the three forms of excess: the overabundance of events and spaces, and the individualization of references – naturally receives it fullest expression. No social analysis can leave out the individual, and no analysis of individuals can fail to consider the spaces through which they move. Despite the apparent contradiction of terms, a geography of nowhere or a geography of non-places and 'half-places' is perhaps already needed.

By the action of time, however, non-places do not remain total non-places. They become elements in an established and broader social context. Ultimately they come to form patterns of behaviour. They, too, are subject to the process that Michel de Certeau (1980) has labelled the 'invention of daily life', whereby they acquire a character of their own. This leads to a recognition of two of the forms of the reappropriation of space, which are characteristic of current conditions but which display a real continuity with the past: the steady, slow transition of non-places to places with a greater identity, the revalorization of ordinary places by a better integration of the older places which are charged with meaning and identity, and established as places of memory.

VI

Must we conclude? It is by no means certain that any definite conclusion can be reached. Indeed, some are emphatic that it cannot. Nonetheless, some ideas do emerge clearly, both at the level of method and regarding the state of the debate. We are privileged to be living through a spectacular intellectual crisis, which has challenged the theoretical bases of the entire modernist orientation in thought. If the term postmodernity already appears to stand out as one of the rallying cries of the 1980s and 1990s, it is very hard to predict what its future evolution will be. Arguably it can be expected to decline, though phenomena as unlikely as the slowness of the circulation of ideas imply that it is bound to crop up again unexpectedly from time to time, in the form of a false innovation or an enigmatic survival. In short, the postmodern appears as a free signifier, paradoxical because it is essentially imaginary, or, if preferred, a conceptual fiction, a category which operates in the way of 'as if …'. It is 'as if' the future had become an empty space. Let's behave 'as if' modernity was over. Just to see …

Offering neither a programme nor activism, the postmodern approach is better understood as a passion for 'weaving alterities', the skeletal outline of which it traces. The model of modernity remains here only as a persistent echo. Hence the condensing of construction, deconstruction and reconstruction into a single action. It is clear why postmodern thought is liable to be treated as a metadiscourse even in its ambition of reaching the heart of experience. This duality is in fact intrinsic to postmodern thought: it is an indicative, 'seismographical' form, especially receptive to the varieties of aesthetic and social sensibility. In its achievements and its failures, it undermines the claim of rational discourse to primacy over what occurs in the real world. The modernity which provided the context for its development is not denied but is modified, so as to safeguard the freedom which had previously fostered creativity.

The question is to know if and how change can be conceived and brought about. It is as if we were confronted for the first time by an authentic practical problem: we are responsible for the changes, but this change occurs so rapidly that an examination of the immediate past enables us to identify and discuss the set of decisions which modifies its operation. This very immediate history which has , in fact, become a permanent criticism of the present, frees us once and for all from the illusions of the *tabula rasa*. All we have to do is observe and imagine the forthcoming state of the world, then ask ourselves if this is what we want, in the knowledge that when barely underway the transformations we seek will have already modified the terms of our intentions. The symbolic retreat of history is accompanied by a curious circularity between aim and praxis. By relating its own experience, by inventing it from day to day, postmodern humanity hopes to be able to shape the meanings. If this turns out to be an illusion, this illusion constitutes a question in its own right.

One of the major questions facing our discipline at present concerns the nature of the complex relationship between the debates within geography and the internal contradictions of modernity. Are the siren calls of postmodernism responsible for the abandonment of research on general theoretical frameworks by so many geographers? Whatever the answer to that question, there is little doubt that geographical thought has been heavily influenced both by modernism, as in for example the 'quantitative revolution', and by postmodernism, with the collapse of theories and a new emphasis on diversity. We are all familiar with the hopes aroused by modernism's compartmentalization of science, morality and art, and its promise of a higher synthesis to be produced at some future date. Fewer and fewer people now believe in that promise; we have witnessed the end of strong consensus around a handful of powerful ideas. Reason is in retreat and science is in crisis. In fact, however, this is a positivist science that sets itself up against narrative. Even in their ostensibly most rational or formal manifestations, the social sciences are based on a certain number of 'founding myths' (Claval, 1980) that can be traced in a number of master narratives. Like other sciences, geography is narrative by nature (Berdoulay, 1988). Pluralism in the discourse of geography is thus needed, something which poses a challenge at the level of epistemological analysis, because the relations between the forms of discourse and meaning are multiple and complex. This extremely 'postmodern' conclusion is echoed by an analogous vision of the developments observed in society, with the atomization of individuals and the retreat into solidarities of change and circumstance. At the level of geographical practices, this is translated by the return to the local, to the plurality of language games – as Lyotard wrote – and thus a valorization of the plurality of places. In this case, however, it is reasonable to be worried – like Habermas – about the danger posed by a power exercised without restriction in such a context of apparent decentralization. At stake here is the whole question of democracy. Geographical thought, for its part, must not shirk its responsibility. The task for geographers is to rediscover the links between places and democratic practices: none of those involved, at the scientific level and in daily life, can avoid the games of discourse: the question, at least in this book, is: modern or postmodern?

References

Adam, B., *Time and Social Theory*, (Cambridge, Polity Press, 1990).

Adam, B. and Allen, S., (eds), *Theorizing Culture. An Interdisciplinary critique after postmodernism*, (London, UCL Press, 1995).

Adorno, Th., *The Culture Industry. Selected Essays on Mass Culture*, (London, Routledge, 1991).

Agnew, J. A. and Duncan, J. S. (Eds), *The Power of Place*, (London, Unwin Hyman, 1989).

Ahmed, A., *Postmodernism and Islam*, (London, Routledge, 1992).

Albertsen, N., 'Postmodernism, post-Fordism, and critical social theory', *Environment and Planning D: Society and Space*, 6, 3, 339–65, (1988).

Allen, J., Lewis, P, and Braham, P., (eds), *The Political and Economic Forms of Modernity*, (Cambridge, Polity Press, 1992).

Amar N., Le Goues, G. and Pradier, G., (eds), *Surmoi II. Les développements postfreudiens*, (Paris, PUF, 1995).

Amin, A., (ed.), *Post-Fordism*, (Oxford, Blackwell, 1994).

Appignanesi, R. and Garatt, C., *Postmodernism*, (Trumpington, Icon Books, 1995).

Arac, J., (ed.), *Postmodernism and Politics*, (Minneapolis, MN, University of Minnesota Press, 1986).

Aschcroft, B., Griffiths, G. and Tiffin, H., (eds), *The Post-Colonial Studies Reader*, (London, Routledge, 1994).

Auge, M., *Non-lieux. Introduction à une anthropologie de la surmodernité*, (Paris, Seuil, 1992).

Auge, M., *Le sens des autres. Actualité de l'anthropologie*, (Paris, Fayard, 1994a).

Auge, M., *Pour une anthropologie des mondes contemporains*, (Paris, Aubier, 1994b).

Baker, S., 'Reflexion, Doubt, and the Place of Rhetoric in Postmodern Social Theory', *Sociological Theory*, 8, 2, 232–45 (1990).

Balandier, G., *Le détour. Pouvoir et modernité*, (Paris, Fayard, 1985).

Balandier, G., *Le désordre. Eloge de mouvement*, (Paris, Fayard, 1988).

Balandier, G., *Le dédale. Pour en finir avec le XXe siècle*, (Paris, Fayard, 1994).

Barnes, T. J. and Curry, M. R., 'Postmodernism in economic geography: methaphor and the construction of alterity', *Environment and Planning D: Society and Space*, 10, 1, 57–68 (1992).

Barnes, T. J. and Duncan J. S., (eds), *Writing Worlds. Discourse, text and metaphor in the representation of landscape*, (London, Routledge, 1992).

Barnett, C., 'Peddling Postmodernism: A Response to Strohmayer and Hannah's "Domesticating Postmodernism"', *Antipode*, 25, 4, 345–58 (1993a).

Barnett, C., 'Stuck in the Post: An Unsympathetic Critique of Andrew Sayers's "Postmodernist Thought in Geography: A Realist View"', *Antipode*, 25, 4, 365–8 (1993b).

Baudrillard, J., 'Modernité', *Encyclopaedia Universalis* 11, 139–41 (1971).

Bauman, Z., 'Sociology and postmodernity', *Sociological Review*, 36, 790–813 (1988a).

Bauman, Z., 'Is There a Postmodern Sociology?' *Theory, Culture & Society*, 5, 2/3, 217–37 (1988b).

Bauman, Z., *Modernity and Ambivalence*, (Cambridge, Basil Blackwell, 1991).

Bauman, Z., *Intimations of Postmodernity*, (Andover, Hants, Routledge, Chapman and Hall, 1992a).

Bauman, Z., 'Simmel, ou l'éclosion de l'expérience postmoderne', *Sociétés, Revue des Sciences Humaines et Sociales*, 35, 3 –16, (1992b).

Beauregard, R. A., 'Between modernity and postmodernity: the ambiguous position of US planning', *Environment and Planning D: Society and Space*, 7, 4, 38 1–395 (1989).

Beck, U., *Risk Society: Towards a New Modernity*, London, Sage, 1992).

Beck, U., *Ecological Politics in an Age of Risk*, (Oxford, Polity Press, 1995).

Becker, J., 'Postmoderne Modernisierung der Socialgeographie', *Geographische Zeitschrift*, 78, 15–33, (1990).

Bell D., *The Coming of Post Industrial Society. A Venture in Social Forecasting*, (New York, Basic Books, 1973).

Belmont, J., *Modernes et postmodernes*, (Paris, Le Moniteur, 1987).

Benjamin, A., (ed.), *The Lyotard Reader*, (Oxford, Basil Blackwell, 1989).

Benjamin, A., (ed.), *The Problems of Modernity, Adorno and Benjamin*, (London, Routledge, 1991).

Benko, G. B., (ed.), *Les nouveaux aspects de la théorie sociale. De la géographie à la sociologie*, (Caen, Paradigme, 1988).

Benko, G. B., *Géographie des technopôles*, (Paris, Masson, 1991).

Berdoulay, V., *Des mots et des lieux. La dynamique du discours géographique*, (Paris, Ed. Du CNRS, 1988).

Berdoulay, V., 'Pluralité du discours et post-modernité', *EspacesTemps*, 40/41, 32–33, (1989).

Berg, L. D., 'Between modernism and postmodernism', *Progress in Human Geography*, 17, 4, 490–507, (1993).

Berman, M., *All that is Solid Melts into Air: The Experience of Modernity*, (New York, Simon and Schuster, 1982).

Bernstein, R. J., (ed.), *Habermas and Modernity*, (Cambridge, Mass., MIT Press, 1985).

Bernstein, R. J., *The New Constellation. The Ethical-Political Horizons of Modernity/Postmodernity*, (Cambridge, Polity Press, 1991).

Berque, A., *Mediance: de milieux en paysage*, (Montpellier, RECLUS, 1990).

Berque, A., 'Le pays où le regard se voit: traditions nippones et postmodernité, *Sociétés, Revue des Sciences Humaines et Sociales*, 35, 17–26 (1992a).

Berque A., 'Les mirages de la cité nippone. Villes, paysages et postmodernité', in Driant, J. C., (ed.), *Habitat et villes: l'avenir en jeu*, (Paris, L'Harmattan, 1992b), 41–49.

Berque, A., *Du geste à la cité*, (Paris, Gallimard, 1993).

Berque, A., *Les raisons du paysage*, (Paris, Hazan, 1995).

Bertaux, D., 1988, 'Individualisme et modernité', *Espaces Temps*, 37, 15–21, (1988).

Bertens, H., *The Idea of the Postmodern*, (London, Routledge, 1994).

Best, S. And Kellner, D., *Postmodern theory: Critical interrogations*, (New York, Guilford Press, 1991).

Beynon, H. and Hudson, R., 'Place and Space in Contemporary Europe: Some Lessons and Reflexions', *Antipode*, 25, 3, 177–90 (1993).

Bhatt, C., *Liberation and purity. Race, new religious movements and the ethics of postmodernity*, (London, UCL Press, 1996).

Bishop, P., 'Rhetoric, memory, and power: depth psychology and postmodern geography', *Environment and Planning D: Society and Space*, 10, 1, 5–22 (1992).

Blanquart, P., 'Sur la piste de l'homme modern', *Espaces Temps*, 37, 64–68, (1988).

Bloch, E., *Heritage of Our Time*, (Cambridge, Polity Press, 1991).

Bocock, R. and Thompson, K., (eds), *The Social and Cultural Forms of Modernity*, (Cambridge, Polity Press, 1992).

Bondi, L., 'Feminism, postmodernism, and geography: space for women?' *Antipode*, 22, 2, 156–167, (1990).

Bondi, L., 'Fragments for geography?', *Antipode*, 24, 1, 73–8, (1992).

Bondi, L. and Domosh, M., 'Other figures in other places: on feminism, postmodernism and geography', *Environment and Planning D: Society and Space*, 10, 2, 199–213 (1992).

Bonnett, A., 'Situationism, geography, and poststructuralism', *Environment and Planning D: Society and Space*, 7, 2, 131–46, (1989).

Bonnett, A., 'Art, ideology, and everyday space: subversive tendencies from Dada to postmodernism', *Environment and Planning D: Society and Space*, 10, 1, 69–86, (1992).

Bordessa, R., 'Geography, Postmodernism, and Environmental Concern', *The Canadian Geographer*, 37, 2, 147–56 (1993).

Boudon, P., 'Un canard décoré', *Les Cahiers de Philosophie*, 6, 85–95 (1988).

Boudon, R., *Le juste et le vrai. Études sur l'objectivité des valeurs et de la connaissance*, (Paris, Fayard, 1995).

'The Art of the Body in the Discourse of Postmodernity', *Theory, Culture & Society*, 5, 2/3, 527–42, (1988).

Boyne, R. And Rattansi, A., (eds), *Postmodernism and Society*, (London, Macmillan, 1990).

Brodribb, S., *Nothing mat(t)ers: a feminist critique of postmodernism*, (Melbourne, Spinifex Press, 1992).

Brown, R. H. 'Rhetoric, Textuality, and the Postmodern Turn in Sociological Theory', *Sociological Theory*, 8, 2, 188–97, (1990).

Brown, S., *Postmodern Marketing*, (London, Routledge, 1995).

Bürger, P., *The Decline of Modernism*, (Cambridge, Polity Press, 1992).

Callinicos, A., *Against Postmodernism. A Marxist Critique*, (Cambridge, Polity Press, 1990).

Carravetta, P., 'On Gianni Vattimo's Postmodern Hermeneutics', *Theory, Culture & Society*, 5, 2/3, 395–7, (1988).

Cenzatti, M., *Los Angeles and the L. A. School: Postmodernism and Urban Studies*, (West Hollywood, CA., Los Angeles Forum for Architecture and Urban Design, Forum Publication no. 10, 1993).

Channell, D., *Science and Postmodernism*, (Oxford, Basil Blackwell, 1993).

Charles, E., 'Temps, musique, post-modernité', *Temps Libre*, 12, 71–8, (1985).

Cheetham, M. A., *La mémoire postmoderne. Essai sur l'art canadien contemporain*, (Saint-Laurent, Que., Liber., 1992)

Chesneaux, J., *De la modernité*, (Paris, La Découverte, 1983).

Chesneaux, J., 'La modernité "ils n'ont que ce mot-là a la bouche"', *La Quinzaine Littéraire*, 456, 1–15 Février, 19–20, (1986).

Chesneaux, J., 'La modernité-monde', *Les Temps Modernes*, 503, 63–77, (1988).

Chesneaux, J., *Modernité-monde*, (Paris, La Découverte, 1989).

Claval, P., *Les mythes fondateurs des sciences sociales*, (Paris, PUF, 1980).

Claval, P., 'Postmodernisme et géographie', *Géographie et Cultures*, 4, 3–24, (1992).

Claval, P., 'Comment présenter l'histoire de la géographie humaine?', (Paris, Univ. de Paris IV, Manuscrit., 1995).

Cloke, P., Philo, C. and Sadler D., *Approaching Human Geography. An Introduction to Contemporary Theoretical Debates*, (London, Paul Chapman, 1991).

Collins, J., *Uncommon Cultures, Popular Culture and Post-Modernism*, (London, Routledge, 1989).

Companion, A., *Les cinq paradoxes de la modernité*, (Paris, Seuil, 1990).

Connor, S., *Postmodernist Culture. An Introduction to Theories of the Contemporary*, (Oxford, Blackwell, 1989).

Conolly, W. E., *Political Theory and Modernity*, (Oxford, Basil Blackwell, 1989).

Cooke, P., 'Individuals, localities and postmodernism', *Environment and Planning D: Society and Space*, 5, 4, 408–12, (1987).

Cooke, P., 'Modernity, Postmodernity and the City', *Theory, Culture & Society*, 5, 2/3, 475–92, (1988).

Cooke, P., *Back to the Future. Modernity, Postmodernity and Locality*, (London, Unwin Hyman, 1990a).

Cooke, P., 'Modern urban theory in question', *Transactions, Institute of British Geographers*, 15, 3, 331–43 (1990b).

Corbridge, S., 'Marxisms, modernities, and moralities: Development praxis and the claims of distant strangers', *Environment and Planning D: Society and Space*, 11, 4, 449–72, (1993).

Corneloup, J., 'Escalades et post-modernité', *Sociétés, Revue des Sciences Humaines et Sociales*, 34, 385–94, (1991).

Cosgrove, D., 'A terrain of metaphore: cultural geography 1988–89', *Progress in Human Geography*, 14, 4, 566–75, (1989).

Cosgrove, D., 'Environmental thought and action: pre-modern and postmodern', *Transactions, Institute of British Geographers*, 15, 3, 344–58 (1990a).

Cosgrove, D., ' Then we take Berlin: cultural geography 1989–90', *Progress in Human Geography*, 14, 4, 560–8, (1990b).

Cosgrove, D., 'Postmodern Tremblings. A Reply to Michael Dear', *Annals of the Association of the American Geographers*, 84, 2, 305–7, (1994).

Couvelakis, E and Vakaloulis, M., 'Entretien avec Fredric Jameson', *Futur Antérieur*, 21, 23–44 (1994).

Crespi, F., 'Sociologie postmoderne/sociologie de l'existence', *Sociétés, Revue des Sciences Humaines et Sociales*, 35, 75–84, (1992).

Cook, S., Pakulski, J. and Waters, M., *Postmodernization. Change in Advanced Society*, (London, Sage, 1992).

Curry, M. R., 'Postmodernism, Language, and the Strains of Modernism', *Annals of the Association of American Geographers*, 81, 2, 210–28, (1991).

Curry, M. R., 'Reply', *Annals of the Association of American Geographers*, 82, 2, 310–12, (1992a).

Curry, M. R., 'The architectonic impulse and the reconceptualization of the concrete in contemporary geography', in Barnes, T. J. and Duncan, J. S. (Eds), *WritingWorlds. Discourse, text and metaphor in the representation of landscape*, (London, Routledge, 1992b), 97–117.

D'Agostino, P. and Tafler, D., (eds), *Transmission. Toward a Post-Television Culture*, [London, Sage, (2nd ed.), 1994].

Dallmayr, F., *Life-world, Modernity and Critique. Paths between Heidegger and the Frankfurt School*, (Cambridge, Polity Press, 1991).

Dandeker, C., *Surveillance, Power and Modernity. Bureaucracy and Discipline from 1700 to the Present Day*, (Cambridge, Polity Press, 1990).

Dear, M. J., 'Editorial: Society and space: an introduction, *Environment and Planning D: Society and Space*, 1, 1, 1–2, (1983).

Dear, M. J., 'Postmodernism and planning', *Environment and Planning D: Society and Space*, 4, 3, 367–84, (1986).

Dear, M. J., 'The postmodern challenge: reconstructing human geography', *Transactions of the Institute of British Geographers*, 13, 262–74, (1988a).

Dear, M. J., 'La reconstruction de la géographie humaine, in Benko, G., (ed.), *Les nouveaux aspects de la théorie sociale. De la géographie a la sociologie*, (Caen, Paradigme, 1988b), 55–75.

Dear, M. J., 'Privatization and the rhetoric', *Environment and Planning D: Society and Space*, 7, 4, 449–62 (1989).

Dear, M. J., 'The premature demise of postmodern urbanism', *Cultural Anthropology*, 6, 538–52, (1991).

Dear, M. J., 'Postmodern Human Geography', *Erdkunde*, 48, 2–13, (1994a).

Dear, M. J., 'Who's Afraid of Postmodernism?: Reflexions on Symanski and Cosgrove;, *Annals of the Association of American Geographers*, 84, 2, 295–300, (1994b).

Dear, M. J., 'Beyond the Post-Fordist City', *Contention*, 5, 1, 67–76, (1995a).

Dear, M. J., 'Prendre Los Angeles au sérieux: temps et espaces dans la ville postmoderne', *Futur Antérieur*, 29, (3), 19–32 (1995b).

Dear, M. J., Jackson, P., Thrift, N. J. and Williams, P. R., 'Cities, consumption, culture, and postmodernism: books in 1986', *Environment and Planning D: Society and Space*, 5, 4, 475–84, (1987).

De Certeau, M., *Invention de quotidien. Arts de faire*, (Paris, Union Générale d'Edition – 10/18, 1980).

De Gandillac, M., *Genèses de la modernité*, (Paris, Cerf, 1992).

Denzin, N. K., '"Blue Velvet": Postmodern Contradictions', *Theory, Culture & Society*, 5, 2/3, 461–73, (1988).

Denzin, N. K., *Images of Postmodern Society. Social Theory and Contemporary Cinema*, (London, Sage, 1991).

Descombes, V., *Philosophie par gros temps*, (Paris, Ed. Minuit, 1989).

Deutsche, R., 'Boys town', *Environment and Planning D: Society and Space*, 9, 1, 5–30, (1991).

Dews, P., *Logics of Disintegration. Post-Structuralist Thought and the Claims of Critical Theory*, (London, Verso, 1987).

D'Haen, T. And Bertens, H., (eds), *Postmodern Fiction in Europe and the Americas*, (Amsterdam, Rodopi, 1988).

Dickens, D. and Fontana, A., (eds), *Postmodernism and Social Inquiry*, (London, UCL Press, 1994).

Doan, L., (ed.), *The Lesbian Postmodern*, (New York, Columbia University Press, 1994).

Doel, M., 'In stalling deconstruction: striking out the postmodern', *Environment and Planning D: Society and Space*, 10, 2, 163–79, (1992).

Doel, M. and Matless, D., 'Editorial: Geography and postmodernism', *Environment and Planning D: Society and Space*, 10, 1, 1–4, (1992).

Doherty, J., Graham, E. and Malek, M., (eds), *Postmodernism and the Social Sciences*, (London, Macmillan, 1992).

Domenach, J-M., *Approaches de la modernité*, (Paris, Ellipses – Ed. Marketing, 1986).

Douzinas, C., Goodrich, P., (eds), *Laws of Postmodernity*, (London, Routledge, 1993).

Douzinas, C., Warrington, R. and McVeigh, S., *Postmodern Jurisprudence. The Law of the Text in the Text of the Law*, (London, Routledge, 1993).

Driver, F., 'Geography's empire: histories of geographical knowledge', *Environment and Planning D: Society and Space*, 10, 1, 23–40, (1992).

Driver, F., 'Histories of the present? The history and philosophy of geography', part III, *Progress in Human Geography*, 20, 1, 100–9, (1996).

Dupas, J-C., 'Le Post-moderne et la Chimère', *Les Cahiers de Philosophie*, 6, 161–75, (1988).

Eadie, W., *Movements of Modernity. The Case of Glasgow and Art Nouveau*, (London, Routledge, 1990).

Eco, U., *Apostille au 'Nom de la rose'*, (Paris, Grasset – Le Livre de Poche, 1985).

Eco, U., 'L'innovation dans le sériel', *Les Cahiers de Philosophie*, 6, 137–59, (1988).

Elam, D., *Romancing the Postmodern*, (London, Routledge, 1992).

Ellin, N., *Postmodern Urbanism*, (Oxford, Blackwell, 1996).

Entrikin, J. N. 'Place, region and modernity', in Agnew, J. A. and Duncan J. S., (eds), *The Power of Place*, (London, Unwin Hyman, 1989), 30–43.

Entrikin, J. N., *The Betweenness of Place. Towards a Geography of Modernity*, (Baltimore, John Hopkins University Press, 1991).

Escobar, A., 'Imagining a post-development era? Critical thought, development and social movements', *Social Text*, 31/32, 20–56, (1992).

Featherstone, M., 'In Pursuit of the Postmodern: An Introduction', *Theory, Culture & Society*, 5, 2/3, 195–215, (1988).

Featherstone, M., *Consommer Culture and Postmodernism*, (London, Sage, 1990).

Featherstone, M., 'Postmodernisme et esthétisation de la vie quotidienne', *Societés, Revue des Sciences Humaines et Sociales*, 35, 37–46, (1992).

Featherstone, M., Lash, S. and Robertson, R., (eds), *Global Modernities*, (London, Sage, 1995).

Fejtö, F., *La fin de démocraties populaires. Les chemins du post-communism*, (Paris, Seuil, 1992).

Fekete, J., (ed.), *Life After Postmodernism. Essays on Value and Culture*, (London, Macmillan, 1988).

Ferguson, M., 'Marshall McLuhan revisited', *Media, Culture and Society*, 1, 71–90, (1991).

Ferrier, J-P., 'Une nouvelle géographie classique pour une modernité du troisième type', *Espaces Temps*, 40/41, 45–9, (1989).

Ferro, M. and Garros, V., (eds), *Russie post-soviétique: la fatigue de l'histoire*, (Paris, PUF, 1995).

Ferry, L., *Philosophie politique, 1. Le droit: la nouvelle querelle des anciens et des modernes*, (Paris, PUF, 1984).

Ferry, L., *Heidegger et les modernes*, (Paris, Grasset, 1988).

Ferry, L., *Le nouvel ordre écologique*, (Paris, Grasset, 1992).

Ferry, L. and Renaut, A., *La pensée 68. Essai sur l'anti-humanisme contemporain*, (Paris, Gallimard, 1988).

Feyerabend, P., *Contre le méthode. Esquisse d'une théorie anarchiste de la connaissance*, (Paris, Seuill, 1979).

Fischer, M. M. J., 'Ethnicity and the post-modern arts of memory', in Clifford, J. and Marcus (G. E., (eds), *Writing Culture: The Poetics and Politics of Ethnography*, (Berkeley, University of California Press, 1986), 194–233.

Flax, J., *Thinking Fragments. Psychoanalysis, Feminism and Postmodernism in the Contemporary West*, (Los Angeles, University of California Press, 1990).

Folch-Serra, M., 'David Harvey and his Critics: The Clash with Disenchanted Women and "Postmodern Discontents"', *The Canadian Geographer*, 37, 2, 176–84, (1993).

Forbes, D. K., 'Geography and development practice: a postmodern challenge?', *Environment and Planning D; Society and Space*, 8, 2, 131–3, (1990).

Fornäs, J. and Bolin, G., (eds), *Youth Culture in Late Modernity*, (London, Sage, 1994).

Foster, H., (ed.), *The Anti-Aesthetic. Esseys on Post-Modern Culture*, (Seattle, B. Press, 1983).

Foster, H., (ed.), *Post-Modern Culture*, (London, Pluto, 1985).

Fougeyrollas, P., *Vers la Nouvelle Pensée. Essai postphilosophique*, (Paris, L'Harmattan, 1994).

Fox, C. J. and Miller, H. T., *Postmodern Public Administration*, (London, Sage, 1995).

Fraser, N. and Nicholson, L. 'Social Criticism without Philosophy: an Encounter between Feminism and postmodernism', *Theory, Culture & Society*, 5, 213, 373–94, (1988).

Friedmann, J., 'Cultural Logics of the Global System: A Sketch', *Theory, Culture & Society*, 5, 2/3, 447–60, (1988).

Friedmann, J., 'The dialectic of reason', *International Journal of Urban and Regional Research*, 13, 2, 217–36, (1989).

Frisby, D., *Fragments of Modernity*, (Cambridge, Polity Press, 1985).

Frug, M. J. *Postmodern Legal Feminism*, (London, Routledge, 1993).

Galletti, J. C., *Aux lieux du bureaux*, (Paris, Ed. Ministère de l'Equipement, 1992).

Gandy, M., 'Crumbling land: the postmodernity debate and the analysis of environmental problems', *Progress in Human Geography*, 20, 1, 23–40, (1996).

Gare, A., *Postmodernism and the Environmental Crisis*, (London, Routledge, 1995).

Gauchet, M., *Le désenchantement du monde*, (Paris, Gallimard, 1985).

Gauthier, A., *La trajectoire de la modernité. Représentations et images*, (Paris, PUF, 1992).

Gellner, E., *Postmodernism, Reason and Religion*, (London, Routledge, 1992).

Giddens, A., 'Modernisme and Postmodernisme', *New German Critique*, 22, 15–18, (1981).

Giddens, A., *The Consequences of Modernity*, (Cambridge, Polity Press, 1990).

Giddens, A., *Modernity and Self-Identity. Self and Society in the Late Modern Age*, (Cambridge, Polity Press, 1991).

Giddens, A., *The Transformation of Intimacy. Sexuality, Love, and Eroticism in Modern Societies*, (Cambridge, Polity Press, 1992).

Giddens, A. and Turner, J., (eds), *Social Theory Today*, (Cambridge, Polity Press, 1987).

Giroux, H., 'Postmodernism and the Discourse of Educational Criticism', *Journal of Education*, 170, 5–30, (1988).

Gitlin, T., 'Postmodernism: Roots and Politics', in Angus, I. And Jhally, S., (eds), *Cultural Politics in Contemporary America*, (New York, Routledge and Kegan Paul, 1988), 47–360.

Glick, T. F., 'History and philosophy of geography', *Progress in Human Geography*, 9, 3, 424–31, (1985).

Glick, T. F., ' History and philosophy of geography', *Progress in Human Geography*, 14, 1, 120–8, (1990).

Goldblatt, D., 'Power, Modernity and Morality in the Long Nineteenth Century', *Theory Culture and Society*, 12, 1, 157–73, (1995).

Gottdiener, M., *Postmodern and Semiotics*, (Oxford, Blackwell, 1995).

Graham, J., 'Post-modernism and marxism', *Antipode*, 20, 1, 60–6, (1988).

Gray, J., *Post-liberalism. Studies in Political Thought*, (London, Routledge, 1993).

Gregory, D., 'Postmodernism and the politics of social theory', *Environment and Planning D: Society and Space*, 5, 3, 245–8, (1987).

Gregory, D., 'La differérenciation, la distance et la géographie post-moderne', in Benko, G., (ed.), *Les nouveaux aspects de la théorie sociale. De la géographie à la sociologie*, (Caen, Paradigme, 1988), 15–37.

Gregory, D., 'A real differentiation and postmodern human geography', in Gregory, D and Walford R., (eds), *Horizons in Human Geography*, (London, Macmillan, 1989a) 67–69.

Gregory, D., 'The crisis of modernity? Human geography and critical social theory', in Peet, R. and Thrift, N., (eds), *New Models in Geography*, (Vol. 2), (London, Unwin Hyman, 1989b), 348–85.

Gregory, D., *Geographical Imaginations*, (Oxford, Blackwell, 1994).

Guattari, F., 'L'impasse post-moderne', *La Quinzaine Littéraire*, 456, 1–15 Février, 21, (1986).

Guattari, F., *Les trois écologies*, (Paris, Galilée, 1989).

Habermas, J., 'Modernity versus postmodernity', *New German Critique*, 22, 314, (1981).

Habermas, J., *The Philosophical Discourse of Modernity*, (Cambridge, Polity Press, 1985).

Hage, J. and Powers, C., *Post-Industrial Lives. Roles and Relationships in the 21st Century*, (London, Sage, 1992).

Hall, S. and Gieben, B., (eds), *Formations of Modernity*, Cambridge, Polity Press, 1992).

Hall, S., Held, D. and McGrew, T., (eds), *Modernity and its Futures*, (Cambridge, Polity Press, 1992).

Hannah, M. and Strohmayer, U., 'Ornamentalism: geography and the labor of language in structuration theory', *Environment and Planning D: Society and Space*, 9, 3, 309–27, (1991).

Hannah, M. and Strohmayer, U., 'Postmodernism (S)trained', *Annals of the Association of American Geographers*, 82, 2, 308–10, (1992).

Harasym, S., (ed.), *The Post-Colonial Critic*, (London, Routledge, 1990).

Harland, R., *Superstructuralism. The Philosophy of Structuralism and PostStructuralism*, (London, Routledge, 1987).

Harris, C., 'Power, Modernity, and Historical Geography', *Annals of the Association of American Geographers*, 81, 4, 671–83, (1991).

Harris, J., Frascina, F., Harrison, C. and Wood, P., *Modernism in Dispute. Art Since the Forties*, (London, Yale University Press, 1993).

Harvey, D., 'Flexible accumulation through urbanization: Reflexions on "postmodernism" in the American city', *Antipode*, 19, 3, 260–86, (1987).

Harvey, D., *The Condition of Postmodernity*, (Oxford, Basil Blackwell, 1989).

Harvey, D., 'Between Space and Time: Reflections on the Geographical Imagination', *Annals of the Association of American Geographers*, 80, 3, 418–34, (1990).

Harvey, D., 'Postmodern morality plays', *Antipode*, 24, 4, 300–26, (1992a).

Harvey, D., 'Social Justice, Postmodernism and the City', *International Journal of Urban and Regional Research*, 16, 4, 588–61, (1992b).

Harvey, D., 'Class relations, social justice and the politics of difference', in Squires, J., (ed.), *Principled Positions. Postmodernism and the Rediscovery of Value*, (London, Lawrence and Wishart, 1993), 85–120.

Harvey, D., 'L'accumulation flexible par l'urbanisation: réflexions sur le " postmodernisme" dans la grande ville américaine', *Futur Antérieur*, 29, (3), 121–45, (1995).

Hassan, I., *The Dismemberment of Orpheus: Towards a Postmodern Literature*, (New York, Oxford University Press, 1971).

Hassan, I., 1987, *The Postmodern Turn. Essays in Postmodern Theory and Culture*, (Columbus, Ohio, State University Press, 1987).

Hassard, J. and Parker, M., (eds), *Postmodernisme and Organisations*, (London, Sage, 1993).

Heckscher, C. and Donnellon, A., (eds), *The Post-Bureaucratic Organization. New Perspectives on Organizational Change*, (London, Sage, 1994).

Held, D. and Thompson, J. B., (eds), *Social Theory of Modern Society. Anthony Giddens and his Critics*, (Cambridge, Cambridge University Press, 1989).

Heller, A., *Can Modernity Survive?*, (Cambridge, Polity Press, 1990).

Heller, A. and Feher, F., *The Post-Modern Political Condition*, (Cambridge, Polity Press, 1989).

Herpin, N., 'Au-delà de la consommation de masse? Une discussion critique des sociologues de la postmodernité', *L'Année Sociologique*, 43, 295–315, (1993).

Hollinger, R., *Postmodernism and the Social Sciences*, (London, Sage, 1994).

Horvath, R. J., 'Between political economy and postmodernism', *Antipode*, 24, 2, 157–62, (1992).

Howell, P., 'Public space and the public sphere: political theory and historical geography of modernity', *Environment and Planning D: Society and Space*, 11, 3, 303–22, (1993).

Hutcheon, L., *A Poetics of Postmodernism. History, Theory, Fiction*, (London, Routledge, 1988).

Inglehart, R., *La transition culturelle dans les sociétés industrielles avancées*, (Paris, Economica, 1993).

Jameson, F., 'Postmodernism, or the cultural logic of late capitalism', *New Left Review*, 146, 53–65, (1984).

Jameson, F., *Postmodernism, or, the Cultural Logic of Late Capitalism*, (London, Verso, 1991).

Jameson, F., 'Postmodernisme et marché', *Future Antérieur*, 12/13, 198–220, (1992).

Jeanniere, A., *Les fins du monde*, (Paris, Aubier, 1987).

Jeanniere, A., 'Qu'est-ce que la modernité?', *Etudes*, 373, 5, nov., 499–510, (1990).

Jencks, C., *The language of post-modern architecture*, (London, New York, Academy/St-Martin's Press, 1977a).

Jencks, C., *Mouvements modernes en architecture*, (Bruxelles, Mardaga, (1977b).

Jencks, C. *What is Post-Modernism?*, (London, New York, Academy, St-Martin's Press, 1986).

Jencks, C., *Heteropolis: Los Angeles, the Riots, and the Strange Beauty of Hetero-Architecture*, (London, Academy Editions, 1993).

Jonas, H., *Le principe responsabilité*, (Paris, Cerf, 1990).

Jones III, J. P., Natter, W. And Schatzki, T. R., (eds), *Postmodern contentions: epochs, politics, space*, (New York, Guilford Press, 1993).

Joron, P., 'Dépense sociale et post-modernité', *Sociétés, Revue des Sciences Humaines et Sociales*, 35, 57–62, (1992).

Kaplan, E. A., (ed.), *Postmodernism and Discontents. Theories, Practices*, (London, Verso, 1988).

Kariel, H. S., *The Desperate Politics of Postmodernism*, (Amherst, MA, The University of Massachusetts Press, 1989).

Kearney, R., (ed.), *Twentieth Century Continental Philosophy*, (Routledge History of Philosophy, Volume 8), (London, Routledge, 1993).

Kellner, D., 'Postmodernism as Social Theory: Some Challenges and Problems', *Theory, Culture & Society*, 5, 2/3, 239–69, (1988).

Kellner, D., *Critical Theory, Marxism and Modernity*, (Baltimore, John Hopkins University Press, 1989).

Kemper, P., (ed.), *Postmodern oder De Kampf um die Zukunft*, (Frankfurt am Main, Fischer Verlag, 1988).

Kling, R., Olin, S. and Poster, M., *Postsuburban California*, (Berkeley, University of California Press, 1991).

Knox, P. L., 'The social production of the built environment: Architects, architecture and the post-Modern city', *Progress in Human Geography*, 11, 3, 354–77, (1987).

Kolb, D., *Postmodern Sophistications: Philosophy, Architecture and Tradition*, (Chicago, University of Chicago Press, 1990).

Kumar, K., *Utopia and Anti-Utopia in Modern Times*, (Cambridge, Basil Blackwell, 1991).

Lagopoulos, A. P., 'Postmodernism, geography, and the social semiotics of space', *Environment and Planning D: Society and Space*, 11, 3, 255–78, (1993).

Lambert, Y., 'Vers une ère post-chrétienne?', *Futuribles*, 200, 85–111, (1995).

Lash, S., 'Discourse or Figure? Postmodernisme as a "Regime of Signification"', *Theory, Culture & Society*, 5, 2/3, 311–36, (1988).

Lash, S., *Sociology of Postmodernism*, (London, Routlege, 1990).

Lash, S. and Friedman, J., (eds), *Modernity and Identity*, (Oxford, Basil Blackwell, 1992).

Lash S. and Urry, J., *Economies of Signs and Space*, (London, Sage, 1994).

Latour, B., *Nous n'avons jamais été modernes. Essai d'anthropologie symétrique*, (Paris, La Decouverte, 1991).

Le Dantec, J-P., *Dédale le héros*, (Paris, Balland, 1992).

Lefebvre, H., *Introduction à la modernité*, (Paris, Minuit, 1962).

Lemert, C., *Sociology After Postmodernism. Twentieth Century Social Theory*, (Cambridge, Basil Blackwell, 1992).

Le Rider, J., *Modernité viennoise et crises de l'identité* (Paris, PUF, 1990).

Le Rider, J., 'La postmodernité', *Commentaire*, 14, 54, 283–91, (1991).

Levin, D. M., T*he Opening Vision. Nihilism and the Postmodern Situation* (London, Routledge, 1988).

Ley, D., 'Modernism, post-modernism, and the struggle for place', in Agnew, J. A. and Duncan, J. S., (eds), *The Power of Place*, (London, Unwin Hyman, 1989) 44–65.

Ley D. And Olds, K., 'Landscape as spectacle: world's fairs and the culture of heroic consumption', *Environment and Planning D: Society and Space*, 6, 2, 191–212, (1988).

Lhomme, A., 'Le Schibboleth des années quatre-vingt?' *Les Cahiers de Philosophie*, 6, 33–54, (1988a).

Lhomme, A., 'Une architecture sans objet?', *Les Cahiers de Philosophie*, 6, 113–36, (1988b).

Lichtblau, K., 'Sociology and the Diagnosis of the Times or: The Reflexivity of Modernity', *Theory, Culture and Society*, 12, 1, 25–52, (1995).

Lipovetsky, G., *L'ère du vide. Essais sur l'individualisme contemporaine*, (Paris, Gallimard, 1983).

Lipovetsky, G., *L'empire de l'éphémère. La mode et son destin dans les sociétés modernes*, (Paris, Gallimard, 1987).

Livingstone, D. N., 'Geography, tradition and the Scientific Revolution: an interpretative essay, *Transactions, Institute of British Geographers*, 15, 3, 359–73, (1990).

Lovering, J., 'Postmodernism, marxism, and locality research: the contribution of critical realisme to the debate', *Antipode*, 21, 1, 1–12, (1989).

Luigi, G., *L'architecture en Europe*, (Paris, Nathan, 1995).

Luke, T. W., *Social Theory and Modernity*, (London, Sage, 1990).

Lyon, D., *Postmodernity*, (Buckingham, Open University Press, 1994).

Lyotard, J-F., *Des dispositifs pulsionnels*, (Paris, Union Générale d'Edition, 1973), 10/18.

Lyotard, J-F., *La condition postmoderne*, (Paris, Ed. Minuit, 1979).

Lyotard, J-F., 'Discussion, ou: phraser "après Auschwitz"', in Lacoue-Labarthe, P. And Nancy, J-L., (eds), *Les fins de l'homme. Autour du travail de Jacques Derrida*, (Paris, Galillée, 1981), 283–315.

Lyotard, J-F., 'Response à la question: qu'est-ce que le postmoderne', *Critique*, 37, 419, 357–67, (1982).

Lyotard, J-F., 'La peinture du secret à l'ère postmoderne, Baruchello', *Traverses*, 30/31, 95–101, (1984).

Lyotard, J-F., *Le Postmoderne expliqué aux enfants*, (Paris, Galilée, 1988a).

Lyotard, J-F., 'Réécrire la modernité', *Les Cahiers de Philosophie*, 5, 193–203 (1988b).

Lyotard, J-F., *Inhuman. Reflexions on Time*, (Cambridge, Polity Press, 1991).

Lyotard, J-F., *Moralités postmodernes*, (Paris, Galilée, 1993).

Lyotard, J-F. and Thebaud, J-L., *Au juste*, (Paris, Bourgois, 1979).

Lyotard, J-F., Van Reijen, W. and Veerman, D., 'Les lumières, le sublime', *Les Cahiers de Philosophie*, 5, 63–98, (1988).

McGowan, J., *Postmodernism and its Critics*, (Ithaca, N.Y., Cornell University Press, 1991).

McHale, B., *Constructing Postmodernism*, (London, Routledge, 1993).

McRobbie, A., *Postmodernism and Popular Culture*, (London, Routledge, 1994).

Maffesoli, M., 'La solidarité post-moderne,' *La Nouvelle Revue Socialiste*, 6, 77–85, (1989).

Marchall, B. K., *Teaching The Postmodern. Fiction and Theory*, (London, Routledge, 1992).

Marchand, M. H. and Parpart, J., (eds), *Feminism/Postmodernism/Development*, (London, Routledge, 1995).

Marcuse, H., *One-Dimensional Man*, (Boston, Beacon Press, 1964).

Marcuse, H., *Eros and Civilisation*, (London, Routledge, 1987).

Marden, P., 'The deconstructionist tendencies of postmodern geographies: a compelling logic?'. *Progress in Human Geography*, 16, 1, 41–57, (1992).

Massey, D., 'Flexible sexism', *Environment and Planning D: Society and Space*, 9, 1, 31–57, (1991).

Matless, D., 'An occasion for geography: landscape, representation, and Foucault's corpus', *Environment and Planning D: Society and Space*, 10, 1, 41–56, (1992).

Mellville, S. W., *Philosophy Beside Itself. On Deconstruction and Modernism*, (Manchester, Manchester University Press, 1986).

Meschonnic, H., *Modernité Modernité*, (Lagrasse, Ed. Verdier, 1988).

Mestrovic, S., *The Barbarian Temperament. Towards a Postmodern Critical Theory*, (London, Routledge, 1993).

Mills, C. A., '"Life on the upslope": the postmodern landscape of gentrification', *Environment and Planning D: Society and Space*, 6, 2, 169–89, (1988).

Mills, D. Q., *L'entreprise post-hiérarchique*, (Paris, InterEditions, 1994).

Morris, M. *The Pirate's Fiancée: Feminism, Reading postmodernism*, (London, Verso, 1988).

Myerson, G., *Rhetoric, Reason and Society. Rationality as Dialogue*, (London, Sage, 1994).

Negri, T., 'Valeur-travail: crie et problèmes de reconstruction dans le postmoderne', *Futur Antérieur*, 10, 30–6, (1992).

Nicholson, L., (ed.), *Feminism/Postmodernism*, (London, Routledge, 1990).

Norris, C., *Deconstruction: Theory and Practice*, (London, Methuen, 1982).

Norris, C., *The Contest of Faculties: Philosophy and Theory after Deconstruction*, (London, Methuen, 1985).

Norris, C., *What's Wrong with Postmodernism: Critical Theory and the ends of Philosophy*, (Baltimore, John Hopkins University Press, 1990).

Norris, C., *Uncritical Theory: Postmodernism, Intellectuals and the Gulf War*, (London, Lawrence and Wishart, 1992).

Norris, C., *The Truth about Postmodernism*, (Oxford, Blackwell, 1993).

Nouss, A., *La modernité*, (Paris, J. Grancher, 1991).

Nouss, A., *La modernité*, (Paris, PUF, 1995).

Nowotny, H., *Time. The Modern and Postmodern Experience*, (Oxford, Polity Press, 1994).

Olsson, G., 'Marxism as a modernism: review essay', *Environment and Planning D: Society and Space*, 2, 2, 241–4, (1984).

Olsson, G., *Lines of power, limits of language*, (Minneapolis, University of Minnesota Press, 1991).

Olsson, G., 'Chiasm of thought-and-action;, *Environment and Planning D: Society and Space*, 11, 3, 279–94, (1993).

Olsson, G., 'Job and the case of the herbarium', *Environment and Planning D: Society and Space*, 12, 2, 221–5, (1994).

O'Neill, J., 'Religion and Postmodernism: The Durkheimian Bond in Bell and Jameson', *Theory, Culture & Society*, 5, 2/3, 493–508, (1988).

O'Neill, J., *The Poverty of Postmodernism*, (London, Routledge, 1994).

Ozuch, C., 'L'attrait pour le ténu', *Les Cahiers de Philosophie*, 6, 5–20, (1988).

Pasquier, D., 'Vingt ans de recherches sur la télévision: une sociologie post lazarsfeldienne, *Sociologie du Travail*, 36, 1, 63–84, (1994).

Paterson, J. M., *Moments post-modernes dans le roman québécois*, (Ottawa, Presses de l'Université d'Ottawa, 1990).

Peet, R. and Watts, M., 'Introduction: development Theory and Environment in an Age of Market Triumphalism', *Economic Geography*, 69, 3/4, 227–253, (1993).

Peet, R. and Watts., (eds), *Liberation Ecologies. Environment, Development, Social Movements*, (London, Routledge, 1996).

Pepper, D., *Eco-socialism. From Deep Ecology to Social Justice*, (London, Routledge, 1993).

Perrez-Gomez, A., *Architecture and the crisis of modern science*, (Cambridge, Mass., MIT Press, 1983).

Perrot M-D., Rist G. And Sabelli, F., *La mythologie programmée. L'économie des croyances dans la société moderne*, (Paris, PUF, 1992).

Petridou, V., 'Un exemple d'architecture postmoderne: Ricardo Bofill', *Les Cahiers de Philosophie*, 6, 105–111, (1988).

Phillipson, M., *In Modernity's Wake: the Ameurunculus Letters*, (London, Routledge, 1989).

Philo, C., 'Reflexions on Gunnar Olsson's contribution to the discourse of contemporary human geography', *Environment and Planning D: Society and Space*, 2, 2, 217–40, (1984).

Philo, C., 'Escaping Flatland: a book review essay inspired by Gunnar Olsson's "Lines of Power/Limits of Language"', *Environment and Planning D: Society and Space*, 12, 2, 229–52, (1994).

Pieterse, J. N., (ed.), *Emancipation – Modern and Postmodern*, (London, Sage, 1992).

Pile, S. and Rose, G., 'All or nothing? Politics and critique in the modernism-postmodernism debate', *Environment and Planning D: Society and Space*, 10, 2, 123–136, (1992).

Pippin, R. B., *Modernism as a Philosophical Problem*, (Oxford, Blackwell, 1991).

Portis, L., 'Autour de la théorie sociale "postmoderniste": clivage des générations, rupture épistémologique et crise historique', *L'Homme et la Société*, 111/112 (1/2), 137–54, (1994).

Portoghesi, P., *Au-delà de l'architecture moderne*, (Paris, L'Equerre, 1981).

Portoghesi, P., *Le post-moderne. L'architecture dans la société post-industrielle*, (Paris, Electa Moniteur, 1983).

Poulat, E., *L'ère postchrétienne*, (Paris, Flammarion, 1994).

Pousin, F., 'Du discours postmoderne en architecture', *Les Cahiers de Philosophie*, 6, 97–104, (1988).

Pratt, G., 1993, 'Reflexions on Poststructuralism and Feminist Empirics, Theory and Practice', *Antipode*, 25, 1, 51–63, (1988).

Pred, A., 'On "Postmodernism, Language and the Strains of Modernism". Straw men Build Straw Houses?', *Annals of the Association of American Geographers*, 82, 2, 305–8, (1992).

Pred, A., *Recognizing European Modernities. A Montage of the Present*, (London, Routledge, 1995).

Pred, A. and Watts, M. J., *Reworking modernity: capitalisms and symbolic discontents*, (New Brunswick, N.J. Rutgers University Press, 1992).

Rabinow, P., 'Representations are social facts: modernity and post-modernity in anthropology', in Clifford, J. And Marcus, G. E., (eds), *Writing Culture: The Poetics and Politics of Ethnography*, (Berkeley, University of California Press, 234–61, (1986).

Racine, J. B., 'Le Métier des géographes: le recours aux sources. Commentaires à propos d'une pensée nouvelle au sein de la géographie française'. *Cahiers de Géographie de Québec*, 38, 88, 51–7, (1989).

Raulet, G., 'L'archipel. Réflexion sur la démocratie post-moderne', *Les Cahiers de Philosophie*, 6, 55–83, (1988).

Reichert, D., 'On boundaries', *Environment and Planning D: Society and Space*, 10, 1, 87–98, (1992).

Reijen, van W., 'The "Dialectic of Enlightenment" Read as Allegory', *Theory, Culture & Society*, 5, 2/3, 409–29, (1988).

Reijen, van W. and Veerman, D., 'An Interview with Jean-François Lyotard', *Theory, Culture & Society*, 5, 2/3, 277–309, (1988).

Relph, E., 'Post-modern Geography', *The Canadian Geographer*, 35, 1, 98–105, (1991).

Ritzer, G., *The McDonaldization of Society*, (Newbury Park, CA./London, Pine Forge Press/Sage, 1993).

Roberts, E., 'Beyond Progress: The Museum and Montage', *Theory, Culture & Society*, 5, 2/3, 543–57, (1988).

Roberts, J., *Postmodernism Politics and Art*, (Manchester, Manchester University Press, 1990).

Robins, K., 'Prisoners of the city: Whatever could a postmodern city be?' *New Formations*, 13, 1–22, (1991).

Rocheleau, D., Thomas-Slayter, B. and Wangary, E., (eds), *Feminist Political Ecology*, (London, Routledge, 1996).

Rogers, A., 'Key Themes and Debates', in Rogers, A., Viles, H. and Goudie, A., *The Student's Companion to Geography*, (Oxford, Blackwell, 1992) 233–52.

Roman, J., *Chronique des idées contemporaines*, (Paris, Bréal, 1995).

Rorty, R., 'Lyotard and Habermas on postmodernity', in Bernstein, R. J., (ed.), *Habermas and Modernity*, (Cambridge, Mass., MIT Press, 1985), 161–75.

Rose, G., 'Architecture to Philosophy – The Postmodern Complicity', *Theory, Culture & Society*, 5, 2/3, 357–71, (1988).

Rose, G., *Feminism and Geography. The Limits of Geographical Knowledge*, (London, Polity Press, 1993).

Rosen, S., *The Ancients and the Moderns. Rethinking Modernity*, (London, Yale University Press, 1987).

Rosenberg, H., *The Tradition of the New*, (Chicago, Chicago University Press, 1960).

Ruby, C., *Le champ de bataille post-moderne, néo-moderne*, (Paris, L'Harmattan, 1990).

Ruby, C., 'Eléments pour une philosophie des victimes. En marge des néo-modernes et des postmodernes', *L'Homme et la Société*, 113, 3, 105–15, (1994).

Russ, J., *La marche des idées contemporaines. Un panorama de la modernité*, (Paris, A. Colin, 1994).

Ryan, M., 'Postmodern Politics', *Theory, Culture & Society*, 5, 2/3, 559–76, (1988).

Sack, R. D., *Place, Modernity, and the Consumer's Word: A Relational Geographical Framework for Geographical Analysis*, (Baltimore, John Hopkins University Press, 1992).

Sandywell, B., 'Forget Baudrillard', *Theory, Culture and Society*, 12, 4, 125–52, (1995).

Sansot, P., 'Modernité et nouvelles métropoles', *Sociétés, Revue des Sciences Humaines et Sociales*, 28, 75–80, (1990).

Sass, L., *Madness and Modernism. Insanity in the Light of Modern Arts, Literature and Thought*, 'New York, Basik Books, 1992).

Savich, H., *Post-Industrial Cities*, (Princeton, N.J., Princeton University Press, 1988).

Sayer, D., *Capitalism and Modernity*, (London, Routledge, 1990).

Sayer, A., 'Postmodernist Thought in Geography: A Realist View', *Antipode*, 25, 4, 320–44, (1993).

Schuurman, F. J. *Beyond the Impasse: New Directions in Development Theory*, (London/New Jersey, Zed Books, 1993).

Scott, A. J., *Metropolis*, (Los Angeles, University of California Press, 1988).

Scott, B. K., (ed.), *The Gender of Modernism. A Critical Anthology*, (Bloomington and Indianapolis, Indiana University Press, 1990).

Scott, J. S. and Simpson-Housley, P., 'Relativizing the relativizers: on the postmodern challenge to human geography', *Transactions, Institute of British Geographers*, 14, 2, 231–36, (1989).

Seidman, S. and Wagner, D. G., *Postmodernism and Social Theory. The Debate over General Theory*, (Oxford, Basil Blackwell, 1992).

Serres, M., *Le contrat naturel*, (Paris, Flammarion, 1990).

Shields, R., 'Social spatialization and built environment: the West Edmonton Mall', *Environment and Planning D: Society and Space*, 7, 2, 147–64, (1989).

Shields, R., *Places on the Margin. Alternative Geographies of Modernity*, (London, Routledge, 1990).

Shields, R., 'Autour des Chutes du Niagara: spatialisation postmoderne?', *Sociétés, Revue des Sciences Humaines et Sociales*, 33, 311–20, (1991).

Shields, R., 'A truant proximity: presence and absence in the space of modernity', , *Environment and Planning D: Society and Space*, 10, 2, 181–98, (1992).

Shusterman, R., 'Postmodernist Aestheticisme: A New Moral Philosophy?', *Theory, Culture & Society*, 5, 2/3, 337–55, (1988).

Silverman, H. J., *Postmodernism – Philosophy and the Arts*, (London, Routledge, 1990).

Simmel, G., *Philosophie de la modernité*, (Paris, Payot, 1923, 1989).

Simons, H. W. and Billig, M., (eds), *After Postmodernism. Reconstructing Ideology Critique*, (London, Sage, 1994).

Slater, D., 'On the borders of social theory: learning from other regions', , *Environment and Planning D: Society and Space*, 10, 3, 307–27, (1992).

Smart, B., *Modern Conditions, Postmodern Controversies*, (London, Routledge, 1992).

Smart, B., *Postmodernity*, (London, Routledge, 1993).

Smith, N., 'Geography redux? The history and theory of geography', *Progress in Human Geography*, 14, 4, 547–59, (1990).

Soja, E. W., 'La réaffirmation de l'espace dans la théorie sociale: la prochaine "fin de siècle"', in Benko, G., (ed.), *Les nouveaux aspects de la théorie sociale. De la géographie à la sociologie*, (Caen, Paradigme, 1988), 1–14.

Soja, E. W., *Postmodern Geographies*, (London, Verso, 1989).

Soja, E. W., 'Aménager dans/pour la post-modernité', *Espaces et Sociétés*, 74/75. 203–14, (1993).

Soper, K., 'Feminism, humanism and postmodernism', *Radical Philosophy*, 55, 11–17, (1990).

Soper, K., 'Postmodernism, subjectivity and the question of value', in Squires, J., (ed.), *Principled Positions. Postmodernism and the Rediscovery of Value*, (London, Lawrence and Wishart, 1993), 17–30.

Sparke, N., 'Escaping the herbarium: a critique of Gunnar Olsson's "Chiasm of thought-and-action"', *Environment and Planning D: Society and Space*, 12, 2, 207–20, (1994a).

Sparke, M., 'The return of the same in geography: a reply to Olsson', , *Environment and Planning D: Society and Space*, 12, 2, 226–28, (1994b).

Spivak, G. C. and Harasym, S., *The Post-Colonial Critic. Interviews, Strategies, Dialogues*, (London, Routledge, 1990).

Squires, J., (ed.), *Principled Positions. Postmodernism and the Rediscovery of Value*, (London, Lawrence and Wishart, 1993).

Starr, K., *Inventing the dream: California through the Progressive era*, (Oxford, Oxford University Press, 1985).

Stauth, G. and Turner B. S., 'Nostalgia, Postmodernism and the Critique of Mass Culture', *Theory, Culture & Society*, 5, 2/3, 509–26, (1988).

Stevenson, N. *Social Theory and Mass Communication*, (London, Sage, 1995).

Stirn, F., *25 livres clés pour comprendre le monde modern*, (Paris, Marabout, 1994).

Strohmayer, U., 'Modernité, post-modernité ou comment justifier un savoir géographique', *Géographie et Cultures*, 6, 75–84, (1993).

Strohmayer, U., 'Beyond theory: the cumbersome materiality of shock', *Environment and Planning D: Society and Space*, 11, 3, 323–47, (1993).

Strohmayer, U. and Hannah, M., 'Domesticating postmodernism', *Antipode*, 24, 1, 29–55, (1992).

Symanski, R., 'Why We Should Fear Postmodernists', *Annals of the Association of American Geographers*, 84, 2, 301–4, (1994).

Taylor, C., *Le malaise de la modernité*, (Paris, Cerf, 1994).

Tester, K., *Life and Times of Post-Modernity*, (London, Routledge, 1993).

Thackaray, J., (ed.), *Design After Modernism*, (London, Thames & Hudson, 1988).

Thompson, J. B., *Ideology and Modern Culture. Critical Social Theory in the Era of Mass Communication*, (Cambridge, Polity Press, 1990).

Thrift, N. J., 'No perfect symmetry', *Environment and Planning D: Society and Space*, 5, 4, 400–7, (1987).

Tibi, B., 'Culture and Knowledge: the Politics of Islamization of Knowledge as a Postmodern Project?', *Theory Culture and Society*, 12, 1, 1–24, (1995).

Tillyard, S., *The Impact of Modernism 1900–1920. The Visual Arts in Edwardian England*, (London, Routledge, 1988).

Torres, F., *Déjà vu. Post et néo-modernisme: le retour du passé*, (Paris, Ramsey, 1986).

Touraine, A., *La société post-industrielle*, (Paris, Denoel, 1969).

Touraine, A., 'Modernité et spécificités culturelles, *Revue Internationale des Sciences Sociales*, 118, 497–511, (1988).

Touraine, A., *Critique de la modernité*, (Paris, Fayard, 1992).

Travers, A., 'Shelf-Life Zero: A Classic Postmodernist Paper', *Philosophy of the Social Sciences*, 19, 291–320, (1989).

Turner, B. S., (ed.), *Theory of Modernity and Postmodernity*, (London, Sage, 1990).

Turner, B. S., *Orientalism, Postmodernism and Globalism*, (London, Routledge, 1994).

Tyler S., 'Post-modern ethnography: from document of the occult to occult document', in Clifford, J. and Marcus, G. E., (eds), *Writing Culture: The Poetics and Politics of Ethnography*, (Berkeley, University of California Press, 1986) 122–40.

Vakaloulis, M., 'Post-capitalisme ou capitalisme post-moderne? Structures fondamentales et facteurs de nouveauté', *Futur Antérieur*, 21, 45–57, (1994a).

Vakaloulis, M., 'Modernité avancée et modernisation "post"-moderne. Note théorique d'une recherche, *L'Homme et la Société*, 113, 3, 5–18, (1994b).

Vattimo, G., *La fin de la modernité. Nihilisme et herméneutique dans la culture post-moderne*, [Paris, Seuil, 1987 (1985)].

Vattimo, G., *the End of Modernity. Nihilism and Hermeneutics in Post-Modern Culture*, (Cambridge, Polity Press, 1988a).

Vattimo, G., 'Hermeneutics as Koine', *Theory, Culture & Society*, 5, 2/3, 399–408, (1988b).

Veerman, D., 'Introduction to Lyotard', *Theory, Culture & Society*, 5, 2/3, 271–5, (1988a).

Veerman, D., 'Développer l'honneur de penser. Remarques sur Lyotard', *Les Cahiers de Philosophie*, 5, 11–34, (1988b).

Venturi, V., Scott-Brown, D. and Izenour, S., *L'enseignement de Las Vegas, ou le symbolisme oublié de la forme architecturale*, (Bruxelles, Mardaga, 1978).

Virilio, P., *L'art du moteur*, (Paris, Galilée, 1993).

Virilio, P., *La vitesse de libération*, (Paris, Galilée, 1995).

Wagner, P., *A Sociology of Modernity. Liberty and Discipline*, (London, Routledge, 1993).

Warf, B., 'Can the Region Survive Post-modernism, *Urban Geography*, 11, 6, 586–93, (1990).

Watson, S. and Gibson, K., *Postmodern Cities and Spaces*, (Oxford, Blackwell, 1994).

Weinstein, D. and Weinstein, M., *Postmodern(ized) Simmel*, (London, Routledge, 1993).

Wellmer, A., 'On dialectic of modernism and postmodernism', *Praxis International*, 4, 337–62, (1985).

Wellmer, A., *In Defence of Modernity*, (Cambridge, Polity Press, 1990).

Wellmer, A., *The Persistence of Modernity. Essays on Aesthetics, Ethics and Postmodernism*, (Cambridge, Polity Press, 1991).

Welody, I. and Williams R., (eds), *Politics and Modernity*, (London, Sage, 1992).

Welsch, W., 'Modernité et Postmodernité', *Les Cahiers de Philosophie*, 6, 21–31, (1988).

Wheale, N., (ed.), *The Postmodern Arts: An Introductory Reader*, (London, Routledge, 1995).

Williams, R., *The Politics of Modernism*, (Oxford, Blackwell, 1989).

Wolch, J. and Dear, M., (eds), *The Power of Geography. How Territory Shapes Social Life*, (Boston, Unwin Hyman, 1989).

Wolin, R., 'Modernism vs. Postmodernism', *Telos*, 62, 9–29, (1984).

Woodiwiss, A., *Postmodernity USA. The Crisis of Social Modernism in Postwar America*, (London, Sage, 1993).

Young, R., *Post-colonial Theory*, (Oxford, Blackwell, 1987).

Zukin, S., 'The Postmodern Debate over Urban Form', *Theory, Culture & Society*, 5, 2/3, 431–46, (1988).

Zukin, S., 'The postmodern invasion', *International Journal of Urban and Regional Research*, 16, 3, 488–95, (1992).

Zurbrugg, N., *The Parameters of Postmodernism*, (London, Routledge, 1993).

PART I

Reasons, Texts and Debates around Postmodernism

Introduction

More than other intellectual debates within the human sciences, it was the eruption of the discussion around "postmodernism" in the 1970s that served as a unifying beacon for academic disputes throughout the 1980s. No matter whether one was sympathetic to the idea or not, the terms of many debates were set with reference to some "postmodernism" or another. Geography was no exception, although it took it until the mid 1980s to digest previous revolutions within its paradigmatic orbit. Hence its relative late arrival at the scene of postmodern discourse.

Since then, if course, much ink has been spilled within geography about the dangers and the possibilities inherent to the "postmodern challenge" (to quote once again from the title of the seminal paper by Michael Dear). The hegemony of reason has been noted and commented upon, alternatives pondered and a newly found epistemological and thematic pluralism has been explored. The root question, however, of whether or not "modernity" has exhausted itself and whether or not some "post"- modern manner of thinking was required, has, if not been ignored, largely been put to rest in the ensuing debates. The following essays hope to rescue this most central of issues from an all too early grave. They highlight the dangers that reside in assuming legitimate answers where we have barely begun to phrase questions.

Paradoxically, one area in which we have yet to formulate convincing questions is the realm of writing. Although the term "discourse" has gained wide currency in the aftermath of the postmodern dawn, do we really know what we mean by this term? A defining element in any science, the enabling properties of writing and discourse have again been largely assumed at the expense of closer investigations into their historically specific coming into being during the early modern period. Geography again is no exception in that it has taken one of its constitutive elements – the *graphos* visibly at work in geography – largely for granted. So what about this material condition of the possibility of (geographical) knowledge? With the book a modern invention, can there be something akin to postmodern publishing? The essays in this part of the book give different answers to these questions. Partly this difference is due to the fact that they explore the question from different angles: Dear's epistemological stance, Peet's ideological analysis and Curry's genealogical perspective do not easily add up to a unified vision of the postmodern. But then, this difference might be as much to do with the problem under scrutiny as a reflection of different approaches to the problem.

1

Postmodern Bloodlines

Michael Dear

The emergence of postmodern thought has provided an important impetus for reconsideration of the role of space in social theory and in the construction of everyday life. Yet critics of postmodernity threaten to erase these gains and return geographical thought to more traditional verities (of various stripes) and thereby reinstate the comfortable hegemonies of old. This would be a mistake. In this essay, I shall focus on continuities and departures in postmodern thinking about space to demonstrate the enduring significance of the issues it raises. To keep this task within manageable proportions, I shall concentrate on two principal texts: Henri Lefebvre's 1974 masterwork *La Production de l'Espace,* available in translation by Donald Nicholson-Smith; and Fredric Jameson's *Postmodernism, or the Cultural Logic of Late Capitalism* (1991).[1] The former will serve as an exemplar of modernist traditions in spatial analysis; the latter provides a perspective on postmodernity (although I shall adjust this oversimple dichotomy later in the discussion). I hope to show that postmodern thought is clearly traceable from modernist "bloodlines;" that it signals equally transparent departures from that heritage; and, hence, that it cannot be dismissed or subsumed without considerable loss.

Space is, in a manner of speaking, nature's way of preventing everything from happening in the same place. Much of Henri Lefebvre's work is essentially a fugue on this simple proposition. Richly embellishing the theme in *The Production of Space,* he identifies the following kinds of space: absolute, abstract, appropriated, capitalist, concrete, contradictory, cultural, differentiated, dominated, dramatized, epistemological, familial, instrumental, leisure, lived, masculine, mental, natural, neutral, organic, original, physical, plural, political, pure, real, repressive, sensory, social, socialist, socialized, state, transparent, true, and women's space. At the end of all this, there can be little doubt that " ... space is never empty: it always embodies a meaning."[2] Most social theorists are by now aware that Lefebvre's project is aimed at a reorientation of human inquiry away from its traditional obsession with time and toward a reconstituted focus on space. There is scarcely a project in theoretical human geography within the past two decades that has remained untouched (consciously or otherwise) by Lefebvre's problematic.[3]

The importance of space in postmodern thought is widely conceded, yet programmatic statements on postmodern spatiality remain rare. Fredric Jameson's 1984 essay "Postmodernism, or the cultural logic of late capitalism" provided the touchstone for a postmodern geography, and it is significant that the essay retains much of its vitality and challenge.[4] He republished this account in a 1991 collection, thus reinforcing his assertion that space is the "supremely mediatory function" in the construction of a postmodern society.[5]

I propose to explicate the concepts of space and spatiality in the texts of Lefebvre and Jameson, and distil therefrom the lineaments of a program for postmodern spatial analysis. My emphasis will be on continuities and discontinuities in their philosophies. In what follows, I shall touch on matters of spatial ontologies, epistemology and method, spatiality and the production of space, and social action. The essay concludes with some reflections on the conformities and departures represented by the two texts.

Ontologies of Space

> Where there is space, there is being
> H. Lefebvre (1991) p. 22

Lefebvre goes back to the beginning in his search for the meaning of space. He is highly critical of previous ontologies that describe space strictly in geometrical terms, as an "empty space." This construct, he asserts, enabled modern epistemologists to adopt the notion of space as a mental thing, capable of absorbing a myriad meanings according to the analyst's whim. Subsequent work in the science of space:

> has produced either mere descriptions which never achieve analytical, much less theoretical, status, or else fragments and cross-sections of space. There are plenty of reasons for thinking that descriptions and cross-sections of this kind, though they may well supply inventories of what *exists in* space, or even generate a *discourse on* space, cannot ever give rise to a *knowledge of* space.[6]

Instead, what we have is an indefinite multitude of spaces, piled one upon the other, each pored over and dissected by analysts from respective disciplines.

Against this, Lefebvre posits the need to uncover the theoretical unity among three fields that are usually apprehended separately: the physical (nature); the mental (logical and formal abstractions); and the social. The loss of an appropriate unitary theory is blamed upon Hegel, whom Lefebvre describes unforgettably as a "sort of [intellectual] Place de l'Etoile."[7] But others, including Heidegger, have contributed to the devaluation of place. Lefebvre turns to Nietzsche as the principal voice maintaining the primordality of space; time may be distinguished from space, but the two cannot be separated:

Time *per se* is an absurdity; likewise space *per se*. The relative and the absolute are reflections of one another: each always refers back to the other, and the same is true of space and time.[8]

Lefebvre is quick to point out that his unitary theory does not imply a privileged language, nor even a metalanguage. Instead, it stresses the dialectical character of spatial decoding:

> The project I am outlining ... does not aim to produce a (or *the*) discourse on space, but rather to expose the actual production of space by bringing the various kinds of space and the modalities of their genesis together within a single theory.[10]

Lefebvre organizes his understanding around separate concepts of space:[10] *absolute space*, which is essentially natural until colonized, when it becomes relativized and historical; *abstract space*, associated with the space of accumulation, in which production and reproduction processes are separated and space takes on an instrumental function; *contradictory space*, where disintegration of the old and generation of the new occur in response to the contradictions inherent in abstract space; and *differential space*, the consequent mosaic of different places. At the core of the Lefebvrian project are the concepts of *production* and the *act of producing* space; i.e. "(social) space is a (social) product."[11] Four precepts are constitutive of this project:[12]

1 *Physical (natural) space is disappearing*, which is not to say it is of diminishing importance.[13]
2 *Every society, every mode of production, produces its own space.*[14] Social space contains, and assigns appropriate places to, the relations of production and of reproduction (including biological reproduction and the reproduction of labor power and social relations). The *process* of creation requires the availability of specialized sites associated with production, prohibition, and repression. As a consequence of this process, dominant spaces are able to mold the subordinate spaces of the periphery.
3 *Theory reproduces the generative process.*[15] If space is a product, our knowledge of it will reproduce and expound the process of production. To move from a concern with things in space to the production of space, additional explanations will be required. Lefebvre emphasizes the dialectical nature of this understanding. He distinguishes among *spatial practices* (our perceptions); *representations of space* (our conceptions); and *representational spaces* (the lived space). Each contributes differentially to the production of space, varying according to local conditions.
4 *The passage from one mode of production to another is of the highest theoretical importance.*[16] Because each mode of production is assumed to have its own particular space, the shift from one mode to another necessarily entails the production of a new space. If this is so, the key issues – greatly exercising students of the putative shift to postmodernity – are exactly how does one identify the emergent spaces, and at what point do they add up to a new mode of production? These determinations are partly a task of determining the appropriate spatial codes (which are often ambiguous), and the proper periodization.[17]

In sum, the Lefebvrian ontology assumes that space is present and implicit in the very act of creation and being, and that the process of life is inextricably linked with the production of different spaces. The production of space is inherently a political project, the consequences of which Lefebvre does not shy from, as we shall see later.

The essence of Jameson's postmodernity is, I believe, a way of seeing. Jameson regards society as a text, and postmodernism as a *periodizing hypothesis*.[18] He is fascinated by the glittering surfaces in the strange new landscape of late twentieth century capitalism, and willing to assume that a new social order is in the making. At the same time, he is appalled by the contradictions in this society, which juxtapose corporate monoliths with homelessness, and the "increasing immiseration of American society" with the "self-congratulatory rhetoric of contemporary political pluralism."[19] He grabs onto the surficial threads and follows them, expecting to find not a labyrinth, but maybe a gulag or a shopping mall. Because we lack an adequate road-map to guide our exploration, Jameson concludes that the challenge lies in making sense of these surfaces – a task that I have characterized as the "geographical puzzle" of unravelling obsolescent modernisms from emergent postmodernisms.[20]

Jameson argues that we needed the term postmodernism without knowing it. Now we cannot not use the term. The "motley crew of strange bedfellows" who embraced the term have coalesced into a new discursive genre – less a "theory," and more a diverse "theoretical discourse."[21] Such a discourse is necessarily imperfect and impure; it is driven to abandon the metaphysical baggage surrounding truth, foundationalism and essentialism. Hence, postmodernism is not something that can be settled once and for all, then used in a noncontroversial manner. Each time it is invoked, Jameson insists: "we are under the obligation to rehearse those inner contradictions and to stage those representational inconsistencies and dilemmas; we have to work all that through every time around."[22]

This is an awesome task, but Jameson suggests that what has happened to *culture* provides important clues for tracking the postmodern. He is quick to point out that social change is not purely a cultural affair; postmodernism is properly to be regarded as the "cultural dominant" of late capitalism. By so contextualizing his analysis, Jameson insists on a concept of postmodernity that is essentially historical rather than merely a disembodied stylistic or aesthetic. This leads him, in turn, to the core of his problematic: that the emergence of a postmodern cultural dominant signals a "radical break" from previous cultures (cf. Lefebvre's emphasis on transitions in the mode of production). Jameson situates this rupture at the end of the 1950s, and associates it with the waning of the 100-year old modern movement. He concedes that granting historical originality to a putative postmodern culture is a risky business, and that self-awareness usually comes later, and then only gradually. But his even greater worry is that:

> period concepts [may] finally correspond to no realities whatsoever, and that whether they are formulated in terms of generational logic, or by the names of

reigning monarchs, or according to some other category or topological and classificatory system, the collective reality of the multitudinous lives encompassed by such terms is unthinkable (or nontotalizable ...) and can never be described, characterized, labelled, or conceptualized.[23]

Jameson escapes this dilemma by situating his inquiry firmly within a Marxian historical materialism. He adheres to Mandel's now-familiar periodization: classical/market capitalism; monopoly capitalism; and multinational/ late capitalism (the term "late capitalism" is not his preferred slogan, because it carries so much ideological and political baggage; he prefers "multinational capitalism" to refer to capitalism's third phase). And, despite his apparent eagerness to kick over the intellectual traces, he is frequently drawn back to what he calls "old friends" in the Marxian grid. For example:

> if modernization is something that happens to the base, and modernism the form the superstructure takes in reaction to that ambivalent development, then perhaps modernity characterizes the attempt to make something coherent out of their relationship.[24]

Most of Jameson's attention is focused on the third phase of capitalist development. He argues that older cities and nation states become obsolete as capital leaps prodigiously beyond them. In the emergent spaces of multinational capital, the suppression of conventional distance and the saturation of remaining voids or empty spaces create a "perceptual barrier of immediacy from which all sheltering layers and intervening mediation have been removed."[25]

Everything in this global space becomes cultural, though not solely in its intent and origins. The subsequent saturated space has become dominated by the USA, giving rise to the "first specifically North American [*sic*] global style."[26] In so forcefully admitting cultural complexity into the analysis, Jameson undermines the notion of the mode of production as a "total system," in the-sense of an all-encompassing explanation for everything.

It is to surfaces that Jameson is irresistibly drawn. For him, postmodern society is characterized by a flatness, or *depthlessness*, a "new kind of superficiality in the most literal sense;"[27] a *waning of affect*, the diminution of feeling, emotion, and subjectivity in postmodern images (Warhol is his archetype);[28] and a *decentering* of the formerly-centered subject or psyche.[29] The consequent *eclipse of the norm*[30] is due to the staggering proliferation of private styles and linguistic fragmentation, marked by the rise of *pastiche*[31] – a neutral, blank parody devoid of parody's satiric impulse. This emptied culture reaches its apex in the *simulacrum*, the identical copy for which no original ever existed, and brought vitally to life in a society where the "the image has become the final form of commodity reification."[32] Postmodern culture is characterized by *fragmentation*.[33] In the final analysis, Jameson attributes these trends to the "universalization of capitalism."[34]

Epistemologies of Space

> Things lie ... in order to conceal their origins
> H. Lefebvre (1991) p. 81

Lefebvre's method in analyzing the production of space is firmly grounded in Marxist thought, and is nourished by the conviction that a proper treatment of space will inevitably revitalize Marxism. What is for me most intriguing about these epistemological voyages is the extent to which Lefebvre travels toward a postmodern consciousness.

Lefebvre wears his Marxism lightly, with no trace of dogma.[35] When he turns to *Capital* for inspiration, it is not "in the sense of sifting it for quotations nor in the sense of subjecting it to the "ultimate exegesis.""[36] He avoids the quicksand of reductionism, and is wary of overemphasizing the economic sphere. His epistemological openness is expressed straightforwardly, in a way that theoretical dogmatists of all persuasions should take to heart: "Marxism should be treated as one *moment* in the development of theory, and not, dogmatically, as a definitive theory."[37] This anti-hegemonic stance is a principal instance of Lefebvre's postmodernism *avant la lettre* (notwithstanding his avowed search for a unitary theory). But in addition, he is extremely critical of the fragmentation brought about by disciplinary fiefdoms, with their predilection for partial representations and occasional arbitrary totalizations.[38] He is particularly hard on traditional philosophy, which "in its decline, stripped now of any dialectical dimension, serves as a bulwark as much for illegitimate separations as for illegitimate confusions."[39]

Lefebvre also betrays a postmodern sensitivity in the matters of language and reading the *text* (of cities, etc.). All the same, he is categorically against the priority-of-language thesis, insisting that Western culture has overemphasized speech and the written word.[40] For him, every language is located in space, and he offers a timely warning to all those who would raise language onto some new epistemological pedestal:

> To underestimate, ignore and diminish space amounts to the overestimation of texts, written matter, and writing systems, along with the readable and the visible, to the point of assigning to these a monopoly on intelligibility.[41]

Lefebvre insists that space is *lived* before it is *perceived*, and *produced* before it can be *read*, which raises the question of what the virtue of readability actually is, especially because the "spaces made (produced) to be read are the most deceptive and tricked-up imaginable."[42] He quotes the example of fascist monumentality, which claims to express the collective will yet masks the will to power and the arbitrariness of its exercise. He concludes that the principal purpose of reading, the decoding of the spatial text, is to help us understand the transition from representational (i.e. lived) spaces to representations (conceptions) of space.

Tolerant of different voices, critical of disciplinary fragmentation, suspicious of hegemonies, and sensitive to language, Lefebvre in these ways reveals himself as a latent postmodernist.[43] Yet, paradoxically, he still abides by certain normal codes of scientific inquiry, seeking to have his theory confirmed by application to other societies, other modes of production.[44] He also concedes that what he seeks could be described by traditional philosophers as a metaphilosophy.[45]

Jameson is quick to emphasize that postmodernism requires new methods. He rejects the modernist mind-set that has "blocked the creative mind with awkward self-consciousness,"[46] and portrayed modernism as "a time of giants and legendary powers no longer available to us."[47] He recognizes multiple, though not infinite, possibilities of explanation (while rejecting the term "undecidability"), and leaves open the question of whether or not it is possible to create an internally self-coherent theory of the postmodern, i.e. an antifoundationalism that truly eschews all foundations, a nonessentialism without the least shred of essence. This fundamental paradox – the desire to break free from modernity's strictures, and yet make sense out of postmodernity's theoretical plenitude – is at the heart of Jameson's (and postmodernism's) epistemological dilemma. Previously, Jameson has argued for a "doctrine of levels" (i.e. different levels of abstraction), whereby incompatible codes and models may be differentiated. In *Postmodernism*, this essentially dialectical approach takes the form of *transcoding*. Jameson abandons "beliefs" about philosophical or political world visions in favor of specific "ideolects" or "ideological codes" which are demonstrably partial languages for understanding the world. Transcoding is about:

> measuring what is sayable and "thinkable" in each of these codes or ideolects and compar[ing] that to the conceptual possibilities of its competitors: this is, in my opinion, the most productive and responsible activity for students and theoretical or philosophical critics to pursue today ... [48]

To be truly free from past traditions, Jameson calls for the production of a theoretical discourse dedicated to generating new codes.

Several important consequences follow from this position. First, no ideology or theory (in the sense of a code or discursive system) is particularly determinant. Second, closure in theoretical debate in unlikely, indeed is better avoided. Third, we can never go far back enough to make primary statements, so that there are no conceptual (but only representational) beginnings, and that the doctrine of foundations is simply a testimony to the inadequacies of the human mind. The consequent theoretical aesthetic excludes philosophical propositions as well as statements about being and truth, because our language is no longer able to "frame utterances in such a way that these categories might be appropriate."[49]

Jameson's theoretical aesthetic is obviously highly demanding. The theorist walks a tightrope, threatened constantly by lapses into obsolete determinisms or stark opinion. Yet the potential gains are enormous. Jameson quotes Rorty, for example:

It is a mistake to think that Derrida, or anybody else, "recognized" problems about the nature of textuality or writing which had been ignored by the [previous] tradition. What he did was to *make the old ways of speaking optional*, and thus more or less dubious.[50]

There are risks associated with this aesthetic. These arise especially when the custodians of existing codes (hitherto presented as nonoptional) take umbrage, and embark on "search-and-destroy" missions on any linguistic misconceptions in their enemy's camp, meanwhile hoping against hope that they will not themselves become the target of such linguistic demystification. What we have then is a discursive struggle of Hobbesian dimensions, a *bellum omnium contra omnes*. To avoid a babel of incommensurable narratives, Jameson (like Lefebvre) discounts the notion that a theoretical code organized around language could have ontological primacy. Such a separation would, he insists, simply create another "named theory" in a world already replete with them.[51]

The Production of Space

> What exactly is the mode of existence of social relationships?
> H. Lefebvre (1991) p.129

The production of social space, according to Lefebvre, begins with "the study of natural rhythms, and of the modification of those rhythms and their inscription in space by means of human actions, especially work-related actions. It begins, then, with the spatio-temporal rhythms of nature as transformed by a social practice."[52] In other words, while social space is a *product* to be used or consumed, it is also a *means of production*.[53]

The shift from former habits of analyzing things in space to a new gaze on the actual production of space is fraught with difficulties:

> (Social) space is not a thing among other things, nor a product among other products: rather it subsumes things produced, and encompasses their interrelationships in their coexistence and simultaneity – their (relative) order and/or (relative) disorder. It is the outcome of a sequence and set of operations, and thus cannot be reduced to the rank of a simple object. At the same time there is nothing imagined, unreal or "ideal" about it as compared, for example, with science, representations, ideas or dreams. Itself the outcome of past actions, social space is what permits fresh actions to occur, while suggesting others and prohibiting yet others.[54]

Social relations exist to the extent that they possess a spatial expression: they project themselves into space, becoming inscribed there, and in the process producing that space itself. Thus, social space is both a *field* of action and a *basis* for action.[55]

The consequent layers of spatial texture interpenetrate and superimpose upon one another, linking the global and the local despite the persistent tendency to fragmentation in socio-economic and intellectual processes. Nothing can be taken for granted in analyzing these spaces: spaces that are meant to be read are in reality often the most opaque; some spaces are overinscribed; others deliberately conceal. Above all, space is multi-faceted and multiply-coded; hence, Lefebvre warns, transparently clear representations of space must be disavowed precisely because they offer an already clarified picture.[56]

In attempting to subordinate space and its contradictions, the capitalist mode of production thereby *produces difference*. The resulting uneven geographical development consists of *dominated* spaces (i.e. those transformed by technology) instead of *appropriated* spaces (i.e. natural space modified to serve the needs and possibilities of a group). Thus, in the spatial logic of capitalism:

> the capitalist "trinity" is established in space – that trinity of land-labor-capital which cannot remain abstract and which is assembled only within an equally tri-faceted institutional space: a space that is first of all *global* ... ; a space, secondly, that is *fragmented*, separating, disjunctive, a space that locates specificities, places or localities, both in order to control them and in order to make them negotiable; and a space, finally, that is *hierarchical*, ranging from the lowliest places to the noblest, from the tattooed to the sovereign.[57]

Deeply embedded at the core of the production of space is the capitalist state. The political apparatuses, while loudly proclaiming themselves to be readable and transparent, are in fact the epitome of opacity. Lefebvre emphasizes the historical importance of state-sanctioned violence and the nation-state. Although he is curiously silent about Max Weber's contribution to these themes, he suggests that misapprehension of the role of space may have led Hegel and Marx to downplay the theory of the state.[58]

Lefebvre uses the city and urbanism as constant touchstones in his analysis, viewing the built environment as a "brutal condensation of social relationships."[59] There is nothing more contradictory than "urbanness," especially the role of planners in effective support of capitalism and the capitalist state.[60] Planners, Lefebvre contends, are perfectly at home in dominated space, sorting and classifying space in service to a class. They deal only with "an empty space, a space that is primordial, a container to receive fragmentary contents, a neutral medium into which disjointed things, people and habitats might be introduced."[61] Lefebvre refers to Haussmann's Paris and Niemeyer's Brasilia as evidence of the consequences of planners' fractured spaces and partial logic. In the production of urban space, state political power dominates at all scales. Power plays a pivotal role in maintaining the dominance of the core over the periphery – Lefebvre's centrality thesis – and in connecting the punctual to the global. Today, centrality aspires to *total* control despite the prevailing anarchy of fragmentation which inhibits the appearance of a new mode of production by the selling of space parcel "by parcel, by a mere travesty of a new space."[62]

Concepts of space are central to the production of Jameson's postmodernism. He offers the following crucial distinction in what he describes as "so spatialized a culture as the postmodern:[63]

> A certain spatial turn has often seemed to me to offer one of the more productive ways of distinguishing postmodernism from modernism proper, whose experience of temporality – existential time, along with deep memory – is henceforth conventional to see as a dominant of the high modern.[64]

In short, categories of space and spatial logic dominate the postmodern in the way time dominated the world of modernism. At the core of Jameson's geography is the assertion that we are experiencing a mutation in built space, i.e. the production of a postmodern "hyperspace." We currently lack the perceptual apparatus to assess this hyperspace, experiencing for the moment little more than a "bewildering immersion" in the new medium.[65] The postmodern hyperspace, Jameson observes:

> has finally succeeded in transcending the capacities of the individual human body to locate itself, to organize its surroundings perceptually, and cognitively to map its position in a mappable external world. It may now be suggested that this alarming disjunction point between the body and its built environment ... can itself stand as the symbol ... of that even sharper dilemma which is the incapacity of our minds, at least at present, to map the great global multinational and decentered communicational network in which we find ourselves caught as individual subjects.[66]

The altered spaces of postmodernity are evident in many sectors. For instance, in the saturated space of multinational capitalism, *place* no longer exists except at a "much feebler level," drowned by other more powerful abstract spaces such as communications networks. The truth of an experience "no longer coincides with the place in which it takes place,"[67] meaning that the structural coordinates of the lived experience are no longer accessible to, or even conceptualizable for, most people. In particular, Nature has been erased from the postmodern by the "essential homogenization of a social space and experience now uniformly modernized and mechanized."[68] At the same time, however, postmodernity includes space for various forms of oppositional culture. According to Jameson, the very term "cultural dominant" implies coexistence with other resistant forces, including Utopian socialists, feminists, and minorities.

In attempting to decode the postmodern hyperspace, Jameson relies greatly upon architecture – the "privileged aesthetic language"[69] – because it possesses a virtually unmediated relationship with the economic. Echoing Jane Jacobs, Jameson credits high modernism with the destruction of the physical fabric of the traditional city and its neighborhood culture, together with an elitism and authoritarianism in contemporary buildings. In contrast, postmodernism is a kind of "aesthetic populism," associated with the emergence of the new texts of mass/commercial culture (including the "degraded" landscapes of schlock and kitsch). The architecture of postmodernism has, in particular, embraced an historicism which "randomly and without principle but with gusto canni-

balizes all the architectural styles of the past and combines them in overstimu-
lating ensembles."[70]

Jameson spends a lot of time in Los Angeles – which he seems to regard as
the ultimate effacement of place – trying to make sense of postmodern architecture.[71] From his examination of John Portman's Bonaventure Hotel and
Frank Gehry's Santa Monica house, he concludes that postmodernism has
abolished the distinction between inside and outside, as well as a great many
other elements of conventional architectural syntax and grammar. The
Bonaventure he describes as a "total space," a "complete world" that does not
wish to be part of the city that surrounds it.[72] Revealing his textual strategy,
Jameson the place-reader observes:

> the words of built space, or at least its substantives, would seem to be rooms,
> categories which are ... related and articulated by the various spatial verbs and
> adverbs – corridors, doorways, and staircases, for example – modified in turn by
> adjectives in the form of paint and furnishings, decoration, and ornament ...
> Meanwhile, these "sentences" – if that indeed is what a building can be said to
> "be" – are read by readers whose bodies fill the various shifter-slots and subject-
> positions; while the larger text into which such units are inserted can be assigned
> to the text-grammar of the urban as such (or perhaps, in a world system, to ever
> vaster geographies and their syntactic laws).[73]

He offers Kevin Lynch's cognitive mapping as a broadly-applicable method
for attaching the "situational representation ... of the individual subject to that
vaster and properly unrepresentable totality ... of society's structures as a
whole."[74] (Jameson draws an analogy with the Althusserian/Lacanian redefinition of ideology as the representation of the subject's Imaginary relationship
to his or her Real conditions of existence.) A global cognitive mapping on a
social and a spatial scale would, he claims, endow the individual with a
heightened sense of place in the global system, as well as clarifying the linkage
between the global and the local.

Jameson's spatial dialectic is not confined to architecture. Directly acknowledging his debt to Lefebvre, Jameson examines the distinctive modes of
production in space. Lefebvre's reassertion of space did more than correct the
modernist imbalance toward time; it also underscored the increasing importance, in daily life and multinational capitalism, of the *urban* and the new
globality of the system. Following Lefebvre, Jameson calls for a revitalized
"spatial imagination capable of confronting the past ... and reading its less
tangible secrets off the template of its spatial structures."[75] Most interestingly,
he incorporates the notion of the "market" into the problematic of postmodernism. For Jameson, the rhetoric of the market has been a fundamental tool
in the conservatives' largely successful ideological struggle to delegitimize the
political claims of the left. Moreover, the concrete reality of the market is as
much about "real markets" as it is about "metaphysics, psychology, advertising,
culture, representations, and libidinal apparatuses."[76] Most ominously, he asks

whether "the practice of consumption has not replaced the resolute taking of a stand and the full-throated endorsement of a political opinion."[77]

The geographical expression of cultural difference is apparently being homogenized by culture's link to global communications and its consequent ability to overcome distance and penetrate into all places. Jameson argues that a new euphoria or intensity accompanies the postmodern cultural experience, especially as a consequence of video – postmodernism's "most distinctive new medium,"[78] and the "most likely candidate for cultural hegemony" in the future.[79] Such developments do not prevent local differences in culture; however, they are strongly implicated in the creation of postmodernity's "saturated space."[80]

From Social Theory to Social Action

> To change life ... we must first change space
> H. Lefebvre (1991) p.190

Within the creative anarchy of capitalist spaces, Lefebvre uncovers his political project, in an immensely skillful and prescient way. Urban conditions tend to uphold a measure of democracy, largely because spatial contradictions allow for a measure of local autonomy. However, these same contradictions pose a continuous threat to the social order. So, Lefebvre asks, with a crucial insight that foreshadows the political fragmentation of the postmodern era: "Might not the spatial chaos engendered by capitalism, despite the power and rationality of the state, turn out to be the system's Achilles' heel?"[81]

Under conditions of modernity, the role of the state has grown to encompass an absolute political space. While relatively few have recognized the extent of this encroachment, fewer still are able to influence it, thus accounting for the silence or passivity of the users of space. Nevertheless, even the powerful experience difficulties in mastering what is "at once their product and the tool of their mastery, namely space."[82] And it is here, in the crucial interstices between locus of power and its reach, that Lefebvre glimpses the emergence of a new politics.

New forms of political struggle including minorities, women, and community-based coalitions, are truly threatening to existing power blocs because they go beyond manipulable tests of ideological purity, and propose counter-spaces. To be successful, the counter-spaces of politics would need to overcome the domination of masculinist principles, and make "the reappropriation of the body, in association with the reappropriation of space, a non-negotiable part of its agenda."[83] Lefebvre, incidentally, has no patience for what he terms the asininity of claims that community-based politics obscure class consciousness.

The political project of postmodernity has been under attack since its inception. The left has tended to view postmodernism as the collapse of any progressive politics; the right sees it as the source of all that is evil in the current malaise of "political correctness" (which rejects diversity and favors the restoration of modernist traditions). Even some of those who initially gained from postmodernism's assault on the authority of existing hegemonies have since retreated from postmodernism's perceived threat to their political programs (this is especially true of feminists). Jameson, however, is in no doubt that postmodernism is about politics: "every position on postmodernism in culture – whether apologia or stigmatization – is also at one and the same time, and *necessarily*, an implicitly or explicitly political stance on the nature of multinational capitalism today."[84]

Jameson holds to the pivotal role of class-based politics, but he concedes that class is confounded by issues of status (referring here to Bourdieu, not to Weber), and that postmodern theorists have yet to provide an account of current class formations. Jameson's steps in this direction are often wonderfully evocative, but hampered by a strange blend of resignation and unfettered optimism. For instance, he speaks of what remains of a residual, unacknowledged "party of Utopia:"

> an underground party whose numbers are difficult to determine, whose program remains unannounced and perhaps even unformulated, whose existence is unknown to the citizenry at large and to the authorities, but whose members seem to recognize one another by means of secret Masonic signals.[85]

Jameson looks ahead optimistically:

> That a new international proletariat (taking forms we cannot yet imagine) will reemerge from this convulsive upheaval it needs no prophet to predict: we ourselves are still in the trough, however, and no one can say how long we still [sic] stay there.[86]

One of Jameson's most telling political insights arises in connection with his treatment of the claustrophobic modernism described in Kafka's *The Trial*. Here, he identifies the crucial nonconformity between the emergence of a "modern (or at least modernizing) economy" and the backdrop of an "old-fashioned political structure."[87] The peculiar overlap between past and future, the resistance of archaic structures to irresistible modernizations, "is the condition of possibility for high modernism." Postmodernism is, then, the situation in which the relict and the archaic have finally been swept away without a trace. If this is indeed so, what does the new postmodern politics look like?

Jameson draws on Laclau and Mouffe's (1985) "overtly postmodern" post-Marxist politics, which emphasizes the proliferation of new social movements based in what Foucault would term a burgeoning micropolitics.[88] Postmodernism includes space for such oppositional cultures, which flourish in the presence of "discursive heterogeneity without a norm."[89] Jameson cites the role of feminism, virtually alone in maintaining a Utopian imagination. Yet for all his admiration of diversity in the new politics, Jameson rejects the claim that such groups have arisen from the void left by the disappearance of social classes.

He dismisses social movements as the basis for a new class politics, because fractured groups are unable to combine in collective action. Ultimately, he joins other Marxist critics in devaluing difference, because it smacks of the "offensive complacencies" of a lugubrious "liberal tolerance."[90]

At the core of Jameson's current political project is the need to overcome the discourse and ideology of the market. This, he claims, is the "most crucial terrain of ideological struggle in our time," because the "surrender to the various forms of market ideology ... has been imperceptible but alarmingly universal." As a consequence, politics has been reduced to the "care and feeding of the economic apparatus."[91] Consensus now dominates representative democracy, through ballots and opinion polls. Conscious ideologies and political opinions have "ceased to be functional in perpetuating and reproducing the system"; consumption has replaced politics.[92] This explains how we can celebrate capitalism at the same time as human misery engulfs us. Jameson again points to cognitive mapping as a way of more fully sketching the lineaments of an emergent postmodern politics, enabling "the coordination of existential data (the empirical position of the subject) with unlived, abstract conceptions of geographic totality."[93] The pedagogical political culture derived from such a mapping should aim to fuse the global with the local, on a social and spatial scale, because: "the incapacity to map spatially is as crippling to political experience as the analogous incapacity to map spatially is for urban experience."[94]

From Lefebvre to Jameson: the Necessity for Postmodernism

> It is impossible ... to avoid the conclusion that space is assuming an increasingly important role in supposedly "modern" societies
>
> H. Lefebvre (1991) p.412

Let me now try to summarize the two problematics and then quickly proceed to emphasize the connections between Lefebvre's ostensible modernism and Jameson's postmodernism. In so doing, I shall hope to convey the utter centrality of the postmodern project in contemporary geographical theory and practice.

The project encompassed by Lefebvre in *The Production of Space* runs counter to many long-entrenched habits of thought.[95] Lefebvre notes that the illusion of transparent/neutral/pure space is slow to dissolve, even though the promise of the new philosophy is great:

> The more carefully one examines space, considering it not only with the eyes, not only with the intellect, but also with the senses, with the total body, the more clearly one becomes aware of the conflicts at work within it, conflicts which foster the explosion of abstract space and the production of a space that is other.[96]

Lefebvre the postmodernist calls for a retreat from the errors and lies of the modernist trio of readability, visibility, and intelligibility. We are teetering on the edge of a science of social space, which

> in no way aspires to the status of a completed "totality,' and even less to that of a "system' or "synthesis.' ... [T]his approach aims both to reconnect elements that have been separated and replace confusion by clear distinctions; to rejoin the severed and reanalyze the commingled.[97]

Lefebvre calls his approach "spatio-analysis" or "spatiology" to distinguish it from the baggage associated with existing disciplinary terminology, but there can be no doubt about the importance of geography in his scheme. The conceptual grid that Lefebvre offers is founded in the connectivity between various levels of analysis: "it discriminates – without sundering them – between a 'micro' level (architecture ...), a 'medium' level (the city ...), and finally a 'macro' level (... land considered in national, global or worldwide terms)."[98] In the final analysis, Lefebvre's science of space is a science of use. It runs counter to the dominant (and dominating) tendency by according *appropriation* a special practical and theoretical status: *for* appropriation and use, and *against* exchange and domination. He suggests that such a science would imply real knowledge about the production of space, but warns against the inevitable counter-challenges of disciplinary chauvinists and reductionists. Lefebvre argues some absolutely fundamental propositions, which extend way beyond the confines of geography, ancient and postmodern: in particular, that the absence of space in human inquiry has led to overemphasis on other dimensions of thought; and that the re-introduction of space will require a recasting of the entire fabric of social theory.

The spatial problematic I have distilled in turn from Jameson's postmodernity is remarkably rich, even though he himself makes no claim to provide such a thing (the closest he gets is in a call for a theory of "separation").[99] But there is little doubt in my mind that Jameson has encouraged a new way of seeing socio-spatial relations. He portrays society as a text, and postmodernism as a periodizing hypothesis. Culture is the key to tracking postmodernity, and to determining whether or not there has been a radical break. Theory, in his scheme, is composed of a broad discourse on diverse ideologies. Contradicting modernist traditions, Jameson eschews foundationalism, theoretical closure, and the notion of a determinant ideology; instead, he identifies transcoding (comparative analysis between theories) as the principal epistemological goal. Space and spatial logic dominate postmodernity, just as time permeated modernity. One urgent task is to discover the coordinates of the new postmodern hyperspace, by exploring the spaces of the built environment, the mode of production, and culture. The techniques of cognitive mapping will assist in this task, as well as in formulating future programs of social action. Social action in postmodernity is confounded by the nonconformity between the emergent economy and an obsolete politics. Localized social movements may be emblematic of a decentered politics, but Jameson argues they do not constitute a new form of class politics. Until we can decipher these politics, he advocates attacking the ideology and practices of the market. In the final analysis, Jameson attributes the fluxes of postmodernity to the universalization of capitalism. He portrays himself as a "relatively enthusiastic consumer of postmodernism,"[100] despite the unresolved ambiguities engendered as he pulls the cloak of Marxism about him:

> I occasionally get just as tired of the slogan "postmodernism" as anyone else, but when I am tempted to regret my complicity with it, to deplore its misuses and its notoriety, and to conclude with some reluctance that it raises more problems than it solves, I find myself pausing to wonder whether any other concept can dramatize the issues in quite so effective and economical a fashion.[101]

Taken together, both Lefebvre and Jameson privilege space as central in their problematics. Lefebvre, perhaps more than any other contemporary philosopher, outlines a basic ontological framework for the study of the production of space. In this, he emphasizes the connectedness of an integrated hierarchy of global and local spaces, which are highly fragmented and multiply-coded. Jameson acknowledges his debt to Lefebvre, but places his primary emphasis on the transition between modes of production. He is also able to address the spatial turn in postmodernity, suggesting that modernism's obsession with time has been usurped by the reassertion of space in postmodern theory.

From an epistemological viewpoint, the continuities between Lefebvre and Jameson are transparent. Both are founded in Marx, although Jameson goes further toward a developed appreciation of difference. Lefebvre is more than prescient in his characterization of Marxism as simply one moment in the development of theory. Yet he remains motivated by the search for science, for a unitary theory that he concedes some would regard as a metaphilosophy. Jameson, writing in a context of greater theoretical diversity, concedes the importance of different voices and the need for a comparative theoretical discourse. But he doubts (along with many others) the possibility of an internally coherent theory of the postmodern, and ultimately seeks refuge among old friends in the Marxist canon. Although both writers are unwilling or unable to sacrifice their allegiance to the totalizations of Marxism, Jameson takes us a step further in realizing the necessity of diversity in theoretical discourse.

The gains made by Jameson are also evident in their respective treatments of the production of space. Once again, Lefebvre seems to have been remarkably contemporary in his analysis of the concrete materialization of social relations. And although Jameson advances the specific concept of a postmodern hyperspace consequent upon the cultural logic of late capitalism, it is clear that his emphasis on culture is (to some extent at least) a reaction against the privileging of the economic sphere that characterizes most previous Marxisms.[102] Here is one case in which intellectual bloodlines are clear, but the dialectic has thrown up an entirely original hypothesis.

The case of politics in Lefebvre and Jameson is very revealing. Both insist (not surprisingly given their points of departure in Marxism) on the primacy of class-based politics, but they also recognize the significance of the political heterogeneity implied in the emergence of locally-autonomous micropowers. Lefebvre uncovers how the spatial contradictions of capitalism allow for a measure of local autonomy in what he terms the counter-spaces. These produce new forms of political struggle which (he suggests) do not obfuscate the potential for a burgeoning class consciousness. Jameson dissents from this view. In drawing particular attention to archaic institutions and the oppositional cultures associated with proliferating social movements, Jameson categorically dismisses such movements as a basis for a new class-based politics. At the same time, he manages to assess the potential for a postmodern politics without once incorporating the state into his analysis. This is in stark contrast to Lefebvre, who has elsewhere developed notions of (for instance) a state mode of production.

In sum, the conformities between what we can now only loosely characterize as Lefebvre's modernism and Jameson's postmodernism are quite transparent. They have to do with the common heritage in Marx, an obsession with a problematic that emphasizes space and transitions in the mode of production, and commitment to social change through a class-based politics. At the same time, the bridges between the modern and the postmodern are also clear, especially because of the remarkably forward-looking nature of Lefebvre's analysis. We can witness this in several dimensions: the sensitivity to difference, the importance of local autonomies in the spatial chaos of capitalism, and the emphasis on the interrelatedness between global and local in the world order.

And yet? And yet, Jameson has categorically identified at least three new emphases that should guide any inquiry into a putatively postmodern society. These are: *hyperspace*, or a radical break in the time/space coordinates of the contemporary world; *culture*, a necessary counter-emphasis to previous obsessions which privileged the sphere of production over the sphere of reproduction; and *transcoding*, which, despite Jameson's own retreat to Marxism, imposes an unavoidable imperative for dealing with the implications of epistemological diversity. To this list, I must append the need to return to the question of *postmodern politics*, because neither Lefebvre nor Jameson deal adequately with this issue from behind the mask of Marxism. I shall conclude this essay by focusing on the unavoidable research agendas posed by these four issues.

Jameson emphasizes space as the key to mapping the emergent hyperspace, via a cognitive mapping of the glittering surfaces of postmodern culture. In this, he would probably concur with Berger that: "Prophesy now involves a geographical rather than historical projection; it is space not time that hides consequences from us;" and with Soja that we need a new ontology, i.e. a "meta-theoretical discourse which seeks to discover what the world must be like in order for knowledge and human action to be possible, what it means to be."[103] Soja has taken us further than Jameson toward an ontology based on space, time, and being. He writes:

spatiality, temporality, and social being can be seen as the abstract dimensions which together comprise all facets of human existence ... Thus the spatial order of human existence arises from the (social) production of space ... Similarly, the temporal order is concretized in the making of history ... [And] the social order of being-in-the-world can be seen as revolving around the constitution of society, the production and reproduction of social relations, institutions and practices.[104]

A large challenge persists with the notion of postmodernism as an epoch, representing a radical break with previous cultures. This ennervating hypothesis emphasizes culture, text, spatiality, theoretical discourse, and the problem of periodization. Jameson asserts that the way to understand differences and discontinuities is to continually rehearse the conditions that lead to change. He ultimately elects an explanation based in the universalization of capital, even though this choice remains unmotivated in his text. His analysis of periodization, for example, has none of the subtlety and lucidity that characterized Webber's investigations of post-Fordist periodizations.[105] In the final analysis, it may matter little that there has been a radical break; what is much more important will be that a new way of seeing has been opened up, and with it, the potential for transcendental social change.

Jameson invokes the homogenized, saturated hyperspace of postmodernity, where place is enfeebled and our cognitive maps so weak that the link between the global and the local is almost entirely obscured. The articulation of these linkages must be regarded as the principal challenge for any postmodern geography.[106] Of special concern is exactly how difference becomes localized in particular places. Soja again offers some important insights, drawing attention to our "existential spatiality," an "original spatialization" implicit in the birth of human consciousness.[107] Subsequently, our being in the world occurs through a distancing (detachment, objectification) that allows us to assume a point of view on our surroundings. Difference in and between places thus becomes a consequence of personal psychology and experience of the lifeworld, and is manifest in many various ways (e.g. labeling, residential differentiation, and land-use planning). Another way of saying this is that culture and human agency are crucial factors in the production and reproduction of spatial relationships. Despite awareness that his work has been criticized for its absence of agency, Jameson makes little headway with the problem, beyond identifying "multinational capital" as a "higher" kind of agency. He nowhere broaches, for example, the structure-institution-agency triptych of Anthony Giddens, and fails to observe how the generic crises of capitalism become spatialized as crises of the locale (as, for example, in the place-specific process of deindustrialization, or in the ghettoization of the homeless).[108] Part of Jameson's (and our) problem lies in the ambiguities and overdetermination associated with the texts of place. The built environment, for example, is much more than an unmediated outcome of the capitalist mode of production; it contains representations of many other authentic human interactions, including the socio-cultural and the political.[109]

In the epistemological realm, postmodernism has resulted in an assault on the authority of modernism. The hegemonic pretensions of the Rational are replaced by an openness, a tolerance for different theories. In its purest form, postmodernism rejects determinant ideologies, theoretical closure, and foundationalism. It is anti-hegemonic, although (of course) it can never escape from the contradictions of its own claims. In Jameson, epistemological openness takes the form of transcoding – an impassioned plea for comparative theoretical analysis. Yet, somewhere along the way, he makes an unannounced retreat into a (Marxian) modernism. Given his political commitments, this is obviously a deliberate decision on Jameson's part, although it may also be fueled by a desire to avoid some of the extremes of postmodern relativism. However, it is achieved only at some cost, most notably a revitalized defense of totalizing discourse, and a repression of difference.[110] Jameson's retreat ironically sacrifices one of postmodernism's greatest gains, i.e. the focus on comparative merits of different theories. The challenge posed by transcoding remains; the voices of the Other (e.g. feminist, multicultural, and postcolonial theorists) are muted, if not totally silenced.

Finally, much has been written about the apparent conservatism of the postmodern movement. But it is impossible to overemphasize the central political lesson of postmodernity, which has taught us that Rationality is not an innocent category upon which to base a political program. Our twentieth-century history of technological industrialization, wars, death camps, and the nuclear threat should have put paid to such naivety. And scholars such as Horkheimer and Adorno revealed that behind Enlightenment rationality lay a logic of domination and repression (as well as academic hegemony). Postmodernism offers a reconstituted vision of the politics of the local, founded in the distribution of micropowers and situated in the fragmented interstices between formal power structures;[111] this vision must necessarily be incorporated with a politics of the global, including revitalized nationalisms, nation-state disintegration, and so on.[112] The frequently-heard complaints (from the left) that postmodernism represents an anti-progressive pluralism, or (from the right) that it imposes a crippling political correctness, amount to little more than nostalgia for past verities; the world has shifted, whether or not we appreciate or approve of its mutations. Equally obviously, the need for moral and political judgements is an inevitable concomitant of everyday life. Postmodernism has not removed the necessity for such judgements; what it has done is to question the status of these judgements.[113] Postmodernism has in itself not disenfranchised any political organization or social movement; what it has done is point to the need for a reconstituted political practice.

The consistencies and nonconformities in the conjoined projects of Lefebvre and Jameson offer profoundly important insights into the *ways of place-making* of the late twentieth century. More than most, Lefebvre allows us to understand the process of place-making; and Jameson shows us new ways of postmodern place-making. Only the foolish would ignore these challenges.

Acknowledgements

I am grateful to Derek Gregory for comments on an earlier version of this essay, and for permitting me to read relevant prepublication chapters from his then forthcoming book, *Geographical Imaginations* (Gregory, 1994). I also thank Catherine Walsh for her assistance in this project.

Endnotes

1. Jameson 1991; Lefebvre 1991.
2. Lefebvre 1991, p. 154.
3. A brief overview of Lefebvre's work is available in Soja (1989, especially Chapter 2).
4. This essay is regarded by Kellner (1989a, p. 2) in his review of Jameson's work, as "probably the most quoted, discussed, and debated article of the past decade." It was originally published in the *New Left Review*, No. 146, 1984, pp. 59–92.
5. Jameson 1991, p. 104.
6. Lefebvre 1991, p. 7.
7. Ibid., p. 21.
8. Ibid., p. 181.
9. Ibid., p.16.
10. Ibid., pp. 48–52.
11. Ibid., p. 26.
12. Ibid., pp. 30–64.
13. Ibid., p. 30.
14. Ibid., p. 31.
15. Ibid., p. 37.
16. Ibid., p. 46.
17. *See also* Lefebvre 1976a.
18. Jameson 1991, p. 3.
19. Ibid., p. 320.
20. Dear 1988.
21. Jameson 1991, p. xvi.
22. Ibid., p. xxii.
23. Ibid., p. 282.
24. Ibid., p. 310.
25. Ibid., p. 413.
26. Ibid., p. xx.
27. Ibid., p. 9.
28. Ibid., p. 10.
29. Ibid., p. 15.
30. Ibid.,p.17.
31. Ibid.
32. Ibid., p. 18; the phrase is Guy Debord's.
33. Ibid., p. 372.
34. Ibid., p. 405.
35. A fact undoubtedly related to his persistent search for a critical Marxism (Lefebvre 1992).
36. Lefebvre 1991, p. 99.

37 Ibid., p. 321.
38 Ibid., pp. 89–91.
39 Ibid., p. 418.
40 Ibid., pp.16, 36.
41 Ibid., p. 62.
42 Ibid., p. 143.
43 This latency is also betrayed by Lefebvre's emphasis on the quotidian (*see* Lefebvre 1992).
44 Lefebvre 1991, p. 41; *See also* Lefebvre 1972, 1993.
45 Lefebvre 1991, p. 405.
46 Jameson 1991, p. 317.
47 Ibid., p. 305
48 Ibid., p. 394.
49 Ibid., p. 392.
50 Ibid., p. 397, my emphasis.
51 Ibid., p. 184.
52 Lefebvre 1991, p. 117.
53 Ibid., p. 85.
54 Ibid., p. 73.
55 Ibid., pp. 182–3, 190–1.
56 Ibid., p. 189.
57 Ibid., p. 282.
58 Ibid., p. 279.
59 Ibid., p. 227.
60 Lefebvre 1976b.
61 Ibid., p. 308.
62 Ibid., pp. 358, 410.
63 Jameson 1991, p. xvi.
64 Ibid., p. 154.
65 Ibid., p. 43.
66 Ibid., p. 44.
67 Ibid., p. 411.
68 Ibid., p. 366.
69 Ibid., p. 37.
70 Ibid., p. 19.
71 Compare with Dear 1991a.
72 Jameson 1991, p. 40.
73 Ibid., p. 105.
74 Ibid., p. 51.
75 Ibid., pp. 364–5.
76 Ibid., p. 264.
77 Ibid., p. 398.
78 Ibid., p. xv.
79 Ibid., p. 69.
80 Ibid., p. 413.
81 Lefebvre 1991, p. 190.
82 Ibid., p. 63.
83 Ibid.
84 Ibid., pp. 166–7.
85 Jameson 1991, p. 3.

86 Ibid., p. 180.
87 Ibid., p. 417.
88 Ibid., pp. 308–9.
89 Ibid., p. 318.
90 Ibid., p. 17.
91 Ibid., p. 341; for further development of Jameson's politics, see Dowling 1984, Jameson 1981, and Kellner 1989b.
92 Jameson 1991, pp. 263–5.
93 Ibid., p. 398.
94 Ibid., p. 53.
95 Ibid., p. 416.
96 For an extended consideration of Lefebvre's oeuvre in the context of French Marxist thought, *see* Gregory (1993).
97 Ibid., p. 391.
98 Ibid., p.413.
99 Ibid., p. 388.
100 Jameson 1991, p. 399.
101 Ibid., p. 298.
102 Ibid., p.418.
103 Lefebvre himself, with his consistent emphasis on the sphere of social reproduction, is a noteworthy exception to this general observation. *See*, for instance, Lefebvre 1976b.
104 Soja 1989, p. 131.
105 Ibid., p. 25.
106 Webber 1991.
107 *See*, for example, Gregory 1989, and Cooke 1990.
108 Ibid., p. 132.
109 The process of localization in the homelessness crisis is examined in Wolch and Dear, 1993.
110 Dear 1986, 1989.
111 Compare with Dear 1991b.
112 Dear 1991a.
113 Some of the new forms of government, in the form of a "shadow state," are discussed in Wolch 1990.
114 Compare Dear (forthcoming).

References

Cooke, P., *Back to the Future: Modernity, Postmodernity, and Locality*, (London, Unwin Hyman, 1990)
Dear, M., 'Postmodernism and Planning', *Society and Space*, 4, 367–84, (1986).
Dear, M., 'The Postmodern Challenge: Reconstructing Human Geography', *Transactions, Institute of British Geographers*, 13, 262–74, (1988).
Dear, M., 'Privatization and the Rhetoric of Planning Practice'. *Society and Space*, 7, 449–62, (1989).
Dear, M., 'Taking Los Angeles Seriously: Time and Space in the Postmodern City', *Architecture California*, 13(2), 36–42 (1991a).
Dear, M,. 'The Premature Demise of Postmodern Urbanism', *Cultural Anthropology*, 6(4), 538–52, (1991b).

Dear, M., 'The Personal Politics of Postmodernity', in Crow, D. (ed.), *Geography and Identity*, (Washington D.C., Maisonneuve Press, 1996).

Dowling, W.C., *Jameson, Althusser, Marx*, (London, Methuen, 1984).

Gregory, D., 'A real Differentiation and Postmodern Human Geography', in Gregory, D. and Walford, R. (eds.), *Horizons in Human Geography*, (London, Macmillan, 1989).

Gregory, D., *Geographical Imaginations*, (Oxford, Blackwell, 1994).

Jameson, F., *The Political Unconscious: Narrative as a Socially Symbolic Act*, (Ithaca, Cornell University Press, 1981).

Jameson, F., *Postmodernism, or the Cultural Logic of Late Capitalism.* (Durham, Duke University Press, 1991).

Kellner, D., 'Jameson, Marxism, and Postmodernism', in Kellner, D. (ed.), *Postmodernism, Jameson, Critique*, (Washington, D.C., Maisonneuve Press, 1989a).

Kellner, D., (ed.), *Postmodernism, Jameson, Critique*, (Washington, D.C., Maisonneuve Press, 1989b).

Laclau, E. and Mouffe, C., *Hegemony and Socialist Strategy*, (London, Verso, 1985).

Lefebvre, H., *Le Droit à la Ville suivi de Espace et Politique*, (Paris, Éditions Anthropos, 1972).

Lefebvre, H., *The Survival of Capitalism*, translated by Frank Bryant, (London, Allison & Busby, 1976a).

Lefebvre, H., 'Reflections on the politics of space', *Antipode.* 8(2), 30–37, 1976b).

Lefebvre, H., *The Production of Space*, translated by Donald Nicholson-Smith, (Cambridge, Blackwell, 1991).

Lefebvre, H., *Critique of Everyday Life*, volume I, Introduction, translated by John Moore with a Preface by Michel Trebitsch, (New York, Verso, 1992).

Lefebvre, H., 'The right to the city', in *Architecture Culture 1943–1968: A Documentary Anthology*, Joan Ockman (ed.), (New York, Columbia Books of Architecture and Rizzoli International Publications, 1993).

Soja, E. W., *Postmodern Geographies: The Reassertion of Space in Critical Social Theory*, (New York, Verso, 1989).

Webber, M., 'The Contemporary Transition', *Society and Space*, 9, 165–82, (1991).

Wolch, S., *The Shadow State: Government and Voluntary Sector in Transition*, (New York, The Foundation Center, 1990).

Wolch, J. and Dear, M., *Malign Neglect: Homelessness in an American City*, (San Francisco, Jossey-Bass, 1993).

2

Social Theory, Postmodernism, and the Critique of Development

---

Richard Peet

The theoretical discourses of modernity, from Descartes, through the Enlightenment, to positivism, saw human reason as the source of progress. Reason produced science and technology, sources of material progress. Norms and values, reasoned rather than divined by magical means from God's intent, could be universally accepted. Normative science enabled emancipation from nature and want and from superstition and ignorance. Considering humans to be "indefinitely perfectible" and all people capable of being guided solely by the light of reason, the Enlightenment found that "reason is the same for all thinking subjects, all nations, all epochs, and all cultures" (Cassirer, 1951: 5, 13–14). In this the Enlightenment was democratic and egalitarian for, as opposed to racism, all people were capable of reason. But the highest forms of reason and freedom were thought to have been attained first in Europe; with this we glimpse the Eurocentrism of the Enlightenment. Thus, in *Sketch for an historial picture of the progress of the human mind*, de Condorcet (1972: 141) expresses both sentiments:

> our hopes for the future condition of the human race can be subsumed under three important heads: the abolition of inequality between nations, the progress of equality within each nation, and the true perfection of mankind. Will all nations one day attain that state of civilization which the most enlightened, the freest, and the least burdened by prejudice, such as the French and the Anglo-Americans, have attained already? Will the vast gulf that separates these peoples from the slavery of nations under the rule of monarchs, from the barbarism of African tribes, from the ignorance of savages, little by little disappear?

Employing a conception of space unified by the rationality of its human inhabitants, but differentiated by differing degress of this common content, an Enlightenment map of the world sees global space divided between a center of knowledge and wisdom in Western Europe and a periphery of ignorance, barbarity, and only potential reason elsewhere. Hegel articulated the idealist tendency latent in this Enlightenment position that, in reaching complete self-consciousness, European civilization achieved the absolute freedom teleologically implicit at the origin of the Western experience (Pippin, 1991: 67, 71). With this the democratic Enlightenment turns into its opposite, the conception of a directed history, a foreordained geography.

This notion of an uneven movement towards rational, democratic perfection, found in the eighteenth century Enlightenment, was carried into the nineteenth and twentieth centuries as a significant theme in Euro-American self-understanding. Whatever its cause, a space of reason opened in Western Europe which modernized a sequence of peripheries, where rational capacity was awakened through contact with the West. The ultimate form was the modernization theory of the 1950s, 1960s, and early 1970s, prevalent in disguised forms today (Parsons, 1966; Eisenstadt, 1973).

Critics of the Enlightenment argue that modernity has consistently generated a variety of victims – peasants, workers, women, the colonized – and a system of disciplinary institutions (jails, hospitals, psychiatric institutions, schools) which must *enforce* reason. *Post*modern social theorists criticize the Enlightenment for its fallacious rationalism, its universalizing and totalizing character, its arrogant claims to supply absolute, universal truth. In particular, postmodern theory criticizes modern theories of representational truth – the position that truth consists in accurately representing reality in symbolic, theoretical form. Postmodern theory takes the relativist position that theories at best provide *partial* perspectives on their objects and that all cognitive representations of the world are historically and linguistically mediated. Some postmodern theory goes further to reject modern assumptions of social coherence and structured causality altogether, in favor of multiplicity, fragmentation, and indeterminacy. Postmodern theory abandons the notion of the rational, unified subject in favor of a socially and linguistically decentered and fragmented subject (i.e. the notion of multiple identities) (Best and Kellner, 1991). And as Young (1990: 9) points out, a special interest of French poststructural philosophy concerns the relation of the Enlightenment, with its universal truth claims, to the universalization of the European power; the new stress on this relation has stimulated a "relentless anatomization of the collusive forms of European knowledge." Hence Derrida (1971, 213): "the white man takes his own mythology, Indo-European mythology, his own *logos*, that is, the *mythos* of his idiom, for the universal form of that he must still wish to call Reason." In brief, postmodernism considers reason to be an historical and regional form of thought rather than a universal potential.

Foucault on Power/Knowledge

Foucault argues the relation between modern knowledge and power in a series of historico-philosophical studies of psychiatry, medicine, punishment, and criminology, which he links with the emergence of the human sciences in "a critique of our historical era" (Foucault, 1984). Foucault was an eclectic thinker drawing on many sources, but especially on earlier critics of Western reason. Nietzsche (1967) was important to postmodern thought in providing a way of "transcending" the Hegelian and Marxian dialectics (Deleuze, 1983). Two positions essential to the trajectory of Foucault's subsequent thought were established by Nietzsche:

1   The will to truth and knowledge is a will to power – Foucault developed this into a critique of liberal humanism and the human sciences.
2   The notion of genealogical histories of unconventional topics, such as reason, madness and the constitution of the subject, again vigorously pursued by Foucault.

With Bataille (1985), by comparison, the ecstatic forces of religious fervor, sexuality, and intoxicated experience were called on to subvert the instrumental rationality and normalcy of bourgeois culture. Against the rationalist outlook of political economy, Bataille sought a transcendence of utilitarian production and needs, celebrating consumption, waste, and expenditure as liberatory.

Drawing on these and other sources, Foucault (1980a) launched an innovative critique of modernity. Rather than emancipatory, he sees the Enlightenment beginning new, powerful modes of domination over human beings. Like Horkheimer and Adorno in *Dialectic of Enlightenment* (1979), Foucault believes modern rationality to be a coercive force, focused on the individual. Reason rationally organizes chaos and disorder, classifying and regulating all forms of experience through a systematic construction of knowledge and discourse making them amenable to administration and control. For Foucault (1972; 1973), discourses have systematic structures which can be analyzed archaeologically (identifying their compositional elements and the relations which form these elements into wholes) and genealogically (the formation of discourses by non-discursive practices, especially by institutions of power). In *Discipline & Punish* and *The History of Sexuality* vol. 1, Foucault (1979; 1980b) argues that the Enlightenment ideal of grounding norms in reason (understood as the human capacity to critically examine, and systemtically order, everything) gave them a strategic directedness and a detail of application, which allow even micro-practices to be dangerously "normalized;" the disciplinary modality of power colonizes other forms of power, linking and extending them, making it possible to bring the effects of power to the most minute and distant elements – i.e. it assures an infinitesimal distribution of power relations. Discipline operates primarily on the body, approaching it as an object to be analyzed, separated into parts, the aim being to make "a docile body that could be subjected, used, transformed and improved" – the idea more generally being to treat humans as objects rather than subjects. Normative social science interacts with a disciplinary technology to produce the docile modern individual.

The control of space is an essential constituent of the disciplinary technologies (Philo, 1992). In modernity, space takes the form of grids with slots in them assigned value; individuals are placed in a pre-ordered, disciplinary space, as for example with military hospitals or factories. Discipline "makes" individuals by this kind of distribution in space, by training, through hierarchical observation, normalizing judgment, examination, documentation, and the sciences; the academic "disciplines" are linked with the spread of disciplinary technologies in the same matrix of power.

Foucault believes global theories such as Marxism (i.e. the dialectical theory of modes of production) to be totalizing, reductionist, coercive, even totalitarian. He attempts to detotalize history and society as wholes governed by a central essence, production in Marxism, world spirit in Hegelian idealism. As opposed to existential phenomenology he decenters the subject as a constitut*ed* consciousness. He sees history as non-evolutionary and society in terms of unevenly developing discourses. Whereas modern theories of emancipation draw on broad, essentialist themes to reach macro-political solutions, Foucault respects difference and favors local criticism in a micro-politics.

Foucauldian. Critiques of Development Theory

Since the middle 1980s postmodern social theory has entered the field of development studies. Many of the arguments relating postmodern skepticism to development extend Foucault's reconceptualization of power, discourse, and knowledge to Western disciplinary and normalizing mechanisms in the Third World (Schuurman, 1992; Peet and Watts, 1993; Watts, 1993; Slater, 1992). Essentially the idea is to see the discourse on development articulating First World knowledge with power in the Third World. Foucault's work on the appropriation of the mind in the West, it is argued, can be extended to the permeation and appropriation of the Third World by Western disciplinary and normalizing processes.

The recent literature uses Foucauldian concepts of power, knowledge and discourse to reexamine development efforts as "uniquely efficient colonizers on behalf of central strategies of power" (Dubois, 1991: 19). The pioneering work, by Escobar (1984–5; 1988; 1992), sees development discourses and practices constituting the "Third World" as the last insidious chapter of the larger history of the expansion of modern, Western reason. Following Foucault he contrasts reason's project of global emancipation with its dark side of domination: i.e. reasoned knowledge using the language of emancipation creates systems of power in a modernized world. Development is one of these languages. Under the political conditions of the Cold War (1945–60), Escobar argues, the West's scientific gaze focused anew on Asia, Africa, and Latin America. Terms like "underdeveloped areas" and "development" invented during this period were components of a new imperialism. Under the hegemony of "development" apparatuses of knowledge-production (the World Bank, planning and development agencies, etc.) established a new political economy of truth, different from that of the Colonial era – the comparison is with Said's (1979: 3) "orientalism" as a Western style for dominating, restructuring, and having authority over the Orient. A vast institutional network defined a perceptual domain, the space of development, that determined what could be said, thought, imagined. From industrialization, through the Green Revolution, to integrated rural development, policies repeated the basic "truth" that development consists of achieving the characteristic conditions of the already-rich societies. The development discourse defined that can be thought, practiced, even imagined, in considering the future of Third World societies:

> development can be described as an apparatus .... that links forms of knowledge about the Third World with the deployment of forms of power and intervention, resulting in the mapping and production of Third World societies .... By means of this discourse, individuals, governments and communities are seen as "under-developed" (or placed under conditions in which they tend to see themselves as such), and are treated accordingly. (Escobar, 1992: 23; *see also* Sachs, 1992).

The deployment of development operates through three more particular strategies:

1   The progressive incorporation of problems as abnormalities to be treated by specific interventions – this results in a field of the intervention of power.
2   The professionalization of development, the recasting by experts of what otherwise would be political problems into neutral "scientific" terms, the aim being a regine of truth and norms, a field of the control of knowledge.
3   The institutionalization of development, the formation of a network of new sites of power knowledge which bind people to certain behaviors and rationalities.

Escobar thus sees a spatial field of power/knowledge expanding outwards from the West. Within this field, networks of sites of power bind people into Western forms of thought and behavior through the device of "development." Development is particularly effective because it appeals to the finest ideals of the Enlightenment (often employing the most idealistic people in air and development agencies) and to the aspirations for a better life by poor people. Development has been "successful" to the extent that it manages and controls populations, that it creates a type of manageable underdevelopment in a more subtle form of management than colonialism. Escobar finds this view of development as a modernist discourse different from the analyses of political economy, modernization, or even alternative development which propose merely modifying the current regime of development.

Highly critical notions like these about development have intersected with the profound sense of disillusionment about developmental practice (e.g. Edwards, 1989) to produce a crises of confidence in development studies, indeed, perhaps, a crisis in progressive thought in general. Again quoting Escobar:

> for some time now, it has been difficult – at times even impossible – to talk about development, protest or revolution with the same confidence and encompassing scope with which intellectuals and activists spoke about these vital matters in our most recent past. It is as if the elegant discourses of the 1960s – the high decade of both development and revolution – had been suspended, caught in mid air as they strove toward their zenith, and, like fragile bubbles, exploded, leaving a

scrambled trace of their glorious path behind .... Hesitantly perhaps, but with a persistence that has to be taken seriously, a new discourse has set in (Escobar, 1992: 20).

Brought on by critical thought's inability to leave behind the imaginary of development, the whole project is said to be sick, dying, gone. Escobar compares this with a powerful social movements discourse which, while unclear about its possible directions, has become a privileged arena for intellectual inquiry and political action. Escobar aims at bridging the two insights of the critique of development and social movements believing:

1   that a critique of the discourse and practice of development can clear the ground for a more radical, collective imagining of alternative futures;
2   that thinking about alternatives to development requires a theoretico-practical transformation which draws on the practices of Third World social movements.

Escobar claims a growing number of scholars in agreement with this prescription who, rather than search for development alternatives, speak about alternatives *to* development. These scholars share: a critical stance with respect to established science; an interest in local autonomy, culture and knowledge; and a position defending localized, pluralistic grassroots movements. We could call the tendency, after the title of Escobar's main articule, "postdevelopmentalism."

Counter-Critique

What might we make of such sweeping condemnations, which seek to undermine the knowledge basis of all established notions about development, destabilize every statement made about it, deconstruct each optimistic expression of Western reason's intervention on behalf of the oppressed people of the world? Is reason to be rejected or *re*-reasoned? Is development outmoded, or *mis*directed? These questions are so important that the postdevelopmentalist discourse itself must be deconstructed, not to synthesize its arguments in mild, sanitized forms into a recast conventional development model (although we can imagine a future World Bank annual report on "postmodern development" – like "sustainable development" in the past), but through critique to draw from it notions for use in a radical practice which might even retain aspects of the idea of development.

Respecting Difference

Postmodernism favors fragmentation and difference except in its own treatment of modern development theory which it portrays in terms of a monolithic hegemony. Hence for Escobar (1992: 26) "critiques of development by dependency theorists, for instance, still functioned within the same discursive space of development, even if seeking to attach it to a different international and class rationality." Thus recent critics have gathered under the rubric "modernist development theory," notions regarded by their proponents as separate, different, even antagonistic. A typical statement lists, as essentially one contemporary discourse, neoclassical development economics, political economy, and social modernization theory. The general positions of this modern paradigm are said to include:

1   A linear view of history in which the West is further along a given path of progress than Third World countries.
2   An agreement that the proximate cause of development is the exercise of human rationality, especially the application of science to production.
3   The advocacy of values like freedom, justice and equality as experienced and defined in the West.
4   An instrumental assumption that means are separable from ends and that moral considerations apply more to ends than to means (Banuri, 1990).

While it might be granted that these criteria describe an apparent similarity between forms of Enlightenment thinking, the deeper question is whether the notion of a single developmental discourse creates an homogenous myth which destroys differences between and within theories crucial to their contents, visions and intentions. Take historial materialism as a case in point.

This notion of a continuous modernist discourse sees Marx as a direct descendant of the Enlightenment. Thus, in *Preface to a Critique of Political Economy*, Marx (1970) finds societal transformation to be driven by developments in the material productive forces which, by coming into periodic conflict with the existing relations of production, create revolutionary ruptures moving society from one mode of production to another. What causes the development of the social forces of production? What propels history? A rationalist version of Marxism (Cohen, 1978: 150–157) finds Marx's "development thesis" resting on the proposition that humans are rational beings, who use their intelligence to relieve material scarcity by expanding their productive powers – i.e. increasing their ability to transform nature. In this rationalist version Marx's theory of history indeed can be read as an elaboration of a central notion of the Enlightenment, i.e. history is the progressive achievement of human reason's control over nature.

But this is one reading of Marx, not the only reading, and not necessarily Marx's final version. Historical materialism was conceived as a critique of the very idea of beginning explanation with consciousness (of which rationality is a part), even in the form of an experientially-based human imagination, and instead beginning with "real active life" i.e. labor and social relations of production. In *Grundrisse*, especially the section on precapitalist societies (Marx, 1973: 471–98), we find another version in which social and natural relations are the basic categories of analysis, production has neither a single logic nor does it have a single objective (such as capital accumulation), history takes multilinear forms, reason multiple forms depending on social relations

(Lefort, 1978; Giddens, 1981). Marx's multilinear, social relational theory does not rest easily in a supposedly singular discourse of development focused on reason as cause stretching from the Enlightenment to the World Bank.

Much the same can be said about "developmentalism" as a hegemonic discourse. This approach has some advantages, such as showing the similarities between capitalist and state-authoritarian economic thought with regard to development. But developmentalism as a mode of thought has long contained critical versions which stem from opposition to the existing forms of development (as with dependency theory), emphasize the different trajectories of development of dependent societies, advocate different logics of development for different societies, passionately favor the empowerment of poor people. Lumping these critical notions and the radical practices guided by them with positivist economics, modernization theory, World Bank policy, into a broad, coherent, "developmentalism" denies fundamental differences and denigrates the efforts of theorist-activists, such as Walter Rodney (Alpers and Fontaine, 1982), who have been far more dangerously involved in praxis than what are admittedly ferocious encounters in the salons of Paris or at the annual meetings of the Modern Languages Association!

This brings a first critical reaction to postmodernism in general and post-developmentalism in particular. Postmodern discourse theory argues for the social construction of meaning, elaborating the institutional bases of discourse, emphasizing the positions from which people speak, the power relations between these positions. This concept indicates constellations of discursive positions which persist over the long term and take a multiplicity of forms. The problem is that in setting up a system of expectations about any theory (i.e. that it may be part of a more general intellectual position), discourse analysis often denies what postmodern philosophy supposedly cherishes – that is, difference, and difference of a fundamental kind. So, the different readings of Marx are said to reveal, still, an essential similarity, whereas it can be argued that *Grundrisse* represents a break from a late Enlightenment emphasis on the manifestation of reason in the social production of existence to a post-Enlightenment emphasis on the social relational contextuality of reason itself. "Discourse" then becomes capable of reconciling even opposing tendencies in theorization. Indeed, there may be a kind of "discursive idealism" in which the category discourse becomes an active force marshaling reluctant ideas into quasicoherent, determining wholes. Perhaps, therefore, we need a more discriminating critique than discourse analysis. Reconstituted theories of ideology might do a better job; or some other conception more directly rooted in social relations.

The critical point here is not to make the easy claim that postmodern critics of development theory overstate their position, but to argue that the analysis of discourse, with its linking of oppositional theoretical traditions just *because* they oppose each other and therefore share a vaguely defined "same discursive space," is prone to this kind of overgeneralization. Why? Exactly because it diverts attention from "international and class rationalities" and material contexts, conflating the different forms and bases of power into a generalized quest for power, merging conflicting positions on development into a single developmental discourse. True to its word about difference, postmodern theory would instead see development as a set of conflictual discourse*s* with imaginary bases in contradictory social relations. In the following section this critique is carried further by linking it with concepts of power and knowledge.

Power/Knowledge/Discourse

In his later work Foucault tried to escape from a structuralist conception of discourses as lumps of ideas determinant in history, and instead concentrate on the material conditions of discourse formation – social practices and power relations. Similarly, Foucauldian postdevelopmentalists, like Escobar, are interested in the institutions which form and spread development theories, models, and strategies. Even so, the power/knowledge/discourse trilogy still has problems. It is never clear what power is. "Power" alternates between a Nietzschean power inherent in all human relations, and specific forms of power such as those cohering in the specific institutions investigated by Foucault. And the positive aspects of power, the ability to get things done, get short shrift, in practice, compared with the negative aspects. Then there is the postmodern critique of "knowledge," modern knowledge as reason, oppressive, disciplining, normalizing, totalizing, essentialist, truth claiming, knowledge thought up in the pursuit of power, caricatures which fail to discriminate between types and potentials of knowledge production, different motives for thinking, the contestations within the social relations of knowledge production, the deposits in knowledge of competing politics. Finally there is the product of power and knowledge in "discourse." Discourse is so powerful it can unite political opposites (the World Bank and Marx); discourse (not capital) has to be abandoned; postdevelopmentalism attacks the *discourse* of development. Postmodern analyses often forget, in practice, the agency behind discourse, or overgeneralize agency as "modernity" or "power." There remain even in analyses following the later Foucault, strong reminders of discursive idealism. Actually, intermediate conceptions, class, gender, state, give more exact descriptions and yield more focused analyses. Let us take the power basis of development theory as an example.

The contemporary notion of "development" emerged as Western policymakers reassessed their positions relative to newly independent states in the Third World during the post-World War II Cold War. From the mid 1940s to the late 1950s the redefinition of foreign policy and the notions of development aid, assistance, food for peace, etc. were repeatedly linked, especially in the newly hegemonic United States – hence the restatement of international control in American terms of the rights of man, rather than European terms of "white man's burden." The culminating triumph of this "development of development theory" is found in the various speeches of John F. Kennedy, president of the United States between 1961 and 1963; as Sorensen (1988: 329) says, "No president before or after Kennedy has matched the depth of his empathy for the struggling peoples of Latin America, Africa and Asia, or the strength of his vow to facilitate their political and economic independence." Read a little more critically, the Kennedy administration managed to contain a fierce anti-Communism within an overall framework of Western humanism in a discourse which drew consciously in the latest in social science. Rostow's *Stages of Economic Growth* (1960) is obviously present in Kennedy's (1988: 365–6) statement that: "The only real question is whether these new nations [in Africa] will look West or East – to Moscow or Washington – for sympathy, help and guidance, in their great effort to recapitulate, in a few decades, the entire history of modern Europe and America."

Thus it quickly becomes apparent that the Kennedy statements on the Third World must be deconstructed to reveal their knowledge sources, motives and power bases. There are excellent critical surveys by political scientists linking US positions on development to broader domestic and foreign policy objectives (Higgott, 1983; Gendzier, 1988), although this literature largely predates the spread of postmodern notions into North American social science, *and* could benefit from Foucauldian techniques of discourse analysis. While necessary, the question, however, is whether discourse analysis is sufficient for the task. Take that culminating moment in postwar history, when an idealistic young president at last expressed the finest sentiments of American generosity towards the world in the one paragraph in Kennedy's Inaugural Address of 1961 dealing with the US relations with the Third World:

> To those people in the huts and villages of half the globe struggling to break the bonds of mass misery, we pledge our best efforts to help them help themselves, for whatever period is required – not because the communists may be doing it, not because we seek their votes, but because it is right. If a free society cannot help the many who are poor, it cannot save the few who are rich
>
> (in Sorensen, 1988: 12).

This speech initiated a renewed US emphasis on development, using the rhetoric of equality and social justice. But Kennedy justified "helping the many who are poor" in terms of "saving the few who are rich." As Foucault would say, the language of emancipation expresses power relations. But this is not an expression of "power" in general, which universalizes the issue, nor power employed by a specific institution, such as a development agency, which confines the resulting critique. It is class and international power – development, anti-poverty programs, welfare, are there to preserve the continued possibility of wealth creation by rich North Americans. The critical analysis of development as discourse is more revealing in terms of motive forces when it is cast in terms of ideology, class, and state. While there is much to learn from it, there are problems with discourse analysis. These problems can be resolved, in part, through a dialogue with Marxism, socialist feminism, and other critical traditions.

Development as Positive Power

Even so, the main issue is postmodernism's negative assessment of modernism, especially its skeptical attitude towards science and material progress. In the

postmodern literature there is a tendency to reject Western models of development and the scientific knowledges which they employ altogether – as Escobar
(1992: 27) puts it: "rather than searching for development alternatives ... [a
growing number of Third World scholars] ... speak about alternatives *to*
development, that is, a rejection of the entire paradigm." The wholesale
rejection of "entire paradigms" stems not only from disgust but from the
clumsiness of Foucauldian discourse analysis which fails to discriminate
between the components of paradigms. There are similar tendencies to deny
that poverty originally existed in the Third World, to romanticize alternatives
to development, to assume a position of reverse snobbery in which indigenous
knowledge systems are automatically superior to Western science.

Then there is the critical, skeptical postmodern attitude towards democratic
ideals and projects of human emancipation. Here the problem with postdevelopmentalism lies in its totalizing criticism, which too readily assumes that
democracy and emancipation are exclusively western, which fails to realize the
positive sides of those aspects of the Western experience that do, actually, realize
(pale versions of) such principles, which denies the Third World what the First
World already has.

Yet we need to look carefully at modernity's accomplishments: the fact that
development has yielded productivity, has enabled back-breaking labor to be
performed by machines, has yielded consumption above basic needs, does give
a margin of safety against natural catastrophes, and so on. Western science *has*
demonstrated its positive power in improving material living standards, albeit
at great environmental and social expense. Indeed, it is exactly the need for
greater material security in Third World countries that empowers Western
images and developmental models. Drawing on this tradition, development
practice involves a real quest for improving the condition of the masses. There
should be a struggle to reorient this practice rather than dismissing the entire
developmental project as a negative power play. We need, therefore, a discriminating analysis which shows how potentials come to be misused, restricted,
exploitative, environmentally dangerous. In other words, we need to replace
the critical category "modernism" with the more discriminating, equally
critical category "capitalism."

Critical political economy takes a different position, seeing science, emancipation, democracy, equality as arenas of contestation fought over in a number
of places and at a number of times rather than as pure products, or even ploys,
of the Enlightenment. For political economy the challenge remains to transform the social relations within which intellectual activity takes place, to
reorient imagination and theoretical practice, and to change the social relations
of the implementation of intellectual endeavors: ie. to make "science" serve the
interests of the oppressed.

The Politics of Fragmentation

The postmodern critique of development theory claims to have, in the notion
of micro-politics, the political capacity to engage with social movements of

resistance in the Third World. This connection is precarious – on a number of grounds. Postmodernism reaches its micro-political position based on a critique of modernism. Yet much of the Third World has yet to experience modernity in all its phases and characteristics. For modernity implies the penetration of reason into all aspects of social existence: individuals regulate their own behavior in a normative order decided through reasonable means. Yet the version of modernity which reaches the Third World is characterized more by forceful state regulation: "freedom of the individual" in the modern sense is a distant dream, beyond practicability, in highly contradictory Third World societies. Much of the postmodern critique is therefore lost to Third World ears. But then postmodern theories are phrased in such complex ways that they are incomprehensible anyway! They assume an education gained in the intellectual capitals of modernity with no expense spared, definitely *not* the conditions under which Third World social movements operate. Postmodernism is as much a Western product as the Enlightenment or development theories it criticizes!

Then, too, there is the suitability of a politics of fragmentation and difference for dealing with powerful Third World states in league with multinational corporations. "Micro-politics" can lead to a fragmented system of localized movements which oppose each other in the face of overwhelming centralized power. Putting the matter in a nastier way than is intended, where would a transnational corporate executive invest his or her money if he/she most wanted to weaken his/her opposition? Surely in a social theory that *advocates* fragmentary social movements! While the notion of geographical difference has potential for a Third World politics of resistance, its corollary "micro-politics" has to be linked with further notions of networks, alliances, broader social movements of resistance, which draw on more traditional left conceptions of class, gender, ethnicity. Again there is a need for dialogue between political postmodernism and the left.

Intellectual Dependency Theory

Postdevelopmentalism, however, is only one critical reaction to the hegemony of Western ideas and practices. Recently it has been argued that, since the colonial encounter, the economic hegemony of the West has been paralleled by academic dependence in which Third World intellectuals, trained in Western knowledge, speak the colonial language, and stress the history of the colonizer over that of the colonized. More than that, the Third World is made dependent on the First for knowledge about itself. Academic dependency entails the export of raw data from the Third World to the First, where its surplus (generalized knowledge) is released, fashioned into theories, and exported back to the Third World as pearls of wisdom (Weeks, 1990). The conditions of this dependence include control of global research funds and scholarly journals by center institutions and the prestige accruing to those who publish in international journals or who are in contact with scholars in core countries.

Since the early 1970s, arguments have been made about the captive minds of Third World scholars, minds which are uncritical and imitative of concepts coming from the West:

> Mental captivity ... refers to a way of thinking that is dominated by Western thought in an imitative and uncritical manner. Among the characteristics of the captive mind are the inability to be creative and raise original problems, the inability to devise original analytical methods, and alienation from the main issues of indigenous society
>
> (Alatas, 1993: 308).

In response, some Third World scholars call for the indigenization of social science, indeed of academic discourse as a whole. Social scientific indigenization goes beyond modifying Western concepts and methods to make them more suitable for non-Western problems. It refers instead to the derivation of scientific theories, concepts, and methodologies from the histories, cultures, and consciousness of non-Western civilizations. For Alatas (1993: 310–11) the aim would be to develop bodies of social scientific knowledge in which theories are derived from culturally- and historically-specific experiences. These, however, would not be restricted in application to the society or civilization from which they were derived. He differentiates this approach from "nativism" – i.e. the tendency for Western and local scholars to "go native" and reject Western science entirely. Instead, Alatas favors encountering, modifying, and combining Western theories with indigenous ones – for him "the call to indigenization is simultaneously a call to the universalization of the social sciences" (Alatas, 1993; 312; *see also* Amin, 1989; Moghadam, 1989).

While positions such as this are not without problems, in particular because they do not point to a convincing array of examples (but *see* Abdel-Malek, 1981), comparison with postmodern arguments is instructive. While highly critical, the indigenization theory does not advocate wholesale rejection of Western science, nor does it abandon notions of common humanity or universal knowledge. Instead it advocates that universal understanding must be based on universal sources, and not the "universalization" of the history of the West. The potential for recasting visions of a better life for Third World peoples based in a renewed, but critical, interest in local knowledge systems is clearly present. Alternatives to postmodernisms have been developed by Third World intellectuals.

Conclusion

A more discriminating critique of development theory sees it produced under definite social relations which guide the discovery and use of knowledge. In this view development has unrealized potential, and radical analysis should be dedicated to extracting those notions from developmentalism which can be used to further the interests of peasants and workers, rather than dismissing the entire venture. What can be extracted, what is worth saving? The idea, present even in liberal versions of development theory, of using production to satisfy needs in a reason*ed* environment, such as planning, where the consequences of action are discussed before action is taken. Specifically, the idea that *development* means using production to meet the needs of the poorest people. Similarly, if we reexamine Marxism, not as a monolith represented by the Soviet Union, not as dinosaur, but as a living tradition of critical thought, what is worth saving? The notion of reproductive democracy, that the people involved in an institution – the workplace, university, or family – should collectively control that institution. Specifically, that workers not only "participate" in management, or research, they *are* the managers, researchers, etc. Putting the two notions together, socialist development means transforming the conditions of reproduction within directly democratic and egalitarian social relations of control so that the needs of the poorest people are met. This is an argument for a critical, democratic Marxism, which engages postmodern notions – for example, the postmodern micro-politics of difference, identity, fragments can be engaged by socialist politics of decentralized control – learns from them, but continues to believe in structure, coherence, reason*ing*, democracy in every sphere of life, and the use of product resources to meet peoples' desperate needs. There is little in the postmodern critique which seriously challenges this vision.

References

Abdel-Malik, A., *Intellectual Creativity in Endogenous Cultures*, (Toyko, The United Nations University, 1981).

Alpers, E. A. and P-M Fontaine, (eds), *Walter Rodney: Revolutionary and Scholar: A Tribute*, (Los Angeles, U.C.L.A. Center for Afro-American Studies, 1982).

Amin, S., *Eurocentrism*, translated by R. Moore, (New York, Monthly Review Press, 1989).

Alatas, S. F., 'On the Indigenization of Academic Discourse', *Alternatives* 18: 307–38, (1993).

Banuri, T., 'Development and the Politics of Knowledge: A Critical Interpretation of the Social Role of Modernization Theories in the Development of the Third World', in F. Apffel Marglin and S. A. Marglin (eds), *Dominating Knowledge: Development, Culture and Resistance*, (Oxford, Clarendon Press, 1990), 29–72.

Bataille, G., *Visions of Excess*, (Minneapolis, University of Minnesota Press. 1985).

Best, S. and Kellner, D., *Postmodern Theory: Critical Interrogations*, (New York, Guilford Press,1991).

Cassirer, E., *The Philosophy of the Enlightenment*, (Princeton, Princeton University Press, 1951).

Cohen, G. A., *Karl Marx's Theory of History: A Defence*, (Princeton, Princeton University Press, 1978).

de Condorcet, M., 'Sketch for a Historical Picture of the Progress of the Human Mind', in L.M. Marsak (ed.), *The Enlightenment*, (New York, John Wiley, 1972), pp. 131–46.

Deleuze, G., *Nietzsche and Philosophy*, (New York, Columbia University Press, 1983).

DuBois, M., 'The Governance of the Third World: A Foucauldian Perspective on Power Relations in Development', *Alternatives* 16, 1–30, (1991).

Derrida, Jacques, 'White Mythology' in *Margins of Philosophy*, (Chicago, University of Chicago Press, 1971).

Edwards, M., 'The Irrelevance of Development Studies', *Third World Quarterly* 11, 116–35, (1989).

Eisenstadt, S.N., *Tradition, Change and Modernity*, (New York, John Wiley, 1973).

Escobar, A., 'Discourse and Power in Development: Michel Foucault and the Relevance of his Work to the Third World', *Alternatives* 10, 377–400, (1984–5).

Escobar, A., 'Power and Visibility: Development and the Invention and Management of the Third World', *Cultural Anthropology*, 3, 428–43, (1988).

Escobar, A., 'Imagining a Post-Development Era? Critical Thought, Development and Social Movements', *Social Text*, 31/32, 20–56, (1992).

Foucault, M., *The Archaeology of Knowledge,*. (New York, Harper and Row, 1972).

Foucault, M., *The Order of Things*, (New York, Vintage Press, 1973).

Foucault, M., *Discipline and Punish: The Birth of the Prison*, (New York, Vintage Books, 1979).

Foucault, M., *Power/Knowledge: Selected Interviews and Other Writings*, (New York, Pantheon Books, 1980a).

Foucault, M., *History of Sexuality*, (New York, Vintage Books, 1980b).

Foucault, M., 'What is Enlightenment?', in P. Rabinow (ed.), *The Foucault Reader*, (New York, Pantheon, 1984).

Gendzier, I., *Managing Political Change: Social Scientists and the Third World*, (Boulder, Westview Press, 1985).

Giddens, A., *A Contemporary Critique of Historical Materialism*, (Berkeley, Univesity of California Press, 1981)..

Higgot, R., *Political Development Theory: The Contemporary Debate*, (New York, St. Martin's Press, 1983).

Horkheimer, M. and Adorno, T., *Dialectic of Enlightenment*, (New York, Seabury, 1972).

Lefort, C., 'Marx: From One Vision of History to Another', *Social Research*, 45, 4,(1978).

Marx, K., (ed.) *A Contribution to the Critique of Political Economy*, (Moscow, Progress Publishers, 1970).

Marx, K., *Grundrisse: Introduction to the Critique of Political Economy*, (Harmondsworth, Penguin, 1973).

Moghadam, V., 'Against Eurocentrism and Nativism: A Review Essay on Samir Amin's *Eurocentrism* and other Texts', *Socialism and Democracy*, 9, 81–104, 1989).

Nietzsche, F., *The Will to Power*, (New York, Random House, 1967).

Parsons, T., *Societies: Evolutionary and Comparative Perspectives*, (Englewood Cliffs, Prentice-Hall, 1966).

Peet, R., and Watts, M., 'Introduction, Development Theory and Environment in an Age of Market Triumphalism', *Economic Geography*, 69, 3, 227–53, (1993).

Philo, C., 'Foucault's Geography', *Society and Space*, 10, 137–61, (1992).

Pippin, R. B., *Modernism as a Philosophical Problem*, (Cambridge, Mass, Blackwell, 1991).

Rostow, W. W., *The Stages of Economic Growth: A Non Communist Manifesto*, (Cambridge, University Press, 1960).

Sachs, W., (ed.), *The Development Dictionary: A Guide to Knowledge as Power*, (London, Zed Books, 1992).

Said, E. W., *Orientalism*, (London, Routledge and Keegan Paul, 1978).

Schuurman, F. J., (ed.), *Beyond the Impasse: New Directions in Development Theory*, (London, Zed Press, 1992).

Slater, D., 'Theories of Development and Politics of the Post-Modern – Exploring a Border Zone', *Development and Change*, 3, 283–319, (1992).

Sorensen, T., (ed.), *'Let the word go forth': The speeches, statements, and writings of John F. Kennedy*, (New York, Delacorte Press, 1988).

Watts, M., 'Development I: Power, Knowledge, Discursive Practice', *Progress in Human Geography*, 17, 2, 257–72, (1993).

Weeks, P., 'Post-Colonial Challenges to Grand Theory', *Human Organization*, 49, 3, 236–44, (1990).

Young, R., *White Mythologies: Writing History and the West*, (London, Routledge, 1990).

3

*Shelf Length Zero: The Disappearance of the Geographical Text**

Michael R. Curry

I take my title, although perhaps not much else, from Andrew Travers's 1989 "Shelf-life zero: A classic postmodernist paper." Travers says that his is a "classic" of the postmodern because it is utterly ephemeral. Now, this may seem counterintuitive, it may appear that he must have his tongue firmly within his cheek. And in contrast, my claim that in the postmodern era the text is coming to have a shelf *length* of zero, may seem quite the opposite, it may seem to be so obvious as not to require discussion. After all, we have been virtually bludgeoned in recent years by claims that we are entering the era of the paperless office, that the book of the future will be on CD-ROM (or its predecessors and successors), and that the development of computer networks like the Internet will make the formal written work obsolete.

But my claim, in fact, may on inspection appear even less obviously true than that which Travers made. For note that I am not asserting simply that *certain* written texts are being replaced by electronic ones, and thus metaphorically have no shelf length, occupy no space. Rather, I am asserting that in this era it is increasingly true that *all* written works have no shelf length. In several important senses, the written work no longer exists as a physical object.

It seems fair to say that this phenomenon has not been widely noted. But why not? In large part it has been obscured by the attention paid to the role of electronic media in the dissolution of the text. Focusing on the printed work as a technological artifact, those considering the nature of changes in such works have operated firmly within a narrow vision of technology, and have as a result looked only at changes in the final form of the object produced. This narrow focus on the most obvious changes has left the wide range of changes

* This work was supported in part by a grant from the Academic Senate of the University of California, Los Angeles. Portions of this work were carried out during a year in residence at the Center for the Critical Analysis of Contemporary Culture at Rutgers University; I should like to thank the members of the Center for their support. Finally, I should like to thank Robert Lake for the reference to the Travers article.

occurring elsewhere outside of the spotlight, and this even though they have been both diverse and large in number.

In this paper I shall point to three ways in which the nature of the geographical work, when viewed more broadly, is changing. First, it is changing as the relationship between the words within the text and the objects and ideas to which those words refer has been reconceptualized. This has happened in several ways. The Adamic view of the natural connection between words and objects was the first to go. Then, it came to be believed that one ought to distinguish between the words on the page and the ideas that they represented, and that the ideas could best be seen as having a different sort of existence, in a mental substance within the author and the reader.

There is a second way in which the scientific work has changed; the very notion of how the written object exists has become transformed. This transformation occurred in two phases. First, where once the book, for example, had been seen only as an object which might be physically owned, the ideas represented within the book came themselves to be seen as the property of the author. In the case of ideas it had long been clear that there was nothing tangible to be possessed, but a second transformation then occurred; the lack of the tangible spread back to the physical work itself. This has meant that ownership can no longer be seen simply as a matter of unconstrained dominion over a substance; it must instead be seen as involving the acquisition of a set of rights and obligations that often quite narrowly circumscribe what can and cannot be done with the work.

Finally, the written work, once seen as an address by the author to the reader, has come to be seen instead as a container of ideas. The titles of books are now labels, and the contents, in turn, refer to other labels. If this has long been the image proffered by those who catalog books, the invention of newer, computer-based indexing systems has made the image all the more real. Indeed, in certain forms of citation analysis similarity of beliefs is both demonstrated and represented by the mapping of clusters of similar citations; in an important sense the written work is seen as a point in conceptual space. At the same time, such works exist as points within a system of authority and status, where they may be counted and otherwise manipulated by name alone, and regardless of the physical form in which they exist.

This last point has itself been subject to a variety of elaborations, but most recently, many have come to believe that one needs always to interpret the "meaning" of a text through a prior analysis of the social, cultural, or other conditions within which the author operated. The written work is, in the end, only a veneer, an image placed by the author in an attempt to define the substance of his or her life.

In each of these ways – the movement of attention from the text to the author to the world, the desubstantialization of the textual object, and the representation of texts as ideational points – the written work has come to lose its physical presence. And it is only against this background that we can truly understand the other, more obvious ways in which it is beginning to lose that presence, as, for example, it begins to be transmitted electronically, or in the case of computer cartography, takes on a different and more fluid form. In what follows I shall comment in more detail of each of these three changes; in the concluding section I shall point to the relationship between these changes and the more obvious technologically driven changes to which I have just referred.

The Object, the Idea, and the Author

What has been termed the "Adamic" view is simply the view that there is, was, or might be a language such that words "naturally" refer to the world.[1] On this view, often associated with the world before the Tower of Babel, there would be perfect communication, because in learning a name we would at once gain knowledge of the object to which it referred. Now, when I say that the Adamic view was the first to go I am, actually, exaggerating. Indeed, we see vestiges of it today. For example, in the early twentieth century, Wittgenstein, in his *Tractatus Logico-Philosophicus*, attempted to develop a theory of meaning which rested on the view that language maps onto the world, and which argued that the logical form of linguistic statements mapped onto the form of the facts which make up the world.[2] Perhaps less abstractly, there is a sense in which we can see the attempt to divise the periodic table in chemistry as involving a similar endeavor to develop such a language. Similarly, we might want to see the attempt to map the human genome as motivated by the same desire, the desire to come up with a natural and transparent vocabulary. In geography much the same motivation has surrounded attempts to develop systems of cartographic representation which will be read without error by everyone; the idea is that if colors or shapes or shades are just designed in the right way the map reader will naturally understand the relationships expressed in the map, and in the world, without the necessity of the intervention of conscious interpretation or analysis.[3]

But if today there are vestiges, even important vestiges, of this Adamic view and if especially in science we can find elements of an attempt to *invent* languages which meet the Adamic ideal, these remain only vestiges, counters to the view that the relationship between language and the world must be

1   The importance of the Adamic view is today a matter of some controversy; some, like Hans Aarsleff and James Knowlson, see it as having been a central concern, while others, like Mary Slaughter, see it as having been less important.
2   Ludwig Wittgenstein, *Tractatus logico-philosophicus*, translated by D. F. Pears and Brian F. McGuinnes, (London, Routledge and Kegan Paul, 1961/1921).
3   *See*, for example, Henry W. Castner and Arthur H. Robinson, *Dot area symbols in cartography: The influence of pattern on their perception*, (Washington, DC, American Congress of Surveying and Mapping, 1969); Borden Dent, "Visual organization and thematic map design,"*Annals of the Association of American Geographers*, 62 (1972), 79–93; and Patricia Gilmartin, "The map context as a source of perceptual error in graduated circle maps," (Lawrence, K. S.: unpublished PhD dissertation, University of Kansas, 1980). In some respects this view is more generally held by mainstream students of cartography, as in Mark Monmonier, *How to lie with maps*, (Chicago, University of Chicago Press, 1991).

contingent at best. In one sense we find this Adamic view as far back as Plato, in the *Cratylus*, where he dismisses the possibility of there being a language in which "a name is an instrument of teaching and of distinguishing natures, as the shuttle of distinguishing the threads of the web,"[4] and concludes that "We must rest content with the admission that the knowledge of things is not to be derived from names. No; they must rather be studied and investigated in their connexion with one another."[5] But we find it more directly at the very fountainhead of modern science, in Descartes and Bacon, where we can see the formulation of the view that the first task of scientists is to see through language, to sidestep language and thereby gain a clearer view of the relationship between concepts and the world.

Bacon argued that "The discoveries which have hitherto been made in the sciences are such as lie close to vulgar notions, scarcely beneath the surface."[6] The reason for the failure to develop a fuller understanding of nature is that people have been entranced by a group of "Idols," those of the marketplace, tribe, cave, and theater. Most important are the idols of the marketplace:

> There are also Idols formed by the intercourse and association of men with each other, which I call Idols of the Market-Place, on account of the commerce and consort of men there. For it is by discourse that men associate; and words are imposed according to the apprehension of the vulgar. And therefore the ill and unfit choice of words wonderfully obstructs the understanding.[7]

These idols "must be renounced and put away with a fixed and solemn determination."[8] Only in this way can one escape the power of the "shadows thrown by words," and avoid being, like Aristotle, "the cheap dupe of words."[9]

If we turn to Descartes we find, as in Bacon, a critique of language as a course of error. But Descartes is more complex than Bacon, and in fact he himself at one point toyed with the idea of a perfect language. In a letter to Mersenne, he rejected a then current proposal, by Des Vallée, which Mersenne had introduced in an earlier letter. The problem, Descartes suggested, was that the author of the proposal had not thought the matter through; the solution to problems with vocabulary will not come, as had been suggested, from the appeal to some more generally acceptable set of words, perhaps a set derived from the historical study of language, and thus closer to some Adamic ideal. Rather, the development of a perfect language requires that one see that:

4 Plato, "Cratylus," 388, in *The dialogues of Plato* (Fourth edition) translated by Benjamin Jowett, 1953.
5 Plato, "Cratylus," 439b.
6 Bacon, "The new organon," XVIII.
7 Bacon, "The new organon," XLIII.
8 Bacon, "The new organon," LXVIII.
9 Francis Bacon, "The masculine birth of time," in *The philosophy of Francis Bacon: An essay on its development from 1603 to 1609, with new translations of fundamental texts*, (ed.), Benjamin Farrington, (1970), pp. 62–3.

Order is what is needed: all the thoughts which can come into the human mind must be arranged in an order like the natural order of the numbers. In a single day one can learn to name every one of the infinite series of numbers, and thus to write infinitely many different words in an unknown language. The same could be done for all the other words necessary to express all the other things which fall under the purview of the human mind ....[10]

At other points, he argued that such a language would not really resolve the fundamental problem, the lack of certainty in science. For that one needed to turn to intuition, which is:

a conception, formed by unclouded mental attention, so easy and direct as to leave no room for doubt in regard to the thing we are understanding .... It is an indubitable conception formed by an unclouded and attentive mind; one that originates solely from the light of reason, and is more certain even that deduction, because it is simpler.[11]

If today we think of intuition as a matter of guesswork, Descartes had a very different image in mind: "We can best learn how mental intuition is to be employed by comparing it with ordinary vision."[12] Hence, the central image of the process of thinking, insofar as it leads to certainty, is one of vision; one grasps the truth with the mind's eye. And this grasping involves the use of a kind of mental vision on the contents of the mind; the mind is represented here as a kind of interior space, a space filled with ideas.

So now, and whatever the outcome of attempts to develop a perfect language, ideas have migrated. After Babel they no longer reside in objects; after Bacon and Descartes neither do they reside in words, and so neither do they reside in the printed page. Rather, they exist in a kind of mental space, in the author and in the reader.

This view, this sundering of the mental and the physical, might very well be seen as one of the defining features of modernism. And all was fine with this modernist view as long as it could be assumed, as with Descartes, that the right method would lead to the correct ideas about the world, for then the fact that ideas were internal and invisible made no difference; they were still in principle accessible. But Kant's Copernican move, which put the order of the universe inside the mind, set the stage for a new phase, a collapse of the view that these ideas could with any certainty be known. Kant, of course, believed that he could know these mental processes[13] with as much certainty as Descartes had known

10 Descartes, Letter to Mersenne, 20 Nov. 1629.
11 Descartes, *Rules*, X, 368.
12 Descartes, *Rules*, X, 400.
13 I use the term here advisedly, and recognize that this colloquial way of characterizing Kant's view obscures and misrepresents certain features of his thought. I am of course referring here to Immanuel Kant, *The critique of pure reason*, translated by Norman Kemp Smith, (New York, St. Martin's Press, 1965/1781, 1787). For alternative interpretations, *see* (to name only two quite extreme examples) P. F. Strawson, *The bounds of sense: An essay on Kant's critique of pure reason*, (London, Methuen, 1966) and Robert Paul Wolff,

the ones that he described. On the other hand, his successors took over the image with a basic change; they believed that these ordering processes varied, by time or place, gender, class, or race. But this issue will turn out to be far more important later in this piece.

The Desubstantialization of the Textual Object

For now, it is important to leave the matter at this, and to note that the development of the view that a work exists in a kind of mental space in the author and the reader, to be read through a process of mental vision, is connected to a second set of issues. These concern the way in which the commodity form of the text came to exist first as a physical object and then as a set of ideas behind the object; this was associated with a reconceptualization of both author and work, and ultimately with a view wherein both can best be seen merely as aspatial armatures, to which are attached sets of rights and responsibilities.

When we think of the ownership of geographical objects today the matter seems straightforward. The objects are actually seen as dual in form. On the one hand, they consist of the actual physical expressions of ideas. These expressions are legally protected, through the law of copyright. The protection, though, is temporally limited, and at the same time is alienable; indeed, in articles and more in the case of maps, the author or creator most often sells his or her rights to a publisher, who may sell them again. On the other hand, the geographer also owns the ideas themselves. If I develop a theory or method it is mine. This form of ownership, of course, is very different from the first, just because it is permanent and cannot be alienated. My work is always mine, for better or worse. Now, this dual form of existence of the scientific and geographical object is a commonplace; it is something about which we seldom feel the need to comment. But there are two things to notice about it. First, it is historically contingent, and rather new. And second, recent developments have begun to recast it.

The relationship between the written work and the author has been considered in a number of recent works, perhaps most notably by Foucault, Rose, and Woodmansee.[14]

Rose's and Woodmansee's works, the first about Britain and the second

Kant's theory of mental activity: A commentary on the transcendental analytic of the Critique of pure reason, (Cambridge, Harvard University Press, 1963). In defense of speaking in this way I would suggest that this is just the way in which his work has been appropriated.

14 Michel Foucault, "What is an author?," in Donald F. Bouchard, (ed.), *Language, counter-memory, practice: Selected essays and interviews,* translated by Donald F. Bouchard and Sherry Simon (Ithaca, New York, Cornell University Press, 1977/1969), pp. 113–38; Mark Rose, *Authors and owners: The invention of copyright,* (Cambridge, Harvard University Press, 1993); Martha Woodmansee, "The genius and the copyright: Economic and legal conditions of the emergence of the "author,"" *Eighteenth Century Studies,* 17 (1984), 425–48.

primarily concerned with developments in Germany, are both concerned with the ways in which the notion of the author developed, and with the relationship between that notion and the notion that the author is the producer of a physical and an intellectual work. Both direct their attention to the eighteenth and especially the early nineteenth centuries, as the eras in which these notions were formalized and codified into law. And both directly address the ways in which formal, legal structures interacted with technical and social changes to produce a series of conceptions of the physical work, the intellectual work, and their interrelations.

At the same time, each begins well after the invention of printing, and well after an important event to which Foucault, albeit briefly, turns his attention. Granting that in the early part of the period discussed by Rose and Woodman-see the modern category of "literature" had yet to be invented, and that the writing of scientists was therefore not seen as disciplinarily distinct from that of others. Foucault points out that it would be a mistake to stop there. In fact, in the era before the invention of printing, and until the invention of modernist science, the scientist was in a sense the author par excellence. That is, the very fact that something had been written by Aristotle, to take the obvious example, guaranteed its truth. So in the pre-modern era the scientist-author had a special sort of authority, and one which only came successfully to be criticized with the rise of modernism.

At the same time, the rise of modernism was the event that gave rise to a new form of the author – and of the work. But this did not easily happen. Certainly key in the development of this form was the printing press. Invented late in the fifteenth century, it immediately made possible a fundamentally different method for the dissemination of knowledge. Whether in the case of the book or the map, it now became possible to produce large numbers of identical objects. If publication produced written and graphic objects which could be easily bought and sold, it had additional effects. For one, it now became possible to engage in textual criticism, and thereby to compare sources, with the view to creating the "best" text.[15] Because they were manufactured objects, their "titles changed from addresses to the reader to become like the labels on boxes."[16] Their very proliferation necessitated the invention of systems by which to catalog them. For the same reason, because they were among the first items in the "age of mechanical reproduction," they began to lose what Walter Benjamin referred to as their "aura."[17]

Perhaps most important, thought, in the case both of books and of maps, it was clear that the production of such objects required the joint collaboration

15 Elizabeth Eisenstein, *The printing press as an agent of change: Communications and cultural transformations in early modern Europe*, (Cambridge, Cambridge University Press, 1979); David Woodward, (ed.), *Five centuries of map printing*, (Chicago, University of Chicago Press, 1975).

16 Walter J. Ong, "System, space, and renaissance symbolism, "*Study on Renaissance Symbolism*, 8 (1956), 229.

17 Walter Banjamin, "The work of art in the age of mechanical reproduction," in *Illuminations* (ed.), Hannah Arendt (New York, Schocken, 1969), pp. 217–51.

of a wide range of people. Books required editors, typesetters, printers, bookbinders, and booksellers; maps required engravers and printers. And as today, the labor required of each was not insubstantial. Arthur Robinson estimates that in the case of maps produced by copperplate, an expert engraver might produce one square inch per day.[18]

This division of labor was reflected in the earliest regulations of the owner-ship of books. They consisted of grants, by governments, to individual booksellers; those grants gave a bookseller a monopoly within a geographic area over a certain category of works. The earliest copyright law, England's 1710 Statute of Anne, was intended to do the same; it was promoted by booksellers who saw their investments in typesetting at risk from literary pirates. What was protected was the right of the bookseller to labor invested in a physical object. Indeed, although now seen as the first copyright statute, there is a sense in which the Statue of Anne was more concerned with physical than with intellectual property.[19]

Still, and notwithstanding the intent of its framers, the Statute came to be interpreted in a way which gradually has led to a more recognizably modern view. As Rose has noted, in England this involved two distinct steps. First, it was necessary that the rights to a work come to be seen as residing – at least in the first instance – in the author, rather than in the bookseller. And second, it was necessary that the physical object come to be seen merely as a set of signs for the "real" work, one which had only a virtual existence.

The first step happened rather quickly. Indeed, one of the very first suits under the Statue of Anne, concerning the translation of a work by a scientist familiar to historians of geography, geologist Thomas Burnet, pressed that point. And by 1735, when a bill for improving the Statute was introduced, it had become clear that "a significant evolution had occurred, in which the focus of the literary-property question shifted from the bookseller to the author."[20]

In England the second step occurred at about the same time. Rose argues that its first manifestation is in a lawsuit brought by Alexander Pope, in 1741. In that suit (Pope v. Curll), Pope argued that he maintained the literary right to letters which he had written, and therefore physically relinquished. In the court's decision, as Rose put it, "the author's words have in effect flown free from the page on which they were written. Not ink and paper but pure signs, separated from any material support, have become the protected property."[21]

The two steps were not, of course, unrelated. In part this is because the

18 Arthur Robinson, "Mapmaking and map printing: The evolution of a working relationship," in David Woodward, (ed.), *Five centuries of map printing*, (Chicago, University of Chicago Press, 1975), p. 14.
19 Rose, 1993, 4–5. *See also* Lyman Ray Patterson, *Copyright in historical perspective*, (Nashville, Vanderbilt University Press, 1968); Harry Ransom, *The first copyright statute: An essay on the Act for the encouragement of learning, 1710*, (Austin, University of Texas Press, 1956); and Peter Jaszi, "On the author effect: Contemporary copyright and collective creativity," *Cardozo Arts and Entertainment Journal*, 10 (1992), 293–320.
20 Rose, 1993, 56.
21 Rose, 1993, 65.

Statute and the common law in which it was embedded were expressive of what after Locke's *Second Treatise* came to be termed the "labor theory of property." There Locke argued that when people mix their labor with portions of the natural world, that portion of the world becomes theirs.[22] Here, as is well known, Locke has assumed that people can be seen as owners or proprietors of their own selves.[23] But the crucial point here is the way in which this view tied in with another view, and one equally popular in the empiricist Britain of the eighteenth century. On that view the mind presents itself to the world as an empty slate. The external world quite literally impresses itself on the mind, and thereby creates impressions. These, in the mind, can be manipulated, as ideas.

In striking contrast to what has since Freud come to seem common sense, for empiricists like Locke and Hume it is possible for one to read one's own thoughts, very much as one would read a book, in the visual way seen in Descartes.[24] Here, then, the creation of a written work is at the same time an act of labor which writes that book into (or onto) one's own mind. So one owns one's own ideas in a way rather more fundamental than the way in which one owns some external object, or to take a favorite case, a piece of land.

This connection, between the ideas which constitute the work and the person, is closer still in the romantic tradition. This is because in the eighteenth century the understanding of writing in terms of adherence to a traditional body of rhetorical rules, an understanding which until then had coexisted uneasily with a notion of writing as motivated by the muse, dropped away.[25] What remained was the muse in a more modern incarnation, in the form of the notion of genuis. Here it became not labor but internal mental qualities which were the source of the work. As Martha Woodmansee has put the matter,

> moments of inspiration move, in the course of time, to the center of reflection on the nature of writing. And as they are increasingly credited to the writer's own genius, they transform the writer into a unique individual uniquely responsible for a unique product. That is, more a (mere) vehicle of preordained truths – truths as ordained either by universal human agreement or by some higher agency – the *writer* becomes an *author* (Lat. *author*, originator, founder, creator).[26]

22   John Locke, "Second treatise of government," in *Two treatises of government* (ed.), Thomas I. Cook (New York, Hafner, 1947/1690).
23   C. B. MacPherson, *The political theory of possessive individualism: Hobbes to Locke*, (Oxford, Oxford University Press, 1962); John R. Wikse, *About possession: The self as private property*, (University Park, Pennsylvania State University Press, 1977).
24   John Locke, *An essay concerning human understanding*, (London, Routledge, nd); David Hume, *Enquiries concerning human understanding and concerning the principles of morals*, Third edition, (Oxford, Oxford University Press, 1975/1777).
25   *See*, for example, Terry Eagleton, "A small history of rhetoric," in *Walter Benjamin, or towards a revolutionary criticism*, (London, NLB-Verso, 1981), pp. 101–13; Brian Vickers, *In defence of rhetoric*, (Oxford, Clarendon Press, 1988); and Charles W. Kneupper, (ed.), *Visions of rhetoric: History, theory, and criticism*, (Arlington, TX, Rhetoric Society of America, 1987).
26   Woodmansee, 1984, 429.

Indeed, by the end of the eighteenth century Fichte, putting a decidedly neo-Kantian cast to the matter, remarked that:

> each individual has his own thought processes, his own way of forming concepts and connecting them .... Now, since pure ideas without images cannot be thought, much less are they capable of representation to others. Hence, each writer must give his thought a certain form, and he can give them no other form than his own, because he has no other. But neither can he be willing to hand over this form in making his thought public, for no one can *appropriate* his thoughts without thereby *altering their form*. This latter thus remains forever his exclusive property.[27]

So in an important sense, by the end of the eighteenth century the physical work of the writer, or the scientist, had lost its aura. But to a certain extent that aura had migrated to the work as an ideal object of ownership and to the author as an owner. Within science this was expressed both in the recognition that there are certain ideas that are clearly the property of those people who discovered or created them; elsewhere we see it in disciplines like history and archaeology where there is a strong sense of one's work as being based within a particular set of facts. In both cases it is common to belive that both the scientist and the ideas deserve special consideration.

At the same time, this romantic view has within the context of an increasingly modernizing and globalizing economy been threatened by an alternative, a Lockean view which attempts to dispense once and for all with the view that we can treat either the author or the idea as special.[28] Codified most forcefully within Anglo-American theory of copyright, this view presses for a system of rights and responsibilities to written works which can in the first instance be operationalized in specifiable ways. For example, the ideal is that rights be of limited and specified duration and that ownership be alienable, in a way that can be clearly delinated within a written context.

It is important here to see that the Lockean view of property developed on a parallel course with a view of the individual. In describing the acquisition of the right to an object as the result of one's having mixed one's labor with that object, Locke appealed to a metaphor of substance. Yet the upshot of that conception was to see the relationship between an individual and that object as one in which with the ownership of the object the individual acquires certain rights and obligations. Indeed, ownership ultimately comes − and especially when what is owned is a mass-produced object − to be seen more and more as only a matter of the holding of such rights and obligations.[29]

---

27 Fichte, "Proof of the illegality of reprinting," pp. 227–28, quoted in Woodmansee, 1984, 445.
28 Lawrence C. Becker, "The labor theory of property acquisition," *Journal of Philosophy*, 73 (1976); David Ellerman, "On the labor theory of property," *The Philosophical Forum*, 16 (1985), 293–326; Edwin C. Hettinger, "Justifying intellectual property," *Philosophy and Public Affairs*, 18 (1989), 3–52; Alfred C. Yen, "Restoring the natural law: Copyright as labor and possession," *Ohio State Law Journal*, 51 (1990), 517–59.

But as Lawrence Friedman has noted, recent times have seen the same view with respect to individuals, as in the last century culture has come to be saturated by law.[30] There have come to be fewer and fewer sites in society which are not seen as possible areas of legal discourse. Friedman argues, in a way reminiscent of Alasdair MacIntyre, that the result has been a society of rules and that this eventuality has followed naturally upon certain technological developments, which have rendered people much more mobile; the result has been the demise of the places which in more traditional societies provided means for the adjudication of disputes short of their being moved into a formal legal system.[31] There seems little doubt that notwithstanding Romantic counter currents this is what has happened in our society.[32] In the context of my comments above, this has meant that one's ownership of one's self has come increasingly to be a matter of seeing one's self as a locus of rights and obligations (although Friedman would argue that there has been little enough recognition of obligations).

If the loss of significant places in the world has led to an increased reliance on rules and instrumentality, this is the same process that we have seen in the modernist project of rethinking language as a set of mental objects which reflect the nature of the world, which have no author, and which come from nowhere. And this rethinking, which in part involved the denigration of the rules of rhetoric which Woodmansee sees as fundamentally associated with the traditional production of the text, is at once a rejection of the tradition which saw language itself as "placed," and the learning of rhetoric a matter of the learning of *topoi*.

And so, with respect to issues surrounding the written work, this means that it is increasingly the case that both author and work are conceptualized as circulating within what amounts to a neutral space. Both are conceptualized as existing outside of those significant places which in the past provided the context for actions which appealed to traditional forms of authority in order to adjudicate disputes. In each of these cases we can see what amounts to an abandonment of the Aristotelian in favor of the Newtonian, of a metaphysics of the concrete in favor of a metaphysics of the abstract, of length zero.

29 Thomas C. Grey, "The disintegration of property," in J. Roland Pennock and John William Chapman, (eds), *Property*, (New York, New York University Press, 1980), pp. 69–85.

30 Lawrence M. Friedman, *The republic of choice: Law, authority, and culture*, (Cambridge, Harvard University Press, 1990).

31 Alasdair C. MacIntyre, *After virtue: A study in moral theory* (Second edition), (Notre Dame, University of Notre Dame Press, 1984); Bruce Kimball, *The "true professional ideal" in America: A history*, (Cambridge, MA, Blackwell, 1992).

32 Jane C. Ginsburg, "French copyright law: A comparative overview," *Journal of the Copyright Society of the USA*, 4 (1989), 269–85; Jane C. Ginsburg, "A tale of two copyrights: Literary property in revolutionary France and America," *Tulane Law Review*, 64 (1990), 991–1031; Benjamin Kaplan, *An unhurried view of copyright*, (New York, Columbia University Press, 1967); Sam Ricketson, *The Berne Convention for the protection of literary and artistic works: 1886–1986*, (London, Centre for Commercial Law Studies, Queen Mary College, 1987).

In the Marketplace of Ideas

There is a final sense in which the written work can be seen as having increasingly had a shelf length of zero. This concerns the ways in which such works have come to be seen simply as pointers within larger systems. Here I shall mention three. First, they have come to be seen as elements within classification systems, which attempt to organize human knowledge. Second, they have become elements within systems of citation and reference. And third, they have become elements within systems of authority in science, and more broadly in society.

Now it would be pointless to attempt to argue that systems of classification of the written work are new. And indeed, this is not what I wish to argue. Rather, support for my position is provided by the very fact that such systems are quite old. There are systems for the organization of knowledge in Plato's *Republic*, in Aristotle's *Metaphysics*, and in Zeno. By AD 305 we find the famous system of Porphyry:

Substance
    Spiritual
    Corporeal
        Celestial
        Terrestrial
            Elementary
        Mixed
            Lifeless
            Living
                Vegetable
                Animal
                    Irrational
                    Rational
                        Man

This system was repeated in later works, and as Richardson points out, strikes us today as "a most interesting suggestion of the modern evolutionary order."[33] Moreover, as the modern age begins there is an efflorescence of such systems of classification; they are developed by Bacon, Descartes, Hobbes, Vico, Kant, Schelling, and Hegel – to name only a few.[34]

If such systems were extremely common, it remains that they were not widely used in the cataloging of books. Indeed, Melvil Dewey created his famed Dewey

---

33 Ernest Cushing Richardson, *Classification: Theoretical and practical*, (New York, H. W. Wilson, 1930), 52.
34 Richardson provides a 110-page listing of such systems. Briefer accounts can be found in Arthur Maltby, *Sayer's manual of classification for librarians* (Fifth edition), (London, Andre Deutsch, 1975/1926) and W. C. Berwick Sayers, *An introduction to library classification* (Sixth edition), (London, Grafton, 1943/1918).

Decimal System in 1876 just because there was such an anarchy of systems; it appeared that almost every library had its own. Of course, there is the "French System," or System of the Paris Booksellers, the basis of which was established in the seventeenth century, and which was codified in the early nineteenth by Jacque Charles Brunet.[35] But the French system, the Dewey system, and the Library of Congress system (1901) precisely demonstrate the point which I wish to make, because none can really be seen as a system based – as were those of Aristotle, Porphryry, Bacon, and Kant – on the organization of knowledge. Rather, they were practical systems, which ordered books themselves, in ways meant to render their use less difficult.

We find much the same when we look to systems developed for the cataloging of maps, although there the logic of organizing maps by region – and by size – imposed itself early enough that it is rare to find attempts to develop conceptually elegant, or even coherent, systems.[36]

In one sense we might want to see this rejection of theoretical models for the classification of knowledge as a recognition that science needs to be seen at the center of a set of social practices, and this would run counter to my thesis. I grant, in fact, that there is a point here. At the same time, though, it seems to me important to recognize that elegant or not, these systems treat books as though they are containers of ideas. Indeed, the difficulty in cataloging books seems to arise not so much from their inherent intractability as from their containing too many ideas. A really small book, a book which contained a single idea, those who classify them seem to say, could be accurately and unambiguously classified; it could be treated as though it occupied only a single point.

If we turn away from classification, we find still another series of ways in which the written products of geography have come increasingly to occupy only a single point in conceptual space. It has been an increasingly common requirement that journal articles be tagged with "keywords," which are expected to represent the subject matter and perhaps methodology of the article. Here, in a sense, we can see the article as merely an expansion of those keywords. Much the same can be said for the development of a requirement that articles be prefaced by abstracts; here, too, the suggestion is that an article can be seen as an expansion of a much smaller set of ideas.

But certainly most important has been the development of new systems of referencing, and of the systems of citation indexing which have attended them. The standards to be used in the writing of scientific papers have in this century been described in a series of style manuals. The earliest of these was general, *Hart's Rules for Compositors and Readers*, published in 1893. But soon thereafter followed the publication of the first manuals directed at scientists, in Britain the 1905 *Notes on the Composition of Scientific Papers*, by Clifford Allbutt, and

35 Maltby, 1975/1926, 111.
36 Christopher Merrett, *Map cataloguing and classification: A comparison of approaches*, (Sheffield, University of Sheffield, Postgraduate School of Librarianship and Information Science, 1976); Jessie B. Watkins, *Selected bibliography on maps in libraries: Acquisition, classification, cataloging, storage, uses*, (Syracuse, Syracuse University Libraries, 1967).

in the United States, Trelease and Yule's 1925 *Preparation of Scientific and Technical Papers.*

Until quite recently it was typical in an article to show one's intellectual sources through the use of footnotes. Trelease and Yule, for example, characterize this – albeit where the items in the reference list are arranged in order of citation – as the preferred method. By contrast, in Trelease's 1947 *The scientific paper: How to prepare it, how to write,* the method of making a citation within the text by author and year (the so-called Harvard system) is argued to be preferable, because it:

> gives the reader the information he wants in the text and enables him to locate the citation easily in the alphabetical list at the end of the paper, or *to use the list independently as a source of literature* [Emphasis added]. This method of reference is most convenient for the author because it allows him to add or delete citations during the revision of the manuscript, without the necessity of repeatedly renumbering the series or inserting interpolated numbers.[37]

Here the way in which such a system renders simpler the task of writing is mentioned as a main argument in favor of the use of this system; a second reason is that it allows the reader to know who is being cited without needing to sort through footnotes. These are obvious and often-mentioned advantages of the system.

But a third reason, less often mentioned, is the one to which I should like to turn my attention. That is that this system allows the reader to read in a different way, to use the text primarily as a source of material for further work, and without even reading it. Where only footnotes are used, without a reference list, or even where they are accompanied by a list sorted by mention in the text, the reader is in a sense forced to attend to the contents of the text. But the new system cuts the references loose from the text, allowing the reader to use them to serve his own purpose. The article itself becomes merely a source.

In the ensuing years the Harvard system of citation has come to be even more widely accepted.[38] Indeed, the author of a recent manual simply advises "Avoid using footnotes … [e]ven if you are writing for a journal that allows [them]."[39] Now it might seem that this practice, which was developed during an era before the personal computer, and hence before the existence of systems for the automatic renumbering of footnotes, has today lost its technological advantage; after all, where footnotes can be easily inserted and deleted, and where typesetting is done by computer, there seems to be little in the way of cost advantages to proscribing their use. Yet they remain unpopular, and

37　Sam F. Trelease, *The scientific paper: How to prepare it, how to write it,* (Baltimore, Williams and Wilkins, 1947).

38　*See,* for example, Sam F. Trelease, *How to write scientific and technical papers,* (Cambridge, MIT Press, 1958); Robert A. Day, *How to write and publish a scientific paper* (Second edition), (Philadelphia, ISI Press, 1983); and Maeve O'Connor, *Writing successfully in science,* (London, Chapman and Hall, 1991).

39　O'Connor, 1991, 92.

journals appear increasingly to be switching to the Harvard system. There is a reason for this, and it concerns an additional way in which the geographical text can be seen to be disappearing.

Thirty years ago Eugene Garfield introduced his *Science Citation Index*. The index, which cross-indexed references within one journal article to other works, was clearly a valuable tool, just because it seemed so obviously to be a means for understanding intellectual lineages and systems of influence. But where citations are dispersed within a text in terms of a system of footnotes the collection of citations is a laborious process. By contrast, the Harvard system makes it much easier. Moreover, if we turn back to Trelease's comment about the ability to "use the list independently as a source of literature" we can see that the citation index supports the very same way of reading scientific literature that is supported by the citation indexes. So whatever the reasons for the continued adoption and use of the Harvard system, there is an important sense in which the two "go together," in a view of science within which the written work exists less as an object to be read than as a virtual armature around which develop a series of activities.

There is a sense, too, in which the system of citation analysis is relevant to the earlier point about the nature of systems of classification. All such formal, or "a priori" schemes, Garfield claimed, rest on a simple error. They organize works on the basis of some simple and explicit set of criteria, and not on criteria that have "real" relevance. The act of citation, though, is at once an act of characterizing a work as relevant to another, which in so doing the author automatically creates a class or group. And this, according to Garfield, is a *real* group, not merely an arbitrary one, like the Dewey Decimal System or like a system based on keywords or on the content analysis of abstracts.[40]

Garfield noted that there was another advantage to the indexes; they may be used for:

> The evaluation of the impact of a paper, a man's works, a journal, material published during specific time intervals, the works of specific teachers, works coming out of a university or department, work financially sponsored by a specific agency....

> It may be used to study journal utilizations, measuring literature habits of scientists, effectiveness of specific journals in reaching specific audiences, purchasing requirements of specific libraries.[41]

Here, too, the written work comes to lose its concrete existence, and to become merely a pointer, a symbol of value or authority within a larger system.

---

40 Eugene Garfield, "'Science citation index' – A new dimension in indexing," *Science*, 144 (1964), 649–54.
41 Quoted in H. Burr Steinbach, "The quest for certainty: *Science citation index*," *Science*, 145 (1964), 143.

The Disappearing Text

There is a third sense in which we can see the written work as an important element within a social system, and one which brings together issues raised in each of the three previous sections. This sense is more directly related to the traditional concerns of the sociology of science. Robert K. Merton, for example, developed a view wherein one could map the relations between the written products of science and the status of their creators.[42] There the content of the work was far less important than its reception.

Now, there has been much recent criticism of Merton, and especially from what might be termed the "postmodern turn" in science studies. Central here has been the view that the Kantian project of understanding people as approaching the world in terms of sets of ordering processes needs to be recast, in order better to recognize that those ordering processes vary widely, and that they create fundamental divisions between groups of people. This has meant yet another turn in the fortunes of the written work, for if the work is seen as reflective of a set of ideas in the author's head, and if those ideas may be very different from one's own, and if at the same time the written work itself no longer contains them, then any attempt to grasp the ideas within the work must now operate at yet another remove.

According to at least one current set of theories, this requires looking at the world itself. The ideas which people hold are themselves expressions of their own interests or positions, and so it is to them that we must look. This is a pervasive view, and I shall mention only two places where it is regularly found. First, several recent works in anthropology have begun to see that discipline, notwithstanding its maintenance of a professional code of ethics demanding support and respect for the groups it studies, as resting fundamentally on a set of oppositions between the author and the object of research. Paul Rabinow, for example, argues that:

> the primary critiques within anthropology ... have been not epistemological, but rather meta-epistemological. By that I mean that they have involved a critique of the Western scientific enterprise, on the grounds that it has fundamentally involved the assertion of an imbalanced power relationship, where the knower, through the scientific text, asserts authority over the known.[43]

As Johannes Fabian put it, this involves a denial that the subject and the anthropologist even inhabit the same time, a denial of "coevalness." And so, just as the physicist sees himself or herself as acting within time, and the world as a place in a sense beyond time, because subject to timeless laws, so too does

42 Robert K. Merton, "The normative structure of science," in *The sociology of science: Theoretical and empirical investigations*, (ed.), Norman W. Storer, (Chicago, University of Chicago Press, 1973/1942), pp. 267–78.
43 Paul Rabinow, "Representations are social facts: Modernity and post-modernity in anthropology," in James Clifford and George Marcus, (eds), *Writing culture*, (Berkeley, University of California Press, 1986), p. 244.

the anthropologist see the subject of research as living outside of time, and hence as not fully human, an Other.[44]

Ironically, it is now argued by Rabinow and others, the traditional realism of anthropological writing had exactly the opposite of the desired effect; it made people less real. James Clifford put the matter in this way, and offered an alternative:

> Every description or interpretation that conceives itself as "bringing a culture into writing," moving from the oral-discursive experience (the natives', the fieldworker's) to a written version of that experience (the ethnographic text) is enacting the structure of "salvage." To the extent that the ethnographic process is seen as inscription (rather than, for example, as transcription, or dialogue) the representation will continue to enact a potent, and questionable allegorical structure.[45]

But according to Rabinow, even this will not work; the postured eclecticism of the anthropologist privileges the critic as "social hero."[46] Indeed,

> Clifford talks a great deal about the ineluctability of dialogue (thereby establishing his authority as an "open" one), but his texts are not themselves dialogic…. Both Geertz and Clifford fail to use self-referentiality as anything more than a device for establishing authority.[47]

And for Rabinow this leads to an additional issue:

> Is it vulgar to ask: would longer, dispersive texts yield tenure? Is it bad taste to remark that, for example, advocates of experimental writing themselves produce texts which are resolutely academic and traditional in form. But these questions are posed in the corridors all the time. They are real.[48]

Hence, according to Rabinow, no matter what the involvement of the subject, no matter how generous the acknowledgements, no matter how much the voice of the subject lives in the text, the anthropological work, ultimately, is a piece of anthropology, written for anthropologists, read by them, and judged by them. After all is said and done, the anthropologist remains an anthropologist, and this means that the anthropologist remains a person with a life and a career,

44   Johannes Fabian, *Time and the other: How anthropology makes its object*, (New York, Columbia University Press, 1983).
45   James Clifford, "On ethnographic allegory," in James Clifford and George Marcus, (eds), *Writing culture*, (Berkeley, University of California Press, 1986), pp. 113.
46   Paul Rabinow, "Discourse and power: On the limits of ethnographic texts," *Dialectical Anthropology*, 10 (1985), 8.
47   Paul Rabinow, "Representations are social facts: Modernity and post-modernity in anthropology," in Clifford and Marcus, (eds), *Writing culture*, 1986, p. 244.
48   Paul Rabinow, "Discourse and power: On the limits of ethnographic texts," *Dialectical Anthropology*, 10 (1985), 12.

and with needs and interests related to them. To read the text, to *really* read the text, requires that one read the anthropologist.

If anthropologists like Rabinow have emphasized the social bases of the practice of anthropology, and hence have seen the text as a sort of epiphenomenon, there has been little – in fact no – anthropology of anthropology. If there has been widespread agreement that the text can be "read" only by reading the anthropologist, the task has not actually been done. This is perhaps not surprising; placing one's gaze on one's colleagues is common enough, but publishing the results can be difficult and dangerous. There is, though, a second set of works which have concerned themselves with the text, and to a degree have engaged in just this analysis. These, works in the sociology of science, have avoided the dangers of the project by focusing on the written works of nonacademics or of those in disciplines far removed from their own.

A quick look at some of the most visible examples of this genre, for example, those by Lynch and Woolgar, Knorr-Cetina, and Latour, may suggest that here the text really *is* being taken seriously, treated as a real and important physical object.[49] After all, Knorr-Cetina goes to great length in analyzing the written work emerging from a laboratory; in her analysis the work is followed from laboratory notes to draft to published article. Similarly, in *Science in Action* Latour goes in some detail into the analysis of written works, dividing them into units as small as the sentence and paragraph and characterizing the arguments to be found.

Yet, even if in both cases the written work begins as an artifact, as a piece of evidence, it comes quickly to disappear. This is in part shown in Knorr-Cetina's characterization of her conclusions. She points to the cognitive operations of science as "constructive" rather than "descriptive," to the "analogical reasoning" which informs research, and to "the webs of social relations in which the scientists situate their laboratory action."[50]

Similarly, Latour writes of the need of the author to "Writ[e] texts that withstand the assaults of a hostile environment."[51] In so doing, he argues,

> The author protects his or her text against the reader's strength. A scientific article becomes more difficult to read, just as a fortress is shielded and buttressed; not for fun, but to avoid being sacked.[52]

> Comparing Hall's and Packer's texts is like comparing a musket with a machine-gun. Just by looking at the differences in prose you can imagine the sorts of worlds they had to write in.[53]

---

49 Karin D. Knorr-Cetina, *The manufacture of knowledge: An essay on the constructivist and contextual nature of science*, (Oxford, Pergamon, 1981); Bruno Latour, *Science in action: How to follow scientists and engineers through society*, (Milton Keynes, Open University Press, 1987); Michael Lynch and Steve Woolgar, (eds), *Representation in scientific practice*, (Cambridge, MIT Press, 1990).

50 Knorr-Cetina, 1981, 152.

51 Latour, 1987, 45.

52 Latour, 1987, 46.

The way in which this involves a turning away from the text can perhaps best be seen in Lynch and Woolgar's characterization of the method involved in several pieces in a recent volume on representation in science.

> "Reflexivity" in this usage means, not self-referential nor reflective awareness of representational practice, but the inseparability of a "theory" of representation from the heterogeneous social contexts in which representations are composed and used. To study representations "sociologically," thus means to come to terms with the socially distributed competencies which establish the theoretic sense and import of any representational device.[54]

That is, even with a powerful theory one cannot deduce from a text the social status or nature of a set of practices, because any theory of representation itself operates in the context of a set of practices which are "heterogeneous." Indeed, it is this impossibility of moving via strictly inferential means between the text and the world which implies that any attempt to determine the import of a text must ultimately turn away from that text, and to the world itself.

Now, one might wish to argue that this is of consequence only to those whose work in the social studies of science is directly motivated by a desire to comprehend the social, and that for those interested simply in understanding the text itself this is quite irrelevant. Yet on one variant of the postmodern turn, the one deriving from Wittgenstein's later work, even an understanding of the *content* of the text itself must ultimately refer back to the sets of practices within which it was written. And so, what began as a splitting of the word from the object, then the word and the idea, has in this century led to a renunciation of the view that the written work can be seen as in itself anything at all. It exists only in its many social uses.

Conclusion

It may seem petulant of me to have waited until the conclusion to say much about the geographical work itself. After all, in a paper nominally about such works I have until now, excepting an occasional aside, devoted my attention to issues much more general than geography. I have done so for a reason; I have done so – as I suggested in the beginning – because there is a sense in which certain geographical works, and here I have in mind geographic information systems, are so patently examples of disappearing texts. After all, the paper map, that repository of notes and data and symbols, seems fast being sucked into the memory systems of computers; when, having been organized and analyzed those data reappear on the screen and then a plotter in the form of a map they are really only a single version of an infinite number of possible versions.

53 Latour, 1987, 49.
54 Lynch and Woolgar, 1990, 12.

Indeed, as I have suggested elsewhere, geographic information systems in a wide range of ways appear implicated in the refiguring of geographical practice. A geographic information system exists as a set of hardware, software, and data, and of their real and potential output. Each of those elements itself raises the very same issues, of existence and meaning, of ownership, and of social context, which I have raised above.[55] But one cannot properly address the issues raised by geographic information systems without having first addressed these same issues in the context of the more traditional practice of geography, and of science more generally.

Without repeating in detail what I have said elsewhere, I would note the following. The move to an understanding of the scientific work which sees it in the last centuries as having developed a shelf length of zero has happened in two related ways. On the one hand, the theoretical understanding of the relationship among text, word, author, and object has increasingly seen each as an isolated individual, floating in a kind of Cartesian space. On the other hand, certain social, and especially legal, practices have rendered this understanding real.

But following Friedman, to conclude that the recasting of culture in terms of individual rights moves us into a strictly Newtonian universe of individuals moving in accord with sets of rules where the rules can themselves be mechanically applied, though, is to miss an important point. If in a sense in traditional societies one can say that decisions happen by habit and custom, the need today to rely on cases and precedents shows that here, too, the application is not built into the rule.

Understanding this helps us to understand two important features of the production of more modern and seemingly more abstract works. First, geographers and other scientists act as though places very much matter. They believe in the places of academic departments and universities; and they believe in the correctness of certain facts of hierarchical organization within those places. They believe in a hierarchy of journals and presses. They believe that there exists a "real" hierarchy within the disciplines, of people who make good articles and maps and people who do not. Each, too, has acted against the background of a socially accepted hierarchy. In each of these cases the Cartesian has become at most a stage on which is being played out what its actors take to be an Aristotelian drama. Very little of this is dependent on the Cartesian and individualistic metaphysics which I have discussed, and the result is, simply, a set of conflicts.

---

55 Michael Curry, "On the inevitability of ethical inconsistency in geographic information systems,' in John Pickles, (ed.), *Representations in an electronic age: Geography, G.I.S., and democracy*, (New York, Guilford Press, 1994); Michael R. Curry, *Progress in Human Geography*; Michael R. Curry, "Rethinking rights and responsibilities in geographic information systems: Beyond the power of the image,' *Cartography and GIS*, 22, 1 (1995).

The second issue is this; if we look, for example, at the production of computer-assisted maps, we find that those engaged in that production tend to be openly skeptical of the possibility of those who are non-practitioners making useful comments about their work. Some of this, no doubt, is a matter simply of turf protection. But then, too, there is an important element of truth in this skepticism. For here, too, those who know the rules may still be unable to apply them – or to apply them in an accepted way. In this they share a great deal with those who attempt in other areas, of the law for example, to apply general rules to particular cases.[56]

Indeed, the point here is one that can be made more generally. To the extent that one is operating with objects which are abstracted, which are defined in terms of sets of criteria, and not operating with objects which are taken to be members of classes simply by virtue of custom and long association, one will be unable to draw firm, acceptable, and reproducible conclusions just from a set of rules, of meaning, ownership, of place in a social system. Ironically, perhaps, as the article becomes more abstract it comes increasingly to gain its very existence from a supporting set of practices and practitioners. As its shelf length approaches zero, it gains its very existence from those who clamor around it. And this explains the postmodern reaction to modernism's disappearing object, for postmodernism is a clamorous movement if ever there was one.

References

Aarsleff, Hans, *From Locke to Saussure: Essays on the study of language and intellectual history*, (Minneapolis, University of Minnesota Press, 1982).

Allbutt, T. Clifford, *Notes on the composition of scientific papers*, (London, Macmillan, 1905).

Bacon, Francis, 'The masculine birth of time', in Farrington, Benjamin, *The philosophy of Francis Bacon: An essay on its development from 1603 to 1609, with new translations of fundamental texts*, (Liverpool, Liverpool University Press, 1970), pp. 59–72.

Bacon, Francis, 'The new organon', in Spedding, James, Ellis, Robert Leslie and Heath, Douglas Denon, (eds), *Works*, (Boston, Taggard and Thompson, 1863) 8, pp. 57–350.

Becker, Lawrence C., 'The labor theory of property acquisition', *Journal of Philosophy*, 73, 653–63, (1976).

Benjamin, Walter, 'The work of art in the age of mechanical reproduction', in Arendt, Hannah (ed.), *Illuminations*, (New York, Schocken, 1969), pp. 217–51.

---

56 Here I am drawing upon my "The architectonic impulse and the reconceptualization of the concrete in contemporary geography,' in James Duncan and Trevor J. Barnes, (eds), *Writing geography: Text, metaphor, and discourse*, (New York, Routledge, 1991b), pp. 97–117 and Michael R. Curry, "Forms of life and geographical method,' *Geographical Review*, 79 (1989), 280–96. These, in turn, draw upon Ludwig Wittgenstein, *Philosophical investigations* (Third edition), translated by G. E. M. Anscombe, (Oxford, Blackwell; New York, Macmillan, 1968/1953).

Castner, Henry W. and Robinson, Arthur H., *Dot area symbols in cartography, The influence of pattern on their perception*, (Washington DC, American Congress of Surveying and Mapping, 1969).

Clifford, James, 'On ethnographic allegory', in Clifford, James and Marcus, George, (eds), *Writing culture: The poetics and politics of ethnography*, (Berkeley, University of California Press, 1986b), pp. 98–121.

Curry, Michael R., 'The architectonic impulse and the reconceptualization of the concrete in contemporary geography', in Duncan, James and Barnes, Trevor J., (eds), *Writing georgraphy: Text, metaphor, and discourse*, (New York, Routledge, 1991b), pp. 97–117.

Curry, Michael R., 'Forms of life and geographical method', *Geographical Review* 79, 3, 280–96, (1989).

Curry, Michael R., 'On the inevitability of ethical inconsistency in geographic information systems', in Pickles, John, (ed.), *Representations in an electronic age: Geography, G.I.S., and democracy*, (New York, Guilford Press, 1994).

Curry, Michael R., 'Image, practice and the hidden impacts of geographic information systems', *Progress in Human Geography*, 18, 4, 441–59, (1994).

Curry, Michael R., 'Rethinking rights and responsibilities in geographic information systems: Beyond the power of the image', *Cartography and GIS*, 22, 1 (1995).

Day, Robert A., *How to write and publish a scientific paper*. 2nd ed., (Philadelphia, ISI Press, 1983).

Dent, Borden, 'Visual organization and thematic map design', *Annals of the Association of American Geographers*, 62, 79–93, (1972).

Descartes, René, *Descartes: Philosophical letters*, (ed.), Anthony Kenny, (Oxford, Clarendon Press, 1970).

Descartes, René, 'Rules for the direction of the mind', in Anscombe, G. E. M. and Geach, Peter, (eds), *Descartes' philosophical writings*, (Indianapolis, Bobbs-Merrill, 1971/1628), pp. 151–80.

Eagleton, Terry, 'A small history of rhetoric', in *Walter Benjamin, or towards a revolutionary criticism*, (London, NLB-Verso, 1981), pp. 101–13.

Eisenstein, Elizabeth, *The printing press as an agent of change: Communications and cultural transformations in early modern Europe*, (Cambridge, Cambridge University Press, 1979).

Ellerman, David, 'On the labor theory of property', *The Philosophical Forum*, 16, 293–326, (1985).

Fabian, Johannes, *Time and the other: How anthropology makes its object*, (New York, Columbia University Press, 1983).

Foucault, Michel, 'What is an author?', in Bouchard, Donald F. (ed.), translated by Donald F. Bouchard and Sherry Simon, *Language, counter-memory, practice: Selected essays and interviews*, (Ithaca, New York, Cornell University Press, 1977/1969), pp. 113–38.

Friedman, Lawrence M., *The republic of choice: Law, authority, and culture*, (Cambridge, Harvard University Press, 1990).

Garfield, Eugene, '"Science citation index" – A new dimension in indexing', *Science*, 144, 649–54, (1964).

Gilmartin, Patricia, 'The map context as a source of perceptual error in graduated circle maps', (unpublished dissertation, Lawrence, KS, University of Kansas, 1980).

Ginsburg, Jane C., 'French copyright law: A comparative overview', *Journal of the Copyright Society of the USA*, 4, 269–85, (1989).

Ginsburg, Jane C., 'A tale of two copyrights: Literary property in revolutionary France and America', *Tulane Law Review*, 64, 991–1031, (1990).

Grey, Thomas C., 'The disintegration of property', in Pennock, J. Roland and Chapman, John William, (eds), *Property*, (New York, New York University Press, 1980), pp. 69–85.

Hettinger, Edwin C., 'Justifying intellectual property', *Philosophy and Public Affairs*, 18, 3–52, (1989).

Hume, David, *Enquiries concerning human understanding and concerning the principles of morals.* 3rd ed., (Oxford, Oxford University Press, 1975/1777).

Jaszi, Peter, 'On the author effect: Contemporary copyright and collective creativity', *Cardozo Arts and Entertainment Journal*, 10, 2, 293–320, (1992).

Kant, Immanuel, *The critique of pure reason*, translated by Norman Kemp Smith, (New York, St. Martin's Press, 1965/1781, 1787).

Kaplan, Benjamin, *An unhurried view of copyright*, (New York, Columbia University Press, 1967).

Kneupper, Charles W., (ed.) *Visions of rhetoric: History, theory, and criticism*, (Arlington, TX, Rhetoric Society of America, 1987).

Knorr-Cetina, Karin D., *The manufacture of knowledge: An essay on the constructivist and contextual nature of science*, (Oxford, Pergamon, 1981).

Knowlson, James, *Universal language schemes in England and France*, (Toronto, University of Toronto Press, 1975).

Latour, Bruno, *Science in action: How to follow scientists and engineers through society*, (Milton Keynes, Open University Press, 1987).

Locke, John, *An essay concerning human understanding*, (London, Routledge, no date).

Locke, John, 'Second treatise of government', in Cook, Thomas I., (ed.), *Two treatises of government*, (New York, Hafner, 1947b/1690).

Lynch, Michael and Woolgar, Steve, (eds), *Representation in scientific practice*, (Cambridge, MIT Press, 1990).

MacIntyre, Alasdair C., *After virtue: A study in moral theory.* 2nd ed., (Notre Dame, University of Notre Dame Press, 1984).

MacPherson, C. B., *The political theory of possessive individualism: Hobbes to Locke*, (Oxford, Oxford University Press, 1962).

Maltby, Arthur, *Sayer's manual of classification for librarians.* 5th ed., (London, Andre Deutsch, 1975/1926).

Merrett, Christopher, *Map cataloguing and classification: A comparison of approaches*, (Sheffield, University of Sheffield, Postgraduate School of Librarianship and Information Science, 1976).

Merton, Robert K., 'The normative structure of science', in Storer, Norman W., (ed.), *The sociology of science: Theoretical and empirical investigations*, (Chicago, University of Chicago Press, 1973/1942), pp. 267–78, [Also published as 'Science and democratic social structure', in *Social theory and social structure*, enlarged edition, pp. 604–15, (New York, The Free Press, 1968). Original, 'Science and technology in a democratic order', *Journal of Legal and Political Sociology.* vol. 1 (1942), 115–26].

Monmonier, Mark, *How to lie with maps*, (Chicago, University of Chicago Press, 1991).

O'Connor, Maeve, *Writing successfully in science*, (London, Chapman and Hall, 1991).

Ong, Walter J., 'System, space, and renaissance symbolism', *Study on Renaissance Symbolism*, 8, 222–39, (1956).

Patterson, Lyman Ray, *Copyright in historical perspective*, (Nashville, Vanderbilt University Press, 1968).

Plato, 'Cratylus', in *The dialogues of Plato*, 4th ed., translated by Benjamin Jowett, vol. III, pp. 1–107, (New York, Oxford University Press, 1953).

Rabinow, Paul, 'Discourse and power: On the limits of ethnographic texts', *Dialectical Anthropology*, 10, 1–13, (1985).

Rabinow, Paul, 'Representations are social facts: Modernity and post-modernity in anthropology', in Clifford, James and Marcus, George, (eds), *Writing culture: The poetics and politics of ethnography*, Berkeley, University of California Press, 1986), pp. 234–61.

Richardson, Ernest Cushing, *Classification: Theoretical and practical*, (New York, H. W. Wilson, 1930).

Ricketson, Sam, *The Berne Convention for the protection of literary and artistic works, 1886–1986*, (London, Centre for Commercial Law Studies, Queen Mary College, 1987).

Robinson, Arthur, 1975, 'Mapmaking and map pringing: The evolution of a working relationship', in Woodward, David, (ed.), *Five centuries of map printing*, (Chicago, University of Chicago Press, 1987), pp. 1–24.

Rose, Mark, *Authors and owners: The invention of copyright*, (Cambridge, Mass., Harvard University Press, 1993).

Sayers, W. C. Berwick, *An introduction to library classification.* 6th ed.,(London, Grafton, 1943/1918).

Slaughter, Mary, *Universal languages and scientific taxonomy in the seventeenth centure*, (Cambridge, Cambridge University Press, 1982).

Steinbach, H. Burr, 'The quest for certainty, *Science citation index'*, *Science*, 145, 142–3, (1964).

Strawson, P. F., *The bounds of sense: An essay on Kant's critique of pure reason*, (London, Methuen, 1966).

Travers, Andrew, 'Shelf-life zero: a classic postmodernist paper', *Philosophy of The Social Sciences – philosophie Des Sciences Sociales* 19, 3, 291–320, (1989).

Trelease, Sam F., *How to write scientific and technical papers*, (Cambridge, MIT Press, 1958).

Trelease, Sam F., *The scientific paper: How to prepare it, how to write it*, (Baltimore, Williams and Wilkins, 1947).

Trelease, Sam F. and Yule, Emma Smart, *Preparation of scientific and technical papers*, (Baltimore, Williams and Wilkins, 1925).

Vickers, Brian, *In defence of rhetoric*, (Oxford, Clarendon Press, 1988).

Watkins, Jessie B., *Selected bibliography on maps in libraries: Acquisition, classification, cataloging, storage, uses*, (Syracuse, Syracuse University Libraries, 1967).

Wikse, John R., *About possession: The self as private property*, (University Park, Pennsylvania State University Press, 1977).

Wittgenstein, Ludwig, *Philosophical investigations.* 3rd ed., translated by G. E. M. Anscombe, (New York, Macmillan, 1968/1953).

Wittgenstein, Ludwig, *Tractatus logico-philosophicus*, translated by D. F. Pears and Brian F. McGuinness, (London, Routledge and Kegan Paul, 1961/1921).

Wolff, Robert Paul, *Kant's theory of mental activity: A commentary on the transcendental analytic of the 'Critique of pure reason'*, (Cambridge, Harvard University Press, 1963).

Woodmansee, Martha, 'The genius and the copyright: Economic and legal conditions of the emergence of the "author"', *Eighteenth Century Studies.* 17, 425–48, (1984).

Woodward, David, (ed.), *Five centuries of map printing*, (Chicago, University of Chicago Press, 1975).

Yen, Alfred C., 'Restoring the natural law: Copyright as labor and possession', *Ohio State Law Journal*, 51, 517–59, (1990).

PART II

Writing Space, Forming Identities

Introduction

A core notion within both modern and postmodern discourses, 'identity' has been a much-contested concept for as long as we can meaningfully speak of – indeed *identify* – Enlightenment discourses. How 'identities' are constructed and who is doing the construction of identities have been questions very much on the agenda of the past centuries. It was only recently, however, that the constitutive role of space in the construction of individual and group identities became theoretically acknowledged.

This new interest in space was instigated by the recognition that many a problem associated with modern construction of identities stems from a largely unreflected prioritization of time over space. Constructed in this manner, 'identities' proved to embody not simply an inbuilt resistance to spatial variations – an issue of geographical interest at best – but were now seen to be responsible for the hegemony of certain identities at the expense of others. The paradigmatic 'white, male and middle class' perspective which had become the role model in the construction of spaceless identities was now increasingly being challenged from a host of different positions.

Geography, for once, was and continues to be at the centre of these debates. Much of what is currently being produced within the redefined realm of 'cultural' geography bears witness to the efforts by geographers and others to redefine 'identity' and 'identities' in spatial manners. Indeed, so often is space acknowledged and evoked these days that it comes as something of a surprise to see the writing *of* space still being largely taken for granted within the human sciences. How do we write when we write about the construction of identities? What language(s) do we employ? And what sorts of questions emanate from the incorporation of 'space', in a more than metaphorical manner into the construction of identities? The following essays will explore some of the issues raised in these and related questions.

With the question of 'identity' directly implicating the 'positionality' of the writing person, it should not come as a surprise that the need for linguistic experimentation is felt most pressingly when exploring the boundaries of identity in general. The oft-invoked characterization of postmodern discourse as involving the 'play of language' stems partly from this need; since any 'play' involves non-directional elements, writing in a modern (and thus by implication teleological) manner is often perceived as missing the point and counter-productive. With issues of space being central to the construction of identities, the question now becomes: how 'spatially' can we write before the resulting narrative ceases to function as a narrative? Can we write about identity without assuming some identity already?

4

Re-Presenting the Extended Present Moment of Danger: A Meditation on Hypermodernity, Identity and the Montage Form

Allan Pred

"Method of this work: literary montage. I have nothing to say, only to show."
Walter Benjamin (1982), 574
as quoted in Susan Buck-Morss (1989), 73.

★★★

"What we [as cosmopolitan intellectuals'] share as a condition of existence ... is a specificity of historical experience and place, however complex and contestable they might be, and a worldwide macro-interdependency encompassing any local particularity. Whether we like it or not, we are all in this situation."
Paul Rabinow (1986), 258.

★★★★★★★

"[T]erritorial place-based identity, particularly when conflated with race, ethnic, gender, religious and class differentiation, is one of the most pervasive bases for both progressive political mobilization and reactionary exclusionary politics."
David Harvey (1993), 4.

★★★★★★★

"The erosion of the nation-state, national economies and national cultural identities is a very complex and dangerous moment."
Stuart Hall (1991), 25.

★★★★★★★

> *"[W]e now have to make sense of a world without stable vantage points; a world in which the observers and the observed are in ceaseless, fluid, and interactive motion, a world where 'human ways of life increasingly influence, dominate, parody, translate, and subvert one another.'"*
>
> Derek Gregory (1994), 9.[1]

****

A conjunction of scary instabilities, bewildering contradictions and numbing tensions. ..."[P]rocesses that cross-cut time frames and spatial zones [and one another] in quite uncontrolled ways."[2]... Political erosion. ... Transnational and global economic integration. ... National and local economic crisis. ... Cultural contestation. ... Simultaneous and immediate. ... Turbulent and frequently vertiginous. ... Coupled with the long march of environmental degradation.

We now have to make sense of, *and act within*, an extended moment of danger which assumes countless local forms, each of which is constituted and transformed through reconfigured articulations between the local and the translocal or global. Each of which almost inevitably modifies the points of intersection between locally coexisting structures of power. None of which can be reduced to the logic and workings of capitalism(s). But very few of which are completely untouched by the logic and workings of capitalism(s), by the ever-shifting web of commodity relations. In the 'East' as well as the 'West.' In the 'South' as well as the 'North.'

****

A moment of danger is also a moment of opportunity to be seized upon.

****

In our writing,
how may we as intellectuals,
      as human geographers,
      as corpo-real beings,
      as knowing, thinking and feeling subjects,
      as self-reflexive women and men,
make sense of the world
    for ourselves and for others;
at one and the same time make the dangerous here and now,
    and its then and there antecedents,
intelligible,
    while still giving artful, art-filled play
    to our imag(e)inations?

1   Gregory is here quoting Clifford (1986), 22.
2   Marcus (1992), 326.

How may we (re)constructively re-present the present,
creatively produce on-the-page images
of our mental images and reflective reworkings
    of the contemporary world(s)
           in which our everyday lives are interwoven,
           in which our observations and hearings are enmeshed,
           from which our categories and metaphors are derived?

How may we critically capture those sounds
     which resonate with the circumstances of hypermodernity,
          with the very condition(ing)s of our lives
             and our writings?

                ★★★★★★★

Have I
in the particular juxtaposing of selected quotes,
in the phrasing of the above questions,
in the selection of words, stops and silences,
in the calculated deployment of indentations, hyphens and parentheses,
already provided a signpost,
         an en route set of indicators,
         an abbreviated inventory of possible destinations,
already suggested an answer
            or two, three, four, ...
already demonstrated that –
    like it or not –
the p(r)o(s)etics of one's textual strategy
are the politics of one's textual strategy?

     ★★★

   "The effect of technology on both work and leisure in the modern metropolis has been
to shatter experience into fragments."
                         Susan Buck-Morss (1989), 23.

   "[The] common theme [of Kurt Schwitters' 'Merz' paintings] was the [modern] city
as compressor, intensifier of experience. So many people, and so many messages: so many
traces of intimate journeys, news, meetings, possession, rejection, with the city renewing
its fabric of transaction every moment of the day and night, as a snake casts its skin,
leaving the pattern of the lost epidermis behind as 'mere' rubbish."
                        Robert Hughes (1991), 64

                ★★★★★★★

Upon situated reflection ...

There is no taking issue
with the denial of a unitary human history,
of a singe history of "man,"
of an unilinear, uninterrupted story of progress,
of a monolithic Euro-centric history,
of history with a capital H.

There is no taking issue
with the rejection of metanarratives,
of narratives which make all other narratives subordinate,
which make claims to the totalistic,
to the completely overarching,
to the all encompassing.

For any one place as well as the world at large, for the present moment as well as any given period of the past, there cannot be one grand history, one grand human geography, whose telling only awaits an appropriate metanarrative. Through their engagement in a multitude of situated practices, through their participation in a multitude of juxtaposed power relations, people make a multitude of histories and construct a multitude of human geographies.

If the appropriateness of metanarratives is readily cast aside, the appropriateness of MEGAnarratives – of narratives which encompass large pieces of all that is ever-becoming – is not so easily denied in a world in which the practices and power relations of patriarchy, capitalism, racism and bureaucratic rationality are extremely widespread, if not all pervasive.

The rejection of metanarratives without any recognition of meganarratives merely "allow[s] those with power to counter the increasingly insistent challenge from those at the margins."[3]

****

Whatever our scale of reference, the contemporary world (or any past world) is neither a completely integrated totality, nor a chaotic pastiche, a free-floating chaos of meaningless flux, a jumble of atomistic, unrelated fragments.

---

3   McDowell (1992), 65. McDowell is critically addressing the postmodernist stance on meganarratives, but not raising the question of what are here termed meganarratives. Her position echoes that of Haraway, Hartsock, Spivak and other key feminist theorists.

The world of individuals and the world of collectivities,
the contemporary social world writ small
    and the contemporary social world writ large,
        cannot be anything but a totality of fragments,
            a totality of corpo-really, structurally and symbolically
                interconnected fragments,
cannot be anything but an assemblage
    of physically and socially encountered fragments,
        none of which stands meaninglessly on its own,
        each of which meaningfully touches upon others,
        almost all of which are associated with power structures,
        all of which are *not*
            bound up in a single structure of power and meaning.

This is so
as human beings are inescapably embodied beings,
as they are always literally in touch
    with (transformed and culturally mediated) nature,
        with the material and the concrete,
as they cannot but trace an uninterrupted path through space and time
    from the moment of their birth to the moment of their death,
as their everyday lives and their entire biographies
    unavoidably course through situated practices,
        through institutionally embedded practices,
whose associated power relations are of varying geographic extent
                and temporal depth,
whose forms of knowledge, language and meaning
    become differently superimposed,
        differently shared.

****

"*The* Passagen-Werk *suggests that it makes no sense to divide the era of capitalism into formalist 'modernism' and historically eclectic 'post-modernism,' as those tendencies have been there from the start of industrial culture. The paradoxical dynamics of novelty and repetition simply repeat themselves anew.*

Modernism and postmodernism are not chronological eras, but political positions in the century-long struggle between art and technology. If modernism expresses utopian longing by anticipating the reconciliation of social function and aesthetic form, postmodernism acknowledges their nonidentity and keeps fantasies alive. Each position thus represents a partial truth; each will recur 'anew' so long as the contradictions of commodity society are not overcome."

Susan Buck-Morss (1989), 359.

****

An -*ism* cannot be identical with an -*ity*, even though they may emerge out of one another. Neither a system of theory or thought, nor a distinctive doctrine or set of ideas – however politically charged – is to be confused with a state of affairs, quality, or condition. 'Postmodernism' and 'postmodernity' – however putatively related – cannot be one and the same thing. The existence of the former is not necessarily synonymous with the existence of the latter.

Neither the demise of various 'high modernisms,'
nor the existence of a 'postmodern' architectural style,
    of a by now trite register of pastiche, eclectical historical borrowing
    and 'double codings,'
nor the existence of a pivotal (but sometimes incompatible) set
    of language-centered 'postmodern' academic discourses calling into
    question the decidability of truth and rejecting the Enlightenment
    project,
is to be conflated with a 'postmodern' world of everyday life,
is to be equated with a 'postmodern' epoch,
is to be confused with a lived and experience 'postmodern' condition.

****

"*Postmodernism is hardly of concern to trade unionists, social workers, health providers, the unemployed or the homeless. Like Rajneesh's religion, postmodernism appears to be the preoccupation of a segment of the privileged classes.*"
David Harvey (1993), 25.

****

It may well be that it matters little, in terms of the "serious threat to traditional standards of disciplinary legitimacy" brought on by "*certain* issues associated with postmodernism," whether or not "their context is relabelled 'late modernism'" or "whether it began at the turn of the century, after World War II, or just recently."[4] However, it matters a great deal whether or not "postmodernity" is an appropriate term for the condition(ing)s of the extended present moment of precariousness. It matters a great deal *if* that term serves to legitimate that which is, *if* the widespread public broadcast and consequent popular usage of that term contributes to the political disarming, paralyzation or incapacitation of people by falsely suggesting distinct epochal breaks and thereby helping to obscure the power-relation workings largely responsible for the nameable and unnameable insecurities, injustices, anxieties, dissatisfactions and dis-eased circumstances collectively and individually encountered with frequency in daily life.

****

4   Strohmayer and Hannah (1992), 29, emphasis added.

"*The modernist project [within the arts] was far from homogeneous, of course, but what its various movements had in common was a displacement and a decentering of those conventional, taken-for-granted, above all respectable representations. Its critical salvos thus contributed to what Lunn calls the 'intellectual bombardment of liberal certainties.'*"

Derek Gregory (1994), 47.[5]

"*[I]t is too easily forgotten that modernism itself was a deeply subversive project.*"

Neil Smith (1992), 63.

"*[We] find ourselves today in the midst of a modern age that has lost touch with the roots of its own modernity.*"

Marshall Berman (1982), 17.

★★★★★★★

The day-to-day and minute-to-minute
    worlds in which we live
are perhaps post-'high modern,'
but difficult to defend as *post*modern;
for,
any placing of the ear to the ground
    of past times and places
would aurally reveal that we are not literally completely beyond the
    modern modes of life that appeared in conjuncture with specific
    forms of industrial capitalism.

    The practices and experiences of everyday life during the modernity of late nineteenth-century European and North American industrial capitalisms were characterized in geographically specific ways by
encounters
with a "ruthless centrifuge of change,"[6]
with the transitory and the apparently fragmented,
with an incessant spectacle of the new,
with repeated material evidence of creative destruction,
with relentlessly expanding commodification,
with fleeting forms of consumption
    and a dreamworld of commodity fetishism,
with constant changes in employment opportunities and circumstances.
All of which were repeatedly subject to popular, artistic and
    intellectual reworkings, to symbolic discontent and cultural struggle.
The practices and experiences in question were further characterized by
encounters

5   Gregory is here quoting Lunn (1985), 39.
6   Schorske (1981), xix.

with ephemeral and disjointed social contacts,
with a densening flow of commercial signs and messages,
with a jumble of local and far-flung distant images produced by ever
    more rapid and spatially extended communications networks,
with the persistent spread of bureaucratic rationality
      and its iron-cage rules,
with powerful new technologies and new technologies of power,
with reconfigured articulations between the local, the national and
    the global,
with reconfigured mediations between the discourse of gender, class
    and 'race' or ethnicity.
All of which were repeatedly subject to popular, artistic and
    intellectual reworkings, to symbolic discontent and cultural struggle.

In short,
these were encounters
with plural complexities,
with shifting heterogeneities and
with shockingly new meanings
    that dislocated and displaced,
    that confirmed rupture,
    that invited or demanded cultural contestation
    by calling the meanings
        of locally preexisting practices and social relations
        into question,
    and thereby calling individual and collective identities
        into question.

****

"[E]mergent 'modernism' has tended to take the specific form of ... a 'reshuffling of the self.' Here historical change not only forces upon the individual a search for a new identity but also imposes upon whole social groups the task of revising or replacing defunct belief systems."

Carl Schorske (1981), xviii[7]

"Both [Marx and Freud] insisted that identity – our sense of ourselves as individuals and as social beings – is constructed through structural processes rather than being innate or pre-given. In so doing, both also implied that there are no necessarily universal or unchanging attributes of human identity, but that differentiation and movement between identities is characteristic of modern societies."

Liz Bondi (1993).

7   Cf. Le Rider (1993).

"[Cultural identity] is not something which already exists, transcending place, time, history and culture. ... Far from being eternally fixed in some essentialized past, [cultural identities] are subject to the continual play of history, culture and power."
Stuart Hall (1989), 70.

"[I]dentity is always mobile and processual, partly self-construction, partly categorization by others, partly a condition, partly a status, a label, a weapon, a shield, a fund of memories, et cetera. It is a creolized aggregate composed through bricolage."
Liisa Malkki (1992), 37.

"[A]ll identity formation is engaged in this habitually bracing activity in which the issue is not so much staying the same, but maintaining sameness through alterity."
Michael Taussig (1993), 129.

****

If everyday life during the modernity of early industrial capitalisms was characterized by fleeting and fragmented encounters with plural complexities, shifting heterogeneities and shockingly new meanings,
then the everyday practices and experiences
    of here and now commodity societies,
    of the 1990s in specific places,
however clearly distinctive they may be,
however radically altered they may have become
        by post-Fordist,
            post-Colonial or
            post-Cold War circumstances,
are best characterized as modernity magnified,
as modernity accentuated and sped up,
as *hyper*modern,
not postmodern.

If this is the case,
if the present moment of prolonged danger is a hypermodern one,
in which 'fast,' 'casino,' 'post-Fordist' and 'flexible-accumulation'
    capitalisms churn with an incessant irregularity,[8]
in which just about everything becomes commodified[9] and national
    economies are persistently eroded,
in which money and information are hypermobile,
in which articulations between the local and the global are constantly
    reconfigured,

8 Cf. Harvey (1989).
9 In various of his writings, Henri Lefebvre emphasizes the colonization of everyday life by the commodity form as a defining characteristic of contemporary life. This 'colonization' is not merely a figure of speech, but a term consciously employed so as to draw upon "the implications of occupation, dispossession and territorialization with which it is freighted" (Gregory, 1994, 403).

in which the mediations between gender, class and 'race' or ethnicity
    are repeatedly altered,
then it is also a moment which is synonymous with hyperdisruption.
It is a moment synonymous
with one disjuncture fading into another disjuncture,
with the emergent more or less quickly becoming the residual
with discordancies and incompatibilities being heaped upon one
    another,
and, consequently,
it cannot be otherwise but that identity repeatedly becomes
    undermined, problematic, an issue,
something to be reworked, reconstructed, retrieved,
    or struggled over in order to reanchor.[10]
Or,
it cannot be otherwise but that identity crises abound, that identity becomes
politicized, that identity becomes a word issued from the lips of the population
at large as well as a preoccupation of countless academics (many of whom write
as if it had never been problematic prior to the appearance of 'postmodernity,'
prior to culture and everyday life having somehow – abracadabra, hocus-pocus,
sim salabim, OPEN SESAME! – having moved totally beyond the modern,
beyond the workings of modern capitalisms and bureaucratic rationalities).

****

"*[T]he idea of a premodern state of unselfconscious localized identity is perhaps
merely wishful thinking. – [I]dentity has never been neatly provided by a naturally
bounded place, but has always been negotiated within a complex and often confusing
mesh of interaction across multiple geographic scales.*"[11]
"*As global forces of political economy have become more fluid, seeming to seep into
every last crack of cultural isolation, localized identities have apparently become more
important – and in some areas more dangerous – to construct.*"

T. S. Oakes (1993), 48, 47.

"*Difference and identity is produced and reproduced within a field of power relations
rooted in interconnected spaces linked by political and economic relations.*"
"*Globalization does not signal the erasure of local difference, but in a strange way
its converse, it revalidates and reconstitutes place, locality and difference.*"

Michael J. Watts (1991), 14, 10.

"*[The core of world history] is no longer the evolution and devolution of world systems,
but the tense, ongoing interaction of forces promoting global integration and forces
recreating local autonomy. This is not a struggle for or against global integration itself,
but rather a struggle over the terms of that integration. The struggle is by no means*

10 As Augé observes, people still demonstrate a remarkable ability to (re)construct anchoring
    identities under the dis-placing conditions of what he terms 'supermodernity,' rather than
    'hypermodernity.'
11 Oakes is here inspired by Feierman (1990).

finished, and its path is no longer foreordained by the dynamics of western expansion that initiated global integration. The world has moved apart even as it has been pulled together, as efforts to convert domination into order have engendered evasion, resistance and struggles to regain autonomy. This struggle for autonomy – the assertion of local and particular claims over global and general ones – does not involve opting out of the world or resorting to autarky. It is rather an effort to establish the terms of self-determining and self-controlled participation in the processes of global integration and the struggle for planetary order.

[These matters lead to] the question of who, or what, controls and defines the identity of individuals, social groups, nations and cultures."

Charles Bright and Michael Geyer
(1987), 69–70 (emphasis added).

"[W]hat one always sees when one examines or opens up ...[a national identity is that it] represents itself as perfectly natural: born an Englishman, always will be, condensed, homogeneous, arbitrary. What is the point of an identity if it isn't one thing? That is why we keep hoping that identities will come our way because the rest of the world is so confusing, everything else is turning, *but identities ought to be some stable points of reference which were like that in the past, are now and ever shall be, still points in a turning world. ... [Even though] Englishness never was and never possibly could be that."*

Stuart Hall (1991), 22 (emphasis added).

****

Any one of the fluid collective or individual identities a person evokes
   in telling stories about herself to herself and others,
does not merely involve the assuming of a position,
the marking out of a space,
the drawing of meaning-filled, meaning-separating boundaries,
   on the inside of which are those
      with whom one shares likenesses,
      with whom one is identical,
   on the outside of which are those marked by difference,
      those who are excluded,
      those *others* who are not identical,
      yet whose otherness tells us of our sameness.

In addition, every dimension of collective or individual identity is intimately interwoven with its own set of flexible, taken-for-granted meanings. More precisely, each dimension of identity is entwined with a set of more or less unreflected recognitions of what is or is not meant by
   particular objects, settings, circumstances, or linguistic expressions,
a set of context-dependent taken-for-granted signs necessary to action, to
   practical and relational engagement in some part of the everyday
   world,
a set of self-evident meanings that is built up or reinforced via
   corpo-real involvement in the situated practices and power relations

of everyday life, and yet simultaneously contributes to the further navigation and negotiation of everyday life.[12]

Thus it is
that forms of collective or individual identity become problematic,
that identity 'crises' appear,
when taken-for-granted meanings of centrality
      become   unmoored,
when unreflected common sense is confronted with $A \neq B$ circumstances,
when the clearly identical is put into question, contradicted, made
      unrecognizable or challenged,
when the highly familiar becomes strange,
as a result of the actual introduction or proposal of new practices
      and their accompaniments –
      new forms of domination, exploitation or subjection,
      new would-be hegemonic discourses,
as a result of long coexisting structures of gender, class, 'race'; and
      sexuality being brought into radically new juxtapositions with one
      another,
as a result of incongruity and rupture being badly encountered,
as a result of disjuncture and discontent being acutely experienced,
as a result of the shocking newness of the invading or occupying new
      making itself all too evident.

★★★★★★★

> "People have undoubtedly always been mobile and identities less fixed than the static and typologizing approaches of classical anthropology would suggest. But today, the rapidly expanding and quickening mobility of people combines with the refusal of cultural products and practices to 'stay put' to give a profound sense of a loss of territorial roots, of an erosion of the cultural distinctiveness of places."
>
> Akhill Gupta and James Ferguson
(1992), 9.

> "Not only has the border [between the West and rest] been punctured porous by the global market and multinational corporations, together with desperate emigration from the South, but the border as cultural artifact has been diffused to cosmic proportion."
>
> "[Through the] intercultural connectedness of image-practice ... [t]he border has dissolved and expanded to cover the lands it once separated such that all the land is borderland."
>
> Michael Taussig (1993), 251, 248–9.

★★★★★★★

12 Cf. Fiske (1992) on "the practices of everyday life within and against the determinate conditions of the social order," the embodiment and performance of difference, and identity construction. Fiske's argumentation draws heavily on Bourdieu's 'habitus.'

No body may become disembodied, may be removed from the present moment, may escape the local situation and its wider, or global, interconnections. No group or individual is immune from the unanchoring of identity elements, from the dissonance arising between deeply engrained experiences and meanings and startingly new experiences and meanings. There is no monopoly on identity crises held by those who are marginalized and oppressed, who are subaltern, who are displaced emigrants or refugees, who belong to the 'wrong' gender or class, who possess the 'wrong' attributes of race or ethnicity, who are outside the male-heterosexual-WASP fold. However intensely jolting their experience of otherness may be, however well justified their politics of recognition and equal rights may be, they are not the only ones subject to the unmooring of identity. Which is not to deny that in interrogating the present moment, there are often strong intellectual or political grounds for focusing on the predicaments of cultural identity experienced by mobile and exiled peoples, by those who are 'guest workers' or who have resettled in the wake of post-colonialism, by those who have been 'uprooted' by national disintegration or are confronted by the prospect of national integration into a larger entity, by those who have been deprived of their sense of place or regional belonging, by those who reside along cultural and national borders, by those who are saturated with hybridity[13] – like "the Korean Buddhist chemical engineer, recently arrived from three years in Argentina, who becomes a Christian greengrocer in Harlem."[14] But to leave matters there, to see identity issues largely or entirely in terms of the subaltern, the territorially displaced and the hybrid is to fail to recognize that these are nothing more or less than key instances of an even more general phenomenon. It is to fail to recognize the even more pervasive destabilization of identities associated with the condition(ing)s of hypermodernity, and especially – but not exclusively – with the constant locational reshuffling of capital investments, with an ever-transforming and more intricate geographical division of labor. Under the condition(ing)s of hypermodernity, under the concrete and relational whirl-swirl of the new and greatly altered, identity problems may show up on anybody's front step. Under the *repeated* restructurings and inconstancies of hypermodernity, identity may *frequently* become problematic for the long settled as well as the recently arrived, for the centrally situated as well as the marginalized, for local power holders as well as local power subjects, for the victimizers as well as the victims of domination, exploitation and subjection.[15] Under the super-fluid circumstances of hypermodernity, the mesh of interactions and power relations within which identities are negotiated has become more intricate, more multi-layered, more extensive, more transitory in composition, more subject to reconfiguration for just about every (situated) body.

13 Cf. Gupta and Ferguson (1992), Malkki (1992), and the literature cited therein.
14 Watts (1991), 11.
15 Of course, this statement, with its emphasis on *repeated* and *frequently*, is not to suggest that power holders have been spared from identity problems in past times and places untouched by hypermodern conditions.

Even for those who would disavow any reality beyond language and the flow of signifiers.

****

If a modernism is an intellectual or artistic reworking or creative rejection of the experiences and condition(ing)s, of modernity, then any self-declared postmodernism is – regardless of its insightfulness and significance – but another modernism,
or, more accurately,
a hypermodernism.[16]
A postmodernism cannot be divorced from its hypermodern context, from the extended moment of danger in which it is enmeshed and to which it contributes.
It does not matter if it rests on a discursive claim that everything turns on language,
on a claim ignoring the mutual and indissoluble embeddedness,
    of language, situated social practices and power relations within
      one another,
on a claim deaf to their mutual constitution,
on a textual obsession nullifying the existence of corpo-real people,
    whose materially real everyday lives are entangled in very real
      relations of domination, exploitation and subjection.
It does not matter if it instead involves an artistic avowal of pastiche and the fragmented "which sees the jumbling of elements as all there is."[17]

****

If there is an extensive 'crisis of representation,'
it is, as much as anything,
a hypermodern,
rather than a postmodern crisis.

****

> "*Whatever else postmodernism may be about, ... it represents an attempt to come to terms with – to find the terms for – this bewilderment of the contemporary; what might be called, with apologies to Edward Said, the dis-orientation of Occidentalism.*"
> Derek Gregory (1994), 139.

> "*I have argued that the emphasis upon ephemerality, collage, fragmentation, and dispersal in ['postmodern'] philosophical and social thought mimics the conditions of flexible accumulation.*"
> David Harvey (1989), 302.

16 It is characteristic of the conditions of hypermodernity that some people have already begun to refer to 'postmodernism' in the past tense (Rosenthal, 1992).
17 Rabinow (1986), 249, rephrasing Jameson (1983). Also note Jameson (1991).

****

If there is a 'crisis of representation'
within academic and literary-criticism worlds,
    a situation where the *only* referent is other sentences,
                        other texts,
                        other printed discourses,
it emerges in some unmeasurable measure from a reworking of the asymmetries
existing between different realms of action and experience.
It emerges in some unmeasurable measure from the asymmetries
    between deeply sedimented,
        largely unexamined and
        unreflectingly reproduced representational practices,
        or, academic and literary-criticism practices that still now
            remain norm-ally unilinear, neatly sequenced
            (even when addressing simultaneous diversity),
and the condition(ing)s of hypermodernity experienced
    outside those academic and literary-criticism worlds.

****

With another *fin-de-siècle* in sight, it remains very much the case that the fleeting and fragmented encounters of everyday life demand response, that they are repeatedly subject to popular, artistic and intellectual reworkings, to symbolic discontent and cultural struggle.[18]

****

    "In the face of radically unstable configurations [between local 'presences' and distant, or global, 'absences'], which seem to defy every conventional cartographic possibility, some writers have turned to postmodernism for inspiration. In their eyes its celebration of the play of difference, of indeterminacy and contingency, seems particularly appropriate to the giddy, kaleidoscopic diversity of the late twentieth-century world."
                                      Derek Gregory (1994), 122.

If there is a 'crisis of representation,' it as much as anything involves
    a refusal of central meanings to stand still,
    a breakdown of identities.
It is a crisis which does *not* simply derive from the ordinary slipping and sliding of meaning that occurs when 'the same word' is reiterated in different more or less familiar context, where there remains some trace of recognizability, where the word paradoxically remains the same only different.[19]

18 *See* Pred and Watts (1992).
19 Cf. Derrida's much elaborated position on difference and *différance* (especially 1973 and
    1982, 1–27).

It is instead a crisis which to a considerable extent derives from those numerous instances when the encountered context is enough different, enough contrary to previous experience, enough at odds with the taken for granted, that the associational links between signifier and signified become suddenly untenable, suddenly without a trace of compatible connections, suddenly twisted beyond recognition, suddenly re-cognized as problematic.

Or, it is a crisis which to a considerable extent derives

from the repeated realignment and revision of the everyday practices
    and power relations in which language and meaning are embedded,
from multiply recurring experiences of incongruity and rupture that
    produce a sense of being out of place.

It is a crisis which to a considerable extent derives

from an accelerated tendency for everyday practices – including those
    involving the international and intercultural circulation of images –
    to be engineered or controlled by nonlocal agents of capital or the
    State,
from a consequently accelerated tendency for the truth of experience
    to no longer coincide with the place – with the socially produced
    spaces – in which it takes place.[20]

****

"The absence of purpose and meaning cannot be championed as an end in itself: [whatever the claims made] there is always some reason for any act of construction, destruction, or simple deconstruction."

Sadie Plant (1982), 148.

Whatever else you or I may choose to say about the matter,
at some level,
including our efforts to re-present the present moment of danger,
involves a reworking of our situated experiences,
and, thereby – like our various identities –
it resonates with particular condition(ing)s of hypermodernity.

****

However much we exert ourselves,
however much we deny it,
there is no abstracting from
    (the multiplicity of differentiating)
power relations characteristic of hypermodernity.

****

20   This final phrase is a rewording of Jameson (1988), 35. As Gregory (1991, 17) notes, by the onset of the twentieth century "such a disassociation between ... structured and lived experienced had been transcoded into a radically new relation between space and place," Also note Gregory (1994).

"[The Condition of Postmodernity] *was written ...from a relatively privileged position* within *the belly of the beast that is capitalism. It was written with the primary intention of giving the beast a belly-ache. But it was also written to try and remind many who seem to have forgotten or mislaid the sense of it, that this particular situatedness is both important and revealing. For this reason, it did indeed emphasize the situatedness of postmodernism within the belly of the capitalist beast.*"

" *... a cogent framework (though not the whole story) for explanation of what postmodernism is all about.*"

David Harvey (1992), 304, 311.

★★★★★★★

A moment of danger is also a moment of opportunity to be seized upon.

★★★★★★★

Why the montage form in meditating upon hypermodernity and identity?

Why, elsewhere, the montage form in re-presenting the particular, in re-presenting critical (geographical hi)stories of the extended present moment of danger?

★★★★★★★

[In his One Way Street (Einbahnstrasse) *and the notes and drafts for his* Arcades Project (Das Passagen-Werk),[21] *in his efforts to critically re-present and de-myth-logize the circulation of commodities]* Benjamin *effectively 'spatialised' time, supplanting the narrative encoding of history through a textual practice that disrupted the historiographic chain in which moments are clipped together like magnets. In practice this required him to reclaim the debris of history from the matrix of [linear, progressive] systematicity in which historiography had embedded it: to blast the fragments from their all-too-familiar, taken-for-granted and, as Benjamin would insist, their mythical context and place them in a new, radically heterogeneous setting in which their integrities would not be fused into one. This practice of montage was derived from the surrealists, of course, who used it to dislocate the boundaries between art and life.*[22]

Derek Gregory (1991), 26.

21 Benjamin (1979) and (1982).
22 As a conscious art form, montage had its apparent origins in the photomontages of Georg Grosz, Hannah Höch, other Berlin Dadaists, and especially John Heartfield, who, during the late twenties and thirties, brought this mode of political collage "to a pitch of polemical ferocity that no artist has since equalled" (Hughes, 1991, 73). Their images "directly cut from the 'reckless everyday psyche' of the press, stuck next to and on top of one another in ways that resembled the laps and dissolves of film editing, ... could combine the grip of a dream with the documentary 'truth' of photography," (Hughes, 1991, 71). Note Buck-Morss (1989, 60–64) on the parallels between Heartfield's work during the thirties and that of Benjamin. Also *see* Bürger (1984, 66 ff.) on Benjamin, avant-garde art and allegory.

"For Benjamin, the technique of montage had 'special, perhaps even total rights' as a progressive form because it 'interrupts the context into which it is inserted' and thus 'counteracts illusion.'"

"When Benjamin praised montage as progressive because it 'interrupts the context into which it is inserted,' he was referring to its destructive critical dimension .... But the task of the Arcades project was to implement as well the constructive dimension of the montage, as the only form in which modern philosophy could be erected."

"[I]f Benjamin threw the traditional language of metaphysics into the junkroom, it was to rescue the metaphysical experience of the objective world, not to see philosophy dissolve into the play of language itself."

Susan Buck-Morss (1989), 67, 77, 223.

****

Not a matter of either/or, but of both/and ...

"[The idea] is formulated in one place, of the work [The Arcades Project] *as pure 'montage,' that is created from a juxtaposition of quotation so that the theory springs out of it without having to be inserted as interpretation."*

"In place of mediating theory, the form of commentary was to have appeared which he defined as interpretation out of the particulars. ... The quotations are instead the material that Benjamin's representation [interpretation and commentary] was to employ."

Theodor Adorno in a letter to Max Horkheimer (May, 1949) and Rolf Tiedemann, editor of the *Passengen-Werk*, as quoted in Susan Buck-Morss (1989), 73–74.

****

Benjamin's "montage" is a highly suggestive point of departure.
A source of intellectual inspiration.
Not a work of art to be mechanically reproduced.

Benjamin's writing resonated with the condition(ing)s of modernity
       in Berlin during his childhood,
          in Berlin and Paris during the twenties and thirties.
Our writings resonate with the condition(ing)s of hypermodernity
       in our particular worlds during the nineties.

Benjamin did not make it over the mountains with his baggage.[23]
We are still carrying ours.
Time to unpack!

---

23 Fleeing Paris in 1940 after it fell to Hitler's troops, Benjamin picked up a US visa in Marseilles and eventually crossed into Spain with some fellow exiles at Port Bou. Confronted by a local official who threatened (for blackmail purposes) to return them in the morning to France and the Gestapo, he took an overdose of morphine. Had he waited until the following day, he actually would have been permitted to proceed to Lisbon.

****

In attempting to (re)constructively re-present the hypermodern present and
its modern antecedents
through the medium of montage,
through the juxtaposing of verbal and visual fragments,
through the juxtaposing of quotations,
       newspaper reports,
       anecdotes,
       jokes,
       other ethnographic evidence of symbolic discontent,
       aphorisms, and
       more conventional summary statements and notes,
with photographs, art reproductions and cartoons,
one may attempt to art-iculate
as well as resonate
at several levels at once.[24]

Through assembling (choice) bits
    and (otherwise neglected or discarded) scraps,
through the cut-and-paste reconstructions of montage,
one may bring alive,
open the text to multiple ways of knowing
    and multiple sets of meaning,
allow multiple voices to be heard,
    to speak to (or past) each other
        as well as to the contexts from which they emerge
           and to which they contribute.

Through deliberately deploying the devices of montage,
one may, simultaneously,
reveal what is most central to the place and time in question,
be confronting the ordinary with the extraordinary,
      the commonplace with the out-of-place,
      the (would-be) hegemonic with the counterhegemonic,
      the ruling with the unruly,
      the power wielders with the subjects of power,
      the margin definers with the marginalized,
      the boundary drawers with the out-of-bounds,
      the norm makers with the 'abnormal,'
      the dominating with the dominated.

24 For initial, groping efforts along these lines *see* Pred (1991, 1992, 1993).

Through the combinatory possibilities of montage,
one may uncover what is otherwise covered over,
and, simultaneously,
bring into significant conjuncture
    what otherwise would appear unrelated,
blast into isolated disjuncture
    what would otherwise would be buried with insignificance,
over and over again
focusing on tiny, seemingly inconsequential details,
    on fragments of no apparent significance,
so as to project the largest possible picture,
so as to provide an intelligible account –
    an array of truthful knowledges –
which is as partial as possible.

Through the calculated arrangements of montage,
one may present – from re-presented particulars –
    a particular interpretation,
and, simultaneously,
allow theory and theoretical position to speak for themselves,
    to emerge from the spatial (juxta)positions of the text,
        from the silent spaces

        which force discordant fragments
        to whisper and SHOUT at each other in polylogue.

Through the de-signing and re-signing designs of montage,
one may confront the reader
    with the possibility of seeing and hearing
        what she would otherwise neither see, nor hear,
    with the possibility of making associations,
        that otherwise would go unmade,
by subtly demanding that the meaning of each fragment
    be enhanced and shifted repeatedly
    as a consequence of preceding-fragment echoes
        and subsequent-fragment contents.

In the end,
through all of these simultaneous strivings,
through the maneuvered configurations of montage,
through the intercutting of a set of (geographical hi)stories,
through a strategy of radical heterogeneity,
through (c)rudely juxtaposing the incompatible and contradictory,
one may attempt to bring component fragments into mutual illumination,
    and thereby startle.

One may, in other words,
attempt to illuminate
    by way of shock,
    by way of a stunning constellation,
attempt to jolt out of position
    by suggesting a totality of fragments,
without insisting upon a closure
    that does not exist.

In the process,
    explicitly and implicity,
raising as many questions
as are answered.

All the while
showing as much about oneself
    as about anything else,
showing as much about one's place in a hypermodern world,
    as about the in-place practices and power relations
        of the hypermodern world itself.

****

> *"There is a contradiction between creativity and socialization. Just as the overriding aim of the former is the creation of the new, so the overriding aim of the latter is the preservation of the old."*
>
> Gunnar Olsson (1991), 28.

Montage is transgression
    of the (hyper)modern condition(ing)s
    out of which it is created.
In demanding new associations,
    new connections that transcend taken-for-granted meanings,
it also demands transgressions
on the part of those who read it.

The well socialized do not comply with transgressive demands.
The creative comply in their own way.

****

> *"Benjamin's heteroclite constellation seems to mine the same historico-geographical vein [as Foucault's archeology]: in both cases 'archeology' is not so much an excavation, bringing buried or hidden objects to the surface, as a way of showing the particular – anonymous, dispersed– practices and the particular – differentiated, hierarchized – spaces through which particular societies make particular things visible."*
>
> Derek Gregory (1991), 36.

****

"Benjamin had, indeed, not made things easy on himself."
Susan Buck-Morss (1989), 23.

****

Lev Kuleshov, the avant-garde Soviet filmmaker and theoretician, referred to his own particular strategy of montage, his rapid interoplicing of differently situated people and urban landscapes, as "creative geography."[25]

References

Augé, Marc, 'Espacio y alteridad', *Revista de Occidente*, (1993).
Benjamin, Walter, *One Way Street and other writings*. (London, New Left Books, 1979).
Benjamin, Walter, *Gesammelte Schriften*, vol. 5, *Das Passagen Werk*, edited by Rolf Tiedemann. (Frankfurt am Main, Suhrkamp Verlag, 1982).
Berman, Marshall, *All that Is Solid Melts into Air: the Experience of Modernity.* (New York: Simon and Schuster, 1982).
Bondi, Liz, 'Locating Identity Politics', in Keith, M. and Pile, J. (Eds.) *Place and the Politics of Identity*, (London: Routledge, 1993).
Bright, Charles and Geyer, Michael, 'For a Unified History of the World in the Twentieth Century', *Radical History Review*, 39, 69–91 (1987).
Buck-Morss, Susan, *The Dialetics of Seeing: Walter Benjamin and the Arcades Project*, (Cambridge, Mass, the MIT Press, 1989).
Bürger. Peter, *Theory of the Avant-Garde*, Minneapolis, University of Minneapolis Press, 1984).
Clifford, James, 'Introduction: Partial Truths', in James Clifford and George E. Marcus, (eds), *Writing Culture: The Poetics and Politics of Ethnography*, (Berkeley, University of California Press, 1986), 1–26.
Derrida, Jacques, *Speech and Phenomena, and other Essays on Husserl's Theory of Signs*, (Evanston: Northwestern University Press, 1973).
Derrida, Jacques, *Margins of Philosophy*, (Chicago, University of Chicago Press, 1982).
Feierman, Steven, *Peasant Intellectuals: Anthropology and History in Tanzania*, (Madison, University of Madison Press, 1990).
Fiske, John, 'Cultural Studies and the Culture of Everyday Life', in Lawrence Grossberg, Cary Nelson and Paula Treichler, (eds), *Cultural Studies*, (New York: Routledge, 1992) 154–73.
Gregory, Derek, 'Interventions in the Historical Geography of Modernity: Social Theory, Spatiality and the Politics of Representation', *Geografiska Annaler*, 73B, 17–44, (1991).
Gregory, Derek, *Geographical Imaginations*, (Oxford: Basil Blackwell, 1994).
Gupta, Akhil and Ferguson, James, 'Beyond Culture: Space, Identity, and the Politics of Difference', *Cultural Anthropology*, 7, 6–23, (1992).
Hall, Stuart, 'Cultural Identity and Cinematic Representation', *Framework*, 36, 69–70, (1989).

25   *See* Levaco (1974).

Hall, Stuart, 'The Local and the Global: Globalization and Ethnicity', in Anthony D. King, (ed.) *Culture, Globalization and the World-System: Contemporary Conditions for the Representation of Identity*. (Binghamton: Department of Art and Art History, SUNY Binghamton, 1991), 19–39.

Harvey, David, *The Condition of Postmodernity. An Enquiry into the Origins of Culture Change*, (Oxford: Basil Blackwell, 1989).

Harvey, David, 'Postmodern Morality Plays', *Antipode*, 24, 300–26, (1992).

Harvey, David 'From Space to Place and Back Again: Reflections on the Condition of Postmodernity', in Jon Bird, Barry Curtis, Tim Putnam, George Robertson and Lisa Tickner, (eds), *Mapping the Futures: Local Cultures, Global Change*. (London, Routledge, 1993), 3–39.

Hughes, Robert, *The Shock of the New*, revised ed. (New York, Alfred A. Knopf, 1991).

Jameson, Fredric, 'Postmodernism and Consumer Society', in Hal Foster, (ed.) *The Anti-Aesthetic: Essays on Postmodern Culture*, (Port Townsend, Wash., Bay Press, 1983), 11–125.

Jameson, Fredric, 'Cognitive Mapping', in Cary Nelson and Lawrence Grossberg, (eds), *Marxism and the Interpretation of Culture*, (Urbana, University of Illinois Press, 1988), 347–60.

Jameson, Fredric, *Postmodernism, or, The Cultural Logic of Late Capitalism*, (Durham, N.C., Duke University Press, 1991).

Le Rider, Jacques, *Modernity and Crises of Identity: Culture and Society in Fin-de-siècle Vienná*, (Oxford, Polity Press, 1993).

Levaco, Ronald, *Kuleshov on Film: Writings by Lev Kuleshov*, (Berkeley, University of California Press, 1974).

Lunn, Eugene, *Marxism and Modernism: An Historical Study of Lukacs, Brecht, Benjamin and Adorno*, (Berkeley, University of California Press, 1982).

Malkki, Lisa 'National Geographic: The Rooting of Peoples and the Territorialization of National Identity Among Scholars and Refugees', *Cultural Anthropology*, 7, 24–44, (1992).

Marcus, George, 'Past, Present and Emergent Identities: Requirements for Ethnographies of Late Twentieth-Century Modernity Worldwide', in Scott Lash and Jonathan Friedman, (eds), *Modernity and Identity*, (Oxford, Blackwell, 1992), 309–30.

McDowell, Linda, 'Multiple Voices: Speaking from Inside and Outside "the Project"', *Antipode*, 24, 56–72, (1992).

Oakes, T. S., 'The Cultural Space of Modernity: Ethnic Tourism and Place Identity in China', *Society and Space*, 11, 47–66, (1993).

Olsson, Gunnar, *Lines of Power/Limits of Language*, (Minneapolis, University of Minnesota Press, 1991).

Plant, Sadie, *The Most Radical Gesture: The Situationist International in a Postmodern Age*, (London, Routledge, 1992).

Pred, Allan 'Spectacular Articulations of Modernity: The Stockholm Exhibition of 1897', *Geografiska Annaler*, 73B, 45–84, (1991).

Pred, Allan, 'Pure and Simple Lines, Future Lines of Vision: The Stockholm Exhibition of 1930', *Nordisk Samhällsgeografisk Tidskrift*, 15, (1992), 3–61.

Pred, Allan, 'Where in the World Am I, Are We? Who in the World Am I, Are We?: The Glob(e)alization of Stockholm, Sweden', *Recognizing European Modernities. A Montage of the Present*, (London, Routledge, 1995), 175–264.

Pred, Allan and Watts, Michael John, *Reworking Modernity: Capitalisms and Symbolic Discontent*. (New Brunswick, N.J., Rutgers University Press, 1992).

Rabinow, Paul, 'Representations Are Social Facts; Modernity and Post-Modernity in Anthropology', in James Clifford and George E. Marcus, (eds), *Writing Culture: The Poetics and Politics of Ethnography*, (Berkeley, University of California Press, 1986), 234–61.

Rosenthal, Michael, 'What Was Postmodernism?' *Socialist Review*, 22, no. 3, 83–105, (1992).

Schorske, Carl, *Fin-de-siécle Vienna: Politics and Culture*, (New York, Vintage Books, 1981).

Smith, Neil, 'Geography, Difference and the Politics of Scale', in Joe Doherty, Elspeth Graham and Mo Malek, (eds), *Postmodernism and the Social Sciences*, (London, Macmillan, 1982) 57–79.

Strohmayer, Ulf and Hannah, Matthew, 'Domesticating Postmodernism', *Antipode*, 24, 29–55, (1992).

Taussig, Michael, *Mimesis and Alterity: A Particular History of the Senses*, (New York, Routledge, 1993).

Watts, Michael, J., 'Mapping Meaning, Denoting Difference, Imagining Identity: Dialectical Images and Postmodern Geographies', *Geografiska Annaler*, 73B, 7–16, (1991).

5

Identity, Space, and other Uncertainties

Wolfgang Natter and John Paul Jones III

Introduction

Any effort to measure the character of the "postmodern" is fraught with difficulty, not the least due to its overlapping and sometimes conflicting meanings. What is more, these meanings have been differentially imported into, and appropriated by, the social sciences and humanities. As a result, and especially during early phases of the debates surrounding postmodernism, one could often find surprising variance in the ways in which "it" was deployed within individual disciplines.[1] Over-and-above this multiaccentual reception – which intersected with a series of new substantive inquiries such as "flexible accumulation," "modes of information," and "orientalism" – a key cross-disciplinary outcome of nearly two decades of engagements with postmodernism has been a rigorous questioning of the certainties that earlier on worked to separate the aims, methods, and objects of various fields. The unsettling of foundational ontologies brought by a postmodern rethinking of power, representation, and disciplinary history has now come to resonate across the "great divide" of the social sciences and the humanities, giving scholars occasion to peer beyond ensconced disciplinary borders.

The resulting uncertainties – the epistemological provocations of which were presaged by much poststructuralist thinking – do more than problematize disciplinary boundaries,[2] they enable inquiry into substantive matters the articulation of which had hitherto been limited by disciplinary circumscription. In this essay, we deploy a poststructural epistemology in an effort to articulate two such substantive domains of current interest to those sympathetic to postmodernism: identity and space. A poststructuralist – or nonessentialist – stance toward identity recognizes both the theoretical impulses that announced the "death of the subject" during the late 1960s, as well as the failures of liberalism and Marxism to usher in a democratic society based on their versions of identity politics. Meanwhile, space has been problematized through postmodernism's attention to context and contingency, as well as through efforts to understand the new social landscapes accompanying the arrival of late, disorganized, or flexible capitalism.

Those attracted to the challenges posed by poststructuralism have raised several questions that apply to identity theory, and these animate the analysis that follows: how does identity arise, how is it differentiated, and how is it maintained? It is a premise of this essay that any answer to these questions must necessarily engage space. Inasmuch as social relations constitute and embed both identities and space, theorizing the linkages between these moments is an important task for social theory. This essay, then, asks the following: can we envision a poststructuralist, or nonessentialist, theory of space that is commensurate with poststructuralist identity theory?

Our efforts to theorize these connections are prefaced with a critical analysis of the "category" – *Der Begriff* – meant both in-and-of itself and in its relation to the process of classification. This discussion is necessary inasmuch as essentialist theories of "identity" and "space" are themselves grounded in essentialist conceptions of the category. Moreover, our critique of essentialist categories bears directly on an ongoing political question: can the identities of social subjects be theorized in ways that are not complicitous with either holistic and hermetic identifications or with the total annihilation of the "social?"

This question is important for those who reject both indifference and foundationalism in thinking about politics. On the one hand, the unwillingness to conjoin difference – for fear that doing so will reintroduce hierarchy and metanarrative – makes politics unpracticable. On the other hand, foundationalism limits in advance the forms of identification through which politics might be practiced. Two forms of contemporary politics underscore the latter point. First, neo-conservatives have offered a version of identity politics that deploys a rhetoric of individuation while wresting from individuals oversight over policies the outcome of which is worldwide submission to corporatist economics. Those on the "left," meanwhile, often confront this individualist rhetoric with their own entrenched and no less essentialist categories of identification, ones that may now have become so instrumentalized as to present obstacles for rethinking democracy. And because identity politics – as everyday practice – finds its ideal types congealed in the social sciences as separate systems of thought, e.g., Marxism versus feminism, feminism versus black feminism, etc., these issues resound with implications for politics within theory itself.

The argument we present is organised as follows. We first explore the complications that arise for identity and identity politics via the "category." We then discuss nonessentialist or poststructuralist identity theory, drawing both upon Laclau and Mouffe's understanding of hegemony – as the process by which identification/identity congeals as apparently fixed, if not natural – and upon Derrida's formulation of the relational process – the constitutive outside – by which all identities are inscribed by the "other" they ostensibly exclude. This in turn leads us to an understanding of space that, like identity, is never fixed, monolithic, and bound, but is open to interventions when theorized through nonessentialist theory. Our aim, in short, is to dislodge remnant essentialisms from spatial thought. This evacuation and rearticulation leads to an examination of the productive uncertainties commensurate with a nonessentialist politics of both space and identity.

The Essentializing Category

Given that any discussion of identity, whether couched in terms of gender, sexuality, race, or class, necessarily involves the question of boundaries – as in where and how identity becomes circumscribed – it seems useful to begin a consideration of the identities thus *identified* by asking what is at stake in the process of categorization itself. First, inchoate and singular events/objects are formed for thought through categories. The resulting representations of events/objects are the necessary precondition for all communication. Thus, even the severe critique of the category found in the *Dialectic of Enlightenment* – written in reaction to a time/place where its always possible misuse had become palpable as a place of terror – already acknowledges the futility of rejecting general concepts, categories, and classification. As Horkheimer and Adorno emphasized, however, critique becomes necessary when socially domi-nant groups employ categories self-identically, as if referring to the "things themselves," instead of being understood as meaning-full representations of them: "Classification is a condition for cognition, and not cognition itself;" moreover, all categories, as representations, are open to scrutiny and reformu-lation, for: "cognition in turn dispels classification."[3]

In the dialectic between cognition and instrumentality that together com-prise Reason, the category is a component of instrumental and not "pure" reason, and thus, though necessary, the category is always revisable. Rather than the mere filling-in of linguistic containers that facilitate communication, the category's role in instrumental reason suggests that it is a purposeful construction that is never neutral in intent nor inconsequential in effect. As Foucault argued, where one encounters the category, one of necessity also finds ordering, hierarchy, and – under the aegis of instrumental reason – tools for social domination.[4] In short, in the category there lurks a particular form of social power: the ability to seize alterity and assign it a social significance.

With respect to identity theory, the power of the category is manifest in the construction of fixed social identifications out of the multiplicity of unnamed alterity. In this process, the category subsumes individual particularity via equivalence. For Horkheimer and Adorno, modern capitalist society's reliance upon equivalence – the basis of exchange value – further enhanced the power of the category to process social objects based on abstractions of their "quali-ties:"

> Bourgeois society is ruled by equivalence. It makes the dissimilar comparable by reducing it to abstract quantities. To the Enlightenment, that which does not reduce to numbers, and ultimately to the one, becomes illusion; modern positiv-ism writes it off as literature.[5]

Given capitalism's tendency to disaggregate "humanity" from human labor and to deploy what is left as an "abstract" value exchangeable in commodity form, it should not be surprising that Horkheimer and Adorno have a particu-larly pessimistic account of the identity assigned Enlightenment subjects:

"[people] were given their individuality as unique in each case, different to all others, so that it might all the more surely be made the same as any other."[6] As a generalizing moment, the category's framing of Identity, abstracted from the multiple qualities which inhere in the identities contained by this frame, is precisely what lends the category a force far and above what the elements themselves might marshal. As these authors depict the reversal from identities to identity: "The identity of the category forbids that of the individual cases ... Now any person signifies only those attributes by which he can replace everybody else: he is interchangeable, a copy."[7]

One possibility for resisting this homogenizing effect – whereby identities are reduced to nothing more than the category that collects them – is to question the accuracy and adequacy of the category to describe the social "objects" brought under its umbrella. In the face of the category's power to stereotype the identities contained within it, one response has been to call for a respecification of the boundaries of the category such that it more precisely aligns with the diversity of identities it contains. Certainly there are cases when this response can form an effective resistance to the domination of the category. For example, the scope of Marxist analysis certainly widened in the wake of feminist critiques of the universality ascribed to its subject; in turn, recognition of the diversity of women's experiences has widened the project of feminism beyond a white, middle-class formulation of its universality.[8] However, the mere assertion of diversity within the category can be problematic, when, for example, instead of rethinking the process of categorization, it merely reinscribes a new system of boundaries around increasingly differentiated subjects. Though this may achieve a more precise encapsulation of Identity, it is ultimately destined to proliferate into a fragmentation of ever more complex social categories. And because these narrower categorical specifications are typically constructed as further differentiated versions of already existing categories, it leaves intact the system of boundaries used to collect alterity in the first place.

One can chart the political implications of differentiating categorical diversity by recalling the fragmentation of left-liberal politics in the United States over the past two decades. The late 1960s witnessed the near-simultaneous coalescence of a diverse set of already politicized social movements – denigrated in the succeeding decades as "interest groups" – organized around racial equality, the elimination of poverty, and women's rights. The possibilities for unifying this multiplicity during the late 1960s were very much enhanced by widespread anger over United States' militarism during the Vietnam War. Moreover, for commentators like Herbert Marcuse, the reaction against militarism also pointed to the possibility of global linkages between the left coalition within the "developed" countries and movements within the "underdeveloped" countries trying to free themselves from colonial oppression.[9] Yet just as quickly as the War ended, the galvanizing force of anti-militarism was lost. The various focuses of the left-liberal coalition in the United States became narrower and – as a result – less effective.

For us, these developments partly explain Reagan's widely recognized ability to fill the growing interstitial political arena created by the receding boundaries of categorically-based politics with a discourse which drew upon a mythologizing sense of national identity and purpose and, simultaneously, a politics of divisiveness: black versus white, men versus women, poor versus rich. The Reagan coalition that captured representational democracy away from left-liberal groups would in the 1980s claim to speak from a position "beyond" the rancor of identity politics, enabling it to denigrate "interest group" positions as being outside the national consensus.

If anything, the experience of United States politics during the past 20 years underscores the fragility of deploying essentialist categories as the basis for political action. Both hegemony and, in a mirror image, counterhegemony, have spoken the language of fixed identity/space. Phrased in terms of the category, it seems to us that the task at hand is to theorize outside an essentialism the polar moments of which are, at one end, a blindness toward diversity, and at the other end, the total disintegration of the category. Given the force of postmodernism's critique of metanarratives, recognition of the value of local knowledges, and various destabilizations of the feminist standpoint, we are unlikely to soon witness the arrival of an overarching category capable of uniting left politics. And as Chantal Mouffe comments in reference to the latter of the polar oppositions, the valorization of all differences – as the postmodern embrace of "heterogeneity, dissemination, and incommensurability" – presents its own dangers to politics, for where "all interests, all opinions, all differences are seen as legitimate," complete indifferentiation and indifference result. [10]

We believe that what may be more helpful just now is a theorization of categories and subjects that refuses either to subsume difference within the homogenizing moment of the category, or to dispense with the category altogether. And importantly, it is not only the end points, but indeed each point in the continuum given parameters by these polar moments that needs to be questioned, for compartmentalizing categories along ever more distinct lines of difference still relies upon the organizing principle of the category that never questions the status of the subject. As Mouffe puts it:

> we would have made no advance at all if we were simply going to replace the notion of a unified and homogeneous subject by a multiplicity and fragmentation in which each of the fragments retains a closed and fully constituted identity. As we have argued ..., such an essentialism of the "elements" remains within the problematic that it tries to displace, because a clear-cut identity pre-supposes a determinate system of relations with all the fragments or "elements" – and what is this but the reintroduction of the category of totality whose elimination was the meaning of the whole operation? [11]

Mouffe's non-embrace of "postmodernism" is underwritten by a poststructuralism that speaks in the name of difference. It invokes an identity theory based on the category of citizenship, an imaginary that reworks categories of class, gender, race, and sexuality for the purpose of a radical and plural democracy. [12] It is to poststructuralist identity theory that we now turn.

Nonessential Identity

Poststructuralist theory operates against both essentialist identity categories and the methodological processes that produce them. In contrast to the view that subjects lie at the center of the categories that encircle and empower them, poststructuralist identity theory starts with an understanding that identity is the product of categorization rather than its raw material. Thus, any essential identity, whether "grounded" in the language of origins or projected toward a telos that substantiates its promise, is an impossible ideal. For some social theorists, to so unhinge identity signals the unravelling of any form of politics. Yet as developed for example by Ernesto Laclau and Chantal Mouffe, recognizing identity as an imaginary construct immediately directs attention to hegemony, as in how hegemonic social power aims to fix identifications around "nodal points" where "identity" can be constructed and policed.[13]

Like hegemony, the constitutive outside directs our attention to the identifications through which composite identity is formed. In addition, it describes a process by which boundaries and categories are constructed and social objects within them are framed. The constitutive outside is a relational process by which the outside – or "other" – of any category is actively at work on both sides of the constructed boundary, and is thus always leaving its trace within the category. Thus, what may appear to be a self-enclosed category maintained by boundaries is found in fact to unavoidably contain the marks of inscription left by the outside from which it seemingly has been separated. As Derrida has shown through the work of deconstruction – beginning with his destabilization of writing and speech as separable practices[14] –the outside of any category is already found to be resident within, permeating the category from the *inside* through its traceable presence-in-absence within the category.

What explains the character of this presence is the fact that the power to make and maintain difference is never undirectional: it always works from both within and outside the category. Though boundaries, through a process of hegemony, *may appear* as rigid and hermetic, the differences so sorted are never neatly *contained*; they are only *maintained*, and this through the force of the category itself. Moreover, while the outside marks the alterity of the inside, fashions its borders, assigns its social significance, and supervises its relations with other boundaries, the constructed inside, which is both agent and victim of this territorializing process, extends beyond itself to become another's outside within.

What implications ensue from the recognition of the processes of hegemony and the constitutive outside? At one level, theory has long acknowledged that race, gender, nationality, ethnicity, and sexuality are *socially constructed* categories.[15] Poststructuralist theory goes further, however, by asserting that as products of hegemony, the categories we take as materially significant not only lack a "natural" basis for grounding identity, but are the very grounds by which identity is produced. It is not just that categories are "social" – hardly a meaningful distinction, unless God is being invoked – but rather that those aspects of alterity that are seized upon and amplified into a system of social differentiation are always contingently productive of subjects in the interest of hegemonic power. "Race," for example, is so widely naturalized as a significant category of identity that we have to be confronted by the hypothetical possibility that eye color could have been the basis for an equally oppressive system of difference for us to fully acknowledge the contingent nature of, say, skin color as a basis for a socially significant category. As Toni Morrison describes the contingency of this boundary-making process:

> These slaves, unlike many others in the world's history, were visible to a fault. And they had inherited, among other things, a long history on the meaning of color; it was that this color "meant" something ... One supposes that if Africans all had three eyes or one ear, the significance of that difference from the smaller but conquering European invaders would have also been found to have meaning.[16]

To focus on the contingent social construction of the category, as opposed to, say, its implications in everyday social practice, might for some seem to imply an inattentiveness to the material effects – conquerors/slaves – of that construction. Precisely the opposite is true: it is only through the linkage of both – the construction of the category (i.e., race *as* representation) and the material effects that conform to and reproduce the category – that we can deconstruct with full force the deep structures that construct difference as meaningful and deploy it in hegemonic projects. Thus to question the social effects of racism without simultaneously asking how the differences collapsed in the category are defined and maintained, will inevitably reinforce the social hierarchy inscribed in and by the category, thus sustaining that hierarchy as inevitable. It is manifestly not a mystification of the material effects of social difference to assert its contingently constructed nature; rather, recognition of hegemony – the precondition for alternative strategies – requires that we ask questions as to how differences arise, are amplified and maintained through power, *and* toward what effect.

Answers to these questions benefit from the addition of an historical dimension, for over time hegemony's rendition of identity as fixed, natural, and inevitable offers grounds for recognition of them as nodal points – temporary locations for social identification. Over time, that hegemony best sustains itself that secures tradition as a seal of its destiny – the desirable culmination of the past in the present, laden with future promise. Whether deployed as a pre-articulation so weighted in the present that its fulfillment is "destined" to arrive, or presented *ex post facto* as a selective ordering of past events which "necessarily" demonstrate the present as a casual link in a past/future teleology – tradition can be used, in Benjamin's words, to buttress the present rulers who are "the heirs of those who conquered before them."[17]

The above argument suggests, first, that counterhegemonic practices work to expose the contingent construction of hegemonically constituted nodal points. This involves an interrogation of the "cultural treasures" put on display by the guardians of tradition wherever and whenever dense cultural capital is at stake. In so doing, theorists will be identifying potential sites of disarticulation so that tradition can be unframed – in Benjamin's sense – and actualized as it always really is: "thoroughly alive and extremely changeable."[18]

Following the disclosure of the cultural moments constituting hegemonically defined identities, the task for an alternative politics is to work towards new cultural practices that subvert and rework dominant nodal points. For Michel Pecheux, one strategy beyond a counterhegemonic reversal of the hierarchies embedded in any categorization is that of disidentification, a relation to the hegemonic that is neither identification – as the fulfillment of hegemony – or anti-identification – as its opposite.[19] The latter strategy, as Rosemary Hennessy notes, is that of the "bad subject" the rebellion of which against hegemonic subject identifications keeps in place the system imposed by hegemonic ideology. Disidentification, by contrast, is a critique that disrupts and rearranges "the pre-constructed categories on which the formation of subjects depend."[20] This subject does not claim to speak from any group identity; rather she exposes by critique the entire system that constitutes identity.

For us, such tactics of resistance are made all the more possible when practiced in recognition of the constitutive outside, because this process bespeaks a recognition that no dominant cultural strategy proves in fact to be so seamless that the trace of exclusion is not in evidence. Facilitating the deconstruction of any identity's claim to an ordinary or self-referential standpoint, the constitutive outside suggests counterhegemonic practices that expose the presence of the outside/other *within* the boundaries of dominant cultural groups. As Toni Morrison describes this process as it operates within American literature, the canon is thoroughly marked with the trace of Africanism necessary to construct the American cultural tradition:

> Explicit or implicit, the Africanist presence informs in compelling and inescapable ways the texture of American literature. It is a dark and abiding presence, there for the literary imagination as both a visible and invisible mediating force. Even, and especially, when American texts are not "about" Africanist presences or characters or narrative or idiom, the shadow hovers in implication, in sign, in line of demarcation. It is no accident and no mistake that immigrant populations (and much immigrant literature) understood their "Americanness" as an opposition to the resident black population.[21]

Thus for Morrison, this ineluctable "dark and abiding" trace in American literature is constitutive of identity itself: "the self-conscious but highly problematic construction of the American as the new white man."[22] But what specific forms of politics accompany the recognition of the constitutive outside? We would offer that this process, far from so decentering the subject that politics is unthinkable, has several advantages for strategies aimed to resist hegemony. First, and as Said has made clear in the case of the European construction of the "Orient,"[23] the relational process so described raised questions as to who has the power to construct the "other," and how such constructions, far from being merely a projection onto the "other," provide the very grounds for constituting the "self." Second, the mutual dependencies derived from this constitutive process can be the basis for articulating alternative nodal point configurations that *rework* (e.g., through disidentification) rather than *reinforce* the surplus of social resistances now demarcated according to gender, sexuality, class, ethnicity, race, ableness, environment, Third World, etc. As Mouffe stresses the difference: "it is not a matter of establishing a mere alliance between given interests but of actually modifying the very identity of these forces."[24] And finally, the constitutive outside also points to the possibility of interweaving and thereby strengthening new nodal points. When, as Mouffe offers, these interconnected social movements are linked by a "chain of equivalence,"[25] rearticulated counterhegemonic subject positions offer a viable alternative to a politics that presents as its choices either the subsumption of difference or its ever increasing fragmentation.

Nonessential Space

We are now posed to consider the question of a spatial theory commensurate with our understanding of the subject as a temporary determination – a provisional nodal point subverted, asserted, and reconstituted through contingent social relations. The construction of such a theory cannot rely solely on a nonessentialist conception of the subject, but requires a similar conception of space. Because subjects achieve and resist their systems of identification in and through social space, it follows that without a nonessentialist conception of space – as an also open, heterogeneous, and indeterminate field – extant spatialities, both in theory and practice, would only reinstate or at the least reinforce an essentializing moment in identity theory. The task is thus to produce a nonessentialist theory of social space.

Partial steps in this direction have already been suggested by theorists attempting to combine the socio-spatial dialectic with identity theory.[26] What makes the socio-spatial dialectic a propitious avenue for spatializing identity theory is that it too makes social relations a central theoretical moment. As Lefebvre repeatedly emphasized, space is produced by social relations that it also reproduces, mediates, and transforms.[27] For him, the materialization of this dialectical interchange is social space itself: the sublation of social relations and space on an uncertain path in a way that is open toward the reformulation of each.

However, it should be emphasized that the socio-spatial dialectic does not in-and-of-itself foreclose an essentialist understanding of social relations, and hence, of identity. There are manifold ways to theorize social relations, and some of these – for example, certain deployments of the concept of Class – offer no guarantees that one does not inscribe an essentialist spatiality, and with it, a fixed and homogeneous politics of space. Therefore, in contrast to a category of space as self-present social essence, it is more useful to start with a conception of space that, like the subject, is a *lack* to be filled, contested, and reconfigured through contingent and partially determined social relations, practices, and meanings.

The manifest danger in an essentialist conception of social space is given by the *strategic* fact that hegemonic cultural practices will always attempt to fix the meaning of space, arranging any number of particularities, disjunctures, and juxtapositions into a seamless unity: the one place, the one identity, as in, for example, the "Nation."[28] Yet hegemony, as the process that naturalizes both space and social relations, is like any form of power: never fixed or inevitable but always open to exposure, confrontation, reversal, and refusal through counterhegemonic or disidentifying practices. Attempts at normalization can never therefore be fully complete, for the same indeterminate and always partially sutured social relations implicated in the construction of identity are – understood through the socio-spatial dialectic – also implicated in the production of space. Space, no less than identity, will always therefore offer the potential for *tactical* refusal and resistance.[29]

Argument against an essentialist understanding of spatiality therefore additionally confronts the structural impulse that undergirds the theorization of space as a stabilized and stabilizing product. As a process that organizes alterity, such stabilizations result in the *appearance* of totalization in the form of a structured coherence of space – discrete units at various scales: neighborhoods, cities, regions, and nations. However, spatial structures elide totalization – except, perhaps, in appearance – for no structure can fully erase difference. Instead, any structure, in this case spatial, simultaneously incarnates alterity and – through configuration and hierarchy – imposes order over it. Though structured space can be *presented* as a totality – in ways that are naturalized via representations of space[30] – such orderings can never thoroughly subsume difference.

This line of argument can be extended to address the production and maintenance of spatial boundaries more generally. All such circumscriptions are based on an ordering of alterity, yet the crucial issue is not simply that the boundaries that result from such an ordering are socially constituted or, for that matter, porous, but rather that this process proceeds by assigning an *origin* around which alterity is structured. The boundaries of any "region" can only be drawn by first constructing an "origin" from alterity, and upon interrogation, such an "origin" always proves to have been set in place in the absence of an a priori foundation. Already ontologically then, any structure implies the potential for a reversal or displacement, that is, the possibility that the origin could in another context be an "other." As a social process, origins are imminently contestable through a displacement in which the structuring locus is lost, or through dissemination, by which the "origin" gives rise to effects over which it has no control.[31]

The structural critique also has implications for the status of such concepts as "center" and "periphery" that have been deployed as organizing principles in structured space. The (social) process of centering entails a structuring moment necessary to perform the ordering, but at the same time any such structuring implies the assignation of a periphery. Assignment to the periphery "provides a home" – one of terror – for "the other," the mere existence of which was both a provocation to, and the raw material for, the center.[32] The power emanating from the center that, on the one hand, peripheralizes alterity, on the other hand incorporates traces of the periphery from which it is constitutively constructed. As in a poststructural theorization of "self" and "other," to speak of a "center" and a "periphery" is already to acknowledge the latter's constitutive power. Accordingly, there is not only – as bell hooks has amplified[33] – a power in the margin, but also, through the constitutive outside, a peripheral power poised to deconstruct any center of which it is a part.

Still another route to unhinging the self-grounding epistemology substantiating space and thereby confirming it as a pre-given articulation, is to conceptualize it as *both* materiality and – through the system of signification contingently adhered to it – as representation.[34] In combining both lines of argument, space is not simply a socially produced materiality but a socially produced – and forceful – object/sign system. This, which we refer to as a "system of representation", does not deny materiality, but rather argues that any materiality is attached to the representation(s) through which that materiality both embeds and conveys social meaning.

To conceive of all spaces as being stamped by signification suggests that we resist the temptation to conceive of "mere" ideology as an intrusion upon our ability to grasp the "essence of space" in its full and unmediated presence. This view – a hangover from the historic tendency to separate materiality from representation[35] – presupposes the ability to call forth, through ideology critique, a space (*die Sache selbst*) purged of hegemony. Such an approach merely reproduces the objectivist and essentialist view of space it seeks to replace, for, as Rosalyn Deutsche points out, it falsely promises the possibility of severing materiality – as full presence – and representation – as ideological overlay.[36]

An appropriate theory of space as representation will, therefore, not only question the apparent unity of the object and sign, but also the possibility of their separation. In this view, the representational can neither be eliminated nor honed to a "correct" specification. Nor can the spatial be rendered apolitical. We are left, then, with space as an always already, but never predetermined, representation. Though materialized in space – for example, in the ideologies embedded in our streets, buildings, monuments, and neighborhoods – the anchors of representation are always open to disruption. Freed from the moorings of a rigidified and fixed spatiality, the social meanings of space can be contested as they actually are: thoroughly open, and never self-identical or outside social processing. Social space, despite its apparent substantive materiality, is thus also characterized by an emptiness, one which social powers work to substantiate with meaning content, truth value, objectivity.

All of this recognizes that space, like identity, is equally subject to the naturalizing processes of hegemony. Just as fixed identities rely upon categories condensed at nodal points, so too does the meaning content, truth value, and objectivity assignable to any spatial object/sign system rely upon its naturalization. Hegemonic spatiality, the categorically ordered possibilities for, and the construction of, meanings about any space, is a representational process that works to tie "readers" – or "operators" – however tentatively, to "texts" – and "space." The common distinctions between public and private space, for example, demonstrate the ability of hegemonic powers to naturalize spatial categories in the vested interests of those benefiting from capitalist property relations. One might ask, however, how much more effective might socio-spatial praxis be if the category "private" were denaturalized, that is, repositioned as a mere temporary categorization the cultural markers of which – the "No Trespassing" sign, the fence – were open to contestation and transgression?

Finally, in thinking space through the constitutive outside, it is apparent that any category representationally adhered to space already bears the marks of the other it aims to exclude. As categories, representations are not sewn seamlessly into the fabric of space; rather, the very process of exclusion that permits the category also permits oppositional moments to insert themselves into the object/sign system. Thus any space, as representation, is an already possible site for deconstruction. Or what is the same, the bar

$$-/-$$

in any object/sign system is never fully continuous.[37]

Practicing Uncertainty

In this section, we consider how to construct a politics capable of confronting the calcifications of both space and identity that emerge from their essentialist formulation. Let us begin with an equation, deeply etched in the fabric of spatial and cultural thought, which has normalized a set of operating assumptions regarding the relations between space and identity:

certain spaces = certain identities

The equation certifies a homologous alignment between space and identity. Historically, it also characterizes entire traditions of modernist (and essentialist) geographies, ranging from the mapping of peoples by cultural and regional geographers to the assumptions about identity built into the theoretical models of scientific and Marxist geographers. It equally has served to provide governing norms for the study of culture in relationship to "the peoples" that produce it (e.g. national literatures). Thought un-essentially, however, the equation immediately prompts questions for social theorists concerning the hegemonic production of identifications in and through space that determine how exactly "certain" spaces and identities come to be equated. Thought un-essentially, the equation also becomes a matter of considerable interest to social actors who must live with its determinate effects.

The generally veiled or "socialized" force of these alignments provokes shock when their dynamic is put on display by the media at moments of violent excess, such as occurred in New York's suburb of Howard Beach. It is important to emphasize, however, that from the perspective of its victims, the violence which structures space/identity is part of everyday life at all scales – from the license of exclusion issued through private property relations and the reinforcement of patriarchy through housing design to the patriotic identities forged in nation states. As we have seen, hegemony not only perpetually processes identifications to which "identity" may then become attached, it does so spatially, by disciplining the meanings and practices associated with any social space. This structuring, historically and geographically, has served the aim of stamping both identity and space with a resolute correspondence: every identity has its place.[38]

When thought through the selection criteria hegemony provides to decide what is "certain" about space and identity, the above equation points not only to the social facts of space/identity alignments, but also to the production of them. The normalizations rendered by the equation suggest that we reflect more carefully on the character of the "certain" in our hypothesis. At this juncture, our argument can profit from an investigation of the dictionary definition of the modifier, "certain." Perhaps when read in a manner that considers the differential meanings attached by the dictionary to "certain," the equation may turn out after all to reflect the relationships between space and identity this essay has sought to explore.

In *Webster's Third New International Dictionary*, the reader learns that certain meanings of "certain" are so differently. Of the six definitions listed, all but the second, to which we return below, form a cluster of meanings that reinforce the stabilizing moments indicated in a normative reading of the equation:

1   fixed, settled, stated, exact, precise;
3   sure, dependable;
4   inevitable, destined;
5   complete assurance and conviction;
6   steadfast.

Leaving aside the slightly different orbits that each of these inscribes (i.e., dependable versus inevitable, steadfast versus fixed), these definitions, when applied to the equation, imply a determined, uncompromised, and teleologically grounded relation between space and identity, one whose certainty is not to be doubted.

Definition (2), by contrast, undermines these certainties through a qualification of their specification and precision, and indeed, of the possibility and desirability of foreclosure in categorization itself. In this definition, certain means:

> particular, of a character difficult or unwise to specify – used to distinguish a person or thing not otherwise distinguished or not distinguishable in more precise terms.

This definition registers a residue of imprecision, introducing into "certain" an *uncertainty* regarding the inevitability and desirability of further specifying the contents of *named* objects (e.g., space and identity). No longer defined by the parameters that determine and fix objects, "certain" unspecificities regarding the moments linked by the equation suggest themselves. First, the boundaries of both the containers "space" and "identity" are, under definition (2), no longer as specified or specifiable as previously held. The uncertainties, specificities, and particularities necessitated by this definition tend to render the equation unstable. Second, the imprecisions invoked by this definition also concern those characteristics of persons or things which it is difficult or unwise to distinguish, raising a question as to what processes were at work in fixing the initial connotation of the term. In other words, what is it about the object and the character of the category that makes further queries concerning its suitability unwise or difficult? Third, and finally, the principle of the constitutive outside is in force. Within its connotative meanings, the boundaries of the generally certain are pierced by the particular within. The exclusion of alterity, as the less than specified and determined, proves never to be total and complete, even in the dictionary.

This analysis, while lexicographically suggesting that no identity can claim "certainty" with regard to space (and vice versa), now points to the question of a social praxis commensurate with both nonessentialist identity and space. That such an opening is *present* in praxis is consistent with our assertion that hegemony is never a closed process, either with regards to space or identity. But what might a praxis that works against both essentialist identity and space look like?

A nonessentialist praxis of identity and space will first of all reject the notion that politics must conform to a telos the destiny of which is the attainment of absolute consensus. This view, common in some "progressive" communitarian formulations, holds the promise that counterhegemony portends a full and total reversal of hegemony. This view, however, merely reinscribes a system of identity and space the grounds of which remain essential and the borders of which self-enclosed. To conceive of identities and spaces as open and plural sites of multiple identifications suggests instead that praxis be conceived as an ongoing project, one activated precisely in recognition of a lack of political guarantees. As Mouffe puts it:

> ... while politics aims at constructing a political community and creating a unity, a fully inclusive political community and a final unity can never be realized since there will permanently be a "constitutive outside," an exterior to the community that makes its existence possible. Antagonistic forces will never disappear and politics is characterized by conflict and division.[39]

For Mouffe, what explains this ever-present antagonism is the impossibility of stabilizing and giving closure to identity. For us, her argument also implies that space be recognized as an open-ended site of social contestation and antagonism. When thought through the constitutive outside, which recognizes that spatial categories are not *fixed* but *made* by the ongoing exclusion of an other that is deferred elsewhere, spatial politics is cut loose from teleological certainties and the apparent stability they guarantee for the present. As an unfixed category, space proves always open to a politics of reconfiguring difference differently.

Second, nonessentialist praxis would attempt to rework both identity and space by reconfiguring the field of socio-spatial relations that maintain dominant meanings and practices in social space. The possibility of transgressing such extant meanings/practices was already articulated by Walter Benjamin in the 1930s drawing upon the new medium of film as an example ready at hand. For him, the impression of a regulated coherence of space is a contingent matter that is open to transformative possibilities:

> Our taverns and our metropolitan streets, our offices and furnished rooms, our railroad stations and our factories appear to have us locked up hopelessly. Then came the film and burst this prison-world asunder by the dynamite of the tenth of a second, so that now, in the midst of its far-flung ruins and debris, we calmly and adventurously go travelling.[40]

Benjamin invokes the moving image's power to cognize otherwise, thereby contervening the extant ontology seemingly substantiated in the materiality of inherited social space. His destabilizations of a spatial epistemology that only seems to have us "locked up" is consistent with our view of spaces as indeterminate, localized, and temporary nodal points that are "essentially" un-fixed and productive of contestory possibilities based on juxtaposition, withdrawal, and dislocation.

A socio-spatial praxis consistent with this understanding will seek to liberate thought and action from the regulated coherence imposed by the ordered and monumentalized spaces of everyday experience. Resisting the power that organizes both social and spatial fields involves disidentifying space from this regulated coherence, and especially from that one opposition that forms the basis for further segmentations, namely, the distinction between "public" and "private" space. A spatial praxis of disidentification would work to disclose and circumvent the processes the verdict of which presumes to seal the fate of social space as private, and, as a corollary, as male, heterosexual, white, militarist, First World, etc.

Various tactics are already being deployed to circumvent dominant assumptions and practices of regulated spaces. These include any defacement, transgression, or occupation of space that: exposes as merely contingent systems of spatial representations; activates the presumably excluded power of the constitutive outside; or breaks through the "certain" alignments of space and identity. Examples of social movements that have practiced such tactics include: the Greenham Common's women's peace group camped at the border of a military installation in the United Kingdom; the interruption of religious services at New York's St Patrick's Cathedral by gay rights activists; and the cross-class, anti-gentrification struggle culminating in the Tompkins Square uprising in New York City in 1988.[41] In each of the above cases, spatial praxis consisted of defacement, transgression, or occupation of dominant space's meanings and practices. These actions served to expose space for what it *is*, a contingent, hegemonically maintained system of representation.

The examples listed above demonstrate that spatial praxis is necessarily site specific. Our choice of them should not, however, imply that social movements should be confined to the "merely" local, or to any boundary imposed by structured space. For in destabilizing the equation between space and identity, our aim is not simply to disidentify "certain" identities from "certain" spaces, but to spatially disidentify praxis itself. This becomes desirable inasmuch as one of the spatial effects of hegemony is the containment of spatial praxis, which locates and localizes resistance, thereby limiting the range of nodal points that can be articulated. The result of these localizations is a centered politics of both space and identity that leaves unrealized potential connections across space to other, similarly bounded, identities. A social movement that works against hegemony in all its forms must not only disidentify from the categories of identity processed by hegemony, it must also disidentify from the spaces in which it has been situated and maintained.

What we have called for "in theory" can already be found in the practices of those social movements and organizations that resist the categorical imperatives of hegemony. An additional example – perhaps a surprising one for those who look to metropolitan areas to provide the settings for such activities – is that of Appalshop, a multimedia, community-based cultural center whose activists have engaged in various forms of activities relevant to our discussion.[42]

Appalshop is located in Whitesburg, Kentucky, a town inhabited by 3,000 people in the Pine Mountain area of Appalachia. The coal industry has deeply etched itself underneath and on the (physical and social) surface of the area's landscape. A century of economic, social, and environmental exploitation in the region has resulted in rates of unemployment, poverty, and illiteracy that climb to over one-half of the population in many counties. Appalshop, which can trace its beginnings to a 1969 federal grant enabling the formation of media studies program for area youth, has produced films, music, plays, and worked with other media in order to document Appalachia's history of social struggle and to otherwise preserve and transmit mountain cultural traditions. This counterhegemonic effort was propelled by a recognition that the identity assigned the region and its inhabitants was forged by the hegemonic production of cultural stereotypes perpetuated to legitimate the theft of land and resources by the coal industry and its political agencies.[43] The image of ignorant, drunken, and duelling "hillbillies" drew upon a familiar nature-culture dichotomy, one which, in colonialism's history, has been activated in various settings to ideologically legitimate the "development" of colonized regions by outsiders, because these region's inhabitants, as "savages," were themselves disqualified. Appalshop productions were directed towards reanimating the region's traditions while refusing such images hegemonically assigned to it over the course of its exploitation. Thought much of Appalshop's productions over the course of the 25 years of its existence have worked to preserve Appalachian music, oral traditions, and other cultural practices – and in this sense have discovered alternative, positive views of "mountain life" – its productions also evidence an ever-increasing body of work that problematizes the very character of what it means to be in or from "Appalachia."[44] This tacit deconstruction of the categories of identity used to mark people and place has ensued in recognition of the diversity of social groups residing within Appalachia. In recent years, Appalshop productions have increasingly reflected the recognition that Appalachia, as a social space, has always been in transit. Appalshop films have imaged the limits on self-enclosure that waves of migration and diaspora have set, while historical excavation has uncovered the African and Native American influences on the area's cultural artifacts (even the quintessential instrument of Bluegrass music – the banjo – has its own history in Africa). Appalshop, while continuing to uncover neglected or nearly forgotten cultural traditions the recovery of which serve to deepen an appreciation of the multiple and multi-cultural identities out of which the region's culture has been shaped, has developed a series of programs which move beyond counterhegemonic resistance to categorically disidentify the region and its inhabitants from a self-enclosed identity.

Appalshop's spatial disidentifications have been furthered recently by its involvement with a series of regional, national and international cross-cultural exchanges. As part of the American Festival Project, for example, Appalshop's Roadside Theater has collaborated with other community-based theaters in the United States (as well as in Guatemala and Russia) which likewise are problematizing notions of identity. Along with the African-American "Junebug Productions" located in New Orleans, with "Taetro Pregones," a Puerto-Rican theater group from the South Bronx of New York, with the feminist African-American dance troupe "Urban Bush Women," also from New York, and with the Pueblo Zuni dancers of New Mexico, members of the Whitesburg community have found that they share with other communities economic and cultural suffering as the outcome of hegemonic disempowerment. These exchanges have not only pointed to how hegemony works by stratifying identifications in diverse locales, they have also demonstrated that global capitalism is each locale's constitutive outside, and, what is the same, that the alterity of areas like Appalachia constitute global capitalism itself.

Thus, "from within," Appalshop has aimed to denaturalize the hegemonic constructs of place-identity that have reinforced the disempowerment of most of the region's citizens. By reworking those extant traces that refuse the hegemonic identifications assigned the region, the area's tradition, has become, as Benjamin would have it, "thoroughly alive and extremely changeable." Towards the world "outside the mountains," meanwhile, Appalshop has pursued a national and international dialogue based on the principle that such dialogue best confronts the intersection of economy and culture at the grass roots level, from one community to another. What might have seemed an unlikely site for plural and multiple identity-constitution has via Appalshop become a promising exemplar of the productive uncertainty of identity/space equivalence.

Conclusion

Our discussion has deployed understandings of both hegemony and the constitutive outside in order to undermine the apparent naturalness, stability, and boundedness of identity. Stressing the inseparability of identity and space through the socio-spatial dialectic, we also have argued a similar understanding for space – both through the structuring processes that organize it and through its status as a disclosable object/sign system. The linkages we have made suggest that the deployment of essentialist categories of either identity or space will only reinforce the other's essentialization.

A nonessentialist stance toward social space – which for us includes space and identity in an ever open dialectic – thus points to a praxis that recognizes that no identity/space is so colonized by hegemony as to remove all traces of its organizing power. The form of resistance most antithetical to hegemony is one that refuses the emplacement of categorically designated identifications, while offering a potentially effective strategy for reconfiguring nodal points of both identity and space. In this regard, disidentification – even while generally thought of as being outside an economy of production – becomes a tactic that enables a refusal of concepts – e.g., the "private" and the "public" – that ground such economies.

The dual disidentification we have called for does not therefore depend upon or involve a "liberation" emanating from either the destruction of extant or the production of new (material) spaces, but an epistemological reconfiguration of "certain spaces" and "certain identities" in terms of their meanings and associated practices. Made more effective by recognition of the dialectical relationships between identity and space, the praxis commensurate with the epistemological transformation this affords will continue to denaturalize, expose, and contest the essentialization of both social and spatial categories. The epistemological recognition that "the postmodern" has definitively etched out in theory and to a considerable extent in academic discourse more broadly is one that can be linked to already extant social movements that have found similar, albeit differently phrased, reasons to reject a politics based either on foundationalism or on indifference. In refusing spatial orderings that reproduce structurally derived social categories, this praxis (and theory) will work to transform the structures and strictures of everyday space, while also reconfiguring the range of social identifications made possible by a politics of space.

Acknowledgments

The authors thank Ulf Strohmayer for his editorial comments on an earlier draft of this chapter, Caron Atlas of Appalshop for helpful discussions, and Sophie, Max, and Joseph for giving us reasons to think about the uncertainties that await.

Notes

1 Any effort to make sense of the character of the 'postmodern' will find it useful to differentiate the elements of its reception within the social sciences and the humanities. See *Postmodern Contentions: Epochs, Politics, Space*, John Paul Jones III, Wolfgang Natter and Theodore R. Schatzki, (eds), (New York, Guilford, 1993).

2 Difficult as it is to date the arrival of any intellectual tradition, it nevertheless seems clear the poststructuralism's emergence as a distinct theoretical shift owes much to the international symposium on 'The Languages and Sciences of Man', held at Johns Hopkins University in the autumn of 1966. The collected proceedings can be found in Richard Macksey and Eugenio Donato, (eds), *The Structuralist Controversy* (Baltimore, Johns Hopkins University Press, 1970).

3 Max Horkheimer, and Theodor Adorno, *Dialectic of Enlightenment*, translated by John Cumming (New York, Continuum, 1991), p. 219–20.

4 Michel Foucault, *The Order of Things* (New York, Pantheon, 1970).

5 Horkheimer and Adorno, *Dialectic of Enlightenment*, p. 7.

6 Horkheimer and Adorno, *Dialectic of Enlightenment*, p. 13.

7 Horkheimer and Adorno, *Dialectic of Enlightenment*, p. 145.

8 For feminist critiques of marxism, *see* Nancy C. M. Hartsock, *Money, Sex and Power* (Boston, Northeastern University Press, 1984); and Lydia Sargent, (ed.), *Women and Revolution: The Unhappy Marriage of Marxism and Feminism* (London, Pluto Press, 1981). For critiques of white feminism, *see*: Patricia Hill Collins, *Black Feminist Thought* (London, Routledge, 1991); bell hooks, *Ain't I a Woman: Black Women and Feminism* (Boston, South End Press, 1981), *Feminist Theory from Margin to Center* (Boston, South End Press, 1983), and *Talking Back: Thinking Feminist, Thinking Black* (Boston, South End Press, 1989).

9 Herbert Marcuse, 'Political Preface, 1966', in *Eros and Civilization* (Boston, Beacon Press, 1966).

10 Chantal Mouffe, 'Democratic Politics Today', in *Dimensions of Radical Democracy: Pluralism, Citizenship, and Community*, Chantal Mouffe, (ed.), (London, Verso, 1992), pp. 1–15, the quote is from p. 13.

11 Mouffe, 'Democratic Politics Today', p. 10–11.

12 For our interpretations of Mouffe's poststructuralist politics, especially as it pertains to 'radical and plural democracy', see, John Paul Jones III and Pamela Moss, 'Democracy, Identity, Space', *Society and Space*, vol. 13, no. 3, (1995), pp. 253–58 and Wolfgang Natter, 'Radical Democracy: Hegemony, Reason, and Time/Space', *Society and Space*, vol. 13, no. 3, (1995), pp. 267–74.

13 Ernesto Laclau and Chantal Mouffe, *Hegemony and Socialist Strategy: Towards a Radical Democratic Politics*, translated by W. Moore and P. Cammack (London, Verso, 1985).

14 Jacques Derrida, *Of Grammatology*, translated by Gayatri Chakravorty Spivak (Baltimore, Johns Hopkins University Press, 1974).

15 Peter Jackson and Jan Penrose, 'Introduction: placing "Race" and Nation', in *Constructions of Race, Place and Nation*, Peter Jackson and Jan Penrose, (eds). (Minneapolis, University of Minnesota Press, 1993), pp. 1–23.

16 Toni Morrison, *Playing in the Dark: Whiteness and the Literary Imagination* (Cambridge, Mass., Harvard University Press, 1992), p. 49.

17 Walter Benjamin, 'Theses on the Philosophy of History', *Illuminations*, Hannah Arendt, (ed.), (New York: Hartcourt, Brace, Jovanovich, 1968), p. 256.

18 Walter Benjamin, 'The Work of Art in the Age of Mechanical Reproduction', in *Illuminations*, p. 223.

19 Michel Pecheux, *Language, Semantics and Ideology* (New York, St. Martin's, 1975).

20 Rosemary Hennessy, *Materialist Feminism and the Politics of Discourse*, (London, Routledge, 1993), p. 96.

21 Morrison, *Playing in the Dark*, pp. 46–7.

22 Morrison, *Playing in the Dark*, pp. 39.

23 Edward Said, *Orientalism*, (New York, Pantheon, 1978).

24 Chantal Mouffe, 'Democratic Citizenship and the Political Community', in *Dimensions of Radical Democracy: Pluralism, Citizenship, and Community*, pp. 225–39; the quote is from p. 236.

25 Chantal Mouffe, 'An Interview with Chantal Mouffe', *disClosure*, no. 3, (1993), pp. 87–104.

26 *see*, for example: Michael Keith and Steve Pile, 'Introduction Part 2: The Place of Politics', in *Place and the Politics of Identity*, Michael Keith and Steve Pile, (eds), (London, Routledge, 1993), pp. 22–40; Doreen Massey, 'Politics and Space/Time', *New Left Review*, no. 196, (1992), pp. 65–84 and 'Thinking Radical Democracy Spatially', *Society and Space*, vol. 13, no. 3, (1995), pp. 267–74; and Wolfgang Natter, 'Radical Democracy: Hegemony, Reason, and Time/Space'.

27 Henri Lefebvre, *the Production of Space*, translated by David Nicholson-Smith (Oxford, Basil Blackwell, 1991). Also *see* Edward Soja, *Postmodern Geographies* (London, Verso, 1989).

28 According to the Russian formalist, Mikhail Bakhtin, verbal signs are never fixed but always an arena of struggle. Though dominant groups may attempt to fix the meaning of words in 'unitary language', all language operates as 'heteroglossia'; this multi-accentuality becomes apparent as various interests clash over the meaning of words. *See* his 'Discourse in the Novel', in *the Dialogic Imagination: Four Essays*, Michael Holquist, (ed.), translated by Caryl Emerson and Michael Holquist (Austin, University of Texas Press, 1981).

29 Our distinction between the *strategy* – a co-ordinated hegemonic assault – and the *tactic* – a resistance rooted in everyday practice – follows Michel de Certeau, *The Practice of Everyday Life* (Berkeley, University of California Press, 1984).

30 Lefebvre, *The Production of Space*, p. 33.

31 Jacques Derrida, 'Structure, Sign, and Play in the Discourse of the Human Sciences', in *the Structuralist Controversy*, pp. 247–65.

32 Horkheimer and Adorno, *Dialectic of Enlightenment*, p. 183. The full quote: 'The mere existence of the other is a provocation. Every "other" person who "doesn't know his place" must be forced back within his proper confines – those of unrestricted terror'.

33 bell hooks, 'Choosing the Margin as a Space of Radical Openness', in *Yearning: Race, Gender, and Cultural Politics* (Boston, South End Press, 1989), pp. 145–53.

34 John Paul Jones III, 'Making Geography Objectively: Ocularity, Representation, and *The Nature of Geography*', in *Objectivity and its Other*, Wolfgang Natter, Theodore Schatzki and John Paul Jones III, (eds), (New York, Guilford, 1995), pp. 67–92.

35 *See* Wolfgang Natter and John Paul Jones III, 'Signposts toward a Poststructuralist Geography', in *Postmodern Contentions: Epoch, Politics, Space*, John Paul Jones III, Wolfgang Natter and Theodore Schatzki, (eds), (New York, Guilford, 1993), pp. 165–203.

36 Rosalyn Deutsche, 'Boys Town', *Society and Space*, vol. 9, no. 1, (1991), pp. 5–30.

37 *See* Gunnar Olsson, 'Signs of Persuasion', in *Objectivity and its Other*, Wolfgang

Natter, Theodore Schatzki and John Paul Jones III, (eds), (New York, Guilford, 1995), pp. 21–32.

38 For a discussion of the alignments of meanings, practices, and identities in space, *see* Tim Cresswell, *In Place/Out of Place*, (Minneapolis. University of Minnesota Press, 1995).

39 Chantal Mouffe, 'Democratic Citizenship and the Political Community', p. 235.

40 Walter Benjamin, 'The Work of Art in the Age of Mechanical Reproduction', in *Illuminations*, Hannah Arendt, (ed.), (New York, Schocken, 1969), p. 236; for further discussion of the epistemological shifts made possible by cinema in reference to social space, *see*: Wolfgang Natter, 'The City as Cinematic Space: Modernism and Place in *Berlin, Symphony of a City*', in *Place, Power, Situation, and Spectacle*, Stuart Aitken and Leo Zonn, (eds), (Lanham, Maryland, Rowman and Littlefield, 1994), pp. 203–27.

41 *See*, respectively: Tim Cresswell, *In Place/Out of Place*; Lee Lucas Berman, 'The Spatial Politics of ACT UP', paper presented at the annual meeting of the Association of American Geographers San Francisco, California, 1994; and Neil Smith, 'New City, New Frontier: The Lower East Side as Wild, Wild, West', in *Variations on a Theme Park*, Michael Sorkin, (ed.), (New York, Noonday, 1992), pp. 61–93.

42 Appalshop is loosely linked to a number of organizations throughout Appalachia that have fought against economic and cultural domination. For descriptions of the activities of other groups, *see*: Stephen L. Fisher, (ed.), *Fighting Back in Appalachia: Traditions of Resistance and Change*, (Philadelphia, Temple University Press, 1993).

43 *See* Herbert Reid, 'Appalachian Policy, Social Values, and Ideology Critique', in *Policy Analysis: Perspectives, Concepts, and Methods*, William Dunn, (ed.), (Greenwich, Connecticut: JAI Press, 1986), pp. 203–22.

44 Recent Appalshop films include: *Fast Food Women*; *Beyond Measure: Appalachian Culture and Economy*; *Fighting for a Breath*; Justice in the Coalfields; and *Evelyn Williams* (a portrait of the African-American grassroots organizer working in West Virginia, Kentucky, and Brooklyn, New York).

6

Belonging: *Spaces of Meandering Desire*

Ulf Strohmayer

Whose mills does this stream activate? Who is utilising its power? Who dammed it? These are the questions which historical materialism asks, and it changes the picture of the landscape by naming the forces which have been operative in it.

Walter Benjamin

Points of Departure, or, the Here and Now of *Beginning*

The following essay seeks to analyse a question that is deceptively easy to phrase: what is the smallest unit of analysis within the human sciences? Or, to paraphrase only slightly, where is the original site of identity? With questions of identity now at the forefront of the agenda everywhere in the human sciences, such a query might need no justification; because no query prescribes the terrain in which one seeks answers, however, some introductory words are in order. For, although the question seems straightforward enough, it also masks one of the most fundamental circles within the human sciences: how can anyone write about identity without always already assuming one form of identity or another? Wherever we start analysing identities, we depart from that particular point only to take its properties for granted. In other words: we no longer question where we come from in order (finally) to begin. The following thoughts try their best to articulate this problem. They will do so by reversing the linearity of reading to which we all have become accustomed: rather than departing from some identity or another, this essay will continuously question its way backward towards its very own point of departure. It thus endeavours to approximate what Derek Gregory once aptly called the 'situation at the start'.[17] For most of us, I assume, this 'situation' comes in the form of a name: a word like the one we find in our letterheads. 'Geography' here formulates but one identity many of us find hard to question. Instead, we take it for granted that there is a world (out there somewhere: 'geos') and the possibility of a written discourse about it (a means to an end: 'graphos'). And more than that, for the unity of both is present as a representational mode of understanding, 'writing …(about) the world'. It was only after 'the postmodern challenge'[18] had been recognized as such that geographers learned fundamentally to question this unity and thus made different forms of knowledge respectable within and outside the discipline.

But critiques or challenges only every go so far. Eager to contribute to an ever-expanding canon of knowledge, the times to think and the spaces to reflect seem precious few. The following essay reclaims both. It argues that what is needed most urgently today is not the reintegration of critiques or challenges into the service of normal science, but a reflection on the roots of such service. Where does it stem from? What are its consequences? And where do we start *asking*?

Should we not start on common ground? *After postmodernism*, this can only mean to accept without further ado that we will not get outside of language: in talking about time, space and people within, we handle texts and act textually. In a word, we interpret the world, knowing full well that us 'the world' constitutes another text. Words, naming the landscape: words, forms of representation the meanings of which dwells on pre-existing traditions separating you and me from some obscure origin of discourse. *After postmodernism*, the myth of a reality 'out there' and hence open to consent turns lucid in the realization that whatever is 'out there' cannot be but words for us: merely words, material words, present to be used, always already, potentially pointing, but pointing in what direction? Where precisely is the geographical interpreter located in his or her everyday labour of signifying 'time' and 'space'?

And, most important, *where does all this take place?* What the following pages seek is consequently not a different answer to the endless quest of legitimizing scientific research, but a different question instead. Who is speaking? Where do we locate the one that speaks? What space does Descartes's *cogito* occupy? In short, what time, what space are we trying to frame, to render meaningful. Where is this space we cannot but take for granted to go anywhere in our quest for knowledge? To be a cause is to become self-sufficient: circular; is to start here and now with the least questioned of all scientific points of departure – the speaking or writing subject. Any wh*eye* implies a reason. *But even so*

Embarkation, or, the Here and Now of *Continuation*

> *some form of difference …is … here, is 'only a trace,'*
> *'(nur eine Spur),'[19] but a trace that has left its mark*
> *of change: like this white paper **here now** no longer is,*
> *human geography becomes another each time we write*
> *(about)it. It is simultaneously more and less than we*
> *would like it to be every time our understanding of*
> *ourselves reflects both upon the world and upon itself in a*
> *most fertile dance of knowledge. Which is why men like*
> *Descartes or Hegel, Marx and Comte, by framing*
> *experience in conceptual epistemologies, had to reveal*

more than they wanted to. As consciousness translates into self-consciousness, as we embark upon knowledge about ourselves, something new emerges. Taming this new has become the task we set ourselves. To think about was to think in – experience, meaning, interpretation. A number of closed circles emerged which are spiced well with prejudice and naturalness and which provided any reflection on the relationship between an individual and his or her experience with a multitude and no answers to the question of being. Trust reigns instead. The confidence in a subject whose coming-into-being is as circular a petitio principii as an inconspicuous 'o' in any 'cogito' tries to hide: an available, spaceless 'I am,' a pregiven but naked form that communication merely has to complete according to circumstances – 'You are ... what? Accountable?' Is that the question? In geography as in other scientific discourses – we ask, someone answers. Someone? Well, he does and she does. They do. Quite obviously the idea of an individual always already **there** *is founded on the discursive capability of that very subject: there is meaning in what the saying is about. By speaking, we distinguish, thus using language as a means of expression. Stated are not experiences, but representations instead – words, divided Saussurian algorithms in a world of 'barter.'[20] 'What did you say? Ah, yes ...', exchange- value. 'What the picture represents is its sense.'[21] Who is listening?*

The point of departure for any analysis in the human sciences, indeed in all of the sciences is thus revealed to be not a point but a circle instead. Inside this circle, someone speaks, writes and listens. But how to comprehend the speaking, the writing and the listening subject? Simply presupposing it won't do because we have recognized the ubiquitous possibility of critique everywhere in the social sciences. And yet, will we not have to presuppose 'the subject', will we not have to take some identity for granted, if only because *beyond* any 'cogito' to-be comprehended there cannot but be another framing and de-framing 'cogito' at work? Is not this presupposition the ultimate limit to knowledge?

Georg Wilhelm Friedrich Hegel thought different. In the context of nineteenth-century Idealism it was he who tried to think beyond the 'naturalness' of framing practices by exposing the necessary Kantian reduction from 'the thing-as-such' to the 'thing-for-us' as a backfiring 'circle of reciprocity'.[22] With ontological trust always entangled in every attempt at circumscribing and using the limits to knowledge, thinking this trust in turn without lapsing back into the mythical identity of a night 'in which ... all cows are black',[23] was to become young man Hegel's quest. It became a tightrope walk on a cracked circle, questioning the **mirror** as the model of representation long before Richard Rorty made this particular metaphor popular with all of us today: Thinking or seeing yourself never is enough because 'yourself' *itself* is merely another representation. A name repeated, a badge to recognize. In this game of substitution, the privileged place is held by the tautological sentence. In itself taught to be no further representation, 'I am I', 'a tree is a tree', or the more abstract 'a = a' all are true by virtue of positive identity – the mirror works, negating a separating space only to create selfsameness as the edge of certain experience: 'A tautology's truth is certain …'.[24] At no scale is knowledge more certain or immediate, nowhere else can serve as a point of departure. However, not even this certainty of the most general of generalities can work on its own spaceless logic. Almost a century before Ferdinand de Saussure thought about the diacritical nature of signs and names, it was Hegel who pointed towards this insufficiency of the tautological phrase. While staring ourselves blind with both eyes on either side of the equality sign, we take for granted the way this symbol works: *giving* identity. 'A proposition, as something posited by reflec- tion, is something limited and conditioned on its own account. It requires another proposition as its foundation, and so on *ad infinitum*.'[25] I am I because I am not You, and any immediate identity falls back into a mere idealism of wishful thinking – 'Ego *ought* to be equal to Ego …':[26] faith as a modern virtue. Beyond this trust, understanding any tautology calls for a rather different way of looking at the equality sign and at the space it grants. 'Being' now becomes a spatial movement *in itself*, a gesture of differences.[27] As experience stretches, the alienation that is built into the fabric of tautological certainty initiates an exceedingly beautiful phenomenological journey through the becoming of dialectical knowledge. Across the skin and into the I. Transformations of the obvious, both Hegel's 'Phenomenology' and 'Logic' set out from the immediate generality of concepts only gradually to unmask their tautological incomplete- ness – in formulating the experience of consciousness and a reflection on being, both these complementary narratives transcend the given realm of identity and the taken-for-granted point of departure. 'Entzweiung', the 'splitting open' of the one that requires another to be recognizably one,[28] is the source of Hegelian discourse. The very moment I think I am, I experience myself different; the conscious act seeking knowledge or certainty negates the immediacy of con- sciousness, 'hebt auf', (annuls). An opposition arises out of an earlier identity; and this *by necessity*: ( ) identity could not sustain itself on its own, but had to breed opposition. Initiated by doubt talking tautology turns out to embrace a mediated process of alienation: consciousness becomes consciousness *of* the self only in **space**. In itself, the subject never is for itself and once the unquestioned hyphen of the 'I' is rearing its behind, subject turns into object – *I* am. Alienated in this generality, I know, with the uniqueness of my, and only my, immediate identity being transformed into the abstractness of the 'genus.'[29] The resulting '*Unhappy Consciousness*' writes Hegel, 'is the consciousness of self as a dual-natured, merely contradictory being'.[30] Foreign in the formality of the I, the tension of difference creates desire, 'Begierde', as the longing for recognition: 'Tell me that I am'. Only this confirmation will translate the alien I into my I, will prove identity in difference or 'the unity of itself in its otherness'. [31] Outside of space and without the other, I am lost. Tautology, in other words, is not a private language but essentially social instead. In space, experiences meet to create knowledge. Transforming the taken-for-granted, the epistemic path of the Hegelian dialectic reveals a split individual, constituting him- or herself time and again anew in her narrative. The discursive subject is the subject of desire: signified by what is lost and unfolding his or her story as they long for the substitute of social recognition. Desire speaks and in language we desire. Representation's recognition. Tell me. Who is performing?

Desidero ergo sum. I desire therefore I am. In desire the speaking subject thus reconciles itself with itself. As the slave realizes his master's dependency on him, desire becomes reason through the labour of the famous third 'Aufhebung'. 'It is man himself who poses God. Man recognizes the master, but that recognition emanates from him. In posing himself as the lowest he is the highest'.[32] Resurrection revisited: Le roi est mort, vive le roi. Far from representing a straightforwardly paradox 'Münchhausen God',[33] this passage comprises Hegel's answer to the question of (individual) identity precisely *because* its logic is satisfying: different I am. Dialectical identity, in other words, here comes home again through the creation of objective contradiction. 'Difference in general is contradiction *in itself*.'[34] Which is to say that the all-embracing generality of the 'I' that experiences alienation 'is' in fact 'itself' throughout the Hegelian journey, rendered possible by an idealized absolute difference, an identical negativity.[35] How else could desire hide reason following the movement of a cracked circle if not connected with a personal pronoun? Ends don't meet directly, but a spiral the path is (not a Tinguely sculpture), a spiral within linear space. Once desire is identified, the subject knows its way about. 'Difference' here functions in the same manner than 'identity' did function earlier. A different scale, a different, albeit now spatial, point of departure, the same logic repeated elsewhere. While the Kantian transcendental reduction of experience could achieve its goal of saving moral freedom only at the price of turning 'terrorist with the ban on thinking the absolute',[36] Hegel followed the opposite path. Instead of arriving at a formulation of valid entities, the general spacelessness of the tautological 'I' by necessity presupposes the stable difference between You and Me: created in the antithetical rupture of consciousness and self-consciousness, desire becomes the symbol of particularity and drive for knowledge in one. It becomes, in other words, a permanent mediator between individual and society; identify your desire and the means are yours to transcend it. Speak. Think. And see what happens to your I (for yours it is). In Hegel, nothing *happens*. A haunting necessity occurs instead: inevitably 'the incoherence of one concept (...) demonstrates the indispensability of the next',[37] not difference, but conceptual negativity forms the focus of speculative thought. 'Aufgehoben' is this particular *only* in meeting the requirement of negative identity, thus entering the logic of what Lyotard once called a 'dialectical syllogism'.[38] Desire expires in submission the moment it is recognized, the moment it contributes to the construction of a recognizable identity in difference, thus ruling out the possibility of truly being different. In his encyclopedic effort, Hegel's 'deification of what is', to quote Adorno,[39] curries favour with its Marxian headstand and positivistic castration in general – 'far from being a denial of external reality, [Hegel's idealism] is the strongest affirmation of it; it not only exists, but necessarily exists'.[40] The question seems pertinent: have we been on this long journey, only to reinforce the Kantian formalism? Have we departed from one commonly accepted identity only to resurrect it through the back door? Not quite, since the difference of experience in Hegel is the difference of a fragile becoming in space, despite its instant drowning in the spirit of a conceptual expression. The problem, as Hyppolite states, is that 'nothing remains'[41] in this teleological knowledge: everything, even desire, has its place.

My desire. Cracked as it is, and thus leaving space for individual alienation, still the Hegelian mirror of representation works, facilitating the identification of desire by means of a speculative discourse. 'In its object, consciousness reaches itself,'[42] not in the form of a Kantian Ding-an-sich, but just the same presupposing a beyond, a tin-foil fitting negative representation. Exiled on Main Street I know my place. To reflect is to see: oneself; is to experience contradiction in experiencing experience – a mesmerism of repetitive representation. When God made Adam, Michelangelo figured, he touched him. A gesture. No repetition. And stories to come. But in the beginning was

Dwelling across space, the merging dialectical geography of discourse thus turns milky the moment it is conceived, conceptually transforming the assumed role of a pure mediator into the constitutive element of my becoming. No language outside of space – and thus no desire either. And yet, we need to ask over and again, what kind of space empowers the unfolding of the dialectical journey of desire, establishing a subject, establishing you and me: any 'I' along its path? Preparing the ground for the permanently feasible homecoming of an alienated consciousness, singular space must be more than just linear space; its linearity must furthermore be a shared one, maintained in language and through time – circularity, never in danger of breaking loose, thus forms an ideal axis of progress around which the trip (the discourse) takes place. In speaking, the alienated I occupies its place, finds it, ᵗ/makes it home. It is important to note that the stage is thus set already before Hegel begins his tale, a stage which facilitates the possibility of a self-identical subject in space. Encompassed, always already, desire is bound to become 'aufgehoben' sooner or later within the frame of shared space. The curtain raises for science to replace the witches, 'the science of Spirit determining itself in itself as a subject for itself,'[43] merely mirroring *topological presence*, the mythical locus of self-reflexivity. 'Importantly, the Hegelian subject is not a self-identical subject who travels smugly from one ontological place to another. It *is* its travels and *is* every place in which it finds *itself.*'[44] This pre-established metaphysical **place**, the **space** every (alienated) individual fits into, can take possession of, from hence allows for a certain conceptualization of meaning: meaning here emerges as a truth which *can* be transported from one stable place to another, and which can thus become the object of scientific interpretation. Outside this place, outside, mind you, not of language but of the personal pronoun, 'the nonidentical remnants' prove to be nothing but – 'accidental',[45] No surprise then, that we find the most faithful re-presentation of the Hegelian discourse in the work of Sigmund Freud. Given his task of legitimizing the scientific nature of working beyond the standards of perceptible, positivistic objectivity, Hegel's conception of **space** *as* **place** prepared the path towards the *sub*conscious. The split 'I' here finds itself thrown into a topography of triads, and reading the text of the patient becomes the task of the analyst who in the process uncovers the waiting truth behind slips of the tongue. Hence Oedipus points towards exile as the place of 'uncertain certainty',[46] of presence (da) in absence (fort), points towards *his place?*

Unmasking the presentations of formal tautology as yet another representation in a world of appearances, both Hegel's and Freud's discourse of the I present: itself. 'Le language est l'être-là de l'esprit,' 'Language is the being-here of the spirit'[47] Là, da, here – a glove to slip in with form fitting place. Fenced in by contradiction, discourse becomes sacrosanct and totalizing. Leftovers turn into chance (a trace in the gutter). Once more the ontology of the borderline claims truth. To trespass is to sin now that the masters have thrown away their ladders. Between claustrophobia and madness the mirror is set: transparent except for the foil behind. Is such the nature of (dialectical) identity? 'Imprisoned again:'[48] 'But that's me,' you say whilst looking into a mirror, thus multiplying your confidence in formal representations. Not only does the mirror work, naming the reflection retains identity, through positive tautology or negative contradiction. 'But that's not me' ...Partners in standardisation, optical trust again meets language, tying together original and replica around a dash.

Plate 6.1 *The Creation of Adam*, Michelangelo Buonarroti. 1508–12. Sistine Chapel, Rome.

A hidden dash, for hardly ever do we think about the foil behind or the Saussurian bar between – on the edge, identity is created and preserved in time. Reap, eat it. And in language you are. What if desire remained silent?

Language, space and desire – such is the frame of our approach to the smallest unit of analysis in the human sciences. Different I am, ever-changing yet unambiguously represented; the form of my I, leaving a footprint wherever I go, and perfectly matching the progressing original. '[D]ifference threatens the subject with annihilation until the subject can discover that difference as an essential moment of itself.'[49] But there's mud on the road to truth, spoiling the very possibility of a Hegelian recognition prior to experience: 'knowing yourself differently' presupposes the discourse about separating distances to keep – both in its signs and symbols – the assumed and necessary linearity of Cartesian space. The resulting idea of language as a mediator, as a tool, a neutral means of expression still was to form the solid base of Hegelian thinking – the art was to make the match perfect, to distil the synthesis out of every dialectical journey, or, to represent in words the loss a subject was experiencing. Once you detected both their unambiguous places inside and outside the mirror, directing desire towards the reconciliation of 'I' and 'Other' could no longer fail to reach its destination. But in language, no subject ever is at home. Once the mutual recognition of consciousness and self-consciousness no longer is conceived as taking place in the idealistic void of a self-identical, metaphysical space, form and identity suddenly encompass choices to be made on either side of the dialectical zeropoint. Both now become firmly tied to questions about the presence ('placeness') of space: Any represented I, be it of tautological positivity or of negative, alienated characteristics, not only is separated from, but furthermore split in, itself. A fundamental instability thus becomes legible, a different conception of the geography of discourse: beyond a granted home, it is precisely *the difference space makes* which carries the 'I', makes it fray, referring to some Other that never will know my place for sure. Not being a neutral stage on which a consciousness could become the alienated consciousness of the self, **space** rather **is constitutive of being and of being differently at the same time,** thus creating a presence in language that 'present' never will be. Without the possibility of speaking to myself, of knowing 'myself' privately ('(...) for what would there be to know?'[50]) does silence become the only place to dwell outside the forever slipping 'lure of spatial identification?'[51]

It starts that way, does it not? Not exactly silent, but nonetheless without a concept of separate identity. Thrown into a world not of his or her own making, the infant still is – unrepresented, beyond the scope of a personal pronoun. Without words to personify needs, the world has to search for an intention behind each particular bodily movement. **When space has no meaning, no subject can be:** *but once 'I' am, once space has established the specificity of my being, the expressed identity of myself in space becomes a place of alienation.* Pushing Hegel's framework to its logical extreme, the attempt of locating a place for desire was to become the lifelong quest for Jacques Lacan. It is not in the emptiness of a philosophical speculation that the discourse of the I comes into being; for Lacan, this journey has a place in language and a time in the unfolding of human ontogenesis: *because* space has no meaning to a new-born human being is there no language and thus no desire either. But the moment the transition into language has been left behind, once the youngster expresses (knows) what he or she wants, it is precisely the meaning attached to space that will henceforth keep desire from being satisfied, aufgehoben. It is literal(ly) space that is separating – me. Creating a social subject is the name of the game, not as a further trait added to a mystical cogito, but as a simultaneous, concurrent creation and alienation in(to) form. A slanting logic, unfolding most conventionally in Lacan's early 1936 speech 'Le stade du mirroir' ('The mirror stage'). What is happening, *taking place*, Lacan pondered, the moment a child recognizes an image in a mirror as a representation of itself? Interestingly, this 'Aha-Erlebnis' of recognition does not occur straight from birth, but only some time thereafter. Sooner or later, the infant suddenly smiles in a moment of 'primary narcissim',[52] moving 'from a fragmented body-image to a form of its own totality',[53] thus recognizing him- or her Self in the mirror. The moment space becomes meaningful ('there!') allows for a view of my distinct totality – compared to experiencing bodily fragments –, but does so at the price of recognizing myself elsewhere ('there?'). Here/there – only by moving **across space** does the infant become a conscious being, 'an experience that leads us to oppose any philosophy directly issuing from the cogito',[54] and disclosing 'an ontological structure of the human world'. [55] Striving to overcome this **constitutive gap** will henceforth motivate the acts of the self. A strive, which becomes desire only after 'the deflection of the specular I into the social I',[56] after the self learns to name the place of identification and 'represents itself by a "stand-in"'.[57] Twofold in space, the now re-presented self becomes an entity, a subject for itself and thus an object for others: *I* am ('Je suis'), but that's *me* in the mirror ('C'est moi – là'). Lacan's point is obvious. Not only – as Hegel has shown – is space necessary for the constitution of any tautological I, even within the resulting dialectical, negative movement, is there no way to eliminate space: the 'origin' is spoiled, always already, and thus little less than – misplaced. Unreconciled but striving, we are thrown into language, alienated into the ego. A place to be, the I becomes a harbour hosting desire only to the point at which acts are interpreted as a series of individual appropriations of specific places in a given context. You are what you are, neuroses included. '[S]ocial relations are fixed in the same process by which the subject is produced, able to predicate an outside. It is ideology which necessitates the limiting of this relation to a specific predicate; it produces a specific articulation which necessitates a certain subject for its meanings.'[58]

Beyond this effective, if arbitrary, fixation into form, is there still a place for truth to be?

Space enough – though never unrepresented. To place the name of the self thus signals the moment when 'consciousness collapses into its double':[59] in and by language, 'the double phenomenon of the division of the subject engenders the unconscious'.[60] Represented I am ... elsewhere, different. And yet, lacking a framed self as my point of origin and smallest unit of analysis, 'elsewhere' cannot be anywhere but $^{1}/_{h}$ere. A distorted image in the mirror of language, the unconscious loses its Freudian box like character, storing avoided remembrances of times past and becomes a language itself, 'composed of signifiers'[61] 'whose "topography" can be defined by the Saussurian algorithm'[62] a place 'beyond tautology'.[63]

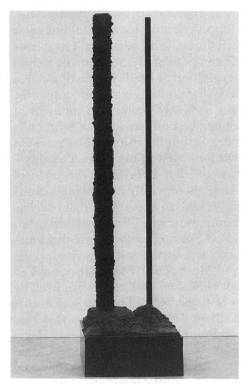

Plate 6.2 *Here I*, Barnett Newman. 1951/62. ©Moderna Museet, Stockholm.

A *place*? 'What one ought to say is: I am not wherever I am the plaything of my thought; I think of what I am where I do not think to think.'[64] Vintage Lacan, this thought, but contrary to common consent 'the subject does not "disappear" in Lacan's hands',[65] rather 'man speaks, ... but it is because the symbol has made him man'[66] – leaving traces in language. **Abandoned places**, are(n)as of alienation, slipping, sliding ..., never matching, since 'the signifier acts separately from its signification and without the subject being aware of it'.[67] 'The identity of the subject, then, is a kind of prosthesis. Something added, something that did not exist at birth that helps you to stand up straight within yourself. It is a carefully located form, the form of the totality of the body, which the child sees for the first time in the mirror. There is no doubt that it finds plenty to laugh about. And there is plenty to laugh about in this farce, specific to the human species. For in obtaining its identity, the child in fact only manages to achieve identification .... The subject will never be truly 'himself'. He will be the son of, the sister of, the cousin of, the lover of, the friend of. He will become stuck in the affections of others, in which he will be not himself but another – an other man, an other woman.'[68]

Mirror-space, space in language – where do we, where do I meet? Where do we depart from every time we seek knowledge? What can we rely upon? Exiled from that place which never was one but a distance between, the symbolic identity of the I becomes a signifier of displacement: a substitute in space and itself replaced time and again anew. Chains of association, metonymical movements – driven by a desire that is 'eternally stretching'[69] for an absent place. It is within substitutions that we think we are, constantly being forced to repeat what never has been the same only to produce fetishes in discourse. **Finally spaceless**, desire can be instrumentalized in the realm of a generalized totality – play it again, Sam, turn the spool. Timeless repetition, the creation of the 'all too evident',[70] preparing the way for what Lacan saw fit to call the Phallus, the Law, the Object, in short, for 'that which denies the lack, that which fills the empty space'.[71]

Pornographic space

Without a place that permanently harbours a subject, discourse now becomes a movement beyond Hegelian certainty. 'There is no truth that, in passing through awareness, does not lie. But one runs after it all the same.'[72] What, then, do we meet in this uncartesian space? Something we would like to call fragments, only to oppose this 'something' to totalities. In other words: traces of truth, potentially incoherent, unsymmetrical and as representations all too open to scientific (mis-)interpenetration. Irreplaceable space, unmatchingly represented – and the circle is broken more than once along the way. Instead of a plain, logical, Euclidean geometry preparing the table for the feast of Descartes, we are now dealing with ' a topology of knots',[73] representations of space that do not allow 'to divide things up into an inner and an outer reality',[74] about which the child laughs. 'Laughter is the quality unique to man.'[75]

As is desire. In lack of a defined goal, unoriginal, desire becomes 'the desire for desire'[76] and thus a threat, rather than a source of motivation, to the speaking self. Constantly kicking the subject out of its social balance, desire makes itself heard between pre-established forms, **between places** and thus forever slipping into discourse. Where no identity remains identical, desire makes us aware of the difference. Truth consequently loses itself constantly in some elsewhere beyond its referential gestures: 'man's desire is the desire of the Other',[77] is truth in the margin, or, ' a truth that has not said its last word',[78] a wit, a dream, grotesque representations of unpresent, possible places. In this movement which permeates both mirror and language, satisfaction is kept in a permanent state of postponement, without a metalanguage to be(come) written in. Yet in no way is desire dumb: 'the first thing to make itself heard is the void';[79] manifesting a different language to listen to, a language beyond the realm of trusted categories, which thus reveals 'those toponymical inscriptions which a geographical map, lest it remain mute, superimposes on its design, and which may become the object of a guessing game: who can find the names chosen by a partner? – noting immediately that the name most likely to foil a beginner will be one which, in large letters spaced out widely across the map, discloses, often without an eye pausing to notice it, the name of an entire country.'[80] 'The nature of language plays with us';[81] once more Martin Heidegger will have been here before, a trace himself, bridging human intentionality. And indeed, it is not by vainly focusing on the centre, but rather by revolving around the edges, that we are likely to meet the framing modalities of a meaningful subject in discourse. The borderline between, the tain of the mirror, Saussure's bar – assumptions hidden behind the spoken, reasonable word: it is against the grain that 'desire must be taken literally';[82] 'ça pense,[83] 'ça parle',[84] filling the space inside a language game.

Skate on. In crossing the bar constantly from either side, in writing the unconscious, what do we write? 'The ethics of a speech'[85] in a finally liberated, mimetical kind of language? Perhaps, and yet: mimetic (authentic) to what? If the idea is to write this so-called souture the best we can, that engendering split into the self, into a representation 'missing from its place',[86] does not the question somehow remain – from what place are we missing? What, again and again, is the original site of this search for a genuine unit of analysis? Is there an exile without a home and has there been a place before the space between? (On the ceiling of the Sistine.)

Over and again our point of departure thus sets about a progressing narrative, encircling a hidden origin – '[T]he real problem is to understand precisely why the child recognises himself and not someone else in his place.'[87] A narcissistic taken-for-granted, bringing progress to the not-yet (but soon-to-be) linguistic realm: perhaps 'Hegel is not so easily dismissed, even by those who claim to be beyond him'.[88] The idea of writing beyond Hegel, writing a possible representation of meaning outside any system of necessity, pushes the question as to how Lacan himself escapes the trap of a 'constant re-absorption'.[89] The difference would seem to be a difference in desire: in Hegel, we are faced with a desire of awareness, *aufgehoben* in the 'conjunction of the symbolic with a real',[90] while in Lacan we read about a suspended desire, which is pointing towards 'the cut in discourse'.[91] On the one side do we find Hegelian indispensability, while Lacan laments 'I would to heaven it were so, but (...) indeed, a number of cracks to be heard confusedly in the great consciousness responsible for some of the outstanding changes in physics remind us that, after all, for this knowledge as for others it is **elsewhere** that the hour of truth must strike'.[92] Our search for identity has thus arrived at the idea of a discontinuous subject, which can be captured only in passing through a discontinuous language, yet whence this idea of 'capturing' at all? Why, in other words, should we (or anyone, for that matter) favour a certain and specifically different way of looking at the world if not in the end to present a better representation of what is? A goal, *mimesis*: caught up again in negativity, belonging to, progressing towards and tracing truth. 'I am ... another'[93] – nothing less than the ontology of desire, or the mirror prior to its expression in terms of **possible spatiality**, is at stake in this act of writing a difference. The aporia of positing: meaningful you are, however non-identical your claims may be? The significance of the signifier reveals structuralist remainders in Lacan: though originally *dis*-placed, Lacan's subject still is able to identify a loss in the traces of *its own* discourse and thus to attach meaning to it. Who is speaking ... in-between, on the bar, what *is* expressed – or, without souture who would be? 'The representative of representation in the absolute condition is at home in the unconscious, where it causes desire.[94] Thus desire can become a carrier of truth, the signifier of a locus of resistance against the self-evidence of a spoken I 'in which the living being would be annihilated, if desire did not preserve its part in the interferences and pulsations that the cycles of language cause to converge on him'.[95] Though placeless, Lacan's space still has a **vanishing point** of orientation. To lose one's Self *there* is eventually to become a real subject, 'aufgehoben' in a coexistence of places and times. No place of departure, yet spaces of destination: 'the female orgasm represents, within the entire body of his work and thought, the absolute culmination: *there* theory ends'.[96] Elsewhere, but stable the world *is not*.

Ent-fernung: fort/da; framing an economy of perception. What's on the canvas, Velázquez? Las Meninas and a stare. No ...not that one, the other one. Stuck in representation, desire always walks, elliptically and quoting and

within 'the scenography that makes representation feasible (...), that is, the architectonics of its theatre, its framing in space-time, its geometric organisation, its props, its actors, their respective positions, their dialogues, indeed their tragic relations, without overlooking the mirror, most often hidden, that allows the subject, to re-duplicate itself, to reflect itself by itself.'[97]

'The *one* of form',[98] the value of presence (or place) 'in the course of time':[99] 'spell and ideology are one and the same':[100] 'forcing, doctoring, abridging, omitting, suppressing, inventing, falsifying'.[101]

But desire there is, is there not? Be it *in* **space** and distanced across places, or *by* **space** and lacking the means to express an impossible home, both the Hegelian and the Lacanian subject trails some form of original identity which will allow its desire to be transformed into a 'transcendental signifier'.[102] '[T]he other will remain the place'[103] where in presence history unfolds as a progressing narrative of (metonymical) substitution. Spreading itself across space – the space of a mirror – the subject gets lost in traceable locations. And desire. there. is. Il y a. Es gibt. What the German everyday language allows to hide, the English reveals: the taken-for-granted possibility of fixing being to a place in presence. There simply is no tradition without some ontology behind: here. there, now and then; the rest is for the witches. A 'topo-logical arrangement',[104] as Derrida once called this kind of guarantor of identities, that allows for a signification that keeps seemingly specific structures intact. Coming from, going to, arkhē and telos, it is indeed the idea of *progress* that

_____*is*. ('*indeed*'). Here? In these lines? Does every text have to be pretentious?

turns problematic in our I's. Embedded in an eschatological framework, progress will have been the progress of prediction and control with the syllogism of logic formulating its credo. Locating and relocating appropriated and from hence fetishized objects ('reducing the other to the Other of the Same',[105] ready to be sold, ready to be copied), the act of whoresipping reliable ready-made™ becomes the prerequisite of writing a progressing history. In other words: we assume identities where thought alone would force us to persist questioning them. 'Men had to do fearful things to themselves before the self, the identical, purposive, and virile nature of man, was formed, and something of that recurs in every childhood. The strain of holding the I together adheres to the I in all stages; and the temptation to lose it has always been there with the blind determination to maintain it.'[106] Progress that never was, a subject which only is (present) elsewhere, asymmetrically represented: if coherence can be obtained only at the cost of violating the non-identical, making it linear and putting it into place – perhaps we shall never be able to talk meaningfully without this act of drawing a borderline? The choice seems to be either to exercise power and, consciously or otherwise, castrate the richness of possibilities into form, or to stay on the margin, concentrating on the place in language wherein that very same power is generated. If a 'choice' it is: 'reality present, then, or reality represented, this alternative is itself derived from a prior model'.[107] No world, no self ever comes unrepresented, and thus the search is for a place beyond the certainty of the I, beyond an ontology that allows us to posit tautologies within dialectical symmetries, beyond that which inevitably leads to 'the serene demonstration of the fact that there are two sides to everything'.[108] On the margin, between difference – this is the site of

Plate 6.3 *Man Pointing*, Alberto Giacometti. 1947. Tate Gallery, London. © DACHS London.

Derrida's *'différance'*,[109] an everslipping and unprogressive concept. Not the positing of 'presence' or 'absence', but the space between, an ambiguous place, framing 'or' and 'and' in one picture (to be looked at elsewhere). What makes a place, if not the palimpsest-like characteristics it is expressing, written 'sous rature' and constantly supplementing …itself with itself and myself with myself. 'Belatedness'[110] (or 'thrownness') formulates the a priori condition of discourse; '3 is what makes 2 into the impossibility of 1 …',[111] which is to say that 'no meaning can be determined out of context, but no context permits saturation'.[112] Always already is there a mirror and thus any attempt at writing beyond it can only formulate another 'negative theology'[113] assigning another original place, when the art would be to write: mirrors. Transitions, footnotes, trying to capture something of that space between, and beyond the formality of a paradox. The place of proof. 'What is.' **'Where is.'** The form of a question already implies an ontology of presence framing the geography of its discourse. But truth does not dwell. No only is there always a possibility for a specific proof not to coincide with the truth it is trying to become, in language is there moreover no measure to experience whether or not they match to start with – the alienation of the scientific proof becomes the signifier of exile. 'Vermessen, entmessen, verortet, entwortet, entwo.'[114] *Difference, not lack or desire is thus the naked and unconditioning condition of possibility of every act of comprehension.* And yet (again). What does it mean to write a fragment capable of tracing an I that will have been 'not here'. Does not the representation of ~~a place~~ in turn become **'a place'**? Thus, necessarily and '[f]or us, différance remains a metaphysical name, and'[115] ' the presentation contained, the event, the "There is" is a secret'.[116] Layers of layers without any 'true essence of difference?'[117] 'The midday-friend, – no, do not ask me who; at midday't was, when one became as two?'[118] Perhaps. The question is not so much whether or not there is an absolute (identity) – for even if there were, its non-placeable characteristics would not be ours to name –, but how we handle the slippery yet fundamental materiality of whatever remains. Once we acknowledge that our initial question whether or not there is a genuine expression of identity is a meaningless one since we cannot access it, once we accept that 'there is no (...) common ground, all we can do [then] is to show how the other side looks from our point of view'.[119] In different words: 'Linguistic quixotry has become obligatory, since the putting-together of each sentence contributes to the decision whether language as such, ambiguous since primeval times, will succumb to commercialism and the consecrated lie that is part of it, or whether it will make itself a sacred text by diffidence towards the sacral element on which it lives.'[120] Writing something resembling a fragment, writing the I, will still form a text, but a text that does not pretend to be a coherent whole, a one-to-one match with some identity or another. Without the illusion of a totality present, the stage is set for the deconstruction of the 're-', signifying the interchangeability of representations in a singular place (or of one representation in different places): repetition. 'It no longer even enters our heads that all these things we have known so long might be different ...'.[121] Homo ludens or homo faber, why should we mutilate the limited means we are given even more ...

Endings

And Geography? 'Denied an "outside", or window looking through representations on to a world beyond it',[122] where do we go from here? Where in fact are we? Even within the pregiven epistemological realm of categories designed to fit the social world, the fit never is perfect and already the slightest modification in scale – be it in space or time – reveals the impotence implied in that very practice. The alternative may be barely legible by now, on the border, in-between – infrastructures; that which changes the landscape of places, disrupts and combines the geography of discourse. Here and there, without an origin: going from, going to, and any road leads to more than one goal. Just like the space of the I never was (itself), 'infrastructural accounting'[123] will not inhabit the pre-established space of logic but rather spread itself across 'a hinge picture that, as it opens out or folds back, physically and mentally, shows us other vistas, other apparitions of the same elusive object'.[124] Traces of difference, the art of writing the world. Outside the categorical presumption, plenty of space for contexts to collide or snuggle up – making room for modes of expression across the destitute division of an independent scientific and artistic realm. Writing: differently, 'it nonetheless posits a thesis'[125] (no picture without a frame, if only for the wall behind), but a thesis that tries to leave space for the inexpressible to become. A modest thesis, a thesis that will not claim. 'Art is magic, delivered from the lie of being truth';[126] why not write a geography that lends its pencils to a pointing gesture towards those abandoned places where truth will have been, a geographical language without (pre-)fixed references. The art is to cut the frame (Modigliani the geographer): 'the invisible is not obscure or mysterious, it is transparent ...'[127] Go slowly. Leave blank, leave ... space for transitions, passages – 'La porte du mystère, une défaillance humaine l'ouvre, et nous voilà dans les royaumes de l'ombre. Il y a dans le trouble des lieux de semblables serrures qui ferment mal sur l'infini',[128] 'the infinity of difference'.[129] Any other place could only be inhabited by nothing but

another. God[130]

'escaping' from Hegel

Acknowledgments

The preceding essay owes its existence to the generosity and patience of Tony Cutler, Peter Gould and Gunnar Olsson. Furthermore, I would like to thank Felix Driver and Tim Cresswell for helpful comments and critiques.

References

Adorno, Th. W. *Negative Dialectics*, [ND],
  e English version – trans. E. B. Ashton. New York: Seabury, 1973.
  g original German version – {'Negative Dialektik'}, Frankfurt am Main: Suhrkamp, ³1982.
Adorno, Th. W. *Minima Moralia*, [MM],
  e – trans. E.F.N. Jephcott, London: New Left Books, 1974.
  g – {dto.}, Frankfurt am Main: Suhrkamp, 1951.
Aragon, L. *Le paysan de Paris*. Paris: Gallimard, 1926.
Asenjo, F. G. *In Between. An essay on Categories*. Washington, D. C.: University Press of America, 1988.
Bär, E. S. 'Understanding Lacan.' In *Psychoanalyse and Contemporary Science*, ed. L. Goldberger and V. H. Rosen, Vol. III. New York: Grore, 1974.

Benjamin, W. *Briefe*, ed. Th. W. Adorno and G. Scholem. Frankfurt am Main: Suhrkamp, 1966.

Benjamin, W. *Charles Beaudelaire. A lyric poet in the era of high capitalism*, trans. H. Zohn. London: New Left Books, 1976.

Benjamin, W. *Das Passagenwerk*, 2 Vols. Frankfurt am Main, 1983.

Berman, R. 'Modern Art and Desublimation.' *Telos* no. 62, 1984/84.

Bernstein, R. *Praxis and Action*. Philadelphia: University of Pennsylvania Press, 1971.

Bloom, H. 'The Breaking of Form.' In *Deconstruction and Criticism*, ed. H. Bloom et.al. New York: Seabury Press, 1979.

Bowie, M. 'Jacques Lacan.' In *Structuralism and Since*, ed. J. Sturrock. Oxford: Oxford University Press, 1979.

Bowie, M. *Freud, Proust and Lacan: Theory as Fiction*. Cambridge: Cambridge University Press, 1987.

Bréton, A. *Premier Manifeste du Surréalisme*. Paris: Gallimard, 1924.

Bryson, N. *Tradition and Desire*. Cambridge: Cambridge University Press, 1984.

Butler, J. *Subjects of Desire. Hegelian Reflections in twentieth-century France*. New York: Columbia University Press, 1987.

Casey, E. S., Woody, J. M. 'Hegel, Heidegger, and Lacan.' In *Interpreting Lacan*, ed. J. H. Smith and M. Kerrigan. (Psychiatry and the Humanities, Vol. 6). New Haven: Yale University Press, 1983.

Celan, P. *Gedichte*. Gesammelte Werke Bd.3. Frankfurt am Main; Suhrkamp, 1983.

Certeau, M. De *Heterologies: Discourse on the Other*, trans. B. Massumi. (Theory and History of Literature 17). Minneapolis: University of Minnesota Press, 1986.

Clément, C. *The Life and Legends of Jacques Lacan*, trans. A. Goldhammer. New York: Columbia University Press, 1983.

Collier, P. 'Surrealist Narrative: Bréton and Aragon.' In *Unreal city. Urban Experiment in Modern European Literature and Art*. ed. E. Timms and D. Kelley. Manchester: Manchester University Press, 1985.

Coward, R., Ellis, J. *Language and Materialism*. London: Routledge & Kegan Paul, 1977.

Dear, M. J. 'The Postmodern Challenge: Reconstructuring Human Geography.' *Transactions*. Institute of British Geographers. **13**, 1988.

Derrida, J. 'The Purveyor of Truth.' *Yale French Studies*, no. 52, 1975.

Derrida, J. 'Living On: Borderlines' trans. J. Hulbert. In *Construction and Criticism*. ed. H. Bloom et al. New York: Seabury Press, 1979.

Derrida, J. *Positions*, trans. A. Bass. Chicago: University of Chicago Press, 1981a.

Derrida, J. *Dissemination*, trans. B. Johnson. Chicago: University of Chicago Press, 1981b.

Derrida, J. *Of Grammatology* trans. G. C. Spivak. Baltimore: John Hopkins Press, 1982a.

Derrida, J. *Margins of Philosophy*, trans. A. Bass. Chicago: University of Chicago Press, 1982b.

Derrida, J. *Glas*, trans. J. P. Leavy and R. Rand, Lincoln: University of Nebraska Press, 1986.

Doel, M. 'In stalling deconstruction: striking out the postmodern' *Environment and Planning D: Society and Space*, **10**, 1992.

Doel, M. 'Deconstruction on the move: from libidinal economy to liminal materialism.' *Environment and Planning A* **26**, 1994.

Eagleton, T. *Walter Benjamin, or, Towards a Revolutionary Criticism*. London: Verso, [3]1988.

Felman, S. 'Turning the Screw of Interpretation.' *Yale French Studies*, no. 55/6, 1977.

Felman, S. *Jacques Lacan and the Adventure of Insight*. Cambridge, Ma.: Harvard University Press, 1987.

Feyerabend, P. *Wissenschaft als Kunst*. Frankfurt am Main: Suhrkamp, 1984.

Frank, M. *Was ist Neostrukturalismus?* Frankfurt am Main: Suhrkamp, 1984.

Friedenburg, L. v., Habermas, J. (Eds). *Adorno-Konferenz, 1983*. Frankfurt am Main: Suhrkamp, 1983.

Gadamer, H. G. 'Die Idee der Hegelschen Logik.' In *Gesammelte Werke*, Bd. 3. Tübingen: J. H. Mohr, 1987.

Gasché. R. *The Tain of the Mirror. Derrida and the Philosophy of Reflection*. Cambridge Ma.: Harvard University Press, 1986.

Gasché. R. 'Postmodernism and Rationality.' *The Journal of Philosophy*, no. 3., 1988.

Gould, P. 'A Critique of Dissipative Structures in the Human Realm.' *European Journal of Operational Research* Vol. 30, no. 2, 1987.

Gregory, D. 'Suspended Animation: The Stasis of Diffusion Theory.' In *Social Relations and Spatial Structures*. ed. D. Gregory and J. Urry. London: MacMillan, 1985.

Haag, K. H. *Der Fortschritt in der Philosphie*. Frankfurt am Main: Suhrkamp, 1985.

Habermas, J. *The Philosophical Discourse of Modernity*, [DIS],
  e - trans. F. Lawrence. Cambridge, Ma.: MIT Press, 1987.
  g - {'Der Philosophische Diskurs der Moderne'}, Frankfurt am Main: Suhrkamp, 1985.

Hannah. M. 'Foucault on Theorizing Specificity.' *Environment and Planning D; Society and Space*, **11**, 3, 1993.

Hannah. M. and Strohmayer, U. 'The Artifice of Conviction, or, Towards an Internal Geography of Responsibility,' *Geographical Analysis*, **27**, 1994.

Hannah. M. and Strohmayer, U. '*Gnostic Materialism. Exploring the Ruins of Social Theory*, (forthcoming).

Hegel, G. W. H. *Science of Logic*, [L],
  e - trans. W. H. Johnston and C. G. Struthers, 2 Vols., Vol. 2. New York: Mac-Millan, 1929.
  g-{'Wissenschaft der Logik'}, Werke Bd. 5 and 6, Bd. 6. Frankfurt am Main: Suhrkamp, 1986.

Hegel, G. W. H. *The Difference between Fichte's and Schelling's System of Philosophy*, [D],
  e - trans. W. Cerf and H. S. Harris. Albany: State University of New York Press, 1977.
  g - {'Differenz des Fichteschen und des Schellingschen System der Philosophie'}, Werke Bd.2. Frankfurt am Main: Suhrkamp, 1986.

Hegel, G. W. H. *Faith & Knowledge*, [F&K],
  e - trans. W. Cerf and H. S. Harris. Albany: State University of New York Press, 1977
  g - {'Glaube und Wissen'}, Werke Bd.2. Frankfurt am Main: Suhrkamp, 1986.

Hegel, G. W. H. *Phenomenology of Spirit*, [PH].
  e - trans. A. V. Miller. Oxford: Clarendon Press, 1977.
  g - {'Phenomenologie des Geistes'}, Werke Bd.3. Frankfurt am Main: Suhrkamp 1986.

Heidegger, M. *Introduction into Metaphysics* [M].
  e - trans. R. Manheim. Garden City: Doubleday, 1961.
  g - {'Einführung in die Metaphysik'}, Tübingen: Max Niemeyer, [4]1976.

Heidegger, M. *What is called Thinking?* [T/D],
  e - trans. J. G. Gray. New York: Harper and Row, 1968.
  g- {Was heißt Denken?'}, Tübingen: Max Niemeyer, 1954.

Horkheimer, M. and Adorno, Th. W. *Dialectics of Enlightenment*, [DIA],
  e - trans. J. Cumming. New York: Seabury Press, 1972.
  g - {'Dialektik der Aufklärung'}, Frankfurt am Main: Fischer, 1969.

Hyppolite, J. *Logique et Existence. Essai sur la Logique de Hegel*, Paris: Presses Universitaires de France, 1953.

Hyppolite, J. *Genesis and Structure of Hegel's Phenomenology of Spirit*, trans. S. Cherniak and J. Heckman. Evanston: Northwestern University Press, 1974.

Irigaray, L. *This sex which is not one*, trans. C. Porter with C. Burke. Ithaka, N.Y.: Cornell University Press, 1985.

Johnson, B. 'The Frame of Reference: Poe, Lacan and Derrida.' In *Literature and Psychoanalysis*, ed. S. Felman. Baltimore: Johns Hopkins University Press, 1982.

Kofman, S. *Lectures de Derrida*. Paris: Gallimard, 1984.

Kojève, A. *Introduction to the Reading of Hegel*, trans. J. H. Nichols. Ithaka, N.Y.: Cornell University Press, 1980.

Kristeva, J. *Desire in Language. A Semiotic Approach to Literature and Art*, trans. T.H. Gora et al. Oxford: Basil Blackwell, 1980.

Lacan, J. *Écrits*, [Éf]. Paris: Édition du Seuil, 1966.

Lacan, J. 'Seminar on "The Purloined Letter",' *Yale French Studies*, no. 48, 1972.

Lacan, J. *Écrits. A Selection*, [Ée], trans. A. Sheridan. New York: Norton, 1977.

Lacan, J. *The four fundamental concepts of psycho-analysis*, [4F], trans. A. Sheridan. London: Hogarth Press, 1977.

Leavy, S. A. 'The Image and the World: Further Reflections on Jacques Lacan.' In *Interpreting Lacan*, ed. J. H. Smith and M. Kerrigan. (Psychiatry and the Humanities, Vol. 6). New Haven: Yale University Press, 1983.

Lemaire, A. *Jacques Lacan*, trans. D. Macey. London: Routledge & Kegan Paul, 1977.

Llewelyn, J. *Derrida on the Threshold of Sense*. London: MacMillan, 1986.

Lyotard, J.-F. 'Presentations.' In *Philosophy in France Today*, ed. A. Montefiore. Cambridge: Cambridge University Press, 1983.

Mehlman, J. 'The "floating signifier": from Lévi-Strauss to Lacan.' *Yale French Studies*, no. 48, 1972.

Menninghaus, W. *Schwellenkunde. Walter Benjamins Passage des Mythos*. Frankfurt am Main: Suhrkamp, 1986.

Nietzsche, F. *Beyond Good and Evil*, [BGE],
  e - trans. O. Levy. Complete Works Vol. 12. New York: Gordon Press, 1974.
  g - {'Jenseits von Gut und Böse'}, Stuttgart: Kröner, [10]1976.

Nietzsche, F. *The Genealogy of Morals*, [GM],
  e - trans. H. Samuel. Complete Works Vo. 13. New York: Gordon Press, 1974.
  g - {'Zur Genealogie der Moral'}, in: {'Jenseits von Gut und Böse'}, Stuttgart: Kröner, [10]1976.

Olsson, G. 'The social space of silence.' *Environment and Planning D: Society and Space*, 5, 1987.

Olsson, G. 'On doughnutting.' In *Possible Worlds in Humanities, Arts and Sciences*, ed. S. Allén, (Proceedings of Nobel Symposium 65), Berlin, New York: Walter de Gruyter, 1989.

Olsson, G. *Lines of Power, Limits of Language*, Minneapolis and Oxford: University of Minnesota Press, 1991.

Olsson, G. 'Heretic Cartographies.' *Ecumene* 1, 3, 1994.

Paz, O. *Marcel Duchamp. Appearance stripped bare*, trans. R. Phillips and D. Gardner. New York: Viking Press, 1978.

Reichert, D. 'Writing around circularity and self-reference.' In *A ground for common search*, ed. R. Golledge et al., Santa Barbara: Santa Barbara Geographical Press, 1988.

Rhees, R. 'Can there be a private language?' In *Wittgenstein. The Philosophical Investigations*, ed. G. Pitchner. Notre Dame: University of Notre Dame Press, 1968.

Richter, H. *Dada. Kunst und Antikunst.* Köln: DuMont, ³1978.

Robertson, R. *Robbie Robertson.* Los Angeles: Geffen Records, 1987.

Ronell, A. *The Telephone Book.* Lincoln, NE and London: University of Nebraska Press, 1989.

Rorty, R. *Philosophy and the Mirror of Nature.* Princeton, N.J.: Princeton University Press, 1979.

Saussure, F. *de Cours de linguistique* générale. Paris: Payot, 1972.

Schneidermann, S. *Jacques Lacan. The death of an intellectual hero.* Cambridge, Ma.: Harvard University Press, 1983.

Shiff, R. 'The Original, the Imitation, the Copy, and the spontaneous Classic: Theory and Painting in nineteenth-century France.' *Yale French Studies*, **66**, 1984.

Strohmayer, U. 'Formalities Too -On Language, Maps and Human Geography.' *GeoJournal*, **30**, 4, 1993a.

Strohmayer, U. 'Beyond Theory. The Cumbersome Materiality of Shock.' *Environment and Planning D: Society and Space*, **11**, 3, 1993b.

Strohmayer, U. 'Modernité, Postmodernité, ou comment justifier un Savoir Géographique.' *Géographie et Cultures*, **6**, 1993c.

Strohmayer, U. and Hannah, M. 'Domesticating Postmodernism.' *Antipode*, **24**, 1, 1992.

Strohmayer, U. and Hannah, M. 'Finite Specificity.' *Limits of Representation*, ed. F. Farinelli, G. Olsson, D. Reichert, Munich: Accedo, 1994.

Taylor, C. *Hegel.* Cambridge: Cambridge University Press, 1975.

Vattimo, G. *Jenseits vom Subject.* Graz, Wien: Böhlau, 1986.

Ver Eecke, W. 'Hegel as Lacan's source for necessity in psychoanalytic theory.' In *Interpreting Lacan*, ed. J. H. Smith and M. Kerrigan. (Psychiatry and the Humanities, Vol. 6.) New Haven: Yale University Press, 1983.

Witte, B. *Walter Benjamin.* Reinbek bei Hamburg: Rowohlt, 1985.

Wittgenstein, L. *Philosophical Investigations*, [PI],
    e - trans. G.E.M. Anscombe. New York: MacMillan, 1953.
    g - {'Philosophische Untersuchungen'}, Werke Bd. 1, Frankfurt am Main: Suhrkamp, 1986.

Wittgenstein, L. *Tractaus logico-philosophicus*, [TLP],
    e - trans. D.F. Pears and B. McGuinnes. London: Routledge & Kegan Paul, 1961.
    g - {dto.}, Werke Bd. 1, Frankfurt am Main: Suhrkamp, 1986.

Wolff, M. 'Über Hegel's Lehre vom Widerspruch.' In *Hegels Wissenschaft der Logik*, ed. D. Henrich. Stuttgart: Klett-Cotta, 1986.

Wollheim, R. The Cabinet of Dr. Lacan.' *The N. Y. Review of Books*, Jan. 25, 1979.

Wright, E. *Psychoanalytic Criticism: Theory in Practice.* London: Methuen, 1984.

Notes

17 Gregory (1985), 320
18 Dear (1988), passim.
19 Hegel [PH], **e**: 16, **g**: 32.
20 Adorno [ND], **e**: 316, **g**: 310.
21 Wittgenstein [TLP], 2.221.
22 Hegel [PH], **e**: 29, **g**: 49. 'This formalism (...) imagines that it has comprehended

and expressed the nature and life of a form when it has endowed it with some determination of the schema as apredicative.' (ibid). The paradoxical quality in the Kantian distinction between phenomena and noumena thus anticipates Wittgenstein's ladder: *in fixing a boundary, you have to pass it.* (Cf. Adorno [ND], e: 381–89, g: 374–81). The act of disguising this deus ex machina characteristic of a 'Real' has been part of positivistic habits ever since.

23 Hegel [PH], e: 9, g: 22.
24 Wittgenstein [TLP], 4.464.
25 Hegel [D], e: 103, g: 36.
26 Hegel [D], e: 82, g: 12.
27 '... for this [tautological] movement, when we look at it more closely, is directly the opposite of itself. That is to say, it posits a difference which is not only *not* a difference for us, but one which the movement itself cancels as a difference' (Hegel [PH], e: 94, g: 126), so 'that truth is complete only in the union of identity with variety, and therefore consists only in this unity.' (Hegel [L], e: 40, g: 42).
28 Hegel [D], g: 20, e: 90.
29 Hegel [PH], e: 109, g: 143.
30 Hegel [PH], e: 126, g: 163. 'Unhappy consciousness expresses subjectivity essentially, it expresses the for-itself as opposed to the in-itself (...). Thus, unhappy consciousness is the culmination of self-certainty's endeavor to be its own truth for itself.' (Hyppolite (1974), 203.
31 Hegel [PH], e: 110, g: 144–45.
32 Hyppolite (1974), 212.
33 Taylor (1975), 101.
34 Hegel [L], e: 58, g: 65. If the term 'objective contradiction' has an oxymoronic ring to us, no reason to believe it affected the same impression in other times, other places. Diderot and Voltaire, for instance, based many of their ideas on this concept, as 'Le neveau de Rameau' (just to mention) clearly indicates.
35 The way |a| in mathematical reflection is supposed not to change when put negative or positive. Hegel thus negatively equated tautology and contradiction similar to the way Wittgenstein did in his Tractatus: by keeping both their identities out of question. (Cf. [TLP], 4.464). In resembling the '0', they cannot be further negated, i.e. they become absolute ('reflexionslogische Substrate).' (Wolff (1986), 118).
36 Adorno [ND], e: 388, g: 381. This 'dead end' of the Kantian transcendental reduction most obviously shows in Kant's third critique, the 'Critique of Judgement,' where finally the aesthetic realm has to be cut out of the development of reason in order to sustain the system.
37 Taylor (1975), 229.
38 Lyotard (1983), 120. There is no better depiction of this submissive trait in Hegel's thoughts than the one presented by Th. W. Adorno in his 'Negative Dialectics'. Cf. [ND], e: 303–30, g: 299–324.
39 Adorno [ND], g: 298, e: 303, translation altered.
40 Taylor (1975), 109.
41 Hyppolite (1953), 197, my translation.
42 Hyppolite (1974), 119.
43 Derrida (1982b), 75.
44 Butler (1987), 8.
45 Adorno [ND], e: 347, g: 340.
46 Derrida (1982b), 21.

47 Hyppolite (1953), 23.
48 Olsson (1989), 77.
49 Butler (1987), 45–6.
50 Rhees (1968), 274. Cf. Wittgenstein [PI], 268.
51 Lacan (Ée], 4.
52 Lacan (Ée], 6.
53 ibid., 4.
54 ibid., 1.
55 Lacan (Ée], 2.
56 ibid., 5.
57 Coward, Ellis (1977), 111.
58 Coward, Ellis (1977), 94.
59 Lemaire (1977), 99.
60 ibid., 77.
61 Lemaire (1977), 99.
62 Lacan (Ée], 163
63 ibid., 165.
64 ibid., 166.
65 Bowie (1979), 131.
66 Lacan (Ée], 65.
67 Lemaire (1977), 38.
68 Clément (1983), 90–1. A train of thoughts that deliberately destroys 'the self-evident that has become an idée reçue' (Lacan (Ée],41)*: 'This ego, whose strength our theorists now define by its capacity to bear frustration, is frustration in its essence.' (ibid., 42).*
69 Lacan (Ée], 65....
70 Lacan (1972), 51
71 Lemaire (1977), 59.
72 Lacan [4F]., pref. vii.
73 Schneidermann (1983), 34.
74 ibid., 33
75 Clément (1983), 87.
76 Jacques Lacan, as quoted in Lemaire (1977), 164.
77 Lacan [Ée], 264. In other words: '... the unconscious has no meaning. The unconscious is not directed towards a goal' (Clément (1983), 33), a move Lacan exemplified in translating the Freudian dictum 'Wo Es war, soll Ich werden' into one of his awkward but beautiful phrases: 'Là où c'était, peut-on dire, là où s'était, (...) c'est mon devoir que je vienne à être, (as quoted in Frank (1984), 374).
78 Lacan (Ée], 60.
79 ibid., 40.
80 Lacan (1972), 66.
81 Heidegger [T/D], **e**: 118, **g**: 83.
82 Lacan (Ée], 256.
83 ibid., 193.
84 Bär (1974), 508.
85 de Certeau (1986), 48.
86 Lacan (1972), 55.
87 Clément (1983), 85.
88 Butler (1987), 175. The problem (*the* problem of contemporary deconstructive philosophy, if that name provides a meaningful frame) is that 'to break with Hegel

and yet to escape being cast into his all-encompassing net of interrelations requires finding a way to be different from Hegel that he himself cannot account for.' (ibid., 184).

89 Lacan (Ée], 296.
90 ibid. Lacan continues: 'What is this real, if not a subject fulfilled in his identity to himself?'
91 ibid., 299.
92 ibid., 296–7.
93 Ver Eecke (1983), 120.
94 Lacan (Ée], 296.
95 ibid., 68.
96 Clément (1983), 64.
97 Irigaray (1985), 75.
98 ibid., 26.
99 Wittgenstein [PI], 141.
100 Adorno [ND], **e**: 349, **g**: 342. Representing more than a simple 'spell', the German 'Verbannung,' used by Adorno in its verbal form ('bannen'), has the additional connotation of fixing something (or indeed someone) in a particular place. Thus the combination with the uprooting prefix 'Ver-' can denote exile as a non-place away from home.
101 Nietzsche [GM], **e**: 196, **g**: 399.
102 Derrida (1981b), 26.
103 Irigaray (1985), 89.
104 Derrida (1982b), 75.
105 Irigaray (1985), 98–9.
106 Horkheimer, Adorno [DIA], **e**: 33, **g**: 40. 'The nearer the sphere of immediate, physical existence is approached, the more questionable progress becomes, a Pyrrhic victory of fetishized production.' (Adorno [MM], Aphorism 75, **e**: 117, **g**: 152).
107 Derrida (1981b), 44.
108 Adorno [MM], Aphorism 152, **e**: 247, **g**: 333. 'Freedom would be not to choose between black and white but to abjure such a prescribed choice,' (ibid., Aphorism 85, **e**: 132, **g**: 172).
109 Derrida (1982b), 1 and passim.
110 Bryson (1984), 21.
111 Johnson (1982), 469. '… [T]he law of the addition of the origin to its representation, of the thing to its image, is that one plus one makes at least three.' (Derrida (1986), 36).
112 Derrida (1979), 81. Therefore 'the supposed "commentary" of the "i.e." or "in other words" has furnished only a textual supplement that calls in turn for an overdetermining "in other words", and so on and so forth.' (ibid., 75).
113 Derrida (1982b), 6.
114 Celan (1983), 123.
115 Derrida (1981b), 26.
116 Lyotard (1983), 132.
117 Gasché (1986), 87.
118 Nietzsche [BGE], **e**: 268, **g**: 236.
119 Rorty (1979), 364.
120 Adorno [MM], Aphorism 142, **e**: 222, **g**: 297.
121 Heidegger [M], **e**: 44, **g**: 41.

122 Bryson (1984), pref. xix..

123 Gasché (1986), 142.

124 Paz (1978), 94.

125 Kristeva (1980), 135. 'A thesis, not of a particular being or meaning, but of a signifying apparatus ...' (ibid.). It is in this act of 'positing,' of course, that a residual and hence fundamental materiality makes its 'presence' felt. On this materiality, see Doel (1994) and Hannah and Strohmayer (1995).

126 Adorno [MM], Aphorism 143, **e**: 222, **g**: 298.

127 Paz (1978), 3.

128 Bréton (1924), 20–1.

129 Hegel [PH], **e**: 107, **g**: 141.

130

7

Spatial Stress and Resistance: Social Meanings of Spatialization[1]

Rob Shields

It is strange that one must resort to a term like *social spatialization* to grasp what a social analysis of 'space' entails. Transfixed by flight into the interplanetary void, the geographical language of space, one of the fundamental axes of life and one of the most essential of resources has been lost: we can no longer speak without confusion about 'space' or even 'social space'. What has been lost in this language? Sensitivity to coding operations on topographical space which materially produce sites and regions, our sense of spatiality and, reflexively, the way in which we perceive geographical space. This topogenetic coding process has been called 'the production of social space' or 'the social production of space' (Soja 1980; Gottdiener 1985; Werlen 1993) but the multiple aspects and reflexive character of the 'production' is often lost. For example, most geographical theorists fail to consider the full range of impacts such a basic category of thought and perception has. Not only is the concern the construction of social regions and the spatializing of social values so that places always have a connotative, value-laden aspect to them. We must also be concerned with the manner in which this constructed spatiality informs our bodily comportment and our 'crowd practice' (Jameson 1984) as we bump into each other in the lines of soup kitchens ...

Bodies are understood and lived spatially as much as are topographical sites in the landscape. Such issues are the logical concerns of social geographers (Werlen 1993: 179 ff.). But to include the social and the body in geographical theory requires that issues of cultural spatiality not be reduced to an empirical notion of objects-in-space.

The juggling act of 'making space' and putting into practice spatial codes is indicative of a larger social quality to spatial coding, to spatial practices, to our representations of this 'space', and to our 'imaginary geography' in which everything has a place and a time. This *social spatialization* is rapidly being deformed and recast, introducing us all to a time of *spatial stress*. Spatializations of social values, that is to say, traditional codings of space were never certain anchoring points for sociocultural norms (*contra* Werlen 1993: 174). They were always contested. But the meanings of social spatializations are now more equivocal, being fractured by new genres of contradiction besides, for example, class and ethnic divisions which produced competing and contested spatializations (from within the spatial envelope of the nation-state) permitting on the one hand a massive and nostalgic effort of spatially recoding social meanings on to new 'geographies of desire' and on the other hand, a popular disinvestment from the certainties of place- and space-based systems of linguistic reference and conceptual shortcuts.

1 The Problem with 'Space'

Failing to examine the nature of space as a cultural 'artifact', the realm of the spatial has often been assumed to be purely neutral and a-political, conferring neither disadvantage, nor benefit to any group. This 'empirical space' is complacently understood to be fully defined by dimensional measurements (height, width and breadth) and by trigonometric descriptions of the geometrical relationships between objects, which are thought to sit in a kind of vacuum. According to this empirico-physics model, 'space' exists (even though it is a 'nothingness';) as a given. Separated off in other disciplines are considerations of the overall ethos or atmosphere of such arrangements, the manner in which assemblage was produced and came into being, the methods and forces by which the objects are held in their positions, and finally the significance attributed to this tableau. While the model of 'empirical space' is sometimes useful, it excludes important cultural and cognitive issues from consideration. These issues direct our attention to the manner in which 'space' is part of a culturally created system of philosophical categories. It is a 'place-holder' when no objects are present and an index of a totality of numerous co-present objects and elements in empirical-spatial relationships.

Yet in everyday life, all such 'spatial relations' (Massey 1984) are constantly overcoded with *social significance*. Except to sociologists and geographers, it comes as no surprise to most people that the *where* and *when* of events are as significant as *what* those events are. This applies to the most important of social activities (including crimes), which may well be empty of meaning or may never take place except for their fortuitous siting and timing. If one still bridles at the idea of a social 'production' or cultural 'making' of 'spaces' then perhaps one might refer to the remaking of empirical space by social groups. This remaking, the make-over of topography takes place almost invisibly, however, because the social categories in which space is conceived and perceived structure the most elementary aspects of our interaction with our physical context and setting. Here, the cognitive structures and topogenetic codes which are the result of material processes of spatialization *precede* physical engagement with 'spaces'.

Even modern geography has been accused as being essentially *spaceless* because relations are conceived of as operating within 'empirical space' which is treated merely as a container. Geography has reified locations and areas (such as 'the city'), making them stand for the social and economic processes and organization which in fact comprise them (Gottdiener, 1985: 121). In the formal literature on 'space' this neglect of *coded spaces* is surely as much an error as it has been the rule. The problem is that these social, coded 'spaces' are usually described just as 'space'. This usage has introduced numerous linguistic difficulties (*see* Soja 1980; Sack 1980; Lefebvre 1991). As Soja has pointed out, 'space' is a difficult term because of its broad meanings and wide semantic field (Soja 1980; *see also* the earlier and somewhat neglected work of Sorokin 1943). It is also difficult because space is an a priori dimension of the epistemologies and ontologies which form the philosophical background for all social theory (Sack 1980). To question 'space' is to question one of the axes along which 'reality' and truth are conventionally defined.

As a result of the wide range of conflicting usages of the word, 'space' will be largely avoided as a term in this chapter. Here, 'a space' denotes a limited area: a site, zone or place characterized by specific social activities with a culturally given identity (name) and image. I will use the term *social spatialisation*[2], to designate the ongoing social construction of the spatial at the level of the social imaginary (collective mythologies, presuppositions) as well as interventions in the landscape (for example, the built environment). This term allows us to name an object of study which encompasses both the cultural logic of the spatial and its expression and elaboration in language and more concrete actions, constructions and institutional arrangements.

2   Spatialization

Invariably social spatializations are the product of what Henri Lefebvre once called a particular 'mode of production of space' under the control of specific groups. Lefebvre uses the term 'spatialization' only once, to refer to inscription of time into space as in a tree-trunk and the contrast with the absorption of time into space in the city, so that time is not seen or understood as time – 'the greatest of all goods' – but is either denied as in the case of phobias or ageing, or displaced into the econometric measurement of labour time:

> Until nature became localized as 'underdevelopment', each place showed its age and, like the rings of a tree trunk, bore the traces of the years over which it had grown. Time was inscribed in space and this 'natural-space' was but the lyrical and tragic writing of 'natural-time' ... But, Time, is disappearing in the social space of modernity ... It is the time of living, time as an irreducible 'good' which eludes the logic of visualisation and of spatialisation, as far as it has a logic. Raised to ontological dignity of philosophers, time is killed by society.[3]
>
> (Lefebvre 1981: 114–15)

The 'spatialization' of the culture of capitalism was something ominous for Lefebvre. Opposed to Harvey's (1989) political-economic arguments that space is being eliminated by time in the transactions of post-Fordism, in 1974 Lefebvre had argued that time was being ontologically and epistemologically 'killed off' in favour of space. This was indeed one of the justifications for his

485 pages of analysis and argument of 'the problem of space'. For Lefebvre the centrality of space was linked with the absorption of time in an alienated and neurotic everyday life under capitalism.

Spatializations are central to cultural hegemony and dominant ideologies as well as what we might call 'dominant practices'. Lefebvre argues that different, coded, spaces are accorded the status of a priori material objects approaching, asymptotically, the features of the natural landscape (Lefebvre, 1976: 89–90). To push this further, I would argue that the natural topography itself is inaccessible except through the mediation of the creative mind's imposition of significance, meanings, and associations on topographical features. This notion has been well addressed under the rubric of the 'social construction of reality' (cf. Berger and Luckman 1967) but Lefebvre's Marxian terminology of the *production* of space has the advantage of grounding the construction of reality and of spatialization in a historical materialist framework. As Lefebvre also acknowledges through a dialectical model, spatializations become tools for the recognition of the environment and thinking of the social and cosmological world. Thus, map-makers and explorers were never content simply to locate rivers and natural features. They continually enlarged upon and embroidered their graphical depictions of territory: '*here be dragons*'.

Naming is one moment at which the elements of spatialization – habitual spatial practices, representations of the world, and a spatial, imaginary geography – are apparent. Samuel Hearse, a European explorer in the subarctic area to the west of Hudson's Bay[4] named the region of peat bog, tundra, and innumerable lakes and ponds where water lies on the surface above an impermeable membrane of permafrost 'The Barren Lands', forming the perception of generations of map-readers ever since. He saw little beauty and found no merit: 'in my opinion, there cannot exist a stronger proof that mankind was not created to enjoy happiness in this world, than the conduct of the miserable beings who inhabit this wretched part of it' (Hearse 1795: 81). The European court of history has been less kind to the viewpoint of the native inhabitants of the region, who resorted to *their* social spatialization of the same space to cross-examine incredulously a Christian missionary's description of Heaven:

> My father, you have spoken well; you have told me that heaven is very beautiful; tell me now one thing more. Is it more beautiful than the country of muskox in summer, when sometimes the mist blows over the lakes, and sometimes the water is blue, and the loons cry very often?
>
> (Saltatha, reported in Warburton Pike 1892: 302)

In this incisive query, Saltatha resorted to an attempt to 'place' Heaven, if not in the Barren Lands, then in a conceptual structure of difference using comparison and contrast. Significantly, this reveals the cross-cultural nature of strategies of differentiation and binary thinking (those natives 'reasoned' as well as any European scholar!) used in spatial cognition. These associations and the structure of difference are not arbitrary, rather, they are split into constituent parts of materially produced, locally grounded spatializations – systems of place and 'spacing-outs' – which have historical specificity.[5]

'Social spatialisation'[6] names the situation which authors such as Sack begin to describe: that it is not just a question of 'Space' but of overlaid 'Spaces' which are made up of multitudinous 'places', good and bad (the 'right' and 'wrong' sides 'of the tracks', 'dangerous' urban areas, ghettos, 'middle class enclaves', public squares, private yards, the sanctified space of a cathedral, the profane space of a tavern) and are criss-crossed by directional 'paths' ranging from natural paths (trails, mountain passes, river routes) through physical pathways (roads, railways, canals) to abstract paths of air-route corridors, frequency delimited microwave transmission beams, electronic, satellite-based trans-border data flows. All these genres of space[7] have the effect of fragmenting any overall vision of the socio-cultural system of spaces in which we live. However, this remains a 'system'– an overarching social spatialization – even though it is broken up by internal contradictions, which are directly implicated in the dilemmas of daily life.

3 The Spatial Problematic

The project of theorizing social spatialization may be conceived of as a new *spatial problematic*. In a looser sense, the general philosophical problematization and redefinition of epistemological borders taken on by theorists such as Derrida (1980) or Deleuze and Guattari (1976) has also been referred to as a spatial problematic (cf. Garden, 1985: 74 ff.). Such proposals through the early to mid-1980s represented the first signs of a growing re-evaluation of importance of spatiality in the North American and British literature (*see also* Werlen 1993). This, however, is more true in the case of those who were interested in social and political theory than those concerned with geography or 'urban studies' *per se*. This disregard forced these latter practitioners into narrower fields of study than they might otherwise have considered. Geographers abandoned the key terrain of theory. Any claim to a 'spatial problematic' is of a central concern. Urban sociologists became virtually extinct when they refused to re-theorize their subdiscipline when it became obvious that 'the urban', their object of study, was not definable as a geographically region. It was phenomenological a *topos*, defined by Lefebvre as simply 'social centrality' (1975). This left 'the urban' to the practical machinations of property developers and planners, and the quixotic interest of literary theorists, philosophers and historians (cf. DeCerteau 1984) who may lack a working appreciation of the social and spatial complexity of the urban milieu, seeing instead only one 'text' to be read.[8]

In a spatial problematic, space, displaced in conventional formulations would be re-centred and probed for its meaning. But this new spatial problematic would not abolish the more traditional problematics [eg. urbanism as in Harvey (1973), or consumption as in Castells (1977)]. As Jameson puts it it transcodes them: it includes urban and daily life under the more general problem of the reproduction of the relations of production in space (Shields 1992a). This is not a re-coding of existing, legitimate, problematics into a new private discipline language. This will be an 'overcoding', which does not seek to abolish the distances and breaks between different levels (practice versus conceptual versus symbolic discourse of space; economic analysis versus cultural analysis) and codes but rather the ideological and illegitimate media- tions and separations between them, bringing them into a unitary framework and allowing the possibility for new syntheses and the overcoming of previously entrenched discipline dichotomies (Jameson 1984; Shields 1992a).

'Social spatialization' is thus a rubric under which currently separated objects of investigation – the mapping of colonial and subaltern spaces and the philosophical theory of space and the topography of physical landscape – will be brought together to demonstrate their interconnectedness and co-ordinated nature. The dichotomies of social theory (public-private; base-superstructure; economy-culture) lead to anomalies that do not fit in either term of the dualism. These can be made intelligible only under a macro-level framework which permits internal paradoxes and divisions. A transcoding of apparently dichotomous problematics into the common problematic of space becomes possible which produces an equation of the cultural and economic. The rhetorical devices, such as the base-superstructure metaphor which Marx resorted to, have been rendered less and less as metaphors and more and more as metonyms by apologists and critics alike. The transcoding process implicit in any examination of spatialization allows, while preserving the place of specific analyses, a view of the diachronic relations between elements, levels and problematics within the transcendent whole of space. Social activity, of course, takes place in space, and, has been argued, at the epistemological level space is implicated in symbolic and conceptual formations. Economic forma- tions emerge as relations and organizations of space at symbolic levels. Such spatial distinctions as right versus left echo through cultural formation inte- grating everything to their taxonomy of 'things of the left' and 'things on the right' posing in turn (tautologically) the imperative 'this belongs on the left' and 'this belongs on the right' (disconcerting to anyone who has ever found themselves inexplicably 'rated' as being 'on the Left', or, 'on the Right'). Similarly, and with greater relevance in the urban context, consider the distinction centre-periphery with all the connotations and cultural 'baggage' implied in statements such as 'being in the centre (of things)'.

Against class-reductionist approaches, which begin with the assumption of the primacy of conflict in the relations between economic groups as the basis for the study of society, a spatial formulation poses anew the disturbing question of people's co-operation, docility and complicitous self-implication in systems of inequality and in the survival and expansion of the capitalist economic system. Most left-orthodoxies have little basis for a response to such 'issues of silence' except for (weak) theories of 'false consciousness' and untheorized notions of the persuasion inherent and necessary to the achieve- ment of cultural hegemony. As a result there is little understanding of and no quarter given to, the deviations of popular cultures from the 'politically correct' or the theoretically orthodox. The spatial problematic draws attention to the politically discounted symbolic and distorted forms of resistance (for example, the riotous mini-rebellions which quickly dissipate in the public areas often planned for riot control) practised through the spatialization itself: eruptions of instability through the carefully spread net of the Cartesian three-dimensional grid of rationality and homogenously empirical spaces of canonical modernity. Yet space and disruptions of the normalcy of this modernist spatial system (Shields 1992b) become themselves at once the medium of compliance and resistance to objectification and to the relations of ruling and dominance which characterize economic exploitation.

4   The Role of Spatialization in Social Reproduction

In social spatialization, spaces are not only overcoded, but physical space itself is 'produced' via classification schemes with various (ideological) divisions as good and bad areas (for example, the 'red-lining' effect on urban districts when banks and mortgage companies refuse to lend money to high-crime or high-bankruptcy areas); ours and theirs; this place and that place; spaces and places for this and that.[9] More than the production of, for example, functional urban environments is at issue here. This 'production' of space also concerns social and cultural reproduction. People learn the comportment associated with their gender and 'know their place in society' as the old saying goes. Ideologies and cosmologics are reproduced through this training of bodies as well as through the tutoring of outlook via images of community, nation and world. These are often expressed in spatial/urban images – the heavenly mountain; the global village. A complex of spatial practices and conceptual assumptions guides, for example, not only the production of the environment and landscape in terms of social norms regarding the allocation of functions and activities to their appropriate spaces, but also the practical use and inhabitation of the resulting spatialization. For example, many will remember being ordered throughout our schooling, 'Don't run; walk!' in the school's corridors, only to feel conspicuous and strange everytime we run in the street or corridor in later life.[10]

As a cognitive and practical *habitus*,[11] social spatialization is a source not only of 'templates' or algorithms (traditional routines) but of allegorical solutions (attempting to solve new problems by metaphorically assimilating them to older, routine difficulties), differentiating images (locating someone's views as 'Right' or 'Left') and conceptual shortcuts (attributing stereotypical qualities to a person from a given region or place). The linkage between the production of cultures, social reproduction and the production of a whole social spatialization is of central importance. Cultural hegemony is reinscribed upon the physical landscape to 'haunt' what Bourdieu (1972) has called *habitus*.

5 Spatialization and Ideology

What then is the status of *social spatialization* with respect to ideology? Latent here is the issue of the appropriateness of the term 'Ideology'. Is the spatialization inscribed at a higher (or deeper, to manipulate the metaphors) level than what is typically understood as 'ideology'? Especially if a 'class position' was taken on ideology (Gramsci) then a spatialization would have to be described as 'other than' ideology. The spatial, in conceptual terms, while 'Ideological' is not just 'Ideology' in the conventional senses of the term. Nietzsche calls this absolute space the ground upon which force and will are etched – the 'substratum, the determinant and the model', of Force (Nietzsche 1967: 293 (Fragment 545) cited in Lefebvre, 1981: 30). An indication of its explanatory importance and unexamined status may be gained from a study of the resort to 'space' as a metaphor in the otherwise seamless logic of the texts of Michel Foucault (esp. 1973; 1979; 1980). He suggests that 'space' is inscribed above the level of ideology (1973: x). Space is always:

> 'that full space in the hollow of which language assumes volume and sizes', in which, ' ... We must place ourselves, and remain once and for all at the level of the fundamental *spatialisation*.'
>
> (Foucault, 1973: x–xi; original stress)

'Classificatory thought gives itself an essential space' in this manner (Foucault, 1973: 9). At its most basic levels, the spatialization clearly crosses class borders, underpinning the socius, providing part of the *glutinum mundi* which binds classes into a cultural, as opposed to merely economic, totality. On the other hand, however, certain performative codes and conceptual use of space are class-specific (Berman 1983). Spatialization thus forms the possibility of the being of classes and of various class and subclass strategies along with the subdivision of society. Especially in our case, a capitalist spatialization is characterized by the reconceiving of 'The Land' in commodity terms as 'lots' and as the most visible index of the private property systems of exclusion and privilege. This spatialization also includes the cutting away of the private sphere from the public and common typical of bourgeois identity formations. It is also, however, itself masked and fractured by class and gender practices, sectoral cleavages and local arrangements.

In Marxian terms, spatialization is a 'superstructural' element which, however, in action assumes the status of a material element of the 'base'. This overthrows the conventional, formalistic (Martins, 1982: 173), attitudes whereby space appears to us as a non-dialectical a priori (a 'contentless abstraction'; an inert container; a neutral void) rather than as only one reflexive moment in a dialectic (Lefebvre, 1981: 337–41).[12] This approach would then displace the historicism where social space is accorded the status of a product of the overall social relations; but, is (problematically) reduced to a reflection of socio-economic features (or lost in the limbo of an enigmatic 'relative autonomy'). It is not a vague 'society-space' dialectic – such as may be found in most realist texts and in much of the Marxian literature – which adds nothing to the possibilities of practice, nor does it aid analysis because of its tendency to occlude the fact that society is spatial as one characteristic of its essential being. 'Space' must be re-examined as only one constituent of the social edifice of 'spatialization'. We must capture both the sense of the social creation of a defined/designed system of space and the achieved artefact (even though it is a conceptual one) which is a fundamental element of *habitus*.

Such an analytic has direct implications for the entire range of social, economic and political analysis. All spatial zones and the debates surrounding them as: 'territorial waters'; the notion of 'open sea'; 'air space'; and offshore fishing grounds are all socio-political constructions ideologically coded into cartographic conventions and reified in socio-cognitive mappings of the world. Again these serve to exemplify the extent to which we live within the territori-alizing and boundary-drawing impulse of the *imaginary geography* of the nation-state which leads us to see the world through the fragmented patterns of state territories. In our politics we deal more hesitantly with the global spaces not allocated to national territory. *Representations of space* such as national air space and the 200-mile limit inform and delimit our *practical* interventions in these spaces.

6   Spatialization in the West

Empirical spatializations have a nominalistic notion of space itself and of the spatiality of 'really-existing' objects at their core. 'Space' is the Cartesian *extensio*. That is, it is simply a three-dimensional void, and 'things' are held to exist only if they occupy a spatial volume. Objects are treated as existing in and of themselves. They are deterritorialized from their surrounding context. While this idea of objects' volume contains a smuggled sense of spatiality, volume is held to be the attribute of objects, not of spaces. If one wishes to speak of space, one must speak of it only through the volumetric discourse. In as much as metrics are essentially an example of temporal cognition, space may be said to be subsumed in time. This causes a series of predicaments, such as the problem of subatomic particles in physics or the debates in the social sciences concerning whether or not society or class can be said to 'exist' and to which Realism is one response (Sayer 1985). Strangely the Cartesian cogito is inverted: not 'I think, therefore I exist' but 'I occupy space therefore I exist'.

This postulate of space-as-a-void is the ontological foundation for a Humean action-by-contact type of causality (Sack, 1980: 20). Like one billiard ball hitting another, cause and effect are relayed through direct contact between objects in time and space. Nothing intervenes between these objects to mediate their causal relationship, for this 'empirical space' is a void in terms of its essence (a contradiction in terms) and null in its causal power. So familiar are we with 'action by contact' and the interconnection between pattern and process that these principles affect every realm of social action. Proof or innocence in a crime, for example, rests on whether such links in space and time can be established between the accused and the victim (Sack, 1980: 11–12). In this spatialization, the only 'effects of space' taken seriously, are the effects of contingent positions and geometric relationships between persons or objects-in-space (expressed via geometry and measurements of distance), not 'space' at all.

Spatial possibilities unthinkable in other spatializations are opened by the Western subsumption of the spatial from the temporal and from the existence of objects-in-space. The interiority of consciousness is simply an extension of the monadic quality of objects which are treated as independent of their environment or context. Thus objects or people may be transferred from one place to another without any acknowledgement of the effect new settings may have. The very belated recognition of environmental impacts and the role of locality and historicity in shaping viewpoints and interests is one corollary of this spatialization. This 'de-territorialization' of objects allows the possibility of asking questions. What if the social order were altered so that land were held differently? What if the village were redesigned, placing this here rather than there ...? These are simply absurd in other spatializations (Sack, 1980: 177) where not only siting but networks of sites and cosmological representations of space are held to alter the qualitative being of an object-in-space.

The pulse of separation and recombination of objects and contexts is not perfect, fragmenting and obscuring links between behaviour and space and between different scales of spatial entities (for example, cities-provinces and nations) leaving open an area where social science may strive to reconstruct chains of cause and effect (Sack, 1980: 17). Symbolic orientations and sitings and aesthetic concerns have the effect of fracturing the simple picture of a purely empirical spatialization. However, these codings tend to be excluded from the all-important domain of volumetric objects which are held to 'really exist'.

This attitude towards spatial separation and recombination is mirrored in concepts of justice and in everyday spatial practice. Certain activities are accorded spatial status, while others are not. Such a spatial status plays a role in determining the status of labour: driving a truck is spatial (hence, work), talking on the phone is less spatial (hence, bureaucratic), and pondering an idea is simply ethereal (Sack, 1980:17) hence, indolent.

7 Globalization and Spatial Stress

Yet, contemporary technology (especially communications) has the effect of disrupting the empirical space of everyday action which can be described by a simple, Euclidean geometry. Indeed, the purpose of such technologies is precisely to transcend such spatial limits. By attenuating and qualitatively shrinking distances, the relationships of empirical reference points (between home and work, between oneself and a distant other) change. The nominalistic vision is constantly challenged by contemporary life. These spatial reference points are part of a larger spatialization, and are imbricated in value-laden, coded, classification schemes, by which the perceptions, social action and attitudes of individuals are co-ordinated. The effect is *spatial stress* at the 'system level' (ie. theoretically) of individual thought as well as at the level of individual action. For example, new associations and *rapprochements* are made between sites which once carried symbolic connotations of mutual opposition, of distance and of otherness and served as conceptual shortcuts of the imagining and discussion of difference (Shields 1992b).

Any social spatialization that could be identified and profiled is not only contested but rapidly being deformed and recast. This quality of arbitrariness and equivocation is a symptom of a new genre of fracture cutting across social spatializations. The meanings of social spatializations are contested at new geographical scales. The nation-state with a modernist spatialization of the global as a frieze of competing nations and states faces the drawing of new borders which fragment nation-states internally (Russia, Yugoslavia, Canada) while at the same time lumping them together into new regional blocs (eg. NAFTA and the European Union). It can be hypothesized that this equivocality permits, on the one hand, a massive and nostalgic effort of spatially recoding social meanings on to new 'geographies of desire' from ethnic homelands to cultural tourist zones of authenticity. On the other hand, a popular disinvestment from the certainties of place- and space-based systems of reference and conceptual shortcuts might be one possible response to this erosion of the authoritative and concrete quality of social spatializations.

Not only is Europe, for example, being 're-imagined', it is being remapped and we all now live in new relationships to that socio-spatial entity called Europe, which in the spatial categories of modernity was supposed to stand for civilized values of progress, universal human rights and dependable justice. As conflicts of the Middle Ages re-erupt into a post-bloc Europe, it is much more difficult to construct Europe as an ongoing spatial signifier of modernity without the actively produced character of this spatialization becoming ever more evident. A cultural sense of 'postmodern' spatial stress and dislocation can thus be grounded in the material framework of new relationships between spatial regions and localities as well as in the 'imaginary geographies' and spatial practices of agents.

More radical restructurings are also possible as global communications media erode or compete with local and indigenous community folk-information structures (for example, gossip) and destabilize old epistemological foundations of cultures in new, unaccustomed, intimacy with each other. The conditions of knowledge change to reflect the non-nominalistic conditions and bases upon which epistemological truth claims may be made. One key dimension of these changes is the importance of new media-borne visions of the world which are difficult to contain within a fact-ideology classification because of their tendency to produce complex representations. Information and entertainment transmitted through communications technology such as television news, a trans-national culture industry, the internationalization of personal financial data flows and corporate information links challenge the spatialization which privileges the space of the nation-state as an 'invisible community' (Anderson, 1983) and demands that the television viewer grasps and practice spatialization articulated on a global basis – the geography of an abstract and unequal community of television viewers and the viewed, of telecommunications subscribers, impoverished and very distant craft and sweatshop producers and relatively wealthy consumers.

A new global ethos arises slowly out of these relationships, even if they are at first based only on the consumer recognition of the global scope of the products in a typical shopping basket and can be said to be truly relationships of super-exploitation. But accommodating this global ethos within the divisions of 'us' and 'them' constructed through the spatialization of the nation-state with its imagined community provokes the need for what Jameson called a new 'cognitive mapping' of the globe. We are in an ethical crisis. Without the ideological scaffolding which legitimated the practices and politics of Eurocentrism, imperialistic expansion and colonial rule, new ideologies of global markets, competitiveness and vacation opportunities have become prominent. Against this, downward economic adjustments have negatively affected the resources of community-based activists to maintain widely dispersed networks. The international networking of movements and agencies concerned with human rights, social justice and the environment is often limited by state policy priorities and dependency on the state for funding. Many labour unions and environmental issue groups practise and articulate a place and nation-based spatialization in which a politics of 'us versus them' (them being immigrants, refugees, those in other regions or cities) erodes their ability to articulate and further develop the coalitional politics of a global ethic.

A global ethic would respond to the problems of spatial stress and global spatialization. It must be elaborated by faulty and poorly informed individuals and groups of human agents both conceptually *and materially* in the practices of everyday life. Attempts towards a global ethic are much manifest in an acute consciousness of the contradictory relationship and responsibilities towards distant and scarcely imaginable others and protests against the adventurism and warfare of the 'new world order'. Attempts toward a global ethic are, however, also reflected in the commercial provision of 'Rastafarian-wanna-be;' beaded hair, the consumption of the aesthetics of Japanese industrial design, and the reactionary politics of ethnic nationalism which attempt to re-establish the nation-state. A new cognitive-mapping is accompanied by a new practical-mapping and a mania for exploration which may re-use the neo-colonial relationships and staged interaction with 'the locals' wrought by cultural tourism (Urry 1990).

8 The Spatial Problematic and the Question of Resistance

Space provides a key to grasping the essential changes in the possibilities for agency and the key fields where social intervention is called for. The mythifying language and obfuscations of popular writers who have proclaimed a 'popular postmodernism' while eliminating its radical potential reduce it to little more than the thrill of novelty and *jouissance* which comes with a born-again and fatalistic consumerism. Against this trend, the spatial problematic highlights the new postmodern 'cast' or form of social spatializations with real, all-pervasive effects which *must* become an area of critical, strategic focus.

However, this spatial is still a neglected and highly significant field for resistance and transformative interventions in social life. The aim of 'resistance' is not revolution but the preservation of the potential for significant social change at a time of confused praxis and rapid restructuring. Spatialized forms of resistance through the tactical appropriation (De Certeau 1984) and 're-functioning' of urban public spaces, and through contestatory comportment and spatial practices in public cannot be dismissed from the repertoire of provisional and immediate responses to totalizing developments and social spatializations by creative actors. Caught in the well-worn grooves of dogmatic Marxism, unreflective theorists continue to doubt, while lesser researchers dismiss resistance as a response to commodity capitalism without any examination of its linkages to wider social change and even to revolutionary upheaval (eg. Anderson 1983). It is in this manner that we may unthinkingly disempower both their own critical research and human agents who must survive and act in the field of everyday life (ie. the banal, trivial content ignored by grand theories of social and class forms) with a 'pedagogy of disapproval' (Jameson 1984). By the same gestures, academics de-link their analyses from the field of everyday life, leaving them in an unethical relationship with their host population, and vulnerable to their spatial critique of academia as a discredited 'ivory tower'.

Notes

1   The paper on which this chapter is based was originally written in 1986. It has been revised and updated, but I have dealt with some of the issues raised here in work published in the early 1990s. The spatialization of presence and absence as proximity and distance is dealt with in 'A Truant Proximity' (Shields 1992b).

2   The term, 'spatialization', defined by the *Oxford Dictionary* as, 'the fact or action of making spatial, or investing with spatial qualities and relations;' better denotes the process by which 'space' is socially constructed, with codes of spatial performance, expectation, and definition which transcend the purely physical realm of action to defend and define whole conceptual and cultural 'worlds', as a materially produced phenomenon. The effect of the verbal 'spatialization' is to shift analytic attention from the synchronic nature of 'space' – a tradition of research handed down to us by bourgeois science which, as demonstrated above, produces a multiplication of fragmentary notions of limited, disconnected, microspaces – to a new emphasis on the diachronic processes by which the spatiality, the social spatialization is materially produced. The clarificatory value of this term is not to be underestimated. It avoids confusing the ambiguous usage of 'space' in a variety of non-social science disciplines as well as overthrowing the common-sense apperception of its value neutrality, and moves beyond the limited discipline-based analytics of 'space' of one type or another. This is essential for the English reader owing to the (ideological) linguistic tradition explicated above which militates against any usage of 'space' as a social concept.

3 Author's translation and bold type. Italics as in original. Compare D. Nicholson-Smith's pioneering and appreciated translation (1991: 96). Lefebvre's polemical wit and characteristic sets of rhetorical questions to the reader are lost in the translation. Admittedly, the central importance of dialectics in Lefebvre's style as much as in the contents of his works (pushed to extremes in eg. *La Somme et le Reste*, 1959) has been little advertised to Anglo-American readers.

4 It is difficult to be complacent about names. Hudson's Bay denotes a body of water but also the expropriation of the natural resources and commercialization of riches of the Canadian north. The Hudson's Bay Company continues to exist as a Canadian retail chain.

5 A similar argument is presented by Durkheim. Indeed, against the neo-Kantian perspective that 'Space' must exist before social groups can be perceived to exist and without even leaving room for the 'pre-cultural' experience of space – as in, for example, the conception of 'up' and 'down' which, in the sense that 'up' and 'down' are the human experience of gravitational forces, transcend the more specifically cultural definitions of space at the level of, for example, 'right' and 'left' – Durkheim audaciously proposed a correspondence between social structure and the societies' notion of space: if, in a primitive society, tribal camps are traditionally laid out in a circle, the notion of cosmological space held by the inhabitants is also often circular. Durkheim argues that 'logical categories derive from social categories', space being one of them (Kern, 1983: 138). In a study of the Zuni Indians of Arizona, Durkheim concluded that their space was nothing else than, 'the site of the tribe, only indefinitely extended beyond its real limits'. Thus, space is heterogeneous, varying not only from place to place, region to region (some being perhaps sacred, others profane); and also varying between societies. This heterogeneity is in turn used to co-ordinate sense data into basic categories. In every society, there is, 'a collective sense of these unique; "spaces", shared by all members of a society', (Kern, 1983: 138) hence this heterogeneous space made up of multiple 'spaces' must have a social origin. Harre's principle of spatial indifference is correct therefore only under the hegemony of Western rationalism. Further, Durkheim suggests that the classification of space into 'spaces' – its territorialization, as Deleuze and Guattari would say – is structurally similar to the social form of the society (Durkheim, 1976: 11–12).

6 The mutability of this spatialization and its susceptibility to poetic licence and witty manipulation demonstrates its 'deep' role in cognition. To choose only one of hundreds of possible literary examples, Solzenhitsyn opens his *Gulag Archipelago* (1977) by playing on the superstructural and ideologically charged 'second-nature' of otherwise explicitly empirical, geographical, 'space'. This shift from the geographical to the social betrays the tensions of power relations and hierarchies of privilege and 'social place':

> And the Kolyma was the greatest and most famous island, the pole of ferocity of that amazing country of Gulag which, though scattered in an Archipelago geographically, was, in the psychological sense, fused into a continent – an almost invisible, almost imperceptible country inhabited by the 'zed' people. And this Archipelago crisscrossed and patterned that other country within which it was located, like a gigantic patchwork, cutting into its cities, hovering over its streets. Yet there were many who did not know of it (1977: 1)

The system of imprisonment and exile exhibits an almost territorial unity and presence which, however, are obscured by the omnipresence of (socially defined) 'reality' – that of empirical landmasses, and natural science-defined notions of space. This 'reality' insists that the carceral system of the Gulag is spatially separate from the civilized heartland of Soviet society. The power of Solzenhitsyn's formulation is to break through the polar opposition of the empirical space of quotidian life on the one hand (that of the positivist geographers, for example), and the supposed non-existence (no-placeness) of the internal prison system on the other. By throwing them against each other, the prison system is made visible, (hence analyseable, visible to the 'eye' of reason, as it were) 'placed' through the giant conceptual metaphor of the 'Archipelago', where before it could not be perceived.

7 Kern dates this development from the promulgation of Einstein's theory of relativity which provided a sense of reasonableness in talking about spaces of this or that with relativity's 'infinite number of spaces, which are in motion with respect to each other'. (Einstein, 1961: 139).

8 For a excellent survey of the anglophone literature and an ultimately unconvincing but instructive effort to resolve this dilemma in favour of the extinction of the urban and an object of study *see* Saunders, 1981.

9 Spatialization is hypothesized to consist not only of spatialization as a noun designating the:

a   physical expression of social order in space, or, even:
b   the privileged and personal investment of places and (micro) spaces in which meaning is invested, *but also* as a functioning *formation* (spatialization as a verb, designating the arranging of elements, the production of space) which:
c   conceptually grounds the 'rationality' of thought through the presence of spatial categories in schemes of causality:
d   'spaces' individuals, placing them in conceptual hierarchies by which they relate to each other and to the society as a whole, thus playing a role informing the identity of individuated subjects:
e   tutors these bodies in spatial performance and crowd practice.
f   forms categories of discourse – those schemes by which it is possible to conceive of things through the metaphoric appropriation of spatial categories.

10 As documented in the work of Kern (1983), it was the peculiar 'culture' of time and space – the cultural attitudes and priorities towards these two fundamental dimensions of existence – that is to be found lying beneath the aspirations and achievements and also the omissions (for instance, the dismissal of the environment on the one hand and the control of epidemic disease; and the lust for empire and domination and the establishment of a global economic system) of Western modernity in this century.

11 I use this term in its more precise etymological sense of 'habitual routine' rather than in Bourdieu's structuralist sense of a set structuring routines which mediate class responses to an economic 'reality' (*see* Bourdieu 1972, compare Maffesoli 1981).

12 Lefebvre may be criticized as propounding an *essentialist* position. His perhaps over-hasty attempt to totalize his theorization of space by integrating what he sees as the historical succession of distinct 'modes of production of space' with a series of 'spatial ages' opens him to the critique made by Hindess and Hirst (1977) of Marxist theory for similar periodicizations based on industrial modes of production. Lefebvre's replacement of periodicized modes of production with periodicized

spatial ages is further open to the substantive criticism that this periodicizing project neglects the non-periodic condition of social spatializations which, through the longevity of the built environment clearly interpenetrate and never disappear but are repressed into limited areas, and may be invoked in rhetoric (through metaphor), and in the built environment through historicizing quotations from archaic architectural styles. Such nostalgic quotations form an important 'theatre' of postmodern activity, based, as they are, on a loss of historicity and the substitution of a temporality of multiple (i.e. schizoid) presents, with corresponding alterations in the concurrent spatialization. By introducing a periodicized historical temporality, Lefebvre closes off the approaches to the postmodern condition by his new theorization of space. This places him firmly within the modernist paradigm as opposed to what could be called a competing, 'postmodern paradigm.' Nonetheless, despite this closure, Lefebvre's work (1972; 1991) provides powerful insights into how one might construct a project to examine the spatialization of postmodernity at both the social and global, cross-cultural, scales.

References

Anderson, B., *Imagined Communities*, (London, Verso, 1983).

Anderson, P. 'Modernity and Revolution' in *New Left Review* 144 (March–April), 96–113, (1983).

Benjamin, W. *Gesammelte Schriften*, R. Tiedemann, H. Schweppenhäuser, (eds), (Frankfurt, Suhrkamp, 1978).

Berger, P. L. and Luckmann, T., *The Social Construction of Reality: a Treatise in the Sociology of Knowledge*, (New York, Anchor, 1967).

Berman, M., 'The Signs in the Streets' in *New Left Review*, 144, 114–23, (1983).

Bourdieu, P., 'The Berber house or the World Reversed' in Mary Douglas (ed.), *Rules and Meanings*, (Harmondsworth, Penguin, 1971), 98–110.

Bourdieu, P., *Esquisse d'une théorie de la pratique* (Paris, PUF, 1972).

Castells, M., *The Urban Question*, (London, Edward Arnold, 1977).

Davis, M., 'Urban Renaissance and the Spirit of Postmodernism' in *New Left Review*, 151, May–June. 106–14, 1985).

DeCerteau, Michel, *The Practice of Everyday Life*, (Berkeley, University of California Press, 1984).

Deleuze, G. and Guattari, F., *The Anti-Oedipus* (Paris, Minuit, 1976).

Derrida, J., *La Carte postale*, (Paris, Flammarion, 1980).

Durkheim, E., *Elementary Forms of the Religious Life*, 2nd ed., (New York, George Allen & Unwin, 1976).

Einstein, A. *Relativity*, (New York, Random House, 1961).

Foucault, M., *The Birth of the Clinic: An Archaeology of Medical Perception*, translated by A.M. Sheridan Smith, (New York, Vintage/Random House, 1973).

Gottdiener, M., *The Social Production of Urban Space*, (Austin, Texas, University of Texas Press, 1985).

Harvey, D., *Social Justice and the City*, (Baltimore, Johns Hopkins University Press, 1973).

Harvey D., *The Condition of Postmodernity*, (Oxford, Basil Blackwell, 1989).

Hearne, S., *A Journey from Prince of Wales Fort in Hudson's Bay to the Northern Ocean in the Years 1769–70–71* (London, no publisher's imprint, 1795).

Jameson, F., 'Postmodernism, or the Cultural Logic of Late Capitalism' in *New Left Review*, 146 (July-August), 53–93, (1984).

Kern, S., *The Culture of Time and Space*, (London, Weidenfeld and Nicolson, 1983).

Jardine, A., *Gynesis*, (Cambridge, Mass. Harvard University Press, 1985).

Lefebvre, H., *La somme et le reste*, 2 vols (Paris, La Nef de Paris, 1959).

Lefebvre, H., *La Pensée marxiste et la ville* (Paris, Casterman, 1972).

Lefebvre, H., *Le Droit la ville*, (Paris, Editions Anthropos, 1975).

Lefebvre, H., 'Reflections on the Politics of Space' in *Antipode*, 8, 31 ff., (1976).

Lefebvre, H., *La Production de l'espace*, 2nd ed. (Paris, Antipode, 1981) originally published 1974

Lefebvre, H., *The Production of Space*, (Oxford, Basil Blackwell, 1991) trans. of Lefebvre 1981.

Lefebvre, H., *Le Temps des Tribus*, (Paris, Méridiens-Klinckseick, 1981).

Martins M. R., 'The Theory of Social Space in the Work of Henri Lefebvre', in R. Forrest, J. Henderson and P. Williams, (eds), *Urban Political Economy and Social Theory*, (Epping, Essex, Gower, 1982). 160–85.

Massey, D., *Spatial Divisions of Labour: Social Structures and the Geography of Production*, (London, Macmillan, 1984).

Nietzsche *Will to Power*, translated by W. Kaufmann (New York, Random House, 1967). Pike, W. (1892)

Sack, R. D., *Conceptions of space in social thought*, (Minneapolis, University of Minnesota Press, 1980).

Saunders, P., *Social Theory and the Urban Question*, (London, Hutchinson, 1981).

Sayer, A., 'The Difference that Space Makes', in Gregory, D. and Urry, J., *Social Relations and Spatial Structures*, (London, Macmillan, 1985) 49–66.

Shields, R., 'Social Spatialisation and the Built Environment: the Case of the West Edmonton Mall;' in *Environment and Planning D: Society and Space* 7: 2 (summer, 1989), 147–64.

Shields, R., 'Social Science and Postmodern Spatialisations: Jameson's Aesthetic of Cognitive Mapping', chapter 2 in Elspeth Graham, Joe Doherty and Mo Malek (eds), *Postmodernism and the Social Sciences*, (Macmillan, London, 1992a), 39–56.

Shields, R., 'A Truant Proximity: Presence and Absence in the Space of Modernity', in *Environment and Planning D: Society and Space* 10:1, 181– 207, (1992b).

Soja, E., 'The Socio-Spatial Dialectic' in *Annals of the American Association of Geographers*, 70: 2, 207–25, (1980).

Solzenhitsyen, A., *The Gulag Archipelago*, (New York, Harper and Row, 1977).

Sorokin, P. A., *Sociocultural Causality, Space, Time* (Durham N.C., Duke University Press, 1943).

Urry, J., *The Tourist Gaze*, (London, Routledge, 1990).

Werlen, Benno, *Society, Action and Space* , (London, Routledge, 1993).

8

Lacan and Geography: the Production of Space Revisited

Derek Gregory

> In advance of the invasion we will hear from the depths of mirrors the clatter of weapons.
>
> Jorge Luis Borges; *The Book of Imaginary Beings*

A Paris fantasy

Imagine. An old philosopher looks out from his apartment in the rue Rambuteau. The real, he believes, resides in the rhythmical, and from his windows, out of the buzz and roar of the great city, he begins to pick out the overlapping, alternating and interpenetrating rhythms of the street below. He can sense the vast invisible circuits of capital that choreograph the ebb and flow of the crowds, the movements of the metallic and carnal bodies: somewhere in this scene is an order that comes from elsewhere, he realizes, from the intricate disciplines of the state and the Bank of France. But there is more to city life than this. Looking down into the street, the windows, the doors, the façades of the bistros and shops seem in a delicate harmony with the gestures and figures that animate the pavements. And yet now, over the way, alien and intrusive, a vast exhibition of metal and solidified piping transcends this human scale and offers itself to the gaze: like a meteorite fallen from a planet ruled by an absolute technocracy. The fabric of everyday life in his little neighbourhood has been shattered by this immense, supra-modern boutique of Beaubourg, the Centre Georges Pompidou, the monumentalized space of which now articulates and conjugates the unrelenting rhythms of an abstracted modernity. The distractions in the surrounding square – the fireaters, the jugglers and the snake men – offer only an illusionary respite from the routinized world of the everyday, prolonging its banalization by other means. But the old philosopher is convinced that it is still possible to hear the muffled murmurs of 'the real', of the traces of an older and somehow more authentic everyday life, by opening

oneself to the music of the city, to rhythms that can never be captured by a sequence of images.

Imagine. Inside Beaubourg, an artwork that is also the staging of an artwork, another French philosopher is at work, putting together a new installation. Beaubourg is a building turned inside-out, with racks of green pipes and blue ducts crawling over its exterior and great glass tubes cutting diagonals through its interior. But it is now being turned inside out again: a giant metallic maze is in place, divided by grey gauze screens, producing an inverted museum. Wandering through its labyrinth, *flâneurs-bricoleurs* are saturated by intimations of a future that is all around them but which they cannot fix, cannot name, cannot map: there is no order of things to which they can appeal, no meta-narrative guiding their reading. No longer spectators, they are dissolved into players in the drama of the postmodern. Their performance begins at 'The Theatre of the Non-Body', a mirrored vestibule, and proceeds in the company of disembodied voices – Barthes, Baudrillard, Derrida; Artaud, Beckett, Kleist – that animate objects, videos, slides, displays: a technoscientific odyssey into what the philosopher calls *Les immatériaux*. Unlike other museums, this does not stage a codification of what has gone before but a disorientating anticipation of what might be. In this peculiar postmodern museum, the philosopher wants to fracture the frozen surfaces of what is conventionally taken to be 'the real', to show that every particular of the taken-for-granted world -- including the embodied self – can be infinitely analysed into a web of processes and relations ('immaterials'). His objective is to confront the traditional Utopia of a single world for identical beings with a postmodern heterotopia of multiple worlds and diverse identities, to reveal a sublime mutability that is enacted through the dispossession of the human body and the dematerialization of space.

In my fantasy, the old philosopher is played by Henri Lefebvre, the younger philosopher by Jean-François Lyotard. But it is only part-fantasy: in the early 1980s Lefebvre did sketch a tantalizing essay contemplating the rhythms he could hear from his apartment overlooking Beaubourg where, in 1985, Lyotard did direct *Les immatériaux*.[1] I don't know whether Lefebvre ever visited Lyotard's installation, though I doubt it; he surely would have seen it as a chamber of horrors, and his unwavering humanism could never accommodate Lyotard's fascination with the 'inhuman'. But imaginatively juxtaposing the two is an economical way of interrupting attempts to treat Lefebvre as a

---

1   I have derived Lefebvre's reflections from Henri Lefebvre, 'Vu de la fenêtre', in *Éléments de rhythmanalyse: introduction à la connaissance des rythmes* (Paris, Syllepse, 1992) pp. 41–53; translated as 'Seen from the window' in *idem, Writings on cities* (Oxford and Cambridge MA, Blackwell, 1995) pp. 219–27; the essay was written in the early 1980s and published posthumously. For the details of Lyotard's *Les immatériaux*, I have drawn on John Rajchman, 'The postmodern museum', originally published (with illustrations) in *Art in America*, October 1985, pp. 110–17, 171 and reprinted in his *Philosophical events of the 80s* (New York, Columbia University Press, 1992) pp. 105–17; and on Paul Crowther, 'The postmodern sublime' in Andrew Benjamin (ed.), *Judging Lyotard* (London, Routledge, 1994) pp. 192–205.

postmodern philosopher *avant la lettre* and, more importantly, identifies the relation between bodies and spaces as a particularly productive site at which Lefebvre confronts one of the most influential visions of the postmodern. In what follows, I propose to (re)construct this site by reading Lefebvre through the *grille* of concepts provided by a third figure: Jacques Lacan. This is not as strange as it might seem; in fact Lefebvre intended his 'rhythmana-lysis' as an alternative to psychoanalysis and, as I want to show, this magisterial account of the production of space depended, in part, on a running critique of Lacan.

Histories of bodies and spaces

Lefebvre's writings represent (for me) one of the most important single sources for the development of a critical understanding of the production of space. In the course of his long life he wrote almost 70 books, but it was those that appeared between 1968 and 1974 that addressed most directly what came to be called 'the urban question'. *La production de l'espace*, which was first published when Lefebvre was in his early seventies, is the climax of that sequence and reveals him at the height of his powers: imaginative, incisive and immensely suggestive.[2] There, Lefebvre sketches two, closely imbricated 'histories of space' which are also 'histories of the body'.

The most prominent is a history of the relations between bodies and spaces which is constructed through a radicalization of Marx's critique of *political economy*. Most commentators fix Lefebvre's intellectual topography by sighting these coordinates, plotting the lines between his Marxism and an eclectic humanism, and I do not mean to diminish their importance. Lefebvre's position within Western Marxism may be singular, but there can be no doubt of his commitment to a reconstructed historical materialism. Indeed, there are suggestive (though I think superficial) parallels between Habermas's theory of communicative action, which he once advertised as a 'reconstruction' of historical materialism, and Lefebvre's account of the production of space. Habermas speaks of the colonization of the life-world by the system, Lefebvre of the colonization of the spaces of 'everyday life' by the production of an abstract space. But Habermas sees this process as a deformation of the project of modernity, which his own work is intended to reclaim, and his argumentation sketches and reconstructive histories are designed to expose the inner logics and circuit diagrams of a transcendent process of rationalization.[3] In contrast, Lefebvre strongly implies that the triumph of functionalist reason is inscribed within the very heart of capitalist modernity. Its impositions and alienations

2   Henri Lefebvre, *La production de l'espace* (Paris, Anthropos, 1974), translated into English by Donald Nicholson-Smith as *The production of space* (Oxford, and Cambridge, Mass., Blackwell, 1991).
3   Cf. Jürgen Habermas, *The theory of communicative action*, vol. 2, *The critique of functionalist reason*, (Cambridge, Polity Press, 1987); this was first published in German in 1981.

are not purely conjunctural or contingent, and Lefebvre offers an alternative history the progressions of which install a dramatically different historicism. From this perspective, the colonization of everyday life has been advanced through a 'logic of visualization' in which the spatialities of a fully human existence have been almost entirely erased: all the remains are traces, feint human geographies in an otherwise abstract geometry. If capitalism is constituted as a particular constellation of power, knowledge and spatiality, as Lefebvre seems to say, then its modernity is inscribed in a decorporealized space.[4]

Although Lefebvre is concerned to chart the historical succession and superimposition of modes of production of space, his project is not a simple extension of Marx's critique of political economy. He remains indebted to Marx's writings, and most particularly to the sketches contained in the *Grundrisse*, but he believes that there is something sufficiently distinctive about the collective production of space under neo-capitalism that makes it necessary to transcend the classical categories of historical materialism. Partly for this reason there is, I think, another history of space in Lefebvre's work, which is derived from the developmental relations between the human body and space – from those phases through which the human being is supposed to move during its passage from infancy to adulthood – and which is constructed through an oblique, and at times almost subterranean critique of Lacanian *psychoanalysis*. In my previous discussions of Lefebvre, like most commentators I ignored his response to Lacan. But it is impossible to read the same book twice, and a re-reading of *La production de l'espace* has since persuaded me of the importance of this psychoanalytic provocation. In what follows, therefore, I want to show how Lefebvre's reworking of historical materialism, and in particular his construction of concepts of spatiality, depend crucially on these unstable foundations.

Lefebvre and Lacan

In many ways, parallels between the two projects are unremarkable. On the one side, Popper castigated both psychoanalysis and historical materialism as pretenders to the throne of Science, as 'pseudo-sciences' with propositions that scrupulously avoided his own criteria of falsification.[5] On the other side, modern French thought has often been preoccupied with conjoining Freud and Marx, libidinal economy and political economy, and there is a vital tradition of what Margaret Cohen has recently described as 'Gothic Marxism' that, from the early twentieth century, sought to appropriate Freud's writings for a renewed historical materialism.[6] According to Mark Poster, Lefebvre was

4   For a fuller discussion, *see* 'Modernity and the production of space', in my *Geographical imaginations*, (Oxford, and Cambridge, Mass., Blackwell, 1994) pp. 348–416.
5   Karl Popper, *The logic of scientific discovery* (London, Hutchinson, 1959); this was first published in German in 1934–35.

probably the first French philosopher to read Freud seriously, but he claims that he did so 'only during his brief interest in surrealism in the 1920s'.[7] Certainly, the surrealists were the first group in France to draw on Freud's work in any sustained and constructive fashion – one writer suggests that Freud was almost unknown in France until surrealists 'discovered' him, though whether this did very much to further Freud's reception is an open question – and there were plainly important connections between psychoanalysis and Breton's 'modern materialism'.[8] But Lefebvre's (critical) interest in surrealism was not eclipsed in the inter-war period; it is vividly present in his writings after 1958 (when he broke with the PCF, the French Communist Party) and in *Production*, written in the wake of May '68, he concedes that 'surrealism appears quite otherwise than it did half a century ago' and that its theoretical promise, although unrealized, remains none the less vital: 'to decode inner space and illuminate the nature of the transition from this subjective space to the material realm of the body and the outside world, and thence to social life'.[9] As I will show, this was, in essence, the object of Lefebvre's own 'spatial architectonics'.

But neither was Lefebvre's interest in psychoanalysis confirmed to Freud, and throughout *Production* he conducts a running skirmish against Lacan's provocative re-reading of Freud. Lefebvre and Lacan were exact contemporaries, both born in 1901. Like Lefebvre, Lacan moved in the circles – sometimes the shadows – of surrealism, and in fact the discussion between Bataille, Caillois and Leiris that led to the foundation of the Collège de Sociologie, a group of dissident surrealists, took place in 1937 in Lacan's Paris apartment. He was drawn to surrealism by its obsessive play with language; as David Macey remarks, surrealism involved an exploration of the production of signification – of what Lacan would later call the symbolic – and was thus, in part, a challenge to conventional conceptions of subjectivity.[10] The surrealists were also among

6   Margaret Cohen, *Profane Illumination: Walter Benjamin and the Paris of surrealist revolution*, (Berkeley, University of California Press, 1993). Closer to our own time, Vincent Descombes has suggested a reorientation in French critical thought, post '68, in which historical materialism was supposed to be revivified 'with an injection of desire and *jouissance*'. He notes the (passing) importance of Herbert Marcuse and hence, indirectly, of the Frankfurt School of critical theory, but pays much more attention to the contributions of Gilles Deleuze and Jean-François Lyotard. *See* Vincent Descombes, *Modern French Philosophy*, (Cambridge, Cambridge University Press, 1980) pp. 171–86.

7   Mark Poster, *Existential Marxism in post-war France: from Sartre to Althusser*, (Princeton, Princeton University Press, 1975) p. 260.

8   Helena Lewis, *The politics of surrealism* (New York, Paragon, 1988) p. x. Freud's response to his 'discovery' was equivocal. 'I am not able to clarify for myself what surrealism is and what it wants', he wrote to Breton, and Cohen suggests that he was disconcerted by Breton's interest in 'statements by Freud that pivot suggestively to Marxist theory'. *See* Cohen, *Profane Illumination*, (1993) pp. 57–61 and, for a further discussion, Elizabeth Roudinesco, 'Surrealism in the service of psychoanalysis', in her *Jacques Lacan & Co. A history of psychoanalysis in France, 1925–1985*, (Chicago, University of Chicago Press, 1990) pp. 3–34.

9   Lefebvre, in *Production*, (1974), p. 18.

10 For an elaboration of the (complex) connections between surrealism and Lacan's own work, see Cohen, *Profane Illumination*, (1993), pp. 147–53 and David Macey, 'Baltimore in the early morning', in his *Lacan in contexts* (London, Verso, 1988) pp. 44–74. The title

the first in France to reclaim Hegel for revolutionary thought, and Lefebvre's involvement with surrealism thus led him not only to Freud, as I have noted, but also to Hegel (and then through him to Marx). Lefebvre's was no simple Hegelian Marxism, and his appropriation was a stubbornly critical one, but the traces of Hegel are indelibly present throughout his work and are particularly prominent in his account of the production of space.[11] The Collège de Sociologie played a part in introducing Lacan to Hegel, whose ideas proved to be a vital spur to the development of his own thesis about the constitution of subjectivity. But both Lefebvre and Lacan, like many others of their generation, were also profoundly influenced by Kojève's recuperation of Hegel's *Phenomenology*, and Macey suggests that if one were to develop a cultural geography of dissident Paris in the 1930s, then 'Kojève's lecture room would lie at its heart'.[12] Lefebvre and Lacan learned different lessons there, to be sure, but where they differed most decisively was over historical materialism. Lacan's earliest political sympathies were with the Right rather than the Left, and, when he was subsequently drawn into a closer association with Marxism, it was with an avowedly structural Marxism that Lefebvre strenuously repudiated. In fact, it was the principal architect of structural Marxism, Louis Althusser, who invited Lacan to move his seminar to the École Normale Supérieure in 1963, and Althusser later used Lacan's work to construct a theory of ideology that was at odds with Lefebvre's humanist inclinations.[13] Many critics have claimed that it was also at odds with Lacan – that no matter how closely Althusser read *Capital*, he did not accord Lacan the same careful study[14] – but it was still the

of Macey's essay is taken from what he regards as Lacan's 'surrealist' image of the unconscious as 'Baltimore in the early morning'.

11 Soja argues that 'Hegel and Hegelianism promulgated a powerful spatialist ontology' that was lost when Marx subsequently 'inverted' Hegel. 'The early expansion of Marxism in France, however, coincided with a major Hegelian revival, a reinvestiture that carried with it a less expurgated sensitivity to the spatiality of social life.' Its leading bearer, so he claims, was Lefebvre. *See* Edward Soja, *Postmodern geographies: the reassertion of space in critical social theory* (London, Verso, 1989) pp. 46–7, 86, For a fuller discussion of the filiations between surrealism, Hegel and Lefebvre – though one which says nothing about spatiality – *see* Martin Jay, 'Henri Lefebvre, the surrealists and the reception of Hegelian Marxism in France', in his *Marxism and totality: adventures of a concept from Lukács to Habermas*, (Cambridge; Polity Press, 1984) pp. 276–99.

12 Macey, *Lacan* (1988) p. 96. For discussions of Kojève's role in the Hegelian revival in France, *see* Judith Butler, *Subjects of desire: Hegelian reflections in twentieth-century France* (New York, Columbia University Press, 1987) and Michael Roth, *Knowing and history: appropriations of Hegel in twentieth-century France,*(Ithaca, Cornell University Press, 1988).

13 I have found Martin Jay particularly helpful on the relations between Lacan and Althusser: see 'Lacan, Althusser and the specular subject of ideology', in his *Downcast eyes: the denigration of vision in twentieth-century French thought* (Berkeley, University of California Press, 1993) pp. 329–80; *see also* Michèle Barrett, *The politics of truth: from Marx to Foucault*, (Cambridge, Polity Press, 1991) pp. 96–110. For the relations between Lefebvre and Althusser, *see* Michael Kelly, *Modern French Marxism*, (Oxford, Basil Blackwell, 1982) and Gregory, 'Modernity', (1994) pp. 355–7.

14 For a summary, *see* Anthony Elliott, 'Psychoanalysis, ideology and modern societies: post-Lacanian social theory', in his *Social theory and psychoanalysis in transition: self and society from Freud to Kristeva* (Oxford, and Cambridge, Mass., Blackwell, 1992) pp. 162–200, especially pp. 164–77.

case that by 1966 Lacan was endorsing Althusser against Sartre, at a time when Lefebvre and Sartre had already established an intellectual *rapprochement* of sorts.[15] By the time the events of May '68 were unfolding on the streets of Paris, Lacan and Lefebvre were on the same side, more or less, and for that matter on the same sidelines, but their positions were none the less different. Both were accused of fanning the flames of student unrest, though neither of them joined the students on the barricades, but Lefebvre was much more sympathetic, and his classes as Nanterre were a rallying-ground for many of the young revolutionaries, whereas Lacan stormed out of a lecture at Vincennes denouncing those who longed for 'a Master'.[16]

These biographical connections and affiliations are important, but none of them discloses the conceptual tensions between Lefebvre and Lacan in any detail. For this reason I want to set out in summary form a series of claims made by Lacan (at various times) from which Lefebvre most conspicuously dissents in *La production de l'espace*. I hope it will be obvious that these spare observations are not – cannot be – a synoptic account of Lacan's work: that would be absurd. They do not constitute a critique of Lacan either, but my presentation of these ideas should not be confused with their endorsement. By sharpening those points which provoke Lefebvre into such vocal disagreement, however, it should be possible to develop a clearer sense of those other, counter-claims that he seeks to advance. It follows that my intentions in this essay are largely expository: I hope that by locating one of the unremarked bases from which Lefebvre constructs his history of space, a more vigorously critical appreciation of his work might be set in train.

Lacan's speculations

Lacan posits three 'orders' – the Real, the Imaginary and the Symbolic – which together form a complex topological space in which, as Malcolm Bowie puts it, 'the characteristic disorderly motions of the human mind can be plotted'. The spatial metaphoric becomes progressively more important in Lacan's work, which is what both attracts and annoys Lefebvre, and Lacan eventually configures this topological space as a Borromean chain (or 'knot'), a complex

15 Lefebvre had dismissed Sartre's *L'Etre et le Néant*, published in 1943, in uncompromisingly hostile terms, but the publication of the first part of his *Critique de la raison dialectique* in 1960 marked both Sartre's philosophical acceptance of Marxism and Lefebvre's (still critical) acceptance of Sartre.
16 It was in fact Foucault, another of Lefebvre's *bêtes noires*, who invited Lacan to conduct his seminar at Vincennes, after the École Normale Supérieure refused to allow him to continue in its own precincts. For a general (though hardly disinterested) discussion of the connections between French philosophy and the events of May 68, *see* Luc Ferry and Alain Renaut, *French philosophy of the sixties: an essay on anti-humanism*, (Amherst, University of Massachusetts Press, 1990); this was originally published in French in 1985. Lefebvre provides his own account of those events in his *The explosion: Marxism and the French Revolution*, (New York, Monthly Review Press, 1969); this was originally published in French in 1968.

figure formed from two separate links joined by a third in such a way that the chain will fall apart if any one of the links is severed.[17]

The Real

The Real is one of Lacan's most elusive concepts, and it also marks the site of one of Lefebvre's most fundamental disagreements with him. As a first approximation, one might say that the Real is 'an anatomical, "natural" order' into which a child is born and through which the child experiences its being as a 'body-in-parts': as a set of unco-ordinated, fragmented 'raw materials' that Lacan calls, in an artfully gendered play on words, *un homelette*. This primal phase is soon organized through the other two orders, the Imaginary and the Symbolic, which correspond to subsequent developmental phases. But there is an interpretative difficulty here. Elizabeth Grosz treats the Lacanian Real as 'a pure plenitude or fullness' exemplified by 'the lack of a lack' – a reading which turns out to be much closer to Lefebvre's inclinations – whereas Bowie suggests that plenitude is approached by 'reading off one by one the interferences between the Symbolic, Imaginary and Real by which "being human" is defined': a claim which clearly accords with Lacan's topological representation of the three orders. Seen in this latter way, the Real is a permanent, 'unrecoverable presence' as it were, caught in a force field of tension and resisting its always unsuccessful re-presentation through the Imaginary and the Symbolic.[18]

It follows that the Real is not to be confounded with 'reality' which is lived and known only through the Imaginary and the Symbolic. Although these other two orders were not developed in this way, they can I think be related to Lacan's invocation of Hegel's *Phenomenology* as a warrant for his own claim that the self can grasp itself only 'through its reflection in, and recognition by, the other person'.[19] But Lacan is not prefiguring any Hegelian synthesis, and the ineluctable imperfections of that 'grasping', and most particularly of attempts to conjure the Real into images and words, need to be stressed, because they help to explain why Lacan's attempts to delineate the Real prove to be so elusive. As Bowie reminds Lacan's frustrated readers, 'allowing the structure of the Real to emerge against the background of a primitive, undifferentiated

17 Malcolm Bowie, *Lacan* (London, Fontana, 1991) pp. 98–9; for examples of Lacan's topologies, *see* Jeanne Granon-Lafont, *La topologie ordinaire de Jacques Lacan,*(Paris, Point hors Ligne, 1985) and Alexandre Leupin, 'Voids and knots in knowledge and truth', in Alexandre Leupin (ed.), *Lacan and the human sciences*, (Lincoln, University of Nebraska Press, 1991) pp. 1–23.

18 Elizabeth Grosz, *Jacques Lacan: a feminist introduction*, (London, Routledge, 1990) pp. 33–4; Bowie, *Lacan*, (1991) p. 99. I am indebted to Steve Pile for clarifying this interpretative puzzle for me.

19 Anthony Elliott, 'The language of desire: Lacan and the specular structure of the self', in his *Social theory and psychoanalysis*, (1992); pp. 123–61; the quotation is from p. 125. I should add that the two concepts were developed at different times: Lacan first presented his ideas about the Imaginary in 1936, though a printed (and revised) version did not appear until 1949, and the Symbolic was originally formalized during the 1950s and '60s.

All is not the same thing as being able to name it, process it symbolically and put it to work for one's own ends'.[20]

The Imaginary

Lacan introduces the Imaginary through an allegory that turns on a developmental phase wholly absent from classical Freudianism: the so-called 'mirror stage'. Lacan claims that somewhere between the ages of six and eighteen months the young child typically develops a sense of wholeness, of bodily integrity and subjective unity, by looking at its own reflection in a mirror. He contrasts the child's 'jubilant assumption of his [*sic*] specular image' to the response of a chimpanzee of the same age, which rapidly tires of playing with the mirror and moves off in search of other distractions. But the point of the comparison is not to celebrate human development. On the contrary:

> [S]omething derisory is going on in front of the mirror. Where the chimpanzee is able to recognise that the mirror-image is an epistemological void, the child has a perverse will to remain deluded. The child's attention is seized (*capté*) by the firm spatial relationships between its real body and its specular body and between body and setting within the specular image; he or she is captivated (*captivé*). But the term that Lacan prefers to either of these, and which harnesses and outstrips their combined expressive power, is the moral and legal *captation*: the complex geometry of body, setting and mirror works upon the individual as a ruse, a deception, an inveiglement. The mirror, seemingly so consoling and advantageous to the infant, is a trap and a decoy (*leurre*).[21]

This pre-verbal register constitutes the Imaginary, and I want to emphasize three features of Lacan's characterization of it.

First, its inherent, constitutive *spatiality*. On this occasion, at least, Lacan is offering more than a metaphor. As Jameson recognizes,

> A description of the Imaginary will therefore on the one hand require us to come to terms with a uniquely determinate configuration of space – one not yet organized around the individuation of my personal body, or differentiated according to the perspectives of my own central point of view – yet which nonetheless swarms with bodies and forms intuited in a different way, whose fundamental property is, it would seem, to be visible without their visibility being the result of the act of any particular observer, to be, as it were, already-seen, to carry their specularity upon themselves like a colour they wear or the texture of their surface. In this ... these bodies of the Imaginary exemplify the very logic of mirror images; yet the existence of the normal object world of adult everyday life presupposes this prior, imaginary experience of space.[22]

20 Bowie, *Lacan*, (1991) p. 95.
21 Bowie, *Lacan*, (1991) p. 23. If celebration is in order, it would be difficult to think of a worthier subject than a chimpanzee that can recognize an 'epistemological void'.
22 Jameson, 'Imaginary and Symbolic', pp. 354–5.

Secondly, the *visuality* of the Imaginary. Lacan was extremely interested in Caillois's work on psychasthenia, in which the relation between the self and its surrounding space is disturbed through a visual fusion, a mimicry so complete that the self is assimilated to space. 'To these dispossessed souls', Caillois wrote, 'space pursues them, encircles them, digests them in a gigantic phagocytosis.' But where Caillois described a crisis of the boundaried self, Lacan was interested in its opposite: in the formation of that self through specular identification.[23] For Lacan, Grosz argues, vision most readily confirms the separation of subject from object, and is also 'the most amenable of the senses to spatialization.' Within the Imaginary, 'space is hierarchically organized and structured in terms of a centralized, singularized point-of-view by being brought under the dominance of the visual'.[24]

Thirdly, its *duplicity*. Lacan plainly distrusts this spatialized, specularized self, which is founded on 'a mirage of coherence and solidity through which the subject is seduced into misrecognition of its own truth'. The key word is 'misrecognition' – what Lacan called *méconnaissance* – which has been accentuated by virtually every commentator: thus 'the capture of the "I" by the reflection in the mirror is inseparable from a misrecognition of the gap between the fragmented subject and its unified image of itself'.[25] Taken together, therefore, one might say that, for Lacan, 'the map of the body, setting and mirror both captivates and consoles the child, but it is an illusion, a trap, a decoy'; [imaginary] geography is the medium of deception, it 'offers "ground truth" but cannot be trusted'.[26]

The Symbolic

What frees the subject from this hall of mirrors – or at any rate prevents its glissade into psychosis – is its passage into the Symbolic. This marks the child's entry into language, and Lacan's preoccupation with language is one of the signal elements of his own work. I mean by this something more than the analytical priority he accords to language, because Lacan's playfulness within language – in his speech and in his writing – is an integral part of his project. If 'Lacan's writing seeks to tease and seduce', as Bowie says, then its multiple

23 Roger Caillois's original essay was published in *Minotaure* in 1935; it has been translated and reprinted as 'Mimicry and legendary psychasthenia', *October* 31 (1984) pp. 17–32; the quotation is from p. 30. My discussion also draws on Jay. 'The specular subject of ideology', pp. 342–3.
24 Grosz, *Jacques Lacan*, (1990), p. 38. These considerations prompt Grosz to implicate Lacan in an ocularcentrism, but her discussion ignores the complex ways in which vision is gendered – even as she indicts Lacan for his phallocentrism – and forecloses Lacan's *critique* of ocularcentrism: see Jay, 'The specular subject of ideology', pp. 353–70.
25 Peter Dews, 'Jacques Lacan: a philosophical rethinking of Freud', in his *Logics of disintegration: post-structuralist thought and the claims of critical theory* (London, Verso, 1987) pp. 45–86; the quotation is from p. 55; Elliott, 'Language of desire', (1992), p. 128.
26 Steve Pile, 'Human agency and human geography revisited: a critique of "new models" of the self', *Transactions of the Institute of British Geographers* 18 (1993) pp. 122–39; the quotation is from p. 135.

'feints, subterfuges, evasions and mimicries' are (im)precisely what Lacan is talking *about*, (in)exactly what he has to *show*: if 'the unconscious is structured like a language', then its irruptions cannot be other than plural, allusive, heterogeneous.[27]

With the installation of the Symbolic as the signifying register, Lacan effectively turns the subject into a series of fleeting events within language: 'the signifier becomes a versatile topological space, a device for plotting and replotting the itineraries of Lacan's empty subject'.[28] This imaginative analytical cartography has two roots (routes?) that reappear, in displaced form, in Lefebvre's spatial architectonics. One is inside the signifying chain and the other is inside the system of intersubjectivity, though these are articulated through one another, and I need to consider each of them in turn.

In the first place, Lacan turns to structural linguistics to identify two modes of connection within the signifying chain: *metaphor*, which is supposed to mark the relation of discourse to the subject, and *metonymy*, which is supposed to mark the relation of discourse to the object. The importance of this manoeuvre is that it treats the unconscious as 'the conjectural sub-text that is required in order to make the text of dreams and conversations intelligible'. It removes the occult quality of the unconscious – makes it accessible to analysis – by identifying these two rhetorical tropes with what Freud took to be the fundamental mechanisms of the dream-work: thus the signifying domain of the dream-work is decoded by identifying metaphor with 'condensation' and metonymy with 'displacement'.[29] More than this, however, Lacan also implies an intricate gendering of the two processes. Metaphor's substitution of one word for another crosses the Saussurean bar between signifier and signified and can be read as an index of (phallic) 'verticality', whereas metonymy's substitution of part for whole remains on one side of the bar and suggests a contiguity of femininity and 'horizontality': thus the object appears 'beyond' or 'on the other side of discourse' as an absence, a lack, which is invested with *desire*.[30]

In the second place, and closely connected to these considerations, Lacan turns to structural anthropology, in particular to Lévi-Strauss's seminal discussion of the incest taboo, to conceptualize the Oedipus complex as a linguistic transaction. Most importantly, he identifies those agencies that place

27 Bowie, *Lacan* (1991), p. 200. Bowie suggests that Lacan 'eroticizes' the language of theory, and interestingly Eagleton makes a similar point about Jameson:

> Discourse must be reinvested with desire, but not to the point where it confiscates the historical realizations of that desire. Jameson's style is a practice which displays such contradictions even as it strives to mediate them.

See Terry Eagleton, 'Fredric Jameson and the politics of style', in his *Against the grain: essays 1975–1985* (London, Verso, 1986) p. 69.
28 Bowie, *Lacan*, (1991) p. 76.
29 Bowie, *Lacan*, (1991) p. 70–1.
30 My understanding of these relations is indebted to Jane Gallop, 'Metaphor and metonymy' in her *Reading Lacan* (Ithaca, Cornell University Press, 1985) pp. 114–32. She is wonderfully successful in conjuring up coexistent and contradictory readings of metaphor and metonymy in Lacan, and in showing that the oppositions between the two terms and their connotations are far from straightforward or stable.

prohibitions on the child's desire for its mother with the 'symbolic father' whose name supposedly initiates the liquid mobility of the signifying chain: with what Lacan calls the Name-of-the-Father, an ascription which in spoken French cleverly blurs the *'Non' du Père* (prohibition) with the *'Nom' du Père* (symbolization).[31] These prohibitions are inscribed within the Symbolic, and by this means Lacan equates entry into language with castration and identifies this loss or lack with the *phallus*, thus:

> [T]hrough his relationship to the signifier, the subject is deprived of something of himself, of his life, which has assumed the value of that which binds him to the signifier. The phallus is our term for the signifier of his alienation in signification. When the subject is deprived of this signifier, a particular object becomes for him an object of desire ...[32]

I should say at once that Lacan's 'phallus' cannot be immediately and directly identified with the penis – it connotes a signifier before a physical organ[33] – and that his primary point is about linguistic or symbolic castration. As Jane Gallop puts it, Lacan's Symbolic means that 'we can only signify ourselves in a symbolic system that we do not command'.[34] And yet this is not a counsel of despair; the burden of Lacan's work – of his teachings and writings – is that it ought to be possible to comprehend our lack of comprehension, to learn from our loss, not to recover some (imaginary) plenitude but to come to terms with the tantalization of language. Gallop's reading strategy turns on this very possibility: hence what one commentator criticizes as her 'insufficient command' of Lacan becomes a central part of her project as she struggles to disclose the ambiguities and evasions that enter into her 'pathology of interpretation'.[35] Delimiting language in this way, signalling its limits, is by definition not confined to the analyst or critic, however, and Lacan accentuates the reflexivity of all intersubjective action, thus:

> Although it may at first appear that the other subject is perpetually hidden 'behind' the wall of language, it becomes apparent that all subjects are on the

31 Jay, 'The specular subject of ideology', p. 352. *See also* Grosz, *Jacques Lacan*, (1990), pp. 101–5.

32 These remarks are taken from Lacan's seminars on *Hamlet*, and are cited in Kaja Silverman, *The subject of semiotics*, (New York, Oxford University Press, 1983), p. 183. As Lacan observes elsewhere, therefore, 'Nothing exists except on an assumed foundation of absence'.

33 Though the two are by no means unconnected: *see* Kaja Silverman, 'The Lacanian phallus', in *differences* 4 (1992) pp. 84–115.

34 Gallop, *Reading Lacan*, (1985), p. 20. This does not absolve Lacan of phallocentrism, however, and Gallop provides a constructively critical account in her 'Reading the Phallus', pp. 133–56; *see also* her *The Daughter's Seduction: feminism and psychoanalysis* (Ithaca, Cornell University Press, 1982). For further discussions, *see* Bowie, 'The meaning of the phallus' in *Lacan* (1991), pp. 122–157 and Jane Flax, *Thinking fragments: psychoanalysis, feminism and postmodernism in the contemporary West* (Berkeley, University of California Press, 1990) pp. 97–107.

35 Gallop, *Reading Lacan*, (1985), pp. 19–21, 131.

same side of this wall, although they are able to communicate only indirectly by means of the echo of their speech upon it.[36]

In general, then, one might conclude that Lacan's project issues in what Gallop calls 'an implicit ethical imperative' to disrupt the Imaginary to reach the Symbolic. His forceful reconstruction of psychoanalysis works through a critique of *ocularcentrism* (of the Imaginary – a shattering of the mirror) which is at the same time far from being an assent to *logocentrism*. It is perfectly true that, on occasion, Lacan seems to privilege the Symbolic over the Imaginary, to exult in the play of language and to break 'the alibi of visual plenitude'.[37] But it is also true that he is immensely suspicious of all such binary oppositions, which he takes to indicate the continued presence and enduring power of the Imaginary: phrasing matters thus, privileging the one over the other, indicates the irruption of the Imaginary into the Symbolic.

Lefebvre's architectonics

In *La production de l'espace* Lefebvre refers directly to Lacan on only four occasions, always in footnotes and never in the body of the text. But his debt to Lacan is much greater than these few citations suggest, and in the introduction he sketches a spatial architectonics derived more or less immediately from Lacan:

> [O]ne might go so far as to explain social space in terms of a dual prohibition: the prohibition which separates the (male) child from his mother because incest is forbidden, and the prohibition which separates the child from its body because language in constituting consciousness breaks down the unmediated unity of the body – because ... the (male) child suffers symbolic castration and his own phallus is objectified for him as part of outside reality.[38]

This is not how Lefebvre constructs his own architectonics, let me say, but what is important about such a psychoanalytics of space, so he argues, is that it prepares the ground for an analysis of the spatial inscription of 'phallic verticality' and horizontal partition. In his history of space he pays particular attention to the phallocentrism of abstract space and to the use of 'walls, enclosures, and façades ... to define both a *scene* (where something takes place) and an *obscene* area to which everything that cannot or may not happen on the

36 Dews, 'Jacques Lacan' 1987, pp. 79–80.
37 The term is from Jay, 'The specular subject', p. 359; Jay goes on to provide an important discussion of the difference (the split) that Lacan proposes between the eye and the gaze. For a particularly imaginative appropriation of Lacan, which speaks directly to Lefebvre's concerns, *see* Kaja Silverman, 'Fassbinder and Lacan: a reconsideration of the gaze, look and image', in her *Male subjectivity at the margins* (New York, Routledge, 1992) pp. 125–156.
38 Lefebvre, *Production*, (1974), pp. 35–6.

scene is relegated'.[39] If Lefebvre's critique of Lacan is discriminating, however, this does not diminish its force. He is most critical of what he takes to be the imperialism of psychoanalysis, and insists that to explain everything in its terms 'can only lead to an intolerable reductionism and dogmatism'. But Lacan's work has a greater influence on Lefebvre's project than these comments imply, because he advances many of his own claims about the production of space through a critical dialogue with psychoanalysis. In many ways, I think that Lefebvre's response to the spatial architectonics sketched in the passage above provides the parameters for his own discussion. He objects that such a schema assumes 'the logical, epistemological and anthropological priority of language over space' and that it puts prohibitions, not productive activity, at the heart of social space.[40] As I now want to show, his own project seeks to reverse these priorities; but in reversing them, his work carries forward, in displaced and distorted form, the same conceptual grid.

'An intelligence of the body'

Lefebvre's style is often as allusive as Lacan's, and he shares a similar exultation *in* language that is at the same time a suspicion *of* language. 'Man does not live by words alone', he declares: 'In the beginning was the Topos', 'long before the advent of the Logos'. What Lefebvre seeks to invoke by this cryptic phrase is a tensely organic spatiality, 'an intelligence of the body', rooted in the taking place of practical activity and bound up with what, in a glancing blow at structural anthropology, he terms 'the elementary forms of the appropriation of nature'.[41] Lefebvre talks of a time, long before the inauguration of either 'historical' or modern, 'abstract' spatialities, when the body's relationship to space had 'an immediacy which would subsequently degenerate and be lost'. He grounds this 'absolute space' in a 'biologico-spatial reality', but it is plainly not a projection of the Lacanian Real on to the plane of society: there is an implication not only of intimacy but of plenitude, inseparable from the dense figuration of absolute space in practices of measurement and representation that 'held up to all

39 Ibid. p. 36; Lefebvre subsequently talks about a 'psychoanalysis of space' in exactly these terms (p. 99).

40 Ibid. p. 36. The emphasis on *production* is vital, not because Lefebvre denies the reality of prohibition – he does not – but because it distances him from any preoccupation with 'space in itself' that would inculpate him in a spatial fetishism: ibid. p. 90. It also enables him to treat social space as 'not only the space of "no", [but] also the space of the body, and hence the space of "yes", of the affirmation of life': ibid. p. 201.

41 Ibid. pp. 117, 174. Cf. Claude Lévi-Strauss, *Les structures élémentaires de la parenté* (Paris, Presses Universitaires de France, 1949) translated into English as *The elementary structures of kinship* (Boston, Mass., Beacon Press, 1969). Lévi-Strauss's relationship to historical materialism was always contentious which is presumably why Lefebvre invokes classical Marxism through 'the appropriation of nature'. Lefebvre subsequently confronts Lévi-Strauss directly: his structural anthropology is another strategy of abstraction, in which space becomes merely 'a means of classification, a nomenclature for things, a taxonomy' quite independent of their content. Lefebvre is also, and in consequence, astonished at Lévi-Strauss's determination to discuss kinship without discussing sexuality, eroticism or desire: Lefebvre, *Production*, (1974) p. 296.

members of a society an image and reflection of their own bodies'.[42] Neither is this a projection of the Lacanian Symbolic on to the plane of society; these 'images' and 'reflections' were not separate from the corporeality of the body or the physicality of the natural world but were fully continuous with them. They formed analogical and cosmological spaces within an absolute space the meanings of which were not assigned to some separate symbolic register: they belonged to a world in which, as Lefebvre displaces Lacan, 'the imaginary is transformed into the real'.[43]

The distorted echoes of Lacan in that phrase are unmistakable, but I propose to sharpen Lefebvre's argument (and to clarify those distortions) by means of a different comparison. Michel Foucault had already suggested that the human body 'is always the possible half of a universal atlas'. He illustrated the claim with a series of vivid vignettes, many of which were unknown to, or even unrecognized by, some of the astonished historians who read *Les mots et les choses*. For example:

> Upright between the surfaces of the universe, [man] stands in relation to the firmament (his face is to his body what the face of heaven is to the ether; his pulse beats in his vein as the stars circle the sky according to their own fixed paths; the seven orifices in his head are to his face what the seven planets are to the sky); but he is also the fulcrum upon which all these relations turn, so that we find them again, their similarity unimpaired, in the analogy of the human animal to the earth it inhabits: his flesh is a glebe, his bones are rocks, his veins great rivers, his bladder is the sea, and his seven principal organs are the metals hidden in the shafts of mines.'[44]

'Man', Foucault wrote, 'transmits these resemblances back into the world from which he receives them.' And for Foucault – though not Lefebvre – 'the space inhabited by immediate resemblances becomes like *a vast open book*': 'The great untroubled mirror in whose depths things gazed at themselves and reflected

---

42 Ibid. pp. 110–11.
43 Ibid. p. 251. For a fuller discussion of the distinctions between the analogical and cosmological spaces of absolute space and the emergence of the symbolic spaces of historical space, *see* Gregory, 'Modernity', (1994), pp. 382–92.
44 Michel Foucault, *Les mots et les choses*, (Paris, Gallimard, 1966), translated into English as *The order of things: an archaeology of the human sciences*, (London, Tavistock, 1970), p. 22. The original French publication coincided with that of Lacan's *Écrits*; Foucault had heard Lacan lecture at the École Normale Supérieure, and psychoanalysis was one of the 'counter-sciences' he discussed in *Les mots et les choses*. Didier Eribon claims that 'Foucault's entire archaeological enterprise was really based on Lacan', but his other biographers – David Macey and James Miller – contend that Foucault had little sympathy with Lacan's project. Certainly, by the time of *La volonté de savoir*, the first volume of his projected *Histoire de la sexualité*, even Eribon agrees that Foucault was 'setting out on a genealogical quest against Lacan': *see* Didier Eribon, *Michel Foucault* (Cambridge, Mass., Harvard University Press, 1991) p. 272; this was originally published in French in 1989. Lacan's close collaborator (and son-in-law) has provided a brief post-mortem discussion of the importance of psychoanalysis in Foucault's writings: *see* Jacques-Alain Miller, 'Michel Foucault and psychoanalysis', in Timothy Armstrong (trans.), *Michel Foucault: Philosopher* (London, Routledge, 1992) pp. 58–63.

their images back to one another is, in reality, filled with *the murmur of words*.'[45]
To be sure, Foucault was describing the episteme of sixteenth-century Europe
(or so he said), whereas Lefebvre conjures up an altogether different culture in
time and space. But these distinctions are more than historico-geographical
markers. If the 'great mirror' of Lefebvre's absolute space also reveals 'the prose
of the world', if its language has also 'been set down in the world and forms
part of it' – I take these phrases from Foucault – it is emphatically not
textualized in the same way and does not privilege the written word.[46] Lefebvre
acknowledges that absolute space was marked by various means, and concedes
that in this sense one might say that 'practical activity writes upon nature'. But
he prefers to speak of the production of *textures* not texts. Analogies between
space and language space 'can only be carried so far', he warns, because space
is 'produced before being read,' marked by demarcations and orientations not
in order to be read – deciphered – but 'rather in order to be *lived* by people
with bodies'.[47]

Lefebvre's history of space reconstructs the degradation of this organic
spatiality, and it should already be apparent that there is something nostalgic
about his project. Its characteristic conjunction of humanism and romanticism
faces in quite the opposite direction to Lacan. Where Lefebvre offers a threnody
for a lost plenitude, and in places seems to hold out the hope that 'authenticity'
and subjectivity can be recovered through a kind of corporeal mimesis, Lacan's
Real always already resists representation and recovery: as Merquior sees it,
from a position that is not dissimilar to Lefebvre's, Lacan is 'the archdenier of
fulfillment, for whom all desire was bound up with the tragedy of lack and
dissatisfaction'.[48] Lefebvre yearns for a return to his 'real', to the fulfilment of
what Marx once described as 'man in the whole wealth of his being', whereas
Lacan bars any such return: that 'wealth' (if I can extend the metaphor) is
invested in all three orders, Real, Imaginary and Symbolic, and human being
necessarily capitalizes on all three.

The tension between the two thinkers is compounded further because
Lefebvre treats the degradation of this organic spatiality as at once 'developmental' and 'historical', and his discussion slips in and out of these different
temporalities. This makes exposition difficult, partly because these slippages
mark sites of ambiguity (and sometimes, I suspect, evasion), but partly because
Lacan's treatment is conducted within the developmental register alone. For

45 Foucault, *Order of things* (1970), p. 27 (my emphases).
46 Ibid. pp. 34–5, 38–9. Lefebvre talks of 'the prose of the world' too, but he has in mind
   buildings which constitute 'the homogeneous matrix of capitalist space' and which he
   reads within the symbolic dimension of spatiality. See Lefebvre, *Production*, (1974), p. 227.
47 Ibid. pp. 118, 132, 143. Lefebvre's distance from Foucault (here and elsewhere) is thus
   considerable. What interests Lefebvre is not space *as* language therefore, or landscape *as*
   text, but rather 'as-yet concealed relations between space *and* language' (p. 17; my
   emphasis).
48 J. G. Merquior, *From Prague to Paris: a critique of structuralist and post-structuralist thought*,
   (London, Verso, 1986) p. 155. I yoke Merquior to Lefebvre through their antipathy to
   structuralism and post-structuralism; Merquior treats Lacan as the principal architect of
   the bridge between structuralism and post-structuralism (p. 149).

Lefebvre, however, the politics of space are inseparable from the history of the body and from the history of space and, as I have said, he pays particular attention to the formation of abstract space through an historical process of decorporealization (which thus becomes the dual of 'abstraction'). Although my continued presentation of Lefebvre will parallel my presentation of Lacan, for these reasons I hope it will be understood if on occasion it becomes necessary to follow tangents which, in some places, will ineluctably turn from clear lines of flight into tangled labyrinths.

'The fruits of dread'[49]

I resume with Lefebvre's own discussion of the mirror, which is clearly provoked by Lacan (and, indirectly, by Althusser's reading of Lacan). Lefebvre complains that psychoanalysis plays too freely with the mirror effect and abstracts it 'from its properly spatial context, as part of a space internalized in the form of mental "topologies"'.[50] This is an objection which, in its more general form, provides the original spur to Lefebvre's project: the inability of other thinkers to eschew 'the basic sophistry whereby the philosophico-epistemological notion of space is fetishized and the mental realm comes to envelop the social and physical ones'.[51] In Lacan's case, Lefebvre remarks that 'the mirror helps to counteract the tendency of language to break up the body into pieces, but it freezes the Ego into a rigid form rather than leading it towards transcendence in and through a space which is at once practical and symbolic (imaginary)'.[52] The elision between 'imaginary ' and 'symbolic' is obviously problematic if these terms are understood in a strictly Lacanian sense, but that is precisely what Lefebvre intends: he wants to establish the double inscription of the two in social space and the materiality of that conjunction. 'Into the space which is produced first by natural and later by social life the mirror introduces a truly dual spatiality: a space which is imaginary with respect to origin and separation, but also concrete and practical with respect to co-existence and differentiation.'[53]

Let me explain this double inscription. Lefebvre begins by using the mirror and mirror-effect to suggest the intimate involvement of the production of social space in the constitution of the self:

> On the one hand, one ... relates oneself to space, situates oneself in space. One confronts both an immediacy and an objectivity of one's own. One places oneself at the centre, designates oneself, and uses oneself as a measure ... On the other hand, space serves as an intermediary or mediating role: beyond each plane

49 The phrase is Tristan Tzara's and refers to mirrors: *see* Lefebvre, *Production*, (1974), p. 184n.
50 Ibid. p. 184n.
51 Ibid. p. 5. Lefebvre's indictment includes Althusser, Barthes, Derrida, Foucault, Kristeva and Lacan.
52 Ibid. p. 185n.
53 Ibid. p. 186.

surface, beyond each opaque form, 'one' seeks to apprehend something else. This tends to turn social space into a transparent medium occupied solely by light, by 'presences' and influences.[54]

The production of social space as duality has profound consequences, for Lefebvre suggests that this shift from 'the space of the body to the body-in-space' facilities the 'spiriting-away' or *scotomization* of the body. The term originated in ophthalmology in the nineteenth century, where it was used to refer to a lacuna in the field of vision, and had been introduced into French psychoanalytic theory in the 1920s; it was later appropriated by Lacan to diagnose a psychosis produced by a particular entanglement of the visual and the linguistic. Lefebvre uses the term in an historical rather than a developmental sense but, as I will show, retains that imbrication of the visual and the linguistic.[55]

Lefebvre argues that space, which was originally known, marked and produced through all the senses – taste, smell, touch, sound and sight – and which was, in all these ways, in intimate conjunction with the 'intelligence of the body', comes to be constituted as a purely visual field. He represents this process as a generalization of the mirror-effect, in which social space itself becomes a collective mirror. Unlike Lacan, however, the importance of the mirror for Lefebvre is not that its reflection 'constitutes my unity *qua* subject' but rather that 'it transforms what I am into the *sign* of what I am'. In much the same way, therefore, Lefebvre suggests that within the 'symbolic imaginary' of social space 'the sign-bearing "I" no longer deals with anything but other bearers of signs'. In effect, 'space offers itself like a mirror to the thinking "subject"', but, after the manner of Lewis Carroll, the "subject" passes through the looking-glass and becomes a lived abstraction'.[56] This collective – and historical – passage marks the transformation from absolute into abstract space.

> By the time this process is complete, space has no social existence independently of an intense, aggressive and repressive visualization. It is thus – not symbolically but in fact – a purely visual space. This rise of the visual realm entails a series of substitutions and displacements by means of which it overwhelms the whole body and usurps its role.[57]

Lefebvre maps what he calls this 'logic of visualization' along two dimensions. The first is *metonymy*, which he treats as an axis of *spectacularization* by means of which 'they eye, the gaze, the thing seen, no longer mere details or parts, are

---

54 Ibid. pp. 182–3.
55 Ibid. p. 201; Jay, 'The specular subject of ideology', pp. 353–7. I am summarizing and simplifying a complicated argument about scotomization here; for a fuller discussion, *see* Carolyn Dean, *The self and its pleasures: Bataille, Lacan and the history of the decentred subject* (Ithaca; Cornell University Press, 1992).
56 Lefebvre, *Production*, (1974), pp. 185 (my emphasis), 311, 313–14.
57 Ibid. p. 286.

now transformed into the totality'. As vision asserts its primacy over the other senses, therefore,

> All impressions derived from taste, smell, touch and even hearing first lose clarity, then fade away altogether, leaving the field to line, colour and light. In this way, a part of the object and what it offers comes to be taken for the whole.[58]

The second is *metaphor*, which he treats as an axis of *textualization* by means of which words substitute for images and the conduct of social life becomes synonymous with 'the mere reading of texts':

> Living bodies, the bodies of 'users' ... are caught up not only in the toils of parcellized space, but also in the web of what philosophers call 'analagons': images, signs and symbols. These bodies are transported out of themselves, transferred and emptied out, as it were, via the eyes.[59]

The parallels and tangents, resonances and dissonances between Lefebvre and Lacan could scarcely be clearer, but Lefebvre prefers to attribute these ideas to Nietzsche. It was Nietzsche who disclosed the historical advance of the visual over the other senses, he notes, and Nietzsche who identified 'the visual aspect predominant in the metaphors and metonyms that constitute abstract thought'.[60] The acknowledgement is significant, not only because it gestures towards Nietzsche's general importance to Lefebvre's project but also because it accentuates the historical specificity of his own account of metaphor and metonymy. He is scathing about those appropriations of psychoanalysis that provide 'homogenizing' explanations which cannot comprehend diversity. In his reflections on 'monuments' and 'buildings', for example, he treats these linguistic operators in ostensibly Lacanian terms and identifies the condensations and displacements which they effect; but he also insists that the Saussurean bar separating 'signifier from signified and desire from its object' is placed differently in different social spaces and that these concepts will not explain very much until they 'address the question of which particular power is in place'.[61] For this reason, it is necessary for me to emphasize that the

---

58 Ibid. p. 286. In speaking of 'spectacularization' Lefebvre is acknowledging his debt to his (once close) collaboration with the Situationist International and, in particular, to Guy Debord, *La société du spectacle* (Paris, Éditions Buchet-Chastel, 1967); this has been translated into English as *The society of the spectacle* (Detroit, Black and Red, 1983). For an imaginative commentary on the periodization of the spectacle, which intersects with Lefebvre's thesis in suggestive ways, *see* Jonathan Crary, 'Spectacle, attention, counter-memory', *October* 50 (1989) pp. 99–107.

59 Lefebvre, *Production*, (1974), p. 98. For a salutary commentary on explicitly spatial metaphors, which takes its cue directly from Lefebvre, *see* Neil Smith and Cindi Katz, 'Grounding metaphor: towards a spatialized politics', in Michael Keith and Steve Pile, *Place and the politics of identity* (London, Routledge, 1993) pp. 67–83. Their central point is Lefebvre's: 'Spatial metaphors are problematic is so far as they presume space is not'.

60 Lefebvre, *Production*, (1984), p. 139.

61 Ibid. pp. 225–7, 248. *See also* Andrew Merrifield, 'Lefebvre, Anti-Logos and Nietzsche: an alternative reading of *The production of space*', *Antipode*, 27 (1995) pp. 294–303.

foregoing discussion concerns the metaphorical and metonymical dimensions of *abstraction* – the materials they work with and the outcomes of their operations in other process-domains will be different – and that Lefebvre is using 'abstraction' in a highly specific way.

Still, notice what has happened: Lefebvre has used the mirror to conjure up what, for Lacan, would be the signifying order. By inscribing the imaginary and symbolic within the same social space, Lefebvre is able to register a double suspicion. First, he warns against *ocularcentrism*;

> Wherever there is illusion, the optical and visual world plays an integral and integrative ... part in it. It fetishizes abstraction and imposes it as the norm. It detaches the pure form from its impure content – from lived time, everyday time, and from bodies with their opacity and solidity, their warmth, their life and their death.[62]

This is at once a developmental and an historical thesis, I take it, and it underwrites Lefebvre's claim that the production of space – most particularly of abstract space – is typically concealed by a (double) illusion of transparency and opacity. Edward Soja has since used and extended these tropes to identify two illusions in the conventional theorization of spatiality: a 'hypermetropic illusion' that 'sees right through the concrete spatiality of social life by projecting its production into an intuitive realm of purposeful idealism and immaterialized reflexive thought' and a 'myopic illusion' that produces 'short-sighted interpretations of spatiality which focus on immediate surface appearances without being able to see beyond them'. These are important and insightful remarks, but Lefebvre's original claim was not a disciplinary or even a trans-disciplinary one. These illusions are by no means confined to the academy – to 'theory' – but enter into the material constitution of social space: into what he calls 'the world-as-fraud'.[63]

Secondly, Lefebvre is wary of *logocentrism*. He distinguishes two orientations towards language. The one is derived from semiotics and structuralism, and involves the exorbitation of language: in its most extreme form it becomes a formalism in which 'everything – music, painting, architecture – is language' – and which is therefore directed to the salvation of 'the Logos'. The other is less elegiac, more tragic: it dwells on the brooding menace of the sign, the 'intimate connection between words and death', and discloses 'the secret of the Logos as foundations of all power and authority'.[64] Lefebvre's own sympathies are much closer to the second:

62 Lefebvre, Production, (1974), p. 97.
63 Ibid. pp. 27–30, 39; Soja, *Postmodern geographies*, (1989), pp. 122–6.
64 Lefebvre, *Production*, (1974), pp. 133–5; I have borrowed 'the exorbitation of language' from Anderson, *Tracks*, pp. 40–1. It seems particularly appropriate here: although Lefebvre represents psychoanalysis as the (dishonest) broker between these two positions, it seems clear that – like Anderson – he identifies Lacan with the first position and pays little attention to what Lacan also has to say from the second position.

This is a lethal zone thickly strewn with dusty, mouldering words. What slips into it is what allows meaning to escape the embrace of lived experience, to detach itself from the fleshly body. Words and signs facilitate (indeed provoke, call forth and – at least in the West – command) metaphorization – the transport, as it were, of the physical body outside of itself. This operation, inextricably magical and rational, sets up a strange interplay between (verbal) disembodiment and (empirical) re-embodiment, between uprooting and reimplantation, between spatialization in an abstract sense and localization in a determinate expanse. This is the 'mixed space' – still natural, yet already produced – of the first year of life, and, later, of poetry and art. The space, in a word, of representations.'[65]

The elision between developmental and historical temporalities is particularly stark in this passage. Lefebvre is implicitly addressing Lacan, and he prefaces these remarks with the suggestion that the unconscious be treated not as 'a source of language' but rather as an interstice between the self-seeking-to-constitute-itself and its body; what then 'slips into the interstice' is 'language, signs, abstraction – all necessary yet fateful indispensable yet dangerous'. But he is also prefiguring an historical thesis, in which the production of space is marked by a progressive and aggressive logocentrism. 'The Logos makes inventories, classifies, arranges: it cultivates knowledge and presses it into the service of power'.[66]

As I have indicated, then, these processes of spectacularization and textualization are implicated in the historical production of an *abstract space*. The term is at once entirely accurate and yet thoroughly deceptive. 'Abstraction passes for an "absence"', Lefebvre cautions, ' as distinct from the concrete "presence" of objects, of things', but 'nothing could be more false.' He says this precisely because abstract space is not a void. In his view, 'signs have something lethal about them; not only because they involve 'devastation and destruction' – in particular, scotomization – but also because *they put in place an apparatus of repression*. This 'visual space of transparency and readability', produced under the sign(s) of capitalist modernity, is one in which 'exchanges between knowledge and power, and between space and the discourse of power, multiply and are regularized'. To forestall misunderstanding, I should say at once that Lefebvre's critique is not limited to the construction of quasi-Foucauldian disciplinary spaces, as this phrasing might imply, to the normalization of a space in which nothing escapes surveillance and where the theoretical and everyday practices of 'reading space' are implicated in discursive technologies of *assujetissement*. These are important matters, to be sure, and Lefebvre does not neglect them (though he does not treat them in the same way as Foucault).[67] But Lefebvre also insists that the violence of abstraction – flattening, plan(n)ing, emptying space – at once unleashes and lures *desire*. 'It presents

65 Lefebvre, *Production*, (1974), p. 203.
66 Ibid. pp. 203, 391–2.
67 Ibid. pp. 282, 289; cf. Michel Foucault, *Discipline and punish: the birth of the prison* (London, Allen Lane 1977); this was originally published in French in 1975.

desire with a "transparency" which encourages it to surge forth in an attempt to lay claim to an apparently clear field.'[68]

The invocation of desire is immensely important, even though Lefebvre does not develop its topographies in any detail, because it means that abstract space cannot be evacuated altogether. On the contrary: 'It demands a truly full object', so Lefebvre argues, a signifier 'which, rather than signifying a void, signifies a plenitude of destructive force – an illusion, therefore, of plenitude, and a space taken up by an "object" bearing a heavy cargo of myth'.[69] This turns out to be the (Lacanian) phallus writ large and physically inscribed in abstract space:

> Metaphorically, it symbolizes force, male fertility, masculine violence. Here again the part is taken for the whole [metonymy]; phallic brutality does not remain abstract, for it is the brutality of political power, of the means of constraint: police, army, bureaucracy. Phallic erectility bestows a special status on the perpendicular, proclaiming phallocracy as the orientation of space, as the goal of the process – at once metaphoric and metonymic – which instigates this facet of spatial practice.[70]

If this is a starker architecture than Lacan had in mind, if its materialism seems too crude in places, this may be because Lefebvre offers only illustrative sketches, signs indicating the sites at which a more subtle argument needs to be developed. But the nature of that project should now be clear: Lefebvre is bringing together three key elements from Lacan – the Eye, the Logos and the Phallus – and using them to gloss, to illuminate (in highly particular ways) the historical production of abstract space. As he puts it with a characteristic flourish, 'King Logos is guarded on the one hand by the Eye' – what he calls, in the same play of words that captivates Lacan, 'the eye of the Father' – and on the other hand by the Phallus. Together these mark, represent and produce 'the space of the written word and the rule of history'.[71]

Lefebvre works with these ideas to disclose and to contest a dominant phallocentrism. He does so through a double argument. In the first place, he constantly accentuates the gendering of Lacan's conceptual trinity and hence establishes the masculinism that is written into this abstract space.

> In abstract space, ... the demise of the body has a dual character, for it is at once symbolic and concrete: concrete, as a result of the aggression to which the body is subject; symbolic, on account of the fragmentation of the body's living unity. This is especially true of the female body, as transformed into exchange value, into a sign of the commodity and indeed into a commodity *per se* ...[72]

68 Lefebvre, *Production*, (1974), p. 97.
69 Ibid. p. 287.
70 Ibid. p. 287.
71 Ibid. pp. 262, 408.
72 Ibid. p. 310.

Lefebvre repeatedly points to the conjunction between the deceptive 'transparency' of abstract space and a masculinist violence, and there are poignant connections between his troubled attempt to come to terms with the symbolic imaginary of this space and Gillian Rose's critique of the masculinism of the geographical imagination in which, in theory and in practice, 'the innocent transparency of the empty street' becomes, for her and for so many other women, 'an aggressive plastic lens pushing on me'.[73] In the second place, Lefebvre tries to show that phallocentrism is so hideously destructive of what it is to be a human being that it has become one of the most powerful media of alienation. 'Over abstract space reigns phallic solitude and the self-destruction of desire', he writes, and its violent severance from the plenitude of the Real is equivalent to castration:

> Abstract space is doubly castrating: it isolates the phallus, projecting it into a realm outside the body, then fixes it in space (verticality) and brings it under the surveillance of the eye. The visual and the discursive are buttressed (or contextualized) in the world of signs.[74]

Histories, archaeologies

Although I have tried to show how Lefebvre's account of the production of space can be illuminated through a consideration of Lacan's psychoanalytic theory, this is plainly not the only way to read it. *La production de l'espace* is constructed from many different materials and there is no single route through all of its passages. One of the most telling differences from Lacan, as I have repeatedly remarked, is that Lefebvre offers a *history* that stands in close, critical proximity to *historical* materialism. In Lefebvre's view, psychoanalysis had a fatal flaw: 'It had a non-temporal view of the causes and effects of a society born in historical time'.[75] The originality of his own work, within Western

---

73 Gillian Rose, *Feminism and geography: the limits of geographical knowledge,* (Cambridge, Polity Press, 1993) p. 143. She has subsequently developed these remarks in a series of luminous reflections on the transparency of space and the transparency of the subject inscribed within phallocentrism: *see* in particular her 'Distance, surface, elsewhere: a feminist critique of the space of phallocentric self-knowledge', *Environment and Planning D: Society and Space* 13 (1995) pp. 761–81. I do not mean to imply that these projects are coincident, however, and neither do I think these affinities protect Lefebvre's project from a feminist critique.

74 Lefebvre, *Production,* (1974), p. 310. Elsewhere Lefebvre refers to 'The Great Castration' (p. 410) which is presumably a play on Foucault's treatment of 'The Great Confinement'.

75 Henri Lefebvre , *The survival of capitalism,* (London, Allison and Busby, 1976), p. 31; this was originally published as *La survieu du capitalisme,* (Paris; Editions Anthropos, 1973). This may well be true of Lacan, and there is undoubtedly a universalizing temper to much of psychoanalytic theory, but such a claim ought not to become a misleading universal in its own right. Kristeva, for example, makes it very clear that the 'signifying economy' operates through the *biographical* subject and recasts him/her as an *historical* subject. Joan Copjec has recently provided a stringent Lacanian critique of historicism that does not deny historicity: *see Read my desire: Lacan against the historicists* (Cambridge, Mass., MIT

Marxism, lies in the connection it proposes between this history of space and the history of the body, however, and it is for precisely this reason that I think an approach through Lacan can be so revealing.[76] But it can also be concealing, and the historicity of Lefebvre's project has three implications that need to be underscored.

First, Lefebvre is adamant that the decomposition of the human body and the decorporealization of social space cannot be 'laid at the door of language alone'. In his view, such a manoeuvre would wrongly exonerate both the Judaeo-Christian tradition, 'which misapprehends and despises the body, relegating it to the charnel-house if not to the Devil', and also the capitalist mode of production and its advanced division of labour, which 'has had as much influence as linguistic discourse on the breaking-down of the body into a mere collection of unconnected parts'.[77] It is for this reason that Lefebvre upholds historical materialism, and in doing so he turns it into something very like David Harvey's historico-geographical materialism. Very like, but scarcely the same. Harvey's recent writings on postmodernity have clearly been inspired by Lefebvre's work, and he has had much to say about images, mirrors and representations; but he has yet to engage with psychoanalysis (except through Jameson's appeal to Lacan, and then only in passing).[78]

Secondly, there is undoubtedly a sense in which Lefebvre's long history of space treats the aggressive advance of a 'logic of visualization' as a meta-narrative: but I believe this is offered for strategic not stipulative purposes. He does not claim that the decorporealization of space is the only important thematic, nor even that it is the one which most inclusively gathers in the other possible narratives and *petits récrits*, but simply that it is one which has been neglected and which has a vital, terrible salience for any critical politics of space. This also allows Lefebvre to speak to questions of gender, sexuality and phallocratic violence – and to their inscriptions in social space – more directly than many other writers of his time. Of course, the logic of visualization was not uncontested, and there were multiple attempts to interrupt or unravel its metanarrative. Lefebvre says little enough about them in concrete terms and prefers to remain at a metaphilosophical level. But he makes much of the 'great struggle' between what Nietzsche called 'the Logos and the Anti-Logos', between what he himself sees as 'the explosive production of abstract space and the production of a space that is other', and his own critique is intended as a challenge to the hegemony of that awful metanarrative.[79]

Press, 1994).

76 Lefebvre, *Production*, (1974), p. 196.

77 Ibid. p. 204.

78 David Harvey, *The condition of postmodernity: an enquiry into the origins of cultural change* (Oxford, and Cambridge, Mass., Blackwell, (1989) pp. 53–4. Cf. Meaghan Morris, 'The man in the mirror: David Harvey's "Condition" of Postmodernity'. *Theory, culture and society* 9 (1992) pp. 253–79. For a detailed discussion of other connections and contrasts between Lefebvre's project and Harvey's historico-geographical materialism, *see* Gregory, 'Modernity', (1994).

79 Ibid. p. 391. Even at this general level, within the realms of reflection and speculation, it

Lefebvre's insistence on contestation is a political claim, deliberately so, and his project locates the bases for resistance – for the construction of authentically human spaces – in the past as well as the present. He is offering, or at least his writings can be made to offer, a 'history of the present' in something like the sense in which Foucault employs the term. John Rajchman suggests that 'a history of the present' has two connotations. In the first place,

> The 'present' refers to those things that are constituted in our current proceedings in ways we don't realize are rooted in the past, and writing a 'history' of it is to lay bare that constitution and its consequences.

Lefebvre's project can certainly be read in this way: the very idea of a history of space has long been ignored by many writers and critics. In the second place, however,

> Foucault does not show our situation to be a lawlike outcome of previous ones, or to have been necessitated by the latest historical conjuncture. On the contrary, he tries to make our situation seem less 'necessitated' by history, and more peculiar, unique or arbitrary.[80]

In so far as Lefebvre's history of space is a historicism, then it is of necessity much less 'singularizing' than this. But it also provides, on occasion, what Benjamin once called a constellation – I can think of no better term – in which it becomes possible for a (forgotten, even repressed) past to irrupt explosively into the present.

Thirdly, therefore, and following directly from this claim, Lefebvre situates his history of space somewhere between anthropology and political economy. His 'anthropology' is the site of another awkward slippage between the developmental and the historical. Lefebvre suggests that the 'history' of space is inaugurated as the plenitude of a 'biologico-spatial reality' is lost, and he evidently believes that non-modern societies and their spaces are somehow closer to 'the intelligence of the body' and its organic spatiality. But he also argues that those biomorphic resonances persist into our own troubled present and provide the distant murmurs of a fully human future:

> Nothing disappears completely ... nor can what subsists be defined solely in terms of traces, memories or relics. In space, what came earlier continues to underpin what follows. The preconditions of social space have their own particular way of enduring and remaining actual within that space ... The task of *architectonics* is thus to describe, analyse and explain this persistence, which is

is possible to provide more detailed counter-histories. I have already drawn on Martin Jay's reconstruction of a persistent critique of ocularcentrism within twentieth-century French philosophy, for example, and I should also like to draw attention to Rosalind Krauss's wonderful reconstruction of art history and her evocation of a counter-modernism that inscribed the corporeality of vision within and against the power of the abstracted eye. *See* Jay, *Downcast eyes*, and Rosalind Krauss, *The optical unconscious* (Cambridge, Mass., MIT Press, 1993).

80 John Rajchman, *Michael Foucault: the freedom of philosophy* (New York, Columbia University Press, 1985), p. 58.

often invoked in the metaphorical shorthand of strata, periods, sedimentary layers ...[81]

This is, in part, what Lefebvre's 'rhythm analysis' was supposed to recover; it would seek to discover those rhythms, those circuits of plenitude as it were, 'whose existence is signalled only through mediations, through indirect effects of manifestations'. He claimed that their presence is registered in the space of dreams, 'where dispersed and broken rhythms are reconstituted', and for this reason he wondered whether rhythm analysis might not 'eventually even displace psychoanalysis'. This turned out to be a vain hope, and it is in any case far from clear, even in Lefebvre's own exposition, what he had in mind.[82] But these muffled rhythms are also registered in the modern sphere of 'everyday life', in the day-to-day practices and representations of modernity, which Lefebvre treats as both 'a parody of lost plenitude and the last remaining vestige of that plenitude'.[83] This may be a more promising avenue of inquiry, though its elegiac romanticism remains extremely troubling, but in any event it seems clear that his project is a thoroughly redemptive one.

Between these three comments, however, is a space of critique that returns me to psychoanalytic theory. Although Lefebvre closes his account of the production of space with a consideration of the 'contradictions' of abstract space and the possibility of a 'differential space' there is, I think, something strangely unyielding about his narrative of loss and redemption. Here I have found the writings of Victor Burgin especially suggestive. He works, creatively and critically, with Lefebvre and with Lacan (among others). For him too, space has a history, one that is intimately connected to the constitution of the subject; but he shows that the 'optical-geometrical spatial regime', 'the panoptical-instrumental space of colonialist capitalist modernity', has always been fissured and constantly called into question by transgressions. Echoing Homi Bhabha, Burgin effectively suggests that the impositions of abstract space have always been *ambivalent* and that – rather than fixing analysis on the proliferation of binary oppositions – it is possible, in these moments of interruption (of sly partiality?), to glimpse a space of inbetweenness, what Bhabha himself calls a 'third space'. Burgin argues that the superimposition of spatial formations never erases those that came before; modern spatialities are 'porous' and through these fissures pasts erupt into the present. These interruptions and displacements reveal – imperfectly and fleetingly – what Burgin sees as 'an image of space latent in all of us': 'a space in which the subject itself is soluble', a space that is at once 'the source of bliss and of terror'.[84]

---

81 Lefebvre, *Production*, (1974), p. 229.
82 Ibid. pp. 205, 209; *see also* Lefebvre *Elements*, (1992).
83 Michael Trebitsch, 'Preface' to Henri Lefebvre, *Critique of everyday life*, vol. 1: *Introduction*, (London, Verso, 1991) p. xxiv; this was first published as *Critique de la vie quotidienne*, (Paris, Grasset, 1947). For a discussion of Lefebvre's account of the 'colonisation of everyday life' and the practical recovery of that 'lost plenitude', *see* Gregory, *Imaginations* (1994), pp. 401–6.
84 Victor Burgin, 'The city in pieces', *New formations* 20, (1993) pp. 33–45; *idem.* 'Geometry

Acknowledgements

A first version of this essay was published in Georges Benko and Ulf Strohmayer (eds), *Geography, History and Social Sciences* (Dordrecht, Kluwer, 1995) and this revised version is published here at the invitation of the editors. I have relied even more than usual on the comments and advice of friends, and it is a pleasure to acknowledge the help of Trevor Barnes, Alison Blunt, Noel Castree, Mike Crang, Heidi Nast, Chris Philo, Geraldine Pratt, Rose Marie San Juan, Matt Sparke, and Bruce Willems-Braun. I am particularly grateful to Steve Pile who commented in wonderfully constructive ways on a draft of the argument and generously shared his insights into Lacan's work with me.

References

Barrett, Michèle, *The politics of truth: from Marx to Foucault*, (Cambridge, Polity Press, 1991).

Bhabha, Homi and Burgin Victor, 'Visualizing theory', in Lucien Taylor (ed.), *Visualizing Theory*, (New York and London, Routledge, 1994), pp. 454–463.

Bowie, Malcolm, *Lacan* (London, Fontana, 1991).

Bukatman, Scott, *Terminal identity: the virtual subject in postmodern science fiction*, (Durham, Duke University Press, 1993).

Burgin, Victor, 'Geometry and abjection', in James Donald (ed.), *Psychoanalysis and cultural theory: threshold*, (London, Macmillan/ICA, 1991) pp. 11–26.

Burgin, Victor, 'The city in pieces', *New formations*, 20, pp. 33–45.

Butler, Judith, *Subjects of desire: Hegelian reflections in twentieth-century France*, (New York, Columbia University Press, 1987).

Caillois, Roger, 'Mimicry and legendary psychasthenia', *October* 31, pp. 17–32, (1984).

Cohen, Margaret, *Profane Illumination: Walter Benjamin and the Paris of surrealist revolution*, (Berkeley, University of California Press, 1993).

Copjec, Joan, *Read my desire: Lacan against the historicists*, (Cambridge, Mass., MIT Press, 1994).

Crary, Jonathan, 'Spectacle, attention, counter-memory', *October* 50, pp. 99–107, (1989).

Crowther, Paul, 'The postmodern sublime', in Andrew Benjamin (ed.), *Judging Lyotard* (London, Routledge, 1994) pp. 192–205.

Dean, Carolyn, *The self and its pleasures: Bataille, Lacan and the history of the decentred subject*, (Ithaca, Cornell University Press, 1992).

Debord, Guy, *The society of the spectacle*, (Detroit, Black and Red, 1983).

Descombes, Vincent, *Modern French Philosophy*, (Cambridge, Cambridge University Press, 1980).

Dews, Peter, *Logics of disintegration: post-structuralist thought and the claims of critical theory*, (London, Verso, 1987).

and abjection', in James Donald, (ed.), Psychoanalysis and cultural theory: thresholds (London; Macmillan/ICA, 1991) pp. 11–26; Homi Bhabha and Victor Burgin, 'Visualizing theory', in Lucien Taylor (ed.) *Visualizing theory* (New York and London; Routledge, 1994) pp. 454–63. If this is indeed the postmodern sublime, then perhaps it is also the space that Lefebvre and Lyotard were evoking, in different ways and from radically different positions, one outside and one inside Beaubourg?

Dowling, William, *Jameson, Althusser, Marx*, (Ithaca, Cornell University Press, 1984).

Eagleton, Terry, *Against the grain: essays 1975–1985* (London, Verso, 1986).

Elliott, Anthony, *Social theory and psychoanalysis in transition: self and society from Freud to Kristeva*, (Oxford, and Cambridge, Mass., Blackwell, 1992).

Eribon, Didier, *Michel Foucault*, (Cambridge, Mass; Harvard University Press, 1991).

Ferry, Luc and Renaut, Alain, *French philosophy of the sixties: an essay on anti-humanism*, (Amherst, University of Massachusetts Press, 1990).

Flax, Jane, *Thinking fragments: psychoanalysis, feminism and postmodernism in the contemporary West*, (Berkeley, University of California Press, 1990).

Foucault, Michel, *The order of things: an archaeology of the human sciences*, (London, Tavistock 1970).

——— , *Discipline and punish: the birth of the prison*, (London, Allen Lane, 1977).

Gallop, Jane, *The Daughter's Seduction: feminism and psychoanalysis*, (Ithaca, Cornell University Press, 1982).

——— , *Reading Lacan*, (Ithaca, Cornell University Press, 1985).

Granon-Lafont, Jeanne, *La topologie ordinaire de Jacques Lacan*, (Paris, Point hors Ligne, 1985).

Gregory, Derek, *Geographical imaginations*, (Oxford and Cambridge, Mass., Blackwell, 1994).

Grosz, Elizabeth, *Jacques Lacan: a feminist introduction*, (London, Routledge, 1990).

Habermas, Jürgen, *The theory of communicative action*, vol. 2; *The critique of functionalist reason*, (Cambridge, Polity Press, 1987).

Harvey, David, *The condition of postmodernity: an enquiry into the origins of cultural change*, (Oxford, and Cambridge, Mass., Blackwell, 1989).

Jay, Martin, *Marxism and totality: adventures of a concept from Lukács to Habermas*, (Cambridge, Polity Press, 1984).

——— , *Downcast eyes: the denigration of vision in twentieth-century French thought*, (Berkeley, University of California Press, 1993).

Kelly, Michael, *Modern French Marxism*, (Oxford, Basil Blackwell, 1982).

Krauss, Rosalind, *The optical unconscious*, (Cambridge, Mass., MIT Press, 1993).

Lacan, Jacques, *Écrits: a selection*, (New York, Norton and Co., 1977).

Lefebvre , Henri, *The explosion: Marxism and the French Revolution*, (New York, Monthly Review Press, 1969).

——— , *The survival of capitalism* (London, Allison and Busby, 1974).

——— , *Critique of everyday life*, vol. 1, *Introduction* (London, Verso, 1991).

——— , *The production of space*, (Oxford, and Cambridge, Mass., Blackwell, 1991).

——— , *Éléments de rythmanalyse: introduction à la connaissance des rhythmes*, (Paris, Éditions Syllepse, 1992).

——— , *Writings on cities*, (Oxford, and Cambridge, Mass., Blackwell, 1995).

Leupin, Alexandre, 'Voids and knots in knowledge and truth', in Alexandre Leupin (ed.), *Lacan and the human sciences*, (Lincoln, University of Nebraska Press, 1991) pp. 1–23.

Lévi-Strauss, Claude, *The elementary structures of kinship* (Boston, Mass., Beacon Press, 1969).

Lewis, Helena, *The politics of surrealism*, (New York, Paragon, 1988).

Lynch, Kevin, *The image of the city*, (Cambridge, MIT Press, 1960).

Macey, David, *Lacan in contexts*, (London, Verso, 1988).

Merquior, J. G., *From Prague to Paris: a critique of structuralist and post-structuralist thought*, (London, Verso, 1986).

Miller, Jacques-Alain, 'Michel Foucault and psychoanalysis', in Timothy Armstrong (trans.), *Michel Foucault: philosopher*, (London, Routledge, 1992) pp. 58–63.

Morris, Meaghan, 'The man in the mirror: David Harvey's "Condition" of Postmodernity', *Theory, culture and society*, **9**, pp. 253–79, (1992).

Pile, Steve, 'Human agency and human geography revisited: a critique of "new models" of the self'. *Transaction of the Institute of British Geographers*, **18**, pp. 122–39, (1993).

Popper, Karl, *The logic of scientific discovery*, (London, Hutchinson, 1959).

Poster, Mark, *Existential Marxism in post-war France: from Sartre to Althusser* (Princeton, Princeton University Press, 1975).

Preziosi, Donald, 'La vi(ll)e en rose: Reading Jameson mapping space', *Strategies*, **1**, pp. 82–99, (1988).

Rajchman, John, *Michel Foucault: the freedom of philosophy*, (New York, Columbia University Press, 1985).

—— , *Philosophical events of the 80s*, (New York, Columbia University Press, 1992).

Rose, Gillian, *Feminism and geography: the limits of geographical knowledge*, (Cambridge, Polity Press, 1993).

—— , 'Distance, surface, elsewhere: a feminist critique of the space of phallocentric self/knowledge', *Environment and Planning D: Society and Space*, **13**, pp. 761–81, (1995).

Roth, Michael, *Knowing and history: appropriations of Hegel in twentieth-century France*, (Ithaca, Cornell University Press, 1988).

Roudinesco, Elizabeth, *Jacques Lacan & Co. A history of psychoanalysis in France, 1925–1985*, (Chicago, University of Chicago Press, 1990).

Silverman, Kaja, *The subject of semiotics*, (New York, Oxford University Press, 1983).

—— , 'The Lacanian phallus', in *differences*, **4**, pp. 84–115, (1992).

—— , *Male subjectivity at the margins*, (New York, Routledge, 1992).

Smith, Neil and Katz, Cindi, 'Grounding metaphor: towards a spatialized politics', in Michael Keith and Steve Pile, *Place and the politics of identity*, (London, Routledge, 1993), pp. 67–83.

Soja, Edward, *Postmodern geographies: the reassertion of space in critical social theory*, (London, Verso, 1989).

PART III

Planning and the Postmodern

Introduction

Arguably one of the defining features of modernity has been the development and proliferation of discourses about and in 'planning'. The idea of planning itself – the conscious structuring of human environments that negates prior passive acceptances of existing spatial relations – grew out of the Enlightenment ideal of human emancipation from both religious and political misuses of reason and remains thus central to our understanding of modern democracy in general. From the individual through the local to the national and global scale, the implementation of planning into a host of culturally different everyday life situations became the hallmark of modern societies. Situated squarely within this tradition, the academic discipline of geography did and continues to derive one of its *raison d'être* from its ability to educate students to perform the tasks necessary for planning the humanly transformed environment.

As with most other traditions within the history of modernity, the concrete uses and goals of planning processes have been criticized from a host of different positions (most damaging in this respect was probably the Marxist critique), but never had the very idea of planning – its condition of possibility – been structurally questioned until the arrival of postmodern ideas. Now, the notions of rationality, of scarcity, geographical stability and the idea of a controllable environment embodied in and expressed through planning processes all came under intense scrutiny. Also questioned was the central place commonly occupied by the nation-state in many analyses leading to conscious changes in the social, economic or political environment. With little less than our human capacity for steering changes that implicate the whole of society at stake, however, what are the alternatives? Do we need to write differently, as Lipietz argues; do we need to rethink our concepts of space, as Soja would have us believe, or is, to argue with Cooke, a more flexible unit of analysis all that is required to account for the postmodern critique launched against the idea of planning?

9

Planning in/for Postmodernity

Ed Soja

In *Postmodern Geographies*, I outlined a series of arguments about the transition from modernity to postmodernity in the contemporary world and attempted to explore the implications of this profound societal and theoretical restructuring at every level of scholarly discourse, from ontology and epistemology to the realms of empirical analysis and political practice.[1] A primary focus for these critical interpretations of postmodernity was the Modern discipline of Geography, an intellectual channel that was simultaneously the source of inspired insight and understanding for what I called "the reassertion of space in critical social theory" and the site of an almost inbred resistance to the challenges raised by the postmodernist critique – the most important source of this reassertion of space -- for the discipline itself. Each step forward made by geographers in the creative spatialization of critical social theory and in the geographical interpretation of postmodernity seemed to be followed by two steps backward, a retreat home to the familiar conventionalities and canons of the still modernist disciplinary cocoon.

Even now, few geographers feel entirely comfortable with being labelled "postmodern." And even fewer, it seems, are content with applying the name "geographer" to postmodern critical thinkers outside the discipline, no matter how geographical their discourses may be. Interpretations of postmodernity are offered by geographers, but the object of interpretation is typically set up as an external and distanciated material world that presents few introspective or reflective challenges to the traditional geographical imagination or to the institutionalized disciplinarity of Modern Geography itself. Postmodernity is "out there" to be studied and analyzed as just another part of our phenomenal world.

Partially as a result of this introversion and distancing, the most exciting and creative work being done today in exploring the intersections of social and spatial theory and in the geographical interpretation of postmodernity is being

---

1   Edward Soja, *Postmodern Geographies: The Reassertion of Space in Critical Social Theory*,(Verso, 1989); *see also* "Postmodern Geographies and The Critique of Historicism," in Jones, Natter, and Schatzki (eds), *Postmodern Contentions: Epochs, Politics, Space* (Guildford, 1993).

done outside the discipline of Geography – and by scholars who, for the most part, adopt an explicitly postmodern, if not postmodernist, perspective. Moreover, there appears to be developing in this transdisciplinary exploration of postmodernity a new mode of critical thinking about space and the spatiality of social life that differs significantly from the locked-in traditional perspectives of the more specialized spatial disciplines, by which I mean not only geography but also architecture and urban design, urban and regional planning, and the more general fields of urban and regional studies. I will return briefly to this alternative view of space in the conclusion to this chapter, which will focus not on geography but on planning theory and the interpretations of postmodernity that have been filtering into (and out from) the fields of urban and regional planning (in which I have been teaching for the past 22 years).

The arguments presented here derive from a paper initially delivered at a joint meeting of the North American Association of Collegiate Schools of Planning (ACSP) and the Association of European Schools of Planning (AESOP) in Oxford in July, 1991. The theme of the conference was "Planning Transatlantic: Global Change and Local Problems." My presentation was in a session on "Claims to Knowledge and Reason," one of many sessions devoted specifically to new developments in planning theory.[2]

In many ways, urban and regional planning, and planning theory in particular, have been even more resistant to postmodernization than Modern Geography, largely because their practical foundations and philosophy, their insistent call for "the translation of knowledge into action in the public domain," have been more explicitly and consciously rooted in the emancipatory projects of post-Enlightenment modernism. In their more inherently pragmatic reactions to postmodernity, planners have had fewer opportunities than geographers or cultural critics to retreat into purely theoretical debate and discourse, or into the warm confines of established traditions, far from the madding and demanding crowds of civil society. It is this constantly challenging commitment to *praxis*, the transformation of theory into action, and its accompanying openness to many different disciplinary perspectives, that makes planning theory a particularly rich context from which to explore the new challenges raised by postmodernity, postmodernization and postmodernism.

Preliminary Observations on the Postmodernization of Planning Theory

The general argument I propose to develop concerning the postmodernization of planning theory can be summarized in three broad observations. First, we must recognize that we live and plan – and theorize about life and planning –

2   A French translation of a slightly modified version of the original presentation will appear in a special edition of *Espaces et Societes*, edited by Vincent Berdoulay.

in an increasingly postmodern world. I emphasize "increasingly postmodern" for the processes of societal restructuring, and hence also the transition to postmodernity, are by no means complete. Modernity and postmodernity, each a heterogeneous mix of forms and expressions, coexist today in a complex state of convergence and divergence, conflict and accommodation. What is becoming increasingly clear, however, is that postmodernity in all its various forms and expressions is on the ascendant in early every sphere of contemporary life. This postmodernization may be deplored and resisted, but it cannot be ignored.

The second observation follows directly from the recognition that the specific reality with which the urban and regional planner must deal is becoming increasingly postmodernized. From the designs of the built environment and the social production of space, place, and locality to the composition of the global economy and its changing spatial divisions of labor, the postmodern restructuring of the contemporary world has been significantly recontextualizing the empirical fields of relevance to the planning profession. This has, in turn, provoked a serious challenge to long-established philosophies, theories, methods, and practices of planning especially those modernist versions that have dominated the profession over the past 100 years. Household and community, town and country, city and region, state and nation, First, Second, and Third worlds have changed so dramatically over the past three decades that they now demand significantly new and different approaches, indeed even new and different definitions, as objects of planning intervention.

The third general observation accentuates the magnitude of the challenges raised by what I have included under the umbrella of societal restructuring and postmodernization. Despite some accomplishments, there is still a long way to go in the adaptation of planning theory and practice to the conditions of postmodernity. Such adaptation requires a much deeper and more disruptive critique than has yet occurred, especially if planning is to maintain the progressive project and emancipatory potential that have always been central to its purpose and development. For planning and planners to take advantage of the new possibilities and opportunities of postmodernity and to avoid its very powerful anti-progressive tendencies and enticing diversions into whimsy, planning theory and planning practice must engage in a far-reaching deconstruction and reconstitution, perhaps a more far-reaching and wrenching conceptual restructuring than has ever occurred before. In the words of my title, we must move from simply planing *in* a postmodern world to actively planning *for* postmodernity, i.e., striving to construct a progressive, emancipatory, and intentionally postmodern planning theory and practice.

Epistemological Questions

These preliminary observations on planning theory and the postmodern transition focus particular attention on epistemological questions, on our claims to knowledge and reason. This is not surprising, for the debates on postmodernity and postmodernism have revolved primarily around a deep epistemological critique, an attack on well-established (modern) ways of knowing: how we obtain practical knowledge of our world, how we distinguish between the "real" and the "imaginary," and especially how we decide "what is to be done" here and now to change the world for the better. To outline the directions being taken by this postmodern deconstruction and reconstitution of epistemology, its radical restructuring, I will discuss first the two epistemological paradigms that have dominated twentieth-century planning theory, and then present some of the key issues that have become part of planning theory's postmodern deconstruction and reconstitution.

The most widely accepted and established epistemology in planning theory and in nearly every other mode of theory-building is what we have come to understand as the "scientific method." In its variously verificationist and falsificationist forms, this modern epistemology of science enables us to make accurate and potentially practical sense of the world and, with appropriate utilitarian intentions, to use this knowledge to improve the quality of life for as many individuals as possible. It is thus, at least potentially, a critical or progressive epistemology and has been such since the Enlightenment. Its way of knowing can be captured in the epistemological metaphor of the mirror, that is, knowledge arises from the ability to comprehend in rational thought the sensible "reflections" emanating from the real empirical world. Its method is designed to sort out the accurate, good, useful information from the accompanying noise, randomness, and distortion. Its familiarity can be taken for granted and requires little further elaboration, for it remains the foundational epistemology of planning theory and practice.

An alternative "critical" epistemology, even more explicitly aimed not simply at knowing the world but also at changing it for the better (and hence even more appealing to the progressive planning theorist and practitioner), developed most systematically in the late nineteenth century. Its metaphorical embodiment is not the mirror but the mask, a belief that the "good" reflections potentially receivable from the sensed world of the real can be blocked by a deceptive shroud of false or counterfeit appearances. Practical knowledge and understanding, from this perspective, require an unmasking, a demystification of surface appearances, a digging for insight beneath the empirical world of directly measurable reflections. Not entirely divorced from the scientific method, this more structuralist and/or hermeneutic form of explanation significantly reshaped the discourse on modernity in the late nineteenth century, influenced the development of urban and regional planning in the first three decades of the twentieth century, and became refocused and more radically critical in the fields of planning beginning in the 1960s. The hardest cutting edge of the transformational structuralist critique has always been Marxist, but even more appealing to the progressive planner in capitalist societies was a milder mix of social anarchism, Utopian socialism, radical advocacy, and social movement politics that opened room for local and regional progressive actions that fell far short of global proletarian revolution. Here, too, the story is a relatively familiar one that needs little further elaboration.

Modern planning theory, by which I mean the body of work since the nineteenth century that theorizes the roles, objectives, methods, designs, practices, and social impacts of planning and the planner, can be roughly divided into two main streams according to the degree of emphasis placed on one or another of these epistemological positions. Within each stream there is significant variation and many, if not most, planning theorists have been comfortable trying to combine both in a practical and strategic mix.[3] In the 1980s, however, a new critique of planning theory began to develop questioning the authority of the "scientific" and of "critical" epistemologies as well as the attempts to achieve some stable synthesis between them. To elaborate further, it is useful to distinguish two levels of this new critique, one reflecting the specific dynamics of what I will call Late Modernism and the other more explicitly postmodernist in its standpoint, insight, and implications.

Towards a New Modernity

The Late Modernist epistemological critique arose, at least in its relation to planning theory, from the turbulent mix of neo-Marxist critiques and social movement politics that had been developing since the 1960s. The pursuit of radical planning from a critical epistemological stance led quickly to an unmasking of sources of oppression, exploitation, domination and impoverishment that went beyond the deep structures of capitalism, and similarly beyond the equally deep theoretical strictures of orthodox Marxism. Each of the social movements to which many activist planners became attached found additional forces other than class antagonisms constraining their actions and reproducing oppression and subordination. Moreover, not only were these structuring forces, such as patriarchy and racism, inadequately theorized in orthodox Marxism and in the liberal social sciences, but the inherited theories and epistemologies themselves appeared to incorporate their own deceptive masks and mystifying silences. Without rejecting entirely these modernist ways of making practical, political, and theoretical sense of the world, a new mode of critical thinking began to develop that opened alternative pathways to radical social change.

Two of these late modernist critiques deserve particular attention. The first was feminist and, with respect to planning and planning theory, it developed not only as an advocacy of the silenced and subordinated, but also as a critique of the white-male domination of the "Master" theories and practices of planning. This feminist critique of planning reflected a larger feminist critique of modernity itself, that is, of the very definition of practical knowledge, of what it means to change the world for the better, of how we know "what is to be done." Feminism, along with the related critiques of racism and neo-colonialism, became fundamentally epistemological critiques that demanded not just

---

3   The most comprehensive recent survey of these planning theory traditions can be found in John Friedmann, *Planning in the Public Domain: From Knowledge to Action*, (Princeton, 1987).

piecemeal reform but a much more radical and transformative restructuring of the very foundations of planning knowledge and action. This deep critique of planning *praxis* gradually shifted radical planning and planners away from the modernist mainstreams, and, if not to postmodernism directly then to something significantly different from the established modernist traditions, whether rooted in Marxism or in the liberal social sciences.[4]

The second movement away from modernism came from a similar series of unmaskings and epistemological critiques of Marxist and liberal social scientific traditions. It involved a specifically spatial turn and emphasis in the new theoretical debates. Feminists were among the first to take this spatial turn, but the movement was joined by a larger group of geographers, sociologists, planners, architectural historians, and cultural critics who together became concerned with the forms of social control, power, and domination embedded in the design of the built environment and, more broadly, in the social production of space and the spatiality of social life. Among the many themes of this new spatial critique were the "entrapment" of women in patriarchal suburban households and segregated job hierarchies, the enclavement of minorities in ghettos and barrios, the destruction of rebellious communities through urban renewal or freeway construction, the disenfranchisement arising from a gerrymandered political organization of space, the redistribution of real income away from the poor that flows from the normal practices of urban planning, the suppression of regional cultures that hides behind the promises of integrated national development plans, and the hidden geographies of postcolonial domination and dependency that block Third World development.

Uncovered in these spatial critiques was another source of oppression, domination, exploitation, and impoverishment, and it frequently was located directly in the realm of planning practice. Like the feminist critique, the spatial critique eventually turned directly to epistemology and sought to understand and root out the critical silences and subordinations implicit in modern planning theory and its inspirational sources. In the search for an appropriate critical perspective to guide this new exploration of the interplay between space, knowledge, and power, increasing attention was given to the works of two of the twentieth century's leading philosophers of space, Henri Lefebvre and Michel Foucault. Both Lefebvre and Foucault, in different ways, centered their critical philosophies on the spatiality of social life and, in particular, on the

---

4   A key work summarizing the impact of feminism of planning theory and the planning
    profession – and in focusing attention on specifically epistemological issues – is Leonie
    Sandercock and Ann Forsyth, "Gender: A New Agenda for Planning Theory," *Working
    Paper* 521, Institute of Urban and Regional Development, (Berkeley, University of
    California, 1990); also published in *Planning Theory Newsletter* 4 (1990), 61–92. *See also*
    the brief statement by Sandercock and Forsyth, "Feminist Theory and Planning Theory:
    The Epistemological Linkages," in *Planning Theory Newsletter* 7/8 (1992), 45–9, an issue
    which contains several additional papers on epistemological questions edited and
    introduced by Robert Beauregard under the heading, "Planning Theories, Feminist
    Theories: A Symposium."

evolving institutional structures of urban and regional planning in France, giving both special relevance to critical planning theory.[5]

In *Postmodern Geographies*, I traced the development of a critical and explicitly postmodern human geography (and by implication a critical and postmodern planning theory) through the contributions of Lefebvre and Foucault. Although neither would have been completely comfortable with the postmodern label, their work provided the most insightful philosophical pathways to the contemporary reassertion of a spatial critique in the human sciences and to an understanding of the double meaning behind my use of the term postmodern geographies. At one level, postmodern geographies refer to the empirical texts and contexts that are the material objects of geographical analysis (and planning practice). These geographies, from the local to the global, have become increasingly postmodernized through a profound sociospatial restructuring in the late twentieth century. This empirical restructuring of geographies, in turn, has had significant repercussions on the discourse and epistemology of geographical analysis and interpretation. At this second, more discursive level, new interpretive geographies, significantly different kinds of critical geographical discourse, have begun to emerge to capture the practical and political meanings of the postmodernization of the contemporary world. These, too, can be described as postmodern geographies.

Although Late Modernist in their origins and viewpoint, the epistemological critiques of feminism and the new critical human geography attacked the very foundations of modern planning theory and presented challenges which could not easily be met by piecemeal adaptive reform. They helped to push contemporary planning theory to the brink of a profound disintegrative crisis, suspended awkwardly between the modernist projects of the past that are still being retained even as they lose much of their legitimacy and impact; and the postmodernist projects of the present and future, attractive and alluring but often incomprehensible and repellent at the same time. The major chronicler of this brinksmanship has been Robert Beauregard.[6] In his introduction to a set of articles on the impact of feminist theory on planning theory he restates his position:

> [P]lanning theory is in an epistemological bind. The modernist planning project no longer seems to apply to the issues before us, but no "postmodernist" project has arisen to take its place. As planning theorists, we seem suspended between outmoded and bankrupt positions of functional rationality, critical distance, universalizing stances, totalizing perspectives, apolitical practices, and a variety of challenges emanating from postmodern, poststructuralist, hermeneutic, de-

5   One of the earliest attempts to apply Foucault and Lefebvre to a critical history of urban planning was Christine Boyer, *Dreaming the Rational City: The Myth of American City Planning*, (Cambridge Mass., MIT Press, 1983).

6   *See* Beauregard, "Between Modernity and Postmodernity: The Ambiguous Position of US Planning," *Environment and Planning D: Society and Space* 7 (1989), 381–95; and "Without a Net: Modernist Planning and the Postmodern Abyss,," *Journal of Planning Education and Research* 10 (1991), 189–94.

constructionist, postcolonial and feminist perspectives. Our epistemological base, our way of knowing, no longer supports our theoretical edifice.[7]

Let me try to explain why a further push is needed, a push that will move planning theory out of its bind and into a more accommodating and productive postmodern terrain. Here again the argument revolves around epistemology, around claims to knowledge and reason. To get to this new terrain, I will borrow a bit from Jean Baudrillard in his writings on *Simulations*.[8]

The Crises of Representation

In Baudrillard's view, a third critical epistemology has been developing along-side the other two in the late twentieth century. Rather than the mirror or the mask, its metaphorical episteme is captured in the concept of the simulacrum, an exact copy or simulated representation of an original that has either been lost or, perhaps, never existed in the first place. The multiplication of simulacra and their increasing empowerment in the contemporary world is playing havoc with our old ways of knowing, our inherited epistemologies. There is what Baudrillard calls a growing "liquidation of all referentials," an unhinging of the signifier from the signified, a growing substitution of images or representations of the real for the real itself. You do not have to visit Greece or Italy, for example. Instead, you can go to their simulated recreations in Disneyworld or, even closer to home, in planned new housing developments that advertise them-selves under the enticements "Welcome to Mykonos!" or "Enjoy Life in a Tuscan Villa." The "precession of simulacra," as Baudrillard describes it, is threatening to make the very difference (and hence our ability to differentiate) between the "true" and the "false," the "real" and the "imaginary," disappear, melt into air. The mirror is blurred and the unmasking reveals only more masks.

Baudrillard often descends into fatalistic submission in his response to the growing power of simulations and simulacra. Without following him all the way into the "bovine immobility" he has occasionally espoused, his formulation of the epistemological crisis of representation can be re-presented as a forceful challenge to all those who are seeking to make practical/political sense of the contemporary world. Stated most simply, what is being argued here is that reality is no longer what it used to be. Our confidence in being able to distinguish what is real from what is imagined, the foundational assumption behind all modernist epistemologies and critical theories, is being shaken by the intrusion of an expansive "alternative reality" that is simultaneously real *and* imagined, a growing realm of *hyper-reality* that is filled with "real fakes" (to use Umberto Eco's term), with simulations that take on the appearances *and effects* of material things and increasingly influence our everyday thoughts

7 *Planning Theory Newsletter* (1992), 9.
8 Jean Baudrillard, *Simulations*, (Semiotext(e), 1983). *See also* Soja, "Postmodern Geographies and the Critique of Historicism."

and actions: who we vote for, where we choose to live, how we fulfill our desires and needs.

Simulations and simulacra have always existed in virtually every human society, especially in systems of religious belief (and some might also add in politics). What is significantly different today is the scale and scope of a more secular hyper-reality. In part arising from the disseminative power of the mass communications media, thicker layers of hyper-reality now blanket the world and reach more deeply into the immediate spaces of our daily lives. Simply "unmasking" these representations of the real to discover a hidden material reality behind them is no longer as revealing as it once was, for the underlying reality increasingly consists of the representations themselves.

This epistemological crisis of representation, this increasing realization that reality is no longer what it used to be, infuses what is now popularly described as the postmodern condition, the growing recognition that *modernity* is not what it used to be. Efforts to respond to the breakdown of modernist episte-mologies and the need to reconstruct our claims to knowledge and reason in light of the widening sphere of hyper-reality have been the source and instiga-tion of the postmodern turn to discourse theory and the methodologies of deconstruction; to the rise of a more flexible, recombinant, and open-ended poststructuralism in reaction to structuralist and to humanist oversimplifica-tions of the relation between structure and human agency; to the appeal of relativism, radical pluralism, eclecticism, pastiche, montage, and other means of putting together in new and different ways the shattered fragments of modern life; to the recognition of an invasive alternative reality and its accom-panying dis-location and de-centering of the concrete subject and its (especially *his*) referents; to the rejection of totalizing, overarching metanarratives and essentialisms; to the substantive attention being given to the media and popular culture as revealing locations for the manufacturing and diffusion of hyper-re-ality; to the search for tactical and strategic niches rather than universal programs for emancipatory social action and progressive politics; and to a greater appreciation of difference and "otherness," to making what was once marginal central and inclusive within a new cultural politics of difference and the redefinition of radical subjectivity.

A right-leaning, neo-conservative postmodernism has successfully capital-ized on these conditions and drawn strength from the epistemological crises of representation. Spin-doctored hypersimulations are increasingly shaping democratic politics and election results, fostering a belief in the annihilation of the progressive projects of modernity, liberal as well as Marxist, in an increasing proportion of the contemporary world. From the initial assertions about the "end of ideology" and the rise of "post-industrial society" to the recently proclaimed "end of history" following upon the "triumph of capitalism" in Eastern Europe and the spontaneous generation of a "new world order" out of the ashes and blood of the Gulf War, so successful has this reactionary postmodernism been that, for many, it has come to define postmodernism itself.

The most insidious effect of this reactionary postmodernism on the planning profession has similarly involved the substitution of strategic and convincing simulations of the real for the real itself. All left-leaning definitions of the progressive projects of modernity are represented either as sadly antiquated or incontinent idealism, or, even worse, as the antecedants to totalitarianism and the terrors of planning as social engineering. Advocacy and affirmative action with regard to race and gender are being increasingly portrayed as racism and sexism in reverse, and attacked with that newest of simulacra, the tarnishing image of undemocratic "political correctness." Radical planning (along with the welfare state that opened room for its practice) is declared dead and, unfortunately, too many radical planners either quietly and tearfully attend the wake or run and hide in increasingly isolated "safe houses," reminiscent of the 1960s, where no traces of the postmodern condition are allowed to enter.

What is left to the progressive planners, it seems, is an exceedingly narrowed array of choices: to operate in that always negotiable space at the public-private interface or the neighboring under-and-over-the-table world of developer agreements and tax subsidies; to engage in the competitive entrepreneurship involved in fighting with other planners in the territorial wars for jobs and dollars, siphoning off public service investments to attract industries, office construction, yuppie boutiques, and shopping malls; or else retreating numbly behind the nostalgic tranquilizer of returning home to the hypersimulated roots of the profession in physical planning, land-use mapping (with GIS, of course) and faux beaux arts or "neo-traditional" urban design. Are they any other alternatives?

Postmodern Strategies

In an increasingly postmodern world, new forms of planning theory and planning practice must be constructed to contend with the growing empowerment of conservative and/or politically accommodative postmodernism. It is not enough to continue to respond to politically reactionary hypersimulations by simply unmasking the hard realities which presumably lie behind them, for in practice the hypersimulations and simulacra have become the hard material realities planners must deal with. Today, rather than responding by reasserting old epistemological truths, planning theorists must attempt to meet the opposition head on, on its own grounds, by creating a critical and progressive postmodernism of resistance and reconstruction, by opening up the possibilities for a planning process and a planning theory that are radically in and for postmodernity rather than outside and against it – or else perilously suspended between.

A comprehensive program for this new postmodern planning theory cannot be outlined here, but it is possible to identify a few strategic (re)directions that might be taken. First, a new planning theory must be built upon a epistemological openness and flexibility that are suspicious of any attempt to formalize a single, totalizing, way of knowing, no matter how progressive it may appear to be. Second, it must make this openness a means of understanding ambiguity, fragmentation, multiplicity, and difference, for these are the material social realities of the contemporary world. This means not only tolerating but encouraging what can be described as *the disordering of difference* (as opposed to the modernist search for order and stability).[9] Such a disordering of difference shifts some needed attention away from epistemology to ontology, to a re-exploration of the very nature of being and becoming, not only with regard to time but also to space. The intent of this ontological restructuring is to redefine radical subjectivity and political consciousness as inherently spatial, rooted in the existential spatiality of human life.

More concretely, I suggest that the reconstitution of postmodern planning theory should draw particular insight and inspiration from a growing cluster of spatially conscious critical scholars whose work centers on the intersections of class, race, and gender and revolves around the reconceptualization of difference and "otherness." Stated somewhat differently, planning theory must shift its primary attention to an understanding of the new cultural politics of identity and empowerment that has been taking shape in the conditionally postmodern contemporary world. It must build, for example, on the concepts of "postmodern blackness" and radical spatial subjectivity that are explored in the writing of bell hooks, Cornell West, Gayatri Spivak, Arjun Appadurai, Trinh T. Minh-Ha, Edward Said, Chandra Mohanty, Homi Bhabha, Gloria Anzaldua; on the increasingly spatialized postmodern feminisms of Iris Marion Young, Jane Flax, Judith Butler, Diana Fuss, Meaghan Morris, Rosalyn Deutsche, Donna Haraway; on the anti-essentialist critiques of postmodern Marxist scholars such as Ernesto Laclau and Chantal Mouffe; and on a critical re-reading of the presuppositional work on space, knowledge, and power by Henri Lefebvre and Michel Foucault.

What is emerging from the insights of these critical scholars is a new interpretation of modernity and postmodernity, of the interpellations of social and spatial theory, and of the practical and strategic translation of (spatial) knowledge into (spatial) action: the very core of urban and regional planning theory. Older traditions of planning theory are not discarded but recast in the context of postmodern culture and cultural studies. As Cornell West proclaims:

> These gestures are not new in the history of criticism … yet what makes them novel – along with the cultural politics they produce – is how and what constitutes difference, the weight and gravity it is given in representation and the way in which highlighting issues like exterminism, empire, class, race, gender, sexual orientation, age, nation, nature, and region at this historical moment acknowledges some discontinuity and disruptions form previous forms of cultural critique. To put it bluntly, the new cultural politics of difference consists of creative

9 *See* Edward W. Soja and Barbara Hooper, "The Spaces That Difference Makes: Some Notes on the Geographical Margins of the New Cultural Politics," in Keith and Pile (eds), *Place and the Politics of Identity*, (Routledge, 1993). *See also* Barbara Hooper, "Split at the Roots: A Critique of the Philosophical and Political Sources of Modern Planning Doctrine," *Frontiers – A Journal of Women Studies*, 13 (1992).

responses to the precise circumstances of our present moment ... in order to empower and enable social action.[10]

At the heart of postmodern cultural politics is a critique of the tendency within modernist politics to construct and essentialize binary definitions of difference and identity, such as those between bourgeoisie and proletariat, man and woman, black and white, the citizen and the state; and to mobilize political struggle within rather than across these categorical polarizations. By deconstructing and disordering these binarisms, the new cultural politics opens up the possibilities for articulation, coalition, and community among all those subject to exploitation, domination, and subjection, that is, to all those peripheralized or marginalized by the workings of socio-spatial power.

Of particular importance to the recasting of planning theory are the explicitly spatial consciousness and praxis that have accompanied the development of postmodern cultural politics. In the writings of the best of the critical scholars I have identified, there is a foregrounding of political action in the spatiality of social life, from the renewed interest in the politics of the body (what Adrienne Rich, the postmodern feminist poet, once called "the geography closest in") to the search for non-oppressive built environments, the revived interest in critical urbanism and regionalism, and the more general debates on the "situated" politics of location, positionality, place, site, and context. In my view, an especially compelling spatial voice among the contemporary critical scholars exploring the new cultural politics comes from bell hooks. Virtually every sentence in the following set of extracts from her writings rings with relevance to the future restructuring of planning theory.

Postmodern culture with its decentered subject can be the space where ties are severed or it can provide the occasion for new and varied forms of bonding. To some extent, ruptures, surfaces, contextuality, and a host of other happenings create gaps that make space for oppositional practices ... A space is there for critical exchange ... [and] this may very well be "the" central future location of resistance struggle, a meeting place where new and radical happenings can occur.

As a radical standpoint, perspective, position, the "politics of location" necessarily calls those of us who would participate in the formation of counter-hegemonic cultural practice to identify the spaces where we begin the processes of re-vision .... For me this space of radical openness is a margin – a profound edge. Locating oneself there is difficult yet necessary. It is not a "safe" place. One is always at risk. One needs a community of resistance.

There is a definite distinction between the marginality which is imposed by oppressive structure and that marginality one chooses as a site of resistance, as

10 Cornell West, "The New Cultural Politics of Difference," in R. Ferguson, M. Gever, T. T. Minh-Ha and C. West (eds), *Out There: Marginalization and Contemporary Cultures*, (Cambridge, Mass., MIT Press 1991); New York: The New Museum of Contemporary Art, p. 20.

a location of radical openness and possibility. It was this marginality that I was naming as a central location for the production of a counter-hegemonic discourse that is not just found in words but in habits of being and the way one lives. As such I was not speaking of a marginality one wishes to lose, to give up, but rather as a site one stays in, clings to even, because it nourishes one's capacity to resist. It offers the possibility of radical perspectives from which to see and create, to imagine alternatives, new worlds.

This is an intervention. A message from that space in the margin that is a site of creativity and power, that inclusive space where we recover ourselves, where we move in solidarity to erase the category colonizer/colonized. Marginality is the space of resistance. Enter that space. Let us meet there.[11]

A Different Conclusion

The words of bell hooks both conclude my brief discussion of the postmodernization of planning theory and opens up a new debate, one having to do with the reconceptualization of spatiality that has been occurring outside the spatial disciplines of urban and regional planning, architecture and urban design, and geography. To many within these spatial disciplines, especially those whose radical spatial subjectivity is unquestioned, the work of the new cultural critics of postmodernity often appears to be exceedingly immaterial, filled with ungrounded metaphorical allusions to space which float perilously above the world of concrete politics and struggle. "Their" spatiality (with some exceptions) is somehow not "ours." It may be well intentioned and literally imaginative, but remains too distanced from "real" geographies and politics. An occasional insight or two can be usefully borrowed and the growing attention to space engendered by their work can be embraced as additional justification for the importance of the spatial disciplines themselves (although "they" never quite get their geography right).

I will conclude with a very different proposal: that embedded in the works of the new cultural critics (especially those emanating from radical women of color), and prefigured in the writings of Henri Lefebvre and Michel Foucault, is a conceptualization of space and spatiality that comprehends the well-established perspectives of the spatial disciplines and creatively and challengingly extends beyond them. In this new mode of critical spatial thinking, there is a fusion of the traditional distinction between objectively defined material geographies (what Lefebvre described as the realm of "spatial practices" or perceived space) and more subjectively defined mental, cognitive, or ideational geographies (Lefebvre's "representations of space" or conceived space); and also the opening up of a *thirdspace*, a combination and extension of the other two that expands further the ontological and empirical significance of human

11 These comments are taken from two chapters, "Postmodern Blackness" and "Choosing the Margin as a Space of Radical Openness," in bell hooks, *Yearning: Race, Gender, and Cultural Politics*, (Boston, South End Press, 1990).

spatiality. Lefebvre calls this, in an intended but too often misunderstood critique of materialism and of idealism, the "spaces of representation" or *lived space*. In these space of representation, the real, the imaginary, and the hyper-real coexist without one being prioritized over the others.

In a short lecture entitled "Of Other Spaces," Foucault followed a similar path of fusion and expansion from the historically binarized alternatives of materialist and/or idealist interpretations of the lifeworld to identify an Other spatiality which closely resembles Lefebvre's spaces of representation in its encompassing complexity and multisidednes. This third mode of critical spatial thinking he named "heterotopology," and he proceed to explore its micro-geographies in nearly all his writings on such "heterotopias" as the asylum, the prison, the clinic, the school, and the body.

In bell hooks's notion of "choosing marginality as a space of radical openness" and Gloria Anzaldua's conception of the "borderlands" (*la frontera*), as well as in Jameson's descriptions of the "hyperspaces" of postmodernity and Baudrillard's precession of simulacra, it is this heterotopological thirdspace, this open-ended, fragmented, limitless *lived* space, filled with representations of power and the power of representations, that is being explored. It is a spatiality that does not fit very comfortably into either of the two ways of thing about space that have dominated – and continue to compartmentalize – the perspectives of the perhaps overly specialized spatial disciplines. Even among geographers, planners, and architects who draw insight and inspiration from these postmodern spatial theorists, there is little recognition that the works they draw upon are posing profound challenges to their established geographical imaginations and demanding a far-reaching deconstruction and reconstitution. As we continue to explore space and social theory and develop further our geographical interpretations of postmodernity, it is well worth keeping this provocative challenge in mind.

10

Warp, Woof and Regulation:
A Tool for Social Science

Alain Lipietz

Styles change in France. Skirt hems rise above and then drop down below the knees, trousers widen into bell-bottoms only later to tighten around the ankles. Social science also has its fashions. When mini-skirts and bell-bottoms were in style in the late 1960s, structuralism held sway. Actions and anticipations of agents were but the reflection of the reproductive requirements of social structures. In the 1980s dress has become stricter and the methodology of social sciences more individualist (which, by the way, demonstrates the relative autonomy of the fashion system). Methodological individualism imposes the idea that structures are but the compositional effect of projects, and practices in turn are a description of the choices of 'rational' agents.

The collapse of structuralist hegemony in the mid-1970s did not, however, lead to the consolidation of a 'dominant methodologically individualist current'. Was that because of an old Keynesian and Durkheimian tradition? Intellectual France did not throw itself, body and soul, into the turnkey model imported from Anglo-Saxon countries by the 'new economists', 'new sociologists', and so on. It withered instead. It seems to me that heterodox currents have remained lively, though dominated by individualist background noise, and that, very early on they distanced themselves from structuralism's excesses. These currents tried to reintroduce into the world the possibility of 'agentless structures', and saw instability and change as consequences of the possible deviance of individuals or social subgroups, without falling prey, nonetheless, to a world of 'structureless agents'.

Owing to the inherent instability of much of what was written in this vain, the resulting 'post'-structuralist era was quite often seen to represent a break with a preceding period which was structured around a stable 'agency' 'structure' axis. This 'superseded' era was, of course, no other than 'modernity', and its successor went by the name of 'postmodernity'. The difference was to be a difference of 'space': largely absent in the former, it was to become everything in the latter. I wonder, though, if the resulting debate about the 'postmodern condition' has really moved us into more productive territory. Partly as a result of this scepticism, the following chapter will largely refuse to dance to the tune of easy classifications. Rather, it will take as its point of departure the widespread recognition, which gained ground after the 1970s, of a problem inherent to traditional ways of theorizing 'structure' and 'agency'.

In economics, new lines of thought, such as the notions of 'accumulation regimes' and 'regulation modes', were an offshoot of this concern. Their power in explaining Fordism and its crisis has been widely acknowledged. Here I would like, as an 'indigenous informer', to take up the theoretical framework underlying the attempt to supersede the sterile opposition 'structuralism/individualism'. My paper will be deliberately introspective. It is a personal view that does not claim to speak for the many researchers who, like myself, have contributed to this current of thought.

It will also be subjective in that it is based, not only on a researcher's experience, but also on pedagogical activity. In the course of preparatory work for a short film project on regulation (Lipietz 1987a), a director asked me to reproduce for him the images I ordinarily sketch on a sheet of paper when I reflect, or draw on a blackboard when I teach. According to his experience, by examining such images one can learn more about the basis for a way of thinking than in a presentation, however didactic the latter may be. I realized on that occasion that I unconsciously lent paradigmatic importance to a metaphor incidentally used in literary terms in the CEPREMAP's (Centre d'etudes prospectives d'economie mathematique appliquées a la planification) report (1977): that of weaving, warp, woof, and heddle (sometimes replaced by the metaphor of streams of water flowing between a bridge's pillars). I became aware that this metaphor already underlay my earlier thoughts about the competitive and monopolistic production of space (Lipietz 1975). It played the same metaphorical role in my report on 'accumulation regimes/values in process' as the 'invisible hand' in Adam Smith. Geographers such as Hägerstand (1970) had used the same metaphor, as had certain sociologists in their efforts to overcome the 'structure/agent' dilemma (for example Pierre Bourdieu and Anthony Giddens). It is actually related to a field of study I came across long ago (and discussed in Lipietz and Rouilleault 1972 and Lipietz 1973) on the nature of human reality as 'objective subject' (Kosik 1968). It is a dialectical approach which obviously goes back as far as Spinoza (naturing nature and natured nature) and even Heraclitus, Karl Marx finding his place in the series as well, of course.

My purpose here is to offer a free-floating and subjective sketch of the usefulness of this metaphor, without a great deal of critical commentary. Many researchers will, I hope, see their own inner schemas in what I say and will easily identify these same schemas in many other works.

I will begin with a brief presentation of the intellectual culture in which regulationist approaches have developed. I will then take up the 'warp/woof' image at a 'deeper' level, after which I will provide two examples by way of application, one economic, the other geographical.

1 Regulation in Context: The Concept and Its Time

In 1975–76, Michel Aglietta organized a discussion of his thesis (1974) in the form of a long seminar which was later to inspire the works of a CEPREMAP team (1977). At that time, much French research in social science was characterized by the domination, but also the exhaustion, of the structural Marxism identified with the school of Louis Althusser. One can summarize its fundamental theses as follows.[1]

(a) Social reality is a fabric, that is, an articulation of relatively autonomous and specific relations that overdetermine each other (even though certain of them are more fundamental than others), that is, 'a whole which is always already given and overdetermined, and which has a dominant feature'.
(b) Each of these social relations is reproduced *qua* result by the action of its 'bearers' ('the structure exists as a result'), but puts the bearers in the position of reproducing it independently of their subjectivity. Jacques Rancière, who has since changed his mind, went so far as to say, in *Reading Capital*, that 'Being mystified is the essential attribute of the subject function'.

Althusser's school (more or less contingently or derivatively) joined to these fundamental methodological theses two further theses that are important for economists:

(c) The 'productive forces' themselves are the materialization of the social relations of production (a theme developed by Balibar and Bettelheim).
(d) The contradictory character of exchange relations is superficial and secondary (a point forcefully made by Althusser and later developed by Balibar).

I will not question the merits of thesis (a) here. For quite some time it sheltered French Marxist thought from the mirages of 'expressive totality' according to which politics, ideology and fashion only 'reflect' the fundamental economic structures. The generalized functionalism underlying, for example, German '*Kapitallogik*' approaches found itself easily used as a weapon for propaganda.

I will not question the merits of thesis (c) either, this latter joining up with those of the Italian 'operaïstes', 'radical' Anglo-Saxons and 'radical' Chinese. Breaking with Stalinist technological determinism – which owed more to nineteenth-century bourgeois ideology than to Marx himself (despite the ambiguities in his 1859 Preface to the *Contribution to the Critique of Political Economy*) – thesis (c) underlies all our work on the Taylorian organization of work, its crisis and its supercession.

Thesis (b), on the other hand, and thesis (d) – which is in reality (b)'s corollary and illustration – constitute the 'seamier side' of Althusserism, that is its submission to a structuralist hegemony which, from Lévi-Strauss to Lacan, sought to deconstruct the subject and his autonomy everywhere, this no doubt as a reaction to the preceding theoretical fashion: existentialism and the philosophy of praxis. Individualism, for example the subjectivism of 'industrial capitalism', actually finds its first illustration (and perhaps its economic determinant) in the existence of market relations, in the autonomy of 'private activities carried out independently' which afterwards must seek social validation (cf. *Capital*, chapter 1!). Yet in throwing Noah's coat over chapter 1, Althusser in one fell swoop censured the subject, contradiction, and market relations. Developing this idea, Balibar was led to deny the existence of structural contradiction at the root of crises: a structure's purpose is simply to ensure its reproduction.

There is but one small step from such a notion to functionalism, that is, thinking that 'everything is made for the purpose of reproducing structures'. Terray (1977) explains this very clearly:

> When thinking about reproduction, the whole outdated arsenal of functionalist interpretations frequently resurfaces. Reproduction is conceived of as a final cause from which the set of structures and institutions analyzed proceed [...]. To avoid this error, one must first recall that reproduction cannot be an end: only a subject can propose an end in itself. But society is not a subject. One must recall above all that what is reproduced is precisely, and first and foremost, a contradiction [...]. Hence, to adopt the point of view of reproduction is to definitively understand how the very cycle of production and distribution constantly encounters two terms of this contradiction constituted by the relation of fundamental production – dominators and dominated, exploiters and exploited – how the former try to ward off crises through which this contradiction could be overcome or resolved, and how the latter more or less consciously attempt, on the contrary, to abolish it or escape from it. Reproduction as a whole is both what is at stake in their encounter and its result.

Retrospectively one can evaluate the importance of the long period of crisis-free Fordist growth in sustaining this functionalist illusion. In reality, Fordism turned out to be devoid of crises 'in circulation', but not in production. 'Circulationism' thus deservedly became an insult in Marxist circles (particularly in Rosa Luxemburg's critique, but also in the analysis of 'center-periphery' relations). The need to focus on the level of production, that is on capital-labour relations, was thus reaffirmed.

Michel Aglietta's thesis followed this latter line: one had to wade through hundreds of pages dedicated to the analysis of capital/labour relations – fortunately divided into two relations, that of the organization of work and that of the distribution of surplus value – before the existence of autonomous capital was mentioned. But this 'division' served the purpose of bringing out the *contradiction* in the reproduction of this complex relation, and thus the possibility of crisis and the problem of *regulation*. It was high time: the crisis of Fordism had just exploded.

The introduction of the term 'regulation' was admittedly not enough to dissipate the functionalist connotations of the term 'reproduction'. In Michael Aglietta's first formulations, in certain publications that came out of CEPREMAP research (1977), 'regulation' simply designated 'what is necessary for reproduction to work, *in spite of underlying contradictions*'. To explain the crisis, one obviously sought to explain Fordism before its crisis. The 'mode of regulation' was thus offered to the public in the form of its result, rather than on the basis of a preliminary discussion about the existence of structurally contradictory relations and the resulting tendency towards crisis (which the mode of regulation is supposed to inhibit for a certain period of time). One could even go so far as to speak of '*ex post* functionalism.'[3]

The term 'regulation' however, had already been introduced into the discourse. It was already seriously weighed down by Canguilhem's famous definition in the *Encyclopedia Universalis*; 'Regulation is the adjustment, in conformity with some rule or set of norms, of a plurality of movements or acts, as well as their effects or products, whereas their diversity or succession at first makes them foreign to each other'.

This definition was irremediably marred by two prejudices, seen in the expressions, 'at first, makes foreign' and 'in conformity with some rule'. First of all, the 'movements' or 'acts' were not perceived as being induced (in their divergence) by the contradiction within a unique relation. Secondly, this definition posited the existence of a teleological norm or finalism which automatically led to functionalism. The 'goal' of adjustment seemed to be the cause of the existence of the regulating apparatus, the assembly of which could be confided to some human or divine architect. The theory of systems – cybernetics – had then only to describe the retroactive regulatory functions.

Even in its cybernetic version, the 'regulationist vogue', which emerged in the 1970s through the work of Atlan, Thom, Prigogine and Attali,[4] represented great progress when compared with structuralism. While the whole set of representations and identities that had become dominant during the Fordist era (that which today I would call the 'hegemonic societal paradigm', cf. Lipietz 1986) crumbled, new social movements came to the fore which seemed to be able to regenerate the social system. Alain Touraine (1978) in a positive vein, and Régis Debray (1978) in a negative one, theorized the capacity of collective actors to modify ossified social systems, leading thereby to new equilibria. For Jean-Pierre Dupuy (1977), 'the autonomy of actors' became the condition for society's 'structural stability'. It was a promising idea, but revealed the limits of such autonomy when confronted with the rigidity of heavy structures inherited from the past and the need to make specifically *institutional* compromises to stabilize the innovations. Nonetheless, the difficulties experienced by successive governments, leftist and rightist, between 1974 and 1986, in proposing compromises allowing for the regulation of a new model of development, paved the way for the triumph of liberal ideologies in society, and at the very least facilitated the progress of methodological individualism and 'microsociology' in the field of social science.[5]

As I mentioned above, this 'progress' by no means amounted to a total triumph. A countertendency could be found in the work of the Ecole des Annales, and especially that of Georges Duby and Fernand Braudel, which influenced a broad public. The work gave a major role to the durability of heavy structures, the weight of norms bearing down on everyday life, and the slight degree of freedom offered to individuals and groups. Similarly, the success of Bourdieu's school has endured: the '*Révoltes logiques*' Collective (1984) affirmed its influence in referring to the 'empire of the sociologist'.

The case of the Bourdieu school is particularly interesting. A widely held view is that its central thesis is akin to Althusser's: the strategies of agents are functions of a '*habitus*', and can therefore contribute only to the reproduction of the structure of the current state of things. To caricature this thesis, we could say: like father, like son; they have the same hopes, ambitions and results. But this begs the question, for the whole problem is precisely that of defining the relative 'power' of strategies and structures! Bourdieu has been systematically criticized on two fronts; as a structuralist and also as a methodological individualist (and even as a 'spontaneist' by Lévi-Strauss![6]). This ambiguity in the critique is quite telling. In reality, the exploration of the concepts 'habitus' and 'strategy' led the Bourdieu school to investigate the same problems as the regulation school, as well as to overlap with the work of certain *Annales* historians like Duby.[7] For example, Boltanski's fine book (1982) shows how, on the basis of slowly changing social structures, the group of 'cadres' (professional workers) gained power from 1930 to 1950, and came to play a central role in 'wage based society' (Aglietta and Brender 1984), in other words the French form of the Fordist model which it helped mould.[8]

Such is the intellectual context, woven of reciprocal exchanges, that has inspired my theoretical and pedagogical reflections on the concept of regulation.

2 Dialectic and Fabric

'Men don't realize how that which varies remains in accord with itself. There is a harmony of opposed tensions, like that of the bow and the lyre'. This famous saying by Heraclitus is the starting point for what our culture calls dialectic, and the image of the bow seems appropriate for an exposé on the contradictory character of social relations. The problem is obviously one of providing an example, without having first dealt with the example in its own right: market relations and wage relations. A convenient short cut can be found in the example of love relationships.

'A' love relationship (a couple's history together) is a social relation in two senses. First of all, it is a relationship between two people, and secondly it is established in accordance with a model, a 'pattern', that is a recognized social form existing prior to any particular couple. The human need to couple is certainly ancient, but the 'love relationship' couple form is rather recent (in France, it became entrenched in the middle classes during the seventeenth century). Individuals must already see themselves as subjects (which is a condition that is overdetermined by the totality of social relations) and feel a lack which can be filled by love relationships; they learn this from their culture, and afterwards from personal experience. *Willingness* to engage in a love relationship thus seems to be a property of an individual but it is, in fact, realized only as an interpersonal relationship – which is social in the first sense – and it follows a 'pattern', that is it is social in the second sense.

The exploration of 'willingness', differing little from Bourdieu's *habitus*, is the domain of psychoanalysis, though the latter finds it difficult to separate the social from the biological. Keeping to the essentials, let us examine Lorenzo da Ponte's view in *Le Nozze di Figaro*, as pronounced by Chérubin:

> You who know what love is
> Women, tell me if I have it in my heart [...]
> I seek something outside myself,
> I know not who has it, nor what it is [...]
> And yet I am pleased to languish so.

Such a search for something outside oneself may be satisfied in a variety of ways: pairing, mysticism, ambition, work, and so on. The social existence of couples in love is in no sense an effect of the composition of individual strategies for finding happiness. It is an historical invention, as I mentioned above. But for *each* individual, the formation and maintenance of a couple is clearly the result of a (more or less co-operative) strategy. Thus, the encounter of two people willing to love provides only the 'material' of a love, its biological *bearers* ('*träger*', as Althusser says). But it is the love relationship that constitutes them as lovers. One hardly worries about what Molière's lovers were like before they met, and there one is perhaps mistaken – I'll come back to this point further on.

Love relationships are no more isolated in this world than are lovers. Before analysing the social relation of love, one must recall [Althusserian thesis (a)] that it is overdetermined by other social relations, beginning with – in the case of heterosexual love relations – relations the bearers of which coincide with those of love relationships, but which are different: so-called phallocratic or 'gender' relations (Guillaumin 1978), and more generally, the set of patriarchal relations (especially those between lovers and their parents). There are, of course, also the social relations of market production and distribution, co-determining the economic independence of individuals, that must be taken into account, not to mention legal relations which can seriously overdetermine choices.

But what is a love relationship? It is a relationship in which each person seeks happiness and self-realization through the other person, there being variable components of giving, identification, and fusion, though they presuppose and imply autonomy of the two partners. In short, a love relationship *unites* and *opposes* lovers, the 'fusion' of the two being the means and the obstacle to each individual's fulfilment'. Like every social relation, a love relationship is a *contradiction*, like market relations. Churches and good-willed sexologists can preach all they like that 'it is in the giving of oneself that one finds oneself', just as liberal economists can repeat that the pursuit of private interest results in collective well-being. Sometimes it's true, and sometimes not. When true, we are 'working within a regime', when false in a moment of 'crisis'.

Let us turn to the image of the bow. One can define a contradiction as a relation which defines two poles in uniting and opposing them.

Figure 10.1 The Bow of Contradiction

The contradictions which are of interest here are social relations, one of which is the love relationship. Every social relation, existing (as overdetermined) in human society (whether we're dealing with a couple or a nation) isolates in this society a system of *places*, hierarchical (capitalist/wage labourers) or non-hierarchical (lovers, co-exchangers). These places are complementary to the relationship that defines them: seen from this vantage point, the relation is a structure. But the places hold in store for the individuals who occupy them a *role* which is more or less in conformity with what they perceive as their interest (in comparison, notably, with other places in the same relation, or other places in other relations, or even physical needs). Whether they 'refuse to play the game' or whether they 'take their places' in trying to 'improve their game', individuals in relation are necessarily opposed. This is true whether the game is a negative or positive sum one! Even the gift is an opposition (for example, the potlatch within exchange relations, and invasive devotion within love relations).

I have termed 'willingness' or 'disposition' (*disponibilité*) the ability to fill a role and to try to improve one's game from that position; I have also identified this disposition with Bourdieu's habitus. There are thus two possibilities: (1) the pursuit of the game, that is, the lived experience of the relationship through time, leads to the dissolution of the relationship – there it is difficult to speak of a social relation (at the very most one could speak of fleeting interaction); or (2) it leads to the reproduction of the relationship, and it is this reproduction of unity that allows us to identify a relation. One can thus represent the reproduction of a relation in time, either from the vantage point of contraction or from that of places:

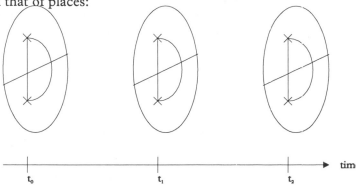

Figure 10.2 Structure over Time

The two 'squares' defined by love relationships have been filled, in the course of time, by Célimène and Alceste, Paul and Virginie, and Colin and Chloé. But from the point of view of the individuals occupying these places, things present themselves differently in every case. They are actors in their love relationships, they fill roles by which the relationships and the places are reproduced. What allows them to fill their roles in such a way as to (and not necessarily 'in order to') reproduce their relation is their disposition and habitus, but also the perceptions they have of the other's intentions, and possibly of external social pressure experienced as an incorporated norm (in Marivaux, for example) or as an explicit institution (for example marriage)?. One must thus take into account:

1   the disposition, habitus, interest and individual desires; and
2   a space of representation of the relation in which the agents are taken up and perhaps hemmed in by an institutional apparatus.

At this point, it makes no difference whether the relation be perceived as egalitarian or hierarchical, as consensual or oppressive, or whether, in the space of representation, a real or assumed power relation be taken into account. In any case, the reproduction of the relation supposes a certain 'agreement', willingly or unwillingly granted, as to the legitimacy of its perpetuation. As Gramsci shows, even exploitative relations imply the consent of those who are dominated: a hegemony 'armor-plated with coercion'. A very serious error of methodological individualism consists in reducing every relation to an agreement between individuals accepting a common norm. It is obvious that such agreements exist, for instance between citizens in a city, and between market exchangers,[9] but reducing any relation to an *inter pares* agreement is illusory.

According to Thucydides, during the Peloponnesian War, the Athenians, when at odds with the people of Melos because they refused to join in the alliance against Sparta – the Melians invoking divine law to justify their right to remain neutral – declared: 'Laws are only valid amongst equals. In the case of unequal powers, power decides'. Such a principle of legitimation clearly can function only on a case-by-case basis. In a stabilized empire, the recognition of hegemony must be materialized in another way, even though power continues to underlie legitimacy. In the case of love relationships, power is absent in theory, but the subjective cost of loss of love (for both Alceste and Célimène) weighs upon each individual like a power relation.

Fig. 10.2 now takes on another meaning. Endowed with their habitus and with the idea they have of their inscription in social life (in a couple or an empire), each agent develops a strategy such that the set of trajectories works to reconstitute the relation, in the course of time. In fig. 10.3, the agent's habitus is represented by a small circle, and his space of representation by a small rectangle or 'map':

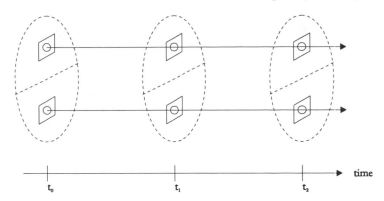

Figure 10.3 Trajectories

It is immediately clear that Figs 10.2 and 10.3 are, in a sense, duals of each other. Epistemologically, it is 'virtually' identical to say that:

1 the love binding Alceste and Célimène forces them, act after act, into their place as lover, despite their character differences and arguments, until the final crisis; or that

2 Alceste and Célimène are two subjects who seduce each other, and weigh up at each moment their interest in continuing the relationship; only the reading of the play confers on their conjoint histories the appearance of a history of 'one' love relationship which, in the end, turns out unhappily.

Depending on one's point of view, one opts for (1) a structuralist or (2) an individualist approach. What seems to me to be objective – that is real – is that there is a relatively stable interwebbing of behaviours. Whether Fig. 10.2 or 10.3 is the most 'real', or whether one gives 'consistency' to the other, is, in my mind, simply a question of 'relevance': it is a property of discourse and not of reality. Let us finally introduce here the metaphor of the weaving of a scarf.

The weaver first lays down the threads of the *warp,* creating a system of transversal places analogous to those in Fig. 10.2. Then the shuttle is passed back and forth through these places, leaving in its wake, as a trace of its trajectory, the threads of the *woof.* The *heddle* moulds the shuttle's trajectory to fit in with the warp's places. Once the fabric is taken out of its frame, what gives it consistancy? Without the warp, the threads of the woof would get tangled. Without the woof, the threads of the warp would simply sag.

I would argue – and this is my basic tendency – that the warp (Fig. 10.2) provides the *form,* and the woof the *matter* of the fabric's substance, in Aristotle's sense. A positivist tendency would argue the contrary (here we leave the metaphor behind) that the only reality observed is the set of trajectories in Fig. 10.3, that is, that the system of places and the structure (that is, form) exist only in the theoretician's mind. In any system of thought (in Althusser's terms) which seeks to reproduce the social fabric in a clarifying way,[10] it is on the other hand difficult to forget that the actors certainly presuppose that they will contribute to the weaving of a love relationship, businesses, state, or whatever. Their whole strategy derives from that. Célimène and Alceste are, moreover, but phantom-like beings (who can coincide with real contingent beings) who give flesh to a schema: that of a particularly contradictory love.[11]

Let us stick to the criterion of relevance: one can narrate history however one likes – it will never be the real, but one must narrate it as well as possible. Despite the seeming legitimacy of its 'positivism', individualism forgets that the 'habitus' and the 'map' at an individual's disposal are the products of a structured social totality which exists prior to their actions. One does not throw oneself into a love relationship when love does not exist, or when couples are linked by elders in their family line to fulfil reproductive strategies.[12] One does not seek to sell oneself as a slave when the only acceptable relation of productive subordination is that of wage-labour. Moreover, one can pursue with one's attention a beloved who does not reciprocate, on the condition that he or she pays attention to you, if only sadistically.[13] Similarly, one can apply for a job because one knows that wage-labour exists, and nevertheless remain unemployed. Thus the analysis of the real social fabric must start from the existence of social forms recognized by agents (even if the theory furnishes a different representation of them than do the actors),[14] locate the institutions which prop up these forms, and account for the willingness of actors to play the required roles.

But one goes beyond the limits of relevance (towards structuralism) when one reduces actors' *ways of acting* to their roles. This amounts to forgetting that each actor has his or her own style.[15] In other words, habitus is not a programme that obliges the individual trivially to act in conformity with the necessities of reproduction. Habitus is a willingness to play the game, but in accordance with autonomous aims, and even to quit playing if the possibility and interest arise. In these senses, habitus not only reproduces reality: it transforms and even engenders it.[16]

The refusal to reduce behaviour and intentions to structural requirements is, as is well known, the point where Marx's 'dialectical' materialism breaks with Feuerbach's 'metaphysical' materialism ('metaphysical' here denoting the hypostasis of immortalized structures): 'The materialist doctrine which takes men as products of circumstances and education, thus taking transformed men as products of other circumstances and a modified education, forgets that it is men themselves who transform circumstances and that the educator himself must be educated [...]. The coincidence of changed circumstances with different human activity or self-change, cannot be considered and rationally understood except as revolutionary practice' (the 3rd These on Feuerbach, 1846).

This position, which led to Bourdieu's break with structuralism (1987, p. 24), goes back a long way and comes out forcefully in all of Marx's work. Beginning with his thesis in philosophy on *The Difference between the Philosophy of Nature of Democritus and that of Epicurus*, the young Marx identified rectilinear fall as the 'relative' existence of the atom, as it is determined 'in itself' through its relation with the rest of space, and its 'angle' as the manifestation of its 'for itself': 'The movement of falling is the movement of non-autonomy [...]. For the atom, declination is, in its heart, that which can struggle and fight'.[17]

In this intellectual schema, the possible divergence, when compared with a tendency determined by the totality, is Lucretius' 'angle' or 'clinamen', its similarity with differential reasoning shown by Michel Serres (1977). I will schematize it as follows:

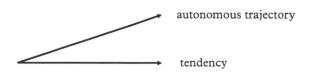

autonomous trajectory

tendency

This same schema appears in the *18th Brumaire of Louis Bonaparte*'s (1852) famous thesis: 'Men make their own history, but on the basis of conditions which are given and inherited from the past', a point of departure claimed by Giddens (1984) when he too attempts to go beyond the structuralism/individualism dilemma. To return to our metaphor, the woof's threads can move away from their predestined place in the warp, creating holes or folds in the fabric! This is why there are crises and why the problem of regulation arises.

Why thus do trajectories diverge? One could answer, 'Why not?', if one believed in human freedom without limits.[18] One could also seek positive reasons for such divergence. These last involve two different orders of equal theoretical legitimacy which take on varying importance in different cases.

Firstly, there are reasons which are external to the relation. In an overdetermined whole, each agent belongs to several structures and is endowed with several 'habituses', belongs to several 'cities', or 'natures' as Boltanski and Thevenot (1987) would say, which all contribute to the definition of his/her 'style'. He/she can thus be led to protest against, and even denounce, the place and role assigned him/her, appealing to other norms and interests. Conversely, the form and history of 'a' concrete relation depend on the styles of willing agents, necessarily adapting themselves to these last as much as adapting these last to themselves. This is why 'one can never step into the same river twice': no two love relationships are alike. Nor are there two identical unskilled workers on an assembly line, this particular form of work organization itself being dependent on the existence of 'conveniently styled' labour, whether involving women, peasants or immigrants, each having their own history and style.[19] The variability of agents' styles is no doubt the most direct vector of the reciprocal overdetermination of structures in which these agents are co-present. A love relationship between yuppies does not have the same dimension of dependency as one between a bourgeois and a non-working 'girl fit to be married off'.

Just as important, if not even more so (in that they lead to the 'possibility', and even the 'necessity' of crises), are the causes of divergence within the relations, that is, those result from the relation's *contradictory character*. Actually, in its plainest form, the *difference* between the terms in relation is the formal operating condition of external causes. But I am speaking now of the *opposition* or *struggle* that unites the terms in relation. Our sketchy definition of love relationships immediately gives rise to an internal cause of divergence: each person is inevitably led to complain that the other doesn't give him/her enough of what she/he lacks. Hence the necessary form of the crisis: the lover's quarrel that recurs in act after act in *Le Misanthrope*, despite Alceste's desire and Célimène's cleverness. They are clearly in love with each other and want the best for each other, but only so as to 'find' or 'realize' themselves individually.[20] In the case of wage relations, the very nature of the relation (extraction/sharing of added value) just as obviously implies struggle and divergence.

Hence the synthesis of Figs 10.2 and 10.3 is more complex than it at first seems. Trajectories tend to veer away from the requirements of reproduction of places, the latter being thus punctuated by 'revamping' and 'readjusting' which I will call 'minor crises'.

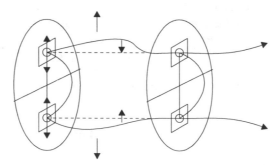

Figure 10.4 Minor crises

During the first few acts of *Le Misanthrope*, the *result* of fighting is to re-establish the unity of the love relationship at issue. Note that 'unity' and 'struggle', two aspects of a contradictory relation, themselves form a contradictory couple. There is a *unity* of 'unity' and 'struggle': struggle maintains unity and unity maintains struggle. Alceste remains misanthropic, Célimène remains flirtatious, and, while each of them satisfies his or her need for the other, they simultaneously prepare new divergences which lead to further fighting. It is this kind of unity – by which 'unity' (of the elements in relation) is maintained despite, and even because of, their 'struggle' – that the dialectician terms *regulation*.

We can see here how this conception goes beyond and engulfs Canguilhem's view. As individuals, Alceste and Célimène were 'at first strangers'. But regulation bears on their relationship only insofar as they are lovers, its result being to smooth over and to contain their differences. These last derive, on the one hand, from the fact that their 'styles' or 'natures' were already different before coming into relation (she is 'worldly' while the other is 'other-worldly', as

Lucien Goldmann might say). On the other hand, the accumulation of differences is also due to the ever contradictory character of love relationships: there is something (a cause) *within* a relationship that poses a problem of regulation. Furthermore, regulation does not result in a transcendental 'norm' nor 'rule': it is immanent, being the very unity of the relationship. Their love is what it is as a result of their incessant fighting.[20]

Here a question arises which we have carefully avoided, that is the finalism, functionalism or intentionality, of the *mode of regulation*: fighting. Well, it depends! For fighting in fact 'eliminates points of contention'; it results in the re-establishment of unity; one might argue that it fulfils this function '*ex post facto*'. It does not fulfil it '*ex ante*': in Act 4, Alceste begins the fight with the intention of breaking up (or so he tells Eliante). But doesn't he suspect deep down that what has already worked so well (a good row) will work again? For Célimène, it is clear that the fight already has a goal of re-establishing unity: it is a foreseen and sch~~~ ~~~ ~ t is the price which has to be paid for holdi~~ ~~~ ~~~ flirtatious. But many lovers *institution-*
a ~~~ ~~~ ging in marriage counselling, being
s~~~ ~~~ le one sees that regulation modes
c~~~ ~~~ e function of regular fighting
(~~~ ~~~ nce of the couple) may remain
c~~~ ~~~ lized in the form of marriage
(~~~ ~~~ through which agents give up –
in~~~ ~~~ m to interrupt their relation or
se~~~ ~~~ ning of its contradictory charac-
te~~~

c~~~ ~~~ ich the formerly institutionalized
re~~~ ~~~ re no longer able to reproduce a
p~~~ ~~~ ?' wins out over 'unity'. For our
A~~~ ~~~ 5. Célimène has gone to far, and
is~~~ ~~~ go on as before': the bowstring

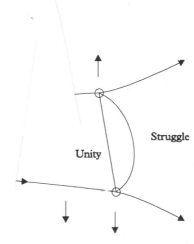

Figure 10.5 The major crisis

Three outcomes are possible:

1   The actors separate, and their trajectories thus no longer partake of the same history. It is the 'final crisis' of the relationship.
2   The form another kind of relationship: 'Let's just be friends'.
3   They renew their relationship, with another institutionalized compromise and another mode of regulation.

Célimène proposes the third solution: marriage. Alceste makes a pretence of negotiating: yes, but in his desert. Give up the world? Célimène cries out, frightened. It's over. Alceste choses the first solution. It is a moving scene, rich in dialectics! In this major crisis, as in the minor ones, the (manifest) external causes must not be allowed to veil the internal ones. If love is destroyed, it is because Alceste and Célimène 'were strangers to too great a degree from the outset' (Canguilhem would say) – their 'natures' were too different (worldly for one and other worldly for the other) and ended up making any agreement or arrangement impossible (as Boltanski and Thévenot would say). This is certainly so, but it would be a bit naïve to be satisfied with such answers. Célimène didn't speak her piece. Alceste 'seized the occasion'. Like the Princess of Clèves who, in the end, refused the Duke of Nemours's hand though her passion had become legitimate, he chose the desert, recognizing the impossibility of absolute love ('You find everything in you, and me wholly in you'). He preferred nothing to institutionalized compromise, arrangements and relative solutions.[21]

Note that the contradiction within a love relationship which necessarily leads to major (though not necessarily final) crises is perceptible only to the literary critic, psychoanalyst or sociologist. The theoretician (or the playwright who takes his or her inspiration from 'love problems') analyses the 'anatomy' of the relation, its 'internal', 'profound' and 'esoteric' schemas.[22] He/she analyses the relation for itself and its contradiction, independently of the agents' 'styles'. This does not mean that he/she must or has the right to neglect these last for there to be a relationship, the agents must want there to be one (or resign themselves to it), and they must monitor it and direct themselves to it. This points to the defect of structuralism, that of abstracting the agents, as if there were love relationships, wars, exchange and wage relations without love strategies, warmongering, job applicants and merchants: just 'place'-holding phantoms.[23] A generic relation, like a particular realization of this relation, exists only as an abstraction or an acutalization of practices, and these practices exist only if need is transformed into projects and practices.

For Alceste and Célimène, there is no love relationship that reproduces itself. There are loving feelings which are deployed as tactics and strategy. Alceste wants Célimène to be his, and for her to be like him (even if we suspect that if she were like him, he wouldn't want her anymore). Célimène wants to hold on to Alceste, she doesn't want him to be like her, but wants to remain as she is. Their strategies turn out to be compatible for four acts (thanks to regulative fighting) but then can no longer keep them 'under the regime'. As long as the love affair lasts, the misanthrope wants to be 'intra-worldy', and not very adeptly acts somewhat 'prudently' notwithstanding. With the help of his friends, Philinte and Eliante, he 'nevertheless' makes a worthy effort not to insult Oronte immediately (for a major crisis immediately set off) and not definitively to lose Célimène. He nevertheless tries to 'play the game', follow suit, apply the codes of worldly life and make a formal display of love; in a word, he follows 'surface', 'exterior' and 'exoteric' 'rules', worldly and gallant codes.[24] The comic element derives from the fact that his nature stops him from carrying them out; but he knows them, and, while cursing them, tries nevertheless to follow them. The problem is that the combination of the codes and his own style leads him to a trajectory that diverges seriously from that of the world around him. For Alceste, as for Célimène, the crisis does not arise from the fact that, structurally, there is no such thing as happy love. It arises because each person 'has gone too far'.

In the duality of the warp and the woof, this story can be read in two different ways. At a profound level, it can be read as a love relationship caught up in the cyclical pulsation of unity and struggle, or in the dialectic of fusion an autonomy. At a superficial level, it can be seen as an external relation between two independent strategies. Fights are the mode of adjusting these strategies into a love 'regime'. But there comes a moment at which the partners' wagers, hopes, reservations and practices turn out to be irremediably incompatible. Love must be transformed or disappear.

3 Values in Process and Regimes of Accumulation

I will now briefly return to the concepts of values in process, accumulation regimes, and the 'warp/wool' duality, as they have been originally used in analyses in terms of regulation, that is, in the CEPREMAP report (1977), and as I have developed them (1979a, 1983a). This will allow us to clarify the link between economic studies and the preceding epistemological considerations.

Rereading *Capital*, Etiènne Balibar stressed the extent to which commodity circulation between capitalists and the proletariat results in the reproduction of the structure of wage relations. The *conditions* of this latter (and of the circulation to which it gives rise) seem, in effect, to be identical to the *result*:

	A →	P^c ...	M ... →	A'	A
Capitalists	Money-capital	Production conditions	Products	Money	Money-capital
Proletarians	Labour power	Money V		Subsistance goods	Labour power
	F →	V	→	M	... F

Figure 10.6 The Reproduction of Wage Relations

Figs 10.2 and 10.3 have been superimposed here, and Althusserians have above all given priority to the 'vertical' dimension (the system of places) therein. Indeed, it suffices to consider the graph 'straight on' (that is, with the time vector pointing towards the reader) instead of longitudinally (with time running left to right) to obtain the famous double circuit of reproduction.[25]

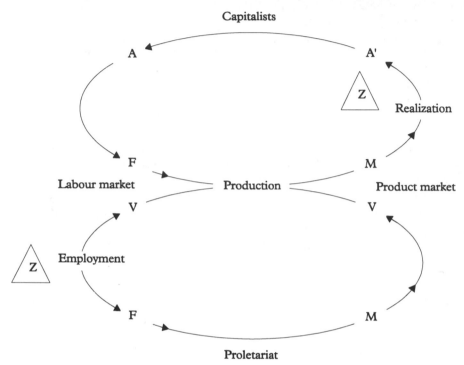

Figure 10.7 The 'Double Circuit'

Seen in this way, reproduction in fact seems to be 'non-contradictory'. All studies done by 'regulationists' can thus be understood as three-fold efforts to show: that capitalist reproduction 'is not self-evident'; why, over long periods of time, it continues 'nevertheless'; and, why, after a certain amount of time, a major crisis breaks out.

Today these points are well known. First of all, the simple reality of market relations, that is, the capitalist producer's uncertainty as to the social validity of the commodities he/she proposes, introduces a radical asymmetry between commodities and money: money is the 'unconditional' general equivalent of commodities, the conversion of commodities into money being, on the contrary, a 'perilous jump', indicated in Fig. 10.7 by the letter 'Z' (for 'dangerous curve'). The flow of commodities from the graph's north-east loop must be correctly correlated (in volume and value) to the demand expressed in the south-east loop, but also to the loops which are not represented – especially the 'accumulation-investment' loop (purchase of production goods by capitalists), and to all the other complications brought about in the socio-economic fabric by the State, other social classes, and so on. Uncertainty, in this sense, constitutes the 'formal possibility' of crises. Its necessity is introduced by accumulation itself which tends to increase the flow from the north-east, while containing growth in the south-east loop. This contradiction is at the core of wage relations. It can be summarized in one sentence: either the exploitation rate is too high and an overproduction crisis will soon loom on the horizon, or it is too low and an underinvestment crisis will arise. This rate is itself a function, on the one hand, of distribution relations (consumption norms) and, on the other, of changes in production (production norms), and in particular of productivity increases and changes in the organic composition of capital.

An accumulation regime is a mode of transformation comprising compatible norms of production and consumption. Such a regime can be described as the repeated given of the production of productive sectors or branches and its corresponding demand: this is what is known as the reproduction schema or macroeconomic structure. We have shown that the 'Fordist' regime could be described as establishing a parallel between the growth of productivity, the consumption norm of wage-earners, and the composition of capital. In other words, it follows a schema of intensive reproduction with a widening of wage-earner consumption such that parallel growth takes place in sector I and II of net product volume, which is related to the number of productive wage-earners. This accumulation regime is thus a possible kind of warp for capitalist reproduction:

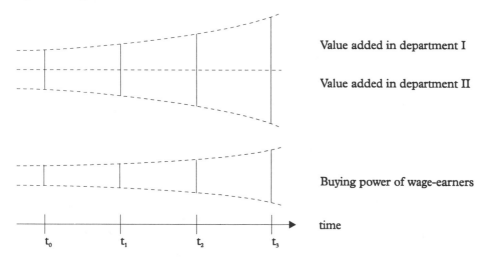

Figure 10.8 Accumulation Regime as Warp

Let us return to Fig. 10.6. The graph's longitudinal dimension must be taken seriously. One can consider agents (capitalists and proletarians) as owners of 'values in process', that is of the 'flows' of value of the respective generic forms:

$$\ldots \quad \rightarrow \quad A \quad \rightarrow \quad P\ldots \quad M \quad \rightarrow \quad A' \quad \rightarrow \quad P'\ldots$$

and $\quad \ldots \quad \rightarrow \quad F \quad \rightarrow \quad S \quad \rightarrow \quad M\ldots \quad F \quad \rightarrow \quad S\ldots$

This concept of 'values in process', changing from one form into another, is introduced in chapter 3 of *Capital* and developed at length throughout the whole of volume II. The millions of individual flows constitute the woof of economic reality, that is, the 'flow' of values in process. In 'everyday life' (*Alltagsleben*), they are in fact the *only* positive reality. In the case of capital, Marx pushes the textile metaphor so far that he shows capital's thread-like structure, composed as it is, of three intertwined strands: the cycles of Money, Commodities and Productive capital (volume II).

Along this stream, values in process change forms, as can be seen if one traces out Fig. 10.7's double circuits over time:

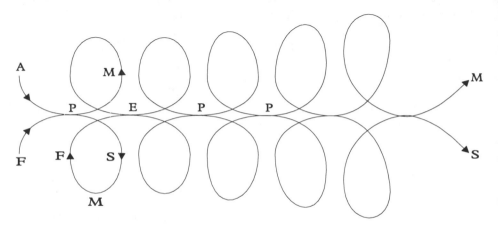

Figure 10.9 The Flow of Values in Process

In reality, the two circuits in this figure are made up of a myriad of individual flows: the flow. '*Ex post*' when the accumulation regime is stabilized, this circuit, in its structure, must exactly match the proportions repeatedly described by the reproduction schema.

The famous Marxian equalities in the reproduction schema outlined in volume II express precisely this duality. The laws governing the flows of nominal value – as expressed in money – are as yet unknown. The laws of money-wage and price formation are 'external connections': they regulate the exchange norms between supposedly independent flows. Knowing normal prices, and putting into play the capitalists' and wage-earners' habituses, agents must direct their value in process so as to respect the accumulation regime. One can interpret the general problem of the transformation of values into production prices as the study of the conditions under which external connections (laws fixing wages and production prices) are compatible with recursive proportions of the accumulation regime in force.[26]

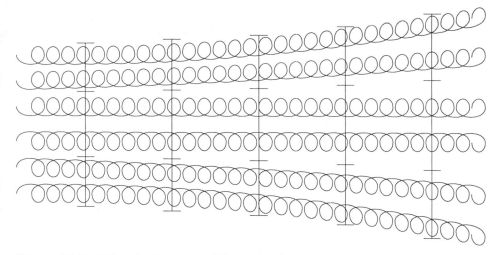

Figure 10.10 Values in Process and Reproduction Schema

This possibility provides no guarantee that things will turn out well. If the laws of nominal wage and profit formation are not adapted to the evolution of production norms, disequilibrium arises. The stream of values in process seems thus to 'overflow' the reproduction schema's growth in value or, on the contrary, to turn out lower than its potential growth. In the economic fabric, folds and holes appear: inflation or overproduction appears. Thus arises the problem of adapting the stream to the regime, the woof to the warp. Adaptation is the effect of the regulation mode in force, which plays, in the weaving metaphor, the role of the loops or ... of Adam Smith's 'invisible hand'.

The purpose of economic research on regulation, and especially of the CEPREMAP report (1977) and its derivatives, was to show that the 'invisible hand' was not a trans-historical mechanism of perfectly pure competition. Modes of regulation (comprising forms of direct and indirect wage determination, inter-company competition and co-ordination, and money management) change over time, as do forms of growth and the self-piloting of values in process. As an accumulation regime itself changes, major crises can arise from the inappropriateness of its regulation mode. Such major crises (like the current crisis, or that of the 1930s) are to be distinguished from cyclical 'minor crises' which are the very form of regulatory action in so-called 'competitive' modes.[27] As for 'intentionality' in the institution of an adapted regulation mode, such as 'monopolistic regulation' in the Fordist regime, these works have shown that, historically, it is most often a question of 'lucky finds' which are consciously consolidated over time by 'Keynesian' theoreticians of Fordist regulation, reformist unions and governments seeking to preserve social consensus.

Conversely, understanding how the major crisis of Fordism (for example) arose, that is, how its 'fabric' was torn, implies a two-fold task. At a profound level, one finds a progressive deformation of the macroeconomic structure: a slowdown in productivity gains, an increase in the organic composition of capital, and rising internationalization. At an 'exogenous' level, one tries to show how the socio-economic actors – in their struggles to 'change the rules of the game' within the logic of that development model, as well as in their attempts to change that model by appealing to a 'nature' which is incompatible with this model – accumulated divergences. Unions tried to make wage increases more and more automatic, and consolidate Welfare State benefits; they thus carried out offensive measures within the model. But wage-earners increasingly resisted alienating forms of the Fordist organization of work. To counter these tendencies, business people tried to increase scale of production, accelerate automation (a strategy within Fordist logic), but also to relocate production in countries with regulation modes that were more favourable to profits, circumventing social legislations by 'polarizing' labour markets: a form of denunciation by flight (exit ...) from Fordist institutionalized compromises.

The result of these divergent strategies is well known. What is important here is to understand that it is not a question of an unfortunate disruption of consensus that a bit of good will could have smoothed over. The contradiction lay within the regime itself.

4 The Fabric of Space-Time

Having already discussed love and capitalist accumulation, I will now take up a third field: human geography. I will also change cultures here: my references will be to Anglo-Saxon critical geography, a still excellent epistemological opus of which can be found in D. Gregory and J. Urry's collection of articles (1985). The problem of establishing a dialogue between cultures because of the language barrier, second-hand knowledge and approximate translations has led to misunderstandings which are really superseded only in Ed Soja's remarkable contribution (1985). Despite ritualistic and often hardly relevant criticism of Althusserism, it is difficult to see what is really new (when compared with Althusserian overdetermination) in 'theoretical realism' – according to which objects have 'causal powers' owing to their internal structures which are realized only as a function of their contingent contextual articulations.[28] Similarly, it is difficult to see where Bourdieu's 'constructivist structuralism' differs from Giddens's 'theory of structuration', but most writers included in the collection (especially Walker 1985) agree that they are the same.

What did attract my attention is the direct use made of the warp-woof metaphor in the mentioned volume. In critical geography, its originator was Hägerstrand (1970), discussed by Giddens (1985) and Gregory (1985). Hägerstrand presents his 'space-time geography' as a micro-sociology, based on routinized 'choreographies' of individual trajectories by agents subject to the constraints of their spatial-temporal materiality. These trajectories combine to form bundles at the 'stations' where they interact. The projection of these trajectories into planar-space produces the structuration of space.

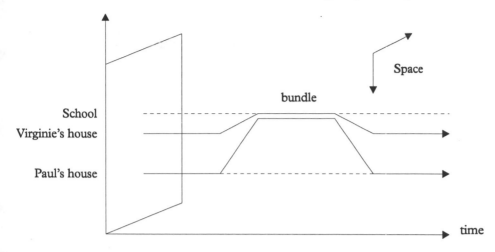

Figure 10.11 Hägerstrand's Choreography

Let us take the example of young villagers (Paul and Virginie) who go to school everyday. We see the 'woof' of trajectories structured by (and structuring) the 'warp': the system of the village's 'stations' (*see* Fig. 10.11). One can even throw this schema into a 'minor crisis'. Paul invites Virginie to play truant in grove B, and gossip soon brings the little devil and his Cinderella back to their normal trajectories. Tattling and sanctions constitute the most primitive forms of social regulation. But the divergence can be developed so far as to set off a major crisis, upon which our love birds will either get engaged and leave school (*see* Fig. 10.12) or be sent to boarding school.

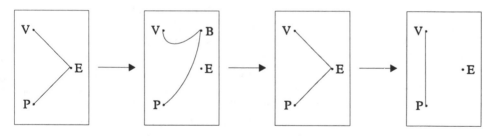

Figure 10.12 Divergence, Minor and Major Choreographic Crises

The operational character of Hägerstrand's 'space-time geography' becomes clear here, as does the way it can lead to methods of urbanist projection, as for example the conception of a transport system [Matzner and Rusch (1976)]. Giddens nonetheless points out its weaknesses. It neglects the origin of 'projects' which guide trajectories, or else views them as caused by the stations themselves which are 'already given'; one thus falls back into the totalitarianism of the 'warp'. Giddens proposes to replace the stations by 'centres' endowed with 'presence availability' which he analyses as Goffman (1959) might have. In our example, one could say that the grove presents the availability of 'girl-chasing', carried out or not depending on the amorous impulses of the village boys. But the grove exists prior to their impulses, and this prohibits any attempt at 'micro-sociological grounding' in localization.[29]

D. Gregory criticizes (in accordance with a theme that must by now be familiar to the reader) the tendency to reduce the spatial warp to the functional necessities of capitalist structure. He distrust just as thoroughly the opposite tendency (based on the chronic instability of structurations, brought on by permanent innovation), seeing in the movement of the woof's threads only an intertwined tangle. He concludes that contradiction and struggle must be understood within structuration itself (another theme with which we are familiar), and D. Gregory introduces here the Sartrian notion of *seriality* which Hägerstrand did not, according to Gregory, get beyond. 'Seriality' (opposed to the state of 'groups in fusion' – Sartre 1960) is the state of individuals behaving like Democritus' determinate atoms, deprived of 'clinamen', and incapable of a collective project leading to the modification of structures. We must therefore be careful not to identify the 'warp' with necessity and the 'woof' with freedom! I'll come back to this point in my conclusion.

For the moment, I would like to discuss two examples from my studies which will allow me to clarify, in other fields of human geography, both the warp-woof distinction and the question of regulation.

The first concerns the regional question, or rather that of inter-regionality, a subject about which I once disagreed intermittently and amicably with Doreen Massey. In a first paper (1974a, taken up again in 1977) I defined French regions for themselves by their genealogies, the histories of the internal social relations which moulded their 'personalities' (in the terms of Vidal de la Blache), and endowed them with availabilities differentiated in terms of the forms of the division of labour that characterized, after 1945, that which I hadn't yet called 'French-style Fordism'. Fordism, as a form of the organization of labour, in fact allows for a disjunction between design, skilled fabrication, and unskilled assembly. France, with its regions highly differentiated in terms of wages, unions, skilled labour and markets, was greatly tempted to deploy the circuits of productive branches over three kinds of labour levels, in conformity with the Fordist tripartition. And it succumbed, with the regions themselves 'calling' for industrial jobs, and the Regional Planning Agency directing the choices of big businesses (a regulation problem I won't go into here). Three types of regions could thus be defined relationally according to branch circuit structures, certain regions, in conformity with their inherited 'styles', coming to take on 'roles' defined within this structure. For example, one finds type I: the greater Paris area; type II: the Nord-Pas de Calais; type III: the West.

D. Massey (1978) criticized the ambiguity stemming from using one approach based on the warp and another on the woof: 'Lipietz's regions seem at times to be defined in themselves – in their genealogy – and at others by their synchronic place at the heart of the inter-regional division of labor'. To Massey only the second alternative is valid – as long as one does not overly simplify the 'warp' of this structure – in recognizing (something I willingly accept) the existence of many forms of labour organization, varying from branch to branch and even within each branch, combining in contingent ways in explaining the fate of each region by the accumulation of 'genealogical layers'. Massey applied this method in her book (Massey and Meegan 1982) in which I immediately detected (1983c) a tendency to reduce geography to industrial organization. How, I objected, can one explain the variable success of different regions faced with industrial restructuring, if on does not take into account the character and availability of regions, inherited from accumulated genealogical 'layers'? A declining skilled industry region can either convert by mobilizing its 'human resources' (for example, the Ruhr area), or by evolving towards unskilled industry (for example, the Lorraine area). The precise path of development depends on many factors, but first and foremost on whether the region forms a political coalition capable of carrying out industrial renovation (Lipietz 1985).

Massey (1985) wholeheartedly agreed with this critique and went so far as to affirm – upon the publication of a balance sheet on developments in industrial geography (very similar to the summary of the 'structure/agency' debate in the first part of this chapter) – the importance of pre-existing spatial realities in the inter-regional restructuration process. 'The unique is back on the agenda' – here again we see the influence of Vidal de la Blache!

I tried to show (in 1985a) that, in the case of international economic relations, the autonomy of national trajectories is even greater (than in the case of inter-regional relations) when compared with the structure of the totality. As opposed to the classical 'centre/periphery' structure, as well as the orthodoxy of the New International Division of Labour inspired by the Fordist tripartition (Frobel, Heinrichs and Kreyes 1980), one must advance the notion of an 'international configuration' (a much softer version of the 'warp'), wherein are traced vague regularities in transfers (of populations, commodities, knowledge, and capital) between autonomous national accumulation regimes (which here play the role of the 'warp'). I even tried to study what the possible forms of regulation for this warp/woof duality and its crises could be, namely commercial agreements, transnational companies, international credit, and so on.

I would, however, here like to raise the question of spatial regulation as a last example. It concerns the transformation of urban neighbourhoods. In a first study, considerably inspired by structuralism, on land rent (1974b), I presupposed the existence of a 'warp': the Spacial Economic Division of Labour (here the workers, there the *petit bourgeois*, over there the superior tertiary sector buildings, and so on). This SEDS is reproduced and transformed by the practice of real-estate agents. But what should they construct in such and such a place? I showed that the mechanism of land prices, as resulting from the pre-existing SEDS (the 'exogenous differential land tribute'), obliges agents to reproduce the social use of a neighbourhood, or at most to locate 'superior' uses in nearby neighbourhoods that were formerly less highly rated. But what can then be said of large-scale urban redevelopment projects which change, in one fell swoop, the social use of a neighbourhood, or which at least are effectuated according to long-term planning co-ordinating several (private and public) sectors? Here, the land rent (said to be 'endogenous intensive differential') must be divided between the agents in accordance with the product of the projected space: the agents internalize the result of their future co-operation, dividing up the fruits of the completed transformation. In a later article (1975), I termed these two forms of spatial reproduction-transformation 'competitive' and 'monopolistic', not yet having the term 'regulation' at my disposal.[30]

Stated otherwise, the 'competitive/monopolistic' couple refers to two modalities used by 'woof' agents to regulate their relations in a warp which changes shape in the course of their practices. Either the 'warp' is viewed as 'already given', and thus the 'map' of their space of representation (here the land prices) allows each of them to make 'rational' decisions contributing to the reproduction of the structure or its slight alteration; or else the 'map' anticipates macro-transformations of the 'warp' which can be brought about by their own explicitly co-ordinated actions, and this collective projected space becomes the economic landscape of individual projects. The spatial-temporal metaphors (and what are those of weaving?) thus close in on themselves ... .

By Way of Conclusion

The preceding argument may be summarized in the following way. There are two different possible points of view about a social process which appears to have a certain regularity. First of all, one can account for it as the reproduction over time of a relation, or of a complex of reciprocally overdetermined relations. Second, one can understand it as the juxtaposition and interaction of individual trajectories of agents (or groups) following their own goals in accordance with a representation of the consequences of their interaction. It is irrelevant here whether this representation be appropriate or not, or whether the coherence of their actions be an unintended effect of their conscious aims. It is also irrelevant whether the relations be hierarchical (oppressive) or co-operative.

As long as all goes well (the phenomenon reproducing itself 'within a regime'), the two interpretations are compatible. Agent's projects and constraints are the products of a habitus and a space of representation generated by the very reproduction of the structure. But the structure is nothing but a conceptualization of the observed compatibility of individual trajectories. The metaphor of the warp (the reproduction of relations) and the woof (individual trajectories), aims at making one see this duality.

This becomes interesting only because the agents 'defined' by relations have the capacity, and even the tendency, to diverge in their actions from the requirements of social reproduction. These divergences are resolved by a mode of regulation, unless they accumulate to the point of setting off a 'major crisis'.

Minor crises ('within' regulation) themselves contribute to altering the structure until a major crisis breaks out.

The existence of divergences and crises in no way leads to the dethroning of structures or actions, some of them simply giving way to others. On the contrary, it points to the autonomy, irreducibility, or reality, as it were, of the two aspects. There can be no divergence without structure (there would in fact be only chaos). There can be no structure without routinized action or without a founding agreement (whether willed or submitted to). One must still account for autonomy, and even for the possible individualization of agents, especially as we have admitted that individuals and groups can function as 'agents'.

The individualization of agents playing a 'role' – in a place defined by the structure, but in accordance with personal 'styles' – poses a first set of problems. A relation can define a system of places which are 'in themselves' individualized: lovers, social classes and regions. But the capacity of these 'individuals' to act 'for themselves' is problematic. When the individuality in question is collective, whether it be that of a class, big business or region, the problem of aggregation obviously arises, that is, that of 'collective consciousness' (for which theories as diverse as those involving class consciousness, delegation, principal agents, and hegemonic block try to account). But when the 'individual' is a human individual, the 'splitting of the subject' (*Ichabspaltung*), dear to psychoanalysis, poses as many problems as aggregation in the understanding of this individual as subject. Alceste is torn between his misanthropic ego and his amorous ego. In short, contradictory relations set in opposition *knots* of contradiction at their poles. A national accumulation regime is a contradiction which is reproduced in time, but it can be considered, within the framework of a worldwide configuration, as an individuality in a contradictory relation with others of the same type. Agents' particular 'styles' are products of the articulated relations that define them, lying both inside and outside of themselves.

An individual is certainly not a class or a nation, but can, no more then they, be reduced to an atom capable of rational individualism ('you don't know what you want!'). One could obviously appeal to the hierarchical organization of the real. But then the question arises of 'internal causes' and 'external causes': must one view a wage-earner as a living contradiction externally overdetermined by his/her relation to capital, or as a place in wage relations, encumbered with a 'style' inherited from outside determinations? This amounts to a relativism that can be resolved only by using the criterion of relevance: does one construct the history as that of the life of Ali, a marabout's son working at Citroën, or as an analysis of problems of human management?

The goal of this first group of questions is to recall the importance of the notion of 'overdetermination'. As 'actors' are involved in many relations, or are themselves a condensation of relations, they enter into the relation which defines them from a certain vantage point with an always already given 'individuality' that *changes* owing to their entering (and remaining) in this relation (loving affection, Imperial England, or the female working class), but which all the same gives specific concrete form to that relation which can modify or transform it: for example, the liberal professions were not incorporated into wage-labour without changing some of the latter's norms.

Once individuality is agreed to, what is one to say of the autonomy of agents in relation to their roles? An easy and generally relevant answer consists in appealing to that aspect of individuality which is not defined by the relation: the participation in a different 'nature' or overdetermination by other relations. Young people refuse Taylorism because they have other areas of interest. Célimène doesn't listen to Alceste because she enjoys fashionable circles. An opposite, and just as relevant, answer appeals to the relation's internal contradiction, and individual's irreducible aspiration to freedom: Taylorism is a negation of human dignity (and perhaps of productive efficiency), and love cannot justify self-effacement (nor can it survive such an eventuality). Behaviour adequate to relations generally prevails, nonetheless, for otherwise the world would be in a terrible mess. And when it prevails, the warp-woof duality identifies actions and structures that can be distinguished only by the methodological point of view, reading, as it does, along the longitudinal (diachronic) and transversal (synchronic) axes.

This is a fundamental point: at the most profound level, the contradiction is *not* between structure and agency. It lies within agency itself, between its routinized, reified and reproductive facet (and thus, by duality, one immediately has the structure) and its potentially divergent, innovative, autonomy, generative and perhaps revolutionary (but at least inciting) one. That is the contradiction Lucretius and Epicurus were aiming at with the ideal of 'clinamen', that Karl Marx was aiming at in his *Theses on Feuerbach*; Karel Kosik in his dialectic of the concrete; Jean-Paul Sartre in his *Théorie des ensembles pratiques*; and Pierre Bourdieu in his definition of 'constructivist structuralism'.[31]

Towards the end of his life – I don't recall exactly where or when – Fernand Braudel explained that the weight of the oldest routines encumber our present like the Amazon's alluvia colour the ocean for hundreds of miles around its estuary. In our history, based on given conditions inherited from the past, humans perhaps have the right to at most a 5 per cent 'clinamen' (or degree of freedom) and a 95 per cent necessity factor. But this 5 per cent calls forth and creates new and perhaps better social forms.

Notes

1 I am writing here only of the ontological theses, not the epistemological ones, and I am considering only 'classical' Althusserism – that of *Reading Capital* (Althusser et al., 1965). For an in-depth discussion *see* Lipietz and Rouilleault (1972) and Lipietz (1973 and 1979a).

2 Aglietta's book (1976) which came out after the seminar, gave first place back to market relations which went on to have increasing importance in his work.

3 I devoted many pages of my book (1979a) to distinguishing my conception of regulation from functionalism, and to grounding regulation in dialectics. In the second edition of his book, Michel Aglietta (1976), like Boyer (1987), confirmed his agreement with my critique of functionalism.

Let me make one comment all the same: students should be warned against functionalism, i.e. the belief that the result of a mechanism or institution is the cause of its existence. At the stage or research, when, for example, one unpacks an unknown apparatus, it is nonetheless helpful to ask two basic functionalistic questions: (a) How does it all work? and (b) What is each piece there for?

4 *See* for example the Organum in the *Encylopaedia Universalis*.

5 *See* M. Guillaume (ed.), 1987.

6 J. Rancière, in his contribution to *L'empire du sociologue*, simply reduces Bourdieu's sociology to his own former position, as express in *Reading Capital*: 'The practical meaning [of agents] is never anything but a ruse of reason ... The system reproduces its existence because it is misunderstood'. Now 'practical meaning', 'habitus' and 'strategy' in Bourdieu's work, which reintroduce agent, action and practice, imply (according to C. Lévi-Strauss) a critique of structuralism 'which winds up everywhere and takes its inspiration from fashionable spontaneism and subjectivism' (cf. Bourdieu 1987, pp. 77–8).

7 *See* 'Le mariage dans la société du haut Moyen-Age' in Duby (1988).

8 While Luc Boltanski, in *Les cadres*, deploys all the generative and even transformational potential borne by the concept of habitus, countering a mechanist view of reproduction, he nonetheless does not forget the exploitative relations (in the Marxist sense of the term) that underlie 'grading struggles', like geology underlies geomorphology. Unfortunately, a more recent work (Boltanski and Thevenot 1987), however adept, suggestive and 'operational' it may be, seems to mark a move towards an exclusively 'external' (exoteric) – and thus individualist – approach to social relations. I will come back to this point. This same movement (in conformity with the general trend) is also present in Aglietta and Orlean (1982), my divergences from whom I have explained in (1983a and b).

9 In their innovative work, Boltanski and Thevenot (1987) take on the task of going beyond the 'methodological individualism/collectivism' dilemma, and more precisely of dealing with 'problem, central to social science, of the possibility of agreement between a society's members, if one takes seriously the question of legitimacy, without abandoning it by adopting an explanation on the basis of contingency, cheating and power'. They thus construct a grammar of the forms of agreement collected in political theory and in good behaviour guides. These agreements correspond to 'cities' and 'natures'. In the first few pages, they observe that the city form is not the only possible (there is the 'cosmos' and 'chaos' which are unaware of the 'common humanity' of those with equal rights, who agree on a social order). But their reservations are progressively forgotten in later pages. The condition of the 'commerce of men' definitively takes the form of interindividual agreement. In reality, this marks a return to a variation of methodological individualism that eliminates conflicts intrinsic to social relations, which takes a back seat when compared with Bourdieu's intention (1987, p. 55) to study 'real situations in which consensual submission comes about in and through conflict'.

10 A word of epistemology here: despite his ritualistic deference to Lenin's critiques of empiro-criticism, Althusser did not confuse the real concrete and the concrete of thought, i.c. he did not think that abstract relations were present within empirical reality, hidden in the gauge? of contingencies. Structuralism leads one, however, to believe in the *existence* of fundamental hidden structures which are *realer* than the mystified behaviour of the agents they 'direct'. I criticized (1985a and b, 1987b)

the dangers of this 'realism of the concept', in my own conceptual formulations as well, such as 'Fordism' and 'peripheral Fordism'.

11 Our theatrical example introduces complications, for the theatre makes for a cascade of interpretations. Starting from a deep narrative schema, present in works as different as the *Misanthrope* and *Gone with the Wind*, writers endow their characters (their place holders) with very different personalities. Directors and actors in turn interpret these personalities with their own styles. One could object, as do narratologists, that literary narratives have their own structures and laws of movement, which differ from those of social reality. I must assume here that, if life is not a novel, Molière's theater is life itself.

12 This is not only the case in the lineage and segmentary societies analysed by Africa scholars, but also in the French nobility of the Middle Ages (Duby 1988) and even in the Bearnais peasantry. The *Misanthrope* constitutes a considerable cultural revolution in that the love relationship appears therein as a 'sociologically pure' form, i.e. independently of lineage relations which were still at the forefront of classical theatre and did not die out until Marivaux (cf. Lipietz 1988).

13 'Your eyes are enough to persuade you
    If only they could look at me for but a moment' (Racine, *Phèdre* II, 5).

14 On the importance of intellectual coding in social relations, i.e. what Bourdieu calls 'effects of theory' (1987, pp. 93 and 164), *see* Lipietz (1985b).

15 My distinction here between 'place', 'role' and 'style' owes a great deal to long and fruitful discussions with Jane Jenson. 'Style' is an actor's own way of playing a role. His/her own characteristic way is not entirely determined by the relation , but by experience and the other 'natures' in which the actor participates.

16 'Why not say habit? Habit is spontaneously taken to be repetitive, mechanical, automatic and more reproductive than productive. Now I mean to insist on the idea that habitus is something that is powerfully generating. Habitus is, briefly stated, a product of conditioning which tends to reproduces the objective logic of conditioning, but in making it undergo transformation; it is a type of transformational machine which makes us "reproduce" the social conditions of our own production, but in a relatively unpredictable way, i.e. in such a way that one cannot simply and mechanically move from knowledge of productive conditions to knowledge of products', Bourdieu (1986, p. 134).

17 K. Marx, *The Difference between Democritus' and Epircurus' Philosophies of Nature*, (French translation, Ducros, Bordeaux, 1970, p. 243).

18 Even in 'cold' societies, accusations or suspicion of 'sorcery' or 'possession' by a demon (who must be exorcized) target deviance which is at times virtually imperceptible (*see* the tiny revolt of a young girl in the film *Remparts d'Argile* by Bertucelli and Duvigaud).

19 Robert Linhart, in *L'établi* (1978), realizes this as soon as he meets his factory friends away from the assembly line. But he also shows that it is not just anyone who can bear assembly line work, and that the line is not designed for everyone. One could go further: in a capitalist economy in which there are skilled workers willing to 'commit themselves', it is not 'efficient', from a capitalistic point of view, to push too far one's recourse to Taylorism.

20 The expression 'to realize oneself' borrowed from a psychology one could describe as 'old-fashioned', is here used on purpose in reference to 'realization', i.e. the validation of commodities in exchange.

20.5 This is why it is better to use the 'game' metaphor with care. As Bourdieu notes (1987, p. 82), (immanent) social *regularities* are not all (transcendental) 'rules of the game', even if there are (customary and juridical) 'laws'. To avoid implying a transcendence of the rules, and thus leave agents the possibility of progressively changing the rules of the game in the course of the game itself, Bowles and Gintis (1986) write of 'recurrent games'. The disadvantage of this is that one thus risks flattening into the same level what we are trying here to distinguish as 'relations', 'regimes', 'regulation modes' and 'trajectories', and thereby no longer understanding how divergence from a regime can lead to crisis, or why the problem of regulation arises. One can imagine, for example, an alternative play in which Alceste would throw himself into Eliante's arms right after the first fight, or Célimène, while upset, would 'drop' Alceste: but it wouldn't be the same story, nor the same love regime, nor perhaps the same relation.

21 In accordance with their non-dialectical conception of agreement, Boltanski and Thevenot (1987, chapter 4) cannot explain the appearance of 'points of contention' or the 'retraction' of agreements, except by the idea that agents participate in several 'natures'. They thus veer towards E. Balibar's structuralist position in *Reading Capital* which can explain crises only by the play of external relations among themselves. Aglietta and Orlean's 'conflictual' methodological individualism, on the contrary, is able to register contradiction and the necessity of crises (and of regulation) at the core of each relation. To do so, they have taken their inspiration from René Girard's work on 'violence and the sacred'. The problem is that Girard himself only abusively generalizes his own research (1961) on the literary treatment of love relationships as described by Da Ponte ('I am seeking something outside myself, I know not who has it, nor do I know what it is'). Transposed into economy, this works rather well for speculation on bonds, but not so well for 'real' economics.

22 The fundamental, though somewhat misunderstood, distinction in Marx's work between esoteric and exoteric is the basis of my book (1983a).

23 'The intellectualist and theorist error permanently threatening social science – i.e. the structuralist error – is the one that consists in saying: "I know better than the indigenous peoples what they are like"' (Bourdieu 1987, p. 114).

24 Sociology, like economy, *must* account for this 'exoteric' world, that of agents' lived experience (this is, for example, the object of book III Capital). It is world in which each agent perceives other agents occupying other places of the same relation, in 'exteriority', like elements of a space of representation with which he will 'interact'. This world has manifest laws which must be inventoried, but without forgetting its bond of dual dependence on the esoteric. 'Sociology is an esoteric science which, however, seems exoteric' (Bourdieu 1987, p. 68). Thence the charm and the temptation to flirt (as I have done throughout this analysis of (*Le Misanthrope*) with Boltanski and Thevenot's terminology. My suspicion is that their terminology of the exoteric does not overlap with any kind of esoteric sociology.

25 We are of course dealing here with a schema that abstracts the 'intercapitalist' accumulation-investment loops, and other social relations tied to the reproduction of wage relations (e.g. patriarchy at the M ... F level).

26 One can show that with constant production norms, and data concerning behaviour and exoteric laws (in this case: equalization of profit rates among branches, the constancy of the sharing rate of value added), the accumulation regime and price system are simultaneously determined (Lipietz 1979b). This demonstration combines Frobenius' theorem and Brouwer fixed point theorem: it is thus simply a theorem of *existence* and not of stability!!

27 In the fourth part of this paper it will become clear why I have proposed this pair of terms – competitive/monopolistic – to distinguish two main types of regulation modes. This terminology may seem unfortunate.

28 Thus Urry (1985, p. 27) criticizes Althusser for neglecting the fact that structures have no effect but through their interdependence, and that 'the degree to which their respective causal powers [more or less Althusser's structural causality] are expressed within particular events is a contingent matter'. Such neglect of Althusser's overdetermination is all the more striking in that his seminal article 'Contradiction and Overdetermination' in *For Marx* (1965), Althusser himself took off from Mao Tse-tung's geopolitical texts! In reality, 'theoretical realism' is so similar to Althusser's position in *For Marx* that it is subject to the same criticism. D. Massey (1985) had already mentioned her worry, in concluding, that economics (= structures) risked being assimilated with necessity, and geography (= overdetermination) with contingence. Advancing this critique of neo-structuralism (even when it respects overdetermination), Saunders and Williams (1986) see therein a 'neo-conservatism': from Althusser to theoretical realism, they think that agency has been reintroduced only to submit agents' acts to the determinism of 'causal powers', tempered by contingency left to empiricism, and to leave aside (as usual) autonomy, agents' projects, etc.

29 The butterfly hunt also exists as a scenario before any interaction takes place (*see* P. Faure and G. Brassens). More generally, the structuration of space which is 'always already given' is an insurmountable obstacle for methodological individualism (*see* Lipietz 1977, chapter 5).

30 These forms of urban transformations have, nevertheless, turned out to be more complicated and ambiguous than I originally thought. *See*, for example, Kaszynski (1982) and Somekh (1987).

31 In his definition of constructivist structuralism (1987, p. 147 ff) one finds an implicit theoretical anthropology similar to that of all these writers, which H. Rouilleault and I (1972) formerly thought we could mobilize against Althusser in conceptualizing transformational action of the masses in history, without losing structuralism's import. The study of society as reproduction or routinized action thus seems to be partially legitimate, e.g. in the academic framework (a 'necessary moment of research' as Bourdieu says). The other, subjective facet of agency requires, on the contrary, participation in, or at least 'sympathy' (in the etymological sense) for, transformational social practices on the theoretician's part (cf. Lipietz 1973, 1977a, Introduction).

Bibliography

Aglietta, M., *Accumulation et régulation du capitalisme en longue période. Exemple des Etats-Unis (1871–1970)*, Dissertation, (Paris, 1974).

—— *Régulation et crises du capitalisme*, (Calmann-Lévy, Paris, 1976).

Aglietta, M. and Brender, A., *Métamorphoses de la société salariale*, (Calmann-Lévy, Paris, 1984).

Aglietta, M., Orlean, *La violence de la monaie*, (PUF, Paris, 1982).

Althusser, Lefebvre., et al., *Lire le Capital*, (F. Maspero, Paris, 1965).

Benko, G. B. and Lipietz, A., (eds), *Les régions qui gagnent. Districts et réseaux: les nouveaux paradigmes de le géographie économique*, (Paris, PUF, 1992). 424 p.

—— 'De la régulation des espaces aux espaces de régulation, in Boyer, R. and Saillard, Y., (eds), *Théorie de la régulation: l'état des savoirs*, (Paris, La Découverte, 1995), 293–303.

Boltanski, L., *Les Cadres*, (Minuit, Paris, 1982).

Boltanski, L. and Thevenot L., 'Les économies de la grandeur'. *Cahiers du Centre d'Etudes sur l'emploi*, no. 31, (PUF, Paris, 1987).

Bourdieu, P. *Questions de sociologie*, (Minuit, Paris, 1980).

—— *Choses dites*, (Minuit, Paris, 1987).

Bowles, S. and Gintis, M. *Democracy and Capitalism*, (Basic Books New York, 1986).

Boyer, R., *La théorie de la régulation: une analyse critique*, (La Découverte, Paris, 1987).

Boyer, R. ' La théorie de la régulation dans les années 1990', *Actuel Marx*, 17, 19–38, (1995).

Boyer, R. and Durand, J-P., *L'après-fordisme*, (Paris, Syros, 1993), 174 p.

Boyer, R. and Orlean, A., 'Les transformations des conventions salariales entre théorie et histoire. D'Henry Ford au fordisme, *Revue Economique*, 42, 2, 233–72, (1991).

—— 'Persistance et changement des conventions', in Orlean, A., (ed.), *Analyse économique des conventions*, (Paris, PUF, 1994), 219–47.

Boyer, R. and Saillard, Y., (eds), *Théorie de la régulation: l'état des savoirs*, (Paris, La Découverte, 1995), 568 p.

CEPREMAP., *Approche de l'inflation: L'exemple français*, report made to CORDES by Benassy, J. P., Boyer, R., Gelpi, R. M., Lipietz, A., Mistral, J., Munoz, J. and Ominami, C., (Paris, 1986), mimeographed.

Collectif 'Révoltes Logiques', *L'empire du sociologue*, (La Découverte, Paris, 1984).

Debray, R., *Modeste contribution aux discours et cérémonies officielles du dixième anniversaire*, (Maspero, Paris, 1978).

Duby, G., *Mâle Moyen-Age*, (Flammarion, Paris, 1988).

Dupuy, J. P., 'Autonomie de l'homme et stabilité de la société', *Economie Appliquée*, no. 1, (1977).

Frobel, F., Heinrichs, J. and Kreyes, O., *The New International Division of Labor*, (Cambridge University Press and the Maison des Sciences de l'Homme Publishers, Paris, 1980).

Giddens, A., *The Constitution of Society*, (Polity Press, 1985).

—— 'Time, Space, and Regionalisation', in Gregory and Urry (eds), *Social Relations and Spacial Structures*, (Macmillan, London, 1985).

Goffman, E., *The Presentation of Self in Everyday Life*, (New York, 1959).

Gregory, D. 'Suspended Animation: The Stasis of Diffusion Theory', in Gregory and Urry (eds), *Social Relations and Spacial Structures*, (Macmillan, London, 1985).

Gregory, D. and Urry, J. (eds), *Social Relations and Spacial Structures*, (Macmillan, London, 1985).

Girard, R., *Mensonge romantique et Vérité romanesque*, (Grasset, Paris, 1961).

Guillaume, M. (ed.), *L'Etat des Sciences Sociales en France*, (Le Découverte, Paris).

Guillaumin, C., 'Pratique du Pouvoir et idée de Nature. L'appropration des femmes', *Questions féministes*, no. 2, February, (1978).

Hägerstrand, T., 'What about people in Regional Sciences?', *Paper and Proceedings of the Regional Science Association*, vol. 24, pp. 7–21, (1970).

Kaszynski, M., *Observation foncière et division économique et sociale de l'espace*, Disseration at Lille I, (1982), mimeographed.

Kosik, K. *La dialectique du concret*, (Maspero, Paris, 1968).

Leborgne, D. and Lipietz, A., 'Idées fausses et questions ouvertes de l'après-fordismé, *Espaces et Sociétés*, 66/67, 39–68, (1991).

—— 'Conceptual Fallacies and Open Questions on Post-Fordism, in Storper, M. and Scott, A. J., (eds), *Pathways to Industrialization and Regional Development*, (London, Routledge, 1992b), 332–48.

Linhart, R., *L'établi*, (Minuit, Paris, 1978).

Lipietz, A., 'D'Althusser à Mao?', *Les Temps Modernes*, November (1973). In Italian: Ed. *Aut Aut*, Milano, 1977.

—— 'Structuration de l'espace, problème foncier et aménagement du territoire'. Intervention at the *Congres de Louvain de I 'A.S.P.R.E.N.O.*, (1974a). Published in *Environment and Planning*, no. 7, (Pion, London, 1975). In English: Carney et al., (eds), *Regions in Crisis*, (Croon Helm, London, 1980).

—— *Le tribut foncier urbain*, (F. Maspero, Paris, 1974b). In Italian: (Feltrinelli, Milano, 1977). In Danish: (Inst. Archi., mimeograph, Copenhagen, 1975).

—— 'Quelques problèmes de la production monopoliste d'espace urbain', *Notes Méthodologigues*, Institute de l'Environnement, no. 5, (1975). In Spanish: *Zona abierta* no. 8, (Madrid, 1976). In Portugese: *Espaço & debates* no. 7, (Sao Paulo, 1982).

—— *Le capital et son espace*, (Paris, F. Maspéro, 1977a), version supplemented in 1983. In Spanish: (Siglo XXI, Mexico).

—— *Crise et inflation: pourquoi?* Tome I: *L'accumulation intensive*, (F. Maspéro, Paris, 1979a).

—— 'Nouvelle solution au problème de la transformation: les cas du capital fixe et de la rente', *Recherches Economique de Louvain*, no. 4, (1979b).

—— *Le monde enchanté. De la valeur à l'envol inflationiste*, (F. Maspéro-La Découverte, Paris, 1983a). In English: (Verso, London, 1985), with (1983b) as an appendix.

—— 'Le débat sur la valeur: bilan partiel et perspectives partiales', intervention at the colloquium of the EHESS for *Le centenaire de Marx*, (December 1983b). Published in Chavance (ed.), *Marx en perspective*, (EHESS publishers, Paris, 1986). In English: added on to (1983a).

—— Book Review on Massey & Meegan (1982), *International Journal of Urban and Regional Research*, p. 302, (1983c).

—— 'Réflection autour d'une fable. Pour un statut marxiste des concepts de régulation et d'accumulation', *Couverture Orange*, CEPREMAP no. 8530, (1985a). In English: *Studies in Political Economy* no. 26, (1988).

—— 'Le national et le régional: quelle autonomie face à la crise capitaliste mondiale?', intervention at the colloquium *Spacial Structures and Social Progress*, Lesbos, (August, 1985b). *Couverture Orange*, CEPREMAP n°8521. In English: Moulaert & Wilson (eds), *Industrial restructuring: Spacial development and the role of the State*, (not yet published). In Spanish: *Cuadernos de Economia*, no. 11, [1987 (U.N. from Columbia)].

—— *Miracles et mirages. Problèmes de l'industrialisation dans le Tiers-Monde*, (La Découverte, Paris, 1985c). In English: (Verso, London, 1987).

—— 'Les conditions de la création d'un mouvement alternatif en France', intervention at the colloquium on 'l'Association d'Etudes et de Recherches Institutionnelles et Politiques', *Les enjeux institutionnels et politiques de mars 1986*, (January, 1986).

—— *Le huit infernal. La régulation économique*, (1987a), scenario and synopsis for a short film directed by Paul Dopf, assistant directed by Christine Crutel, a co-production by Cité de Sciences and Production 108.

—— 'Regulation: les mots et les choses', *Revue Economique* no. 5, (September, 1987b).

—— 'Phèdre: identification d'un crime. D'un vers d'Hippolyte à un livre d'Irigaray', *Les Temps Modernes*, (June, 1988).

—— *Choisir l'audace*, (Paris, La Découverte, 1989).

—— 'Après-fordisme et démocratié, *Les Temps Modernes*, 45, 524, (March 1990a), 97–121.

—— 'Le national et le régional: quelle autonomie face à la crise capitaliste mondiale?', Benko, G. B., (ed.), *La dynamique spatiale de l'économie contemporaine*, (La Garenne-Colombes, Editions de l'Espace Européen, 1990), 71–103.

—— *Toward a New Economic Order*, (Oxford, Polity Press, 1992).

—— 'Social Europe, legitimate Europe: the inner and outer boundaries of Europe, *Environment and Planning D: Society and Space*, 11, 5, 501–12, (1993a).

—— 'The local and the global: regional individuality or interregionalism?', *Transactions, Institute of British Geographers*, 18, 1, 8–18, (1993b).

—— 'De l'approche de la régulation a l'écologie politique: une mise en perspective historiqué, (interview de G. Cocco, F. Sebaï, C. Vercellone), *Future Antérieur*, n° hors série, 71–99, (1994).

—— *Green Hopes*, (Oxford, Polity Press, 1995a).

—— 'De le régulation aux conventions: le grand bond en arrière?', *Actuel Marx*, 17, 39–48. (1995b).

Lipietz, A. and Rouilleault, *Sur les pratiques et les concepts prospectifs du matérialisme historique*, (D.E.S. Paris I, 1972), Mimeographed.

Massey, D., 'Regionalism: some current issues', *Capital and Class*, no. 6, (1978).

—— 'New Directions in Space;, in Gregory and Urry (eds), *Social Relations and Spacial Structures*, (Macmillan, London, 1985).

Massey, D. and Meegan, R., *The Anatomy of Job Loss*, (1982).

Matzner, E. and Rusch, G. (eds), *Transport as an instrument for allocating space and time, A social science approach*, (Institute of Public Finance, Technical Univ. in Vienna, 1976).

Sartre, J. P., 'Théorie des ensembles pratiques' in *Critique de la raison dialectique*, (Gallimard, Paris, 1960b).

Saunders, P. and Williams, P. R., 'The new conservatism: some thoughts on recent and future developments in urban studies', *Society and Space*, vol. 4, pp. 393–9, (1986).

Sayer, A., 'The Difference that Space Makes', in Gregory and Urry (eds), *Social Relations and Spacial Structures*, (Macmillan, London, 1985).

Serres, M., *La naissance de la physique dans le texte de Lucrèce*, (Minuit, Paris, 1977).

Soja, E., 'The Spaciality of Social Life: Towards a Transformative Retheorisation', in Gregory and Urry (eds), *Social Relations and Spacial Structures*, (Macmillan, London, 1985).

Somekh, N., A *(des)verticallzacao de Sao Paulo*, (Mestrado FAUUSP Sao Paulo, (1987), mimeographed.

Terray, E., 'De l'exploitation. Eléments d'un bilan critique', *Dialectiques* no. 21, (1977).

Touraine, A., *La voix et le regard*, (Seuil, Paris, 1978).

Urry, J., 'Social Relations, Space and Time', in Gregory and Urry (eds), *Social Relations and Spacial Structures*, (Macmillan, London, 1985).

Walker, R., 'Class, Division of Labor and Employment in Space', in Gregory and Urry (eds), *Social Relations and Spacial Structures*, (Macmillan, London, 1985).

11

Institutional Reflexivity and the Rise of the Region State

Phil Cooke

Introduction

At a conference held in Bologna, Italy in May 1994 on the subject of 'Industrial Districts and Local Economic Development', one of the first remarks made by the President of the Emilia-Romagna Regional Government in his opening address was that 'atmosphere' is crucial to economic success. Later, Sebastiano Brusco, **doyen** of theorists of the industrial districts of Italy, also stressing the centrality of culture to economy and economy to cultural identity, reported how in 1987 Bill Clinton came to see him. He wanted to know about the local policy of **'real services'** business support successfully provided to small firms in Carpi, a knitwear town near Bologna. In February 1994, Clinton told the G7 group of world economic leaders meeting in Detroit about this encounter and advocated industrial districts as a solution to global economic crisis. If not a sign of desperation, this was at least a somewhat postmodern inversion of 'normal' global-local economic policy guidance.

In this chapter I want to explore this inversion through the reflexive lens of an earlier analysis of postmodernism, that I shall here refer to as the 'Back To The Future' (BTTF) analysis (Cooke, 1990). This differed from some of the other spatially informed books of the time such as those of Harvey (1989) and Soja (1989). These books were sombre in their forebodings about the breakup of old certainties and established hierarchies, whether of class or knowledge. BTTF was rather welcoming of the anticipated demise of the centralization and hierarchization of modern political, business and cultural arrangements, and sceptical of the simplistic elision of postmodernism and neoconservatism that the other authors espoused. For BTTF, the 'Emilian model' represented a polycentric or decentralized socialist practice, at once more humane and effective than the softer variants of democratic centralism practised in most of Western Europe during various interludes in the modern era.

So, in what follows there will be a brief reprise of, especially, the key dimensions of, first, the 'truth as local discourse' approach associated with

Rorty (1989) which gives rise to what, subsequently, we called 'the network paradigm' (Cooke and Morgan, 1993). Second, another look will be given to the notion of **proactivity**, as the necessary ingredient for solidarity, as modern remnants of the pre-modern social form we call 'community' disappear. BTTF argued that conscious reinvention of communitarianism was fundamentally **local** discourse. How this is being done by 'intelligent regions' will be described as a postmodern process of **reflexivity**. This has recently been examined by Lash and Urry (1994) but in a markedly abstracted way. Here, the chapter will develop a more institutionalist version of reflexivity based on practices presently evident in two 'intelligent regions': Baden-Württemberg in Germany and Emilia-Romagna in Italy. Conclusions, pointing to the diffusion of such reflexivity throughout the world, will be drawn and supported by the regionalist insights of Ohmae (1993).

The Back To The Future Analysis

The argument in 1988, when BTTF was written, as to why modernity and its institutions were under attack from a multiplicity of directions, can be summarized in five sets of binary oppositions.

- **the local and the global**: practically throughout history people have lived in communities. These need not have been **geographically** fixed (nomadic communities etc.) but were, by and large, **socially** fixed to a large extent in terms of kinship and intergenerational linkages. Modernity disrupted these processes, especially through its twin forces of massive and rapid urbanization and industrialization. Only in a few, new industrial areas, classically in coal-mining communities, as described in Emil Zola's *Germinal*, which were, to a large extent, isolated from the major cities, did new forms of social solidarity among people from different geographical areas and even countries, come into existence. Now, the postmodern era has seen the demise of these, too, in the German Ruhrgebiet, Dutch and Belgian Limburg, French Lorraine and Nord Pas de Calais, Wales, Scotland and northern England in the United Kingdom. The force responsible for this is **globalization** of market relations and the deregulation of national economies in favour of free competition. Markets, unleashed in the way they have been again in the 1980s–90s as they were in the *laissez-faire* era a century before, are inimical to community. Labour is either forced to migrate or is superfluous and only the cities offer, albeit less-skilled, worked opportunities for redundant industrial labour (Sassen, 1988). Hence, the **local** runs the danger of being swamped by the **global** forces of deregulated market competition. People turn inwards to a privatistic, familial or lone existence, linked to the world by the global imagery of the television and video simulacrum (Baudrillard, 1983).
- **reactivity and proactivity**: it could be said that the communities of the past, especially those geographically fixed in **localities**, arose unconsciously, or to use a phrase coined in a different context, 'in a fit of absent-mindedness'. By this I mean that **time** enters into the analysis with great explanatory force in considering the origin of traditional, say, agricultural communities. Until the nineteenth century, generations of families shared the same settlement space and economic networks

(Braudel, 1976) and, where modern capitalism did not unduly disrupt those networks, they persisted until later. But there were no obvious 'policies' of the governance system aimed at achieving this objective. The sedimentations of time had settled the institutional forms of religion, property, language, social hierarchy into an apparently changeless scene. To that, the person could mostly only **react**, reflexivity was not yet itself institutionalized except inwardly through the medium of the church. But now, after modernity's disruptions and after modernity itself, the institutions are less stable, religion is absolutely weaker, property more generalized, language a global, not merely local, means of communication and social hierarchy transmuted into its new, more marketized but also democratized forms. Now, communities of interest are formed proactively to protect or pursue rights, identities, and projects that may be geographically specific or general (local or global environmental protection) or may not be particularly geographic at all (feminism, the peace movement, bioethics). **Proactivity** is the distinguishing feature of contemporary solidarities.

- **diktat and discourse**: under modern social or cultural, let alone economic, relations, the masses (Benjamin, 1973) were in the sway of 'experts'. The modern era gave birth to the concept of expertise as the premodern era gave rise to *noblesse oblige*. Thus, look at art: the work of Picasso and Braque, 'climbing the mountain of cubism tethered together for safety like mountaineers' as Braque put it, was so strange, so outlandish that it could be interpreted, explained, understood and given aesthetic value, also monetary value, only by experts. Though a peasant might not have got much chance to appreciate art in the premodern era, except in church, the whole point of that art was precisely to communicate with the illiterate. Cubism and its successors sought to create a new, deconstructionist, language that by definition was exclusive, distant, hermetic. The architecture of Corbusier and Mies Van der Rohe had effectively the same mission as did the atonal music of Webern, Schönberg and Stockhausen. In challenging the pastoral canon of the past they originated by **diktat** a new aesthetic discourse in which few could join but many had to endure. Now that approach is itself the subject of massive critique, to the point where – for about one year in 1993 a serious cultural debate occurred in the United Kingdom about whether Bob Dylan was a better poet than John Keats – so, now, the postmodern mood is inclusive, discursive, bringing the margins to the centre (Rorty, 1989). Top novelists are women, ethnic minority or magic realist. 'Dead, white, males' are no longer the centrepiece of the literary canon, the 'canon' itself does not exist. Art is minimalist, music global, culture in fragments but more than ever the subject of animated discourse rather than lofty **diktat**.
- **hierarchy and network**: in business and government as in culture, there is less faith in the superiority of, say, top civil servants and their advisors, let alone politicians or business heads, as solvents of economic disease. When Bill Clinton advocates small-firm subcontracting as a global palliative in the home city of Ford and General Motors, it should be taken, as meant, as a sign that the monopoly of wisdom in business affairs may have migrated from the corridors or corporate or governmental power. When General Motors and IBM filed some of the biggest corporate losses in economic history in the early 1990s, this was a measure of their weakness in the face of, largely, Japanese corporate success. But Japanese corporations arc also large, so scale is not obviously the source of the problem. Rather it is management style. While Ford, GM and IBM were designed on a military model, Toyota, Sony and the like were designed on a **network** model. Flattened hierarchies, empowerment, intrapreneurship, teamwork, down-sizing have become the **corpo-**

rate graffiti (Kellaway, 1994) of Western management, seeking to capture the societal rather than military model of **networked** organization that underpins Japanese, and, as we shall see, some German and Italian, economic success. An example of the change in the inner being (Japanese *kokoro*) of an organization in its treatment of others in society is given in the example of Nordstrom, the successful Seattle-based store: ' ...at Nordstrom each ridiculous (customer) request is an opportunity for an "heroic act" by an employee – like the San Francisco woman who got up early one morning to fetch a pair of shoes in my size from a different branch several miles away' (Lorenz, 1994, citing Richard Pascale, 1993).

- **competition and collaboration**: capitalism was founded upon cutthroat competition. In its early competitive era, massive instability was the norm as employees suffered wage cuts, longer working time or sudden, enforced redundancy owing to the unregulated nature of competition. Investors suffered their losses as the competitive ethic nearly destroyed the burgeoning mode of production, ushering in the popular backlashes that stimulated the revolutionary outbursts of 1848 and, successively to 1917, in Russia and 1948 in China. Competition in its rawest form was seen even by governments and intergovernmental organizations as socially and politically unacceptable during the late modern era up to the 1970s. Then, neo-conservative pressures in the 1980s led to a governmental and intergovernmental relaxation of the rules of competition, washing away the modern impedimenta and with it worker protection, wage legislation, trade union recognition and various 'labour market rigidities'. Now, in the 1990s, many firms, large and small, find they cannot function acceptably in such circumstances. They are turning away from stand-alone competition, seeking the embrace of sympathetic others and engaging in various forms of collaborative activity. While this is not the same as the 'trust' and cartel formation of the last century, for that is still officially illegal, the new pre-competitive collaboration, strategic alliance building, joint-venturing and consortium creation are signs of the imperative to collaborate as well as to compete. Among small and large enterprises in the successful economies of the recent past, collaborative and networking practices have been pronounced. It is a recognition that stand-alone competition is difficult if not impossible in a globalized, postmodern world economy.

The Intelligent Region Analysis and Institutional Reflexivity

The 'intelligent region' analysis can be stated briefly as a prelude to elaboration below. The definition is taken from Cooke and Morgan (1991), and consists in the following argument. In the European Union the twin effects of the reform of the Structural Funds in the context of the Single European Market and the growing internationalization of economies mean that regions must:

1   become more proactive towards the European Community (now Union);
2   develop close links with their business and institutional community;
3   elaborate policies to enhance regional innovation potential;
4   engage increasingly in information-sharing partnerships;
5   establish mechanisms for self-monitoring and continuous policy improvement.

Thus, in a very real sense, regional administrations need to become more 'intelligent' in all the meanings of the word. They need to recognize the full importance of learning. Learning can take many forms, from simple 'learning by doing' and 'learning by using' (e.g. taking a policy developed elsewhere, adapting and implementing it) through 'learning by interacting' (with other internal or external institutions – *see* Lundvall, 1988; Cooke and Morgan, 1990) to the ultimate position as elaborated by Stiglitz (1987), 'learning by learning' where the self-monitoring of the learning process already engaged in is the stimulus for further knowledge-enhancement. Intelligence also implies, as it were, 'letting-go' of competences which may not be of core concern, especially where these may better be able to be discharged by other, more specialist institutions. Lastly, regions usually have data deficits, a lack of the business or other information services usually supplied by the market in strong regions. Where, as noted, these deficits exist, regional authorities must substitute for the market. The ability of a regional administration to display these learning competences will be an index of its collective 'intelligence'. The flexibility to move quickly into new spheres of policy concern and action will be an indicator of its quick-footedness derived from the quality of its self-monitoring capacity. But perhaps the two most important features of the 'intelligent region' are the ability to promote innovation on the one hand and the commitment to social justice on the other (Cooke & Morgan, 1991).

This learning disposition is precisely what characterizes the kind of local or global environmental and other issue-based movements that were discussed before. They have 'intelligence' in all its meanings; they are aware, have good antennae, members with good interpersonal skills; institutional networkers, they monitor events, processes and decisions outside as they affect them inside. They change policies if necessary and are wedded to the principles of continuous improvement and permanent innovation. They are collaborative rather than competitive, and their success is built on a politics of inclusion rather than exclusion. They take advantage of the creative insight that, for example, a tighter environmental regulatory regime can create employment rather than destroy it or that a socially just measure, such as providing universal child-care, can be an economically advantageous step to take because it releases a whole host of new skills into the labour market, the skilled strata of which are seldom oversupplied.

This, in its political, movement-based, form and in its administrative 'intelligent region' form is **institutional reflexivity**. Reflexivity, as such, is picked out in the recent book of Lash and Urry (1994) as the defining characteristic of the postmodern economy and society of signs and spaces. In this interpretation, however, which draws sustenance also from the writing of macro-social theorists, such as Giddens (1990) and Bourdieu (1984) as well as geographers such as Scott (1988), Storper and Walker (1989), and discusses the regions which will be discussed here, there is an absence of close attention to the mechanisms of institutional reflexivity which must underpin their otherwise interesting concept of **reflexive accumulation**. Lash and Urry's analysis rather swings from the individualistic level to the structural, thereby undervaluing the richness to be found in the institutional learning and innovation which produce socioeconomic reflexivity.

Let us summarize the Lash-Urry analysis of reflexive accumulation before going on to critique and improve upon it. Taking, as a touchstone, Ulrich Beck's (1992) assertion that today's world is a '**risk society**' which is both caused by and causes human reflexivity, Lash and Urry say ' ... contemporary life is premised upon the social organization of reflexivity' (Lash and Urry, 1994, 10). This interesting, if debatable, proposition is based, however, on a perceived heightening of individualization and decline of institutions associated with Beck's *risk society*. The proposition is interesting because it points to the generalization of a 'learning' predisposition in the postmodern life-world. But it is debatable where, to the extent that market motivations have triumphed over those of planning, spontaneity is valued more highly, indeed becomes more necessary, than considered, reflective, collective or social reason.

Having registered approval as well as some scepticism of Lash and Urry's macro-social synthetic project, their concept of **reflexive accumulation** deserves attention. Modern institutions become disorganized (cf. Lash and Urry's earlier, *The End of Organized Capitalism*, 1987) in postmodernism. But despite this ' ... Nothing is fixed, given and certain, while everything rests upon much greater knowledge and information, on **institutionalised reflexivity**' Lash and Urry, 1994, 11, emphasis added). This is promising and a useful corrective to the individualist tone of some of what follows. In elaborating upon reflexive accumulation, however, the idea of institutionalized reflexivity is dealt with in an over-abstracted and allusive manner which is unconvincing. It is not unreasonable to say that, having introduced an interesting concept, the authors over-theorize its setting – reflexive accumulation – and lose the idea of actually **reflexive** institutions almost completely.

Following exegesis of **reflexive subjects**, drawn from Beck and Giddens, where, among other useful insights, the notion of anorexia nervosa as a 'pathology of reflexive self-control' (Giddens, 1991) provokes in this author's mind an interesting analogy with the current business obsession with *lean production* (*see* below and, for a recent treatment, Womack and Jones, 1994), the conclusion is drawn that, in industry, the shift from vertical integration to vertical disintegration – where instead of **making** the product in-house, firms **buy** components from outside and only **assemble** the product **in-house** – represents a situation in which the organization of production has itself become reflexive. To the extent such organization relies on spontaneous response to market signals, it is questionable; after all, this is how pre-Fordist production was organized. To the extent **institutionalized learning** is included, it is postmodern.

There are three key characteristics to reflexive accumulation:

- **knowledge** and information are of central economic importance. Of especial importance is knowledge for dealing with complexity and uncertainty through monitoring and design;

- **individualization** is crucial in the determination of consumption norms and behaviour. Consumer identities are constructed through process of self-reflexion. To meet these norms production must be small-batch and customized while services are increasingly provided professionally as 'expert systems';
- **communication** structures are key conveyors of information in production and consumption. In services, communication between producer and user increasingly **is** the service.

This threefold conceptual structure is then used as a guide to explaining differences in reflexive accumulation among Japan, Germany and America/UK production systems. Japanese accumulation is **collectively** reflexive (e.g. within autonomous work groups, between firms, shareholders, employees and their firms). Germany is exemplified by self-monitoring of a **practically** reflexive kind (craft and corporatist production administration). Education, profession or craft skill, and status are important focuses of reflexivity. American and UK reflexivity is **discursive**, less formal; knowledge is more abstract and mobility of labour and capital are high. *Reflexive accumulation* is, conceptually, an expression of the postmodern imbrication of culture and economy. Crucially, the **national** declines as a structural decision-frame while the **global** and the **local** rise as structuring frames for reflexive society.

What becomes very clear in the empirical verification of the theory is that, despite the occasional (and decreasing) references to institutional reflexivity in a generic way, the fundamentals in the analysis are intra- and inter-firm labour process and production organization relations. Moreover – and here there is only space to discuss their treatment of Japan and Germany – while **learning** is briefly mentioned as the most crucial distinguishing feature of the three systems, little use is made of this insight except in the relatively narrow, job-focused dimension of the labour process. In the section on Japan, learning, strangely, given the apparent depth of treatment given to the concept of reflexivity in postmodern life, is treated mostly mundanely in terms of, essentially reproductive, training systems. There is little sense of the variety of types of learning even there, and overall, a rather instrumentalist approach to the notion with surprisingly little attention given to learning in the context of **change**, uncertainty and complexity characterized earlier as definitive features of the context of reflexive accumulation.

In discussing the German case, there is, again, a strong labour-process emphasis in the analysis, but, as in the discussion of Japan, little on the institutional setting, other than passing allusions, to pin down the nature of the learning predisposition outside the skill- or craft reproduction dimension. Moreover, once again, there is surprisingly little on learning and monitoring in contexts of **change**. Finally, the discussion turns to the core of this chapter's theme – institutional reflexivity at the sub-state level – in a section on **industrial districts**. Baden-Württemberg is taken as the paradigm case, with Emilia-Romagna mentioned as another important regional exemplar. In the case of Baden-Württemberg where it is asserted that – for technology-transfer initiatives, for example – the federal level of government is less important than the regional or local, the account, while not wholly inaccurate, completely misses the reflexive learning disposition of the institutional system as it has been forced to confront and anticipate the prospect of change. Thus, innovation and technology policies are described in terms of 'displacement' from 'extensive' to 'intensive' phases with little explanation as to why this should have occurred, nor what the political-economic project was that underlay it. As we shall see, the description of the further development of this policy in terms of another 'displacement', as a developing process of almost cybernetic steering capability on a basically unchanging landscape, leaves much to be desired.

In other words, Lash and Urry have produced an interesting macro-social theorization of social reproduction rather than social change. The concepts of **'reflexive accumulation'**, **'institutional reflexivity'**, and **'learning'** are sketched in rather than painted. Thus, they fail to capture the depth of institutionalized intelligence necessary to cope successfully with the pressures and duress caused for leading industrial systems by the need for permanent innovation and continuous improvement in a context of change and uncertainty of the kind alluded to, but not really explored, in *Economies of Signs and Space*. Nevertheless, this book comes closer than most to opening up for discussion new institutional ways of managing crisis and change. Were the book to miss this point, much less space would have been devoted to a critique of some aspects of it here. In the next two sections an attempt will be made to colour in some of the neglected features of Lash and Urry's (1994) nevertheless estimable outline.

Baden-Württemberg: Crisis Region of the 1990s

Baden-Württemberg was once one of Germany's poorest regions. It lacked industrial resources, it was remote from the main urban centres, its products of timber and agriculture were subject to severe competition. Many migrated from this poor land to the United States and elsewhere, and in general, as is often said, 'all we have is our wits' meaning diligence, intelligence, precision and willingness to work hard (Späth, 1990). Nowadays, the *Land's* promotional material stresses the ingenuity of home-grown *tüftler* or tinkerers such as Dornier, Daimler, Benz, Porsche and Bosch, all of whom began as small firms (*Mittelstand*) in Baden-Württemberg. Their ability to do so was aided by the synthesis of mercantilism and economic liberalism in the Württemberg industrial policy of the mid-nineteenth century. This, building upon an established regional system of local savings and loan banks dating from 1818, received a boost when in 1848 a Central Bureau of Trade and Commerce was set up to promote private business. This was directed by Ferdinand Steinbeis, bureau head from 1855, and provided support by hiring foreign experts to teach business people, exhibiting foreign technology and providing trade exhibitions and means to travel to international ones. Moreover, Steinbeis developed an organized vocational training system (Semlinger, 1993).

After World War II, this was an attractive environment to which hundreds of

Mittelstand businesses could migrate, especially from Saxony (in former German Democratic Republic), which had, until then, been the most densely industrialised small-firm area of Germany. Reconstruction and consolidation of capital goods, engineering and textile business around this long-established business support infrastructure from 1945 to 1973 comprised the **first stage** of what could be summarized as a **three-stage** developmental trajectory in post-war Baden-Württemberg. The modern **Land** was formed only in 1952 and even then only after a second vote, the first having produced a 'no' result from Baden in 1950. Even at that time, the main industry of the region was textiles. As this industry entered decline, the economy was encouraged to move more towards capital goods industries which were already present but capable of expansion, not least because of the high skill content of the work-force. In addition, during the period, the **Land** government sustained a Regional Loans Bank and a Security Bank as well as establishing, in 1952, a Regional Trade Bureau with a special mission to encourage co-operation between *Mittelstand* firms. Finally, in 1968 a unique set of 59 Committees for Further Training was established to co-ordinate programmes and forecast future needs.

Then in 1973, came the oil shock. This seriously threatened Baden-Württemberg's automotive and machine-tool economy. It was a defining moment in the mature modernization of the industrial system. Already, as early as 1971, a foundation named in honour of Ferdinand Steinbeis had been established as a strictly non-profit technology-transfer organization. This reflected particularly the crisis in the textile and textile-machinery industries. Changes in organization at the **firm** and **institutional** levels occurred. Subcontracting developed and spread as ' ... a matter of brute necessity' (Sable, Herrigel, Kazis and Deeg, 1989). This extended to other sectors, as Bosch in automotive components, for example, also created its supplier network at this time. At the **institutional** level, technical consulting rose by 40 per cent and **doubled** in the public sector. Added to this was an increase in quality and extent of training as the co-ordinated system got into its stride, and this included significant upgrading of the courses provided by *Berufsschulen*, or professional training schools, which began to overlap with *Fachhochschulen* or polytechnics. The latter were also upgrading their skills provisions. In 1974, university-level *Berufsakademien* were set up in Stuttgart and Mannheim. In other words, and in a crisis-responsive rather than fully reflexive way, the Baden-Württemberg industrial system was **adjusting** to crisis by developing a **regionalized** industrial policy.

This received a further boost in the early 1980s, by which time the CDU government of Lothar Späth had become ensconced and his government saw the need, after the second oil shock, to entrench the regional state (Ohmae, 1993). The approach sought lay in 'a new leadership structure for Baden-Württemberg' (Späth quoted in Sörgel, 1986). Sörgel explains this through another quote from Späth:

> The currently growing need for policy to be better informed and to bring together the various social interests to a viable consensus makes necessary the estab-

lishment of new structures of leadership and communications. The administration must therefore acquire ... the competence to deal with and integrate differentiated areas of knowledge and from that process to secure information that can be used to give leadership.

(Sörgel, 1986; *see* Cooke and Morgan, 1994).

Technology transfer received the first push in 1982 with the *Land* appointment of a Commissioner for Technology Transfer, directly responsible to Minister President Späth, and, since 1983, also head of the Steinbeis Foundation. The latter took responsibility for technology transfer from the older Regional Trade Bureau (*Landesgewerbeamt*) and benefited from a massive upgrading of capital equipment from its host institution, the *Fachhochschulen*. In 1985 the commission set up to develop the **leadership** and **intelligence** functions of the regional state, reported. It, the Bulling commission, called for: the creation of seven new ministries (including Environment and Economics); each ministry to be networked to the 'supreme basic division' located in the Minister President's office; a '*Land* system concept' to link the whole *Land* administration in an IT network; a new administrative college to train the *Land* **èlite**; and the establishment of Japanese 'vision circles' to engage in 'foresight' to anticipate future social and economic changes.

In brief, the Bulling commission report, not all implemented but much of it now in place, represented one of the world's first subnational-level examples of **institutional reflexivity**. It represented an attempt to fashion a new governance system, one based on modernist discourse between experts aimed at steering an extremely complex system through uncertainty in a period of serious structural change. Even so, the trade and business associations, chambers of commerce and research infrastructure (14 Max Planck Institutes, 14 Fraunhofer Institutes and 9 universities) maintained a significant hold on this steering process, fearing too-close control of the system by industry. By 1992 Späth was gone, dragged down by a mercantilist scandal involving kickbacks from Bosch, but the stage had been set for a method of intelligent monitoring through industrial governance by self-regulating groups, which was not to go away.

Hence, Stage 3 of the development of **institutional reflexivity** in Baden-Württemberg built upon the strengths as well as on the weaknesses of the reflexive-monitoring and discourse-mediation arrangements established in the 1970s and consolidated in the 1980s.

By the end of the 1980s, the Baden-Württemberg system was showing signs of strain. At the Federal level, reunification had added to a new and more difficult context composed of:

- **Public Deficits** – £60–£70 billion per year expenditure in the former German Democratic Republic, resulting in high real **interest rates** and high investment costs throughout Germany in consequence;
- **Production Costs** – added to already high tax, wage and construction costs, tax increases the interest-rate hikes meant Germany became uncompetitive as a **production** location;

- **Export Problems** – these cost constraints made domestic markets tougher to control and export markets more difficult to penetrate;
- **Globalization** – foreign competition and high interest and production costs caused German firms to source and locate more globally.

The Baden-Württemberg (CDU) government set up a ***Zukunftskommission*** (Future Commission) to look into the new problems faced by business in the ***Land***. The report ***Economy 2000*** was published in 1993. It pointed to crucial problems caused by:

- **International Competition**: Japanese imports had 25 per cent of the German machinery market, 30 per cent lower costs and better service;
- **Innovation Deficits**: Baden-Württemberg firms are strong in innovation for mature, mechanical engineering products, weak in **informatics** and **telematics** which are replacing them;
- **Production Costs**: even within Germany, the **Land** is expensive. The SPD Party recommended incentives, the CDU 'necessary sacrifices'.

The report advocated: **competition measures** to make Baden-Württemberg firms, especially smaller ones, more competitive; **innovation measures** with a now-established 45-person Technology Foresight Innovation Board composed of industry, academic and governance representatives; and **production measures** – i.e. '**lean production**'.

This has brought forth some quick, co-ordinated response. Some firms have worked together to improve their innovation capacity by engaging in joint research and development, their know-how protected by partnering with a third-part (Fraunhofer) institute. Others have instituted cost-control measures based on Japanese-style **cost targeting** which judges what the market will bear rather than what the producer can insist upon as a cost basis. Yet others now engage in **value-engineering** to take cost out of production by measuring the skill content of the labour process more carefully. Some are beginning to engage in **simultaneous engineering**, where production is organized in teams composed of marketing, engineering and design functions working on a project basis rather than in a Taylorist division of labour. All are looking far more closely at achieving **lean production** norms.

There have been casualties in the process. Large numbers of workers have been made redundant and others have found alternative employment in less-skilled and less-well-paid jobs. Unemployment is 300,000 or nearly 10 per cent of the work-force, an unheard-of level. The **monitoring** and **guidance** procedures are now well-embedded and respected by all the social partners, however. This means that social instability has been avoided and firms have responded in ways they might not have been able to if left to their own devices (Cooke and Morgan, 1994).

The Baden-Württemberg system functions as a **system**, animated and facilitated by concertation between business and governance institutions to produce guidance of an intelligent, institutionally reflexive rather than self-reflexive or structurally reflexive kind.

Emilia-Romagna: Upgrading the Districts

Rather as Baden-Württemberg can be seen to have passed through three stages of development towards its presently intelligent institutional reflexivity, based on learning from elsewhere as well as from the regional economy's own past performance, so Emilia-Romagna in Italy has a threefold recent developmental logic. This has been summarized by Brusco (1990) as the passage from a Mark 1 Marshallian (1919) industrial district based on organic inter-firm linkages and associated 'industrial atmosphere', or cultural identity capable of transformation into collective enterprise, to a Mark 2 stage in the 1980s. In the Mark 2 stage, what had hitherto been unreflective social norms of behaviour became embodied in the **'real services'** centres which so impressed Bill Clinton. These were local in origin but funded by the regional government and organized collectively. Where innovation was in demand, this was met by networking with sympathetic Italian national research institutes. Now, a third phase has been reached, because this successful system of **real service** provision is no longer sufficient to meet the threat of competition in the 1990s.

In a different, but related triptych, Patrizio Bianchi and his NOMISMA (a Bologna political economy research institute) collaborators (e.g. Bianchi and Giordani, 1993) anatomized the development of the Emilian industrial districts in the way outlined below.

Phase 1

This begins in the 1960s and lasts up to the end of the 1970s. Emilia-Romagna, like many northern Italian regions, had many small firms providing basic products for a local market. A case in point would be agricultural machinery and repairs which had long existed side by side with the large agricultural and foodstuffs industries. Many of these small firms were artisan firms, officially classified as such and represented by artisan's associations such as CGA (General Confederation of Artisans) or CNA (the National Confederation of Artisans). In the 1960s, large firms inside, but mostly outside, the region were seeking buffer suppliers because of increasing variations in demand. Artisan firms in the machinery industry were targeted by such firms seeking to deal with quantitative instability. In textiles, the trajectory was different. Carpi, the main textile industrial district had been a centre for straw-hat making. When the industry collapsed in the 1940s, agricultural homeworking – the main source of production – dried up. Artisans, however, used their contacts with large firms to begin selling (not making) cheap clothing. Later, some began producing T-shirts, using the homeworking tradition in the area. Later, as agricultural work declined, more labour was taken on in small and medium firms expanding into factory production. Large firms often directly or indirectly influenced the course followed by small medium enterprises (SMEs) in this phase.

Phase 2

By the end of the 1970s and into the 1980s, the SMEs that had become established as subcontractors or independent producers began to show flexibility in the quantity and, importantly, the quality of their output. This coincided with a major crisis in the early 1980s in which large firms experienced a severe decline in demand for their products. This recession signified something of a change in the nature of markets for final consumer goods. It marked the ending of the era when fundamentally standardized, mass-produced goods of average quality could easily be sold on mass markets. For one thing, less-developed countries were forced by the debt crisis induced by the anti-inflationary interest-rate hikes of Western government to engage in export drives. These were often of such a scale, rapidity and intensity that, for clothing in particular, they posed real problems for both mass producers and SMEs. For the latter, they posed the problem of very rapid emulation of fairly down market products, forcing a more up-market posture on the part of those industrial district firms in direct competition. Many larger firms also vacated markets to cheap imports where they could no longer compete. Hence the SMEs responded faster and more flexibly to the demand crisis. Large multinationals were not in a position to erect barriers to SME entry. The small-firm sector had gained an advantage which larger firms could neither match nor prevent.

Phase 3

The third phase of development in the Emilian SME sector has occurred since the beginning of the 1990s. It is the most difficult period faced by the firms of the industrial districts, provoked in part by the reactions of large firms to the success of the SMEs in the 1980s. But this crisis is also a product of the emerging single European market and trends towards globalization of production more generally.

Faced by heightened global competition, large firms have responded in ways comparable to those of the SMEs a decade earlier. They have engaged in more intensive product and process innovation, and have developed more flexibility in their management of the product cycle. Instead of producing for the mass market, they have focused upon more rapid turnaround in more diversified and quality-conscious markets. An innovation of particular importance has been the move by large firms in the machinery, garments and food-processing industries to control distribution networks. This is consistent with one of the effects of economic integration and the globalization of production, namely the necessity to gain access to the markets of competitor firms. Not infrequently this is achieved by the formation of complementary strategic alliances or joint ventures with other large companies. Small and medium-sized enterprises find this form of competition difficult to deal with. Fundamentally, they tend to be price and product takers or followers. They react to the innovations of others. When the price and product leaders 'leave the room', as it were, this works. But if, as may now be the case, leaders are seeking to introduce oligopolistic rule, especially through the control of distribution chains, it is a less viable strategy. The issue for SMEs is whether they can re-organize to become innovators; if so, which form is most appropriate given that there has to be a high degree of collaborative effort; and what is the best role for regional and local-government institutions in assisting SME innovation. These are the key issues facing the industrial district firms of Emilia-Romagna, and the ones that are the focus of a lengthy period of political and administrative reflection within the regional government and its development agency ERVET.

The New Phase in the Industrial Districts

The problem faced by the industrial districts is a threefold one involving:

1   inducing new start-up SMEs to recreate the industrial dynamism of the earlier phases;
2   inducing co-operation among existing SMEs to enable them to become product and process innovators;
3   enabling continuous upgrading of SMEs to occur so that improved quality is constantly being sought.

In each of these cases the solution to the problem has involved a mixture of reliance upon the existing networks, experience and information present in the communities, and developing innovative new policies and institutions – often of a governmental nature – to overcome weaknesses in the private part of the local productive system.

It is exceptionally important not to consider the localized 'intelligence' of the actors in the local productive system as merely a 'soft' or intangible element of the inherited success of the Emilian industrial districts. Moreover, it is equally important to recognize that this traditional strength has also turned into something of a weakness. Many experts on the Emilian districts consider that efforts have to be made to create 'new subjects'. This means helping to recreate the local social solidarities that were the main strength upon which the industrial districts were built, to deal with the new competitive realities of innovative, internationalized competition. One view of the districts is that their real externalities rest in the community. It is widely considered that 'social blockages' are a major impediment to the restructuring of the industrial districts.

The manner in which this is to be done is by the restructuring of the regional state so that, instead of funding through ERVET going to support firms through real services centres for an indefinite period, each centre and indeed each activity must be bid for as **a project**. This is a way of heading off criticism from business about the efficiency of the system while ensuring that the best aspects of the regional industrial policy are preserved and the weakest are replaced with more innovative solutions. Under Berlusconi and the Lega too, tighter financial controls, albeit more regionally determined, may be expected to be instituted.

Concluding Remarks

In this chapter, an attempt has been made to explore, in concrete terms, the postmodern forms of organization of socio-economic relations. Of great geographic importance to this argument has been the observation that in an increasingly borderless postmodern world ' ... the nation state has become an unnatural, even dysfunctional, unit for organizing human activity and managing economic endeavour ... It represents no genuine, shared community of economic interests, it defines no meaningful flows of economic activity. In fact, it overlooks the true linkages and synergies that exist among often disparate populations by combining important measures of human activity at the wrong level of analysis' (Ohmae, 1993).

The Back To The Future analysis was outlined in developing the argument because it posited precisely this demise, not necessarily in the grip of the old nation states, but the relevance of that grip for cultural and socio-economic innovation in an era of global deregulation and market hegemony. In such a context, proactivity by regional and local groups acting reflexively upon and through re-invented institutions of governance (*see*, on this, Osborne and Gaebler, 1992), was conceived to be a likely force for intelligent anticipation of events and appropriate collective policy guidance. A key part of this would be the rise of discursive will formation as a replacement for rule by experts alone. The modernist era was characteristically hierarchical in its mode of system guidance, the postmodernist could be expected to be network form in its guidance logic. Finally, such new modes of interest intermediation were less likely to be driven by a logic of competition alone and more by a logic of collaboration to secure continuous improvement in the nature and quality of social and economic life.

The intelligent region, as a key node in the network of postmodern, socio-economic spaces of innovation and creativity will thus be **institutionally reflexive** in nature. Unlike modern forms of guidance which were deterministic in their guidance philosophy, postmodern forms will be learning organizations capable of intelligently anticipating and meeting problems and identifying appropriate, discursively inclusive, solutions.

To some extent, these ideas were picked up by Lash and Urry (1994). In an otherwise exemplary exegesis, however, key aspects of the **institutional** and **learning** propensities of the postmodern guidance and accumulation arrangements at a subnational or subcentral level were left unexplored. Thus, what purported to be a meta-societal theory of change was unsatisfactorily transformed into a theory of reproduction with surprisingly conservative overtones.

In detailed examples taken from Baden-Württemberg and Emilia-Romagna, it was shown that successful contemporary soci-economic spaces are indeed characterized by **institutional reflexivity** which is built on a **learning propensity** derived from the formal application of **discursive intelligence** to the socio-economic problems of the day.

Acknowledgements

I would like to thank the following for their help in compiling this chapter. In Baden-Württemberg, Dietrich Munz, Gunter Meyerhöfer, Dieter Klumpp, Joachim Edelmann. In Emilia-Romagna, Annaflavia Bianchi, Patrizio Bianchi, Nicola Bellini and Mario Pezzini. Elsewhere, Werner Sengenberger, Frank Pyke, Gerhard Bräunling, Jörg Meyer-Stamer, Hans-Joachim Braczyk, Kevin Morgan and Adam Price. They bear no responsibility for the results of their advice.

References

Baudrillard, J., *Simulations*, (New York, Semiotext(e), 1983).
Beck, U., *Risk Society: Towards a New Modernity*, (London, Sage, 1992).
Benjamin, W., *Illuminations*, (London, Fontana, 1973).
Bianchi, P. and Giordani, M., 'Innovation Policy at the Local and National Levels: the case of Emilia-Romagna', *European Planning Studies*, 1, 25–42.
Bourdieu, P., *Distinction*, (London, Routledge, 1984).
Brusco, S., 'The Idea of the Industrial District: its Genesis', in F. Pyke, G. Becattini and W. Sengenberger, (eds), *Industrial Districts and Inter-Firm Cooperation in Italy*, (Geneva, IILS, 199).
Braudel, F., *L'identité de la France*, (Paris, PUF, 1976).
Cooke, P., *Back to the Future*, (London, Unwin Hyman, 1990).
Cooke, P. and Morgan, K., 'Learning Through Networking', *Regional Industrial Research Report 5*, (Cardiff, CASS, 1990).
Cooke, P. and Morgan, K., 'The Intelligent Region', *Regional Industrial Research Report 7*, (Cardiff, CASS, 1991).
Cooke, P. and Morgan, K., 'The Network Paradigm: New Departures in Corporate and Regional Development', *Society and Space*, 11, 543–64, (1993).
Cooke, P. and Morgan, K., 'The Regional Innovation System in Baden-Württemberg', *International Journal of Technology Management*, 9, 1–36, (1994).
Giddens, A., *The Consequences of Modernity*, (Cambridge, Polity, 1990).
Giddens, A., *Modernity and Self-Identity*, (Cambridge, Polity, 1991).
Goss, T., Pascale, R. Athos, 'Reinvention Roller Coaster: Risking the Present for a Powerful Future', *Harvard Business Review*, Jan/Feb, 1–12, (1993).
Harvey, D., *The Condition of Postmodernity*, (Oxford, Blackwell, 1989).
Kellaway, L., 'Time to Walk the Talk', *Financial Times*, 4 Feb., 11, (1994).
Lash, S. and Urry, J., *The End of Organized Capitalism*, (Cambridge, Polity, 1987).
Lash, S. and Urry, J. *Economies of Signs and Space*, (London, Sage, 1994).
Lorenz, C., 'Change is Not Enough', *Financial Times*, 12 Jan. 11, (1994).
Lundvall, J., 'Innovation as an Interactive Process', in G. Dosi, (ed.), *Technical Change and Economic Theory*, (London, Francis Pinter, 1988).
Marshall, A., *Industry and Trade*, (London, Macmillan, 1919).
Ohmae, K., 'The Rise of the Region State', *Foreign Affairs*, 72, 78–87, (1993).

Osborne, D. and Gaebler, T., *Reinventing Government*, (Reading, Addison-Wesley, 1992).

Rorty, R., *Contingency, Irony and Solidarity*, (Cambridge, CUP, 1989).

Sabel, C., Herrigel, G., Deeg, R. and Kazis, R., 'Regional Prosperities Compared: Massachusetts and Baden-Württemberg in the 1980s', *Economy and Society*, **18**. 374–403, (1989).

Sassen, S., *The Mobility of Labour and Capital*, (Cambridge, CUP, 1988).

Scott, A., *New Industrial Spaces*, (London, Pion, 1988).

Semlinger, K., 'Economic Development and Industrial Policy in Baden-Württemberg: Small Firms in a Benevolent Environment', *European Planning Studies*, 1, 435–64, (1993).

Soja E., *Postmodern Geographies*, (London, Verso, 1989).

Sörgel, A., 'Daimler-Benz: Der Multi im Musterländle', *Working Paper 3*, (Bremen, Institute for Economic Research, 1986).

Späth, L., *Unser Baden-Württemberg*, (Stuttgart, DVA, 1990).

Stiglitz, J., 'Learning to Learn, Localized Learning and Technological Progress', in P. Dasgupta and P. Stoneman (eds), *Economic Policy and Technological Performance*, (Cambridge, CUP, 1987).

Storper, M. and Walker, R., *The Capitalist Imperative*, (Oxford, Blackwell, 1989).

Womack, J. and Jones, D., 'From Lean Production to the Lean Enterprise', *Harvard Business Review*, March/April, 93–103, (1994).

PART IV

The Politics of Difference

Introduction

Of the many words that gained a wider currency during the 1980s and well into the 1990s, 'difference' would seem to beat them all in terms of acceptance within the community of scholars. Today, even the most classically modern of scientists within the human sciences and within geography pay at least lip service to some 'difference' or another. Here the arrival of 'postmodern' discourses was of importance primarily because it opened the long-shut door towards a recognition of Hegelian philosophy in the pioneering work of Edward Said and Gayatri Spivak. 'Difference', long since the neglected sibling of the construction of identity, now begot its own research agendas. In the work of Jacques Derrida, this 'different' research agenda even produced its own terminology ('différance') and was in turn subjected to constantly differentiating efforts at destabilizing any resulting relationship between 'identity' and 'difference' ('deconstruction').

With Hegel, it was acknowledged in the resulting work that, while the creation of some difference might well be philosophically inevitable, the geography of this conception – and what else is geography but the analytic stabilization of spatial configurations of identities and differences – was, and continues to be, decided within the political realm. It was the analysis of the mechanisms controlling this geography in the work of Michel Foucault that consequently became influential during this period both in geography and elsewhere in the human sciences. Possibly even more powerful than the influence of Foucault, however, was the growth of feminism as a result of the recognition of difference. In fact, the case of feminism demonstrates how a decidedly modernist and emancipatory tradition was adopted by and through postmodern discourses.

The essays that follow illuminate different aspects of both the construction of differences and of the ensuing geographies. As such, they circumscribe possible avenues for future research within geography, research that no longer treats the margins that result from each and every construction of identity with contempt but, rather, elevates these margins to the status of centres in their own right.

12

Postmodern Becomings: From the Space of Form to the Space of Potentiality

Julie Kathy Gibson-Graham

> Writing has nothing to do with signifying. It has to do with surveying, mapping, even realms that are yet to come.
> G. Deleuze and F. Guatarri, *A Thousand Plateaus: Capitalism and Schizophrenia.*

In the language of contemporary feminist, postmodernist and poststructuralist theory, discursive space is 'occupied', speaking positions are 'located' or 'situated', 'boundaries' are 'transgressed' and 'territory' is 'deterritorialized'. Theory flows 'inside' and 'outside' a conceptual landscape that must be 'mapped', producing 'cartographies' of desire and 'spaces' of enunciation. It seems that we are all geographers now.

The spatialization of theoretical discourse owes much to Foucault[1] and Deleuze and Guatarri,[2] as it also does to pre-poststructuralist theorists such as Althusser and Gramsci, and the Marxian tradition to which they belong.[3] Indeed, the spatial metaphors associated with Marxian analysis – 'colonization', 'penetration', 'core and periphery', 'terrains of struggle' – are not dissimilar to those of poststructuralism. Both types of theory represent space constituted by, or in relation to, 'identity'. While poststructuralist theories are concerned with the performance space of multiple and non-specific identities, Marxian theory has generally been focused upon the performance space of one type of Form – the mode of production, or more particularly, Capitalism.

After struggling for so long to erect and strengthen the ramparts of an academic identity in the shadow of more established disciplines, geographers now find all sort of strange beings camped outside or scaling the battlements eager to assume the uniform/language of geography, though not to take up

---

1 *See*, for example, Foucault (1980) and Soja's (1989) discussion of Foucault's interest in geography.
2 E.g., Deleuze and Guattari (1987).
3 *See* Smith (1984) for a discussion of the Marxian references to space.

positions in its defence. For one who has dwelt protected within the disciplinary space of geography, this 'invasion' is welcome. Indeed, it is the wordy invaders who have kindled in me, for the first time, an interest in 'space' – a core, even foundational, concept within my professional dwelling place. But while 'we' all might be geographers – or at least explorers – now, some disciplinary geographers (despite feeling partially vindicated) are worried.

Massey (1993: 66) is concerned that the proliferation of metaphorical usages of spatial terms has buried important distinctions between different meanings of space. And Smith and Katz are alarmed at the free-floating abstractions of contemporary social and cultural (not exclusively poststructuralist) theory that take as their unexamined grounding a seemingly unproblematic, common-sense notion of space as a container, a field, a simple emptiness in which all things are 'situated' or 'located'.[4] The danger of this particular usage, as they see it, is that attempts to contextualize, relativize and de-universalize speaking positions inadvertently invoke a unique standpoint at a set of coordinates, a location in a naturalized, absolute and asocial conception of space. Absolute space, they caution, is *itself* socially produced and historically specific. In fact, for them, any absolute location is only ever a location relative to all the others produced by capitalism, patriarchy and imperialism.[5] By essentializing our situated positions in absolute space, and failing to recognize the social relationality of those positions, we become prey to an '[i]dentity politics (which) too often *becomes* mosaic politics' (1993: 77, emphasis theirs), that is, a politics of competition and fragmentation.[6]

In *The Production of Space* Henry Lefebvre, the Marxist theorist of space/spatiality, expresses a related but more extreme disapproval of the appropriation of spatial metaphors by philosophers, especially poststructuralist ones:[7]

4 They identify this as a version of Newton's *absolute space*, which was the 'dominant representation of space between the seventeenth and nineteenth centuries' (Smith and Katz, 1993:75). *See* Smith (1984: 67–78) for a discussion of the origins of this notion of absolute space.

5 Thus any one location in *absolute space* is at the same time a location in *relative space* [*see* Smith (1994: 66–96) for a discussion of the difference between absolute and relative space]. Note that *relative space* is also known as *differential space* or *abstract space* [*see* Harvey (1973, 1969) for a discussion of the term *differential space*]. It is worth noting that Lefebvre uses the terms absolute space and abstract space slightly differently than the traditional usage adopted in geography. For Lefebvre, absolute space is a naturalistic, prehistorical space which forms the bedrock of relativized, historical or what he calls, abstract, space (1987: 48–9).

6 This depiction bears some affinity to Laclau and Mouffe's (1985: 104) discussion of the essentialism of the fragments; when the structural essence of the social (e.g., the capitalist mode of production) is discursively displaced by a heterogeneous multiplicity of social sites and practices – as, according to Laclau and Mouffe, it is in the work of Hindess and Hirst – the essentialism of the totality is effectively replaced by an essentialism of the elements; in other words, each part of the 'disaggregation' takes on a fixed and independent identity rather than being relationally defined. In an overdeterminist Althusserian conception, by contrast, 'far from there being an essentialist *totalization*, or a no less essentialist *separation* among the objects, the presence of some objects in others prevents any of their identities from being fixed' (104).

7 In particular, he was concerned with the spatial language of the poststructuralists

> Consider questions about space, for example: taken out of the context of practice, projected onto the place of a knowledge that considers itself to be 'pure' and imagines itself to be 'productive' (as indeed it is – but only of verbiage), such questions assume a philosophizing and degenerate character. What they degenerate into are mere general considerations on intellectual space – on 'writing' as the intellectual space of a people, as the mental space of a period, and so on.
>
> (Lefebvre, 1991: 415).

Suspecting the dissociation of conceptual space from 'lived' space (which he identifies as a pre-discursive terrain of production), Lefebvre see philosophers' production of mental space as only 'apparently' extra-ideological (1991: 6). While poststructuralist theorists might imagine themselves to be undertaking transgressive acts via their work, Lefebvre remains convinced that this work, by conflating mental/conceptual space with social/material space, is unwittingly open to ideological manipulation. The insinuation is that only out of the dialectic of practice and reflection, that is, at the intersection of language and social action, will a true (read revolutionary) spatial understanding be generated.

While Lefebvre berates philosophers and cultural theorists for their failure to recognize the lived materiality of space as the basis of all discursive representations in mental space, Smith and Katz warn against the failure to situate absolute space in an historically materialist (and therefore relative) frame. Together they are concerned that discursivity and materiality be made to touch (the social production of material space must form the foundation of conceptual space) lest spatial metaphors be rendered apolitical, if not out of control (Smith and Katz, 1993: 80), or worse, open to control by the 'dominant class' (Lefebvre, 1987: 6).

For Marxists and geographers alike, there appears to be a concern that the materiality, sociality and produced nature of space might be ignored by those who so readily employ spatial metaphors in their poststructuralist discourse. This concern is traced to the worrying political implications of somehow disregarding 'reality'. Without a true grounding in the material social world, how can spatial representations not be ideological, that is, prey to the desires and manipulations of the 'ruling class'?[8]

Foucault, Derrida, Kristeva and Lacan, and their promotion of 'the basic sophistry whereby the philosophico-epistemological notion of space is fetishized and the mental realm comes to envelop the social and physical ones' (1991: 5).

8   This is a question that is interestingly parallel in structure to one often posed to feminist poststructuralists: without a true grounding in the materiality of women's experience, how can poststructuralist feminist theoretical interventions avoid functioning in service of a dominant masculinism? In the current context it is the dangers of fragmentation (for the left and for feminism) that opens 'us' up to the enemy – revealing the modernist vision of resistance and organization that provides the foundations of this critique. Not all geographers or feminists are worried by the prospect of fragmentation, however (*see* Gibson-Graham, 1995). Soja and Hooper, for example, welcome the proliferation of discursive spatialities and the new 'postmodernized and spatialized' politics of difference (1993: 184).

As battles between metaphor and materiality, discourse and reality rage in and around us, and 'the enemy' infiltrates our disciplined boundaries, what better time might there be for a jump into space? This chapter confronts some of the political and epistemological concerns around the relationship between discursivity, materiality, politics and space that have arisen out of clashes between modern and postmodern feminist and urban discourses. It explores the possibilities of thinking from the outside in, both from the poststructuralist encampments into the protected dwelling of geography, and from the space of formlessness into the space of Form.

> The outside, insinuates itself into thought, drawing knowledge outside of itself, outside what is expected, producing a hollow which it can then inhabit – an outside within or as the inside.
>
> (Grosz, 1994: 9).

Examining the spatial metaphors that have been employed in feminist analyses of the body and the city, the chapter traces the political effects of privileging the materiality of women's experience and capitalist social relations. At the same time, it gestures towards the political potential of an alternative conceptualization in which discourse and other materialities are effectively intertwined.

Rape space, modern space

Recent feminist theorizations of the body employ and also challenge a number of familiar spatial metaphors, such as 'inside/outside', 'surface/depth', 'empty/full', 'dwelling'. Spatial knowledges of women's bodies and female sexuality have philosophical and activist origins. For the moment, I would like to explore feminist knowledge of the body gained through women's activism around rape. In Lefebvre's frame, it is knowledge gained in and through an interaction between 'reality' and 'reflection' that affords 'scientific understanding'.[9]

The feminist language of rape situates it as a fixed reality of women's lives – a reality founded upon the assumed ability of the rapist physically to overcome his target (Marcus, 1992: 387). Creating a public knowledge of rape as a 'reality' has been one of the projects of anti-rape activists and policy makers, and making rape visible in the community constitutes a significant victory for feminist politics. Sharon Marcus is a feminist who challenges the self-evidently progressive and productive nature of this understanding born of action and experience (a so-called engagement with the real). She argues that the cost of

---

9 This process of knowledge production is contrasted to that which involves analysis of texts/writing alone – a process that is destined, in Lefebvre's view, to reproduce an ideological understanding.

feminist success has been the unquestioned acceptance of a language of rape which

> ... solicits women to position ourselves as endangers, violable, and fearful and invites men to position themselves as legitimately violent and entitled to women's sexual services. This language structures physical actions and responses as well as words, and forms, for example, the would-be rapist's feelings of powerfulness and our commonplace sense of paralysis when threatened with rape.
>
> (Marcus, 1992: 390).

More importantly for the argument being developed here, this 'rape script' portrays women's bodies and female sexuality in spatial terms as an empty space waiting to be invaded/taken/formed:

> The rape script describes female bodies as vulnerable, violable, penetrable, and wounded; metaphors of rape as trespass and invasion retain this definition intact. The psychological corollary of this property metaphor characterizes female sexuality as inner space, rape as the invasion of this inner space, and anti-rape politics as a means to safeguard this inner space from contact with anything external to it. The entire female body comes to be symbolized by the vagina, itself conceived as a delicate, perhaps inevitably damaged and pained inner space.
>
> (Marcus, 1992: 398).

This knowledge of women's body space is not an artefact of purely philosophical reckoning but is a representation of the 'reality' of women's bodies *vis-à-vis* men's. That this representation is informed by a movement from the concrete experience of rape victims and rapists to the abstract positioning of woman space as absence/negativity and man space as presence/positivity would attest to its legitimacy as true knowledge in Lefebvre's frame of reference. Marcus's point, though, is that this language of rape positions and confines practical intervention to the post-rape events of reporting, reparation and vindication, thereby blocking an active strategy of rape prevention.[10] Thus, feminist knowledge of rape is bound by the language it employs to a perpetuation of victim status for women.

Marcus argues that the 'truth' of victimhood should not be accepted but should be resisted and undermined. Her argument points up the problems with Lefebvre's view that

> ... space (is) *produced* before being *read* ... (it is produced) in order to be *lived* by people with bodies and lives in their own particular urban context.
>
> (1991: 143).

10 That is, prevention beyond the legal deterrence of laws that are supposedly designed to persuade men not to rape, or measures such as better street lighting which are designed to increase the public surveillance of male sexuality (Marcus, 1992: 388).

According to Marcus, lived space is as much discursively as materially produced. She urges us to produce a different discourse of female spatiality/
sexuality, thus enabling a different female materiality/liveability.

A parallel construction of woman's body and female sexuality is evident in
feminist knowledges of the city. Again, these knowledges are based upon the
experience of women in the city and on contemporary theories of urban
structure. From behavioural geographic research into gendered activity patterns and social networks, a picture has been developed of women inhabiting
certain spaces of the city – domestic space, neighbourhood space, local commercial space while men are more prevalent inhabitors of the central city,
industrial zones and commercial areas.[11] In feminist urban studies, women are
situated within the theoretical spaces of consumption, reproduction and the
private, all of which are mapped on to the suburb (Wilson, 1991; Saegert, 1980;
England, 1991). As vacuous spaces of desire that must be satisfied by consumption, women are positioned in one discourse as shoppers, legitimately entering
the economic space of the city to be filled before returning to residential space
where new and ultimately insatiable consumer desires will be aroused
(Swanson, 1994). As hallowed spaces of biological reproduction, women's
bodies are represented in another urban discourse as empty, needful of
protection in the residential cocoon where they wait, always ready to be filled
by the function of motherhood (Saegert, 1980).[12] Vacant and vulnerable,
female sexuality is something to be guarded within the space of the home.
Confined there, as passive guardians of the womb-like oasis that offers succour
to active public (male) civilians, women are rightfully out of the public gaze
(Marcus, 1993).

In feminist urban theory, the spatiality of women's bodies is constituted in
relation to two different, but perhaps connected, Forms, that of the Phallus
and that of Capital. Feminist discourses of gender difference and capitalist
development associate 'woman' with lack, emptiness, ineffectiveness, the
determined. As we have already seen in the rape script which is articulated
within the broader hegemonic discourse of gender, woman is differentiated
from man by her otherness, her passivity, her vulnerability, ultimately her
vacuousness. She is indeed the symbol of 'absolute space', a homogeneous
inert void, a container, something that can only be spoken of in terms of the
object(s) that exist(s) within it.[13] Inevitably, the object that exists within/
invades/penetrates the inert void – bringing woman into existence – is the
Phallus. Woman is necessarily rape space in the phallocentric discourse of
gender.

---

11 *See* Rose (1993) for an excellent critical summary of this literature.
12 In an intriguing reading of the film and novel *Rosemary's Baby*, Marcus (1993) alludes to
    the punishment that might befall any woman who deserts the fecundity and safety of the
    suburbs and the single-family house for the sterility and danger of the inner city and
    apartment living, yet proceeds to get pregnant and have a baby. (The devil takes such an
    out-of-place women, or at least her child).
13 This is the Newtonian notion of space as a void and the 'plenum of matter' (Kern, 1983:
    153; Smith and Katz, 1993: 75).

In the urban script which is articulated within the broader hegemonic discourse of Capitalism, woman is constituted as an economic actor allocated to the subordinate functions of the capitalist system. As consumer she is seen to participate in the realization of capitalist commodities, putting them to their final, unproductive uses: under the influence of capitalist advertising and mood manipulation she translates her sexual desire into needs which must be satisfied by consumption. This transfiguration of private into public desire is enacted in consumption spaces – the shopping mall, the high street, and department store – horizontal, sometimes cavernous, 'feminized' places within the urban landscape. Represented as maker and socializer of the future capitalist work-force, woman plays a part in the dynamic of social reproduction. In her role of bearing children, ministering to their needs and assisting the state in their education and social training, woman is portrayed as an unpaid service worker attending to the requirements of capital accumulation. Within her limited field of action in the sphere of reproduction, resistance is seen as possible – she may organize around local community and consumption issues – but the real rules are made by capital.

In this urban discourse woman is represented as an active player rather than a passive container; she is a crucial constituent of capitalist social relations, though not situated at the centre of accumulation, nor cast as the subject of history.[14] The discourse of Capitalism renders the space of woman no longer homogeneous and void. Instead woman space is 'relative space', given form by multiple (subordinated) roles, each situated in relation to capitalist production. Women's economic bodies are portrayed as complements to men's economic bodies, adjuncts with important reproductive, nurturing and consumption functions. Indeed, woman becomes 'positive negative space', a background that 'itself is a positive element, of equal importance with all others' (Kern, 1983: 152). Like the structured backgrounds of cubist painting, woman space as relative space is more visible, less empty, more functional than is absolute space.[15] But woman space is still defined in terms of a positivity that is not its own. Whether as absolute or relative space, woman is presented as fixed by, or in relation to, an Identity/Form/Being – the Phallus or Capital.

In an attempt to address women's oppression, feminists may celebrate shopping, birth, homemaking, the fecund emptiness of woman's body, the shopping mall; the suburban home, the caring and nurturing functions, the woman space. But in doing so they accept the boundaries of difference and

14 This role is taken by man as the producer of commodities, the producer of surplus value, situated in the sphere of production, as a member of the working class. Of course, recent episodes of industrial restructuring have altered the gendered face of the capitalist work-force. Women are increasingly occupying the sphere of production and the vertical concrete and glass spaces of economic power (McDowell, 1994). However, a new urban discourse has yet to emerge which dislodges the extremely gendered code that is mapped on to the suburb/sphere of reproduction/space of consumption.

15 Kern argues that absolute space has more in common with the insignificant backgrounds of classical portraiture which serve only to contain and set off the foregrounded subject (1983).

separation designated by the discourses of capitalism and binary gender. Another feminist strategy has been to attempt to reverse the binarisms by claiming back men's economic and urban space as rightfully theirs. Women (particularly female-headed households) have begun to desert the suburbs and, as one of the main groups involved in gentrification, have reasserted their right to a central location in the inner city (Rose, 1989).[16] Women have successfully fought for child-care centres, vacation programmes for school-age children, better community care for the elderly and disabled so that they can temporarily free themselves from the role of carer and claim a rightful place in the capitalist paid work-force. Indeed, the fact that such services are better provided for in the inner city contributes to the feminization of households in inner-city areas. Significant though all these changes have been for women in the city, these strategies rest upon the assumption that women remain the carers, the supplementary workers in a capitalist system, who, if they undertake labour in the productive spheres of the economy, must also provide the reproductive labour. The inner city is one space that allows the exhausted (capitalist) superwoman to function – it has become the site of a new 'problem that has no name.[17]

Similar strategies of reversal are represented in 'Take back the night' rallies and other urban actions where women have claimed their right to the city streets, pressing for better lighting, better policing of public transport, guarded parking areas and other mechanisms of public surveillance of men's behaviour (Worpole, 1992). As the geography of women's fear has been made visible, so has the 'reality' of male sexuality and the 'inevitability' of violence against women been accepted. While greater public surveillance is advocated, women are simultaneously warned not to trespass into public space where, on the streets at night or on public transport after work hours, they are most certainly 'asking' to become players in a rape script.[18]

Feminist strategies of celebration and reversal are all contributing to changes in the liveability of urban space for women. But what might be the cost of these changes if they rest upon the unquestioned acceptance of both the Phallus and Capital as the 'identities' which situate women/space, and if they force women/space into the victim role that the sexual rape script allocates and the adjunct role that the economic urban script allocates? What potentialities are suppressed by such a figuring of women/space? Perhaps we can answer these questions only by looking to alternative notions of identity to see how they might configure women/space, as well as other possibilities they might entail.

16 Even in the face of foreboding and paranoid cautionary fables such as *Rosemary's Baby*.
17 Marcus (1993) notes that after the publication of her bestseller, *The Feminine Mystique*, Betty Friedan was able to move out of the suburbs, the condemned site of women's unnamed oppression, and into an apartment in Manhattan. In the 1960s, unlike the 1990s, such an inner-city location represented an escape from the 'problem that had no name'.
18 In exposing the contradictions associated with this geography of fear, feminists have broken down the inside/outside distinction citing the higher incidence of rape inside the home compared to outside of it (Valentine, 1992).

Rethinking the space of form: 'air against earth'

Both absolute and relative conceptions of space rely upon the logic of identity, presence or Form to give meaning to space. Absolute space is the emptiness which is the 'plenum of matter' (Kern, 1983: 153), 'a passive arena, the setting objects and their interactions' (Massey, 1992: 76). Absolute space invokes a stable spatial ontology given by God, the Phallus, Capital, in which objects are fixed at an absolute location. Relative space comes into existence via the interrelations of objects (Massey, 1992: 77). It invokes a fluid spatial ontology, continually under construction by the force fields established between objects. In Marxist formulations, all locations in absolute space are rendered relative by the fluid, historical structuring and restructuring of capitalist patriarchy and racist imperialism (Smith, 1984: 82–83; Smith and Katz, 1993: 79).

Not only is relative space historically and socially constructed, but space has its own effectivity:

> Could space be nothing more than the passive locus of social relations, the milieu in which their combination takes on body, or the aggregate of the procedures employed in their removal? The answer must be no. Later on I shall demonstrate the active – the operational or instrumental – role of space, as knowledge and action, in the existing mode of production
>
> (Lefebvre, 1991: 11).

Massey's development of Lefebvre's geological metaphor of sedimentation and layering has been influential in theorizing the effectivity of socially produced space (1993, 1984):

> ... no space disappears completely, or is utterly abolished in the course of the process of social development – not even the natural place where that process began. 'Something' always survives or endures – 'something' that is not a *thing*. Each such material underpinning has a form, a function, a structure – properties that are necessary but not sufficient to define it.
>
> (Lefebvre, 1991: 403).

What is interesting in all these spatial conceptions is the prevalence of the image of space as ground or earth (Lefebvre's 'material underpinning') – something which gives the ahistorical Identity located in absolute space a 'place to stand' or the historically grounded Identity of relative space a 'terrain' to (re)mould. But what effect does this reliance upon Identity and the metaphor of grounding have? What violence might it do to space?

Among other poststructuralist theorists who challenge the metaphysics of presence in Western Enlightenment thought, Deleuze and Guattari employ a spatiality that appears divorced from the positivity of Identity. Rather than earth, ground and fixity in a location grid, this space evokes air, smoothness and openness:

The space of nomad thought is qualitatively different from State space. Air against earth. State space is 'striated' or gridded. Movement in it is confined as by gravity to a horizontal plane, and limited by the order of that plane to preset paths between fixed and identifiable points. Nomad space is 'smooth', or open-ended. One can rise up at any point and move to any other. Its mode of distribution is the *nomos*: arraying oneself in an open space (hold the street), as opposed to the *logos* of entrenching oneself in a closed space (hold the fort).

(Massumi, 1987: xiiii).

In the wild productions of rhizome thought, Identity is splintered into disorder, chaos, multiplicity, heterogeneity, rupture and flight. It is mapped and not traced:

The map is open and connectable in all of its dimensions; it is detachable, reversible, adapted to any kind of mounting, reworked by an individual, group, or social formation.

(Deleuze and Guattari, 1987: 12).

And mapping, as Carter has argued, is not about discovery (of already established identity), but about exploration and invention:

To be an explorer was to inhabit a world of potential objects with which one carried on an imaginary dialogue.

(Carter, 1987: 25).

These images of space as air and openness, enabling exploration and potentiality, evoke feminist and postmodern uses of *chora* to represent space (Grosz, 1994a; Lechte, 1994):[19]

... chora is fundamentally a space. But it is neither the space of 'phenomenological intuition' nor the space of Euclidean geometry, being closer to the deformations of topological space. Indeed, the chora is prior to the order and regulation such notions of space imply. It is an unordered space. Although Kristeva herself says that the chora 'preceded' nomination and figuration, this is not meant in any chronological sense. For the chora is also 'prior' to the ordering of chronological time. The chora, therefore, is not an origin, nor is it in any sense a cause which would produce predictable effects. Just the reverse: the chora, as indeterminacy, is a harbinger of pure chance.

(Lechte, 1993: 119–20).

19 Having assumed the status of a 'master term' within French poststructuralist thought, *chora* is of interest because of the way in which it cannot be contained within the logos of any text under examination but is, nevertheless, necessary to the operations of that text. For Derrida and Kristeva, such a term highlights the limits or excess of a system of thought, the vulnerable point at which to focus the most productive deconstruction (Grosz, 1994a: 54).

Chora is the term Plato uses to denote the space of movement between being and becoming – 'the mother of all things and yet without ontological status', 'that space (between being and becoming) that produces their separation and thus enables their co-existence and interchange' (Grosz, 1994a: 58).

> Chora then is the space in which place is made possible, the chasm for the passage of spaceless Form into a spatialized reality, a dimensionless tunnel opening itself to spatialization, obliterating itself to make others possible and actual.
>
> (Grosz, 1994a: 58).

The inherent femininity of chora lies in its immanent productiveness. But it is this very quality that Grosz argues has been undermined by phallogocentrism. Within phallocentric thought, chora became appropriated as the space of production/Form/the father – the space which is the condition of man's self-representation and the condition of Identity. Chora as the space of indeterminacy/enabling/engendering/the mother was denigrated, represented 'as an abyss, as unfathomable, lacking, enigmatic, veiled, seductive, voracious, dangerous and disruptive' (Grosz, 1994a: 66), cast out with name or place.

Feminist poststructuralists have been keen to point out the violence that has been done to women, and now to space, by phallocentric modernist discourse:

> (the) enclosure of women in men's physical space is not entirely different from the containment of women in men's conceptual universe either: theory, in the terms in which we know it today, is also the consequence of a refusal to acknowledge that other perspectives, other modes of reason, other modes of construction and constitution are possible. Its singularity and status, as true and objective, depend on this disavowal.
>
> (Grosz, 1994a: 65).

How might we proceed now to reclaim the feminine aspect of chora, to conceptualize a pregnant space, a space of air, a space of potentiality and overdetermination?

> In order for [sexual] difference to be thought and lived, we have to reconsider the whole problematic of *space* and *time* ... A change of epoch requires a mutation in the perception and conception of *space-time*, the *inhabitation of place* and the *envelopes of identity*.
>
> (Irigaray, quoted in Grosz, 1994a: 63).

> Becomings belong to geography, they are orientations, directions, entries and exits.
>
> (Deleuze and Parnet, 1987: 3).

Feminist theorists urge us to think woman and space outside of that discourse in which Identity, or the Phallus, gives meaning to everything – to think outside the discourse in which woman can be given shape only by Man and in which space is an empty container that can be given shape only by matter. To this urging can be added the encouragement, offered by anti-essentialist Marxism, to think economic and space outside the discourse in which Identity, or Capital, give meaning to everything – to think outside the discourse of woman's economic subordination to Man and of urban women operating in a terrain defined by capitalist social relations.

Pregnant space, postmodern space

Impressionism and Cubism are two interrelated art movements that mirror the possibilities and potentialities of, as well as the impossibilities and barriers to, thinking a postmodern pregnant space. In the paintings of the Impressionists, space was, for the first time, constitutive – the background, full of haze, mist, smoke, light, crowded in on the subject, claiming equal status and attention from the painter and gazer (Kern, 1983: 160). Cubism took one step further, instating space with geometric form, leveling space and material object to the point of complete interpenetration. In this genre, Form was both disintegrated and re-Formed in every constituent space (Kern, 1983: 161–2).

Cubism, however, evokes a closed system of determination in which space is defined by the presence of a positive Being, no matter how fragmented and indistinct. This is the space of modernism, of phallocentrism and capitalism. In the discourse of hegemonic Capitalism, for example, space is constituted by the operations of capital:

> It is not Einstein, nor physics and philosophy, which in the end determine the relativity of geographical space, but the actual process of capital accumulation.
> (Smith, 1984: 82–3).

> The new space that thereby emerges [in the moment of the multinational network, or what Mandel calls 'late capitalism'] involves the suppression of distance ... and the relentless saturation of any remaining voids and empty places, to the point where the postmodern body ... is now exposed to a perceptual barrage of immediacy from which all sheltering layers and intervening mediations have been removed.
> (Jameson, 1991: 412–13).

Although 'we gotta get out of this place',[20] we are caught in the space of no escape.

By contrast, the space of the Impressionists represents one of those points of excess within modernism – space constituted by the random distribution, disorder and chance of smoke, streams of sunlight, steam and clouds (Lechte, 1993: 121). Here we see space as an open system of disequilibrium and indeterminacy, space as a random but productive process (Serres, cited in Lechte, 1994). In this chora-like image of positive immanence and potentiality,

20 *See* Grossberg (1992).

it might be possible to see postmodern becomings that are not devoid of political in/content.

How might we, for example, appreciate differently the spatiality of female sexuality and potential new ways for women to dwell in urban space? Marcus provides some guidance.

> One possible alternative to figuring female sexuality as a fixed spatial unit is to imagine sexuality in terms of time and change ... Rather than secure the right to alienate and own a spatialized sexuality, antirape politics can claim women's right to a self that could differ from itself over time without then having to surrender its effective existence as self.
> (Marcus, 1992: 399–400).

Marcus appears to be arguing for a multiplicity of female sexualities that may coexist within any one individual. In her vision, the spatiality of female sexuality can be dissociated from the notion of a fixed, immobilized cavity defined in relation to the inevitably invading, violent penis. Instead, female sexual space can be conceived in multiple ways – as surface, as active, as full and changing, as many, as depth, as random and indeterminate, as process.

How might this respatialization of the body generate new geographies for women in the city? It might lead us to identify the multiple urban spaces that women claim, but not solely in the name of consumer desire or reproductive/biological function. Here one could think of the heterotopias of lesbian space, prostitution space, bingo space, club space, health spa, body building and aerobics space, nursing home space, hobby space – all terrains of public life in which women's agency is enacted in an effective, if indeterminate manner.[21] One could identify the ways in which such spaces are regulated and ordered by dominant discourses of heterosexuality, health, youth, beauty and respectability, and influenced by discourses of transgression. One could explore and map an urban performance space of women that is defined in terms of positivity, fullness, surface and power. But for such a reinscription not to fall back into simply celebrating woman space in the city,[22] theoretical work must continually and repeatedly displace (rather than reverse) the binary hierarchy of gender.

One strategy of displacement might lead us to deconstruct and redefine those consumption and reproductive spaces/spheres that are the designated woman space in the discourse of urban capitalism. Within geography, for example, the urban restructuring literature points to the massive involvement of women in the paid work-force where they are active in a variety of economic roles apart from that of final consumer or reproducer of the capitalist labour-force.

---

21 Some of this work is currently being done by feminist geographers. Many of the early studies in feminist geography have, however, reproduced a phallocentric discourse by accepting the representation of women's bodies as vulnerable and women's spaces as subordinate (*see* Rose, 1993: 117–36).

22 As Soja and Hooper (1993: 198) suggest, the task is not to 'assert the dominance of the subaltern over the hegemon' but to 'break down and disorder the binary itself'.

Feminist geographers and sociologists are researching women in office space (Pringle, 1988), in finance space (McDowell, 1994), in retail space (Dowling, 1994), in ethnic small business (Alcorso, 1993), in industrial space (Phizacklea, 1990) – again all public arenas in which women's agency is enacted. In some texts we may even see glimmers of spaces beyond or outside capitalism, where women operate in non-capitalist spaces of production and contribute to the reproduction of non-capitalist economic forms.[23]

Despite these glimmers, what characterizes much of the restructuring literature is an overriding sense of 'capitalocentrism' in that women's entry into the paid labour-force is seen primarily in terms of the desire of capital for cheaper, more manipulable labour. Capital has positioned the super-exploited female worker just as it has produced women's roles as reproducers (of the capitalist work-force) and consumers (of capitalist commodities). Any attempt to destabilize woman's position and spatiality within urban discourse must dispense with the Identity of Capitalism as the ultimate container[24] and constituter of women's social and economic life/space.

It would seem that the rethinking of female sexuality and the creation of alternate discourses of sexuality and bodily spatiality are way in advance of the rethinking of economic identity and social spatiality (Grosz, 1994c). Indeed, even the most innovative cultural and poststructuralist theorists leave this terrain untouched:

> Individuals do not appear to appropriate capital but to be appropriated to it. People are caught in its circuits, moving in and out of its paths of mobility, seeking opportunistic moments (luck, fate, fame or crime) which will enable them, not to redistribute wealth, but to relocate themselves within the distributional networks of capital.
>
> (Grossberg, 1992: 328).

> It is here that we can begin to see the relation between capitalism and the construction of everyday life as a transit-mobility which constructs the space for the free movement of capital and for the capitalization, rather than the commodification, of everyday life. For within that transit-space, people are not the producers of wealth but a potential site of capital investment. People become capital itself. And within these circuits, the only thing that they can be sure of is that capitalism is going first-class.
>
> (Grossberg, 1992: 328).

The capitalist relation consists of four dense points – commodity/consumer, worker/capitalist – which in neoconservative society are effectively superposed in every body in every spacetime coordinate. When capital comes out, it surfaces as

---

23 *See*, for example, Katz and Monk (1993) and Gibson(1992).

24 So that household labour and self-employment (which are outside capitalist relations of production) are seen as somehow taking place 'within capitalism', as are non- capitalist forms of commodity production (e.g., independent or communal production).

a fractal attractor whose operational arena is immediately coextensive with the social field.

(Massumi, 1993: 132).

Despite the postmodern interest in chora, in nomadology and smooth space, the identity of Capital confronts us wherever we turn. Do we only ever dwell in a capitalist space? Can we ever think outside the capitalist axiomatic?

The economy constitutes a worldwide axiomatic, a 'universal cosmopolitan energy which overflows every restriction and bond,' (Marx) a mobile and convertible substance 'such as the total value of annual production.' Today we can depict an enormous, so-called stateless, monetary mass that circulates through foreign exchange and across borders, eluding control by the States, forming a multinational ecumenical organization, constituting a supranational power untouched by government decisions.

(Deleuze and Guatarri, 1987: 453).

Here Deleuze and Guattari are difficult and elusive. The capitalist axiomatic is all-pervasive and innovative, seemingly able to co-opt and re-territorialize all lines of flight out of its territory into new opportunities for self-expansion, able to set and repel its own limits (1987: 472). At the same time, they reserve a space for the minority, the becoming everybody/everything outside the total-izing flow of capital:

The undecidable is the germ and locus par excellence of revolutionary decisions. Some people invoke the high technology of the world system of enslavement: but even, and especially, this mechanic enslavement abounds in undecidable propo-sitions and movements that, far from belonging to a domain of knowledge reserved for sworn specialists, provides so many weapons for the becoming of everybody/everything, becoming-radio, becoming-electronic, becoming-mo-lecular ... Every struggle is a function of all these undecidable propositions and constructs revolutionary connections in opposition to the conjugations of the axiomatic.

(1987: 473).

In the footnote to this statement the authors mention the domain of 'alternative practices' such as pirate radio stations, urban community networks, the alter-native to psychiatry (1987: 572). Here we catch a minimal glimpse of what might lie outside the flows of capital. The capitalist axiomatic closes and defines – in the sense of fully inhabiting – social space (evoking the closure and definition of Cubism), yet it is also in motion, providing a space of becoming, of undecidability. This space is reminiscent of the constitutive (pregnant) space of the impressionists. It is a space of mists and vapours, of movement and possibility, of background that might at any moment become foreground – a 'space of excess' and indeterminacy within the modern space of fullness and closure.

If we are to take postmodern spatial becomings seriously, then it would seem that we must claim chora, that space between the Being of present Capitalism and the Becoming of future capitalisms, as the place for the indeterminate potentiality of non- capitalisms.[25] In this space we might identify the range of social practices that are not subsumed to capital flows. We might see the sphere of (capitalist) reproduction as the space of non-capitalist class processes that deterritorialize and divert capitalist flows of surplus value (Gibson, 1992). We might see the sphere of (capitalist) consumption as the space of realization and consumption of commodities produced under a range of productive relations – co-operative, self-employed, enslaved, communal as well as capitalist. What violence do we do when we interpret all these spaces as existing in Capitalism, as cohering within the coded flows of axiomatic capital? We risk relegating space/life to emptiness, to rape, to non-becoming, to victimhood.

References

Alcorso, C., '"And I'd like to thank my wife": women in ethnic small business', *Australian Feminist Studies*, (1993).

Carter, P., *The Road to Botany Bay*, (London, Faber and Faber, 1987).

Colomina, B, (ed.), *Sexuality and Space*, (New York, Princeton, Architectural Press, 1992).

Deleuze, G. and Guattari, F., *A Thousand Plateaus: Capitalism and Schizophrenia*, translated by B. Massumi, (Minneapolis, University of Minnesota Press, 1987).

Deleuze, G. and Parnet, C., *Dialogues*, translated by Hugh Tomlinson and Barbara Habberjam, (New York, Columbia University Press, 1987).

Dowling, R., 'Femininity, place and commodities: a retail case study', *Antipode*, 25, 4, 295–319, (1993).

England, K. 'Gender relations and the spatial structure of the city', *Geoforum* 22, 2, 135–47, (1991).

Foucault, M., 'Questions in geography' pp. 63–77 in C. Gordon (ed.), *Power/Knowledge: Selected Interviews and Other Writings 1972–1977*, (New York, Random House, 1980).

Gibson, K. 'Hewers of cake and drawers of tea: women, industrial restructuring, and class processes on the coalfields of central Queensland', *Rethinking Marxism* 5, 4, 29–56, (1992).

Gibson-Graham, J. K., 'Beyond capitalism and patriarchy: reflections on political subjectivity', in R. Pringle and B. Caine (eds), *Transitions: New Australian Feminisms*, Sydney, Allen and Unwin (1995).

Gibson-Graham, J. K., *The end of capitalism (as we know it)*, (London, Blackwell, 1996).

Grossberg, L., *We Gotta Get Out of this Place*, (London, Routledge, 1992).

Grosz, E. 'Bodies-cities' pp. 241–54 in B. Colomina (ed.), *Sexuality and Space*, (New York, Princeton, Architectural Press, 1992).

Grosz, E. 'Women, chora, dwelling', pp. 47–58 in S. Watson and R. Gibson (eds), *Postmodern Cities and Spaces*, (London, Blackwell, 1994a).

Grosz, E. 'Architecture from the outside;', unpublished manuscript, (Centre for Women's Studies, Monash University, Clayton, VIC3187, Australia, 1994b).

25 Here we may enter a space resembling the 'thirdspace of political choice' depicted by Soja and Hooper (1993: 198–9) (drawing on Foucault's notion of heterotopia) which is a place of enunciation of a 'new cultural politics of difference'.

Grosz, E., *Volatile Bodies: Toward a Corporeal Feminism*, (Bloomington IN, Indiana University Press, 1994c).

Harvey, D., *Explanation in Geography*, (London, Blackwell, 1969).

Harvey, D., *Social Justice and the City*, (London, Blackwell, 1973).

Harvey, D., *The Condition of Postmodernity*, (London, Blackwell, 1989).

Jameson, F., *Postmodernism, or the Cultural Logic of Late Capitalism*, (Durham, Duke University Press, 1991).

Katz, C. and Monk, J. (eds), *Full Circles: Women Over the Life Course*, (New York, Routledge, 1993).

Kern, S., *The Culture of Time and Space 1880–1918*, (Cambridge MA, Harvard University Press, 1983).

Laclau, E. and Mouffe, C., *Hegemony and Socialist Strategy*, (London, Verso, 1985).

Lechte, J., '(Not) belonging in postmodern space', pp. 99–111 in S. Watson and K. Gibson (eds), *Postmodern Cities and Spaces*, (London, Blackwell, 1994).

Lefebvre, H., *The Production of Space*, translated by D. Nicholson-Smith, (London, Blackwell, 1991).

McDowell, L., 'Working in the city: spaces of power', paper presented at the annual meeting of the Association of American Geographers, San Francisco, (1994).

Marcus, S., 'Fighting bodies, fighting words: a theory and politics of rape prevention', pp. 385–403 in J. Butler and J. Scott (eds), *Feminists Theorize the Poltical*, (London, Routledge. 1992).

Marcus, S., 'Placing *Rosemary's Baby*', *Differences: A Journal of Feminist Cultural Studies*, 5, 3, 121–53, (1993).

Massey D., *Spatial Divisions of Labor*, (New York, Methuen, 1984).

Massey, D., 'Politics and space/time', *New Left Review*, 196, 65–84, (1993).

Massumi, B., 'Translator's foreword: pleasures of philosophy', pp. ix–xv in Deleuze, G. and Guattari, F., *A Thousand Plateaus: Capitalism and Schizophrenia*, translated by B. Massumi, (Minneapolis, University of Minnesota Press, 1987).

Massumi, B., *A Reader's Guide to Capitalism and Schizophrenia: Deviations from Deleuze and Guattari*, (Cambridge MA, MIT Press, 1993).

Phizacklea, A., *Unpacking the Fashion Industry*, (London, Routledge. 1990).

Pringle, R., *Secretaries Talk: Sexuality, Power and Work*, (Sydney, Allen and Unwin, 1988).

Rose, D., 'A feminist perspective on employment and gentrification: the case of Montreal', in J. Wolch and M. Dear (eds), *The Power of Geography: How Territory Shapes Social Life*, (Boston, Unwin and Hyman, 1989).

Rose, G., *Feminism and Geography: the Limits of Geographical Knowledge*, (Cambridge, Polity Press, 1993).

Saegert, S., 'Masculine cities and feminine suburbs', *Signs* 5, 3, 96–111, (1980).

Smith, N., *Uneven Development*, (Oxford, Basil Blackwell, 1984).

Smith, N., and Katz C., 'Grounding metaphor: towards a spatialized politics', (pp. 67–83 in S. Pile and M. Keith (eds), *Place and the Politics of Identity*, (London, Routledge. 1993).

Soja, E., *Postmodern Geographies: The Reassertion of Space in Critical Social Theory*, (London, Verso, 1989).

Soja, E. and Hooper, B., 'The space that difference makes: some notes on the geographical margins of the new cultural politics', pp. 183–203 in S. Pile and M. Keith (eds), *Place and the Politics of Identity*, (London, Routledge. 1993).

Swanson, G. '"Drunk with glitter": consuming spaces and sexual geographies', pp. 80–98 in S. Watson and K. Gibson (eds), *Postmodern Cities and Spaces*, (London, Blackwell, 1994).

Valentine, G., 'Images of danger, women's sources of information about the spatial distribution of male violence', *Area*, 1, 22–9, (1992).

Watson, S. and Gibson, K. (eds), *Postmodern Cities and Spaces*, (London, Blackwell, 1994).

Wilson, E., *The Sphinx in the City: Urban Life, the Control of Disorder, and Women*, (London, Virago Press, 1991).

Worpole, K., *Towns for People: Transforming Urban Life*, (Buckingham, Open University Press, 1992).

13

Geopolitics and the Postmodern: Issues of Knowledge, Difference, and North-South Relations

David Slater

Within the realms of critical geographical enquiry, debates on the postmodern still retain a strong Western orientation. This is not only specific to geography, because it has been remarked elsewhere that much discussion of the postmodern displays the features of a customary 'Western conversation'. The themes, agents and practices of knowledge are circumscribed within the heartlands of Euro-America, and are invested with an implicit self-containing viability. At the same time, there is often little apparent awareness of the particularity of the West, and a self-contained matrix of knowledge is projected out for consumption by other worlds. Nevertheless, the peculiarities of Euro-Americanist modes of thought, largely through the impact of post-colonial writings, are beginning to be dissected and destabilized in forms which hitherto were absent from critical agendas. In this newer context, it is important to single out the relevance of the geopolitics of power and knowledge, and ask ourselves to what extent the postmodern turn has stimulated a break from older exclusionary lines of interpretation. In this context, I shall use the term geopolitics to denote a certain spatiality of power that flows across and transgresses international boundaries. The power over other societies is not only a phenomenon connected to violent incursions, military invasions, colonial conquests and externally administered governance; it also expresses a relation of knowledge that posits a Western superiority over the non-West. I shall further suggest that the postmodern sensibility, in relation to the questions of imperial politics as well as the power of knowledge, and in particular the agents of knowledge, remains at best highly ambivalent, and certainly not beyond the limits of Western ethnocentrism.

As has been recently suggested, 'the virtue of ideas from elsewhere is that they can unblock intellectual and cultural formations' (Carter, Donald and Squires, 1993, p. xv), and in an era characterized by 'time-space compression' and intensifying global imagery, one might imagine that the construction and dissemination of theoretical knowledges would be increasingly globalist in nature. Just as one of the orientations of postmodern thinking can invite us to welcome the dissolution of centre-periphery splits and North-South divides, we might imagine that new theoretical debates in the West are less prone to an implicit self-containing agenda than was traditionally the case in earlier times. In today's global times, it is possible to envisage an increasing de-territoriali-zation of knowledge, with the rapid flow of ideas, concepts, and information across cyberspace. Similarly, given the assumption that the postmodern insinu-ates a European recognition that, in cultural terms, it is no longer the unquestioned and dominant centre of the world (Young, 1990, p. 19), we might be encouraged to sustain the position that the postmodern sensibility an-nounces if not the end then at least the beginning of the need of Eurocentrism. Certainly, if we subscribe to the notion that the postmodern invokes plurality, difference, heterogeneity and hybridity, then we might well expect an emerging symbiosis between the post-colonial and postmodern modes of interpretation. We might be emboldened to anticipate the eclipse of Eurocentric or Euro-Americanist contextualizations of political and cultural theory. The agents of knowledge will no longer reside only or predominantly inside the imperial heartlands of the West; there will be an overlapping and an intertwining of knowledges and of different theoretical agendas and experiences; a series of mutually enhancing dialogues and conversations across the North-South divide will emerge with increasing impact. Now, while I do not wish to deny the existence of these sorts of trends, at the same time I want to emphasize here that the postmodern turn does not necessarily imply the end of Western ethnocentrism, and that there is a whole series of issues concerning the geopolitics of power and knowledge which requires much further analysis and discussion.

In contemporary cultural studies, one can discern an increasing interest in the question of the constitution of an inside and an outside, and this is clearly related to the impact of post-colonial literature. Grossberg (1992, p. 24), in his exploration of popular conservatism and postmodern culture, suggests that British cultural studies have been marked by a limited polysemy, a restricted range of voices. More significantly it has frequently been the case, as in the work of Raymond Williams, that the national culture is treated as if it were constructed entirely *within* the nation. As a result, there has been a strong tendency to fail to appreciate that the 'national-popular' is produced in the field of international relations through which there have been continuing efforts to appropriate, resist and control diverse other practices and popula-tions. For Grossberg, then, the colonial and imperial encounters are crucially constitutive of the national-popular and ought to belong at the core of cultural studies, either in Britain or presumably in any other First World society. Thus, for example, a related point can be made for the Untied States in the sense that there also there has been an orienting inclination to analyse American culture in isolation from Empire. As Kaplan (1993) expresses it, cultural studies have been 'left alone with America', and furthermore, in some of the writing around the post-colonial, the possible meanings and impact of imperial politics have tended to be bypassed. Can we, in the context of the United States, talk of a 'post-imperialist' as well as 'post-colonial' culture?

If we focus on the 'inside/outside' nexus, it is possible to make a distinction between two sorts of discussions. First, we can raise the question of the relationship between postmodern thinking as it has been developed inside the West and the analysis of imperial and colonial encounters. To what extent are such encounters represented and interrogated within the textual configurations of postmodern accounts, and how would we situate the possible absence of these signs of disruption? Second, in the context of the geopolitics of knowledge, does the postmodern sensibility carry with it a broadening out of the agents of knowledge and the terrain of analysis; do other themes and agendas from non-Western worlds find their way into these new ostensibly more subversive and heterogeneous frames of interpretation? Has the postmodern interruption displaced that traditionally widespread nostrum, held in the West, that it still strikes us as a paradox to consider an idea of knowledge, especially theoretical knowledge, that is not in the end of occidental origin.

In a passing, but assertive observation, Grewal and Kaplan(1994, p. 9), in their treatment of feminist theories and postmodern interventions, underscore the significance of developing new critiques of Eurocentrism, and write that 'it is impossible to analyse postmodernity without an understanding of geopolitics'. In a related series of thoughts on the 'predicament of culture', the critical anthropologist Clifford (1988, pp. 6–7) has also stressed the importance of geopolitical questions. He contends, for instance, that in any challenging of the dominant narratives of Western identity, the political issue of history as emergence becomes inescapable. The relations between West and non-West, and the origins of occidental power over other non-Western societies need to be seen as formative in the construction of political identities and dispositions.

Jameson (1992), as a well-known exponent of postmodern ideas, develops a similar argument in which he gives more attention to geopolitics in the context of cinema, aesthetics and power. A worthwhile differentiation is made between the First and Third Worlds; it is stated that First World thoughts and dreams about the Third World can have nothing in common with what the Third World is required to know about the First – being subaltern carries the possibility of knowledge with it, whereas domination entails forgetfulness and repression (Jameson, 1992, p. 199). We have here the idea that imperial culture engenders a geopolitical amnesia; that inside the citadels of Empire an essentialized vision of colonized lands erases the fact of conquest and represses the history of domination. Conversely, because of being subaltern, Third World peoples are induced to acquire knowledge about the First World; they are not permitted the luxury of being able to dream nor of forgetting the everyday implications of their geopolitical condition. Although there is an important insight in this position, at the same time, it is necessary to pursue a more nuanced portrayal of these two counterposed worlds. In another connected passage, Jameson writes that the very term 'Third World' seems to have become an embarrassment at a time when the 'realities of the economic have seemed to supplant the possibilities of collective struggle' ... 'human agency and politics seem to have been dissolved by the global corporate institutions we call late capitalism' (Jameson, 1992, p. 86). We have in these connected passages the idea that, while the Third World is oppressed by the First, the power of the economic, an implicit reference to the impact of neo-liberal policies in the South, appears to have stifled the possibility of collective struggle and political opposition. In one sense, Jameson, in contrast to a range of other contemporary thinkers of a postmodern persuasion, does put on to the agenda the continuing issue of the domination involved in North-South relations, but, like many others, he tends to create a homogeneous image out of the apparent lack of resistance. It is not only necessary to recall the subtle often subterranean forms of opposition skilfully documented by Scott (1990), but also to emphasize the heterogeneity, complexity and multidimensional nature of social movements within a whole range of Third World societies (Alvarez and Escobar, 1992; Wignaraja, 1993). The discussions around identity, subjectivity, power and difference so resonant in the societies of the North during the last decade or so have also been taking place in the societies of the South, and testify to the multiple and often perplexing nature of political change inside these societies.

In other instances where resistance is associated with Third World conditions, there has sometimes been an inclination to limit the nature of social struggle to the emergence of 'reactionary governments and sometimes bloody regimes'. Lyotard (1989, pp. 25–26), in debating the place of the Third World in considerations of the universal, suggests that poverty and the struggles of the poor are not conditions of universalization but rather conditions of localization and a return to traditional identities. Referring to the Algerian war of independence, he suggests that, although it was clear that this struggle would not lead to socialism, on an ethical basis the struggle for a new identity deserved support, even though Lyotard himself could not agree with the politics of that struggle. In contrast to Lyotard, the political philosopher Castoriadis (1991, p. 218) offers the view that the countries of the Third World still perhaps contain the possibility of making 'positive, original contribution to the necessary transformation of world society'. Referring to 'traditional cultural forms', Castoriadis notes that, while it is well known that these forms went together with exploitation, poverty and a whole range of negative factors, they also preserved a certain type of 'sociability and of socialization, and a certain type of human being'. According to Castoriadis, the solution to the present problems of humanity will have somehow to link together this element of sociability with what the West can contribute. If Western technique and knowledge can be transformed so as to contribute to the preservation and development of these authentic forms of sociability, in return it might be possible for Western peoples to 'learn something ... that they have forgotten, how to become inspired to revive truly communitarian forms of living' (ibid.).

Without romanticizing the non-Western other, Castoriadis introduces an often neglected theme of how we might learn from different practices, forms of social organization and interaction, and ethical attitudes present in the societies of the periphery. His point is not elaborated, and in invoking notions of community, it is important to avoid positive essentializations which contrast ideas of the selfish possessive individual with a collectively oriented spirit of mutual co-operation, solidarity and trust. These values might well be there but not as the necessary embodiment of all communities, just as possessiveness and individualism do not exhaust the complexity of the individual, for the psychic space of individuality is much more heterogeneous and polysemic. Inspired by a postmodern sensibility, one might expect a greater degree of openness and flexibility when we come to characterize North-South relations and the meanings attached to 'North' and to 'South'. The issues involved are contentious and the terrain is marked by controversy and the overlapping of dissonant positions, sometimes in the texts of the same author.

As one example, we can examine some of Baudrillard's interventions which, on the question of the characterization of the non-West or the Third World, exhibit a variety of oscillations. As I have indicated elsewhere (Slater 1992 and 1994), in the 1970s Baudrillard usefully pointed to the Western ethnocentrism of Marxist theory, whereas by the late 1980s, in works on *America* and *Cool Memories* a strong Eurocentric prejudice seems to have influenced his portrait of other Third World lands. In a later text, however, while still retaining an overly homogeneous, if not caricatured, image of the Third World as being lost to social movements and the hybridities of social action, Baudrillard develops a significantly critical view on the West's relation to alterity. In a section entitled the 'melodrama of difference', it is remarked that we in the West are engaged in an orgy of discovery, exploration and 'invention' of the Other, and Baudrillard connects the quest of alterity to the law of supply and demand; it has fallen under the law of the market, whereby our everyday universe 'is in thrall to a wild speculation on ... otherness and difference' (Baudrillard 1993a, p. 124). These critical remarks are followed by the suggestion that we can posit a salient difference between Western culture and other cultures in the following way. For Baudrillard, all other cultures are exceptionally hospitable; 'whereas we waver between the other as prey and the other as shadow ... other cultures still retain the capacity to incorporate what comes to them from without, including what comes from a Western universe, into their own rules of the game' (Baudrillard 1993a, 142). Nevertheless, those other cultures still tend to be inscribed under the sign of the 'primitive', just as Lyotard (1988) and Vattimo (1991) also tend to locate non-Western cultures. This contrasts with the approach more visible in post-colonial writing in which there is an emphasis on mixing, and the intermingling of 'modern' and 'traditional' within which the meanings of these categories become stretched and refashioned into a new assemblage. It might also be countered that Baudrillard is engaging in a form of positive essentialization because the capacity for hospitality might not be equally distributed across all other cultures. Also to what extent does the Western 'we' only encapsulate the other as either prey or shadow? Before taking these points a little further, let us also refer to another of Baudrillard's texts where the question of racism is directly tackled.

In his analysis of symbolic exchange and death, Baudrillard makes an instructive link between conceptualizations of universality and the emergence of racism. He argues, for example, that the progress of humanity and culture is the chain of discriminations with which the Others can be stigmatized with inhumanity, and consequently with nullity. Accordingly, the definition of the 'Human' contracts in relation to the succession of cultural developments, and so each step towards the universal is associated with an ever more stringent limitation so that eventually humanity's definitive universality will coincide with the excommunication of all people – 'the purity of the concept alone in the void'. It is precisely in this context that Baudrillard avers that 'racism is modern' ... 'previous races or cultures were ignored or eliminated but never under the sign of a universal Reason ...' ... 'it is our undifferentiated concept of man that gives rise to discrimination'. Further, 'it is due to the extent of our progress that we have since become racists, and not only towards Indians and cannibals: the increasing hold of rationality on our culture has meant the successive extradiction of inanimate nature, animals and inferior races into the Inhuman, while the cancer of the Human has invested the very society it claimed to contain within its absolute superiority' (Baudrillard 1993b, pp. 125–6). I have quoted at some length from these passages because they are particularly relevant to my argument. Equally they also make a general point that tends to be forgotten, namely that racism does not belong to some premodern, or pre-rational, or pre-Enlightenment time – it is immanently present within the project of Western progress and scientific expansion. Moreover, these passages are strangely ironic in the sense that, originally written in French in the mid-1970s, they echo Baudrillard's earlier critique of Marxist schemas but severely jar with his later patronizing remarks on Third World peoples, referred to above. Nor is there a necessary time 'progression' because his work on the 'transparency of evil' was also written in the late 1980s.

Irony and vacillation aside, I should like to propose that there is a number of enabling elements in Baudrillard's perspective. His critique of universalism, shared by Lyotard and Vattimo, is formulated in a way that provides a linked understanding of racism. The discursive constructions of notions of mission and manifest destiny, of the spreading and implanting of a way of life which has been posited as superior, are often neglected or belittled in their historical and geopolitical impact. In addition his reference to the 'hospitality' of other cultures, although perhaps overgeneralized, can be added to the comment made by Castoriadis concerning sociability and ethico-political sensibilities still not corroded by one-dimensional market economics. The emergence of the imperialist imperative in Europe as well as in the United States does not give the only content to ethnocentrism and racism but, as the Cuban poet and artist Mosquera (1993, p. 530) indicates, Eurocentrism is different from ethnocentrism because the former refers to the fact that the global hegemony of European culture 'has imposed its own ethnocentrism as a universal value, which other cultures have long since internalized'. This is an important point because obviously it is the case that not only do ethnocentrism and racism assume a variety of historical forms and geopolitical locations, but also the fact of conquest and the subjugation of peoples are not just Western proclivities. Rather, what is being argued here is that the scale, intensity and universalist ambition of the West's imperial project express its uniqueness. Despite their necessary distinction and the complex array of different forms that they have exhibited, colonialism and imperialism do share a commonality in being rooted in the invasive discourse of Western modernity. Invasive because the universalizing intent of 'progress', 'modernity' 'rationality' and 'development' carried and implanted these practices into a wide constellation of peripheral countries. Such a universalizing intent was founded on a binary vision of the world that posited 'peoples with history and those without' or 'civilized as opposed to barbaric nations'; and the diffusion of the sense of mission was coupled to a belief that all peoples would benefit from the spread of Western civilization. Western universalism can be viewed in this context in relation to a number of connected beliefs, which are concisely drawn out for us by Dussel (1993), in his critique of modernity and the West.

Firstly, European civilization understands itself as the most developed and the superior civilization, and this ethos of supremacy induces it to civilize, uplift and educate the more primitive, barbaric and underdeveloped civilizations and cultures. The pathway for such progress and development should be that already followed by Europe in its own history, and in those instances where the primitive opposes the civilizing process, the carriers of modernity are justified in the last instance in resorting to the violence necessary to remove any obstacles to development and modernization. This violence, which produces victims, can take on an almost ritualistic character in the sense that the 'civilizing hero' invests his victims with the character of being participants in a process of redemptive sacrifice. Consequently, from the point of view of Western modernity, the primitive or barbarian is in a state of guilt for resisting the civilizing process; this then permits the bearers of modernity to present themselves as the emancipators or redeemers of the victims from their own guilt. Finally, given the fact that the civilizing and redemptive character of modernity is stressed, the suffering and costs of modernization imposed on less-advanced, traditional peoples can be presented as inevitable and necessary. Running through this interrelated set of contentions and driving assumptions we can locate father/child and male/female images which have been connected to notions of paternal leadership of 'child-like' peoples and the necessary penetration of passive peoples in need of 'civilization'. From the nineteenth-century philosophical writings of Hegel and John Stuart Mill to this century's Ortega y Gasset and Husserl, Western philosophy has effectively sedimented such views in the inner reaches of First World thought and culture.

Critchley (1995) has taken up this theme in a stimulating discussion of the relations between imperialist thought and Western philosophy. He argues, for example, that philosophy tells itself a story that affirms the link between individuality and universality by embodying that link through defining the European philosopher as the 'functionary of humanity'. Philosophy demands universal validity and yet it always seems to begin and end in Europe. It would appear that 'no other culture could be like us, because we have exclusive rights to philosophy, to the scientific-theoretical attitude'. And yet, as Critchley, following Said, suggests 'such philosophical sentiments do not seem far from the core belief of imperialism ... that it is the responsibility or *burden* of the metropolitan powers to bring our universal values to bear on native peoples, ... to colonize and transform other cultures according to our own world-view and to conceal oppression under the cloak of a mission' (p. 20). Critchley goes on to remark that if we provisionally admit that there is a racist or imperialist logic in philosophy – 'then could it ever be otherwise?' (ibid.).

What is then suggested is the beginnings of a de-sedimentation of tradition within which the forgetfulness of origins is remembered. To challenge the origins of a tradition, to indicate why and where the founding moments of an interpretative enterprise come into being is to begin to interrogate the pre-given and potentially open the way for a more critical and heterogeneous tradition – or to replace the imputed singularity of tradition with a plurality of trajectories. In deconstructing tradition we can also welcome the possibility of the hybridity of knowledges, and move away from the historical and geopolitical sovereignty of European thought. Rather than follow Foucault (1973, pp. 376–7) in positing a Hegelian distinction between 'societies with history' and those without, of preserving the idea that it is only in the West that the 'mode of pure theory' is possible, we might want to explore the multiple origins of critical knowledges and employ our geopolitical imaginations to help de-sediment the occidental enclosure of knowledge and theoretical reflection. When Foucault refers to the 'unconscious processes that characterize the system of a given culture', and the 'double articulation of the history of individuals upon the unconscious of culture, and of the historicity of those cultures upon the unconscious of individuals' (pp. 379–80), we may want to incorporate into our studies the analysis of the geopolitical unconscious of the West that tends to occlude the history of imperial encounters. Adopting an enabling element of the postmodern, we may want to invert the primacy of Western thought, or subject it to a playful mixing with its others on the territory of knowledge and power. But this does not have to be constituted through a celebration of the other or a romanticization of difference. Making the non-Western other equivalent to the 'noble savage' in contemporary form, or constructing an essentialized vision of indigenous peoples, as de Certeau (1989, p. 231) tends to do with his statement that 'it is the same Indian communities which were oppressed and eclipsed by the Western "democracies" that are now proving to be the only ones capable of offering modes of self-management ... ', inclines us towards simply reversing the uniformity of imagery. It is perhaps symptomatic of a widespread reading of the non-West, particularly common in anthropological texts, that the agents of contemporary knowledge predominantly reside in the West, and that the non-West is made to signify the strange, the ritualistic, the traditional and the exotic.

When we move into a consideration of the postmodern, we can also discern the same tendency, as if again it is only in the West that this new problematic has relevance. On another occasion, I have dealt in some detail with the way this feature of the politics of knowledge expresses a continuity between the modern and the postmodern (Slater, 1994). Moreover, it would be precipitate to imagine that this relates only to debates inside the West, since Lee (1994), in his excursion into postmodernism and the Third World, tacitly adheres to the view that postmodern thought is a Western creation; writing from Malaysia, he associates the Third World with modernization and post-colonial writing, whereas the First World is used as a context to explore some of the main ideas of the postmodern turn. This is not meant to be a criticism because availabilities of literatures across the different worlds of the South are known to be a crucial problem. At the same time, the kinds of modernizations, and the relations with metropolitan countries vary enormously across these same worlds, and so the contexts of intellectual debates and the types of issues that are prioritized tend not to escape such underlying variations, which does not mean to say that there have been no common concerns, since in the 1970s, the influence of dependency perspectives stretched across Africa, Asia and Latin America.

Heterogeneity within the Third World can also prompt us to signal the need for some attention to the differences inside the First World; differences, that is, in the context of colonial encounters and imperial politics. Two points can be mentioned here. First, it is frequently the case that the 'West' or the 'North' is implicitly based on the assumed realities of Britain, France, Germany and the United States, and the southern European countries of Spain, Portugal and Italy tend to be amalgamated to a 'Northern template', The specificity of Spanish and Portuguese colonialisms in Latin America, and the differential impact on the evolving social and cultural structures of those lands since the fifteenth century are often absent themes in the discussion of Eurocentric projects and practices. In those cases the association of colonialism with merchant as opposed to industrial capital, and the much earlier attainment of constitutional Independence from the early nineteenth century onwards generated a series of different experiences of political configurations. Second, although the United States is rightly included under the general rubric of being an imperialist power, together with European states, the historical specificity of US–Latin American encounters, set as they were in the last century and into this in the framework of invasion, interventions and missions of progress, is commonly occluded. A key difference was the ambivalence of US imperial politics, which is to be explained in terms of the amalgam of the original anti-colonialist sentiments of the early founding struggles for the nation with the sense of imperial mission and manifest destiny which legitimized the subversion of other nations' sovereignties. When engaging in analyses of de-sedimentation, and the re-activation of suppressed histories, these kinds of differentiation need to be kept in mind.

At the beginning of these interpretative notes and reflections, I posed a number of questions around the meanings of the postmodern. Two of these questions are often separated but in a revealing way they can be fruitfully linked, as in fact I have tried to do so far. The situation of colonial and imperial encounters, the location of their significance, do not seem to vary dramatically across the 'modern/post-modern divide'. While Baudrillard, Lyotard and Vattimo all intermittently refer to aspects of imperialism, Jameson assigns the most significance to this theme, perhaps someone might argue because more than other writers associated with the postmodern persuasion, he is still working within a critical Marxist frame that lends force to this kind of position. In contrast, Rorty (1991) has championed the presumed superiority of Western liberal democracy, arguing that, although imperialism may well be rooted in the West's historical project, it has also been inside the West that the critiques of imperialism have emerged. This, of course, then raises again the issue of the agents of knowledge, and the need to challenge the posited 'historical sovereignty of European thought'.

In the development of post-colonial literary theory, Bhabha (1994) has pursued a line of analysis that illuminates the new forms of ethnocentric positioning in postmodern writing, but avoids following a Jameson-style late-Marxist critique. Instead, he emphasizes hybridity and the intermingling of texts and practices, seeing colonialism in a somewhat more nuanced form – the frontal assaults of a Said are absent. But in another territory of theory, in Latin America, the continuing awareness of 'imperial ethnocentrism' (García Canclini, 1993) is combined with other lines of investigation that take us into the domains of identity, subjectivity, culture and hybridity. In this zone of thought, the work of Nelly Richard is particularly emblematic.

In a short but illustrative essay on postmodern appropriations and counter-appropriations, Richard (1993) tackles the question posed by the Euro-Americanist hegemony over international theory – the problem, for example, that theory constructed in the West is inscribed with a universality which is diffused through a series of international channels of communication, and contrasted, implicitly or explicitly with descriptive, empirical narratives produced in the South, or, if there is theory, then it is enframed as being localized and fragmented in significance. Richard (1993, pp. 453–4) writes that 'for any periphery dependent on circuits of international organization, distribution and circulation of metropolitan knowledge, the theoretical challenge is how to interpret the problem of *cultural transference*' ... 'how are we to make use of international theoretical conceptualizations – knowing that they form part of the systematic normative standards of the center – but without, for all that, yielding to its grammar of authority?' And further, 'how are we to take advantage of theoretical-conceptual categories put into circulation by its networks of discourse without adhering to its hierarchizations of culture power?' In one partial answer to these kinds of perplexing questions, an answer that parallels some of Bhabha's interpretations, Richard suggests that postmodernity's themes of discontinuity, fragmentation and ephemerality could be taken up peripherally as a postcolonial instrument of decolonization insofar, she adds, as they promise to liberate us from subjection to hierarchical totalities. Later on Richard (p. 458) argues that it ought to be possible to open oneself to a dialogue with the centre that 'could violate the geopolitical borders created by metropolitan control through our own complicities with its counter-hegemonic voices – those which interest themselves, democratically, in the others of the Other, in the differences of Otherness'.

There is in Richard and in other Latin American writers an attitude of ambivalence towards the postmodern. On the one hand, it can be regarded as enabling in its destabilization of the meta-narratives of Western progress and modernization, but, on the other, in its tendency to dissolve centre-periphery divisions and in its evasiveness with regard to global inequalities in power and income, it must be regarded as collusive with the contemporary practices of neo-liberalism. Richard's work must not be taken as constituting the main or most influential current of Latin American thought on the postmodern because there are other writers, such as Reigadas (1988), for example, who are far more hostile to the postmodern and link it much more closely to the latest wave of Western truth on culture and development. Nor does the discussion which Richard highlights exhaust the debates taking place in Latin America, because these also relate to issues of the politics of identity, culture hybridization and the rethinking of democracy and modernity (Brunner, 1994).

Above all, perhaps Richard's intervention does foreground the recurrent issue of the interweaving of inside and outside, in the context of international relations and power conflicts, and with regard to the geopolitics of knowledge. She takes a distance from the politics of authenticity, or of the recapturing of the 'traditional', and critically welcomes the potential of hybrid knowledge. If the global in the arena of theory is to be empowering, then a move away from the symbols of separation and uniformity ought to be seen as constructive.

In terms of re-imagining our own patterns of thought and interpretation, I have suggested, in a very brief and schematic way, that the geopolitics of power and knowledge, as contextualized with reference to the postmodern debate, assumes a double meaning. First, we can be encouraged to think more about the function of forgetfulness; retracking imperial politics and spatial power can help us to reactivate hidden meanings that have been quite fundamental in the constitution of our own societies, and unavoidably in their relation with others. Second, when endeavouring to map out new terrains of reflection and critical engagement, we can perhaps connect more fully with those border crossings of knowledge and theory that do not necessarily offer up immediate or tangible solutions but perhaps do have the potential to broaden the frame of our understanding. In one sense, the post-colonial turn embraces this possibility and one feels that the crossroads of the postmodern and the post-colonial will come to be a new site of intellectual creativity. The potential activity at this crossroads will, I hope, help to bring about the further breaking up of the occidental enclosure of knowledge.

References

Alvarez, S. and Escobar, A., *The Making of Social Movements in Latin America,*(Boulder, Westview Press, 1992).

Baudrillard, J., *The Transparency of Evil*, (London and New York, Verso Book, 1993a).

Baudrillard, J., *Symbolic Exchange and Death*, (London, Sage, 1993b).

Bhabha, H., *The Location of Culture*, (London and New York, Routledge, 1994).

Brunner, J., *Bienvenidos a la Modernidad*, (Santiago de Chile, Editorial Planeta, 1994).

Carter, E., Donald, J. and Squires, J., Introduction, in Carter, E., et.al (eds), *Space and Place – theories of identity and location*, (London, Routledge, 1993), pp. vii–xv.

Castoriadis, C., *Philosophy, Politics, Autonomy*, (Oxford, New York and London, Oxford University Press, 1991).

Certeau, M. de, (1989). *Heterologies*, (Minneapolis, University of Minneapolis Press 1989).

Clifford, J., *The Predicament of Culture*, (Cambridge, Mass. and London, Harvard University Press, 1988).

Critchley, S., 'Black Socrates?', *Radical Philosophy*, Jan/Feb., no. 69, pp. 17–26, (1995).

Dussel, E., 'Eurocentrism and Modernity', *Boundary 2*, vol. 20, no. 3, Fall, pp. 65–76, (1993).

Foucault, M., *The Order of Things – the archaeology of the human sciences*, (New York, Vintage Books, 1973).

García-Canclini, N., *Transforming Modernity*, (Houston, University of Texas Press, 1993).

Grewel, I., and Kaplan C., 'Introduction: Transnational Feminist Practices and Questions of Postmodernity' in Grewal, I and Kaplan C., (eds), *Scattered Hegemonies*, (Minneapolis, University of Minnesota Press, 1994), pp. 1–33.

Grossberg, L., *We Gotta Get Out of This Place – popular conservatism and postmodern culture*. (London and New York, Routledge, 1992).

Jameson, F., *The Geopolitical Aethestic*, (Bloomington and Indianapolis, Indiana University Press, 1992).

Kaplan, A., '"Left Alone with America": The Absence of Empire in the Study of American Culture', in Kaplan, A., and Pease, D. E., (eds), *Cultures of United States Imperialism*, (Durham and London, Duke University Press, 1993), pp. 3–21.

Lee, R. L. M., 'Modernization, Postmodernism and the Third World', *Current Sociology*, vol. 42, no. 2, summer, (1994), pp. 1–66.

Lyotard, J-F., *The Differend – phrases in dispute*, (Manchester, University of Manchester Press, 1988).

Lyotard, J-F., 'Defining the Postmodern' in Appignanesi, L., (ed.), *Postmodernism*, (Institute of Contemporary Arts, 1989), pp. 7–10.

Mosquera, G., 'The Marco Polo Syndrome: A Few Problems Surrounding Art and Eurocentrism', *The South Atlantic Quarterly*, vol. 92, no. 3, summer, pp. 529–42, (1993).

Reigadas, M., 'Neomodernidad y Postmodernidad: preguntado desde América Latina' in Mari, E., (ed.), ¿Postmodernidad?, (Buenos Aires, Editorial Biblos, 1988), pp. 113–45.

Richard, N., 'Cultural Peripheries: Latin America and Postmodernist De-Centering', *Boundary 2*, vol. 20, no. 3, fall, pp. 156–61, (1993).

Rorty, R., *Objectivity, Relativism and Truth*, Philosophical Papers vol. 1, (Cambridge, Cambridge University Press, 1991).

Scott, J., *Domination and the Arts of Resistance*, (New Haven and London, Yale University Press, 1990).

Slater, D., 'Theories of Development and Politics of the Post-Modern – exploring a border zone', *Development and Change*, vol. 23, no. 3. pp. 283–319, (1992).

Slater, D., 'Exploring Other Zones of the Postmodern: Problems of Ethnocentrism and Difference across the North-South Divide' in Rattansi, A. and Westwood, S. (eds), *Racism, Modernity and Identity*, (Cambridge, Polity Press, 1994), pp. 87–125.

Vattimo, G., *The End of Modernity*, (Cambridge, Polity Press, 1991).

Wignaraja, P., (ed.), *New Social Movements in the South: empowering the people*, (London, Zed Books, 1993).

Young R., *White Mythologies: Writing History and the West*, (New York and London, Routledge, 1990).

14

Postmodern Space and Japanese Tradition

Augustin Berque

The rise of Japan, facing the relative decline of Western nations, shakes the foundations of modernity. It is indeed no mere coincidence that a power stemming from a non-European culture asserts itself at a time when the question of postmodernity is of general concern. Inasmuch as modernity has expressed the hegemony of the modern-classical Western paradigm – that of the scientific revolution of the seventeenth century, symbolized by the names of Bacon (experiment), Galileo (the end of geocentrism), Descartes (dualism), Newton (universal space) – the progressive disrepute of this paradigm can naturally appear as a condemnation of its author and propagator, the Occident, on which non-Western cultures seem now to be getting their own back: traditional world views, such as those of Taoism and Zen, would have known postmodern enlightenment immediately, without need to go through modernity, that Western Utopia. As is well known, such views have not been lacking in prophets, from Pop Zen California to New Science Andalusia.

I intend here to stress that these views are simplistic. Not in the name of the modern-classical Western paradigm, which Europe itself started to attack in the first half of the nineteenth century, since Riemann and non-Euclidean geometrics; but by showing that postmodernity is more than a denial of (Western) modernity. To do so, I shall select some similarities between Japanese traditions and postmodern themes, and argue that, if such similarities do exist, they do not mean that Japan was already postmodern before its occidentalization: postmodernity is a global trend which leads us beyond any modern or non-modern, Western or non-Western culture. Yet Japanese traditional culture is certainly one of those which can give us a hint of what postmodernity might be.

Quotation and *mitate*

Postmodernism is probably, above all, a way of seeing which asserts the rights of sensitivity, or even the rights of aesthetics, against the rigours of rationalism. Indeed it is an art, architecture, which has most clearly illustrated the disrepute of the modern paradigm by rejecting the Newtonian space of the so-called international style: that homogeneous, isotropic and infinite − in a word, neutral − space in which similarly rectangular buildings have mushroomed all over the world, regardless of any locality. To this universal space in which the *Zweckrational ität* (instrumental rationality) of modern architecture extolled itself, postmodernism opposed the right to enjoy forms just for themselves, forms which the modern movement has subordinated to function. Still more: the right to play with forms in the apparent absence of any function.

The intense consumption of forms which was entailed thereof could not but rely heavily on the catalogue of past or foreign styles. This made quotation a characteristic of postmodernism. Correlatively − at least in Europe − flourished the neo-vernacular style of vacation houses which, by referring to local traditions, is also a kind of quotation. In the 1970s, all our built environment seemed on the verge of passing from the era of functionalism to that of formal games − to the era of simulacra, according to a rather widely held opinion, which is not far from seeing there the end of Meaning, if not that of the world.

Such a disenchantment may be avoided if one considers that Japan has systematically practised, throughout its entire history, and without any harm for semantics, a real ecology of quotation. Not only did Japan make nothing of transplanting foreign models on its own soil − it goes from the Chinese pattern of ancient capitals to the *sake nûbô* (nouveau, after the fashion of Beaujolais) which made its début in the autumn of 1990 − but, under the name of *mitate* ('seing as'), transposition was even instituted as a major process of Japan's aesthetics. The *mitate* concerns all domains of art: it can be used as well in literature as in gardens, in clothes as well as in cooking; and its pith is precisely to be appreciated as a passage from one domain to another. Accordingly, Isozaki Arata's postmodernistic stance, when he transposed and inverted the Roman Capitol to Tsukuba (for that city's civic centre), was nothing else than the continuation of a trend with which any Japanese can feel at home.

Italians would certainly not have deemed it aright, had Paolo Portoghesi transposed the form of the Alcazar from Seville to Rome, for his mosque, even if he had inverted it. Indeed, the Europeans − be it on account of their irreclaimable substantialism, or be it a remnant of modern functionalism − eventually could not stomach postmodernistic quotation, at least to the same degree as the Japanese (or, for that matter, Americans as well) who, from a long past, have been prone to consider and transfer forms as such (transferring substances is another matter). If postmodernity is to be the age of form (modernity having been that of substance and function), then one can probably find some clues to its logic in the mechanisms of *mitate*.

Decentring and *sugoroku*

If the new mosque of Rome could not be an imitation of the Alcazar, this is, of course, because there remain in Europe things with which one cannot play.

A certain moral tradition made Portoghesi consider a transcendence and a context, that is, a determining ground that he had to translate into original forms. To transpose existing forms from elsewhere would have flouted this need for authenticity. What the Europeans, today, do not even tolerate for their vacation houses (displacing forms regardless of the place), all the more so, could not be acceptable in sacred architecture.

There lies a profound difference between the ephemeral infatuation for postmodernistic quotation in the West, on the one hand, and on the other hand, the tenacious bent of the Japanese for *mitate*. If, in Japan, 'seing as' (*mitateru*) is admitted as a matter of course, it is because no transcendence, no ideal essence compels forms to express a ground or a substance which would anchor and subordinate them. Forms have a value of their own, wherever they may be. They are not transformed by submitting to the perspective of an invariable point of view. On the contrary, it is the point of view which displaces itself and which 'sees as' if it were the eye of another, elsewhere. Lake Biwa will be seen as if the observer were in central China (facing the original Eight views of the Xiang and the Xiao, *Shô-Shô hakkei*, of which Lake Biwa is supposed to offer a replica), or a ski slope in Hokkaidô will be seen as if one were in Switzerland.

This is more than the mere evocation of an image. The observing subject seems to be transposed to another place, by dint of a decentring process. In fact, the physical organization of space, in traditional Japan, abounded in such decentrements. Except where Chinese models had been deliberately imitated, there were very few cardinal orientations, symmetries, enfilades through which the subject could secure a centrality comparable with that of the modern subject in Europe. Was this disorder? Certainly not; but rather a bent for limited and piecemeal orders, as opposed to general ones. In Shitamachi Edo, even the principle of orthogonal street planning was piecemeal: it was applied like a sort of mosaic, the pieces of which were topologically orientated according to various beacons, *sono ba sono ba* ('from place to place', i.e. from hand to mouth), it seems. The spatial organization of this huge city has indeed been compared to *sugoroku*, a kind of snakes and ladders, in which the cast of the dice made you go from one place to another, without a constant orientation. In fact, some of these games – and this is no coincidence – represented the famous places (*meisho*) of the city.

In such an organization of space, it is not the places which conform to the integrative and stable point of view of the (modern) subject. On the contrary, it is the subject itself which shifts to places and conforms to them.

Land art and *chô-geijutsu*

On account of the laws of perspective, modernity had established an irretrievable distance between presence (that of the real environment in which the subject looking at a picture is placed) and representation (that of the illusive landscape shown by the picture). When looking at a landscape drawn according to these laws, the observer is definitely outside of it. But the disparagement of the modern-classical Western paradigm has questioned this separation; first with the abandonment of the laws of perspective in 'modern' art (e.g. in Cézanne's landscapes, which for that matter were already postmodern); and more radically on the eve of World War I, when the Italian Futurists declared that they would place the spectator inside the picture.

This is indeed what was realized by the practice of 'happening', through which the spectator effectively participates in the accomplishment of the work of art; and more specifically by land art, which completely abolishes the distance between environment (presence) and the work of art (representation). When facing a work of land art, neither dualism nor perspective – those tokens of modernity – are relevant anymore: here the subjective image is the real world, the picture is incorporated into the thing itself instead of being detached from it, and the modern subject's distanciation from the environment is annihilated.

Is land art only cosmetic (a sham environment), instead of cosmic or cosmogenetic? Asking such a question is to defer to the paradigm of modernity, which poses that the subject and the object have respectively a stable, substantial and distinct identity. In such a view, one must not identify any entity with another, which it is not. This entails that make-ups and cosmetics are not modern, because they change identity: mocking substance, they make that Being *becomes*. No Cartesian *cogito* can exist in such conditions; only feeling – the sensation of being another. This is why, in the lawful structure (*costruzzione legittima*, as Alberti called perspective) of modernity, make-up belongs to bagatelle, to feminine fickleness, or to that unfunctional 'decoration' which the modern movement, in architecture, abhorred.

This is to say that land art is essentially postmodern. In that respect, it is interesting to learn that Japan, as early as the twelfth century, practised a kind of landscaping that evokes land art: *gyaku mitate*, or 'reverse seing as'. In the normal way, *mitate* consists, for instance, in transposing a landscape into a garden, from full scale to reduced scale. When reversed, this process will consist in transposing a garden scenery into a full-size environment. Taira no Kiyomori, for example, had a *gyaku mitate* carried out at Miyajima (Itsukushima), following a garden he was fond of, in Kyôto.

Of course, in practice, *gyaku mitate* was not so frequent as *mitate*, because it needed considerably more material means. Normal 'seing as' is definitely less expensive, because it is fundamentally a metaphor (e.g. a literary trope). Metaphors enable one to enjoy more than one representation at a time. They multiply landscapes, among others. In present-day Japanese cities, where land prices are too high to allow for much practical landscaping, people have invented many devices which rely on this principle. One of these is *tomason* (or *chô-geijutsu*, i.e. 'super art'), things which have attained pure gratuity because the rapid change of the city has deprived them of any function; such as these 'pure staircases' (*junsui kaidan*) which lead to nothing because a wall replaced the door; these porch roofs which remain although their porch has disappeared, etc. No need for an architect, and even less for a building contractor: environment here becomes a fantastic landscape all by itself, the real becomes a work of art before any artistic intervention.

One certainly could find *tomason* elsewhere (in fact, this is more or less what the situationists were advocating in France, in the 1960s), but to appreciate it fully, one had better live in a city like Tôkyô, where there is no evident landscape at first glance. You must discover, or rather create it, by changing the ordinary way of looking at the city. If the city, such as Paris, has already been conceived and built as a landscape, art is plenty, and super art is no fun.

Golf and *kata*

The cult of the body is probably another attribute of postmodernity. Modern Man, as for him, had subordinated his body to the accomplishment of serious tasks. For this, he had straightened it, washed it, disciplined it, dressed it in grey, and drilled it in interrupted coition. For certain, he left it some loopholes, like sport or vacation, but these were mainly conceived of as functional (to maintain the work-force), and anyway they were not generally granted before the twentieth century , when the paradigm of modernity was in fact already disintegrating. The fact is that, through these loopholes which, for the sake of hygiene, had been drilled into the lawful structure of modernity, the wind of a strange law soon started to blow: that of the body, of the senses, which modern rationality had turned out ... Today, it is no secondary duty to go to one's vacation house; it has even become a prime necessity to be able to surf and ski, or at least to maintain one's body in a state of virtual glide, with a sun-tanned cheek, a flat belly, and firm breasts under one's leotard. *Sentio, ergo sum*: isn't my body in form?

To be sure, much of this is play; but people observe the rules of the game all the more strictly as it is a matter of form, the form of one's own body. What could be more pressing? And though forms beget formalism – this is, forgetting substance altogether for the sake of form – most worshippers of the body practise their cult in earnest. They are confident that duly performing the rites will give them substance, i.e. physical ability to perform real feats.

With the notions of *shugyô* (ascetic exercise) and of *kata* (martial forms), Japan has institutionalized quite similar principles in various traditional fields. This has something to do with the fact that, today, people in this country are so fond of golf. Indeed golf is a sport where the observance of forms is of prime importance: performing the proper gesture with the proper furniture, much more than physical gifts, is the key to substance (success, and even the mere pleasure to play). This fits exactly the traditional Japanese bent for codified gestures. In martial arts such as *karate*, the perfect observance of a *kata* is supposed to give the utmost efficacy. This is why people indefinitely polish their *kata*. On the same grounds, a Japanese salaryman, on weekdays, while waiting for the next train on an underground platform, will mimic a golf gesture with his umbrella in the guise of a club, and on weekends he will practise inside a net in the guise of a course. Maybe some day, in some higher function, he will go to a real course and eventually perform the feats which those forms should entail; but this is not really the problem. Nor is it the problem, in *karate*, really to kill someone. If it were so, then all these exercises would be no more than a modern functionalization of the body; which they definitely are not. These forms have their own ends in themselves; that is, in the moves of one's proper body. And this is precisely why, in the Japanese version of postmodernity, the golfer's body does not need a wide course, nor that of the surfer a big wave, to celebrate its own cult in due form; polishing the matrix of virtual feats will do.

A distant look at oneself

The dynamics of modernity relied on what has been called the 'withdrawal of the subject'; that is, the process through which the individual subject established a distance between itself and its whole environment, things and other people alike, which from thereon were objectified. This objectifying process made possible modern natural sciences, and later (because objectifying humankind itself was more difficult) the social sciences.

According to the modern classical Western paradigm, a complete separation of the subject from the object is possible and desirable. In fact, the very development of the sciences which were based on this dualism eventually has led to the idea that pure duality is only theoretical. In the social sciences, in particular, there is no such thing as a genuine object: the observer (the subject) always participates in some way in the reality he or she is observing; or, to say it the other way round, the observer, at least partially, is instituted in his/her very subjectiveness by the reality he/she is supposed to objectify.

Acknowledging that pure objectivity is impossible, and that reality is always subjective to some degree – a phenomenon which has been called 'the comeback of the subject' – does not mean a return to the premodern indistinction of the objective and the subjective. On the contrary, it implies a growing objectivity (not to be confused with positivism and dualism). In fact, the modern withdrawal of the subject has not ceased; but it has come to a point where the subject objectifies itself as a subject – not an object, as positivism and scientism (e.g. in Spencer's social Darwinism) had wrongly assumed. The postmodern subject, so to speak, has become able to observe its own moves on the scene of its own subjectivity.

This amounts to saying that environment is not only constituted of objects (as in the modern view). It is also a landscape, into which the subject itself is engaged with all its senses. One of the most conspicuous symptoms of this changing world view is the disrepute of the modern movement in architecture. We have come to understand that human beings cannot live in a strictly functional environment. They need what Zhuangzi called 'the usefulness of the useless' (*muyô no yô* in Japanese): all those things which modernism had neglected or rejected and which, under the name of amenities, have come to be felt as necessary. For instance, efficient sewage facilities are not enough; our cities also need beautiful riversides.

That this subject has become able to handle (to some extent) its own subjectivity poses the question of self-reference – the postmodern theme *par excellence*. Indeed, from cybernetics to ecology (e.g. Lovelock's Gaia hypothesis), but also to logic (e.g. Gödel's theorems) and to psychology, our age is dominated by this idea.

Self-reference, to put it simply by way of an image, consists in looking at oneself from the outside of oneself. In this respect, it is striking to remember that, five centuries ago, Zeami (1364–1443) used quite similar images when speaking of the art of the *nô* actor. He coined such expressions as *riken no ken* ('the look of distant look') or *kensho no ken* ('the look from the place looked at') to show that the true actor should be conscious of his own figure as if he were the public, able to observe himself even from his own back. Zeami opposed this distant look (*riken*) to the look issuing from the ego proper (*gaken*).

This distinction between *gaken* and *riken* seems quite analogous to that between *intuitus* (Descartes' word for the look of the modern subject on to the object) and the postmodern *mise en abyme* of the subject by itself. Is this enough to say that fifteenth-century Japan already possessed the key to postmodernity?

Though we can certainly find plenty of inspiration in such Japanese traditions to free ourselves from the deadlocks of the modern classical Western paradigm, we must be conscious that Zeami's *riken* cannot be truly postmodern. It is definitely not beyond modernity, and it cannot, as such, be a solution to our problems, because it does not refer whatsoever to what the modern subject's *intuitus* on the world actually has been. Invoking *riken* – or tradition in general – as such cannot cure the plight of our world. This plight has arisen from the proper logic of modernity, and consequently, it can be cured only if we transcend this logic. Denying or ignoring it is not enough.

In my view, transcending modernity can be done only by fully reckoning what has been its essential deed, the discovery of the physical world as such; that is, the possibility of knowing objectively the laws of nature, by observing it from outside the phenomenal world in which all cultures, before modernity, had been entrapped. This also can be understood as a *riken no ken*. It was first conceived of in abstract terms when Copernicus, then Galileo, showed that the Earth moves around the Sun, not the reverse. Modernity's illusion, or Utopia, has been to assume that this physical or objective world, as opposed to the phenomenal world (in which it is the sun that moves in the sky), was the only real world. But, towards the end of modernity, in the twentieth century, we have come to understand that reality was no less phenomenal than physical. In other words, the world exists only inasmuch as it is both objective and subjective.

This latter discovery was symbolized by the astronauts who, looking at the Earth from the Moon, said that it was beautiful and irreplaceable. By doing so, they expressed in sensible terms the postmodern synthesis of the physical (Earth as a celestial body) and the phenomenal (Earth as the abode of humanity), which modernity had dissociated.

It is interesting to note that this symbol – looking at the Earth from the Moon – is no other than a distant look of humanity on its own world. I like to think of it as the *riken no ken* which opened the age of postmodernity.

References

Akasegawa, Genpei, *Chôgeijutsu tomason,* (Tokyo, Hakuya Shobô, 1985).

Ashihara, Yoshinobu, *Kakureta chitsujo. Nijûisseiki no toshi ni mukatte,* (Tokyo, Chûôkôronsha, 1986).

Berque, Augustin, *Kûkan no Nihon bunka,* (Tokyo, Chikuma Shobô, 1985).

Berque, Augustin, *Fûdo no Nihon. Shizen to bunka no tsûtai,* (Tokyo, Chikuma Shobô, 1988).

Berque, Augustin, *Nihon no fûkei, Seiô no keikan, soshite zôkei no jidai,* (Tokyo, Kôdansha, 1990).

Berque, Augustin, *Le Sauvage et l'artifice,* (Paris, Gallimard, 1986); engl. transl. *Nature, Artifice and Japanese Culture,* (London, Pilkington, 1996).

Berque, Augustin, *Du Geste à la Cité,* (Paris, Gallimard, 1993); engl. transl. *From Gesture to the City. Urban Form and Social Link in Japan,* (London, Pilkington, forthcoming).

Berque, Augustin, *Etre humains sur la Terre. Principes d'ethiques de l'ecoumène.* (Paris, Gallimard, 1996)

Imada, Takatoshi, *Modân no datsu-kôchiku. Sangyô shakai no yukue,* (Tokyo, Chûôkôronsha, 1987).

Inoue, Mitsuo, *Nihon kenchiku no kûkan,* (Tokyo, Kajima Shuppankai, 1969).

Jinnai, Hidenobu, *Edo-Tôkyô no mikata shirabekata,* (Tokyo, Kajima Shuppankai, 1989).

Karaki, Junzô, *Nihonjin no koro no rekishi,* 2 vols, (Tokyo, Chikuma Shobô, 1976).

Maki, Fumihiko, *Miegakure suru toshi,* (Tokyo, Kajima Shuppankai, 1980).

Matsuba, Kazukiyo, *Posuto-modân no zahyô,* (Tokyo, Kajima Shuppankai, 1987).

Nakamura, Yûjirô , *Basho (toposu),* (Tokyo, Kôbundô, (1989)

Yamazaki, Masakazu, *Henshin no bigaku – Zeami geijutsu-ron. Nihon no meicho, 10, Zeami,* (Tokyo, Chûôkôronsha, 1969).

15

Imperfect Panopticism: Envisioning the Construction of Normal Lives.

Matt Hannah

The term "panopticism" is now common currency among critical social theorists, and much valuable work has been inspired and informed by Foucault's resurrection and analysis of Bentham's prison design in *Discipline and Punish* (1979).[1] There are two related senses in which much of this work has been unnecessarily limited, however. First, it has tended to remain preoccupied almost exclusively with the exercise of power in institutional settings; and second, to the extent that it does venture beyond institutional walls, it employs the image of the panopticon more as a motif or mood setter and a vague guide to selecting important questions than as a source of particular analytical tools. Responsibility for both of these limitations can be laid for the most part at Foucault's doorstep. Although his later work on "governmentality" certainly brought the issue of disciplinary power out into the amorphous space of trans-institutional society as a whole, he never precisely spelled out the ways in which the panoptic logic of visibility had to change to operate effectively in an environment where its subjects did not suffer continuous confinement.

In this essay I will attempt to show in detail how the basic logic of the panopticon operates to maintain normality among the already normal. My hope in so doing is not only to provide more flexible tools of social-geographic interpretation, but also to highlight the common patterns linking control of the "marginalized" with control of the "mainstream." While I do not mean to suggest that free citizens suffer as much under imperfect panopticism as do prisoners and asylum inmates under institutional panopticism, I do wish to discourage the opposite conclusion, namely that the lives of the institutionalized are fundamentally incomparable to the lives of the free. If we see the two as different points on a continuum, we are more likely to develop a healthy discomfort with some of the possibilities of social control looming in the near

---

1   *See* especially Felix Driver, *Power and Pauperism: the Workhouse System*, 1834–1884 (Cambridge, Cambridge University Press, 1993).

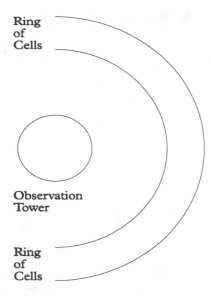

Ring
of
Cells

Observation
Tower

Ring
of
Cells

Figure 15.1 Plan of the Panopticon

future, and also to discern a commonality of interest with the more obviously oppressed.

I will begin with a brief summary of the panoptic logic and its implications for the exercise of control within institutions. This will follow Foucault's analysis in broad outline, and thus may be familiar to some readers; however, I introduce some differences in interpretation which will turn out to be crucial in the second part of the essay. Part 2 will present a refitting of the panoptic logic to demonstrate how it works in a trans-institutional setting, as well as a brief discussion of the conditions of possibility allowing it to do so. The final part will consist of a speculative survey of the possibilities for research opened up by this new perspective on social order, directions in which it still needs to be elaborated or altered, etc.

Part 1

The Panopticon as envisioned by Bentham is a multistoried annual building with a tower at the center of the circular inner space (Figs 15.1 and 15.2). The cells in the outer ring each faces the tower with a completely open barred front. The outer end of each cell is open to light from the outside. Thus, from the central tower, each prisoner (confined one to a cell) is backlit in every daytime activity.

The tower itself, however, is dark, with venetian blinds over the windows. The prisoners never know whether or not they are being watched, but the *threat* is ever present, and, combined with the capability for immediate punishment,

Figure 15.2 View from a cell
Source: Foucault, *Discipline and Punish*

constantly discourages irregular behavior (for example, cursing, masturbating, and especially communicating with other prisoners). Thus described, the carceral situation embodies the rudiments of a relation between human object and authoritative subject which throws everyday life in the modern West into a revealing light.[2]

2   For a fuller appreciation of how the Panopticon project (and its historical failure) related
    to the context of interests and struggles in contemporary England, *Discipline and Punish*

Prisoners as human objects are visible as individuals: each one is distinguishable from all others; each irregular activity is assignable to a specific person. All prisoners are potentially visible in all activities; they are completely limned by light. None can escape punishment as an automatic consequence of abnormal behavior. The watchers in the tower have direct control of the means of punishment through a hierarchical structure of command unifying what I will call the three "moments" of control: *observation, judgement* and *enforcement* of behavior.[3] Again, while watching is only sporadic, the threat of being watched never ceases. Negligence and leniency on the part of the watchers are discouraged by their vigilant superiors who, in turn, are watched, and so on up to the prison director. The whole hierarchy is completely invisible and anonymous to the prisoners; they themselves are the only identifiable people involved in the correctional process.

The immediate goal of the panoptic subject/object relation is normalization of prisoner behavior. The social ends served by normalization may vary somewhat in their specifics but all basically call for the production of people capable of functioning economically and socially without threatening other free citizens. The ideal rehabilitated prisoner is one who reenters society with the conviction that proportional punishment or censure *inevitably* follows every significant behavioral irregularity. Transgressions seem to create and enact their own punishments through neutral and anonymous institutional mechanisms.

To transform aberrant behavior, the panoptic "normalizing machine" must first confine each human being in a strictly separate space. This initial condition allows the three moments of panoptic functioning (observation, judgement, and enforcement) to proceed *infallibly*: there is no confusion as to who perpetrates abnormality, and punishment is meted out *only* to the perpetrator.[4] Any mistaken punishment would suddenly throw the prison hierarchy into

---

should be supplemented with a reading of Michael Ignatieff, *A Just Measure of Pain: the Penitentiary in the Industrial Revolution, 1750–1850,* (New York, NY, Penguin, 1978). Ignatieff places the Panopticon within what might be called a "current affairs of the past," while Foucault reads its "internal" logic in order to produce a "history of the present."

3 This tripartite division is adapted from Foucault's list of three "instruments" of disciplinary power: "hierarchical observation, normalizing judgment and their combination in a procedure that is specific to it, the examination" (Foucault, *Discipline and Punish,* p. 170). Since Foucault is analyzing a prison, he can assume a tight link between judgment and enforcement, both of which are subsumed under the category "normalizing judgment," as well as the unification of the whole process in the examination. In a broader social context, judgment and enforcement are not automatically coordinated, while the examination plays a less central role.

4 Since at the time, Bentham envisioned the Panopticon more as a manufactory than as an instrument of moral reform, with prisoners working up to 16 hours a day in separate cells, he preferred to allow the market and its requirement for a healthy labor force to determine the nature and severity of punishment for abnormal behavior. Around this time, the turn of the nineteenth century, no new consensus had been formed as to how abnormal behavior within prisons should be punished. Although by the late nineteenth century, the transition from such measures as whipping, putting in irons and diet-reduction, to more subtle and unobtrusive punishments (e.g., denial of exercise or visiting privileges), was more or less complete; in Bentham's time punishments varied unpredictably from prison to prison (*see* Ignatieff, *A Just Measure of Pain,* pp. 109–13).

stark relief, destroying its anonymity and the accompanying illusion that the prisoner is the only component of the system free to make responsible or irresponsible choices. Only by denying prisoners *all* anonymity can the prison hierarchy achieve its own complete anonymity and the attendant infallibility.

The power exercised in the hypothetically successful panoptic "community" is *politically efficient* in the sense that the prison authorities do not expose themselves to resentment or blame by exercising it. Even when punishment is necessary, it reflects badly only on prisoners; indeed, *reflection* is a fitting term for the function performed by the dark windows of the central tower. The tower and its hierarchy ceaselessly hold up a mirror to each prisoner, a mirror that reflects responsibility and prevents its assignment to any other person.

On the other hand, punishment is usually not even necessary. The more omniscient, automatic, and infallible the panoptic mechanism, the more preventive its effect. The added labor expense of punishment (as a departure from observational routine) is minimized the more constantly prisoners are aware of their observability. Punishment, or even just the reporting of irregularities, requires the hierarchy to devote inordinate attention to an individual, temporarily lowering its *economic efficiency*.

The goal is to maintain the most effective possible normalization with the least expenditure of effort, so the hierarchy must strive to uphold its image of omniscience with a minimum of actual observation. There is no need for constant watching if the appropriate level of random and sporadic observation can achieve the same prevention of abnormality. Beyond conscious promotion of a rudimentary paranoia, the hierarchy is not much interested in the *inner* workings of individual psyches. Panoptic control is an external method directed at the homogenization of *external* behavior regardless of personal psychological quirks. The private space of motivations is left to itself, but a house of mirrors is constructed "just across the border" in the public space of visible activity. It frames the only human presence at work in an otherwise mechanical power relation. The prisoner acquires a new freedom/responsibility: the freedom/responsibility to be normal.

Panoptic power, then, brings together a completely visible, distinguishable, and precisely punishable human object, and a unified, infallible, omniscient, and anonymous authoritative subject. The latter exercises power preventively, with the utmost economic and political efficiency, while the human object is led to believe that *it* alone exercises the privilege of choice and carries the burden of responsibility.[5] This "anonymization" of authority, as Foucault and Ignatieff both point out, is in stark contrast to the grisly images and practices of punishment which lost prestige during the eighteenth century and all but disappeared during the nineteenth century.

5   Compare my comments here with James B. Rule, *Private Lives and Public Surveillance*, (New York, NY, Schocken Books, 1974), chapter 1.

Part 2

Foucault's analysis of the panoptic situation, slightly different from the fore-going, has already produced a wealth of insights into the functioning of institutions devoted to normalization or the confinement of abnormal individuals. But why are "the rest of us" so normal to begin with? How can we each feel so unique and at the same time be so uncomfortable when faced with abnormality or irregularity in our daily lives? Have we each freely chosen this seemingly magical blend of public normality and private uniqueness? Such questions have been asked before, of course, but have hardly been addressed from the perspective of panopticism.[6] In what follows I will focus on the concept of *visibility* as it plays a part in the maintenance of normality among the already normal.

The idea of a life-path was introduced by Torsten Hägerstrand as a way to represent, and to *some extent* understand, peoples' day-to-day movements through time and space. As a representational device it is fairly straightforward (Fig. 15.3). The Earth's surface is represented (ignoring topography) by two horizontal dimensions, while time is shown by the third, vertical, dimension. Movement through time-space is represented by an arrow, the life-path.[7] The movements and stases of an individual or group can be represented in this way at any spatio-temporal scale, from movements within a house during one hour, to migrations of whole peoples over millennia. Hägerstrand's original life-path construct was far more than just the perceptual aid described above, and numerous writers (most notably Derek Gregory and Allan Pred) have critiqued and extended its concepts and applications over the years. At present, however, it is necessary to grasp it only as a representational (not an interpretive) tool.[8]

Consider the life-path of a prisoner in the panopticon: it is largely vertical and *completely visible* to the authoritative subject. It does not mingle with the life-paths of other prisoners (Fig. 15.4). By contrast, our life-paths, the spatio-temporal movements of "ordinary citizens" are *not* completely visible to authorities. Nonetheless, I would like to portray the image and analysis of the panoptic prisoner as the limit case or hypothetically complete extension of a set of power relations to which we are at present only imperfectly subjected. Normal citizens are most reliably normal in the activities for which their life-paths are publicly visible.

Probably the most important difference between modern citizens and panoptic prisoners is that the former are not strictly confined, but spatially free. Thus, we may mingle with others and gain a certain anonymity, as for instance

---

6   *See* Poster, *Critical Theory, and Poststructuralism*, pp. 105–23, for the only extended treatment I have found.

7   While the person whose life-path is being described remains in one place, the arrow is vertical; any movement over space gives the arrow a finite slope, which decreases with increasing speed of movement. Projection of the life-path onto to the horizontal X–Y plane gives an atemporal map of the individual's movements.

8   *See* especially Allan Pred, "The Choreography of Existence: Comments on Hägerstrand's Time Geography and its Usefulness," *Economic Geography*, 53, (1977): 207–21.

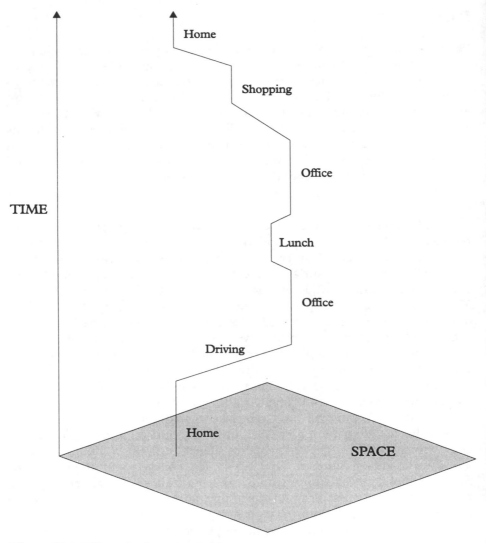

Figure 15.3 Life-path of a normal citizen

while using public transportation, watching a play, or attending a sporting event. We may pass audible wind, boo, scream obscenities, or even throw things if we are so inclined. In such situations our life-paths are bundled so closely together with others that they become indistinguishable, and our chances of being held individually responsible for deeds usually considered abnormal are slim. Some portions of our life-paths are kept invisible for the moment by tradition of law: the privacy of the home, the privacy of the bedroom or bathroom within the home, etc.

Not only observation, but judgment and enforcement as well remain imper-

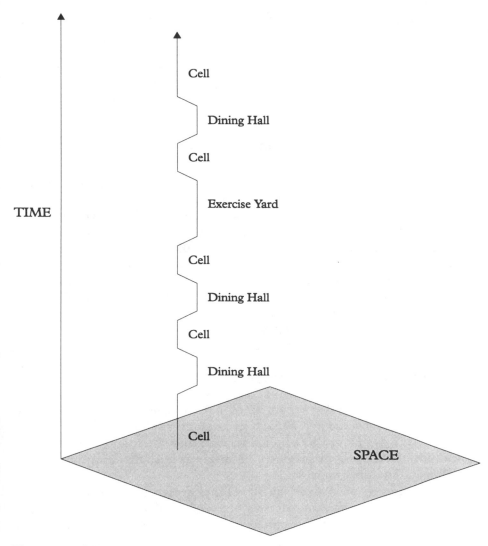

Figure 15.4 Life-path of a prisoner

fect in everyday life. We usually drive 5–10 mph over the speed limit, confident in the knowledge that the law does not have the enforcement power to judge everything technically abnormal as worthy of punishment. Thus, there is some "give" to the definition of normality. It is not too uncommon to neglect payment of speeding tickets received in other states because we are aware of the limited coordination of enforcement.

Briefly, as human objects, mainstream citizens are less spatially fixed and individually distinguishable than the panoptic prisoner. We do not suffer as constant a threat of observation, and judgment and enforcement are not strictly automatic. Despite such differences, however, we share much with the confined. Although the body of the modern citizen is not fixed in place, personal property usually is, and this greatly enhances punishability. One's permanent address is required on most forms, and allows authorities to levy fines or seize property as a last resort in punishment for financial or other irregularities. For example, David Burnham points out that the Inland Revenue Service has a special dispensation to seize property immediately and without notification if it suspects that a tax delinquent intends to leave the country.[9] In this sense, private property at a permanent address, or financial assets in a (non-Swiss) bank account, is a functional substitute for physical confinement. Failure to carry a driver's license or to have car insurance, that is, failure to be readily identifiable, carries a penalty in many countries.

While our life-paths are not entirely visible, many activities are, as in the Panopticon, regulated as much by the *threat* of observation as by actual surveillance: the threat of a tax audit, the possibility of a speed trap for those pushing the 10 mph margin of leniency, the threat of the teacher's gaze for a child taking an exam in a large classroom. And despite only imperfect success, all of these authorities strive for the same economic and political efficiencies of power embodied in the Panopticon. Judgment must seem automatic and impartial, responsibility lies as completely as possible with the perpetrator. In sum, then, the modern citizen is objectified in a life-path comprised of information, as a "spatialized dossier."[10] Some of this information is gathered through direct observation by others, some of it exists as numerical or textual records of financial transactions, use of services. etc. For the average "free" citizen the life-path of information traces is full of gaps, but retains its unity through the matchability of names, permanent addresses, social security numbers, etc. It is a far more complicated affair than the continuous, relatively vertical line of the panoptic prisoner, but messy as it is, it promotes normality according to the same principles.[11]

The incomplete, "patchwork" quality of the average life-path can be attributed largely to the characteristics of our vigilant authorities. While such authoritative subjects as the panoptic hierarchy, God, Big Brother, and Santa

---

9   David Burnham, "The Abuse of Power," *The New York Times Magazine*, 3 September 1989, pp. 26–7, 50, 61.

10 It is in this sense that the human subject is socially constructed. This is *not* the same as saying that there is no autonomous individuality, only that all aspects of an individual's existence that are publicly intelligible must, of necessity, take a form translatable for others (e.g., information or language). This view does not rule out "specificity," only the possibility of preserving it *as such* in communication. To the authorities, a life-path *is* a person, but this does not mean that the person's "essence" is exhausted by the life-path. Cf. Kenneth C. Laudon, *Dossier Society: Value Choices in the Design of National Information Systems,* (New York, NY, Columbia University Press, 1986).

11 Richard Sennett, *Authority*, (New York, NY, Random House, 1981), pp. 95–97, notes that (as in the Panopticon), in modern totalitarian societies, normality is not seen as a basis for self-possessed autonomy, but rather as the best possible state of being *in and of itself*. I wonder how "totalitarian" our democracies are in this sense ... do we still see normality as a means, or is it now an end?

Claus ("He knows when you are sleeping ... ") are unified, omniscient and always capable of punishment, in "real" life we face a variety of normalizing machines, imperfectly coordinated, and each with imperfect powers. Unlike the panoptic hierarchy, these vigilant authorities are often fragmented, either vertically in relation to a particular activity, or horizontally according to different activities. By "vertical fragmentation" I mean that, for a given activity, the three moments in the process of normalizing surveillance (receipt of information traces, judgment and enforcement of normality) may all take place in different organizations with only imperfect communication. Use of a credit card leaves information that banks can acquire to decide whether to loan money to the user, but banks may not be able to obtain information about, say, payment of telephone or utility bills.

"Horizontal fragmentation" refers to the fact that different activities may leave information traces with different organizations, and that these organizations may not be capable, for legal or technological reasons, of exchanging and matching information regarding different activities. Government agencies, employers, financial institutions, etc. collectively hold pictures of our visible life-paths, but coordination is far from perfect, so it would be misleading to view authority as singular, unified, and effectively omniscient. The many authoritative subjects are also not entirely anonymous. In addition to a right of privacy, we can (at least in dealing with the United States government) demand to know what information is held about us or take legal action against misuse of information. We have some leeway to protest, appeal, and complain about the exercise of normalizing authority. We may demand a certain degree of balance between our visibility and that of the vigilant authorities.

Fragmented though they are, it is important to note here that vigilant authorities are becoming more coordinated in horizontal and in vertical dimensions. Credit card firms now regularly provide information to law enforcement agencies, for example, and motor vehicle administrations nationwide share information with insurance companies. Federal regulations now require all US banks to microfilm all personal checks paid, and to retain the films for five years so that federal officials may scrutinize them if they deem it necessary.[12] For the moment, it suffices to reiterate the claim that our public normality coincides with our public visibility. As *human objects* we maintain our individual unities by virtue of our awareness that some of our activities can be watched and assigned to the same person. We experience our visible life-paths as unified representations of ourselves which can, in a sense, be used against us. The unity of the authoritative subject is incomplete at best, but importantly, *complete unity of the authoritative subject is unnecessary for the reasonably successful enforcement of normality in today's society*. Only the achievement of complete visibility would require a completely unified authoritative subject. There are two deterrents to such a goal, however. First, within the Western liberal tradition

---

12 James Rule, Douglas McAdam, Linda Stearns and David Uglow, "Documentary Identification and Mass Surveillance in the United States," *Social Problems*, 31 (1983): 222–34.

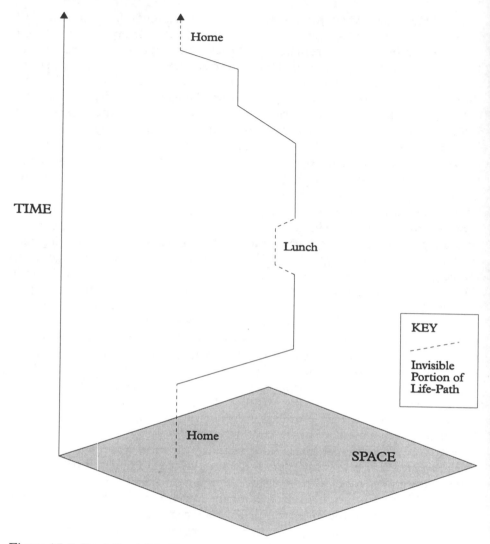

Figure 15.5 Partially visible life-path

since Adam Smith, the idea of total control has been in tension with the notion of a natural and *in principle* unknowable realm of constructive disorder not limited purely to the market.[13] The idea that this latter realm should be exempted from the exhaustive scrutiny has limited the reach of the state, although today, private organizations are increasingly capable of covering the

13 Colin Gordon, "Governmental Rationality: An Introduction," in Graham Burchell, Colin Gordon and Peter Miller, (eds), in *The Foucault Effect*, (Chicago, IL, Univ. of Chicago Press, 1991), pp. 14–15.

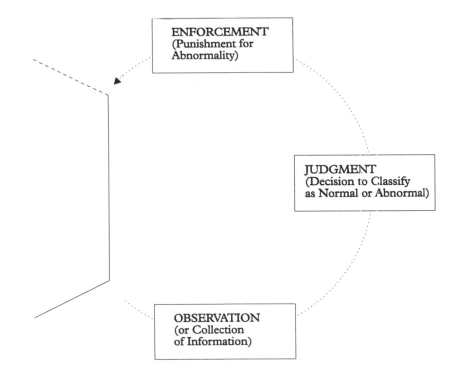

Figure 15.6 Cycle of social control

remaining ground. More important to the present argument is the ubiquity of *insurance technologies*, which protect against and profit from disorder. Panopticism may not achieve perfect coverage of individual lives, but the damages and instabilities resulting from vestigial disorder can be predicted using aggregate social statistics, and security sold (at a profit). In a sense, insurance fills the gaps in knowledge of individual lives by interpolation: the knowledge that is available (e.g. age, sex, driving record, income bracket, etc.) allows a projection of *risk* into those areas about which there is no knowledge (the future, private habits, etc.).[14]

Viewing modern social normality as a result of *imperfect panopticism* suggests numerous reinterpretations of familiar ideas. To give some formal coherence to these reinterpretations, it will be helpful to unify the ideas presented so far through an elaboration of the life-path diagram (Fig. 15.5). Let the solid segments of the life-path shown in Figure 15.5 represent publicly visible activities; dashed segments depict activities not subject to authoritative gazes. Each particular *visible activity* can be seen to anchor a *cycle of social control* (Fig. 15.6). A visible activity occupies a specific, finite time-space segment betrayed

14 *See* Francois Ewald, "Insurance and Risk," translated by Colin Gordon, in Graham Burchell, Colin Gordon and Peter Miller, (eds), *The Foucault Effect*, (Chicago, IL, Univ. of Chicago Press, 1991), pp. 197–210.

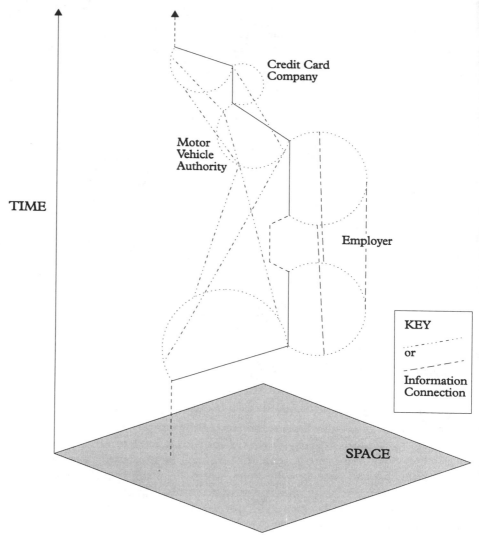

Figure 15.7 Sheath of authority

by information traces in the form of direct physical observations or data. The information may or may not be processed by a judging authority, and, even if it is judged, and judged to betray unacceptable actions, the judgment may or may not lead to punishment. Once again, the cycle does not have to be activated, *or even to exist*, to be effective; our awareness of its potential existence and activation usually suffices to prevent abnormalities.

The life-path of a typical individual fairly bristles with cycles of normalization similar to the one described above, forming a (figurative) *sheath of authority* around the core of physical movement (Fig. 15.7). Cycles intermesh in numberless ways, as different activities may share the same media of observation, judgment, or enforcement. Single cycles may involve numerous organizations, and single organizations may play roles in a variety of cycles. The sheath of authority is woven together through the exchange of information vertically between moments of the cycle and horizontally between cycles. The visible life-path and its woven sheath together paint a picture of normalizing power, a graphic portrayal of the way normality is maintained among normal people.

Part 3

Incomplete and provisional though it is, this view of social control can serve as an interpretive departure point for, or at least an additional window on, a number of different research projects. Before surveying its uses, however, the *status* of the logic of imperfect panopticism needs to be clarified. At the most fundamental, *epistemological* level, it is a framework constructed through human thought and imposed on a social reality which, though possibly unknowable in the strict sense, does not seem to rule out imperfect panopticism as a plausible partial explanation. Once the inherent uncertainty encountered at the epistemological level is bracketed, and the assumption made that a social ontology is possible,[15] the logic of imperfect panopticism can be situated in more familiar ways.

First, it is a "logic" because the various instances in which it appears embody in different ways a fairly stable *reasoning* about how control is to be achieved, the relative benefits of achieving it through observation, judgment, and enforcement as opposed to, say, corporal punishment, etc. The relative pervasiveness of this logic in "modern" societies is not an intended product of a unified, deliberate program, but rather an emergent condition, an aggregate product of similar, but not very interdependent, developments in various spheres of life. Second, imperfect panopticism is not the most basic or fundamental characteristic of modern society (Jürgen Habermas and Charles Taylor misunderstood Foucault on this point).[16] It is not even the only form of social control we live with and through; it lies somewhere in the middle of a continuum running from cooperatively produced social norms and ideology through the legal system to physical confinement and finally military sources of control. As Foucault's work makes clear, panopticism is not entirely separate from these other types, but it certainly does not serve as their common essence. Not only do all these mechanisms of control coexist, but many of them

15 It would of course be irresponsible to presume unreflectively that the ways in which human knowledge is questionable do not apply to *logos* about *onta*. *See* U. Strohmayer and M. Hannah, "Domesticating Postmodernism," *Antipode*, 24:1 (1992), 29–55.
16 J. Habermas, *The Philosophical Discourse of Modernity*, (Cambridge, MA: MIT Press, 1987), pp. 266–93; Charles Taylor, "Foucault on Freedom and Truth," in D. Couzens Hoy, (ed.), *Foucault: A Critical Reader*, (Oxford, Basil Blackwell, 1986), pp. 51–68.

(imperfect panopticism included) are not simply and unambiguously *bad*. This is the third point to be stressed. Some ordering mechanisms *allow* as well as constrain various activities; in particular, many of the systems rendering modern citizens visible simultaneously facilitate important activities (for example, ATMs facilitate access to cash).

There are two broad areas in which further concrete research on imperfect panopticism could enrich our understanding of social worlds: the historical trajectory of this type of social control, and the ways it has been used, by societies in which it is already established, to control other societies. Regarding the historical trajectory of imperfect panopticism, more has been done to unearth its relatively distant origins than to trace it through the first half of the twentieth century; discussions of its immediate future are easier to find.[17] The reasons for considering it an urgent issue come to the fore especially in research dealing with the near future and with the uses to which techniques of visibility have been put in episodes of imperialism. I have explored the role of rudimentary imperfect panopticism in the United States government's administration of an American Indian reservation during the 1870s, and have thereby also been able to clarify some of its spatial prerequisites in modern societies as well. Robinson and Overton have examined similar systems of control operated by imperial powers in South Africa and turn-of-the-century Kenya, respectively, albeit without attempting to pursue the theoretical implications of their "empirical" work. Taken together, these projects barely begin to scratch the surface of the vast mountain of documentary resources left behind by imperial episodes worldwide.

A focus on imperfect panopticism could impact two related *theoretical* problematics as well: the relationship between state and economic power, and the general problem of the nature and identification of classes in late capitalism. The use of refitted life-path diagrams as an instrument of analysis would allow a much clearer anatomy of the constitutive links between larger social forces and individuals. It could also bring into sharper outline the distribution of the tasks of social control between, on the one hand, state institutions and legal structures, and on the other, economic institutions, the changing forms of money, and the ownership of private property. The "authoritative sheath," or web of connections between cycles of social control discussed above, probably has fairly stable topographies for large groups of people, so some general conclusions could be drawn about the relative importance of particular authorities.

It is no doubt possible to distinguish not only typical topographies of the authoritative sheath, but also systematic differences in the *degree* of visibility between groups of people. There is a stable disparity, for instance, between the financial visibility of people and organizations who can afford to pay for

---

17 Rule, McAdam, Stearns and Uglow, "Documentary Identification", (1983); Laudon, *Dossier Society*, (1986); Oscar H. Gandy, Jr., "The Surveillance Society: Information Technology and Bureaucratic Social Control," *Journal of Communication*, 39, (1989), 61–76.

accountants, and that of people who cannot. Expert intervention mediates between actual activities and reported or observable versions of them in ways that allow disguise or deception not available to most low- and middle-income individuals. This, combined with relatively weak per capita expenditure (in countries like the United States) on enforcement of corporate financial regulations, suggests a socio-economic stratification in the dimension of visibility.[18]

Insofar as the notion of imperfect panopticism proves useful to geographers, it will tend to contribute to the complication of interpretive work. Individual lives are in a sense the smallest possible "localities," and thus naturally most likely to be situated and constituted in the most contingent and variable ways by combinations of social forces and processes. As a result, we tend to dismiss them as largely inaccessible to social-geographic analyses. If the framework presented here can introduce some (extremely partial) stability into interpretations at that level of contingency, it may help to expand the purview of social-geographic research.

---

18 See Robert Sherrill, "S&Ls, Big Banks and Other Triumphs of Capitalism," *The Nation*, 251:17, (Nov. 19, 1990), pp. 589–623. Given some empirical flesh, this line of thinking might add an important facet to debates about class and class processes.

16

Imagining the Nomad: Mobility and the Postmodern Primitive

Tim Cresswell

Everyone is travelling in the field of 'theory' today. Metaphors of movement parade across the pages of cultural theorists, social theorists, geographers, artists, literary critics. Mobility is the order of the day. Nomads, migrants, travellers and explorers inhabit a world where nothing is certain or fixed. Tradition and rootedness have the smell of death. Diaspora is everything. Monumentalism, the edifice, the rooted and bound are firmly placed in the museum of modernity. In this essay I examine this romanticization of the nomad as the geographic metaphor *par excellence* of postmodernity. I argue that imaginations of the nomad are central to postmodern social and cultural theory in a number of ways. Through an examination of Deleuze and Guatarri, Iain Chambers and Michel de Certeau I demonstrate the centrality of the nomad metaphor to their understandings of the postmodern world.[1] Secondly, I connect the nomad metaphor to a number of theoretical concerns that have traversed the plain of postmodern theory – particularly the futility of rationality. Thirdly, I undertake an archaeology of the nomad metaphor by digging into pre-postmodern uses of the metaphor in the work of Mayhew, Eliot, Hoggart and Williams. Towards the end of the paper I critique the postmodern embrace of all things mobile through a consideration of who travels and why.

The Traveller, the Migrant and the Nomad

In his intriguing essay 'Travelling Cultures'[2] James Clifford proposes the task of considering travelling as a way of doing ethnography. Ethnography, he argues, has frequently shed its own mobility in a futile search for rootedness,

---

1 All of these authors, in one way or another, have been associated with the critique of modernity and positing of something new in its place. This is not to say that they all embrace postmodernity in all its forms.
2 James Clifford, 'Travelling Cultures' in Grossberg, L., et al. (eds), *Cultural Studies*, (London, Routledge, 1992) pp. 96–112.

authenticity and place (dwelling). Geography is surely subject to the same historical process. Geographers have consistently insisted that the discipline concerns the creation of a human dwelling on the face of nature. Geography, as the study of 'Earth as the home of people', rarely takes mobility as seriously as it does place, space, landscape and territory. Mobility is often the implicit underbelly of the place-roots-authenticity-dwelling lexicon. Even in such a mobility-centred subfield as migration studies, movement is always the result of push and pull factors in places labelled A and B. Clifford takes on the metaphor of 'traveller' as an appropriate one for a more mobile theorization in anthropology. He acknowledges that such a metaphor (together with its hotels, airport lounges and designer luggage) is polluted with interests of First World privilege – it reminds us, he says, of the 'older form of gentlemanly Occidental travel, when home and abroad, city and country, East and West, metropole and antipodes, were more clearly fixed' (page 105). Travel, he says is clearly marked by issues of gender, class, ethnicity and culture. It is not just the heroic male travellers of old, but the contemporary middle-class adventure-traveller, the middle- and upper-class Victorian ladies who made heroic journeys and the artistic elite who romanticized the outcast in the figure of the *flâneur* – all of these valorizations of travel are indicative of privileged positions.[3]

Somewhat differently Edward Said considers the figure of the *migrant* as an apt metaphor for (post)modernity. In *Culture and Imperialism* Said[4] ends with an engagement with the theme of exile and dispossession. The contemporary world (for Said, still in limbo between the modern and the postmodern), he argues, is one in which the state of exile is the norm rather than the exception. The crossing of boundaries and resistance to (en)closure are the mark of modern literature. But it is not just theory and literature that grabs Said's attention, the history of people on the move is also foregrounded.

> ... surely it is one of the unhappiest characteristics of the age to have produced more refugees, migrants, displaced persons, and exiles than ever before in history, most of them as an accompaniment to and, ironically enough, as afterthoughts of great post-colonial and imperial conflicts. As the struggle for independence produced new states and new boundaries, it also produced homeless wanderers, nomads, vagrants, unassimilated to the emerging structures of institutional power, rejected by the established order for their intransigence and obdurate rebelliousness.[5]

> ... it is no exaggeration to say that liberation as an intellectual mission, born in the resistance and opposition to the confinements and ravages of imperialism, has now shifted from the settled, established, and domesticated dynamics of culture to its unhoused, decentered, and exilic energies, energies whose incarnation today is the migrant, and whose consciousness is that of the intellectual and artist in exile ... And while it would be the rankest Panglossian dishonesty to say

3   Importantly Clifford finds the metaphor of the nomad less appealing than that of the traveller. He thinks of it as a thoughtless appropriation on non-Western experience.
4   Edward Said, *Culture and Imperialism*, (London, Vintage, 1994).
5   Edward Said, *Culture and Imperialism*, (London, Vintage, 1994), page 403.

that the bravura performances of the intellectual exile and the miseries of the displaced person or refugee are the same, it is possible, I think, to regard the intellectual as first distilling them articulating the predicaments that disfigure modernity – mass deportation, imprisonment, population transfer, collective dispossession, and forced immigrations.[6]

Despite his words of warning not to conflate the migrant experience with migrant thought, Said suggests that (post)modern consciousness is delightfully migratory in its subjectivity. For Said, culture can be unitary, allegedly rooted, linear and subsuming, or it can be complex and challenging. The latter, favoured, view, he describes as migrant, exilic and nomadic.

Before going too much further it is perhaps wise to note some differences between modes of metaphorical movement in late- and postmodern writing. Clifford attempts to mobilize theory with reference to the obviously privileged figure of the traveller while Said focuses instead on the migrant and the nomad. Clearly the last two are substantially less privileged than the first. Yet differences remain between the migrant and the nomad. The migrant experience is one which revolves around the dialectic of home and away – a sense of longing for a place of home whether in the past or future. The migrant experience (and the experience of diaspora more generally) is one that concerns the questions of 'where you're from' and 'where you're at'.[7] The nomad, on the other hand, is one whose home is on the move, who has no *place* in which meaning and identity can rest. The nomad is subject to the disciplinary discourse which attempts to 'place' the nomadic subject blind to the fact that there is no place but the place of movement itself. While the traveller and the migrant have been well discussed by Clifford on the one hand and theorists of diaspora of the other, the nomad has remained the subject of vast generalizations and misguided metaphorical play. Let us, then, explore the use of the nomadic figure in postmodern theory.

The Nomad as a Central Figure in Postmodern Thought

De Certeau and the Pedestrian Hero(ine)

Michele de Certeau, in the *Practice of Everyday Life*[8] enjoys the nomad metaphor. For him, power is about territory and boundaries – asserting what he calls a proper place. The weapons of the strong are what he calls *strategies* – classification, delineation, division. The strong depend on the certainty of mapping. The weak, on the other hand, are left with furtive movement to contest the territorialization of urban space. The cunning of the nomadic allows

6   Edward Said, *Culture and Imperialism*, (London, Vintage, 1994), page 403.
7   *See* Paul Gilroy, 'It Ain't Where You're From, It's Where You're At ... The Dialectics of Diasporic Identification' *Third Text* 13, winter 1990/91, pp. 3–16 and Ien Ang. 'On Not Speaking Chinese: Postmodern Ethnicity and the Politics of Diaspora' *New Formations*, 24, winter 1994, pp. 1–18.
8   Michel de Certeau *The Practice of Everyday Life*, (Berkeley, University of California Press, 1984).

pedestrians to take short cuts, to tell stories through the routes they chose. These *tactics* refuse the neat divisions and classification of the powerful and, in doing so, critique the spatialization of domination. Thus, the ordinary activities of everyday life, such as walking in the city, become acts of heroic everyday resistance. The nomad is the hero(ine).

Tactics do not 'obey the laws of the place, for they are not defined or identified by it'.[9] The tactic never creates or relies upon the existence of some place for its identity and power. The tactic is consigned to using the space of the powerful in cunning ways. The tactics of the weak are a form of consumption – never producing 'proper places' but always using and manipulating these places. The world of production is confronted with:

> an entirely different kind of production, called 'consumption' and characterised by its ruses, its fragmentation (the result of the circumstances), its poaching, its clandestine nature, its tireless but quiet activity, in short its quasi-invisibility, since it shows itself not in its own products (where would it place them) but in the art of using those imposed on it.[10]

Thus, the tactic is the ruse of the weak – the mobile drifting through the rationalized spaces of power. The tactic is not the action of the knowing and privileged traveller nor the migration of the diasporic identity. The tactic has no place to be 'at'. The tactic is thus the art of the nomad – an art which will 'circulate, come and go, overflow and drift over an imposed terrain like the snowy waves of the sea slipping in among the rocks and defiles of an established order'.[11] De Certeau's hero(ine)s are essentially urban beings. The furtive figure of the nomad takes his/her place on the streets of the city and is the direct descendant of the modern *flâneur*. Thus, de Certeau's most evocative portrayal is of the thousands of pedestrians *making their way* below the masterly view from the World Trade Center in New York. De Certeau's nomad is a pedestrian. Pedestrian is a word which, in the English language, means 'boring', 'slow' and 'of no special interest'. De Certeau takes this very everydayness and makes it into an heroic act of resistance against the disciplinary machinations of the city. It is not in de Certeau, however, that the heroism of the nomad reaches its pinnacle. The metaphor is developed much further in the work of Gilles Deleuze and Felix Guattari.

Deleuze and Guattari and Nomad Science

In the complicated theorizations of Deleuze and Guattari (*see Nomadology*),[12] the nomad is once more valorized.[13] They distinguish between the machina-

9 Michel de Certeau *The Practice of Everyday Life*, page 29.
10 Michel de Certeau *The Practice of Everyday Life*, page 31.
11 Michel de Certeau *The Practice of Everyday Life*, page 34.
12 Gilles Deleuze and Felix Guattari, *Nomadology: The War Machine*, (New York, Semiotext(e), 1986).
13 James Clifford refers to nomadology as the 'postmodern primitive'.

tions of the state (Royal science), which are ordered and hierarchical, and the inventions of the 'war machine' (nomad science/art). While nomads are the conveyors of 'vague essences; (here vague is connected to 'vagabond'). They illustrate these difficult distinctions with reference to journeymen (*compagnonnages*) – nomadic labourers involved in the building Gothic cathedrals. Deleuze and Guattari write of the travelling labourers building cathedrals across Europe 'scattering construction sites across the land, drawing on an active and passive power (*puissance*) (mobility and the strike) that was far from convenient for the State'.[14] The State, in response, managed the construction of cathedrals, created divisions of labour such as mental and manual, theoretical and practical and proceeded to govern the nomads.

> We know about the problems States have always had with journeymen's associations, or *campagnonnages*, the nomadic or itinerant bodies of the type formed by masons, carpenters, smiths etc. Settling, sedentarizing labor-power, regulating the movement of the flow of labour, assigning it channels and conduits, forming corporations in the sense of organisms, and, for the rest, relying on forced manpower recruited on the spot (corvee) or among indigents (charity workshops) – this has always been one of the principal affairs of the State, which undertook to conquer both a *band vagabondage* and a *body nomadism*.[15]

To Deleuze and Guattari the nomad is constituted by lines of flight rather than by points and nodes. While the migrant goes from place to place, moving with place in mind, the nomad uses points and locations to define paths. While sedentary people use roads to 'parcel out a closed space to people',[16] nomadic trajectories 'distribute people in an open space'.[17] The nomad is never re-territorialized, unlike the migrant who slips back into the ordered space of arrival. The metaphorical space of the nomad is the desert, flat, smooth, curiously isotropic. The nomad shifts across this tactile space making the most of circumstance, not unlike the rhizomic vegetation that shifts location with changes in the weather.

The State, on the other hand, is the metaphorical enemy of the nomad, attempting to take the tactile space and enclose and bound it. It is not that the State opposes mobility but that it wishes to control flows – to make them run through conduits. It wants to create fixed and well-directed paths for movement to flow through. Deleuze and Guattari use the nomad as a metaphor for the undisciplined – rioting, revolution, guerrilla warfare – for all the forces that resist the fortress of State discipline.

> Nomads provide new models for existence and struggle. The nomad-self breaks from all molar segments and cautiously disorganizes itself. Nomad life is an experiment in creativity and becoming, and is anti-traditional and anti-conform-

14   Gilles Deleuze and Felix Guattari, *Nomadology: The War Machine*, page 29.
15   Gilles Deleuze and Felix Guattari, *Nomadology: The War Machine*, page 29.
16   Gilles Deleuze and Felix Guattari, *Nomadology: The War Machine*, page 50
17   Gilles Deleuze and Felix Guattari, *Nomadology: The War Machine*, page 51.

ist in character. The postmodern nomad attempts to free itself of all roots, bonds and identities, and thereby resist the state and all normalizing powers.[18]

As with de Certeau and Chambers, Deleuze and Guattari locate their nomads in urban space. Urban space in their lexicon is space where 'smooth space' and 'striated space' play off one another in a constant dialectic tension – 'the city is the smooth striated space per excellence: ... the city is (also) the force of striation that reimparts smooth space'.[19] Smooth space is the space of the nomad – of horizontality that resists and threatens the striations of power. This smooth space is 'sprawling temporary, shifting shantytowns of nomads and cave dwellers, scrap metal and fabric, patchwork, of which the striations of money, work, or housing are no longer even relevant.[20] The nomad, then, moves over this smooth space while power is realized in the striated spaces of money and influence. Within the city, the two impulses are in constant tension, with the nomads never being totally incorporated into the striated spaces of power.

The nomad is but one of Deleuze and Guattari's metaphorical ruses. In addition, they develop social understandings through the metaphors of the rhizome and the schizo, each of which is a mobile alternative to the fixed and the rational(ized).[21] Like de Certeau, though in a more sustained way, Deleuze and Guattari mobilize the nomad as a figure of resistance to the bounded spatiality of modern discipline. A more cultural celebration of the nomad infuses and enthuses the work of Iain Chambers.

Iain Chambers in the Mobile Metropolis

Perhaps the most passionate embrace of the metaphorical nomad comes from Ian Chambers. In a spirited defence of Derrida, Chambers argues for continued disruptions of the presumed coherence of ideology. Rather than relying in an 'abstract morality injected from "outside"',[22] we should live 'inside the signs' – engaging in the pleasure of the metropolis and its (popular) culture.

> Extending our knowledge through these details and their sense of the possible, the previous totality of sense offered by ideology (including Marxism) is 'deconstructed', and its elements relocated in a more detailed, more complex, more specific and more open (i.e. transforming and transformable) perspective.[23]

18 Steven Best and Douglas Kellner, *Postmodern Theory: Critical Interrogations*, (New York, Guilford Press, 1991), page 103.
19 Gilles Deleuze and Felix Guattari, *A Thousand Plateau, Capitalism and Schizophrenia*, (Minneapolis, University of Minnesota Press, 1988), page 481.
20 Gilles Deleuze and Felix Guattari, *A Thousand Plateau, Capitalism and Schizophrenia*, (Minneapolis, University of Minnesota Press, 1988), page 481.
21 Just as the nomad is a problematic romanticization of a marginal figure, the schizo is also a deeply problematic metaphor.
22 Iain Chambers, *Popular Culture: The Metropolitan Experience*, (London, Methuen, 1986), page 212.
23 Iain Chambers, *Popular Culture: The Metropolitan Experience*, (London, Methuen, 1986), page 212.

Chambers asks us to refuse the logic of the deep structure and its 'mechanisms of totality' and replace it with 'A horizontal vista of mobile meanings, shifting connections, temporary encounters, a world of inter-textual richness and detail … '[24] The location for such mobile thought is the metropolis. In the city, Chambers insists, we are forced to recognize the diversity of connection and difference. 'Knowledge' he goes on, 'is no longer monumental and monolithic but differentiated and nomadic.'[25] In a remarkable appreciation of urban confusions, Chambers idolizes the codes of dress, music and design that inhabit the modern city. Through such devices as the Walkman, the certainties of old are broken down.

> Inside this mobile collage a democracy of aesthetic and cultural populism becomes possible. The previous authority of culture, once respectfully designated with a capital C, no longer has an exclusive hold on meaning.[26]

A sense of bewilderment, wonder and uncertainty reveals a nomadic culture in which we each move with our particular baggage and histories.[27]

Perhaps Chambers's nomadic vision find its fulcrum in the world of the international airport:

> With its shopping malls, restaurants, banks, post-offices, phones, bars, video games, television chairs and security guards, it is a miniaturised city. As a simulated metropolis it is inhabited by a community of modern nomads: a collective metaphor of cosmopolitan existence where the pleasure of travel is not only to arrive, but also not to be in any particular place.[28]

Here Chambers makes the connection explicitly between nomadism as the metaphor *par excellence* of postmodern life and the use of nomadism as a metaphor for postmodern thought. The experiences of the airport traveller and the contemporary Western intellectual, he suggests, are not dissimilar. The *flâneur* becomes the *planeur*. The bounded and rationalized space of the modernist intellectual become the 'journeys in postmodernity' of Iain Chambers's postmodern nomad.

> For the nomadic experience of language, wandering without a fixed home, dwelling at the crossroads of the world, bearing our sense of being and difference,

24 Iain Chambers, *Popular Culture: The Metropolitan Experience*, (London, Methuen, 1986), page 213.
25 Iain Chambers, *Popular Culture: The Metropolitan Experience*, (London, Methuen, 1986), page 193.
26 Iain Chambers, *Popular Culture: The Metropolitan Experience*, (London, Methuen, 1986), page 194.
27 Iain Chambers, *Border Dialogues: Journeys in Postmodernity*, (London, Routledge. 1990), page 114.
28 Iain Chambers, *Border Dialogues: Journeys in Postmodernity*, (London, Routledge. 1990), page 57–8.

is no longer the expression of a unique tradition or history, even if it pretends to carry a single name. Thought wanders. It migrates, requires translation.[29]

In Chambers's work, as in much of the growing postmodern canon, the nomad becomes an exhilarating character. Everywhere the nomad goes new freedoms and opportunities follow. Modernist thought, the doomed search for Truth established through the mythical 'view from nowhere', is characterized by stabilities and certainties. The familiar dualisms of man/women; white/black; true/false are all tethered to the geography of here and there. The movements of the nomad, on the ground and in the head, cannot help but transgress such simplicities.

The Postmodern Imagines the Premodern

It is clear, then, that the nomad plays a central role in the critical imagination of a number of people who have labelled themselves or been labelled 'postmodern.' Before moving on to a critique of this process, it is worthwhile to ask why the nomad has been such a positive figure for the postmodern theorist.

Perhaps most obviously, nomads are seen to agitate against the fixity of spatial order. If order is created (at least partly) through the division and pulverisation of space,[30] the delineation of territory and the policing of boundaries,[31] and the purification of neighbourhoods,[32] then mobility, fluidity and dynamic flow present a constant state of transgression – evidence of the impossibility of total discipline. Many of the theorists postmodernists take most seriously emphasize the constant incompleteness of power-in-space. The discussions of carnival in Bakhtin's theorizations of medieval carnival are translated straight into the postmodern world. Carnival is the essentially mobile refusal of the strict spaces of official culture. Michel de Certeau writes of the constant mobile manoeuvres of the pedestrian, denying the ability of the planner and strategist to determine their movements. Deleuze and Guattari employ the nomad as a figure who resists the rational spatializations of the state. In Chambers's work, the nomad is the personification of a popular culture which mobilizes meaning out of the straight-jackets of the museum, the gallery and the university.

In addition to the spatial transgression of fixity, the mobility of nomadism, it is argued, mitigates against the dualizing tendency of rationalistic thought.[33]

29 Iain Chambers, *Migrancy, Culture, Identity*, (London, Routledge, 1994), page 4.
30 Henri Lefebvre, *The Production of Space*, (Oxford, Blackwell, 1991).
31 Robert Sack, *Human Territoriality: Its Theory and History*, (Cambridge, Cambridge University Press, 1986).
32 David Sibley, 'The Purification of Space', *Environment and Planning D: Society and Space*, 6, 1988, pp. 209–41.
33 Interestingly travel has been a dominant metaphor for rational thought in pre-postmodern theory from Montaigne to Rousseau. *See* Georges Van Den Abbeele, *Travel as Metaphor*, (Minneapolis, University of Minnesota Press, 1992).

Perhaps Deleuze and Guattari exemplify this best. In *A Thousand Plateaus* they discuss the arborescent system of thought – the characteristic shape of Enlightenment thought – an organizing principle that systematizes and hierarchalizes through the creation of branches and is based on a firm foundation of roots.

> These allow arborescent culture to build vast conceptual systems that are centered, unified, hierarchical, and grounded in a self-transparent, self-identical, representing subject. The leaves that flower on such trees have names like Form, Essence, Law, Truth, Justice, Right, and Cogito.[34]

In contrast to that, Deleuze and Guattari promote rhizomatics – a process which sets about the destruction of binary logic and the tree that grows on it. The metaphor of the rhizome undermines the solidity and rootedness of the tree – it pluralizes and breaks dualisms. The rhizome is essentially mobile and de-territorialized; it is in their terms, a kind of nomad thought that opposes the totalizing discipline of state thought.

De Certeau make a similar argument in his discussion of strategies and tactics. In *The Practice of Everyday Life* he makes the leap from observations of pedestrians in the rational city to a wider discussion of the consumption of rational spaces by the unpredictable consumer:

> Unrecognised producers, poets of their own affairs, trailblazers in the jungle of functionalist rationality, consumers produce something resembling the '*lignes d'erre*' described by Deligny. They trace 'indeterminate trajectories' that are apparently meaningless, since they do not cohere with the constructed, written, and prefabricated space through which they move. They are sentences that remain unpredictable within the space ordered by the organising techniques of systems. Although they use as their *material* the *vocabularies* of established languages (those of television, newspapers, the supermarket or city planning), although they remain within the framework of prescribed *syntaxes* (the temporal modes of schedules, paradigmatic organizations of places, etc.), these 'traverses' remain heterogeneous to the systems they infiltrate and in which they sketch out the guileful ruses of *different* interests and desires. They circulate, come and go, overflow and drift over an imposed terrain like the snowy waves of the sea slipping in among the rocks and defiles of an established order.[35]

The tactics of the consumer indicate the impossibility of total strategic control. The strategy has its spatial correlate in the proper place and the territory while the tactic is the mobile ruse of the urban nomad. Thought, too, is strategic or tactical. Strategic thought, like the trees of Deleuze and Guattari, forms the basis of modern rationality, while tactical thought represents a more practical and ultimately ungovernable logic that takes short cuts and makes connections.

34 Steven Best and Douglas Kellner, *Postmodern Theory: Critical Interrogations*, (New York, Guilford Press, 1991), page 99.
35 Michel de Certeau, *The Practice of Everyday Life*, page 34.

The Nomad as a Central Figure in Modern(ist) Thought

Nomads have not always been so vogue. My aim here is to place the nomad metaphor in some historical lineage through an investigation of some earlier figures in cultural studies and social theory. Patricia Price-Chalita[36] has suggested that geographers might be profitably employed in examinations of the spatial metaphors in cultural studies literature. How has the nomad metaphor been deployed?

Henry Mayhew and the Wandering Tribes

In distinction to the romance of the nomad in postmodern theory, modernist social and cultural thought consistently mobilized the nomad as a figure of threat and disruption to the 'good life'. Henry Mayhew, in his investigations of London's poor, described the unsavable outcasts of the city as the 'wandering tribes'. Mayhew's investigations of darkest London were influenced by the writings of Dr Andrew Smith, Deputy Inspector General of Hospitals, in the *Philosophical Magazine*.[37] In his series of papers on the 'Origin and History of the Bushmen' Smith suggested that 'civilised' (settled) people were always surrounded by a peripheral nomadic group of wanderers. These wandering tribes were the object of moral scorn whether in South Africa or London. Descriptions of them painted them as the epitome of social disorganization.

> The little intercourse that they have with each other, and the absence of almost any kind of property, render them quite strangers to the great objects of law, and consequently unconscious of the benefits of a regular Government.[38]

> They are deeply versed in deceit, and treacherous in the extreme, being always prepared to effect by guile and perfidy what they are otherwise unable to accomplish.[39]

> The disposition to laziness so decidedly characteristic of the Hottentots, is equally developed in the Bushmen; and were it not for the absolute necessity of daily exertion to procure the scanty means of subsistence, they would doubtless pass their time in indolent practices similar to those pursued where resources are more certain and productive.[40]

Such descriptions form part of a wider distinction between the civilized self and the savage other.[41] Lack of government and law, forms of cruelty and

---

36 Patricia Price-Chalita 'Spatial Metaphor and the Politics of Empowerment: Mapping a Place for Feminism and Postmodernism in Geography', *Antipode*, 26/3, 1994, pp. 236–54.
37 Andrew Smith, 'Observations relative to the origins and history of the Bushmen', *Philosophical Magazine*, New Series 9, 1831, pp. 119–26.
38 ibid. page 122.
39 ibid. page 124.
40 ibid. page 127.

extreme laziness are all given as marks of the savage other. The wandering status of the savage other is itself a source of uneasiness, perhaps the root cause of all the alleged other traits. These observations from South Africa (and elsewhere) are reflected in Mayhew's descriptions of the 'wandering tribes' of London. For Mayhew, the poor of London are split into the familiar distinction of worthy and savable poor and the unsavable poor whom he describes as the wandering tribes. These wanderers are distinguished from the settled poor.

> ... by his repugnance to regular and continuous labour – by his want of provi-dence in laying up stores for the future ... – by his passion for stupefying herbs and roots, and, when possible, for intoxicating fermented liquours ... – by his love of libidinous dances ... – by the looseness of his notion of property – by the absence of chastity among his women, and his disregard for female honour – and lastly, by his vague sense of religion.[42]

> In the continual warfare with the force, they resemble many savage nations, for the cunning and treachery they use ... Their love of revenge too, is extreme – their hatred being in no way mitigated by time ...[43]

Smith, too, wrote of the lust for revenge which he believed constituted one of the main characteristics of people without property and thus formal (and impartial) law. The language of Smith and Mayhew are almost identical. Mayhew transcribes the observations of Smith (and other colonial texts) on to the topography of London, and the wanderers become the 'other' of civilization in all its locations.

Henry Mayhew's writings are a key series of texts which formed part of the origins of contemporary sociology. His journalistic social survey inspired Robert Park and the Chicago School in their ethnographic studies of deviance in the city. In his writings, then, we see the nomad as a figure present right at the birth of modern social sciences. The metaphorical nomad did not go away.

T. S. Eliot and the Threat of Mass Education

One figure widely regarded as a grandfather of cultural studies is T. S. Eliot. His *Notes Towards the Definition of Culture*[44] is one of the key texts in the conservative 'Culture and Society' tradition alongside those of Matthew Arnold and F. R. Leavis. In this text, Eliot advances the argument that Culture (with a big C) can be preserved only through the maintenance of class hierarchy and a strong attachment to region. Without the stability provided by these frame-

41 *See* Miles Ogborn, 'Love-state-ego: 'centres' and 'margins' in 19th century Britain', *Environment and Planning D: Society and Space*, 10/3, 1992, pp. 287–306.
42 Henry Mayhew, quoted in Stallybrass, P. and White A., *The Poetics and Politics of Transgression*, (Ithaca NY, Cornell University Press, 1986), page 128.
43 Henry Mayhew, *Mayhew's London (selections from London Labour and London Poor)*, (London, Spring Books, 1851), page 42.
44 T S Eliot, *Notes Towards the Definition of Culture*, (London, Faber and Faber, 1948).

works (class and region) all hell will break loose. One danger Eliot saw was in the threatened introduction of universal education.

> For there is no doubt that in our headlong rush to educate everybody, we are lowering our standards, and more and more abandoning the study of those subjects by which the essentials of our culture – or that part of it which is transmissible by education – are transmitted; destroying our ancient edifices to make ready the ground upon which the barbarian nomads of the future will encamp in mechanised caravans.[45]

Eliot's nomads are clearly metaphorical. Here he is discussing education not nomadism. The question arises as to what the nomads and their mechanized caravans represent. Undoubtedly the metaphor is pejorative. The nomads are contrasted with *edifices* – monuments, stable and deeply rooted certainties. The nomads represent the threat of chaos brought about by the fracturing of class lines and regional loyalty. People will no longer know their place socially or geographically. For Eliot this would signal the death knell of culture. Eliot's definition of culture is very much a definition of roots and tradition.

> Certainly, an individual may develop the warmest devotion to a place in which he was not born, and to a community with which he has no ancestral ties. But I think we should agree that there would be something artificial, something a little too conscious, about a community of people with strong local feeling, all of whom had come from somewhere else ... On the whole, it would appear to be for the best that the great majority of human beings should go on living in the place in which they were born. Family. class and local loyalty all support each other; and if one of these decays, the others will suffer also.[46]

Eliot's metaphorical nomads quickly become literal in his text. Eliot, himself a fairly mobile intellectual (traveller or migrant but no nomad) removed from his place of birth, sees the contours of culture as firmly attached to the contours of region. The metaphorical nomads represent the threat of universal education but Eliot is also disturbed by people who move in a literal sense. Culture, for Eliot, depends on a lack of movement, on stability, rootedness and continuity. In addition to considering the place-boundedness of his Culture, he considers the 'problems' of those who move (again ignoring himself).

> The colonization problem arises from migration. When peoples migrated across Asia and Europe in pre-historic and early times, it was a whole tribe, or at least a wholly representative part of it, that moved together. Therefore, it was a total culture that moved. In the migrations of modern times, the emigrants have come from countries already highly civilised ... The people who migrated have never represented the whole of the culture of the country from which they came, or they have represented it in quite different proportions. They have transplanted

45 ibid. page 108.
46 ibid. page 52.

themselves according to some social, religious, economic or political determination, or some peculiar mixture of these ... The people have taken with them only a part of the total culture in which, so long as they remained at home, they participated.[47]

Culture and 'home' (defined as a region) belong together in Eliot's mind so the movement of people can be seen only as a 'problem' and threat to cultural distinctiveness. So we can see that Eliot's reference to the mechanized nomads of mass education and culture is linked to beliefs about mobility and place that are far from metaphorical.

The 'culture and society' tradition that Eliot has been associated with was roundly critiqued by the leftist protagonists of the new 'cultural studies' discipline who sought to establish a more democratic and inclusive view of culture. E. P. Thompson, Richard Hoggart and Raymond Williams are widely believed to be the most important figures in the early development of cultural studies as we know it today. Much of their early writing involved a critique of Arnold, Leavis and Eliot. As well as a break from the culture and society tradition, there were elements of continuity. Raymond Williams often wrote positively of Leavis's influence on his thinking. One continuity has been the threat of mobility to 'culture'.

Raymond Williams and the Threat of Industrial Capital

Raymond Williams wrote in 1985, in an essay on the Miners' Strike:

> Yet there is the implacable logic of the social order which is now so strongly coming though: the logic of a new nomad capitalism which exploits actual places and people and then (as it suits it) moves on. Indeed, the spokesmen of this new nomad capitalism have come less and less to resemble actual human beings, and more and more to look and talk like plastic nomads: offering their titles to cash at a great distance from any settled working and productive activity, ... Back in the shadow of their operations, from the inner cities to the abandoned mining villages, real men and women know that they are facing an alien order of paper and money, which seems all-powerful. It is to the lasting honour of the miners, and the women, and the old people, and all the others in the defiant communities, that they have stood up against it, and challenged its power.[48]

> We need not worry about the plastic nomads who hold our own nominal nationality. They will move on, or draw their heavily protected profits from elsewhere. The rest of us, here and needing to stay here, will have to find an alternative economic order if we are to continue to have any real society ...[49]

47 ibid. pp. 62–3.
48 Raymond Williams, 'Mining the Meaning: Keywords in the Miners Strike' in *Resources of Hope*, (London, Verso, 1989), page 124.
49 ibid. pp. 124–5.

While Eliot's nomads represent the threat of mass culture to his ideal rooted and stratified Culture, Williams's nomads are those of twentieth-century industrial capitalism, profiteers who roam the Earth taking what they can and giving little back. While it is easier to sympathize with Williams's vision (at least for this author), the implications of the nomad metaphor are surprisingly similar. For Williams, as for Eliot, culture is a fairly sedentary thing, linked to the continuities of place and community. Note that 'the rest of us' (non-plastic nomads) have to 'stay here' in 'defiant communities' represented by places such as inner cities and mining villages. Williams's moral geography is one of mobile threats to rooted struggling communities. This moral geography is not confined to his Miners' Strike paper – it pervades his work. His point of departure, more often than not, is the place he grew up in on the borders of England and Wales in the Black Mountains. In his cultural criticism and in his imaginative writing, this proves to be a stable point of certainty against which much else is judged.

Williams's evocative novel, *Border Country*, concerns the thoughts and actions of Matthew Price as he returns to the place of his childhood and adolescence in the Welsh Border Country to look after his dying father. The novel consists of Matthew's memories of a Welsh valley as the whole world. As the novel progresses, members of the community leave the village and the valley for places such as Cardiff (jut 30 miles distance). Matthew himself eventually left the village to take his place at Oxford University. Part of returning is to discover that the place he remembered had changed. It was no longer the centre of everything but part of a wider system:

> this place is finished, as it was. What matters from now on is not the fields, not the mountains, but the road. There'll be no village, as a place of its own. There'll just be a name you pass through.[50]

As the story progresses, the cohesion and solidarity of village life is torn apart by the general strike in which the railwaymen of the village are a part. A central figure in the strike, Morgan Rosser, starts a food-delivery business and, a third of the way through the novel, he starts to deliver food to strikers in the next valley. This action of dealing widens his world but is frowned upon by the striking signalmen. In the novel, as in the literary and cultural criticism, Williams is deeply nostalgic for a certain and rooted past of community and place. Williams's work has been seen as a sustained engagement with the importance of human connectedness to political struggle. His work is shot through with living communities that draw strength from tradition and the human bonds with place. To Williams, progressive political movements are based on similarities of experience in time and place.

Just as the miners' communities were threatened (and now, it seems, extinguished) by the nomads of capitalism, Matthew Price's home town changed from a place of companionship and struggle to a point in a journey

50 Raymond Williams, *Border Country*, (London, Chatto and Windus, 1960), page 242.

symbolized by the road. While being far from straightforward, the moral implications of this transformation naggingly imply the inherent value of roots and community and an inherent distaste for mobility and rootlessness.

To Eliot, attachment to place serves to ensure a conservative, hierarchical culture with everyone in their place: to Williams the maintenance of place and community serve to ensure the continuation of progressive struggle against the nomadic machinations of capital. While we may agree with one of the other in a political sense, the two visions are joined by the metaphor of the furtive nomad constructed as negative and threatening.

Richard Hoggart and the Threat of Mass Entertainment

Another of the founders of contemporary cultural studies was Richard Hoggart whose *The Uses of Literacy* is cited as one of the key texts in the fledgling discipline. Hoggart's discussions of working-class culture mirror those of Williams. Hoggart's book details the features of a working-class culture he identifies with and the threats to it.

> The more we look at working-class life, the more we try to reach the core of working-class attitudes, the more surely does it appear that the core is a sense of the personal, the concrete, the local: it is embodied in the idea of, first, the family and, second, the neighbourhood.[51]

Like Williams, Hoggart appears firmly rooted in the closely knit neighbourhoods of his upbringing. All that is good about working-class culture is encapsulated in snug family living rooms with open fires and cluttered mantelpieces. Everyone knows one another, shopkeepers are polite, people help their neighbours when it snows. Working-class life and culture are firmly attached to place, and value continuity and tradition.

> Unless he gets a council house, a working-class man is likely to live in his own local area, perhaps even in the house he 'got the keys for' the night before his wedding, all his life. He has little call to move on if he is a general labourer, and perhaps hardly more if he is skilled, since his skill is likely to be in a trade for which several nearby works ... provide vacancies ... He is more likely to change his place of work than his place of living; he belongs to a district more than one works.[52]

The life of the working-class individual as presented by Hoggart is determinedly local. Movement is over a small distance and repeated as part of a routine – home, work, pub. T. S. Eliot would be assured that these people were staying put:

51 Richard Hoggart, *The Uses of Literacy*, (London, Penguin, 1957), page 33.
52 ibid. page 62.

the speed and extent of his travel are not much different from what they would have been thirty years ago. The car has not reduced distance for him: the trains are no faster than they were three quarters of a century ago. True, he will usually travel by bus if he has to travel, but the point is that he normally has to undertake very little travel except within a mile or two.[53]

To Hoggart's rather nostalgic vision of a valuable working-class culture re-volved around home and place. This is coupled with the observation that working-class people simply didn't often travel anywhere other than for the occasional funeral or wedding. These observations are matched by Hoggart's more metaphorical loathing of the threat to this rooted culture posed by the 'bandwagon' of mass entertainment.

So the wagon loaded with its barbarians in wonderland, moves irresistibly forward: not forward to anywhere, but simply forward for forwardness's sake.[54]

Opposed to the snug living room of working-class culture with its glorious profusion of ornaments and nick-nacks is the glitzy, shallow temptation of popular music, magazines and cheap novels. While the old working-class culture is symbolized by the cosiness of the pub, the new bandwagon is symbolized by the 'milkbar' with its 'glaring showiness' and 'odour of boiled milk' in which customers live a 'myth world' taken to be 'American' consisting of slicked-back hair and endless streams of milk shakes. But Hoggart is still hopeful about the survival of a full and rich working-class culture.

Fortunately the success of 'progressivism' is still much qualified. The persistent if subdued mistrust of science has been strengthened by the latest revelations of its power to harm. Sometimes the objection is to ... its excessive speed ... . The view is ... that it is very good to keep on going on, but that 'They' should take care not to get us into a speed wobble.[55]

Mass entertainment is curiously coupled with science in the metaphor of speed gone wrong. 'Progress' to Hoggart is a word that encapsulates the various threats to the world of the home and neighbourhood. Progress replaces local pubs with 'American' milk bars.

Put simply the working-class culture that Hoggart values is small scale, close knit and family based – it is stable and, for the most part, unchanging. The aspects of mass entertainment that Hoggart feels it is necessary to warn us against are foreign (mostly American), rapidly changing and unattached to place. Progress implies movement, and Hoggart's repudiation of 'Progressiv-ism' is couched as a warning against 'speed' and its dangers. His evocation of working-class life is one of motionless continuity, and his more symbolic description of threats to it are laced with references to movement and speed.

53 ibid. page 62.
54 ibid. pp. 193–4.
55 ibid. page 194.

Hoggart's morality play is essentially one of stability vs. mobility. The forces of mass entertainment are to be prevented from opening up an Americanized 'Candy-floss world' of chrome and depthlessness full of barbarians (always the nomadic threat to civilization's order) on bandwagons and buses:

> The hedonistic but passive barbarian who rides in a fifty-horse-power bus for threepence, to see a five-million-dollar film for one-and-eightpence, is not simply a social oddity; he is a portent.[56]

The Modern Imagines the Premodern

Despite their considerable differences in politics and philosophy, Mayhew, Eliot, Hoggart and Williams are united in their respect for roots and their use of metaphors of mobility to suggest threat. Mass education, mass entertainment and industrial capital are all painted as nomadic and alien, threatening the integrity of cosy regions, towns and neighbourhoods within which lie the virtues of culture in all its manifestations. To the modernist imagination the figure of the nomad is one of threat. These writers mobilize the nomad as a symbol of transience that disrupts the bounded value systems that they have invested with moral worth. It was in this guise that the nomad took his/her place right at the birth of the modern social sciences and cultural studies. It was the certainties of place and region that were embraced by these pre-post-modern thinkers. Just as the postmodern theorists enjoy the disruption of boundaries that the nomad necessitates, the modernists feel nausea at such a threat. The postmodern embrace of the apparently antirational also finds its mirror image in the modern repugnance for the mobile threat to right thinking. To British proto-anthropologists and to Henry Mayhew, the wandering tribes were always the unspeakable threat to the certainties of 'civilization' – people who did not understand rational systems of law and labour. These nomads are reborn in Eliot's mechanized nomads of mass education and Hoggart's 'barbarians' of American (and thus rootless) culture. The lineage is a complicated one, but one that can be traced. It is a history linked to the modern quest for certainty and authenticity in a world which increasingly 'melted into air'.

Conclusions

Ien Ang has identified a 'formalist, postmodern tendency to overgeneralise the global currency of the so-called nomadic, fragmented and deterritorialized subjectivity'.[57] She argues that the use of nomad metaphors often serve to

---

56 ibid. page 250.

'decontextualize and flatten out difference, as if "we" were all in fundamentally similar ways always-already travellers in the same postmodern universe, the only difference residing in the different itineraries we undertake'.[58] This is the issue I want to raise in these concluding remarks. Deleuze and Guattari, Chambers and de Certeau all use the figure of the nomad to posit new freedoms and movements. These nomads are situated in radically unlocated spaces – in the airport terminal, in the 'city' and on the 'street'. The pedestrian in New York, the intellectual in JFK or Heathrow and the uncontrollable postmodern citizen are all collapsed into the body of the nomad – the very being who was described in earlier times as a hopeless barbarian, who had land taken away and was subjected to the twin disciplinary strategies of slaughter and civilization.

The nomad in these texts is a metaphorical one – one for which its meaning therefore rests on assumed similarity with such things as academics attending conferences. Such metaphorical reductions can serve only to negate the very real differences which exist between the mobile citizens of the postmodern world and the marginalized inhabitants of other times and places.

The postmodern nomad is a remarkably unsocial being – unmarked by the traces of class, gender, ethnicity, sexuality and geography. They are nomads who appear as entries on a census table, or dots on a map – abstract, dehistoricized and undifferentiated – a mobile mass.

A recent, distinctly postmodern, book on design in New York subtitled 'Nomadic Design' aptly illustrates the vacuous generalizations to which the nomad has been subjected.[59] In the Introduction to the pages of glossy photos, the editors make the argument that New York is a nomadic city where the nomadic world of the horizontal contests the vertical skyscraper world of power and money. They suggest that in New York 'everything crosses over'. The pictures that make up the majority of the text focus on the design of New York, juxtaposing the work of guerrilla artist, urban graffiti campaigns and anti-homelessness activism on the one hand with the designer spaces of the Investment Banking Partnership, the Cleary, Gottleib, Steen and Hamilton Law Offices and the offices of Island Records. All are linked (in the editors' eyes) by their expression of nomadic desire. The book is a beautiful book that makes even homelessness appear to be aesthetically seductive. Yet to place the protests of the homeless next to the lush million dollar interiors of New York's hyper-privileged eradicates the differences between them through a philosophical and aesthetic deceit that singularly fails to point out the other, less pleasing,

57 Ien Ang, 'On Not Speaking Chinese: Postmodern Ethnicity and the Politics of Diaspora', *New Formations*, 24 winter 1994, page 4.
58 Ien Ang, 'On Not Speaking Chinese: Postmodern Ethnicity and the Politics of Diaspora', *New Formations*, 24 winter 1994, page 4.
59 Ronald Christ and Dennis Dollens, *New York: Nomeadic Design*, (Barcelona, Gustavo Gili, 1993).

connections between huge private spaces of the wealthy and the colourful protests of the homeless.

Here, as in other uses of the nomadic in the postmodern lexicon, no or little attention is paid to the historical conditions which produce specific forms of movement which are radically different . Moving subjects – travellers, migrants and nomads – are all partially fixed by who they are.

Smith and Katz[60] have argued that the use of geographical metaphors in contemporary social theory needs to be subject to scrutiny. In an uncertain world, they argue, everything but space is thrown into chaos while simple geography remains unquestioned and taken for granted. This, they suggest, is the reason for the proliferation of geographical metaphors in contemporary theory. A note of caution should be introduced here as it is clear that at least one of these metaphors – that of the nomad – has a longer history than that which is encapsulated by the short memory of postmodern theory. Nevertheless I agree that there is a need to interrogate the history of spatial metaphors such as the nomad.

Janet Wolff has gone some way to contextualizing the moving subjects of postmodern discourse.[61] She describes how these metaphors are gendered in a way which is usually unacknowledged. Her argument is that the actual practices of travel which serve to exclude women are reflected in the androcentric tendencies of theoretical travel. In her paper she focuses on the Western middle-class idea of travel as a form of leisure, and the way in which metaphors of travel reproduce the masculine identity of this travel:

> the problem with terms like 'nomad', 'maps' and 'travel' is that they are not usually located, and hence (and purposely) they suggest ungrounded and unbounded movement – since the whole point is to resist selves/viewers/subjects. But the consequent suggestion of free and equal mobility is itself a deception, since we don't all have the same access to the road.[62]

In addition to the gendering of travel metaphors, there is the problem of romanticizing the marginal(ized) other. David Sibley[63] has suggested that dominant cultural groups tend to have a schizophrenic reaction to their marginalized others. On the one hand, they are romanticized, and on the other, they are labelled deviant. Theorists appear to be no exception. Just as real-life nomads and semi-nomads are trampled on the one hand and glorified on the other as romantic outcasts, free from the shackles of normality, metaphorical nomads are either a generalized threat to civilization or generalized heroic figures resisting the confines of a disciplinary society.

---

60 Neil Smith and Cindi Katz, 'Grounding Metaphor: Towards a Spatialized Politics' in Michael Keith and Steve Pile (eds), *Place and the Politics of Identity*, (London, Routledge, 1993), pp. 67–83.

61 Janet Wolff 'On the Road Again: Metaphors of Travel in Cultural Criticism', *Culture Studies*, 7/2 May 1993, pp. 224 –39.

62 Janet Wolff, 'On the Road Again', (1993), page 253.

63 David Sibley, *Outsiders in Urban Society*, (Oxford, Blackwell, 1981).

In many ways, this theoretical appropriation of the premodern illustrates Said's[64]

64 Edward Said, *Orientalism*, (New York, Vintage, 1979). important discussion of 'orientalism' in which he describes the West's simultaneous disgust and desire for the Eastern 'other'. As well as travel metaphors being predominantly masculine, they are also profoundly Eurocentric – incorporating and appropriating a predominantly non-Western experience for the benefit of more Western theory. The history of the nomad metaphor in social and cultural theory is one of disgust and desire which refused to locate, situate and contextualize. My suggestion, then, is to refuse the disgust of the modern and the romance of the postmodern, and provide situated and provisional accounts of movement which do not gloss over the real differences in power that exist between the theorist and the source domain of the metaphors of mobility. The constant decontextualization of mobility, whether modern or postmodern, needs to be corrected.

Conclusion

17

Forget the Delivery, or, What Post are We Talking About?

Ulf Strohmayer

> ... and everything was once again an allusion to something else; one would think that before modernity there would already have been a postmodernity. The emptiness of these phrases.
>
> Cees Nooteboom, *Berliner Notizen*

And so, after much deliberation, where do the preceding readings of different spaces and of 'postmodernism' and its consequences for the human sciences leave us? What have we gained? The image we are left with clearly is one of conflicting accounts and contrasting interpretations, rather than of harmonious discourse. 'Modernism' and 'postmodernism' emerge as thoroughly contested concepts which are created to serve specific purposes. Discerning these strategic goals, or, the strategic connection between the construction of concepts like 'modernism' (or 'postmodernism') and their respective usefulness within specific arguments, is what most of the critical discourses we encounter are all about. The oft-anticipated conclusion, however, that we should give up on the idea of ever arriving at some form of consensus over what precisely is characteristic of the time we live in, is counterproductive. We still seem to require ideals, if only as regulative ideas.

It might well be that we have to learn to place less trust in the 'regulative ideas' that motivate us all. Critical self-awareness, or continuous radical honesty, could well be a necessary step in a right direction. In this manner, the often self-undermining – and what else is radical critique but the willingness to risk one's convictions? – question 'where did I depart from?' might yet gain ground on the seemingly more sensible query 'what have we gained?'. What follows is largely motivated by the desire to make the former question a more respectable one within the human and social sciences and thus to move the discussion in the direction of a more consciously self-aware positioning of arguments: not to do battle with other, competing 'positions', but to clarify what could be involved should we want to continue or finally to start opening ourselves up to critique.

Which Modernity?

Awareness of the positionality of one's arguments would seem to entail the twin tasks of accepting that no argument, including one's own, originates out of nowhere, and of refusing to privilege the resulting 'origin' to the point that it functions in the traditional comforting manner. In a word, then, positional awareness must go hand in hand with a sense of radical responsibility for the resulting argument. Every possible 'origin' of an argument becomes an event once it has left a trace somewhere – if mainly on paper: it *happened* and is thus available for further arguments. Recognizing the implications of this is the third task, and is equally dependent on a commitment to honest self-critical awareness on the part of those making or assuming an argumentative proposition.

The necessary attempt to clarify the regulative ideal of 'modernity' and of 'postmodernity', for instance, could opt to depart from a phrase, written in 1848, and (if with the questionable benefit of hindsight) destined to leave a rather remarkable trace, to become a classic: 'A phantom is haunting Europe,' wrote Karl Marx and Friedrich Engels, 'it is the phantom of communism'. Today, almost 150 years later, the alleged phantoms of yesteryear are no more, but living without them has proven to be rather more difficult than was imagined before. Another maxim, moulded into Marxist terminology by Lenin (who borrowed it from Chernyshevsky) still awaits a convincing answer: *What, we continue to ask, is to be done?* Formulated at the turn of our century, we can today discern in this latter question one of the more fundamental problems underlying not just Marxist thought but all of 'modernity' in general. If ever a question captured the theme of an age, this is it. For, official authorship notwithstanding, every '*What is to be done?*' is based on two separate, if contingently related, pillars that allow us to distinguish a 'modern age' from preceding epochs. The first of these is the possibility of a public discourse about a future that is unknown but changeable; the second pillar involves the possibility of identifying and evaluating different responses to Lenin's question, through the public use of reason. Together, as we shall see, they form the indispensable, if problematic, foundation for many contemporary debates.

It is within this admittedly unusual framework that I would like to respond to some of the questions raised in the debates around postmodernism and geography (and the human sciences in general). These debates have been important primarily because they point towards some of the epistemological premises underlying a majority of geographic research and thinking. But it is time to complement this discursive critique with broader considerations about the possibility and the necessity of a genuinely human science in a world that has changed in a multitude of aspects, often beyond recognition. For, as I hope to demonstrate here, the questions surrounding a rather diffuse notion of 'postmodernity' are, at the same time, questions that have become pertinent since the fall of the Wall in Berlin. Postmodernism and 'the fall of communism,' or, the end of ideologies: we will have to think what all of this implies for human geography and for the social and human sciences.

The concept of 'postmodernism' itself, as has been argued by most commentators, originated within architecture (*see* Dear 1988 and Claval 1992; more generally Bertens 1995). Here postmodern architecture signifies first and foremost a return of the ornament and the end of modern transparency. On the one side, we are shown Le Corbusier and the *Charter of Athens*; on the other Vincent Venturi and the celebration of formal chance known as Las Vegas; and between the two a watershed that goes by the name of Baudelaire (Harvey 1989, esp. 174–8; Gregory 1991 and 1994). We need to ask, however, if this separation between 'modernism' and 'postmodernism',' commonly accepted and evident though it is, is indeed as meaningful as it seems. In other words, we will need to ask whether the transparent straightforwardness or lack of ornamentation which we commonly attribute to 'modern architecture' is indeed 'modern' in character. The hunch is that it is not: our identification of transparency with 'the modern' all too often came to mask little more than a reduction in the potentially infinite number of answers to the question '*What needs to be done?*', thus allowing only answers which 'no longer know anything but straight lines, vertical planes or horizons, and right angles' (Claval 1992, 4, my translation). 'The Real' thus became manageable and transparent at a price: its potential complexity was short circuited in such a manner as no longer to represent what the ancient Moderns sought to render lucid in the first place.

The above hiatus is legible in the word itself: transparency, clarity or *clarté*. It is decidedly not without reason that today the word *clarté* is still largely synonymous with the name of Voltaire. If today we call Diderot, d'Alembert, and Rousseau – to mention but a few – 'philosophers of the Enlightenment' we do so because first and foremost we want to evoke the clash between Reason and religious or absolutist conceptions of the world over the means to explain (read: to render as lucid) a given complexity. Immanuel Kant summarized this essential conflict in his phrase *Sapere Aude*, or, 'have the courage to know (and to use your own faculties of judgement)'. This maxim, the most transparent of Enlightenment imperatives, was to change the world profoundly: it was to provide one of the conditions of possibility for the emergence of a genuinely public sphere of discourse, what I have depicted earlier as one of the two pillars of modern thought. But to have or not to have 'courage', as Kant knew well, is one thing, whereas the status of knowledge is always contested terrain. Once tied to a public realm, knowledge thus had to become justifiable within that very sphere; it had to become capable of satisfying more than predetermined audiences like the clergy and the aristocracy. To achieve this goal, knowledge necessarily had to be knowledge *in general*.[1]

Kant's idea of a priori categories would thus already denote the fundamental conflict that would accompany modernity to this very day: knowledge about a constitutionally *historical* world could affirm its status *as* 'knowledge' only by claiming an *ahistorical* position for itself. It is because of this inherent tension that modernity was to remain, in the word of Paul Claval, 'elusive' (1992, 18). But although the conflict itself was, and continues to be, an integral one for every definition of modernity since the days of Kant, the justification given for its resolution (or *'Aufhebung'* in the Hegelian sense) cannot but fall back into pre-modern manners of reasoning. In other, more pointed, words: a modernity that claims the capability to eliminate this friction in the name of a general knowledge loses nothing less than its 'modern' distinction.

The preceding analysis, albeit unfamiliar, allows us to understand differently the time-honoured reference to architecture that still serves as a beacon in every discussion of 'postmodernity'. By insisting on the importance of a non-negotiable conflict between the two constitutive elements of any knowledge, namely a conditioning historicity on the one hand and a no-less necessary claim towards generality on the other, it becomes possible to think the majority of what passes as 'modern architecture' as a rejection of an ideal but distinctive characteristic of modernity in general. The insistence of this architecture on the formulation of universal solutions, its aiming for an 'international style', especially after World War II, is thus nothing less than a betrayal of modernity by so-called modernists. A betrayal, we need to add, that is not without its rationale; the world 'solution' itself is testimony to a most understandable desire to formulate definitive and justifiable responses to problems that continue to haunt humankind, as do notions like 'method' and 'epistemology'. Within architecture, this moral dimension of the Kantian problem became most obvious in the shift, so prevalent in the 1920s, away from the design of individual residences to the construction of apartment houses for the swelling masses of urban centres. And yet, far too many well-argued and justified responses have proven not to be solutions at all but, rather, have turned out to involve problems of often even higher magnitudes than the difficulties they set out to solve. And we can all too often trace the kernel of contemporary problems back to a neglect of historical particularity in the justification of a general claim to knowledge, answering, in one form or another, Lenin's question. *What needs to be done* is hence, first and foremost, a reversal, a deconstruction of the commonly accepted interpretation of modernity: rather than providing answers, modernity questions. It was not without reason that Kant's major works bore the title of *Critiques*; it was they that inaugurated a tradition of rational and self-conscious criticism and thereby opened the door towards a mode of critique that was recognized as potentially ubiquitous first in the writings of Nietzsche (Horkheimer and Adorno 1969) and later in those of Heidegger and poststructuralist philosophers (Soja 1989, Bauman 1990). It should therefore not come as a surprise that we can recognize traces of the above hiatus in the

---

1   This account, of course, is a highly speculative sociological rendering of late Enlightenment thinking. For an internal reading of the emergence of 'general knowledge' *see* Strohmayer and Hannah (1992); an historical rendering of this highly important passage in modern thought is provided in Hannah and Strohmayer (1995).

accomplishments of 'Modernists' (the figure of the 'stranger' both in Georg Simmel and Albert Camus), 'Quasi-Modernists' (the 'everyday' in Michel de Certeau and Maurice Blanchot), and 'Postmodernists' (the notions of '*différance*' in Jacques Derrida and of '*episteme*' in Michel Foucault) alike. Communication between 'generalities' and 'particularities' (or 'historical specificity') is necessarily disrupted; there is neither a *post* or postmen in those spheres pertaining to knowledge.

Quid postmodernity? The term itself is modern in its insistence on an essential, indeed non-circumventable historicity and betrays, again in a 'modern' manner, 'modernity' by denying a just as fundamental and necessary general character of knowledge. Indeed, is it not startling to realize that the best works of both 'modern' *and* 'postmodern' architecture are largely marginal works outside the accepted canon of definitions? The 'modern' chapel designed by Le Corbusier in Ronchamps, France, but also the 'postmodern' *Staatsgalerie* devised by James Sterling in Stuttgart, Germany, labour to express an architectural solution which is utterly historical and unabashedly universal at the same time. Even 'functionality,' long since held to be the distinctive mark of 'modernism', can hide underneath rather different clothes: once materialized into a '*Unité de Habitation*', it resurfaces later in the form of 'Caesar's Palace'. Small wonder, to continue David Harvey's insights on this point, that a large number of so-called 'postmodern' buildings constructed between 1980 and 1989 were museums, rather than residential buildings. Here 'the postmodern' is indeed functional. 'Which,' as the inimitable Henri Lefebvre once phrased it, 'brings forth contradictory, even chaotic effects. According to some, it is necessary to run ahead on this technologically defined path. Among others, nostalgia wins over and against the hope in a future full of astonishing inventions. Continuities and discontinuities thus interlock to form a confusion which translates into spatial disorder' (1981, 94, my translation).[2] Different times, different spaces, different forms deemed functional.

Which Space?

Far from being exhausted by the above analysis, the conflict between the historicity of each and every spatio-temporal event and its ever-possible generalization can be uncovered in a multitude of other embodiments. Within human geography, we can think of the well-known tension between 'nomothetic' and 'idiographic' modes of analyses, but we are no less familiar with other dualisms like those between 'aesthetics' and 'functionality', or between 'determinism' and 'freedom'. Postmodernism, and here even critics agree, has finally prepared the ground for a legitimate critique of these and other dualisms (Sayer 1991). And yet, as I have argued earlier, it is not the dualisms as such

---

2   Lefebvre continues: 'Could there be another path passing between a hard and absurd 'reality' and all those compensations, vain protests, those subjective illusions and lyrical impulses of regret? Such a path is all the more difficult to outline ...'

that are of importance, *or even avoidable*, but rather the role they play within particular claims to knowledge. The importance of postmodernism accordingly lies not in the nihilistic revocation of the possibility of knowledge that some commentators mention (e.g. Sayer 1993), but in the demonstration of a *generally* neglected *particular* historicity by 'Modernists'. Along this path, the first aim of postmodernism was consequently to subvert the justification of general answers to the quintessential question *What needs to be done?*, modes of that justification that were often concealed behind those 'convictions, manners of thinking, ideologies, programs and visions of the world' that have flourished over the last two centuries, as the conservative German poet Botho Strauss phrased it (1992, 44, my translation). But to criticize a neglect is not the same as to offer alternatives. And while it is certainly true that the imperative demanding alternatives is itself modern in substance, we need to ask what, exactly, could be meant by a 'modern imperative' today, more than two centuries after Kant? From the present point of view, such an imperative implies little less than an individual's assent to the idea of an impossible reconciliation between social demands (the enlightened necessity to justify our convictions) and individual conditions of possibility (the historicity of our finite capacities). In the insistence that the reconciliation remains impossible, we are thus touching on what Augustin Berque once called 'this occidental utopia' (1992, 17), a Utopia or ideal that remains functionally necessary even though it can never demonstrably be realized.

In other words, the recognition of the ineffectiveness (or the potential harmfulness) of general explanations will not alone render them obsolete. For one, as Matthew Hannah and I have tried to demonstrate elsewhere (1993), it remains an epistemological impossibility to deal with 'particularities' (or historical specificity) other than as 'generalities'. Analytically speaking, the difference between the two exists primarily as a different in trust. Furthermore, we are, and we will remain, children of the Enlightenment and of the French Revolution, and only an open embrace of dictatorial 'solutions' will make our participation in public discourses, and the obligations that come with this choice, obsolete. In fact, without readily available generalities at our disposal, these latter discourses will certainly tend to be more democratic in nature – with all of the perennial risks implied by this 'democratisation' (Raulet 1988, 58–9).

To remain loyal to rational ideals without succumbing to their tendential arrogance – what does this involve, in more concrete terms, for the humanities, the social sciences, and for geography? Such a loyalty will first and foremost entail a politicization of each and every scientific analysis within the human sciences, a 'politicization' that promises a radical liberation of public spaces from ideological blinkers. Naked but alive and eager to know, the social sciences will become radically public sciences without specialists. And who, frankly, will miss their absence?

What is this 'new public space'? Liberated from an habitual power of persuasion that accompanies accepted generalities, public space will no longer be 'this homogenous, isotrophical, and infinite space out of which we constructed the bars of our suburban environments' (Berque 1992, 18, my translation). Rather, modern space will become a material space without coordinates, a space which no longer locks into opposition 'game' and 'function', a space, finally, at once immanent and open. And if this proposition has itself the air of a paradox, it is nonetheless a rather familiar one. What has changed, however, is that today we no longer possess the *rational* means to maintain self-inflicted illusions. This new space is hence an everyday space, not more, not less, and thus not deprived of modern perspectives (Cosgrove 1984, Crary 1990), but, on the contrary, immersed in a plurality of perspectives, none of which is defined a priori.

A space without predefined positions – is not this, finally, a postmodern celebration of chaos and disorder? Not at all: it signifies the return of collective sincerity, the resurgence of a 'faculty for self-criticism' (Claval 1992, 10), which had been lost during the forced instrumentalization of the social sciences. The year 1989, lest we forget, did not merely symbolize the end of a decade of greed and egotism for those with the means to pay, but also the end of the Cold War and its accompanying, relative stability. And while we have only barely begun to think of all of these events, we are today in a position *sans pareil* to start thinking because we no longer have to act 'as if' our analyses were tied into such a limited and limiting range of larger ideological structures. Which is not to say that these structures no longer exist – the current rise of nationalism and a renewed vigour of conservative 'answers' especially in the United States alone would suffice to dispute that claim – but rather to insist on the need and on the possibility of another, initially unrestricted mode of thinking.

Which Geography?

It is in this manner that an architecture called 'postmodern' becomes important for all of the social and human sciences: for the first time since the Age of Enlightenment it is impossible today to continue to deny the existence of a fundamental *choice*. As in architecture, we in the human sciences can no longer frame the concept of rationality according to our momentary needs for justification. Rationality, too, is historical in the sense that it cannot but participate in a temporal and interminable unfolding of events. Reason, in other words, is neither result nor conclusion but always in constitution. The Ancients knew it: *there is no rational mode by which to detach reason from those means of expression without which reason is nothing*. In forgetting this existential truth, we found it quite easy to construct a separate sphere called 'aesthetics', and to forget that that independence of this sphere was, in fact, the direct result of a former 'postmodernism' at the turn of the nineteenth century, that we still call 'Romanticism' today. Another dualism, this time between 'beauty' and 'functioning', is in dire need of deconstructive labour. We have to choose, less between modernity and postmodernity, but between abandoning and remaining loyal to reason. In the manner in which they have been constructed for us, neither 'modernity' nor 'postmodernity' will leave the latter of these choices an option; loyalty to reason and to the complexities of modernity implies, more than anything else, the labour of thinking each and every event *as if* it were radically singular (Nancy 1988 and 1990).

Geography itself seems well poised to play a significant role in this process of thinking: we have always known, if at times forgotten, that a change in scale can always alter one's access to reality. This change in scale, to mention just the possibility of a 'vertical' displacement, is itself nothing less than the ubiquitous and indeed *modern* potential of critique, constantly juxtaposing generalities and particulars into ever new constellations. Let us thus think of geography as historical in substance: *there is but one geography and this geography will be historical or it will not be at all*. To be sure, this expression symbolizes the fact that we do not have access to geographical elements other than by entering 'late' into a space where we can be with them (Strohmayer and Hannah 1992). But this 'lateness', which has been one of the central problems of modernity from its beginning, carries likewise an omnipresent possibility of new interpretations. We have to labour to formulate them. And I use this word consciously: 'labour' denotes not merely one of the more fertile concepts within the Marxist tradition, it is also the *leitmotiv* of the cultural social sciences. *Cultura* or *cultivare* always imply an element of labour for a future to be constructed.

Within the academic world at large, geography could thus become a noted discipline: it could remind academic communities that modernity is never finished with labouring through its internal contradictions. At once general, regional, and local, geography as undisciplined discipline could thus bring the human sciences closer together; a task which would be, quite possibly, less satisfying than the construction of theories, although certainly more necessary. And is this not what the best works within geography, both 'modern' and 'postmodern', have always achieved? Changes in the world at large should induce us consciously to subscribe to such a notion of geography, a geography that reminds all of us of the vanity implied in attempting to store answers to the question *What needs to be done?* within the human sciences. Once again, it is up to us to raise the blinkers we have become accustomed to, and to profit from insights that are at once old and sceptical. Samuel Beckett once was here, as was Albert Camus. As was Montaigne, another geographer in spirit: 'Our disputes are purely verbal. I ask what is 'nature'. 'pleasure', 'circle', 'substitution'. The question is one of words, and is answered in the same way. 'A stone is a body.' But if you pressed on: 'And what is a body?' – 'Substance' – 'And what is substance?' And so on, you would finally drive the respondent to the end of his lexicon. We exchange one word for another word, often more unknown. I know better what is man that I know what is animal, or mortal, or rational. To satisfy one doubt, they give me three; it is the Hydra's head. '(*Essays*, Book III, Chapter xiii, 'Of Experience'). Whether we are Modernists or Postmodernists, this head will not cease looking at us.

References

Bauman, Zygmunt, 'Modernity and ambivalence', *Theory, Culture & Society*, 7, 2–3: 143–69, (1990).

Becker, Jürgen, 'Postmoderne Modernisierung der Sozialgeographie', *Geographische Zeitschrift*, 78: 15–33, (1990).

Berque, Augustin, 'Les pays où le regard se voit: traditions nippones et postmodernité', *Société*, 35, 17–26, (1992).

Bertens, Hans, *The Idea of the Postmodern. A History*, (London and New York, Routledge, 1995).

Bloch, Ernst, *Erbschaft dieser Zeit*, (Frankfurt am Main, Surkamp, 1962).

Claval, Paul, 'Postmodernisme et géographie', *Géographie et Cultures*, 4, 3–24, (1992).

Cosgrove, Denis, *Social formation and symbolic landscape*, (Totowa, NJ, Barnes & Noble, 1984).

Crary, Jonathan, *Techniques of the observer. On vision and modernity in the nineteenth century*, (Cambridge, MA and London, MIT Press, 1990).

Dear, Michael, 'The postmodern challenge, reconstructuring human geography', *Transactions of the Institute of British Geographers*, 13, 262–74, (1988).

Derrida, Jacques, *Points de suspension*, (Paris, Galilée, 1992).

Graham, Julie, 'Postmodernism and marxism', *Antipode*, 20, 1: 60–6, (1988).

Graham, Julie, 'Theory and essentialism in marxist geography', *Antipode*, 22,1: 53–66, (1990).

Graham, Julie, 'Fordism/Post-Fordism, Marxism/Post-Marxism: the second cultural divide?' *Rethinking Marxism* 4, 1: 39–58, (1991).

Graham, Julie, 'Anti-essentialism and over determination – a response to Dick Peet', *Antipode*, 24, 2: 141–56, (1992).

Gregory, Derek, 'Interventions in the historical geography of modernity: social theory, spatiality, and the politics of representation', *Geografiska Annaler* 73B: 17–44, (1991).

Gregory, Derek, *Geographical Imaginations*,(Oxford, Blackwell, 1994).

Hannah, Matthew, and Strohmayer, Ulf, 'Ornamentalism: geography and the labour of language in structuration theory', *Environment and Planning D: Society and Space*, 9, 3: 309–26, (1991).

Hannah, Matthew, and Strohmayer, Ulf, 'Postmodernism (s)trained', *Annals of the Association of American Geographers*, 82, 2: 308–10, (1992).

Hannah, Matthew, and Strohmayer, Ulf, 'The Obsolescence of Labor. Reference and Finitude in Barnett and Sayer', *Antipode*, 25, 4: 359–64, (1993).

Hannah, Matthew, and Strohmayer, Ulf, 'The artifice of conviction, or, an internal geography of responsibility', *Geographical Analysis*, 27, 4: 339–59, (1995).

Harvey, David, *The condition of postmodernity*, (Oxford, Blackwell, 1989).

Heidegger, Martin, *Sein und Zeit*, (Tübingen, Max Niemeyer).

Horkheimer, Max and Adorno, Theodor W., *Dialektik der Aufklärung*, (Frankfurt am Main, Fischer, 1969).

Jackson, Peter, *Maps of Meaning*, (London, Unwin Hyman, 1990).

Kern, Stephen, *The Culture of Space and Time*, (Cambridge, Ma., Harvard University Press, 1983).

Lefebvre, Henri, *Critique de la vie quotidienne* vol. III, *De la modernité au modernisme (Pour une métaphilosophie due quotidien)*, (Paris, L'Arche, 1981).

Livingstone, David N., *The Geographical Tradition*, (Oxford and Cambridge, Ma., Blackwell, 1992).

Marx, Karl and Engels, Friedrich, *Manifest der Kommunistischen Partei*, [Stuttgart, Philipp Reclam, 1848 (1962)].

Montaigne, Michel de, *Essais, Ouevres Complètes*, (Paris, Gallimard, Editions de la Pléiade, 1962).

Nancy, Jean-Luc, *La communauté désœuvrée*, (Paris, Christian Bourgois, 1986).

Nancy, Jean-Luc, *L'expérience de la liberté*, (Paris, Galilée, 1988).

Nancy, Jean-Luc, *Une pensée finie*, (Paris, Galilée, 1990).

Negri, Antonio, *The politics of subversion: A manifesto for the twenty-first century*, (Cambridge, Polity Press, 1989).

Nooteboom, Cees, *Berliner Notizen*, (Frankfurt am Main, Suhrkamp, 1991).

Olsson, Gunnar, *Antipasti*, (Göteborg, Korpen, 1990).

Olsson, Gunnar, *Lines of power, limits of language*, (Minneapolis, University of Minneapolis Press, 1991).

Pred, Allan, *Lost words and lost worlds: modernity and the language of everyday life in late nineteenth century Stockholm*, (Cambridge, Cambridge University Press, 1990).

Pred, Allan, 'Spectacular articulations of modernity: The Stockholm Exhibition of 1897', *Geografiska Annaler*, 73B: 45–85, (1991).

Pred, Allan and Watts, Michael, *Reworking Modernity: capitalism and symbolic discontent*, (New Brunswick, NJ, Rutgers University Press, 1992).

Raulet Gérard, 'L'archipel. Réflexions sur la démocratie post-moderne', *Les Cahiers de Philosophie*, 6: 55–83, (1988).

Reichert, Dagmar, 'Writing around circularity and self-reference' in R. Gollege et al. (eds), *A ground for common search*, (Santa Barbara, Santa Barbara Geographical Press, 1988).

Reichert, Dagmar, 'On boundaries', *Environment and Planning D: Society and Space*, 10, 1: 87–97, (1992).

Rose, Gillian, 'Architecture to Philosophy – The Postmodern complicity', *Theory, Culture & Society*, 5, 2–3: 357–72, (1988).

Sayer, Andrew, 'Behind the locality debate: deconstructing geography's dualisms', *Environment and Planning A*, 23, 2: 283–308, (1991).

Sayer, Andrew, 'Postmodernist Thought in Geography: A Realist View', *Antipode*, 26 4: 320–44, (1993).

Shields, Rob, 'A truant proximity: presence and absence in the space of modernity', *Environment and Planning D: Society and Space*, 102: 181–98, (1992).

Sloterdijk, Peter, *Eurotaoismus. Zur Kritik der Politischen Kinetik*, (Frankfurt am Main, Suhrkamp, (1989).

Soja, Edward, *Postmodern geographies. The reassertion of space in critical social theory*, (London Verso, 1989).

Strauss, Botho, *Beginnlosigkeit*, (München, Wien, Carl Hanser, 1992).

Strohmayer, Ulf, 'Beyond theory. The cumbersome materiality of shock', *Environment and Planning D: Society and Space*, 11, 3, (1993).

Strohmayer, Ulf and Hannah, Matthew, 'Domesticating postmodernism', *Antipode*, 24, 1: 29–55, (1992).

Strohmayer, Ulf and Hannah, Matthew, 'Finite Specificity', in F. Farinelli, G. Olsson and D. Reichert (eds), *The Limits of Representation*. (1994, Munich, Accedo).

Watts, Michael, 'The shock of modernity: money, protest, and fast capitalism in an industrializing state', *The Wallace A. Atwood Lecture Series 6* (Worcester, Mass., The Graduate School, Clark University, 1991).

Index